Acura TL Automotive Repair Manual

by Rob Maddox
and John H Haynes

Member of the Guild of Motoring Writers

Models covered:

Acura TL - 1999 through 2008

ABCDE
FGHIJ.
KLMNO
PQRST

Haynes Publishing Group

Sparkford Nr Yeovil
Somerset BA22 7JJ England

Haynes North America, Inc

861 Lawrence Drive
Newbury Park

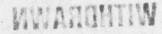

Acknowledgements

Wiring diagrams originated exclusively for Haynes North America, Inc. by Solution Builders. Technical writers who contributed to this project include Joe Hamilton, Mike Stubblefield, Jay Storer and John Wegmann.

© Haynes North America, Inc. 2009

With permission from J.H. Haynes & Co. Ltd.

A book in the Haynes Automotive Repair Manual Series

Printed in the U.S.A.

ISBN-13: 978-1-56392-744-7
ISBN-10: 1-56392-744-6

Library of Congress Control Number 2008943364

Contents

Haynes mechanic and photographer with a 2004 Acura TL

About this manual

Its purpose

The purpose of this manual is to help you get the best value from your vehicle. It can do so in several ways. It can help you decide what work must be done, even if you choose to have it done by a dealer service department or a repair shop; it provides information and procedures for routine maintenance and servicing; and it offers diagnostic and repair procedures to follow when trouble occurs.

We hope you use the manual to tackle the work yourself. For many simpler jobs, doing it yourself may be quicker than arranging an appointment to get the vehicle into a shop and making the trips to leave it and pick it up. More importantly, a lot of money can be saved by avoiding the expense the shop must pass on to you to cover its labor and overhead

costs. An added benefit is the sense of satisfaction and accomplishment that you feel after doing the job yourself.

Using the manual

The manual is divided into Chapters. Each Chapter is divided into numbered Sections, which are headed in bold type between horizontal lines. Each Section consists of consecutively numbered paragraphs.

At the beginning of each numbered Section you will be referred to any illustrations which apply to the procedures in that Section. The reference numbers used in illustration captions pinpoint the pertinent Section and the Step within that Section. That is, illustration 3.2 means the illustration refers to Section 3 and Step (or paragraph) 2 within that Section.

Procedures, once described in the text, are not normally repeated. When it's necessary to refer to another Chapter, the reference will be given as Chapter and Section number. Cross references given without use of the word "Chapter" apply to Sections and/or paragraphs in the same Chapter. For example, "see Section 8" means in the same Chapter.

References to the left or right side of the vehicle assume you are sitting in the driver's seat, facing forward.

Even though we have prepared this manual with extreme care, neither the publisher nor the author can accept responsibility for any errors in, or omissions from, the information given.

NOTE

A **Note** provides information necessary to properly complete a procedure or information which will make the procedure easier to understand.

CAUTION

A **Caution** provides a special procedure or special steps which must be taken while completing the procedure where the Caution is found. Not heeding a Caution can result in damage to the assembly being worked on.

WARNING

A **Warning** provides a special procedure or special steps which must be taken while completing the procedure where the Warning is found. Not heeding a Warning can result in personal injury.

Introduction

These models are available in a four-door sedan body style. The transversely mounted V6 engines used in these models are equipped with electronic fuel injection. The engine drives the front wheels through

either a six-speed manual or a four- or five-speed automatic transaxle via independent driveaxles. Independent suspension, featuring coil spring/shock absorber units, is used on all four wheels. The power-assisted rack-

and-pinion steering unit is mounted behind the engine. The brakes are disc at the front and at the rear, with power assist standard. All models are equipped with Anti-lock Braking Systems (ABS).

Vehicle identification numbers

Modifications are a continuing and unpublicized process in vehicle manufacturing. Since spare parts manuals and lists are compiled on a numerical basis, the individual vehicle numbers are essential to correctly identify the component required.

Vehicle Identification Number (VIN)

This very important identification number is stamped on a plate attached to the dashboard inside the windshield on the driver's side of the vehicle (see illustration). It can also be found on the certification label located on the driver's side door post. The VIN also appears on the Vehicle Certificate of Title and Registration. It contains information such as where and when the vehicle was manufactured, the model year and the body style.

VIN engine and model year codes

Two particularly important pieces of information found in the VIN are the body/engine code and the model year code. Counting from the left, the body/engine code letter designations are the 4th through 6th digits and the model year code letter designation is the 10th digit.

On the models covered by this manual the body/engine codes are:

2001 and earlier models

UA5 .... J32A1 (3.2L V6)

2002 through 2003 models

UA5 .... J32A1 (3.2L V6, 225 HP engine)

UA5 .... J32A2 (3.2L V6, 260 HP engine)

2004 through 2006 models

UA6 .... J32A3 (3.2L V6 engine)

2007 and later models

UA6 .... J32A3 (3.2L V6 engine)

UA7 .... J35A8 (3.5L V6 engine)

On the models covered by this manual the model year codes are:

X	1999
Y	2000
1	2001
2	2002
3	2003
4	2004
5	2005
6	2006
7	2007
8	2008

Certification label

The certification label is attached to the driver's door post (see illustration). The plate contains the name of the manufacturer, the month and year of production, the Gross Vehicle Weight Rating (GVWR), the Gross Axle Weight Rating (GAWR) and the certification statement.

Engine identification numbers

The engine serial number can be found on the front side of the engine (see illustration).

The Vehicle Identification Number (VIN) is located on a plate on top of the dash (visible through the windshield)

The vehicle certification label is located on the driver's door post

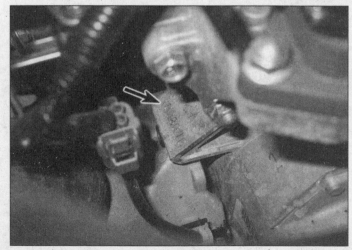

The engine serial number is located on the front side of the block, near the transaxle

Recall information

Vehicle recalls are carried out by the manufacturer in the rare event of a possible safety-related defect. The vehicle's registered owner is contacted at the address on file at the Department of Motor Vehicles and given the details of the recall. Remedial work is carried out free of charge at a dealer service department.

If you are the new owner of a used vehicle which was subject to a recall and you want to be sure that the work has been carried out, it's best to contact a dealer service department and ask about your individual vehicle - you'll need to furnish them your Vehicle Identification Number (VIN).

The table below is based on information provided by the National Highway Traffic Safety Administration (NHTSA), the body which oversees vehicle recalls in the United States. The recall database is updated constantly. For the latest information on vehicle recalls, check the NHTSA website at www.nhtsa.gov, or call the NHTSA hotline at 1-888-327-4236.

Recall date	Recall campaign number	Model(s) affected	Concern
May 01, 2001	01V161000	2002 Acura TL	Sedans equipped with an "auto-up" power window feature on the driver's door. The driver's side power window control unit can fail, and depending on the failure mode, the window could become inoperative, open or close independent of switch activation, or the auto reverse system may not operate. The auto-reverse system failure could result in occupant injury.
Aug 09, 2001	01V166002	2001 Acura TL	The following vehicles were repaired with incorrect parts: 2002 Acura 3.2TL sedans with replacement buckles installed per recall 01V-166001; certain 2000 Acura 3.2TL vehicles with replacement buckles installed as product update repairs; and certain 2000-2002 Acura 3.2TL vehicles with replacement buckles installed as warranty or collision repairs. Repairs were made from March 9 through July 27, 2001. Some of the noncompliant buckles were mislabeled and redistributed to Acura dealers to be used as recall repair parts. Also, incorrect front seat belt buckle replacement parts were used for some product update repairs of 2000 Acura 3.2TL vehicles, and warranty or collision repairs of 2000-2002 3.2TL vehicles. These seat belt buckles may not comply with requirements of FMVSS no. 209, "Seat Belt Assemblies." In the event of a crash, the seat occupant may not be properly restrained.

Recall date	Recall campaign number	Model(s) affected	Concern
Mar 12, 2002	02V080000	2000 Acura TL	On certain passenger vehicles, a component in the inflator of some passenger airbag modules was not welded properly. As a result, the affected airbags may not deploy correctly in a crash, increasing the risk of injury to a front seat passenger.
May 13, 2002	02V120000	1999 Acura TL	On some vehicles, electrical contacts in the ignition switch can degrade due to the high electrical current passing through the switch when the vehicle is started. Worn contacts could cause the engine to stall without warning, increasing the risk of a crash.
Aug 21, 2002	02V226000	2003 Acura TL	On some vehicles, a timing belt tensioner pulley on the water pump is misaligned and could cause the timing belt to contact a bolt on the cylinder head. Eventually the belt could be damaged and fail. If the timing belt breaks, the engine will stall, increasing the risk of a crash.
Oct 24, 2003	03V423000	1999 Acura TL	On some vehicles, the ignition switch may wear excessively and prevent proper interlock operation, making it possible to turn the ignition key to the "OFF" position and remove the key without shifting the transmission to "PARK." If the vehicle operator does not shift to "PARK" before removing the key and fails to engage the parking brake, the vehicle could roll and a crash could occur.
Apr 13, 2004	04V176000	2001 Acura TL	On some vehicles, certain operating conditions can result in heat build-up between the countershaft and secondary shaft second gears in the automatic transmission, eventually leading to gear tooth chipping or gear breakage. gear failure could result in transmission lockup, which could result in a crash.
Jan 27, 2005	05V025000	1999, 2000 Acura TL	On some vehicles, the interlock operation of the ignition switch may not function properly, making it possible to turn the ignition key to the "OFF" position and remove the key without shifting the transmission to "PARK". If the driver does not shift to "PARK" before removing the key and fails to engage the parking brake, the vehicle could roll and a crash could occur.
Mar 29, 2005	05V132000	2005 Acura TL	On some vehicles, a loose terminal in the main fuse box may cause the fuel pump to lose power. If the fuel pump becomes inoperative, the engine may not start. If the fuel pump loses power while driving, the engine could stall without warning which could result in a crash.

Recall date	Recall campaign number	Model(s) affected	Concern
Nov 02, 2005	05V510000	2006 Acura TL	On some vehicles, on the frontal airbag system where the two external impact sensors are mounted, near the front headlights, the front impact sensor bolts were not properly torqued. If the bolts loosen or fall out, the sensor may fail to properly detect a crash, possibly resulting in delayed or non-deployment of the front airbag, increasing the risk of injury.
Jul 25, 2006	06V270000	2006 Acura TL	On some vehicles, the owner's manuals contain incorrect contact information for the National Highway Traffic Safety Administration's (NHTSA) vehicle safety hotline. The language in the owner's manuals is not in accordance with the current mandatory requirements.
Mar 13, 2007	07V097000	2005 Acura TL	On certain vehicles, a coil wire inside the fuel pump relay may break, causing the fuel pump to lose power. If the fuel pump becomes inoperative, the engine may not start. If the fuel pump loses power while driving, the engine could stall without warning, and a crash could occur.
Feb 26, 2008	08V091000	2004, 2005, 2006, 2007 and 2008 Acura TL	On some 2004-2008 Acura TL vehicles, prolonged high under-hood temperatures may cause the power steering hose to deteriorate prematurely, causing the hose to crack and leak power steering fluid. Power steering fluid leaking onto a hot catalytic converter will generate smoke and possibly lead to an under-hood fire.
Feb 26, 2008	08V092000	2004 and 2005 Acura TL	On some 2004-2005 Acura TL vehicles, if water enters the windshield wiper motor breather port, which is designed to allow the motor to vent warm air during normal operation, it can result in corrosion inside the motor housing. This could cause a failure of the electrical circuit breaker inside the motor housing. If the circuit breaker fails, it will cause the windshield wiper motor to become inoperative, which can increase the likelihood of a crash in certain conditions.

Buying parts

Replacement parts are available from many sources, which generally fall into one of two categories - authorized dealer parts departments and independent retail auto parts stores. Our advice concerning these parts is as follows:

Retail auto parts stores: Good auto parts stores will stock frequently needed components which wear out relatively fast, such as clutch components, exhaust systems, brake parts, tune-up parts, etc. These stores often supply new or reconditioned parts on an exchange basis, which can save a considerable amount of money. Discount auto parts stores are often very good places to buy materials and parts needed for general vehicle maintenance such as oil, grease, filters, spark plugs, belts, touch-up paint, bulbs, etc. They also usually sell tools and general accessories, have convenient hours, charge lower prices and can often be found not far from home.

Authorized dealer parts department: This is the best source for parts which are unique to the vehicle and not generally available elsewhere (such as major engine parts, transmission parts, trim pieces, etc.).

Warranty information: If the vehicle is still covered under warranty, be sure that any replacement parts purchased - regardless of the source - do not invalidate the warranty!

To be sure of obtaining the correct parts, have engine and chassis numbers available and, if possible, take the old parts along for positive identification.

Maintenance techniques, tools and working facilities

Maintenance techniques

There are a number of techniques involved in maintenance and repair that will be referred to throughout this manual. Application of these techniques will enable the home mechanic to be more efficient, better organized and capable of performing the various tasks properly, which will ensure that the repair job is thorough and complete.

Fasteners

Fasteners are nuts, bolts, studs and screws used to hold two or more parts together. There are a few things to keep in mind when working with fasteners. Almost all of them use a locking device of some type, either a lockwasher, locknut, locking tab or thread adhesive. All threaded fasteners should be clean and straight, with undamaged threads and undamaged corners on the hex head where the wrench fits. Develop the habit of replacing all damaged nuts and bolts with new ones. Special locknuts with nylon or fiber inserts can only be used once. If they are removed, they lose their locking ability and must be replaced with new ones.

Rusted nuts and bolts should be treated with a penetrating fluid to ease removal and prevent breakage. Some mechanics use turpentine in a spout-type oil can, which works quite well. After applying the rust penetrant, let it work for a few minutes before trying to loosen the nut or bolt. Badly rusted fasteners may have to be chiseled or sawed off or removed with a special nut breaker, available at tool stores.

If a bolt or stud breaks off in an assembly, it can be drilled and removed with a special tool commonly available for this purpose. Most automotive machine shops can perform this task, as well as other repair procedures, such as the repair of threaded holes that have been stripped out.

Flat washers and lockwashers, when removed from an assembly, should always be replaced exactly as removed. Replace any damaged washers with new ones. Never use a lockwasher on any soft metal surface (such as aluminum), thin sheet metal or plastic.

Fastener sizes

For a number of reasons, automobile manufacturers are making wider and wider use of metric fasteners. Therefore, it is important to be able to tell the difference between standard (sometimes called U.S. or SAE) and metric hardware, since they cannot be interchanged.

All bolts, whether standard or metric, are sized according to diameter, thread pitch and length. For example, a standard 1/2 - 13 x 1 bolt is 1/2 inch in diameter, has 13 threads per inch and is 1 inch long. An M12 - 1.75 x 25 metric bolt is 12 mm in diameter, has a thread pitch of 1.75 mm (the distance between threads) and is 25 mm long. The two bolts are nearly identical, and easily confused, but they are not interchangeable.

In addition to the differences in diameter, thread pitch and length, metric and standard bolts can also be distinguished by examining the bolt heads. To begin with, the distance across the flats on a standard bolt head is measured in inches, while the same dimension on a metric bolt is sized in millimeters (the same is true for nuts). As a result, a standard wrench should not be used on a metric bolt and a metric wrench should not be used on a standard bolt. Also, most standard bolts have slashes radiating out from the center of the head to denote the grade or strength of the bolt, which is an indication of the amount of torque that can be applied to it. The greater the number of slashes, the greater the strength of the bolt. Grades 0 through 5 are commonly used on automobiles. Metric bolts have a property class (grade) number, rather than a slash, molded into their heads to indicate bolt strength. In this case, the higher the number, the stronger the bolt. Property class numbers 8.8, 9.8 and 10.9 are commonly used on automobiles.

Strength markings can also be used to distinguish standard hex nuts from metric hex nuts. Many standard nuts have dots stamped into one side, while metric nuts are marked with a number. The greater the number of dots, or the higher the number, the greater the strength of the nut.

Metric studs are also marked on their ends according to property class (grade). Larger studs are numbered (the same as metric bolts), while smaller studs carry a geometric code to denote grade.

It should be noted that many fasteners, especially Grades 0 through 2, have no distinguishing marks on them. When such is the case, the only way to determine whether it is standard or metric is to measure the thread pitch or compare it to a known fastener of the same size.

Standard fasteners are often referred to as SAE, as opposed to metric. However, it should be noted that SAE technically refers to a non-metric fine thread fastener only. Coarse thread non-metric fasteners are referred to as USS sizes.

Since fasteners of the same size (both standard and metric) may have different strength ratings, be sure to reinstall any bolts, studs or nuts removed from your vehicle in their original locations. Also, when replacing a fastener with a new one, make sure that the new one has a strength rating equal to or greater than the original.

Tightening sequences and procedures

Most threaded fasteners should be tightened to a specific torque value (torque is the twisting force applied to a threaded component such as a nut or bolt). Overtightening the fastener can weaken it and cause it to break, while undertightening can cause it to eventually come loose. Bolts, screws and studs, depending on the material they are made of and their thread diameters, have specific torque values, many of which are noted in the Specifications at the beginning of each Chapter. Be sure to follow the torque recommendations closely. For fasteners not assigned a

Grade 1 or 2   Grade 5   Grade 8

Bolt strength marking (standard/SAE/USS; bottom - metric)

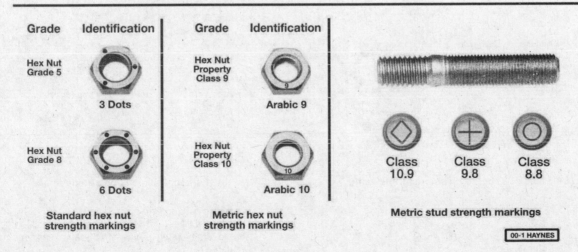

Grade	Identification
Hex Nut Grade 5	3 Dots
Hex Nut Grade 8	6 Dots

Standard hex nut strength markings

Grade	Identification
Hex Nut Property Class 9	Arabic 9
Hex Nut Property Class 10	Arabic 10

Metric hex nut strength markings

Class 10.9   Class 9.8   Class 8.8

Metric stud strength markings

00-1 HAYNES

specific torque, a general torque value chart is presented here as a guide. These torque values are for dry (unlubricated) fasteners threaded into steel or cast iron (not aluminum). As was previously mentioned, the size and grade of a fastener determine the amount of torque that can safely be applied to it. The figures listed here are approximate for Grade 2 and Grade 3 fasteners. Higher grades can tolerate higher torque values.

Fasteners laid out in a pattern, such as cylinder head bolts, oil pan bolts, differential cover bolts, etc., must be loosened or tightened in sequence to avoid warping the component. This sequence will normally be shown in the appropriate Chapter. If a specific pattern is not given, the following procedures can be used to prevent warping.

Initially, the bolts or nuts should be assembled finger-tight only. Next, they should be tightened one full turn each, in a criss-cross or diagonal pattern. After each one has been tightened one full turn, return to the first one and tighten them all one-half turn, following the same pattern. Finally, tighten each of them one-quarter turn at a time until each fastener has been tightened to the proper torque. To loosen and remove the fasteners, the procedure would be reversed.

Component disassembly

Component disassembly should be done with care and purpose to help ensure that

Metric thread sizes	Ft-lbs	Nm
M-6	6 to 9	9 to 12
M-8	14 to 21	19 to 28
M-10	28 to 40	38 to 54
M-12	50 to 71	68 to 96
M-14	80 to 140	109 to 154
Pipe thread sizes		
1/8	5 to 8	7 to 10
1/4	12 to 18	17 to 24
3/8	22 to 33	30 to 44
1/2	25 to 35	34 to 47
U.S. thread sizes		
1/4 - 20	6 to 9	9 to 12
5/16 - 18	12 to 18	17 to 24
5/16 - 24	14 to 20	19 to 27
3/8 - 16	22 to 32	30 to 43
3/8 - 24	27 to 38	37 to 51
7/16 - 14	40 to 55	55 to 74
7/16 - 20	40 to 60	55 to 81
1/2 - 13	55 to 80	75 to 108

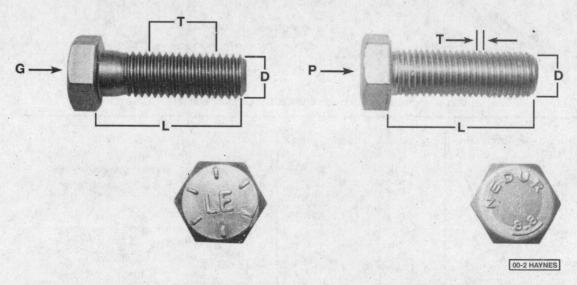

Standard (SAE and USS) bolt dimensions/grade marks

G   Grade marks (bolt strength)
L   Length (in inches)
T   Thread pitch (number of threads per inch)
D   Nominal diameter (in inches)

Metric bolt dimensions/grade marks

P   Property class (bolt strength)
L   Length (in millimeters)
T   Thread pitch (distance between threads in millimeters)
D   Diameter

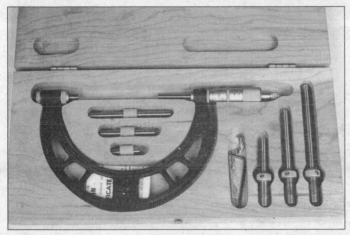

Micrometer set

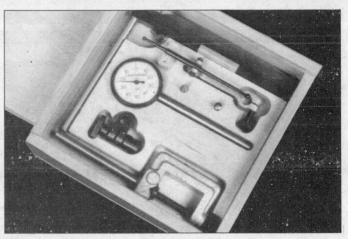

Dial indicator set

the parts go back together properly. Always keep track of the sequence in which parts are removed. Make note of special characteristics or marks on parts that can be installed more than one way, such as a grooved thrust washer on a shaft. It is a good idea to lay the disassembled parts out on a clean surface in the order that they were removed. It may also be helpful to make sketches or take instant photos of components before removal.

When removing fasteners from a component, keep track of their locations. Sometimes threading a bolt back in a part, or putting the washers and nut back on a stud, can prevent mix-ups later. If nuts and bolts cannot be returned to their original locations, they should be kept in a compartmented box or a series of small boxes. A cupcake or muffin tin is ideal for this purpose, since each cavity can hold the bolts and nuts from a particular area (i.e. oil pan bolts, valve cover bolts, engine mount bolts, etc.). A pan of this type is especially helpful when working on assemblies with very small parts, such as the carburetor, alternator, valve train or interior dash and trim pieces. The cavities can be marked with paint or tape to identify the contents.

Whenever wiring looms, harnesses or connectors are separated, it is a good idea to identify the two halves with numbered pieces of masking tape so they can be easily reconnected.

Gasket sealing surfaces

Throughout any vehicle, gaskets are used to seal the mating surfaces between two parts and keep lubricants, fluids, vacuum or pressure contained in an assembly.

Many times these gaskets are coated with a liquid or paste-type gasket sealing compound before assembly. Age, heat and pressure can sometimes cause the two parts to stick together so tightly that they are very difficult to separate. Often, the assembly can be loosened by striking it with a soft-face hammer near the mating surfaces. A regular hammer can be used if a block of wood is placed between the hammer and the part. Do

not hammer on cast parts or parts that could be easily damaged. With any particularly stubborn part, always recheck to make sure that every fastener has been removed.

Avoid using a screwdriver or bar to pry apart an assembly, as they can easily mar the gasket sealing surfaces of the parts, which must remain smooth. If prying is absolutely necessary, use an old broom handle, but keep in mind that extra clean up will be necessary if the wood splinters.

After the parts are separated, the old gasket must be carefully scraped off and the gasket surfaces cleaned. Stubborn gasket material can be soaked with rust penetrant or treated with a special chemical to soften it so it can be easily scraped off. **Caution:** *Never use gasket removal solutions or caustic chemicals on plastic or other composite components.* A scraper can be fashioned from a piece of copper tubing by flattening and sharpening one end. Copper is recommended because it is usually softer than the surfaces to be scraped, which reduces the chance of gouging the part. Some gaskets can be removed with a wire brush, but regardless of the method used, the mating surfaces must be left clean and smooth. If for some reason the gasket surface is gouged, then a gasket sealer thick enough to fill scratches will have to be used during reassembly of the components. For most applications, a non-drying (or semi-drying) gasket sealer should be used.

Hose removal tips

Warning: *If the vehicle is equipped with air conditioning, do not disconnect any of the A/C hoses without first having the system depressurized by a dealer service department or a service station.*

Hose removal precautions closely parallel gasket removal precautions. Avoid scratching or gouging the surface that the hose mates against or the connection may leak. This is especially true for radiator hoses. Because of various chemical reactions, the rubber in hoses can bond itself to the metal spigot that the hose fits over. To remove

a hose, first loosen the hose clamps that secure it to the spigot. Then, with slip-joint pliers, grab the hose at the clamp and rotate it around the spigot. Work it back and forth until it is completely free, then pull it off. Silicone or other lubricants will ease removal if they can be applied between the hose and the outside of the spigot. Apply the same lubricant to the inside of the hose and the outside of the spigot to simplify installation.

As a last resort (and if the hose is to be replaced with a new one anyway), the rubber can be slit with a knife and the hose peeled from the spigot. If this must be done, be careful that the metal connection is not damaged.

If a hose clamp is broken or damaged, do not reuse it. Wire-type clamps usually weaken with age, so it is a good idea to replace them with screw-type clamps whenever a hose is removed.

Tools

A selection of good tools is a basic requirement for anyone who plans to maintain and repair his or her own vehicle. For the owner who has few tools, the initial investment might seem high, but when compared to the spiraling costs of professional auto maintenance and repair, it is a wise one.

To help the owner decide which tools are needed to perform the tasks detailed in this manual, the following tool lists are offered: *Maintenance and minor repair, Repair/overhaul* and *Special.*

The newcomer to practical mechanics should start off with the *maintenance and minor repair* tool kit, which is adequate for the simpler jobs performed on a vehicle. Then, as confidence and experience grow, the owner can tackle more difficult tasks, buying additional tools as they are needed. Eventually the basic kit will be expanded into the *repair and overhaul* tool set. Over a period of time, the experienced do-it-yourselfer will assemble a tool set complete enough for most repair and overhaul procedures and will add tools from the special category when it is felt that the expense is justified by the frequency of use.

Dial caliper

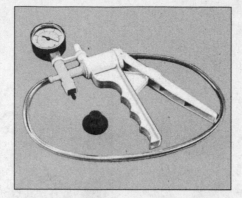

Hand-operated vacuum pump

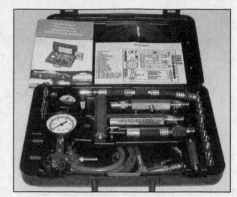

Fuel pressure gauge set

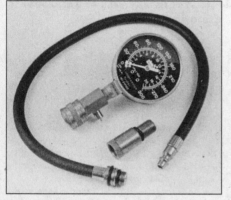

Compression gauge with spark plug
hole adapter

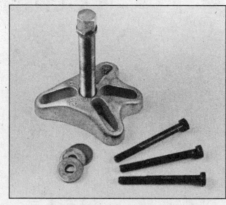

Damper/steering wheel puller

General purpose puller

Hydraulic lifter removal tool

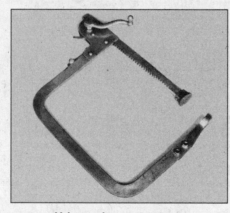

Valve spring compressor

Valve spring compressor

Ridge reamer

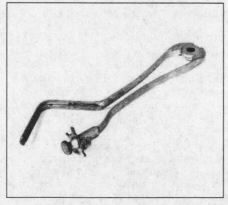

Piston ring groove cleaning tool

Ring removal/installation tool

Ring compressor

Cylinder hone

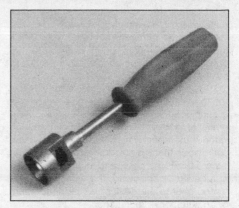

Brake hold-down spring tool

Torque angle gauge

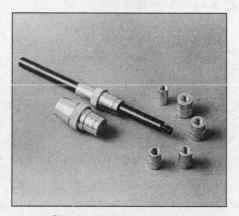

Clutch plate alignment tool

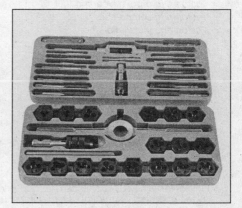

Tap and die set

Maintenance and minor repair tool kit

The tools in this list should be considered the minimum required for performance of routine maintenance, servicing and minor repair work. We recommend the purchase of combination wrenches (box-end and open-end combined in one wrench). While more expensive than open end wrenches, they offer the advantages of both types of wrench.

> Combination wrench set (1/4-inch to 1 inch or 6 mm to 19 mm)
> Adjustable wrench, 8 inch
> Spark plug wrench with rubber insert
> Spark plug gap adjusting tool
> Feeler gauge set
> Brake bleeder wrench
> Standard screwdriver (5/16-inch x 6 inch)
> Phillips screwdriver (No. 2 x 6 inch)
> Combination pliers - 6 inch
> Hacksaw and assortment of blades
> Tire pressure gauge
> Grease gun
> Oil can
> Fine emery cloth
> Wire brush
> Battery post and cable cleaning tool
> Oil filter wrench
> Funnel (medium size)
> Safety goggles
> Jackstands (2)
> Drain pan

Note: *If basic tune-ups are going to be part of routine maintenance, it will be necessary to purchase a good quality stroboscopic timing light and combination tachometer/dwell meter. Although they are included in the list of special tools, it is mentioned here because they are absolutely necessary for tuning most vehicles properly.*

Repair and overhaul tool set

These tools are essential for anyone who plans to perform major repairs and are in addition to those in the maintenance and minor repair tool kit. Included is a comprehensive set of sockets which, though expensive, are invaluable because of their versatility, especially when various extensions and drives are available. We recommend the 1/2-inch drive over the 3/8-inch drive. Although the larger drive is bulky and more expensive, it has the capacity of accepting a very wide range of large sockets. Ideally, however, the mechanic should have a 3/8-inch drive set and a 1/2-inch drive set.

> Socket set(s)
> Reversible ratchet
> Extension - 10 inch
> Universal joint
> Torque wrench (same size drive as sockets)
> Ball peen hammer - 8 ounce
> Soft-face hammer (plastic/rubber)
> Standard screwdriver (1/4-inch x 6 inch)

> Standard screwdriver (stubby - 5/16-inch)
> Phillips screwdriver (No. 3 x 8 inch)
> Phillips screwdriver (stubby - No. 2)
> Pliers - vise grip
> Pliers - lineman's
> Pliers - needle nose
> Pliers - snap-ring (internal and external)
> Cold chisel - 1/2-inch
> Scribe
> Scraper (made from flattened copper tubing)
> Centerpunch
> Pin punches (1/16, 1/8, 3/16-inch)
> Steel rule/straightedge - 12 inch
> Allen wrench set (1/8 to 3/8-inch or 4 mm to 10 mm)
> A selection of files
> Wire brush (large)
> Jackstands (second set)
> Jack (scissor or hydraulic type)

Note: *Another tool which is often useful is an electric drill with a chuck capacity of 3/8-inch and a set of good quality drill bits.*

Special tools

The tools in this list include those which are not used regularly, are expensive to buy, or which need to be used in accordance with their manufacturer's instructions. Unless these tools will be used frequently, it is not very economical to purchase many of them. A consideration would be to split the cost and use between yourself and a friend or friends. In addition, most of these tools can be obtained from a tool rental shop on a temporary basis.

This list primarily contains only those tools and instruments widely available to the public, and not those special tools produced by the vehicle manufacturer for distribution to dealer service departments. Occasionally, references to the manufacturer's special tools are included in the text of this manual. Generally, an alternative method of doing the job without the special tool is offered. However, sometimes there is no alternative to their use. Where this is the case, and the tool cannot be purchased or borrowed, the work should be turned over to the dealer service department or an automotive repair shop.

Valve spring compressor
Piston ring groove cleaning tool
Piston ring compressor
Piston ring installation tool
Cylinder compression gauge
Cylinder ridge reamer
Cylinder surfacing hone
Cylinder bore gauge
Micrometers and/or dial calipers
Hydraulic lifter removal tool
Balljoint separator
Universal-type puller
Impact screwdriver
Dial indicator set
Stroboscopic timing light (inductive pick-up)
Hand operated vacuum/pressure pump
Tachometer/dwell meter
Universal electrical multimeter
Cable hoist
Brake spring removal and installation tools
Floor jack

Buying tools

For the do-it-yourselfer who is just starting to get involved in vehicle maintenance and repair, there are a number of options available when purchasing tools. If maintenance and minor repair is the extent of the work to be done, the purchase of individual tools is satisfactory. If, on the other hand, extensive work is planned, it would be a good idea to purchase a modest tool set from one of the large retail chain stores. A set can usually be bought at a substantial savings over the individual tool prices, and they often come with a tool box. As additional tools are needed, add-on sets, individual tools and a larger tool box can be purchased to expand the tool selection. Building a tool set gradually allows the cost of the tools to be spread over a longer period of time and gives the mechanic the freedom to choose only those tools that will actually be used.

Tool stores will often be the only source of some of the special tools that are needed, but regardless of where tools are bought, try to avoid cheap ones, especially when buying screwdrivers and sockets, because they won't last very long. The expense involved in replacing cheap tools will eventually be greater than the initial cost of quality tools.

Care and maintenance of tools

Good tools are expensive, so it makes sense to treat them with respect. Keep them clean and in usable condition and store them properly when not in use. Always wipe off any dirt, grease or metal chips before putting them away. Never leave tools lying around in the work area. Upon completion of a job, always check closely under the hood for tools that may have been left there so they won't get lost during a test drive.

Some tools, such as screwdrivers, pliers, wrenches and sockets, can be hung on a panel mounted on the garage or workshop wall, while others should be kept in a tool box or tray. Measuring instruments, gauges, meters, etc. must be carefully stored where they cannot be damaged by weather or impact from other tools.

When tools are used with care and stored properly, they will last a very long time. Even with the best of care, though, tools will wear out if used frequently. When a tool is damaged or worn out, replace it. Subsequent jobs will be safer and more enjoyable if you do.

How to repair damaged threads

Sometimes, the internal threads of a nut or bolt hole can become stripped, usually from overtightening. Stripping threads is an all-too-common occurrence, especially when working with aluminum parts, because aluminum is so soft that it easily strips out.

Usually, external or internal threads are only partially stripped. After they've been cleaned up with a tap or die, they'll still work. Sometimes, however, threads are badly damaged. When this happens, you've got three choices:

1) *Drill and tap the hole to the next suitable oversize and install a larger diameter bolt, screw or stud.*
2) *Drill and tap the hole to accept a threaded plug, then drill and tap the plug to the original screw size. You can also buy a plug already threaded to the original size. Then you simply drill a hole to the specified size, then run the threaded plug into the hole with a bolt and jam nut. Once the plug is fully seated, remove the jam nut and bolt.*
3) *The third method uses a patented thread repair kit like Heli-Coil or Slimsert. These*

easy-to-use kits are designed to repair damaged threads in straight-through holes and blind holes. Both are available as kits which can handle a variety of sizes and thread patterns. Drill the hole, then tap it with the special included tap. Install the Heli-Coil and the hole is back to its original diameter and thread pitch.

Regardless of which method you use, be sure to proceed calmly and carefully. A little impatience or carelessness during one of these relatively simple procedures can ruin your whole day's work and cost you a bundle if you wreck an expensive part.

Working facilities

Not to be overlooked when discussing tools is the workshop. If anything more than routine maintenance is to be carried out, some sort of suitable work area is essential.

It is understood, and appreciated, that many home mechanics do not have a good workshop or garage available, and end up removing an engine or doing major repairs outside. It is recommended, however, that the overhaul or repair be completed under the cover of a roof.

A clean, flat workbench or table of comfortable working height is an absolute necessity. The workbench should be equipped with a vise that has a jaw opening of at least four inches.

As mentioned previously, some clean, dry storage space is also required for tools, as well as the lubricants, fluids, cleaning solvents, etc. which soon become necessary.

Sometimes waste oil and fluids, drained from the engine or cooling system during normal maintenance or repairs, present a disposal problem. To avoid pouring them on the ground or into a sewage system, pour the used fluids into large containers, seal them with caps and take them to an authorized disposal site or recycling center. Plastic jugs, such as old antifreeze containers, are ideal for this purpose.

Always keep a supply of old newspapers and clean rags available. Old towels are excellent for mopping up spills. Many mechanics use rolls of paper towels for most work because they are readily available and disposable. To help keep the area under the vehicle clean, a large cardboard box can be cut open and flattened to protect the garage or shop floor.

Whenever working over a painted surface, such as when leaning over a fender to service something under the hood, always cover it with an old blanket or bedspread to protect the finish. Vinyl covered pads, made especially for this purpose, are available at auto parts stores.

Jacking and towing

Jacking

The jack supplied with the vehicle should only be used for raising the vehicle for changing a tire or placing jackstands under the frame. **Warning:** *Never crawl under the vehicle or start the engine when the jack is being used as the only means of support.*

All models are supplied with a scissors-type jack. When jacking the vehicle, it should be engaged with the rocker panel flange, in the area indicated by an arrow stamped into the flange (see illustration).

The vehicle should be on level ground with the wheels blocked and the transmission in Park. Pry off the hub cap (if equipped) using the tapered end of the lug wrench. Loosen the lug nuts one-half turn and leave them in place until the wheel is raised off the ground.

Place the jack under the side of the vehicle in the indicated position. Use the supplied wrench to turn the jackscrew clockwise until the wheel is raised off the ground. Remove the lug nuts, pull off the wheel and install the spare.

With the beveled side in, install the lug nuts and tighten them until snug. Lower the vehicle by turning the jackscrew counterclock-

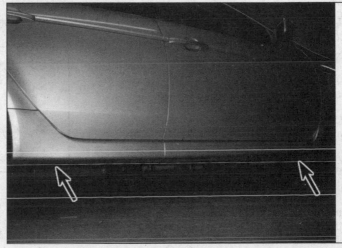

The jack fits over the rocker panel flange (there are two jacking points on each side of the vehicle)

wise. Remove the jack and tighten the nuts in a diagonal pattern to the torque listed in the Chapter 1 Specifications. If a torque wrench is not available, have the torque checked by a service station as soon as possible. Install the hubcap by placing it in position and using the heel of your hand or a rubber mallet to seat it.

Towing

The manufacturer states that the only safe way to tow these vehicles is with a flatbed-type car carrier. Other methods could cause damage to the drivetrain.

Booster battery (jump) starting

Observe the following precautions when using a booster battery to start a vehicle:

a) *Before connecting the booster battery, make sure the ignition switch is in the Off position.*
b) *Turn off the lights, heater and other electrical loads.*
c) *Your eyes should be shielded. Safety goggles are a good idea.*
d) *Make sure the booster battery is the same voltage as the dead one in the vehicle.*
e) *The two vehicles MUST NOT TOUCH each other.*
f) *Make sure the transmission is in Neutral (manual) or Park (automatic).*
g) *If the booster battery is not a maintenance-free type, remove the vent caps and lay a cloth over the vent holes.*

Connect the red jumper cable to the positive (+) terminals of each battery.

Connect one end of the black cable to the negative (-) terminal of the booster battery. The other end of this cable should be connected to a good ground on the engine block **(see illustration)**. Make sure the cable will not come into contact with the fan, drivebelts or other moving parts of the engine.

Start the engine using the booster battery, then, with the engine running at idle speed, disconnect the jumper cables in the reverse order of connection.

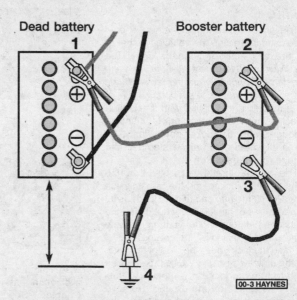

Make the booster battery cable connections in the numerical order shown (note that the negative cable of the booster battery is NOT attached to the negative terminal of the dead battery)

Automotive chemicals and lubricants

A number of automotive chemicals and lubricants are available for use during vehicle maintenance and repair. They include a wide variety of products ranging from cleaning solvents and degreasers to lubricants and protective sprays for rubber, plastic and vinyl.

Cleaners

Carburetor cleaner and choke cleaner is a strong solvent for gum, varnish and carbon. Most carburetor cleaners leave a dry-type lubricant film which will not harden or gum up. Because of this film it is not recommended for use on electrical components.

Brake system cleaner is used to remove brake dust, grease and brake fluid from the brake system, where clean surfaces are absolutely necessary. It leaves no residue and often eliminates brake squeal caused by contaminants.

Electrical cleaner removes oxidation, corrosion and carbon deposits from electrical contacts, restoring full current flow. It can also be used to clean spark plugs, carburetor jets, voltage regulators and other parts where an oil-free surface is desired.

Demoisturants remove water and moisture from electrical components such as alternators, voltage regulators, electrical connectors and fuse blocks. They are non-conductive and non-corrosive.

Degreasers are heavy-duty solvents used to remove grease from the outside of the engine and from chassis components. They can be sprayed or brushed on and, depending on the type, are rinsed off either with water or solvent.

Lubricants

Motor oil is the lubricant formulated for use in engines. It normally contains a wide variety of additives to prevent corrosion and reduce foaming and wear. Motor oil comes in various weights (viscosity ratings) from 0 to 50. The recommended weight of the oil depends on the season, temperature and the demands on the engine. Light oil is used in cold climates and under light load conditions. Heavy oil is used in hot climates and where high loads are encountered. Multi-viscosity oils are designed to have characteristics of both light and heavy oils and are available in a number of weights from 0W-20 to 20W-50.

Gear oil is designed to be used in differentials, manual transmissions and other areas where high-temperature lubrication is required.

Chassis and wheel bearing grease is a heavy grease used where increased loads and friction are encountered, such as for wheel bearings, balljoints, tie-rod ends and universal joints.

High-temperature wheel bearing grease is designed to withstand the extreme temperatures encountered by wheel bearings in disc brake equipped vehicles. It usually contains molybdenum disulfide (moly), which is a dry-type lubricant.

White grease is a heavy grease for metal-to-metal applications where water is a problem. White grease stays soft under both low and high temperatures (usually from -100 to +190-degrees F), and will not wash off or dilute in the presence of water.

Assembly lube is a special extreme pressure lubricant, usually containing moly, used to lubricate high-load parts (such as main and rod bearings and cam lobes) for initial start-up of a new engine. The assembly lube lubricates the parts without being squeezed out or washed away until the engine oiling system begins to function.

Silicone lubricants are used to protect rubber, plastic, vinyl and nylon parts.

Graphite lubricants are used where oils cannot be used due to contamination problems, such as in locks. The dry graphite will lubricate metal parts while remaining uncontaminated by dirt, water, oil or acids. It is electrically conductive and will not foul electrical contacts in locks such as the ignition switch.

Moly penetrants loosen and lubricate frozen, rusted and corroded fasteners and prevent future rusting or freezing.

Heat-sink grease is a special electrically non-conductive grease that is used for mounting electronic ignition modules where it is essential that heat is transferred away from the module.

Sealants

RTV sealant is one of the most widely used gasket compounds. Made from silicone, RTV is air curing, it seals, bonds, waterproofs, fills surface irregularities, remains flexible, doesn't shrink, is relatively easy to remove, and is used as a supplementary sealer with almost all low and medium temperature gaskets.

Anaerobic sealant is much like RTV in that it can be used either to seal gaskets or to form gaskets by itself. It remains flexible, is solvent resistant and fills surface imperfections. The difference between an anaerobic sealant and an RTV-type sealant is in the curing. RTV cures when exposed to air, while an anaerobic sealant cures only in the absence of air. This means that an anaerobic sealant cures only after the assembly of parts, sealing them together.

Thread and pipe sealant is used for sealing hydraulic and pneumatic fittings and vacuum lines. It is usually made from a Teflon compound, and comes in a spray, a paint-on liquid and as a wrap-around tape.

Chemicals

Anti-seize compound prevents seizing, galling, cold welding, rust and corrosion in fasteners. High-temperature ant-seize, usually made with copper and graphite lubricants, is used for exhaust system and exhaust manifold bolts.

Anaerobic locking compounds are used to keep fasteners from vibrating or working loose and cure only after installation, in the absence of air. Medium strength locking compound is used for small nuts, bolts and screws that may be removed later. High-strength locking compound is for large nuts, bolts and studs which aren't removed on a regular basis.

Oil additives range from viscosity index improvers to chemical treatments that claim to reduce internal engine friction. It should be noted that most oil manufacturers caution against using additives with their oils.

Gas additives perform several functions, depending on their chemical makeup. They usually contain solvents that help dissolve gum and varnish that build up on carburetor, fuel injection and intake parts. They also serve to break down carbon deposits that form on the inside surfaces of the combustion chambers. Some additives contain upper cylinder lubricants for valves and piston rings, and others contain chemicals to remove condensation from the gas tank.

Miscellaneous

Brake fluid is specially formulated hydraulic fluid that can withstand the heat and pressure encountered in brake systems. Care must be taken so this fluid does not come in contact with painted surfaces or plastics. An opened container should always be resealed to prevent contamination by water or dirt.

Weatherstrip adhesive is used to bond weatherstripping around doors, windows and trunk lids. It is sometimes used to attach trim pieces.

Undercoating is a petroleum-based, tar-like substance that is designed to protect metal surfaces on the underside of the vehicle from corrosion. It also acts as a sound-deadening agent by insulating the bottom of the vehicle.

Waxes and polishes are used to help protect painted and plated surfaces from the weather. Different types of paint may require the use of different types of wax and polish. Some polishes utilize a chemical or abrasive cleaner to help remove the top layer of oxidized (dull) paint on older vehicles. In recent years many non-wax polishes that contain a wide variety of chemicals such as polymers and silicones have been introduced. These non-wax polishes are usually easier to apply and last longer than conventional waxes and polishes.

Conversion factors

Length (distance)

Inches (in)	X	25.4	= Millimeters (mm)	X	0.0394	= Inches (in)
Feet (ft)	X	0.305	= Meters (m)	X	3.281	= Feet (ft)
Miles	X	1.609	= Kilometers (km)	X	0.621	= Miles

Volume (capacity)

Cubic inches (cu in; in³)	X	16.387	= Cubic centimeters (cc; cm³)	X	0.061	= Cubic inches (cu in; in³)
Imperial pints (Imp pt)	X	0.568	= Liters (l)	X	1.76	= Imperial pints (Imp pt)
Imperial quarts (Imp qt)	X	1.137	= Liters (l)	X	0.88	= Imperial quarts (Imp qt)
Imperial quarts (Imp qt)	X	1.201	= US quarts (US qt)	X	0.833	= Imperial quarts (Imp qt)
US quarts (US qt)	X	0.946	= Liters (l)	X	1.057	= US quarts (US qt)
Imperial gallons (Imp gal)	X	4.546	= Liters (l)	X	0.22	= Imperial gallons (Imp gal)
Imperial gallons (Imp gal)	X	1.201	= US gallons (US gal)	X	0.833	= Imperial gallons (Imp gal)
US gallons (US gal)	X	3.785	= Liters (l)	X	0.264	= US gallons (US gal)

Mass (weight)

Ounces (oz)	X	28.35	= Grams (g)	X	0.035	= Ounces (oz)
Pounds (lb)	X	0.454	= Kilograms (kg)	X	2.205	= Pounds (lb)

Force

Ounces-force (ozf; oz)	X	0.278	= Newtons (N)	X	3.6	= Ounces-force (ozf; oz)
Pounds-force (lbf; lb)	X	4.448	= Newtons (N)	X	0.225	= Pounds-force (lbf; lb)
Newtons (N)	X	0.1	= Kilograms-force (kgf; kg)	X	9.81	= Newtons (N)

Pressure

Pounds-force per square inch (psi; lbf/in²; lb/in²)	X	0.070	= Kilograms-force per square centimeter (kgf/cm²; kg/cm²)	X	14.223	= Pounds-force per square inch (psi; lbf/in²; lb/in²)
Pounds-force per square inch (psi; lbf/in²; lb/in²)	X	0.068	= Atmospheres (atm)	X	14.696	= Pounds-force per square inch (psi; lbf/in²; lb/in²)
Pounds-force per square inch (psi; lbf/in²; lb/in²)	X	0.069	= Bars	X	14.5	= Pounds-force per square inch (psi; lbf/in²; lb/in²)
Pounds-force per square inch (psi; lbf/in²; lb/in²)	X	6.895	= Kilopascals (kPa)	X	0.145	= Pounds-force per square inch (psi; lbf/in²; lb/in²)
Kilopascals (kPa)	X	0.01	= Kilograms-force per square centimeter (kgf/cm²; kg/cm²)	X	98.1	= Kilopascals (kPa)

Torque (moment of force)

Pounds-force inches (lbf in; lb in)	X	1.152	= Kilograms-force centimeter (kgf cm; kg cm)	X	0.868	= Pounds-force inches (lbf in; lb in)
Pounds-force inches (lbf in; lb in)	X	0.113	= Newton meters (Nm)	X	8.85	= Pounds-force inches (lbf in; lb in)
Pounds-force inches (lbf in; lb in)	X	0.083	= Pounds-force feet (lbf ft; lb ft)	X	12	= Pounds-force inches (lbf in; lb in)
Pounds-force feet (lbf ft; lb ft)	X	0.138	= Kilograms-force meters (kgf m; kg m)	X	7.233	= Pounds-force feet (lbf ft; lb ft)
Pounds-force feet (lbf ft; lb ft)	X	1.356	= Newton meters (Nm)	X	0.738	= Pounds-force feet (lbf ft; lb ft)
Newton meters (Nm)	X	0.102	= Kilograms-force meters (kgf m; kg m)	X	9.804	= Newton meters (Nm)

Vacuum

Inches mercury (in. Hg)	X	3.377	= Kilopascals (kPa)	X	0.2961	= Inches mercury
Inches mercury (in. Hg)	X	25.4	= Millimeters mercury (mm Hg)	X	0.0394	= Inches mercury

Power

Horsepower (hp)	X	745.7	= Watts (W)	X	0.0013	= Horsepower (hp)

Velocity (speed)

Miles per hour (miles/hr; mph)	X	1.609	= Kilometers per hour (km/hr; kph)	X	0.621	= Miles per hour (miles/hr; mph)

Fuel consumption*

Miles per gallon, Imperial (mpg)	X	0.354	= Kilometers per liter (km/l)	X	2.825	= Miles per gallon, Imperial (mpg)
Miles per gallon, US (mpg)	X	0.425	= Kilometers per liter (km/l)	X	2.352	= Miles per gallon, US (mpg)

Temperature

Degrees Fahrenheit = (°C x 1.8) + 32

Degrees Celsius (Degrees Centigrade; °C) = (°F - 32) x 0.56

*It is common practice to convert from miles per gallon (mpg) to liters/100 kilometers (l/100km), where mpg (Imperial) x l/100 km = 282 and mpg (US) x l/100 km = 235

DECIMALS to MILLIMETERS

Decimal	mm	Decimal	mm
0.001	0.0254	0.500	12.7000
0.002	0.0508	0.510	12.9540
0.003	0.0762	0.520	13.2080
0.004	0.1016	0.530	13.4620
0.005	0.1270	0.540	13.7160
0.006	0.1524	0.550	13.9700
0.007	0.1778	0.560	14.2240
0.008	0.2032	0.570	14.4780
0.009	0.2286	0.580	14.7320
		0.590	14.9860
0.010	0.2540		
0.020	0.5080		
0.030	0.7620		
0.040	1.0160	0.600	15.2400
0.050	1.2700	0.610	15.4940
0.060	1.5240	0.620	15.7480
0.070	1.7780	0.630	16.0020
0.080	2.0320	0.640	16.2560
0.090	2.2860	0.650	16.5100
		0.660	16.7640
0.100	2.5400	0.670	17.0180
0.110	2.7940	0.680	17.2720
0.120	3.0480	0.690	17.5260
0.130	3.3020		
0.140	3.5560		
0.150	3.8100		
0.160	4.0640	0.700	17.7800
0.170	4.3180	0.710	18.0340
0.180	4.5720	0.720	18.2880
0.190	4.8260	0.730	18.5420
		0.740	18.7960
0.200	5.0800	0.750	19.0500
0.210	5.3340	0.760	19.3040
0.220	5.5880	0.770	19.5580
0.230	5.8420	0.780	19.8120
0.240	6.0960	0.790	20.0660
0.250	6.3500		
0.260	6.6040		
0.270	6.8580	0.800	20.3200
0.280	7.1120	0.810	20.5740
0.290	7.3660	0.820	21.8280
		0.830	21.0820
0.300	7.6200	0.840	21.3360
0.310	7.8740	0.850	21.5900
0.320	8.1280	0.860	21.8440
0.330	8.3820	0.870	22.0980
0.340	8.6360	0.880	22.3520
0.350	8.8900	0.890	22.6060
0.360	9.1440		
0.370	9.3980		
0.380	9.6520		
0.390	9.9060		
		0.900	22.8600
0.400	10.1600	0.910	23.1140
0.410	10.4140	0.920	23.3680
0.420	10.6680	0.930	23.6220
0.430	10.9220	0.940	23.8760
0.440	11.1760	0.950	24.1300
0.450	11.4300	0.960	24.3840
0.460	11.6840	0.970	24.6380
0.470	11.9380	0.980	24.8920
0.480	12.1920	0.990	25.1460
0.490	12.4460	1.000	25.4000

FRACTIONS to DECIMALS to MILLIMETERS

Fraction	Decimal	mm	Fraction	Decimal	mm
1/64	0.0156	0.3969	33/64	0.5156	13.0969
1/32	0.0312	0.7938	17/32	0.5312	13.4938
3/64	0.0469	1.1906	35/64	0.5469	13.8906
1/16	0.0625	1.5875	9/16	0.5625	14.2875
5/64	0.0781	1.9844	37/64	0.5781	14.6844
3/32	0.0938	2.3812	19/32	0.5938	15.0812
7/64	0.1094	2.7781	39/64	0.6094	15.4781
1/8	0.1250	3.1750	5/8	0.6250	15.8750
9/64	0.1406	3.5719	41/64	0.6406	16.2719
5/32	0.1562	3.9688	21/32	0.6562	16.6688
11/64	0.1719	4.3656	43/64	0.6719	17.0656
3/16	0.1875	4.7625	11/16	0.6875	17.4625
13/64	0.2031	5.1594	45/64	0.7031	17.8594
7/32	0.2188	5.5562	23/32	0.7188	18.2562
15/64	0.2344	5.9531	47/64	0.7344	18.6531
1/4	0.2500	6.3500	3/4	0.7500	19.0500
17/64	0.2656	6.7469	49/64	0.7656	19.4469
9/32	0.2812	7.1438	25/32	0.7812	19.8438
19/64	0.2969	7.5406	51/64	0.7969	20.2406
5/16	0.3125	7.9375	13/16	0.8125	20.6375
21/64	0.3281	8.3344	53/64	0.8281	21.0344
11/32	0.3438	8.7312	27/32	0.8438	21.4312
23/64	0.3594	9.1281	55/64	0.8594	21.8281
3/8	0.3750	9.5250	7/8	0.8750	22.2250
25/64	0.3906	9.9219	57/64	0.8906	22.6219
13/32	0.4062	10.3188	29/32	0.9062	23.0188
27/64	0.4219	10.7156	59/64	0.9219	23.4156
7/16	0.4375	11.1125	15/16	0.9375	23.8125
29/64	0.4531	11.5094	61/64	0.9531	24.2094
15/32	0.4688	11.9062	31/32	0.9688	24.6062
31/64	0.4844	12.3031	63/64	0.9844	25.0031
1/2	0.5000	12.7000	1	1.0000	25.4000

Safety first!

Regardless of how enthusiastic you may be about getting on with the job at hand, take the time to ensure that your safety is not jeopardized. A moment's lack of attention can result in an accident, as can failure to observe certain simple safety precautions. The possibility of an accident will always exist, and the following points should not be considered a comprehensive list of all dangers. Rather, they are intended to make you aware of the risks and to encourage a safety conscious approach to all work you carry out on your vehicle.

Essential DOs and DON'Ts

DON'T rely on a jack when working under the vehicle. Always use approved jackstands to support the weight of the vehicle and place them under the recommended lift or support points.

DON'T attempt to loosen extremely tight fasteners (i.e. wheel lug nuts) while the vehicle is on a jack - it may fall.

DON'T start the engine without first making sure that the transmission is in Neutral (or Park where applicable) and the parking brake is set.

DON'T remove the radiator cap from a hot cooling system - let it cool or cover it with a cloth and release the pressure gradually.

DON'T attempt to drain the engine oil until you are sure it has cooled to the point that it will not burn you.

DON'T touch any part of the engine or exhaust system until it has cooled sufficiently to avoid burns.

DON'T siphon toxic liquids such as gasoline, antifreeze and brake fluid by mouth, or allow them to remain on your skin.

DON'T inhale brake lining dust - it is potentially hazardous (see *Asbestos* below).

DON'T allow spilled oil or grease to remain on the floor - wipe it up before someone slips on it.

DON'T use loose fitting wrenches or other tools which may slip and cause injury.

DON'T push on wrenches when loosening or tightening nuts or bolts. Always try to pull the wrench toward you. If the situation calls for pushing the wrench away, push with an open hand to avoid scraped knuckles if the wrench should slip.

DON'T attempt to lift a heavy component alone - get someone to help you.

DON'T *rush or take unsafe shortcuts to finish a job.*

DON'T allow children or animals in or around the vehicle while you are working on it.

DO wear eye protection when using power tools such as a drill, sander, bench grinder, etc. and when working under a vehicle.

DO keep loose clothing and long hair well out of the way of moving parts.

DO make sure that any hoist used has a safe working load rating adequate for the job.

DO get someone to check on you periodically when working alone on a vehicle.

DO carry out work in a logical sequence and make sure that everything is correctly assembled and tightened.

DO keep chemicals and fluids tightly capped and out of the reach of children and pets.

DO remember that your vehicle's safety affects that of yourself and others. If in doubt on any point, get professional advice.

Steering, suspension and brakes

These systems are essential to driving safety, so make sure you have a qualified shop or individual check your work. Also, compressed suspension springs can cause injury if released suddenly - be sure to use a spring compressor.

Airbags

Airbags are explosive devices that can **CAUSE** injury if they deploy while you're working on the vehicle. Follow the manufacturer's instructions to disable the airbag whenever you're working in the vicinity of airbag components.

Asbestos

Certain friction, insulating, sealing, and other products - such as brake linings, brake bands, clutch linings, torque converters, gaskets, etc. - may contain asbestos or other hazardous friction material. Extreme care must be taken to avoid inhalation of dust from such products, since it is hazardous to health. If in doubt, assume that they do contain asbestos.

Fire

Remember at all times that gasoline is highly flammable. Never smoke or have any kind of open flame around when working on a vehicle. But the risk does not end there. A spark caused by an electrical short circuit, by two metal surfaces contacting each other, or even by static electricity built up in your body under certain conditions, can ignite gasoline vapors, which in a confined space are highly explosive. Do not, under any circumstances, use gasoline for cleaning parts. Use an approved safety solvent.

Always disconnect the battery ground (-) cable at the battery before working on any part of the fuel system or electrical system. Never risk spilling fuel on a hot engine or exhaust component. It is strongly recommended that a fire extinguisher suitable for use on fuel and electrical fires be kept handy in the garage or workshop at all times. Never try to extinguish a fuel or electrical fire with water.

Fumes

Certain fumes are highly toxic and can quickly cause unconsciousness and even death if inhaled to any extent. Gasoline vapor falls into this category, as do the vapors from some cleaning solvents. Any draining or pouring of such volatile fluids should be done in a well ventilated area.

When using cleaning fluids and solvents, read the instructions on the container carefully. Never use materials from unmarked containers.

Never run the engine in an enclosed space, such as a garage. Exhaust fumes contain carbon monoxide, which is extremely poisonous. If you need to run the engine, always do so in the open air, or at least have the rear of the vehicle outside the work area.

The battery

Never create a spark or allow a bare light bulb near a battery. They normally give off a certain amount of hydrogen gas, which is highly explosive.

Always disconnect the battery ground (-) cable at the battery before working on the fuel or electrical systems.

If possible, loosen the filler caps or cover when charging the battery from an external source (this does not apply to sealed or maintenance-free batteries). Do not charge at an excessive rate or the battery may burst.

Take care when adding water to a non maintenance-free battery and when carrying a battery. The electrolyte, even when diluted, is very corrosive and should not be allowed to contact clothing or skin.

Always wear eye protection when cleaning the battery to prevent the caustic deposits from entering your eyes.

Household current

When using an electric power tool, inspection light, etc., which operates on household current, always make sure that the tool is correctly connected to its plug and that, where necessary, it is properly grounded. Do not use such items in damp conditions and, again, do not create a spark or apply excessive heat in the vicinity of fuel or fuel vapor.

Secondary ignition system voltage

A severe electric shock can result from touching certain parts of the ignition system (such as the spark plug wires) when the engine is running or being cranked, particularly if components are damp or the insulation is defective. In the case of an electronic ignition system, the secondary system voltage is much higher and could prove fatal.

Hydrofluoric acid

This extremely corrosive acid is formed when certain types of synthetic rubber, found in some O-rings, oil seals, fuel hoses, etc. are exposed to temperatures above 750-degrees F (400-degrees C). The rubber changes into a charred or sticky substance containing the acid. *Once formed, the acid remains dangerous for years. If it gets onto the skin, it may be necessary to amputate the limb concerned.*

When dealing with a vehicle which has suffered a fire, or with components salvaged from such a vehicle, wear protective gloves and discard them after use.

Troubleshooting

Contents

This section provides an easy reference guide to the more common problems which may occur during the operation of your vehicle. These problems and their possible causes are grouped under headings denoting various components or systems, such as Engine, Cooling system, etc. They also refer you to the chapter and/or section which deals with the problem.

Remember that successful troubleshooting is not a mysterious black art practiced only by professional mechanics. It is simply the result of the right knowledge combined with an intelligent, systematic approach to the problem. Always work by a process of elimination, starting with the simplest solution and working through to the most complex - and never overlook the obvious. Anyone can run the gas tank dry or leave the lights on overnight, so don't assume that you are exempt from such oversights.

Finally, always establish a clear idea of why a problem has occurred and take steps to ensure that it doesn't happen again. If the electrical system fails because of a poor connection, check the other connections in the system to make sure that they don't fail as well. If a particular fuse continues to blow, find out why - don't just replace one fuse after another. Remember, failure of a small component can often be indicative of potential failure or incorrect functioning of a more important component or system.

Engine

1 Engine will not rotate when attempting to start

1 Battery terminal connections loose or corroded (Chapter 1).
2 Battery discharged or faulty (Chapter 1).
3 Automatic transmission not completely engaged in Park (Chapter 7) or clutch not completely depressed (Chapter 8).
4 Broken, loose or disconnected wiring in the starting circuit (Chapters 5 and 12).
5 Starter motor pinion jammed in flywheel ring gear (Chapter 5).
6 Starter solenoid faulty (Chapter 5).
7 Starter motor faulty (Chapter 5).
8 Ignition switch faulty (Chapter 12).
9 Starter pinion or flywheel teeth worn or broken (Chapter 5).

2 Engine rotates but will not start

1 Fuel tank empty.
2 Battery discharged (engine rotates slowly) (Chapter 5).
3 Battery terminal connections loose or corroded (Chapter 1).
4 Leaking fuel injector(s), faulty fuel pump, pressure regulator, etc. (Chapter 4).
5 Fuel not reaching fuel rail (Chapter 4).

6 Ignition components damp or damaged (Chapter 5).
7 Worn, faulty or incorrectly gapped spark plugs (Chapter 1).
8 Broken, loose or disconnected wiring in the starting circuit (Chapter 5).
9 Broken or stripped timing belt (Chapter 2).
10 Defective fuel pump relay and/or harness at relay (Chapter 4)

3 Engine hard to start when cold

1 Battery discharged or low (Chapter 1).
2 Malfunctioning fuel system (Chapter 4).
3 Injector(s) leaking (Chapter 4).

4 Engine hard to start when hot

1 Air filter clogged (Chapter 1).
2 Fuel not reaching the fuel injection system (Chapter 4).
3 Corroded battery connections, especially ground (Chapter 1).
4 Malfunctioning EVAP system (Chapter 6)

5 Starter motor noisy or excessively rough in engagement

1 Pinion or flywheel gear teeth worn or broken (Chapter 5).
2 Starter motor mounting bolts loose or missing (Chapter 5).

6 Engine starts but stops immediately

1 Loose or faulty electrical connections at coil or alternator (Chapter 5).
2 Insufficient fuel reaching the fuel injector(s) (Chapters 1 and 4).
3 Vacuum leak at the gasket between the intake manifold and throttle body (Chapters 1 and 4).

7 Oil puddle under engine

1 Oil pan gasket and/or oil pan drain bolt washer leaking (Chapter 2).
2 Oil pressure sending unit leaking (Chapter 2).
3 Valve cover(s) leaking (Chapter 2).
4 Engine oil seals leaking (Chapter 2).

8 Engine lopes while idling or idles erratically

1 Vacuum leakage (Chapters 2 and 4).
2 Defective EGR valve (Chapter 6).

3 Air filter clogged (Chapter 1).
4 Fuel pump not delivering sufficient fuel to the fuel injection system (Chapter 4).
5 Fuel pulsation damper faulty (Chapter 4)
6 Leaking head gasket (Chapter 2).
7 Timing belt and/or sprockets worn (Chapter 2).
8 Camshaft lobes worn (Chapter 2).
9 Problem in Engine Mount Control System (Chapter 2).

9 Engine misses at idle speed

1 Spark plugs worn or not gapped properly (Chapter 1).
2 Vacuum leaks (Chapter 1).
3 Uneven or low compression (Chapter 2).

10 Engine misses throughout driving speed range

1 Fuel filter clogged and/or impurities in the fuel system (Chapter 1).
2 Low fuel pressure (Chapter 4).
3 Faulty or incorrectly gapped spark plugs (Chapter 1).
4 Faulty emission system components (Chapter 6).
5 Low or uneven cylinder compression pressures (Chapter 2).
6 Weak or faulty ignition system (Chapter 5).
7 Vacuum leak in fuel injection system (Chapter 4), intake manifold (Chapters 2A), fuel injection air control valve (Chapter 6) or vacuum hoses.

11 Engine stumbles on acceleration

1 Spark plugs fouled (Chapter 1).
2 Fuel injection system faulty (Chapter 4).
3 Fuel filter clogged (Chapters 1 and 4).
4 Incorrect ignition timing (Chapter 5).
5 Intake air leak (Chapters 2 and 4).

12 Engine surges while holding accelerator steady

1 Intake air leak (Chapter 4).
2 Fuel pump faulty (Chapter 4).
3 Loose fuel injector wire harness connectors (Chapter 4).
4 Defective ECU or information sensor (Chapter 6).

13 Engine stalls

1 Fuel filter clogged and/or water and impurities in the fuel system (Chapters 1 and 4).
2 Faulty emissions system components (Chapter 6).

3 Faulty or incorrectly gapped spark plugs (Chapter 1).
4 Vacuum leak in the intake manifold or vacuum hoses (Chapters 2 and 4).
5 Valve clearances incorrectly set (Chapters 1 and 2).

14 Engine lacks power

1 Faulty or incorrectly gapped spark plugs (Chapter 1).
2 Fuel injection system malfunction (Chapter 4).
3 Faulty coil(s) (Chapter 5).
4 Brakes binding (Chapter 9).
5 Automatic transaxle fluid level incorrect (Chapter 1).
6 Clutch slipping (Chapter 8).
7 Fuel filter clogged and/or impurities in the fuel system (Chapters 1 and 4).
8 Emission control system not functioning properly (Chapter 6).
9 Low or uneven cylinder compression pressures (Chapter 2).
10 Obstructed exhaust system (Chapter 4).

15 Engine backfires

1 Emission control system not functioning properly (Chapter 6).
2 Fuel injection system malfunctioning (Chapter 4).
3 Vacuum leak at fuel injector(s), intake manifold, air control valve or vacuum hoses (Chapters 2 and 4).
4 Valve clearances incorrectly set and/or valves sticking (Chapters 1 and 2).

16 Pinging or knocking engine sounds during acceleration or uphill

1 Incorrect grade of fuel.
2 Fuel injection system faulty (Chapter 4).
3 Improper or damaged spark plugs (Chapter 1).
4 EGR valve not functioning (Chapter 6).
5 Vacuum leak (Chapters 2 and 4).

17 Engine runs with oil pressure light on

1 Low oil level (Chapter 1).
2 Short in wiring circuit (Chapter 12).
3 Faulty oil pressure sender (Chapter 2).
4 Worn engine bearings and/or oil pump (Chapter 2).

18 Engine diesels (continues to run) after switching off

Excessive engine operating temperature (Chapter 3).

Engine electrical system

19 Battery will not hold a charge

1 Drivebelt defective (Chapter 1).
2 Battery electrolyte level low (Chapter 1).
3 Battery terminals loose or corroded (Chapter 1).
4 Alternator not charging properly (Chapter 5).
5 Loose, broken or faulty wiring in the charging circuit (Chapter 5).
6 Short in vehicle wiring (Chapter 12).
7 Internally defective battery (Chapters 1 and 5).

20 Alternator light fails to go out

1 Faulty alternator or charging circuit (Chapter 5).
2 Drivebelt defective (Chapter 1).
3 Alternator voltage regulator inoperative (Chapter 5).

21 Alternator light fails to come on when key is turned on

1 Warning light bulb defective (Chapter 5).
2 Fault in the printed circuit, dash wiring or bulb holder (Chapter 12).

Fuel system

22 Excessive fuel consumption

Dirty or clogged air filter element (Chapter 1).

23 Fuel leakage and/or fuel odor

1 Leaking fuel feed or return line (Chapters 1 and 4).
2 Tank overfilled.
3 Evaporative canister filter clogged (Chapters 1 and 6).
4 Fuel injector internal parts excessively worn (Chapter 4).

Cooling system

24 Overheating

1 Insufficient coolant in system (Chapter 1).
2 Radiator core blocked or grille restricted (Chapter 3).
3 Thermostat faulty (Chapter 3).
4 Electric coolant fan circuit problem (Chapter 3).
5 Radiator cap not maintaining proper pressure (Chapter 3).

25 Overcooling

1 Faulty thermostat (Chapter 3).
2 Inaccurate temperature gauge sending unit (Chapter 3).
3 Electric coolant fan circuit problem (Chapter 3).

26 External coolant leakage

1 Deteriorated/damaged hoses; loose clamps (Chapters 1 and 3).
2 Water pump defective (Chapter 3).
3 Leakage from radiator core or coolant reservoir bottle (Chapter 3).
4 Engine drain or water jacket core plugs leaking (Chapter 2).

27 Internal coolant leakage

1 Leaking cylinder head gasket (Chapter 2).
2 Cracked cylinder bore or cylinder head (Chapter 2).

28 Coolant loss

1 Too much coolant in system (Chapter 1).
2 Coolant boiling away because of overheating (Chapter 3).
3 Internal or external leakage (Chapter 3).
4 Faulty radiator cap (Chapter 3).

29 Poor coolant circulation

1 Inoperative water pump (Chapter 3).
2 Restriction in cooling system (Chapters 1 and 3).
3 Thermostat sticking (Chapter 3).

Clutch

30 Pedal travels to floor - no pressure or very little resistance

1 No fluid in reservoir (Chapter 1).
2 Faulty clutch master cylinder, release cylinder or hydraulic line (Chapter 8).
3 Broken release bearing or fork (Chapter 8).

31 Unable to select gears

1 Faulty transaxle (Chapter 7).
2 Faulty clutch disc (Chapter 8).
3 Release lever and bearing not assembled properly (Chapter 8).

4   Faulty pressure plate (Chapter 8).
5   Pressure plate-to-flywheel bolts loose (Chapter 8).

32 Clutch slips (engine speed increases with no increase in vehicle speed)

1   Clutch plate worn (Chapter 8).
2   Clutch plate is oil soaked by leaking rear main seal (Chapter 8).
3   Warped pressure plate or flywheel (Chapter 8).
4   Weak diaphragm spring (Chapter 8).
5   Clutch plate overheated. Allow to cool.

33 Grabbing (chattering) as clutch is engaged

1   Oil on clutch plate lining, burned or glazed facings (Chapter 8).
2   Worn or loose engine or transaxle mounts (Chapters 2 and 7).
3   Worn splines on clutch plate hub (Chapter 8).
4   Warped pressure plate or flywheel (Chapter 8).
5   Burned or smeared resin on flywheel or pressure plate (Chapter 8).

34 Transaxle rattling (clicking)

1   Release lever loose (Chapter 8).
2   Clutch plate damper spring failure (Chapter 8).
3   Low engine idle speed (Chapter 1).

35 Noise in clutch area

1   Fork shaft improperly installed (Chapter 8).
2   Faulty bearing (Chapter 8).

36 Clutch pedal stays on floor

1   Faulty clutch master or release cylinder (Chapter 8).
2   Broken release bearing or fork (Chapter 8).

37 High pedal effort

1   Piston binding in bore of clutch master or release cylinder (Chapter 8).
2   Pressure plate faulty (Chapter 8).

Manual transaxle

38 Knocking noise at low speeds

1   Worn driveaxle constant velocity (CV) joints (Chapter 8).
2   Worn driveaxle bore in differential case (Chapter 7A).*

39 Noise most pronounced when turning

Differential gear noise (Chapter 7A).*

40 Clunk on acceleration or deceleration

1   Loose engine or transaxle mounts (Chapters 2 and 7A).
2   Worn differential pinion shaft in case.*
3   Worn driveaxle bore in differential case (Chapter 7A).*
4   Worn or damaged driveaxle inboard CV joints (Chapter 8).

41 Clicking noise in turns

Worn or damaged outboard CV joint (Chapter 8).

42 Vibration

1   Rough wheel bearing (Chapters 1 and 10).
2   Damaged driveaxle (Chapter 8).
3   Out of round tires (Chapter 1).
4   Tire out of balance (Chapters 1 and 10).
5   Worn CV joint (Chapter 8).

43 Noisy in neutral with engine running

1   Damaged input gear bearing (Chapter 7A).*
2   Damaged clutch release bearing (Chapter 8).

44 Noisy in one particular gear

1   Damaged or worn constant mesh gears (Chapter 7A).*
2   Damaged or worn synchronizers (Chapter 7A).*
3   Bent reverse fork (Chapter 7A).*
4   Damaged fourth speed gear or output gear (Chapter 7A).*
5   Worn or damaged reverse idler gear or idler bushing (Chapter 7A).*

45 Noisy in all gears

1   Insufficient lubricant (Chapter 7A).
2   Damaged or worn bearings (Chapter 7A).*
3   Worn or damaged input gear shaft and/or output gear shaft (Chapter 7A).*

46 Slips out of gear

1   Worn or improperly adjusted linkage (Chapter 7A).
2   Transaxle loose on engine (Chapter 7A).
3   Shift linkage does not work freely, binds (Chapter 7A).
4   Input gear bearing retainer broken or loose (Chapter 7A).*
5   Worn shift fork (Chapter 7A).*

47 Leaks lubricant

1   Driveaxle oil seals worn (Chapter 7).
2   Excessive amount of lubricant in transaxle (Chapters 1 and 7A).
3   Loose or broken input gear shaft bearing retainer (Chapter 7A).*
4   Input gear bearing retainer O-ring and/or lip seal damaged (Chapter 7A).*

48 Locked in gear

Lock pin or interlock pin missing (Chapter 7A).*
* Although the corrective action necessary to remedy the symptoms described is beyond the scope of the home mechanic, the above information should be helpful in isolating the cause of the condition so that the owner can communicate clearly with a professional mechanic.

Automatic transaxle
Note: *Due to the complexity of the automatic transaxle, it is difficult for the home mechanic to properly diagnose and service this component. For problems other than the following, the vehicle should be taken to a dealer or transmission shop.*

49 Fluid leakage

1   Automatic transmission fluid is a deep red color. Fluid leaks should not be confused with engine oil, which can easily be blown onto the transaxle by air flow.
2   To pinpoint a leak, first remove all built-up dirt and grime from the transaxle housing with degreasing agents and/or steam cleaning. Then drive the vehicle at low speeds so air flow will not blow the leak far from its source. Raise the vehicle and determine where the leak is coming from. Common areas of leakage are:

a) *Dipstick tube (Chapters 1 and 7)*
b) *Transaxle oil lines (Chapter 7)*
c) *Speed sensor (Chapter 7)*

50 Transaxle fluid brown or has a burned smell

Transaxle fluid burned (Chapter 1).

51 General shift mechanism problems

1   Chapter 7, Part B, deals with checking and adjusting the shift linkage on automatic transaxles. Common problems which may be attributed to poorly adjusted linkage are:
a) *Engine starting in gears other than Park or Neutral.*
b) *Indicator on shifter pointing to a gear other than the one actually being used.*
c) *Vehicle moves when in Park.*
2   Refer to Chapter 7B for the shift linkage adjustment procedure.

52 Transaxle will not downshift with accelerator pedal pressed to the floor

Since these transmissions are electronically controlled, check for any diagnostic trouble codes stored in the PCM. The actual repair will most likely have to be performed by a qualified repair shop with the proper equipment.

53 Engine will start in gears other than Park or Neutral

Transmission range switch malfunctioning (Chapter 6).

54 Transaxle slips, shifts roughly, is noisy or has no drive in forward or reverse gears

There are many probable causes for the above problems, but the home mechanic should be concerned with only one possibility - fluid level. Before taking the vehicle to a repair shop, check the level and condition of the fluid as described in Chapter 1. Correct the fluid level as necessary or change the fluid and filter if needed. If the problem persists, have a professional diagnose the cause.

Driveaxles

55 Clicking noise in turns

Worn or damaged outboard CV joint (Chapter 8).

56 Shudder or vibration during acceleration

1   Excessive toe-in (Chapter 10).
2   Incorrect spring heights (Chapter 10).
3   Worn or damaged inboard or outboard CV joints (Chapter 8).
4   Sticking inboard CV joint assembly (Chapter 8).

57 Vibration at highway speeds

1   Out of balance front wheels and/or tires (Chapters 1 and 10).
2   Out of round front tires (Chapters 1 and 10).
3   Worn CV joint(s) (Chapter 8).

Brakes

Note: *Before assuming that a brake problem exists, make sure that:*
a) *The tires are in good condition and properly inflated (Chapter 1).*
b) *The front end alignment is correct (Chapter 10).*
c) *The vehicle is not loaded with weight in an unequal manner.*

58 Vehicle pulls to one side during braking

1   Incorrect tire pressures (Chapter 1).
2   Front end out of line (have the front end aligned).
3   Front, or rear, tires not matched to one another.
4   Restricted brake lines or hoses (Chapter 9).
5   Malfunctioning caliper assembly (Chapter 9).
6   Loose suspension parts (Chapter 10).
7   Loose calipers (Chapter 9).
8   Excessive wear of pad material or disc on one side.

59 Noise (high-pitched squeal when the brakes are applied)

Front disc brake pads worn out. The noise comes from the wear sensor rubbing against the disc (does not apply to all vehicles). Replace pads with new ones immediately (Chapter 9).

60 Brake roughness or chatter (pedal pulsates)

1   Excessive lateral runout (Chapter 9).
2   Uneven pad wear (Chapter 9).
3   Defective disc (Chapter 9).

61 Excessive brake pedal effort required to stop vehicle

1   Malfunctioning power brake booster (Chapter 9).
2   Partial system failure (Chapter 9).
3   Excessively worn pads (Chapter 9).
4   Piston in caliper stuck or sluggish (Chapter 9).
5   Brake pads contaminated with oil or grease (Chapter 9).
6   New pads installed and not yet seated. It will take a while for the new material to seat against the disc.

62 Excessive brake pedal travel

1   Partial brake system failure (Chapter 9).
2   Insufficient fluid in master cylinder (Chapters 1 and 9).
3   Air trapped in system (Chapters 1 and 9).

63 Dragging brakes

1   Incorrect adjustment of brake light switch (Chapter 9).
2   Master cylinder pistons not returning correctly (Chapter 9).
3   Restricted brakes lines or hoses (Chapters 1 and 9).
4   Incorrect parking brake adjustment (Chapter 9).

64 Grabbing or uneven braking action

1   Malfunction of proportioning valve (Chapter 9).
2   Malfunction of power brake booster unit (Chapter 9).
3   Binding brake pedal mechanism (Chapter 9).

65 Brake pedal feels spongy when depressed

1   Air in hydraulic lines (Chapter 9).
2   Master cylinder mounting bolts loose (Chapter 9).
3   Master cylinder defective (Chapter 9).

66 Brake pedal travels to the floor with little resistance

1   Little or no fluid in the master cylinder reservoir caused by leaking caliper piston(s) (Chapter 9).
2   Loose, damaged or disconnected brake lines (Chapter 9).

67   Parking brake does not hold

Parking brake linkage improperly adjusted (Chapters 1 and 9).

Suspension and steering systems

Note: *Before attempting to diagnose the suspension and steering systems, perform the following preliminary checks:*

a) *Tires for wrong pressure and uneven wear.*
b) *Steering universal joints from the column to the steering gear for loose connectors or wear.*
c) *Front and rear suspension and the steering gear assembly for loose or damaged parts.*
d) *Out-of-round or out-of-balance tires, bent rims and loose and/or rough wheel bearings.*

68   Vehicle pulls to one side

1   Mismatched or uneven tires (Chapter 10).
2   Broken or sagging springs (Chapter 10).
3   Wheel alignment (Chapter 10).
4   Front brake dragging (Chapter 9).

69   Abnormal or excessive tire wear

1   Wheel alignment (Chapter 10).
2   Sagging or broken springs (Chapter 10).
3   Tire out of balance (Chapter 10).
4   Worn shock absorber (Chapter 10).
5   Overloaded vehicle.
6   Tires not rotated regularly.

70   Wheel makes a thumping noise

1   Blister or bump on tire (Chapter 10).
2   Worn shock absorber (Chapter 10).

71   Shimmy, shake or vibration

1   Tire or wheel out-of-balance or out-of-round (Chapter 10).
2   Loose or worn front hub or wheel bearings (Chapters 1, 8 and 10).
3   Worn tie-rod ends (Chapter 10).
4   Worn lower balljoints (Chapters 1 and 10).
5   Excessive wheel runout (Chapter 10).
6   Blister or bump on tire (Chapter 10).

72   Hard steering

1   Lack of lubrication at balljoints and tie-rod ends (Chapters 1 and 10).
2   Front wheel alignment (Chapter 10).
3   Low tire pressure(s) (Chapters 1 and 10).

73   Poor returnability of steering to center

1   Lack of lubrication at balljoints and tie-rod ends (Chapters 1 and 10).
2   Binding in balljoints (Chapter 10).
3   Binding in steering column (Chapter 10).
4   Lack of lubricant in steering gear assembly (Chapter 10).
5   Front wheel alignment (Chapter 10).

74   Abnormal noise at the front end

1   Lack of lubrication at balljoints and tie-rod ends (Chapters 1 and 10).
2   Damaged shock absorber mount (Chapter 10).
3   Worn control arm bushings or tie-rod ends (Chapter 10).
4   Loose stabilizer bar (Chapter 10).
5   Loose wheel nuts (Chapters 1 and 10).
6   Loose suspension bolts (Chapter 10)

75   Wander or poor steering stability

1   Mismatched or uneven tires (Chapter 10).
2   Lack of lubrication at balljoints and tie-rod ends (Chapters 1 and 10).
3   Worn shock absorber/coil spring assemblies (Chapter 10).
4   Broken or sagging springs (Chapter 10).
5   Wheels out of alignment (Chapter 10).

76   Erratic steering when braking

1   Front hub bearings worn (Chapter 10).
2   Broken or sagging springs (Chapter 10).
3   Leaking caliper (Chapter 10).
4   Warped discs (Chapter 10).

77   Excessive pitching and/or rolling around corners or during braking

1   Loose stabilizer bar (Chapter 10).
2   Worn shock absorber/coil spring assemblies or mountings (Chapter 10).
3   Broken or sagging springs (Chapter 10).
4   Overloaded vehicle.

78   Suspension bottoms

1   Overloaded vehicle.
2   Worn shock absorber/coil spring assemblies (Chapter 10).
3   Incorrect, broken or sagging springs (Chapter 10).

79   Cupped tires

1   Front wheel or rear wheel alignment (Chapter 10).
2   Worn shock absorber/coil spring assemblies (Chapter 10).
3   Wheel bearings worn (Chapter 10).
4   Excessive tire or wheel runout (Chapter 10).
5   Worn balljoints (Chapter 10).

80   Excessive tire wear on outside edge

1   Inflation pressures incorrect (Chapter 1).
2   Excessive speed in turns.
3   Front end alignment incorrect (excessive toe-in). Have professionally aligned.
4   Suspension arm bent or twisted (Chapter 10).

81   Excessive tire wear on inside edge

1   Inflation pressures incorrect (Chapter 1).
2   Front end alignment incorrect (toe-out). Have professionally aligned.
3   Loose or damaged steering or suspension components (Chapter 10).

82   Tire tread worn in one place

1   Tires out of balance.
2   Damaged or buckled wheel. Inspect and replace if necessary.
3   Defective tire (Chapter 1).

83   Excessive play or looseness in steering system

1   Front hub bearing(s) worn (Chapter 10).
2   Tie-rod end loose (Chapter 10).
3   Steering gear loose or worn (Chapter 10).
4   Worn or loose steering intermediate shaft (Chapter 10).

84   Rattling or clicking noise in steering gear

1   Steering gear loose (Chapter 10).
2   Steering gear defective.

Chapter 1
Tune-up and routine maintenance

Contents

Specifications

Recommended lubricants and fluids

Note: *The fluids and lubricants listed here are those recommended by the manufacturer at the time this manual was written. Vehicle manufacturers occasionally upgrade their fluid and lubricant specifications, so check with your local auto parts store for the most current recommendations.*

Engine oil

Type .... API "Certified for gasoline engines"

Viscosity

2001 and earlier models .... SAE 5W-30

2002 and later models .... SAE 5W-20

Fuel type .... Unleaded gasoline, 91 octane or higher

Automatic transaxle fluid

1999 and 2000 models .... Honda Premium Formula ATF or equivalent

2001 and later models .... Honda ATF-Z1 or equivalent

Manual transaxle fluid .... Acura Manual Transmission Fluid or equivalent

Brake fluid type .... DOT 3 brake fluid

Clutch fluid type .... DOT 3 brake fluid

Power steering system fluid .... Honda power steering fluid or equivalent

Engine coolant .... Acura Long Life Antifreeze/Coolant Type 2 or equivalent 50/50 mixture of non-silicate antifreeze and water (the genuine Acura antifreeze is a pre-mixed solution - don't add water to it)

Capacities*

Engine oil (including oil filter) .... 4.6 quarts (4.4 liters)

Automatic transaxle fluid (drain and refill)** .... 3.0 quarts (2.8 liters)

Manual transaxle fluid .... 2.3 quarts (2.2 liters)

Cooling system

2002 and earlier models

Routine coolant change .... up to 1.50 gallons (5.6 liters)

After engine overhaul .... up to 2 gallons (7.3 liters)

2003 and later models

Routine coolant change

Manual transaxle .... up to 1.69 gallons (6.4 liters)

Automatic transaxle .... up to 1.72 gallons (6.5 liters)

After engine overhaul

Manual transaxle .... up to 2.11 gallons (8.0 liters)

Automatic transaxle .... up to 2.17 gallons (8.2 liters)

* All capacities approximate. Add as necessary to bring to appropriate level.

** If you want to flush the converter during a fluid change, purchase twice the amount of fluid listed here.

Ignition system

Spark plug type and gap
Type

2003 and earlier Premium models .... NGK: PZFR5F-11 or
DENSO: PKJ16CR-L11

2002 and 2003 Type S models .... NGK: PZFR6E-11 or
DENSO: PKJ20CR-M11

2004 and later models .... NGK: IZFR5K-11 or
DENSO SKJ20DR-M11

Gap .... 0.040 inch (1.1 mm)
Engine firing order 1-4-2-5-3-6

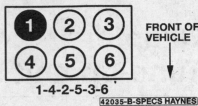

1-4-2-5-3-6

42035-B-SPECS HAYNES

Cylinder locations

Engine idle speed (in Park or Neutral)

2001 and earlier models .... 680+/-50 rpm
2002 and later models .... 750+/-50 rpm

Brakes

Disc brake pad lining thickness (minimum), front or rear .... 1/16-inch (1.6 mm)

Torque specifications

Note: *One foot-pound (ft-lb) of torque is equivalent to 12 inch-pounds (in-lbs) of torque. Torque values below approximately 15 foot-pounds are expressed in inch-pounds, because most foot-pound torque wrenches are not accurate at these smaller values.*

	Ft-lbs (unless otherwise indicated)	Nm
Engine oil drain plug	29	39
Drivebelt tensioner mounting bolts		
2003 and earlier models	96 in-lbs	12
2004 and later models		
10 x 1.5 mm bolt	33	44
8 x 1.25 mm bolt	16	22
Drivebelt tensioner pulley bolt		
2003 and earlier models	28	38
2004 and later models	59	80
Automatic transaxle		
Drain plug	36	49
Filler plug	33	44
Manual transaxle		
Check plug	108 in-lbs	12
Drain plug	29	39
Filler plug	33	44
Spark plugs	156 in-lbs	18
Wheel lug nuts	80	108

1 Maintenance schedule

The maintenance intervals in this manual are provided with the assumption that you, not the dealer, will be doing the work. These are the minimum maintenance intervals recommended by the factory for vehicles that are driven daily. If you wish to keep your vehicle in peak condition at all times, you may wish to perform some of these procedures even more often. Because frequent maintenance enhances the efficiency, performance and resale value of your car, we encourage you to do so. If you drive in dusty areas, tow a trailer, idle or drive at low speeds for extended periods or drive for short distances (less than four miles) in below freezing temperatures, shorter intervals are also recommended.

When your vehicle is new, follow the maintenance schedule to the letter, record the maintenance performed in your owners manual and keep all receipts to protect the new vehicle warranty. In many cases, the initial maintenance check is done at no cost to the owner.

Every 250 miles (400 km) or weekly, whichever comes first

Check the engine oil level (Section 4)
Check the engine coolant level (Section 4)
Check the windshield washer fluid level (Section 4)
Check the brake or clutch fluid level (Section 4)
Check the power steering fluid level (Section 4)
Check the automatic transaxle fluid level (Section 4)
Check the tires and tire pressures (Section 5)
Check the operation of all lights
Check the horn operation

Every 3000 miles (4800 km) or 3 months, whichever comes first

All items listed above plus:
Change the engine oil and oil filter (Section 6)
Check the manual transaxle fluid level (Section 4)

Every 7500 miles (12,000 km) or 6 months, whichever comes first

All items listed above plus:
Inspect (and replace, if necessary) the windshield wiper blades (Section 7)
Check and service the battery (Section 8)
Check the cooling system (Section 9)
Rotate the tires (Section 10)
Check the seat belts (Section 11)
Inspect the brake system (Section 12)

Every 15,000 miles (24,000 km) or 12 months, whichever comes first

All items listed above plus:
Inspect the suspension and steering components (Section 13)*

Inspect and replace, if necessary, all underhood hoses (Section 14)
Replace the air filter (Section 15)*
Replace the interior ventilation filter (Section 16)
Inspect the fuel system (Section 17)
Check the exhaust system (Section 18)
Check the driveaxle boots (Section 19)

Every 30,000 (48,000 km) miles or 24 months, whichever comes first

All items listed above plus:
Check the engine drivebelts (Section 20)
Replace the brake fluid (Section 21)
Change the automatic transaxle fluid (Section 22)**

Every 45,000 miles (72,400 km) or 36 months, whichever comes first

Service the cooling system (drain, flush and refill) (Section 23)

Every 105,000 miles (169,000 km) or 84 months, whichever comes first

Replace the spark plugs (see Section 24)
Check and adjust, if necessary, the engine idle speed (Section 25)
Check and adjust, if necessary, the valve clearance (see Chapter 2A)
Replace the timing belt, and inspect the water pump (see Chapter 2A and Chapter 3)

*This item is affected by "severe" operating conditions as described below. If your vehicle is operated under "severe" conditions, perform all maintenance indicated with a * at 7500 mile/6 month intervals. Severe conditions are indicated if you mainly operate your vehicle under one or more of the following conditions:
Operating in dusty areas
Towing a trailer
Idling for extended periods and/or low speed operation
Operating when outside temperatures remain below freezing and when most trips are less than five miles

**If operated under one or more of the following conditions, change the automatic transaxle fluid every 15,000 miles:
In heavy city traffic where the outside temperature regularly reaches 90-degrees F (32-degrees C) or higher
In hilly or mountainous terrain

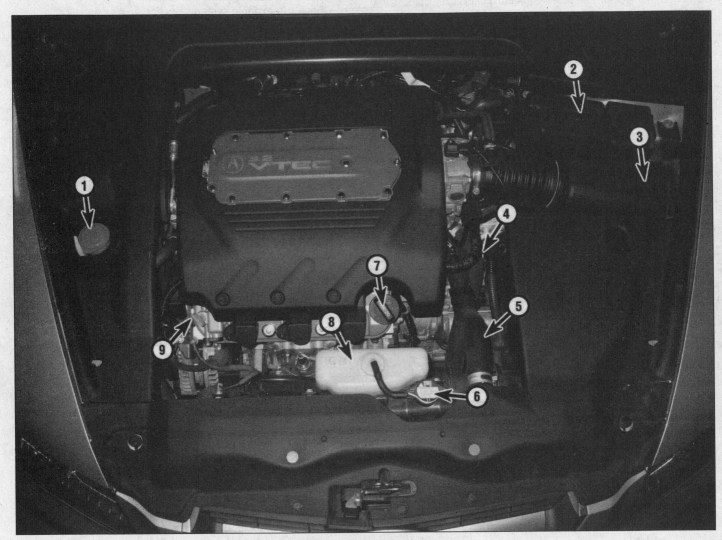

Typical engine compartment layout

1	Windshield washer fluid reservoir	4	Automatic transaxle fluid dipstick	7	Engine oil filler cap
2	Fuse/relay block	5	Upper radiator hose	8	Engine coolant reservoir
3	Air filter housing	6	Radiator cap	9	Engine oil dipstick

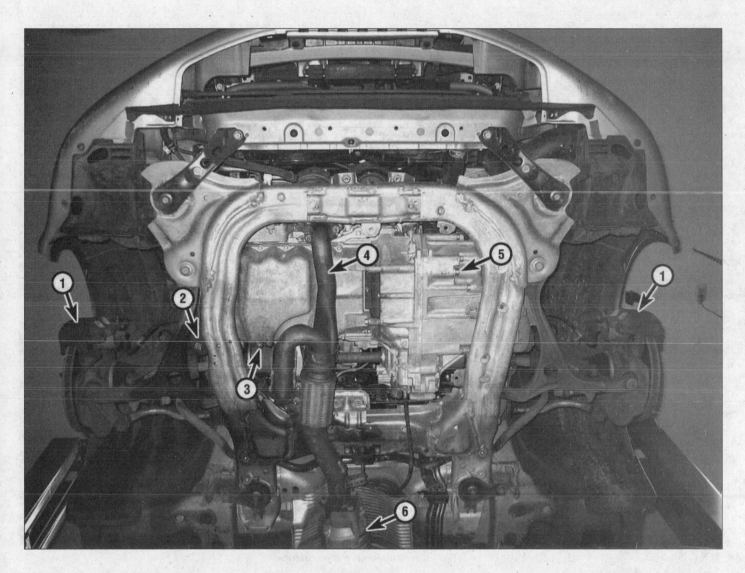

Typical front underside components

1	Front disc brake caliper	3	Engine oil drain plug	5	Automatic transaxle drain plug
2	Engine oil filter	4	Exhaust pipe	6	Catalytic converter

Typical rear underside components

1	*Muffler*	3	*Shock absorber*	5	*Fuel tank*
2	*Rear disc brake caliper*	4	*Exhaust pipe*		

2 Introduction

This Chapter is designed to help the home mechanic maintain the Acura TL with the goals of maximum performance, economy, safety and reliability in mind.

Included is a master maintenance schedule, followed by procedures dealing specifically with each item on the schedule. Visual checks, adjustments, component replacement and other helpful items are included. Refer to the accompanying illustrations of the engine compartment and the underside of the vehicle for the locations of various components.

Servicing the vehicle, in accordance with the mileage/time maintenance schedule and the step-by-step procedures will result in a planned maintenance program that should produce a long and reliable service life. Keep in mind that it is a comprehensive plan, so maintaining some items but not others at the specified intervals will not produce the same results.

As you service the vehicle, you will discover that many of the procedures can - and should - be grouped together because of the nature of the particular procedure you're performing or because of the close proximity of two otherwise unrelated components to one another.

For example, if the vehicle is raised for chassis lubrication, you should inspect the exhaust, suspension, steering and fuel systems while you're under the vehicle. When you're rotating the tires, it makes good sense to check the brakes since the wheels are already removed. Finally, let's suppose you have to borrow or rent a torque wrench. Even if you only need it to tighten the spark plugs, you might as well check the torque of as many critical fasteners as time allows.

The first step in this maintenance program is to prepare yourself before the actual work begins. Read through all the procedures you're planning to do, then gather up all the parts and tools needed. If it looks like you might run into problems during a particular job, seek advice from a mechanic or an experienced do-it-yourselfer.

Owner's Manual and VECI label information

Your vehicle owner's manual was written for your year and model and contains very specific information on component locations, specifications, fuse ratings, part numbers, etc. The Owner's Manual is an important resource for the do-it-yourselfer to have; if one was not supplied with your vehicle, it can generally be ordered from a dealer parts department.

Among other important information, the Vehicle Emissions Control Information (VECI) label contains specifications and procedures for applicable tune-up adjustments and, in some instances, spark plugs (see Chapter 6 for more information on the VECI label). The information on this label is the exact maintenance data recommended by the manufac-

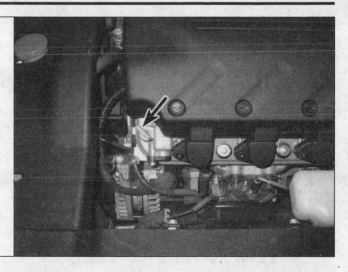

4.2 The engine oil dipstick is located at the front side of the engine

turer. This data often varies by intended operating altitude, local emissions regulations, month of manufacture, etc.

This Chapter contains procedural details, safety information and more ambitious maintenance intervals than you might find in manufacturer's literature. However, you may also find procedures or specifications in your Owner's Manual or VECI label that differ with what's printed here. In these cases, the Owner's Manual or VECI label can be considered correct, since it is specific to your particular vehicle.

3 Tune-up general information

The term tune-up is used in this manual to represent a combination of individual operations rather than one specific procedure.

If, from the time the vehicle is new, the routine maintenance schedule is followed closely and frequent checks are made of fluid levels and high wear items, as suggested throughout this manual, the engine will be kept in relatively good running condition and the need for additional work will be minimized.

More likely than not, however, there will be times when the engine is running poorly due to lack of regular maintenance. This is even more likely if a used vehicle, which has not received regular and frequent maintenance checks, is purchased. In such cases, an engine tune-up will be needed outside of the regular routine maintenance intervals.

The first step in any tune-up or diagnostic procedure to help correct a poor running engine is a cylinder compression check. A compression check (see Chapter 2B) will help determine the condition of internal engine components and should be used as a guide for tune-up and repair procedures. If, for instance, a compression check indicates serious internal engine wear, a conventional tune-up will not improve the performance of the engine and would be a waste of time and money. Because of its importance, the compression check should be done by someone

with the right equipment and the knowledge to use it properly.

The following procedures are those most often needed to bring a generally poor running engine back into a proper state of tune.

Minor tune-up

Check all engine related fluids (Section 4)
Clean, inspect and test the battery (Section 8)
Check the cooling system (Section 9)
Check all underhood hoses (Section 14)
Check the air filter (Section 15)
Check the drivebelt (Section 20)

Major tune-up

All items listed under minor tune-up, plus . . .

Replace the air filter (Section 15)
Check the fuel system (Section 17)
Replace the spark plugs (Section 24)
Check the idle speed (Section 25)

4 Fluid level checks (every 250 miles [400km] or weekly)

1 Fluids are an essential part of the lubrication, cooling, brake, clutch and other systems. Because these fluids gradually become depleted and/or contaminated during normal operation of the vehicle, they must be periodically replenished. See *Recommended lubricants and fluids* and *Capacities* at the beginning of this Chapter before adding fluid to any of the following components. **Note:** *The vehicle must be on level ground before fluid levels can be checked.*

Engine oil

Refer to illustrations 4.2, 4.4 and 4.6

2 The engine oil level is checked with a dipstick located at the front side of the engine **(see illustration)**. The dipstick extends through a metal tube from which it protrudes down into the engine oil pan.

3 The oil level should be checked before the vehicle has been driven, or about 5 min-

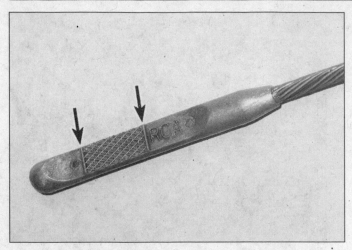

4.4 The oil level should be in the safe range

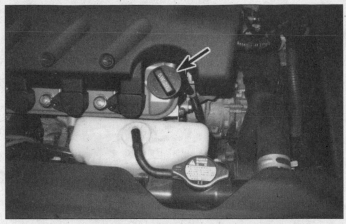

4.6 The oil filler cap is located on the front valve cover - always make sure the area around the opening is clean before unscrewing the cap to prevent dirt from contaminating the engine

utes after the engine has been shut off. If the oil is checked immediately after driving the vehicle, some of the oil will remain in the upper engine components, producing an inaccurate reading on the dipstick.

4   Pull the dipstick from the tube and wipe all the oil from the end with a clean rag or paper towel. Insert the clean dipstick all the way back into its metal tube and pull it out again. Observe the oil at the end of the dipstick. At its highest point, the level should be between the upper and lower marks **(see illustration)**.

5   It takes one quart of oil to raise the level from the lower mark to the upper mark on the dipstick. Do not allow the level to drop below the lower hole or oil starvation may cause engine damage. Conversely, overfilling the engine (adding oil above the upper mark) may cause oil fouled spark plugs, oil leaks or oil seal failures.

6   Remove the threaded cap from the valve cover to add oil **(see illustration)**. Use an oil can spout or funnel to prevent spills. After adding the oil, install the filler cap hand tight. Start the engine and look carefully for any small leaks around the oil filter or drain plug. Stop

the engine and check the oil level again after it has had sufficient time to drain from the upper block and cylinder head galleries.

7   Checking the oil level is an important preventive maintenance step. A continually dropping oil level indicates oil leakage through damaged seals, from loose connections, or past worn rings or valve guides. If the oil looks milky in color or has water droplets in it, a cylinder head gasket may be blown or the oil cooler could be leaking. The engine should be checked immediately. The condition of the oil should also be checked. Each time you check the oil level, slide your thumb and index finger up the dipstick before wiping off the oil. If you see small dirt or metal particles clinging to the dipstick, the oil should be changed (see Section 6).

Engine coolant

Refer to illustration 4.9

Warning: *Do not allow antifreeze to come in contact with your skin or painted surfaces of the vehicle. Flush contaminated areas immediately with plenty of water. Don't store new coolant or leave old coolant lying around*

where it's accessible to children or pets - they're attracted by its sweet smell. Ingestion of even a small amount of coolant can be fatal! Wipe up garage floor and drip pan spills immediately. Keep antifreeze containers covered and repair cooling system leaks as soon as they're noticed.

8   All vehicles covered by this manual are equipped with a pressurized coolant recovery system. A coolant reservoir, located at the front of the engine compartment, is connected by a hose to the base of the radiator filler neck. If the coolant heats up during engine operation, coolant can escape through the pressurized filler cap, then through the connecting hose into the reservoir. As the engine cools, the coolant is automatically drawn back into the cooling system to maintain the correct level.

9   The coolant level in the reservoir should be checked regularly. It must be between the MAX and MIN lines on the tank. The level will vary with the temperature of the engine. When the engine is cold, the coolant level should be at or slightly above the MIN mark on the tank. Once the engine has warmed up, the level should be at or near the MAX mark. If it isn't, allow the fluid in the tank to cool, then remove the cap from the reservoir **(see illustration)** and add coolant to bring the level up to the MAX line. **Warning:** *Do not remove the radiator cap to check the coolant level when the engine is warm!* Use only the recommended coolant and water in the mixture ratio listed in this Chapter's Specifications. Do not use supplemental inhibitors or additives. If only a small amount of coolant is required to bring the system up to the proper level, water can be used. However, repeated additions of water will dilute the recommended antifreeze and water solution. In order to maintain the proper ratio of antifreeze and water, it is advisable to top up the coolant level with the correct mixture.

10   If the coolant level drops within a short time after replenishment, there may be a leak in the system. Inspect the radiator, hoses,

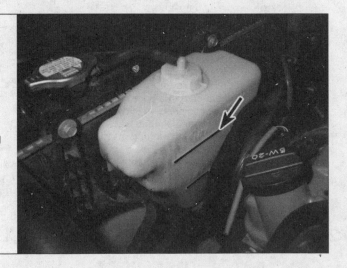

4.9 The coolant reservoir is located at the front of the engine compartment, the level should be at or near the MAX mark

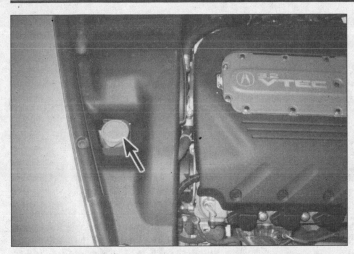

4.14 The windshield/rear window washer fluid reservoir is located in the right front corner of the engine compartment

4.16 The brake fluid level should be kept at the MAX mark on the translucent plastic reservoir

engine coolant filler cap, drain plugs and water pump. If no leak is evident, have the radiator cap pressure tested. **Warning:** *Never remove the radiator cap or the coolant reservoir cap when the engine is running or has just been shut down, because the cooling system is hot. Escaping steam and scalding liquid could cause serious injury.*

11   If it is necessary to open the radiator cap, wait until the system has cooled completely, then wrap a thick cloth around the cap and turn it to the first stop. If any steam escapes, wait until the system has cooled further, then remove the cap.

12   When checking the coolant level, always note its condition. It should be relatively clear. If it is brown or rust colored, the system should be drained, flushed and refilled. Even if the coolant appears to be normal, the corrosion inhibitors wear out with use, so it must be replaced at the specified intervals.

13   Do not allow antifreeze to come in contact with your skin or painted surfaces of the vehicle. Flush contacted areas immediately with plenty of water.

Windshield washer fluid

Refer to illustration 4.14

14   Fluid for the windshield washer system is stored in a plastic reservoir which is located along the right side of the engine compartment **(see illustration)**. Check the fluid level by detaching the cap and pulling up the dipstick. In milder climates, plain water can be used to top up the reservoir, but the reservoir should be kept no more than 2/3 full to allow for expansion should the water freeze. In colder climates, the use of a specially designed windshield washer fluid, available at your dealer and any auto parts store, will help lower the freezing point of the fluid. Mix the solution with water in accordance with the manufacturer's directions on the container. Do not use regular antifreeze. It will damage the vehicle's paint.

Brake and clutch fluid

Refer to illustration 4.16

15   The brake master cylinder is located on the driver's side of the engine compartment firewall, under a plastic cover **(see illustrations 4.38a and 4.38b).** The clutch master cylinder fluid reservoir is located right next to it on the firewall, behind the left shock tower. They both use the same type of fluid.

16   The level should be maintained at the MAX mark on the reservoir **(see illustration).**

17   If additional fluid is necessary to bring the level up, use a rag to clean all dirt off the top of the reservoir. If any foreign matter enters the master cylinder when the cap is removed, blockage in the brake system lines can occur. Also, make sure all painted surfaces around the master cylinder are covered, since brake fluid will ruin paint. Carefully pour new, clean brake fluid into the master cylinder. Be careful not to spill the fluid on painted surfaces. Be sure the specified fluid is used; mixing different types of brake fluid can cause damage to the system. See *Recommended lubricants and fluids* at the beginning of this Chapter or your owner's manual.

18   At this time the brake fluid and the master cylinder can be inspected for contamination. If deposits, dirt particles or water droplets are seen in the fluid, the system should be drained and refilled with fresh fluid (see Section 21).

19   Reinstall the master cylinder cap.

20   The brake fluid in the master cylinder will drop slightly as the brake pads at each wheel wear down during normal operation. If the master cylinder requires repeated replenishing to keep the level up, it's an indication of leaks in the brake system, which should be corrected immediately. Check all brake lines and connections, along with the brake calipers and booster (if there's fluid in the booster, the master cylinder is leaking) (see Chapter 9 for more information on the brake system). As the clutch wears, the fluid level in

the clutch master cylinder reservoir will rise. Unless there is a leak in either system, fluid additions shouldn't be necessary.

21   If you discover that the reservoir is empty or nearly empty, the brake (or clutch) system should be filled, bled (see Chapters 8 or 9) and checked for leaks.

Power steering fluid

Refer to illustration 4.23

22   Check the power steering fluid level periodically to avoid steering system problems, such as damage to the pump. **Caution:** *DO NOT hold the steering wheel against either stop (extreme left or right turn) for more than five seconds. If you do, the power steering pump could be damaged.*

23   The power steering reservoir, located under a cover at the right side of the engine compartment **(see illustration),** has MIN and MAX fluid level marks on the side. The fluid level can be seen without removing the reservoir cap.

24   Park the vehicle on level ground and apply the parking brake.

4.23 The power steering fluid reservoir is located at the right front corner of the engine compartment, under a plastic cover

4.32a The transaxle dipstick is located on the left side of the engine compartment, near the battery

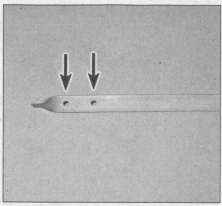

4.32b The automatic transaxle fluid level should be between the two holes in the dipstick - if it isn't, add enough fluid to bring the level to or near the upper hole

4.34 Automatic transaxle fill plug location

25   Run the engine until it has reached normal operating temperature. With the engine at idle, turn the steering wheel back and forth about 10 times to get any air out of the steering system. Shut the engine off with the wheels in the straight-ahead position.
26   Note the fluid level on the side of the reservoir. It should be between the two marks.
27   Add small amounts of fluid until the level is correct. **Caution:** *Do not overfill the reser-voir. If too much fluid is added, remove the excess with a clean syringe or suction pump.*
28   Check the power steering hoses and connections for leaks and wear.

Automatic transaxle fluid

Refer to illustrations 4.32a, 4.32b and 4.34

29   The level of the automatic transaxle fluid should be carefully maintained. Low fluid level can lead to slipping or loss of drive, while overfilling can cause foaming, loss of fluid and transaxle damage.
30   The transaxle fluid level should only be checked when the transaxle is hot (at its normal operating temperature). If the vehicle has just been driven over 10 miles (15 miles in a frigid climate), and the fluid temperature is 160 to 175-degrees F, the transaxle is hot. **Caution:** *If the vehicle has just been driven for a long time at high speed or in city traf-fic in hot weather, or if it has been pulling a trailer, an accurate fluid level reading cannot be obtained. Allow the fluid to cool down for about 30 minutes.*
31   If the vehicle has not just been driven, park the vehicle on level ground, set the parking brake and start the engine. While the engine is idling, depress the brake pedal and move the selector lever through all the gear ranges, beginning and ending in Park. The engine should not be allowed to warm up longer than the time it takes the radiator fan to come on twice.
32   Turn the engine off, remove the dipstick from its tube (**see illustration**). Check the level of the fluid on the dipstick (**see illustra-tion**) and note its condition. **Note:** *The fluid level should be checked within 60 to 90 sec-onds from the time the engine is turned off.*
33   Wipe the fluid from the dipstick with a clean rag and reinsert it back into the tube until the cap seats.
34   Pull the dipstick out again and note the fluid level. The fluid level should be in the operating temperature range (between the upper and lower mark). If the level is at the low side of either range, add the specified automatic transmission fluid through the dip-stick tube (1999 and 2000 models) or through the fill plug opening (2001 and later models) (**see illustration**).
35   With the engine off, add just enough of the recommended fluid to fill the transaxle to the proper level. It takes about one pint to raise the level from the low mark to the high mark when the fluid is hot, so add the fluid

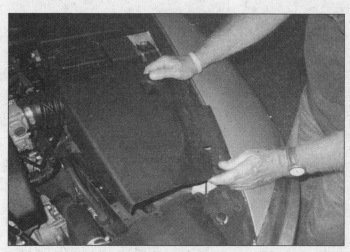

4.38a Remove the left side engine cover . . .

4.38b . . . and the left rear cover

a little at a time and keep checking the level until it is correct. **Caution:** *It's important to not overfill the transaxle.*

36   The condition of the fluid should also be checked along with the level. If the fluid at the end of the dipstick is black or a dark reddish brown color, or if it emits a burned smell, the fluid should be changed (see Section 22). If you are in doubt about the condition of the fluid, purchase some new fluid and compare the two for color and smell.

Manual transaxle fluid

Refer to illustrations 4.38a and 4.38b

Note: *It isn't necessary to check this lubricant weekly; every 3000 miles (4800 km) or 3 months will be adequate.*

37   The manual transaxle does not have a dipstick. To check the fluid level, raise the vehicle and support it securely on jackstands. **Note:** *Be sure the vehicle is level.* On the side of the transaxle housing, remove the fluid check plug (it's the upper of the two plugs; the lower one is the drain plug). If the lubricant level is correct, it should be up to the lower edge of the hole.

38   If the transaxle needs more lubricant (if the level is not up to the hole), remove the left side and left rear engine covers **(see illustrations).**

39   Remove the air filter housing (see Chapter 4).

40   Remove the battery and battery tray (see Chapter 5).

41   Remove the fill plug and washer. The fill plug has a square-drive recess; use a ratchet and an extension to unscrew it.

42   With the fill plug removed, add just enough of the recommended fluid to fill the transaxle. Add the fluid a little at a time until the fluid overflows from the check plug hole. Stop filling the transaxle when the lubricant begins to run out of the hole.

43   Install the plugs and tighten them securely.

44   Installation is the reverse of the removal procedure.

45   Drive the vehicle a short distance, then check for leaks.

---

5   Tire and tire pressure checks (every 250 miles [400 km] or weekly)

Refer to illustrations 5.2, 5.3, 5.4a, 5.4b and 5.8

1   Periodic inspection of the tires may spare you from the inconvenience of being stranded with a flat tire. It can also provide you with vital information regarding possible problems in the steering and suspension systems before major damage occurs.

2   Normal tread wear can be monitored

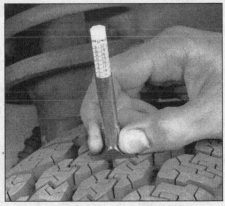

5.2 A tire tread depth indicator should be used to monitor tire wear - they are available at auto parts stores and service stations and cost very little

with a simple, inexpensive device known as a tread depth indicator **(see illustration).** When the tread depth reaches the specified minimum, replace the tire(s).

3   Note any abnormal tread wear **(see illustration).** Tread pattern irregularities such as cupping, flat spots and more wear on one side than the other are indications of front end alignment and/or balance problems. If any of these conditions are noted, take the vehicle to a tire shop or service station to correct the problem.

UNDERINFLATION

CUPPING

Cupping may be caused by:
- **Underinflation and/or mechanical irregularities such as out-of-balance condition of wheel and/or tire, and bent or damaged wheel.**
- **Loose or worn steering tie-rod or steering idler arm.**
- **Loose, damaged or worn front suspension parts.**

OVERINFLATION

INCORRECT TOE-IN OR EXTREME CAMBER

FEATHERING DUE TO MISALIGNMENT

5.3 This chart will help you determine the condition of your tires, the probable cause(s) of abnormal wear and the corrective action necessary

5.4a If a tire loses air on a steady basis, check the valve core first to make sure it's snug (special inexpensive wrenches are commonly available at auto parts stores)

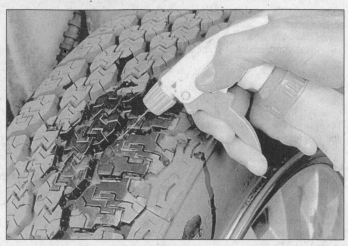

5.4b If the valve core is tight, raise the corner of the vehicle with the low tire and spray a soapy water solution onto the tread as the tire is turned slowly - slow leaks will cause small bubbles to appear

5.8 To extend the life of your tires, check the air pressure at least once a week with an accurate gauge (don't forget the spare!)

4   Look closely for cuts, punctures and embedded nails or tacks. Sometimes a tire will hold its air pressure for a short time or leak down very slowly even after a nail has embedded itself into the tread. If a slow leak persists, check the valve core to make sure it is tight **(see illustration)**. Examine the tread for an object that may have embedded itself into the tire or for a "plug" that may have begun to leak (radial tire punctures are repaired with a plug that is installed in a puncture). If a puncture is suspected, it can be easily verified by spraying a solution of soapy water onto the puncture area **(see illustration)**. The soapy solution will bubble if there is a leak. Unless the puncture is inordinately large, a tire shop or gas station can usually repair the punctured tire.

5   Carefully inspect the inner side of each tire for evidence of brake fluid leakage. If you see any, inspect the brakes immediately.

6   Correct tire air pressure adds miles to the lifespan of the tires, improves mileage and enhances overall ride quality. Tire pres-sure cannot be accurately estimated by looking at a tire, particularly if it is a radial. A tire pressure gauge is therefore essential. Keep an accurate gauge in the glovebox. The pressure gauges fitted to the nozzles of air hoses at gas stations are often inaccurate.

7   Always check tire pressure when the tires are cold. "Cold," in this case, means the vehicle has not been driven over a mile in the three hours preceding a tire pressure check. A pressure rise of four to eight pounds is not uncommon once the tires are warm.

8   Unscrew the valve cap protruding from the wheel or hubcap and push the gauge firmly onto the valve **(see illustration)**. Note the reading on the gauge and compare this figure to the recommended tire pressure shown on the tire placard on the left door jamb. Be sure to reinstall the valve cap to keep dirt and moisture out of the valve stem mechanism. Check all four tires and, if necessary, add enough air to bring them up to the recommended pressure levels.

6.2 These tools are required when changing the engine oil and filter

1   *Drain pan -* *It should be fairly shallow in depth, but wide in order to prevent spills*

2   *Rubber gloves -* *When removing the drain plug and filter, it is inevitable that you will get oil on your hands (the gloves will prevent burns)*

3   *Breaker bar -* *Sometimes the oil drain plug is pretty tight and a long breaker bar is needed to loosen it*

4   *Socket -* *To be used with the breaker bar or a ratchet (must be the correct size to fit the drain plug)*

5   *Filter wrench -* *This is a metal band-type wrench, which requires clearance around the filter to be effective*

6   *Filter wrench -* *This type fits on the bottom of the filter and can be turned with a ratchet or beaker bar (different size wrenches are available for different types of filters)*

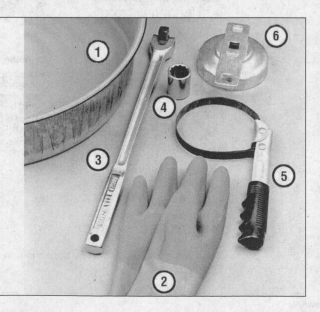

6.7 Use a proper size box-end wrench or socket to remove the oil drain plug and avoid rounding it off

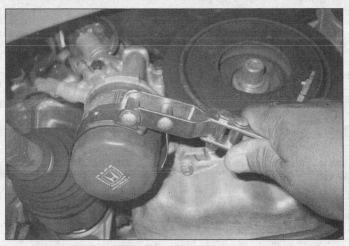

6.12 Use an oil filter wrench to remove the filter

9   Don't forget to keep the spare tire inflated to the specified pressure (consult your owner's manual). Note that the air pressure specified for the compact spare is significantly higher than the pressure of the regular tires.

6   Engine oil and oil filter change (every 3000 miles [4800 km] or 3 months)

Refer to illustrations 6.2, 6.7, 6.12 and 6.14

1   Frequent oil changes are the best preventive maintenance the home mechanic can give the engine, because aging oil becomes diluted and contaminated, which leads to premature engine wear.

2   Make sure you have all the necessary tools before you begin this procedure **(see illustration)**. You should also have plenty of rags or newspapers handy for mopping up any spills.

3   Access to the underside of the vehicle is greatly improved if the vehicle can be lifted on a hoist, driven onto ramps or supported by jackstands. **Warning:** *Do not work under a vehicle which is supported only by a bumper, hydraulic or scissors-type jack.*

4   If this is your first oil change, get under the vehicle and familiarize yourself with the locations of the oil drain plug and the oil filter. The engine and exhaust components will be warm during the actual work, so try to anticipate any potential problems before the engine and accessories are hot.

5   Park the vehicle on a level spot. Start the engine and allow it to reach its normal operating temperature. Warm oil and sludge will flow out more easily. Turn off the engine when it's warmed up. Remove the filler cap from the valve cover.

6   Raise the vehicle and support it securely on jackstands. **Warning:** *Never get beneath the vehicle when it is supported only by a jack. The jack provided with your vehicle is designed solely for raising the vehicle to remove and replace the wheels. Always use jackstands to support the vehicle when it becomes necessary to place your body underneath the vehicle.*

7   Being careful not to touch the hot exhaust components, place the drain pan under the drain plug in the bottom of the pan and remove the plug **(see illustration)**. You may want to wear gloves while unscrewing the plug the final few turns if the engine is hot.

8   Allow the old oil to drain into the pan. It may be necessary to move the pan farther under the engine as the oil flow slows to a trickle. Inspect the old oil for the presence of metal shavings and chips.

9   After all the oil has drained, wipe off the drain plug with a clean rag. Even minute metal particles clinging to the plug would immediately contaminate the new oil.

10   Clean the area around the drain plug opening, reinstall the plug and tighten it securely, but do not strip the threads.

11   Move the drain pan into position under the oil filter.

12   Loosen the oil filter **(see illustration)** by turning it counterclockwise with an oil filter wrench. Once the filter is loose, use your hands to unscrew it from the block. Keep the open end pointing up to prevent the oil inside the filter from spilling out. **Warning:** *The exhaust system may still be hot, so be careful.*

13   With a clean rag, wipe off the mounting surface on the block. If a residue of old oil is allowed to remain, it will smoke when the block is heated up. Also make sure that none of the old gasket remains stuck to the mounting surface. It can be removed with a scraper if necessary.

14   Compare the old filter with the new one to make sure they are the same type. Smear some clean engine oil on the rubber gasket of the new filter **(see illustration)**.

15   Attach the new filter to the engine, following the tightening directions printed on the filter canister or packing box. Most filter manufacturers recommend against using a filter wrench due to the possibility of overtightening and damaging the seal.

16   Remove all tools, rags, etc. from under the vehicle, being careful not to spill the oil in the drain pan, then lower the vehicle.

17   Add new oil to the engine through the oil filler cap in the valve cover. Use a funnel, if necessary, to prevent oil from spilling onto the top of the engine. Pour four quarts of fresh oil into the engine. Wait a few minutes to allow the oil to drain into the pan, then check the level on the oil dipstick (see Section 4). If the oil level is at or near the upper mark on the dipstick, install the filler cap hand tight, start the engine and allow the new oil to circulate.

18   Allow the engine to run for about a minute. While the engine is running, look under the vehicle and check for leaks at the oil pan drain plug and around the oil filter. If either is leaking, stop the engine and tighten the plug or filter.

19   Wait a few minutes to allow the oil to trickle down into the pan, then recheck the level on the dipstick and, if necessary, add enough oil to bring the level to the upper mark on the dipstick.

6.14 Lubricate the oil filter gasket with clean engine oil before installing the filter on the engine

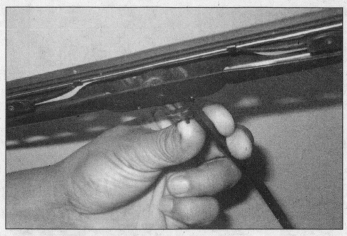

7.5a To release the blade holder, push the release lever . . .

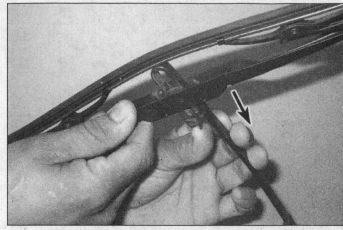

7.5b . . . and pull the wiper blade in the direction of the arrow to separate it from the arm

20   During the first few trips after an oil change, make it a point to check frequently for leaks and proper oil level.

21   The old oil drained from the engine cannot be reused in its present state and should be disposed of. Check with your local auto parts store, disposal facility or environmental agency to see if they will accept the oil for recycling. After the oil has cooled it can be drained into a container (capped plastic jugs, topped bottles, milk cartons, etc.) for transport to one of these disposal sites. Don't dispose of the oil by pouring it on the ground or down a drain!

7   Windshield wiper blade inspection and replacement (every 7500 miles [12,000 km] or 6 months)

Refer to illustrations 7.5a and 7.5b

1   The windshield wiper and blade assembly should be inspected periodically for damage, loose components and cracked or worn blade elements.

2   Road film can build up on the wiper blades and affect their efficiency, so they should be washed regularly with a mild detergent solution.

3   The action of the wiping mechanism can loosen bolts, nuts and fasteners, so they should be checked and tightened, as necessary, at the same time the wiper blades are checked.

4   If the wiper blade elements are cracked, worn or warped, or no longer clean adequately, they should be replaced with new ones.

5   Lift the arm assembly away from the glass for clearance, press on the release lever, then slide the wiper blade assembly out of the hook at the end of the arm **(see illustrations).**

6   Attach the new wiper to the arm. Connection can be confirmed by an audible click.

8   Battery check, maintenance and charging (every 7500 miles [12,000 km] or 6 months)

Refer to illustrations 8.1, 8.6a, 8.6b, 8.7a and 8.7b

Warning: *Certain precautions must be followed when checking and servicing the battery. Hydrogen gas, which is highly flammable, is always present in the battery cells, so keep lighted tobacco and all other open flames and sparks away from the battery. The electrolyte inside the battery is actually diluted sulfuric acid, which will cause injury if splashed on your skin or in your eyes. It will also ruin clothes and painted surfaces. When removing the battery cables, always detach the negative cable first and hook it up last!*

1   A routine preventive maintenance program for the battery in your vehicle is the only way to ensure quick and reliable starts. But before performing any battery maintenance,

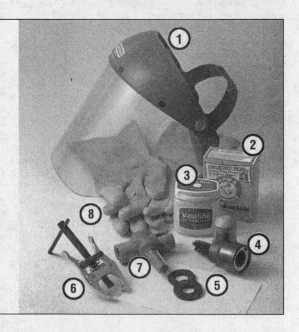

8.1 Tools and materials required for battery maintenance

1   *Face shield/safety goggles -* *When removing corrosion with a brush, the acidic particles can easily fly up into your eyes*

2   *Baking soda -* *A solution of baking soda and water can be used to neutralize corrosion*

3   *Petroleum jelly -* *A layer of this on the battery posts will help prevent corrosion*

4   *Battery post/cable cleaner -* *This wire brush cleaning tool will remove all traces of corrosion from the battery posts and cable clamps*

5   *Treated felt washers -* *Placing one of these on each post, directly under the cable clamps, will help prevent corrosion*

6   *Puller -* *Sometimes the cable clamps are very difficult to pull off the posts, even after the nut/bolt has been completely loosened. This tool pulls the clamp straight up and off the post without damage*

7   *Battery post/cable cleaner -* *Here is another cleaning tool which is a slightly different version of number 4 above, but it does the same thing*

8   *Rubber gloves -* *Another safety item to consider when servicing the battery; remember that's acid inside the battery!*

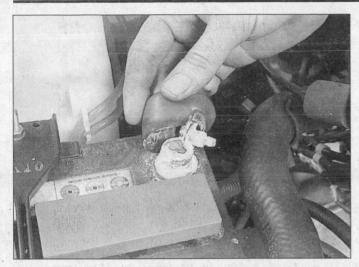

8.6a Battery terminal corrosion usually appears as light, fluffy powder

8.6b Removing a cable from the battery post with a wrench - sometimes a pair of special battery pliers are required for this procedure if corrosion has caused deterioration of the nut hex (always remove the ground [-] cable first and hook it up last!)

make sure that you have the proper equipment necessary to work safely around the battery (see illustration).

2   There are also several precautions that should be taken whenever battery maintenance is performed. Before servicing the battery, always turn the engine and all accessories off and disconnect the cable from the negative terminal of the battery (see Chapter 5, Section 1).

3   The battery produces hydrogen gas, which is both flammable and explosive. Never create a spark, smoke or light a match around the battery. Always charge the battery in a ventilated area.

4   Electrolyte contains poisonous and corrosive sulfuric acid. Do not allow it to get in your eyes, on your skin on your clothes. Never ingest it. Wear protective safety glasses when working near the battery. Keep children away from the battery.

5   Note the external condition of the battery. If the positive terminal and cable clamp on your vehicle's battery is equipped with a rubber protector, make sure that it's not torn or damaged. It should completely cover the terminal. Look for any corroded or loose connections, cracks in the case or cover or loose hold-down clamps. Also check the entire length of each cable for cracks and frayed conductors.

6   If corrosion, which looks like white, fluffy deposits (see illustration) is evident, particularly around the terminals, the battery should be removed for cleaning. Loosen the cable clamp bolts with a wrench, being careful to remove the ground cable first, and slide them off the terminals (see illustration). Then disconnect the hold-down clamp bolt and nut, remove the clamp and lift the battery from the engine compartment.

7   Clean the cable clamps thoroughly with a battery brush or a terminal cleaner and a solution of warm water and baking soda (see illustration). Wash the terminals and the top of the battery case with the same solution but

make sure that the solution doesn't get into the battery. When cleaning the cables, terminals and battery top, wear safety goggles and rubber gloves to prevent any solution from coming in contact with your eyes or hands. Wear old clothes too - even diluted, sulfuric acid splashed onto clothes will burn holes in them. If the terminals have been extensively corroded, clean them up with a terminal cleaner (see illustration). Thoroughly wash all cleaned areas with plain water.

8   Make sure that the battery tray is in good condition and the hold-down clamp fasteners are tight. If the battery is removed from the tray, make sure no parts remain in the bottom of the tray when the battery is reinstalled. When reinstalling the hold-down clamp bolts, do not overtighten them.

9   Information on removing and installing the battery can be found in Chapter 5. If you disconnected the cable(s) from the negative and/

or positive battery terminals, see Chapter 5, Section 1. Information on jump starting can be found at the front of this manual. For more detailed battery checking procedures, refer to the Haynes Automotive Electrical Manual.

Cleaning

10   Corrosion on the hold-down components, battery case and surrounding areas can be removed with a solution of water and baking soda. Thoroughly rinse all cleaned areas with plain water.

11   Any metal parts of the vehicle damaged by corrosion should be covered with a zinc-based primer, then painted.

Charging

Warning: When batteries are being charged, hydrogen gas, which is very explosive and flammable, is produced. Do not smoke or allow open flames near a charging or a

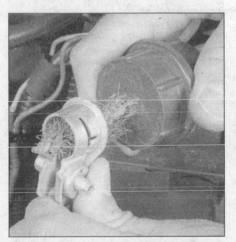

8.7a When cleaning the cable clamps, all corrosion must be removed (the inside of the clamp is tapered to match the taper on the post, so don't remove too much material!)

8.7b Regardless of the type of tool used to clean the battery posts, a clean, shiny surface should be the result

Check for a chafed area that could fail prematurely.

Check for a soft area indicating the hose has deteriorated inside.

Overtightening the clamp on a hardened hose will damage the hose and cause a leak.

Check each hose for swelling and oil-soaked ends. Cracks and breaks can be located by squeezing the hose.

9.4 Hoses, like drivebelts, have a habit of failing at the worst possible time - to prevent the inconvenience of a blown radiator or heater hose, inspect them carefully as shown here

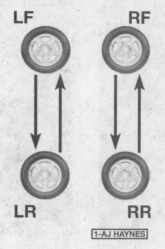

10.2a The recommended rotation pattern for directional radial tires

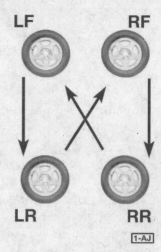

10.2b The recommended rotation pattern for non-directional radial tires

recently charged battery. Wear eye protection when near the battery during charging. Also, make sure the charger is unplugged before connecting or disconnecting the battery from the charger.

12   Slow-rate charging is the best way to restore a battery that's discharged to the point where it will not start the engine. It's also a good way to maintain the battery charge in a vehicle that's only driven a few miles between starts. Maintaining the battery charge is particularly important in the winter when the battery must work harder to start the engine and electrical accessories that drain the battery are in greater use.

13   It's best to use a one or two-amp battery charger (sometimes called a "trickle" charger). They are the safest and put the least

strain on the battery. They are also the least expensive. For a faster charge, you can use a higher amperage charger, but don't use one rated more than 1/10th the amp/hour rating of the battery. Rapid boost charges that claim to restore the power of the battery in one to two hours are hardest on the battery and can damage batteries not in good condition. This type of charging should only be used in emergency situations.

14   The average time necessary to charge a battery should be listed in the instructions that come with the charger. As a general rule, a trickle charger will charge a battery in 12 to 16 hours.

9   Cooling system check (every 7500 miles [12,000 km] or 6 months)

Refer to illustration 9.4

1   Many major engine failures can be attributed to a faulty cooling system. The cooling system also cools the transaxle fluid and thus plays an important role in prolonging transaxle life.

2   The cooling system should be checked with the engine cold. Do this before the vehicle is driven for the day or after the engine has been shut off for at least three hours.

3   Remove the radiator cap by turning it to the left until it reaches a stop. If you hear a hissing sound (indicating it's still pressure in the system), wait until it stops. Now press down on the cap with the palm of your hand and continue turning to the left until the cap can be removed. Thoroughly clean the cap, inside and out, with clean water. Also clean the filler neck on the radiator. All traces of corrosion should be removed. The coolant inside the radiator should be relatively transparent. If it's rust colored, the system should be drained and refilled (see Section 23). If the coolant level isn't up to the top, add additional

antifreeze/coolant mixture (see Section 4).

4   Carefully check the large upper and lower radiator hoses along with the smaller diameter heater hoses which run from the engine to the firewall. Inspect each hose along its entire length, replacing any hose which is cracked, swollen or shows signs of deterioration. Cracks may become more apparent if the hose is squeezed **(see illustration)**. Regardless of condition, it's a good idea to replace hoses with new ones every two years.

5   Make sure that all hose connections are tight. A leak in the cooling system will usually show up as white or rust colored deposits on the areas adjoining the leak. If wire-type clamps are used at the ends of the hoses, it may be a good idea to replace them with more secure screw-type clamps.

6   Use compressed air or a soft brush to remove bugs, leaves, etc. from the front of the radiator or air conditioning condenser. Be careful not to damage the delicate cooling fins or cut yourself on them.

7   Every other inspection, or at the first indication of cooling system problems, have the cap and system pressure tested. If you don't have a pressure tester, most gas stations and repair shops will do this for a minimal charge.

10   Tire rotation (every 7500 miles [12,000 km] or 6 months)

Refer to illustrations 10.2a and 10.2b

1   The tires should be rotated at the specified intervals and whenever uneven wear is noticed. Since the vehicle will be raised and the tires removed anyway, check the brakes (see Section 12) at this time.

2   Radial tires must be rotated in a specific pattern **(see illustrations)**. Most models are equipped with non-directional tires, but some models may have directional tires, which have a different rotation pattern. When rotating tires, examine the sidewalls. Directional tires

12.6a You will find an inspection hole like this in each caliper through which you can view the thickness of remaining friction material for the inner pad (front caliper shown, rear caliper similar)

12.6b The outer pad is more easily checked at the edge of the caliper

have arrows on the sidewall that indicate the direction they must turn.

3   Refer to the information in *Jacking and towing* at the front of this manual for the proper procedures to follow when raising the vehicle and changing a tire. If the brakes are to be checked, do not apply the parking brake as stated. Make sure the tires are blocked to prevent the vehicle from rolling.

4   Preferably, the entire vehicle should be raised at the same time. This can be done on a hoist or by jacking up each corner and then lowering the vehicle onto jackstands placed under the frame rails. Always use four jackstands and make sure the vehicle is firmly supported.

5   After rotation, check and adjust the tire pressures as necessary and be sure to check the lug nut tightness. Ideally, lug nuts should be tightened to the torque listed in this Chapter's Specifications with a torque wrench, and rechecked after 25 miles of driving.

6   For further information on the wheels and tires, refer to Chapter 10.

11   Seat belt check (every 7500 miles [12,000 km] or 6 months)

Warning: *Some models are equipped with seat belt pre-tensioners, which are pyrotechnic (explosive) devices that tighten the seat belts during an impact of sufficient force. Always disable the airbag system before working in the vicinity of any restraint system component to avoid the possibility of accidental deployment of the airbag(s) and seat belt pre-tensioners, which could cause personal injury (see Chapter 12).*

1   Check seat belts, buckles, latch plates and guide loops for obvious damage and signs of wear.

2   See if the seat belt reminder light comes on when the key is turned to the Run or Start position. A chime should also sound. On passive restraint systems, the shoulder belt should move into position in the A-pillar.

3   The seat belts are designed to lock up during a sudden stop or impact, yet allow free movement during normal driving. Make sure the retractors return the belt against your chest while driving and rewind the belt fully when the buckle is unlatched.

4   If any of the above checks reveal problems with the seat belt system, replace parts as necessary.

12   Brake system check (every 7500 miles [12,000 km] or 6 months)

Warning: *The dust created by the brake system is harmful to your health. Never blow it out with compressed air and don't inhale any of it. An approved filtering mask should be worn when working on the brakes. Do not, under any circumstances, use petroleum-based solvents to clean brake parts. Use brake system cleaner only!*

Note: *For detailed photographs of the brake system, refer to Chapter 9.*

1   In addition to the specified intervals, the brakes should be inspected every time the wheels are removed or whenever a defect is suspected.

2   Any of the following symptoms could indicate a potential brake system defect: The vehicle pulls to one side when the brake pedal is depressed; the brakes make squealing or dragging noises when applied; brake pedal travel is excessive; the pedal pulsates; or brake fluid leaks, usually onto the inside of the tire or wheel.

Disc brakes

Refer to illustrations 12.6a and 12.6b

3   Disc brakes can be visually checked without removing any parts except the wheels. Remove the hub caps (if applicable) and loosen the wheel lug nuts a quarter turn each.

4   Raise the vehicle and place it securely on jackstands. **Warning:** *Never work under a vehicle that is supported only by a jack!*

5   Remove the wheels. Now visible is the disc brake caliper which contains the pads. There is an outer brake pad and an inner pad. Both must be checked for wear.

6   Measure the thickness of the outer pad at each end of the caliper and the inner pad through the inspection hole in the caliper body **(see illustrations).** Compare the measurement with the limit given in this Chapter's Specifications; if any brake pad thickness is less than specified, then all brake pads must be replaced (see Chapter 9).

7   If you're in doubt as to the exact pad thickness or quality, remove them for measurement and further inspection (see Chapter 9).

8   Check the disc for score marks, wear and burned spots. If any of these conditions exist, the disc should be removed for servicing or replacement (see Chapter 9).

9   Before installing the wheels, check all the brake lines and hoses for damage, wear, deformation, cracks, corrosion, leakage, bends and twists, particularly in the vicinity of the rubber hoses and calipers.

10   Install the wheels, lower the vehicle and tighten the wheel lug nuts to the torque given in this Chapter's Specifications.

Brake booster check

11   Sit in the driver's seat and perform the following sequence of tests.

12   With the brake fully depressed, start the engine - the pedal should move down a little when the engine starts.

13   With the engine running, depress the brake pedal several times - the travel distance should not change.

14   Depress the brake, stop the engine and

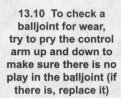

13.10 To check a balljoint for wear, try to pry the control arm up and down to make sure there is no play in the balljoint (if there is, replace it)

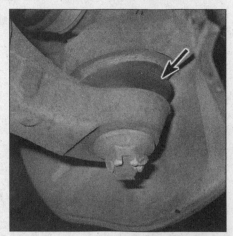

13.11 Push on the balljoint boot to check for tears and grease

hold the pedal in for about 30 seconds - the pedal should neither sink nor rise.

15   Restart the engine, run it for about a minute and turn it off. Then firmly depress the brake several times - the pedal travel should decrease with each application.

16   If your brakes do not operate as described, the brake booster has failed. Refer to Chapter 9 for the replacement procedure.

13   Steering and suspension check (every 15,000 miles [24,000 km] or 12 months)

Note: *For detailed illustrations of the steering and suspension components, refer to Chapter 10.*

With the wheels on the ground

1   With the vehicle stopped and the front wheels pointed straight ahead, rock the steering wheel gently back and forth. If freeplay is excessive, a front wheel bearing, steering shaft universal joint or lower arm balljoint is worn or the steering gear is out of adjustment or broken. Refer to Chapter 10 for the appropriate repair procedure.

2   Other symptoms, such as excessive vehicle body movement over rough roads, swaying (leaning) around corners and binding as the steering wheel is turned, may indicate faulty steering and/or suspension components.

3   Check the shock absorbers by pushing down and releasing the vehicle several times at each corner. If the vehicle does not come back to a level position within one or two bounces, the shocks/struts are worn and must be replaced. When bouncing the vehicle up and down, listen for squeaks and noises from the suspension components.

4   Check the struts and shock absorbers for evidence of fluid leakage. A light film of fluid is no cause for concern. Make sure that any fluid noted is from the struts or shocks and not from some other source. If leakage is noted, replace the struts or shocks as a set.

5   Check the struts and shocks to be sure

they are securely mounted and undamaged. Check the upper mounts for damage and wear. If damage or wear is noted, replace the struts or shocks as a set (both front or both rear).

6   If the struts or shocks must be replaced, refer to Chapter 10 for the procedure.

Under the vehicle

Refer to illustrations 13.10 and 13.11

7   Raise the vehicle with a floor jack and support it securely on jackstands. See *Jacking and towing* at the front of this book for the proper jacking points.

8   Check the tires for irregular wear patterns and proper inflation. See Section 5 in this Chapter for information regarding tire wear and Chapter 10 for information on wheel/hub bearing replacement.

9   Inspect the universal joint between the steering shaft and the steering gear housing. Check the steering gear housing for lubricant leakage. Make sure that the dust seals and boots are not damaged and that the boot clamps are not loose. Check the steering linkage for looseness or damage. Check the tie-rod ends for excessive play. Look for loose bolts, broken or disconnected parts and deteriorated rubber bushings on all suspension and steering components. While an assistant turns the steering wheel from side to side, check the steering components for free movement, chafing and binding. If the steering components do not seem to be reacting with the movement of the steering wheel, try to determine where the slack is located.

10   Check the balljoints for wear by trying to move each control arm up and down with a prybar **(see illustration)** to ensure that its balljoint has no play. If any balljoint does have play, replace it. See Chapter 10 for the balljoint replacement procedure.

11   Inspect the balljoint boots for damage and leaking grease **(see illustration).** Replace the balljoints with new ones if they are damaged (see Chapter 10).

12   At the rear of the vehicle, inspect the suspension arm bushings for deterioration. Additional information on suspension components can be found in Chapter 10.

14   Underhood hose check and replacement (every 15,000 miles [24,000 km] or 12 months)

Warning: *Replacement of air conditioning hoses must be left to a dealer service department or air conditioning shop that has the equipment to depressurize the system safely. Never remove air conditioning components or hoses until the system has been depressurized.*

General

1   High temperatures under the hood can cause deterioration of the rubber and plastic hoses used for engine, accessory and emission systems operation. Periodic inspection should be made for cracks, loose clamps, material hardening and leaks.

2   Information specific to the cooling system hoses can be found in Section 9.

3   Most (but not all) hoses are secured to the fittings with clamps. Where clamps are used, check to be sure they haven't lost their tension, allowing the hose to leak. If clamps aren't used, make sure the hose has not expanded and/or hardened where it slips over the fitting, allowing it to leak.

PCV system hose

4   To reduce hydrocarbon emissions, crankcase blow-by gas is vented through the PCV valve in the rocker arm cover to the intake manifold via a rubber hose (on most models). The blow-by gases mix with incoming air in the intake manifold before being burned in the combustion chambers.

5   Check the PCV hose for cracks, leaks and other damage. Disconnect it from the valve cover and the intake manifold and check the inside for obstructions. If it's clogged, clean it out with solvent.

Vacuum hoses

6   It's quite common for vacuum hoses, especially those in the emissions system, to

15.1a Remove the screws securing the two halves of the air filter housing

15.1b Pull the cover out of the way . . .

be color coded or identified by colored stripes molded into them. Various systems require hoses with different wall thickness, collapse resistance and temperature resistance. When replacing hoses, be sure the new ones are made of the same material.

7   Often the only effective way to check a hose is to remove it completely from the vehicle. If more than one hose is removed, be sure to label the hoses and fittings to ensure correct installation.

8   When checking vacuum hoses, be sure to include any plastic T-fittings in the check. Inspect the fittings for cracks and the hose where it fits over each fitting for distortion, which could cause leakage.

9   A small piece of vacuum hose (1/4-inch inside diameter) can be used as a stethoscope to detect vacuum leaks. Hold one end of the hose to your ear and probe around vacuum hoses and fittings, listening for the "hissing" sound characteristic of a vacuum leak. **Warning:** *When probing with the vacuum hose stethoscope, be careful not to come into contact with moving engine components such as drivebelts, the cooling fan, etc.*

Fuel hose

Warning: *Gasoline is flammable, so take extra precautions when you work on any part of the fuel system. Don't smoke or allow open flames or bare light bulbs near the work area, and don't work in a garage where a gas-type appliance (such as a water heater or clothes dryer) is present. Since fuel is carcinogenic, wear fuel-resistant gloves when there's a possibility of being exposed to fuel, and, if you spill any fuel on your skin, rinse it off immediately with soap and water. Mop up any spills immediately and do not store fuel-soaked rags where they could ignite. The fuel system is under constant pressure, so, if any fuel lines are to be disconnected, the fuel pressure in the system must be relieved first (see Chapter 4 for more information). When you perform any kind of work on the fuel system, wear safety glasses and have a Class B type*

15.1c . . . and lift the element out

fire extinguisher on hand.

10   The fuel lines are usually under pressure, so if any fuel lines are to be disconnected, be prepared to catch spilled fuel. **Warning:** *Your vehicle is equipped with fuel injection and you must relieve the fuel system pressure before servicing the fuel lines. Refer to Chapter 4 for the fuel system pressure relief procedure.*

11   Check all flexible fuel lines for deterioration and chafing. Check especially for cracks in areas where the hose bends and just before fittings, such as where a hose attaches to the fuel pump, fuel filter and fuel rail.

12   When replacing a hose, use only hose that is specifically designed for your fuel injection system.

13   Spring-type clamps are sometimes used on fuel return or vapor lines. These clamps often lose their tension over a period of time, and can be "sprung" during removal. Replace all spring-type clamps with screw clamps whenever a hose is replaced. Some fuel lines use spring-lock type couplings, which require a special tool to disconnect. See Chapter 4 for more information on this type of coupling.

Metal lines

14   Sections of metal line are often used for fuel line between the fuel pump and the fuel

injection unit. Check carefully to make sure the line isn't bent, crimped or cracked.

15   If a section of metal fuel line must be replaced, use seamless steel tubing only, since copper and aluminum tubing do not have the strength necessary to withstand vibration caused by the engine.

16   Check the metal brake lines where they enter the master cylinder and brake proportioning unit (if used) for cracks in the lines and loose fittings. Any sign of brake fluid leakage calls for an immediate thorough inspection of the brake system.

---

15   Air filter replacement (every 15,000 miles [24,000 km] or 12 months)

Refer to illustrations 15.1a, 15.1b and 15.1c

1   The air filter is located inside a housing at the left (driver's) side of the engine compartment under a cover **(see illustration 4.38a)** To remove the air filter, disconnect the throttle cable or wiring harness from the air filter housing cover, remove the screws securing the two halves of the air filter housing together, then separate the cover halves and remove the air filter element **(see illustrations).**

16.3a Release the tabs at the sides of the filter door

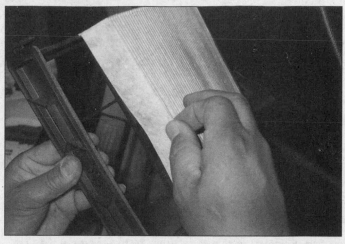

16.3b Slide the filter from the housing, and remove it from its holder

2   Inspect the outer surface of the filter element. If it is dirty, replace it. If it is only moderately dusty, it can be reused by blowing it clean from the back to the front surface with compressed air. Because it is a pleated paper type filter, it cannot be washed or oiled. If it cannot be cleaned satisfactorily with compressed air, discard and replace it. While the cover is off, be careful not to drop anything down into the housing. **Caution:** *Never drive the vehicle with the air cleaner removed. Excessive engine wear could result and backfiring could even cause a fire under the hood.*

3   Wipe out the inside of the air cleaner housing.

4   Place the new filter into the air cleaner housing, making sure it seats properly.

5   Installation of the housing is the reverse of removal.

16   Interior ventilation filter replacement (every 15,000 miles [24,000 km] or 12 months)

Refer to illustrations 16.3a and 16.3b

Warning: *The models covered by this manual are equipped with a Supplemental Restraint System (SRS), more commonly known as airbags. Always disable the airbag system before working in the vicinity of any airbag system component to avoid the possibility of accidental deployment of the airbag, which could cause personal injury (see Chapter 12).*

1   These models are equipped with an air filtering element in the air conditioning system, located in a housing next to the evaporator, under the right side of the instrument panel.

2   Refer to Chapter 11 for removal of the glove box.

3   Release the tabs at the sides of the filter door and remove the filter **(see illustrations).**

4   Installation is the reverse of the removal procedure.

17   Fuel system check (every 15,000 miles [24,000 km] or 12 months)

Warning: *Gasoline is flammable, so take extra precautions when you work on any part of the fuel system. Don't smoke or allow open flames or bare light bulbs near the work area, and don't work in a garage where a gas-type appliance (such as a water heater or clothes dryer) is present. Since fuel is carcinogenic, wear fuel-resistant gloves when there's a possibility of being exposed to fuel, and, if you spill any fuel on your skin, rinse it off immediately with soap and water. Mop up any spills immediately and do not store fuel-soaked rags where they could ignite. When you perform any kind of work on the fuel system, wear safety glasses and have a Class B type fire extinguisher on hand. The fuel system is under constant pressure, so, before any lines are disconnected, the fuel system pressure must be relieved (see Chapter 4).*

1   If you smell gasoline while driving or after the vehicle has been sitting in the sun, inspect the fuel system immediately.

2   Remove the fuel filler cap and inspect it for damage and corrosion. The gasket should have an unbroken sealing imprint. If the gasket is damaged or corroded, install a new cap.

3   Inspect the fuel feed line for cracks. Make sure that the connections between the fuel lines and the fuel injection system. **Warning:** *Your vehicle is fuel injected, so you must relieve the fuel system pressure before servicing fuel system components. The fuel system pressure relief procedure is outlined in Chapter 4.*

4   Since some components of the fuel system - the fuel tank and the fuel lines, for example - are underneath the vehicle, they can be inspected more easily with the vehicle raised on a hoist. If that's not possible, raise the vehicle and support it on jackstands.

5   With the vehicle raised and safely supported, inspect the gas tank and filler neck for punctures, cracks and other damage. The connection between the filler neck and the tank is particularly critical. Sometimes a rubber filler neck will leak because of loose clamps or deteriorated rubber. Inspect all fuel tank mounting brackets and straps to be sure that the tank is securely attached to the vehicle. **Warning:** *Do not, under any circumstances, try to repair a fuel tank (except rubber components). A welding torch or any open flame can easily cause fuel vapors inside the tank to explode.*

6   Carefully check all hoses and lines leading away from the fuel tank. Check for loose connections, deteriorated hoses, crimped lines and other damage. Repair or replace damaged sections as necessary (see Chapter 4).

18   Exhaust system check (every 15,000 miles [24,000 km] or 12 months)

Refer to illustration 18.2

1   With the engine cold (at least three hours after the vehicle has been driven), check the complete exhaust system from the engine to the end of the tailpipe. Ideally, the inspection should be done with the vehicle on a hoist to permit unrestricted access. If a hoist isn't available, raise the vehicle and support it securely on jackstands.

2   Check the exhaust pipes and connections for evidence of leaks, severe corrosion and damage. Make sure that all brackets and hangers are in good condition and tight **(see illustration).**

3   At the same time, inspect the underside of the body for holes, corrosion, open seams, etc. which may allow exhaust gases to enter the passenger compartment. Seal all body openings with silicone or body putty.

4   Rattles and other noises can often be traced to the exhaust system, especially the mounts and hangers. Try to move the pipes,

18.2 Check the exhaust system for rust, damage, or worn rubber hangers

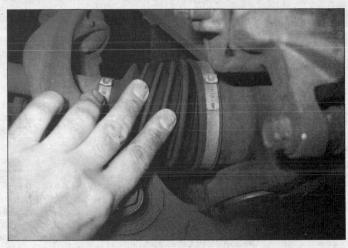

19.2 Flex the driveaxle boots by hand to check for tears, cracks and leaking grease

muffler and catalytic converter. If the components can come in contact with the body or suspension parts, secure the exhaust system with new mounts.

5   Check the running condition of the engine by inspecting inside the end of the tailpipe. The exhaust deposits here are an indication of engine state-of-tune. If the pipe is black and sooty or coated with white deposits, the engine may need a tune-up, including a thorough fuel system inspection and adjustment.

19 Driveaxle boot check (every 15,000 miles [24,000 km] or 12 months)

Refer to illustration 19.2

1   The driveaxle boots are very important because they prevent dirt, water and foreign material from entering and damaging the constant velocity (CV) joints. Because it constantly pivots back and forth following the steering action of the front hub, the outer CV boot wears out sooner and should be inspected regularly.

2   Inspect the boots for tears and cracks as well as loose clamps **(see illustration)**. If there is any evidence of cracks or leaking lubricant, they must be replaced as described in Chapter 8.

20 Drivebelt check and replacement (every 30,000 miles [48,000 km] or 24 months)

Accessory drivebelt

1   A single serpentine drivebelt is located at the front of the engine and plays an important role in the overall operation of the engine and its components. Due to its function and material make up, the belt is prone to wear and should be periodically inspected. The serpentine belt drives the alternator, power steering pump, water pump and air conditioning compressor.

Check

Refer to illustrations 20.3 and 20.4

2   With the engine stopped, inspect the full length of the drivebelt for cracks and separation of the belt plies. It will be necessary to turn the engine (using a wrench or socket and bar on the crankshaft pulley bolt) in order to move the belt from the pulleys so that the belt can be inspected thoroughly. Twist the belt between the pulleys so that both sides can be viewed. Also check for fraying, and glazing which gives the belt a shiny appearance. Check the pulleys for nicks, cracks, distortion and corrosion.

3   Note that it is not unusual for a ribbed belt to exhibit small cracks in the edges of the belt ribs, and unless these are extensive or very deep, belt replacement is not essential **(see illustration)**.

4   The drivebelt tension is adjusted by an automatic tensioner. Look at the wear indica-

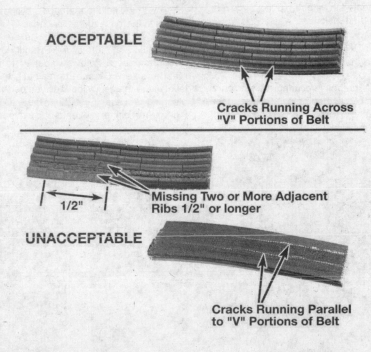

ACCEPTABLE

Cracks Running Across "V" Portions of Belt

1/2"

Missing Two or More Adjacent Ribs 1/2" or longer

UNACCEPTABLE

Cracks Running Parallel to "V" Portions of Belt

20.3 Here are some of the more common problems associated with ribbed drivebelts (check the belts very carefully to prevent an untimely breakdown)

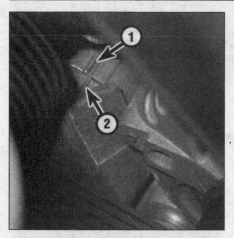

20.4 Details of the drivebelt tensioner

1   *Standard range (belt OK)*
2   *Belt length indicator*

tor on the tensioner **(see illustration)**. The marks should be within the specified range; if not, the belt will have to be replaced.

Replacement

Refer to illustration 20.5

5   Note how the drivebelt is routed, then remove the belt from the pulleys. Use a wrench on the tensioner pulley center bolt and turn the tensioner counterclockwise to release the drivebelt tension **(see illustration)**.
6   Fit the new drivebelt onto the crankshaft, alternator, power steering pump and air conditioning compressor pulleys, as applicable, then turn the tensioner and locate the drivebelt on the pulley. Make sure that the drivebelt is correctly seated in all of the pulley grooves, then release the tensioner.

Tensioner replacement

7   Remove the drivebelt as described previously.
8   Remove the bolts securing the tensioner to the engine block, then detach the tensioner from the engine. **Note:** *The tensioner pulley*

can be replaced separately, if necessary.
9   Installation is the reverse of removal. Be sure to tighten the tensioner (and pulley, if replaced) bolts to the torque listed in this Chapter's Specifications.

21   Brake fluid change (every 30,000 miles [48,000 km] or 24 months)

Warning: *Brake fluid can harm your eyes and damage painted surfaces, so use extreme caution when handling or pouring it. Do not use brake fluid that has been standing open or is more than one year old. Brake fluid absorbs moisture from the air. Excess moisture can cause a dangerous loss of braking effectiveness.*
Note: *Used brake fluid is considered a hazardous waste and it must be disposed of in accordance with federal, state and local laws. DO NOT pour it down the sink, into septic tanks or storm drains, or on the ground.*
1   At the specified intervals, the brake fluid should be drained and replaced. Since the brake fluid may drip or splash when pouring it, place plenty of rags around the master cylinder to protect any surrounding painted surfaces.
2   Before beginning work, purchase the specified brake fluid (see *Recommended lubricants and fluids* at the beginning of this Chapter).
3   Remove the cap from the master cylinder reservoir.
4   Using a hand suction pump or similar device, withdraw the fluid from the master cylinder reservoir.
5   Add new fluid to the master cylinder until it rises to the base of the filler neck.
6   Bleed the brake system as described in Chapter 9 at all four brakes until new and uncontaminated fluid is expelled from the bleeder screw. Be sure to maintain the fluid level in the master cylinder as you perform the bleeding process. If you allow the master cylinder to run dry, air will enter the system.

7   Refill the master cylinder with fluid and check the operation of the brakes. The pedal should feel solid when depressed, with no sponginess. **Warning:** *Do not operate the vehicle if you are in doubt about the effectiveness of the brake system.*

22   Automatic transaxle fluid change (every 30,000 miles [48,000 km] or 24 months)

Refer to illustration 22.6
1   The automatic transaxle fluid should be changed at the recommended intervals.
2   Before beginning work, purchase the specified transmission fluid (see *Recommended lubricants and fluids* at the front of this Chapter).
3   Other tools necessary for this job include jackstands to support the vehicle in a raised position, wrenches, a drain pan capable of holding at least four quarts, newspapers and clean rags.
4   The fluid should be drained immediately after the vehicle has been driven. Hot fluid is more effective than cold fluid at removing built up sediment. **Warning:** *Fluid temperature can exceed 350-degrees F in a hot transaxle. Wear protective gloves.*
5   After the vehicle has been driven to warm up the fluid, raise the front of the vehicle and support it securely on jackstands. **Warning:** *Never work under a vehicle that is supported only by a jack!*
6   Place the drain pan under the drain plug and remove the fill plug **(see illustration 4.34)** and the drain plug **(see illustration)**. Be sure the drain pan is in position, as fluid will come out with some force. Once the fluid is drained, reinstall the drain plug, tightening it to the torque listed in this Chapter's Specifications. Measure the amount of fluid drained and write down this figure for reference when refilling.
7   Lower the vehicle.

20.5 Use a wrench on the tensioner pulley center bolt and turn the tensioner counterclockwise to release the drivebelt tension

22.6 Automatic transaxle drain plug location

23.3 The drain fitting is located at the bottom of the radiator

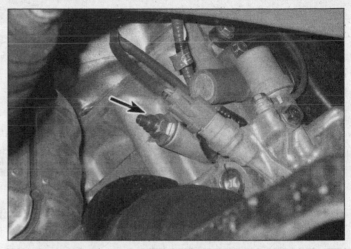

23.4 The engine has a coolant drain plug located on the rear side of the engine

8   With the engine off and the fill plug removed, add new fluid to the transaxle (see *Recommended lubricants and fluids* for the recommended fluid type). Begin the refill procedure by initially adding 1/3 of the amount drained. Then, with the engine running, add 1/2-pint at a time (cycling the shifter through each gear position between additions) until the level is correct on the dipstick.

9   If desired, repeat Steps 5 through 8 once to flush any contaminated fluid from the torque converter.

23 Cooling system servicing (draining, flushing and refilling) (every 60,000 miles [96,000 km] or 36 months)

Warning: *Do not allow antifreeze to come in contact with your skin or painted surfaces of the vehicle. Rinse off spills immediately with plenty of water. Antifreeze is highly toxic if ingested. Never leave antifreeze lying around in an open container or in puddles on the floor; children and pets are attracted by its sweet smell and may drink it. Check with local authorities about disposing of used antifreeze. Many communities have collection centers which will see that antifreeze is disposed of safely. Never dump used antifreeze on the ground or pour it into drains.*

1   Periodically, the cooling system should be drained, flushed and refilled to replenish the antifreeze mixture and prevent formation of rust and corrosion, which can impair the performance of the cooling system and cause engine damage. When the cooling system is serviced, all hoses and the radiator cap should be checked and replaced if necessary.

Draining

Refer to illustrations 23.3 and 23.4

Warning: *The engine must be completely cool before beginning this procedure.*

2   Apply the parking brake and block the wheels. Turn the ignition switch On. If the vehicle is equipped with automatic climate control, set the system to 90-degrees F (32-degrees C). On other models, turn the heater control to maximum heat. Now turn the ignition switch Off.

3   Move a large container under the radiator drain to catch the coolant. The radiator drain plug is located on the bottom of the radiator **(see illustration)**. Unscrew the drain plug until coolant starts flowing from the drain hole (a pair of pliers may be required to turn it).

4   Remove the radiator cap and allow the radiator to drain, then, move the container under the engine. Loosen the engine block drain plug and allow the coolant in the block to drain **(see illustration)**. While the coolant is draining, check the condition of the radiator hoses, heater hoses and clamps (refer to Section 9, if necessary).

5   Remove the coolant reservoir (see Chapter 3) and drain the coolant, then reinstall the reservoir.

6   Replace any damaged clamps or hoses. Tighten the drain plug securely.

Flushing

Refer to illustration 23.9

7   Once the system is completely drained, remove the thermostat from the engine (see Chapter 3), then reinstall the thermostat housing without the thermostat. This will allow the system to be thoroughly flushed.

8   Turn the heating system controls to Hot, so that the heater core will be flushed at the same time as the rest of the cooling system.

9   Disconnect the upper radiator hose from the radiator, then place a garden hose in the upper radiator inlet and flush the system until the water runs clear at the upper radiator hose **(see illustration)**.

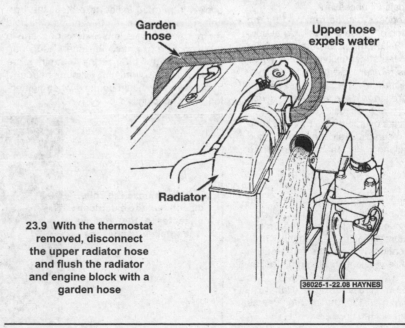

Garden hose

Upper hose expels water

Radiator

23.9 With the thermostat removed, disconnect the upper radiator hose and flush the radiator and engine block with a garden hose

36025-1-22.08 HAYNES

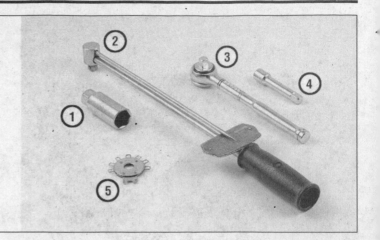

24.2 Tools required for changing spark plugs

1   **Spark plug socket -** *This will have special padding inside to protect the spark plug porcelain insulator*
2   **Torque wrench -** *Although not mandatory, use of this tool is the best way to ensure that the plugs are tightened properly*
3   **Ratchet -** *Standard hand tool to fit the plug socket*
4   **Extension -** *Depending on model and accessories, you may need special extensions and universal joints to reach one or more of the plugs*
5   **Spark plug gap gauge -** *This gauge for checking the gap comes in a variety of styles. Make sure the gap for your engine is included*

24.5 Spark plug manufacturers recommend using a wire-type gauge to check the spark plug gap - if the wire doesn't slide between the electrodes with a slight drag, adjustment is required

10   In severe cases of contamination or clogging of the radiator, remove the radiator (see Chapter 3) and have a radiator repair facility clean and repair it if necessary.

11   Many deposits can be removed by the chemical action of a cleaner available at auto parts stores. Follow the procedure outlined in the manufacturer's instructions. **Note:** *When the coolant is regularly drained and the system refilled with the correct antifreeze/water mixture, there should be no need to use chemical cleaners or descalers.*

12   Remove the overflow hose from the coolant recovery reservoir. Drain the reservoir and flush it with clean water, then reconnect the hose.

Refilling

13   Reconnect the upper radiator hose and reinstall the thermostat.

14   Fill the cooling system with the proper type and mixture of antifreeze (see this Chapter's Specifications), up to the base of the radiator cap filler neck. Install the radiator cap loosely.

15   Start the engine and run it at approximately 1500 rpm until the radiator fan comes on two times. Feel the upper radiator hose - it

should be warm, indicating the thermostat has opened.

16   Turn off the engine and let it cool down. Slowly remove the radiator cap and check the coolant level, adding as necessary. **Warning:** *If you hear a hissing sound as you unscrew the cap, STOP. Let the engine cool down longer.*

17   Tighten the radiator cap, then start the engine, allow it to reach normal operating temperature and check for leaks.

24 Spark plug check and replacement (every 105,000 miles [169,000 km] or 84 months, whichever comes first)

Refer to illustrations 24.2, 24.5, 24.8, 24.10, 24.12a and 24.12b

1   The spark plugs are located in the center of each cylinder head.

2   In most cases the tools necessary for spark plug replacement include a spark plug socket which fits onto a ratchet (this special socket is padded inside to protect the porcelain insulators on the new plugs and hold them in place), various extensions and a feeler gauge to check the spark plug gap **(see illustration).** Since these engines are equipped with aluminum cylinder heads, a torque wrench should be used when tightening the spark plugs.

3   The best approach when replacing the spark plugs is to purchase the new spark plugs beforehand, check the gaps and then replace each plug one at a time. When buying the new spark plugs, be sure to obtain the correct plug for your specific engine. This information can be found in the Specification Section at the front of this Chapter, or in your owner's manual.

4   Allow the engine to cool completely before attempting to remove any of the plugs. During this cooling off time, each of the new spark plugs can be inspected for defects and the gaps can be checked.

5   The gap is checked by inserting the proper thickness gauge between the electrodes at the tip of the plug **(see illustration).** The gap between the electrodes should be as listed in this Chapter's Specifications or in your owner's manual. **Caution:** *The manufacturer recommends against adjusting the gap on platinum- or iridium-tipped spark plugs; if the gap is out of specification, replace the plug.* Also, at this time check for cracks in the spark plug body (if any are found, the plug must not be used).

6   Cover the fender to prevent damage to the paint. Fender covers are available from auto parts stores but an old blanket will work just fine.

7   Remove the engine cover and the ignition coil cover (see Chapter 2A).

8   Remove the ignition coils **(see illustration).**

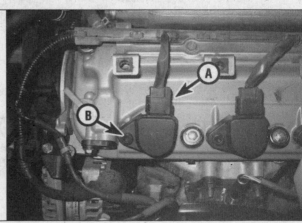

24.8 To remove the coils, disconnect the electrical connector (A) then remove the retaining screw (B)

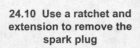

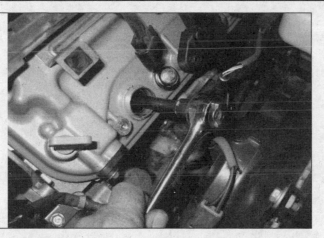

24.10 Use a ratchet and extension to remove the spark plug

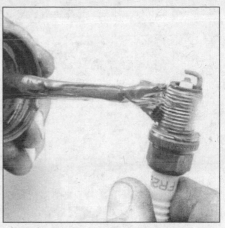

24.12a Apply a thin coat of anti-seize compound to the spark plug threads - DO NOT get any on the electrodes!

9   If compressed air is available, use it to blow any dirt or foreign material away from the spark plug area. **Warning:** *Wear eye protection!* The idea here is to eliminate the possibility of material falling into the cylinder through the spark plug hole as the spark plug is removed.

10   Place the spark plug socket over the plug and remove it from the engine by turning it in a counterclockwise direction **(see illustration)**.

11   Compare the spark plug with the chart on the inside back cover of this manual to get an indication of the overall running condition of the engine.

12   Apply a small amount of anti-seize compound to the spark plug threads **(see illustration)**. Install one of the new plugs into the hole until you can no longer turn it with your fingers, then tighten it with a torque wrench (if available) or the ratchet. It is a good idea to slip a short length of rubber hose over the end of the plug to use as a tool to thread it into place **(see illustration)**. The hose will grip the plug well enough to turn it, but will start to slip if the plug begins to cross-thread in the hole - this will prevent damaged threads and the accompanying repair costs.

13   Attach the coil to the new spark plug using a twisting motion until it is firmly seated on the end of the spark plug. Tighten the mounting bolts securely.

14   Repeat the procedure for the remaining spark plugs.

---

25 Idle speed check and adjustment (105,000 miles [169,000 km] or 84 months)

Check

1   Engine idle speed is the speed at which the engine operates when no accelerator pedal pressure is applied, as when stopped at a traffic light. The speed is critical to the performance of the engine itself, as well as many subsystems.

2   Set the parking brake firmly and block the wheels to prevent the vehicle from rolling. Place the transaxle in Park.

3   Connect a hand-held tachometer in accordance with the tool manufacturer's instructions.

4   Disconnect the two-pin electrical connector from the EVAP purge valve (see Chapter 6).

5   Start the engine and run it at 3000 rpm until it warms up to normal operating temperature (the cooling fan comes on).

6   Slowly release the accelerator until the idle drops to normal speed. Make sure all accessories are turned off and the transaxle is in Neutral.

7   Note the idle speed on the tachometer and compare it to that listed on the VECI label or in this Chapter's Specifications. **Note:** *If the idle speed listed on the VECI label is different than that listed in this Chapter's Specifications, use the specification shown on the VECI label.*

Adjustment

Refer to illustration 25.9

Note: *This adjustment procedure applies to 2003 and earlier models only. If the idle speed is incorrect on other models, a Honda Diagnostic Scan tool is required to perform the PCM idle learn procedure.*

8   Before adjusting the idle speed, make sure the engine cooling fan is off.

9   If the idle speed is too low or too high, remove the plug from the throttle body and turn the idle speed adjusting screw to obtain the specified idle speed **(see illustration)**. Make changes only in quarter-turn increments. Allow the idle to stabilize for one minute and recheck the idle speed.

10   Turn off the engine and disconnect the tachometer. Reconnect the EVAP solenoid.

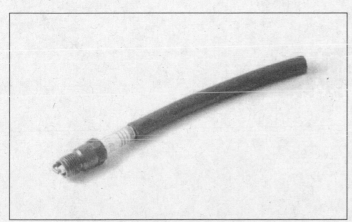

24.12b A length of snug-fitting rubber hose will save time and prevent damaged threads when installing the spark plugs

25.9 Remove the plug from the throttle body and use a small screwdriver to turn the idle adjustment screw

Notes

Chapter 2 Part A
Engines

Contents

Specifications

General

Cylinder numbers (timing belt end-to-transaxle end)
Rear (firewall) side	1-2-3
Front (radiator) side	4-5-6
Firing order	1-4-2-5-3-6
Bore (3.2L and 3.5L engines)	3.50 inches (89.0 mm)

Stroke
3.2L	3.39 inches (86.0 mm)
3.5L	3.66 inches (93.0 mm)

Displacement
3.2L	196 cubic inches
3.5L	212 cubic inches

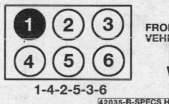

1-4-2-5-3-6

FRONT OF VEHICLE

42035-B-SPECS HAYNES

Cylinder locations

Valve adjustment

Intake	0.008 to 0.009 inch (0.20 to 0.24 mm)
Exhaust	0.011 to 0.013 inch (0.28 to 0.32 mm)

Camshaft and rocker arms

Camshaft-to-holder oil clearance
    Standard.. 0.0020 to 0.0035 inch (0.050 to 0.089 mm)
    Service limit... 0.006 inch (0.15 mm)
Camshaft lobe height
    1999 models
        Intake
            Primary.. 1.3628 inches (34.615 mm)
            Mid.. 1.4280 inches (36.272 mm)
            Secondary... 1.2279 inches (31.188 mm)
        Exhaust... 1.4203 inches (36.076 mm)
    2000 through 2003 models
        Intake
            Primary.. 1.3676 inches (34.737 mm)
            Mid.. 1.4348 inches (36.445 mm)
            Secondary... 1.3748 inches (34.919 mm)
        Exhaust
            J32A-1 engine.. 1.4302 inches (36.326 mm)
            J32A2 engine.. 1.4326 inches (36.389 mm)
    2004 and later models
        J32A3 engine (3.2L)
            Intake
                 Primary.. 1.3796 inches (35.041 mm)
                Mid.. 1.4348 inches (36.445 mm)
                Secondary... 1.3891 inches (35.284 mm)
            Exhaust... 1.4302 inches (36.326 mm)
        J35A8 engine (3.5L)
            Intake
                 Primary.. 1.3824 inches (35.112 mm)
                Mid.. 1.4328 inches (36.394 mm)
                Secondary... 1.3824 inches (35.112 mm)
            Exhaust... 1.4326 inches (36.389 mm)
Camshaft endplay
    Standard.. 0.002 to 0.008 inch (0.05 to 0.20 mm)
    Service limit... 0.008 inch (0.20 mm)
Camshaft runout limit (total indicator reading)......................... 0.001 inch (0.03 mm)
Rocker arm-to-shaft oil clearance
    1999 through 2007 models
        Intake
            Standard... 0.0010 to 0.0026 inch (0.026 to 0.067 mm)
            Service limit.. 0.0026 inch (0.067 mm)
        Exhaust
            Standard... 0.0010 to 0.0030 inch (0.026 to 0.077 mm)
            Service limit.. 0.0030 inch (0.077 mm)
    2008 models
        With automatic transmission
            Intake
                 Standard... 0.0010 to 0.0026 inch (0.026 to 0.067 mm)
                Service limit.. 0.0026 inch (0.067 mm)
            Exhaust
                 Standard... 0.0010 to 0.0030 inch (0.026 to 0.077 mm)
                Service limit.. 0.0030 inch (0.077 mm)
        With manual transmission
             Intake
                 Standard... 0.0010 to 0.0026 inch (0.026 to 0.067 mm)
                Service limit.. 0.0026 inch (0.067 mm)
            Exhaust
                 Standard... 0.0010 to 0.0026 inch (0.026 to 0.067 mm)
                Service limit.. 0.0026 inch (0.067 mm)

Cylinder head warpage

Warpage less than 0.002 inch (0.05 mm)............................... No resurfacing required
Warpage between 0.002 inch (0.05 mm) and 0.008 inch (0.2 mm) .... Resurface the head (maximum of 0.008 inch [0.02 mm])

Oil pump

Outer rotor-to-body clearance
    1999 through 2007 models .... 0.006 to 0.007 inch (0.14 to 0.19 mm)
    2008 models.. 0.004 to 0.007 inch (0.10 to 0.19 mm)
Outer rotor-to-inner rotor clearance.. 0.002 to 0.006 inch (0.04 to 0.16 mm)
Housing-to-rotor axial clearance.. 0.001 to 0.003 inch (0.02 to 0.07 mm)

Torque specifications

Note: *One foot-pound (ft-lb) of torque is equivalent to 12 inch-pounds (in-lbs) of torque. Torque values below approximately 15 foot-pounds are expressed in inch-pounds, because most foot-pound torque wrenches are not accurate at these smaller values.*

	Ft-lbs (unless otherwise indicated)	Nm
Camshaft thrust plate bolts	16	22
Camshaft sprocket bolts	68	92
Coolant passage	16	22
Crankshaft pulley bolt	48	65
Cylinder head bolts		
Models with 6-point bolts		
Step 1	29	39
Step 2	51	69
Step 3	72	98
Models with 12-point bolts		
Step 1	22	30
Step 2	Tighten an additional 90-degrees	
Step 3	Tighten an additional 90-degrees	
Step 4 (with **new** head bolts only)	Tighten an additional 90-degrees	
Drivebelt tensioner mounting bolts	16	22
Drivebelt tensioner pulley bolt	59	80
Driveplate bolts	54	74
Exhaust converter-to-head mounting nuts	23	31
Exhaust converter heat shield nuts	86 in-lbs	9.8
Flywheel bolts	76	103
Intake manifold cover bolts	104 in-lbs	12
Intake manifold bolts (upper manifold and lower manifold)	16	22
Oil pan bolts	106 in-lbs	12
Oil pick-up/screen mounting bolts	106 in-lbs	12
Oil pump housing mounting bolts	106 in-lbs	12
Rocker arm shaft bolts	18	24
Subframe mounting bolts	See Chapter 10	
Timing belt adjuster bolt	19	26
Timing belt tensioner bolts	104 in-lbs	12
Timing belt idler pulley bolt (new)	33	44
Timing belt cover bolts	106 in-lbs	12
Rear main oil seal retainer bolts	106 in-lbs	12
Valve cover bolts	106 in-lbs	12

1 General information

This Part of Chapter 2 is devoted to in-vehicle repair procedures for the 3.2L and 3.5L V6 engines. Since these procedures are based on the assumption that the engine is installed in the vehicle, many of the steps outlined in this Part of Chapter 2 will not apply if the engine has been removed.

A "VTEC" system is used on all models. The VTEC system is Honda's design for Variable Valve Timing and Lift Electronic Control. Refer to Chapter 6 for additional information.

The engine in all models is of 60-degree V6 design, with aluminum cylinder heads using four valves per cylinder. Most models have a variable vane intake manifold system (IMRC or IMT) to improve torque. Refer to Chapter 6 for additional information.

Information concerning engine removal, installation and overhaul can be found in Chapter 2, Part B.

2 Repair operations possible with the engine in the vehicle

Many major repair operations can be accomplished without removing the engine from the vehicle.

Clean the engine compartment and the exterior of the engine with some type of degreaser before any work is done. It will make the job easier and help keep dirt out of the internal areas of the engine.

When working on the engine, cover the fenders to prevent damage to the paint. Special pads are available, but an old bedspread or blanket will also work.

If vacuum, exhaust, oil or coolant leaks develop, indicating a need for gasket or seal replacement, the repairs can generally be made with the engine in the vehicle. The intake and exhaust manifold gaskets, oil pan gasket, crankshaft front oil seal and cylin-

3.5 Align the TDC mark (the white mark) on the crankshaft pulley with the pointer

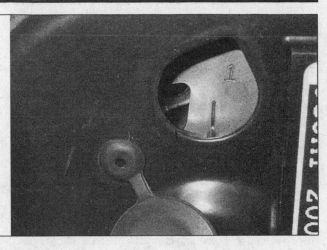

3.6 Position the inspection hole cover aside and check the alignment of the camshaft sprocket timing mark with the mark on the timing belt cover (there is an inspection hole on each cylinder bank) - the numeral 1 is visible when the number 1 piston is at TDC

der head gaskets are all accessible with the engine in place.

Exterior engine components, such as the intake and exhaust manifolds, the oil pan, the oil pump, the water pump (see Chapter 3), the starter motor, the alternator, the ignition coils (see Chapter 5) and the fuel system components (see Chapter 4) can be removed for repair with the engine in place.

Since the cylinder heads can be removed without pulling the engine, valve component servicing can also be accomplished with the engine in the vehicle. Replacement of the camshafts, timing belt and sprockets is also possible with the engine in the vehicle.

In extreme cases caused by a lack of necessary equipment, repair or replacement of piston rings, pistons, connecting rods and rod bearings is possible with the engine in the vehicle. However, this practice is not recommended because of the cleaning and preparation work that must be done to the components involved.

3　Top Dead Center (TDC) for number one piston - locating

Refer to illustrations 3.5 and 3.6

1　Top Dead Center (TDC) is the highest point in the cylinder that each piston reaches as it travels up-and-down during crankshaft rotation. Each piston reaches TDC on the compression stroke and again on the exhaust stroke, but TDC generally refers to piston position on the compression stroke.

2　Positioning the piston(s) at TDC is an essential part of certain repair procedures discussed in this manual.

3　Before beginning this procedure, be sure to place the transaxle in Neutral and apply the parking brake or block the rear wheels. Remove the spark plugs, as this will make the crankshaft much easier to turn (see Chapter 1). On models so equipped, remove the right engine compartment panel for access to the crankshaft pulley.

4　In order to bring any piston to TDC, the crankshaft must be turned using one of the methods outlined below. When looking at the front of the engine, normal crankshaft rotation is clockwise. **Warning:** *If method b) or c) is used, disable the fuel system (see Chapter 4, Section 2).*

a) *The preferred method is to turn the crankshaft with a socket and ratchet attached to the bolt threaded into the front of the crankshaft.*

b) *A remote starter switch, which may save some time, can also be used. Follow the instructions included with the switch. Once the piston is close to TDC, use a socket and ratchet as described in the previous paragraph.*

c) *If an assistant is available to turn the ignition switch to the Start position in short bursts, you can get the piston close to TDC without a remote starter switch. Make sure your assistant is out of the vehicle, away from the ignition switch, then use a socket and ratchet as described in Paragraph a) to complete the procedure.*

5　Turn the crankshaft until the TDC notch (white mark) on the crankshaft pulley is aligned with the pointer on the timing belt lower cover **(see illustration)**.

6　Locate the camshaft sprocket timing mark on the front cylinder bank. Look through the hole in the timing belt cover to check that the camshaft sprocket timing mark (a "1") is aligned with the mark on the rear cover **(see illustration)**. If no mark is present, rotate the crankshaft clockwise one full revolution and realign the marks.

7　When the crankshaft pulley timing marks are aligned, and the camshaft sprocket timing marks are aligned, the number one piston is at TDC on the compression stroke.

8　After the number one piston has been positioned at TDC on the compression stroke, TDC for any of the remaining pistons can be located by turning the crankshaft and following the firing order, aligning the cylinder number on the camshaft sprocket with the pointer on the timing belt cover (they're arranged in the firing order).

4　Valve covers - removal and installation

Removal

Refer to illustrations 4.10a and 4.10b

1　Disconnect the cable from the negative terminal of the battery (see Chapter 5, Section 1).

2　Remove the ignition coils (see Chapter 5).

3　Remove the engine oil dipstick.

4　Remove the intake manifold (see Section 6).

5　Remove the strut brace between the two shock towers (see Chapter 10).

6　Detach the PCV hose from the valve cover.

7　At the rear valve cover, remove the bolt retaining the power steering hose bracket and move the hose aside, if necessary.

8　Remove the harness bracket bolts at each valve cover and set the harness aside.

9　On 2003 and earlier models, disconnect the electrical connector at the IMRC (Intake Manifold Runner Control) then unbolt and set aside the IMRC with its cable still attached.

10　Remove the retaining bolts **(see illustrations)**, then lift the valve cover off. If the cover is stuck to the head, bump the end with a block of wood and a hammer to jar it loose. **Caution:** *Don't pry at the cover-to-head joint or damage to the sealing surfaces may occur, leading to oil leaks after the cover is reinstalled.*

11　Remove the original gasket and seal washers and clean the mating surfaces of the cylinder head and valve cover. If you removed the front valve cover, remove and inspect the PCV valve (see Chapter 1).

Installation

Refer to illustration 4.13

12　Position a new gasket in the groove and install new sealing washers on the bolts.

13　Install the cover and tighten the bolts, a little at a time, to the torque listed in this Chapter's Specifications. Follow the correct torque sequence **(see illustration)**.

4.10a Valve cover retaining bolts (rear valve cover)

4.10b Valve cover retaining bolts (front valve cover)

14   The remainder of the installation is the reverse of removal. Run the engine and check for oil leaks.

5   Valve clearance - check and adjustment

Check

1   The valve clearance generally does not need adjustment unless valvetrain components have been replaced or a valve job has been performed, or if the valves are noisy.
2   The simplest check for proper valve adjustment is to listen carefully to the engine running with the hood open. If the valvetrain is noisy, adjustment is necessary.
3   The valve clearance must be checked and adjusted with the engine cold.

Adjustment

Refer to illustrations 5.6, 5.7 and 5.9

4   Remove the valve covers (see Section 4).

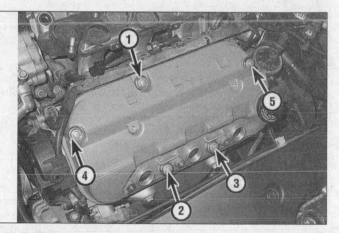

4.13 Valve cover tightening sequence - front shown, rear valve cover tightening sequence is identical

5   Rotate the crankshaft clockwise and position the number one piston at TDC (see Section 3). When positioned correctly at TDC, the pointer on the front timing belt cover will align with the sprocket mark **(see illustration 3.6)**.
6   In this position, adjust the valves for cylinder number one **(see illustration)**. There are four valves for each cylinder.
7   Starting with the intake valve, insert a feeler gauge of the correct thickness (see this Chapter's Specifications) between the valve stem and the rocker arm **(see illustration)**. Withdraw it; you should feel a slight drag. If there's no drag or a heavy drag, loosen the

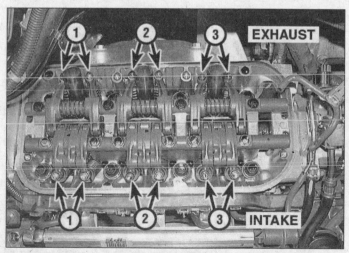

5.6 Valve layout for the rear cylinder head

5.7 Insert a feeler gauge between the valve stem and the rocker arm, loosen the locknut with a box-end wrench and adjust the clearance with a screwdriver

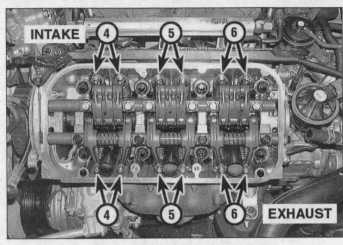

5.9 Valve layout for the front cylinder head

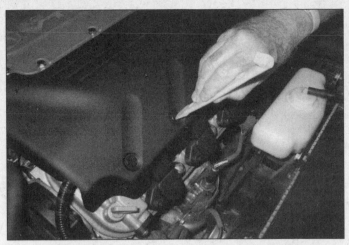

6.2a Rotate the locking tabs a quarter-turn counterclockwise to release the engine cover from the intake manifold

adjuster nut and back off the adjuster screw. Carefully tighten the adjuster screw until you can feel a slight drag on the feeler gauge as you withdraw it.

8   Hold the adjuster screw with a screwdriver to keep it from turning and tighten the locknut. Recheck the clearance to make sure it hasn't changed. Repeat the procedure in this Step and the previous Step on the other intake valve, then on the two exhaust valves.

9   Rotate the crankshaft pulley clockwise until the number "4" on the camshaft sprocket is aligned with the pointer on the timing belt cover (see illustration 3.6). Check and adjust the number four cylinder valves (see illustration).

10   Rotate the crankshaft pulley clockwise until the number "2" cylinder is at TDC. Check and adjust the number two cylinder valves.

11   Rotate the crankshaft pulley clockwise until the number "5" shows at the camshaft cover and adjust the number five cylinder valves.

12   Rotate the crankshaft pulley clockwise until the number "3" shows at the camshaft cover and adjust the number three cylinder valves.

13   Rotate the crankshaft pulley clockwise until the number "6" shows at the camshaft cover and adjust the number six cylinder valves.

14   Refer to Section 4 and install the valve covers.

6   Intake manifolds - removal and installation

Warning: *Wait until the engine is completely cool before beginning this procedure.*

Upper intake manifold

Refer to illustrations 6.2a, 6.2b, 6.10, 6.11, 6.12, 6.13a, 6.13b and 6.13c

1   Relieve the fuel system pressure, then disconnect the cable from the negative terminal of the battery (see Chapter 5, Section 1).

2   Remove the engine cover (see illustra-

tions). On some models it simply snaps onto the intake manifold with clips, while on other models it is secured by bolts to the top of the intake manifold.

3   Remove the air filter housing and the air intake duct (see Chapter 4), then disconnect the accelerator cable (earlier models), vacuum hoses and other connections from the throttle body (see Chapter 4). **Note:** *Early models are equipped with an accelerator cable, while later models are equipped with the Electronic Throttle Control (ETC) system, which does not use a cable, but which instead utilizes an electronically controlled throttle body. There is one large electrical connector at the ETC throttle body.*

4   Remove the EVAP hose and the transaxle vent hose mounting bracket, if equipped.

5   Clamp-off the coolant hoses to the throttle body, then detach them. Be prepared for a little coolant spillage.

6   Disconnect the brake booster hose and the PCV hoses from the intake manifold.

7   Remove the engine harness connectors

6.2b Pull up to remove the engine cover

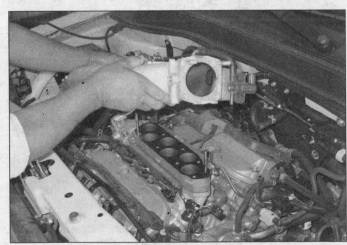

6.10 Lift the upper intake manifold from the engine . . .

6.11 . . . then remove the spacer plate, if equipped

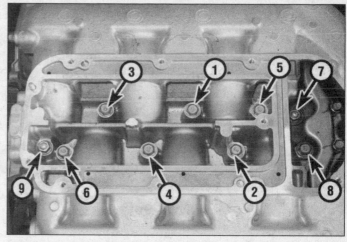

6.12 Upper intake manifold bolt tightening sequence

from their respective components. Label each connector with tape to insure correct reassembly.

8 Unbolt and set aside the Engine Mount Control solenoid at the firewall side of the manifold.

9 Remove the intake manifold cover. **Note:** *Follow the reverse order of the tightening sequence* **(see illustrations 6.13b and 6.13c).**

10 Following the reverse of the tightening sequence **(see illustration 6.12),** remove the bolts and nuts and remove the manifold **(see illustration).**

11 If equipped, remove the spacer plate and gaskets **(see illustration).**

12 To install the upper manifold, clean the mounting surfaces of the upper and lower manifold and remove all traces of the old gasket material or sealant. Install the new gasket over the studs on the lower manifold, then install the spacer (if equipped) and upper intake manifold. Tighten the nuts and bolts in sequence **(see illustration)** to the torque

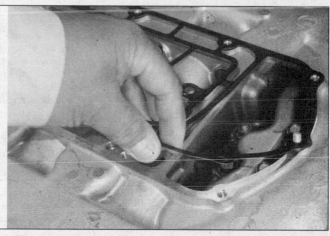

6.13a Install a new intake manifold cover gasket on the upper intake manifold

listed in this Chapter's Specifications.

13 Install the intake manifold cover and tighten the bolts in sequence **(see illustrations)** to the torque listed in this Chapter's Specifications.

14 The remainder of the installation is the reverse of removal. Check the coolant level and add some, if necessary (see Chapter 1).

15 Run the engine and check for fuel, vacuum and coolant leaks.

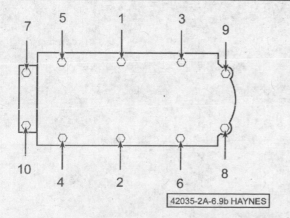

42035-2A-6.9b HAYNES

6.13b Intake manifold cover bolt tightening sequence (2003 and earlier models)

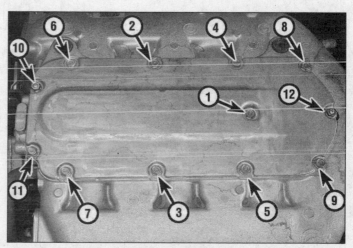

6.13c Intake manifold cover bolt tightening sequence (2004 and later models)

6.18 Location of the lower intake manifold mounting nuts - the four corner nuts are hidden from view

7.3 Location of the engine splash shield fasteners - some hidden from view

Lower intake manifold

Refer to illustration 6.18

16   Remove the upper intake manifold.

17   Remove the fuel rails from the lower intake manifold (see Chapter 4).

18   Remove the mounting nuts and bolts, then detach the two lower intake manifold sections from the cylinder heads **(see illustration)**. If they are stuck, don't pry between the gasket mating surfaces or damage may result.

19   Carefully use a scraper to remove all traces of old gasket material and sealant from the manifold and cylinder heads, then clean the mating surfaces with lacquer thinner or acetone.

20   Install new gaskets, then position the lower manifolds on the cylinder heads. Make sure the gaskets and manifolds are aligned over the dowels in the cylinder heads and install the nuts/bolts. **Note:** *The front and rear halves of the manifold each have their own gasket. Do not mix up the two during installation.*

21   Tighten the fasteners, a little at a time, to the torque listed in this Chapter's Specifications. Work from the center out towards the ends to avoid warping the manifolds.

22   Install the upper intake manifold, using a new gasket.

23   The remainder of the installation is the reverse of the removal procedure. Check the coolant level and add some, if necessary (see Chapter 1). Run the engine and check for fuel, vacuum and coolant leaks.

7   Exhaust manifolds - removal and installation

Warning: *The engine must be completely cool before beginning this procedure.*

Note: *Acura TL models from 1999 through 2003 are equipped with exhaust manifolds. Later models are not equipped with separate exhaust manifolds but instead use catalytic converter assemblies bolted directly to the*

7.4 Disconnect the exhaust pipe from the manifolds (2003 and earlier models shown)

cylinder heads. Refer to Chapter 6 for additional information.

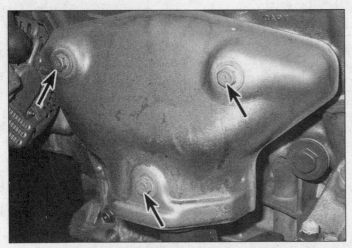

7.5a Remove the heat shield bolts and the heat shield (2003 and earlier models)

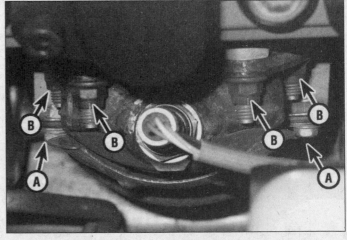

7.5b Heat shield bolts (A) at catalytic converter - catalytic converter mounting bolts (B) (2004 and later models)

7.6 Location of the exhaust manifold mounting bolts at the front cylinder head (models through 2003)

Removal

Refer to illustrations 7.3, 7.4, 7.5a, 7.5b and 7.6

1   Disconnect the cable from the negative terminal of the battery (see Chapter 5, Section 1).

2   Spray penetrating oil on the exhaust manifold/converter/shield fasteners and allow it to soak in.

3   Block the rear wheels to prevent the vehicle from rolling. Set the parking brake and place the transaxle in Park. Raise the front of the vehicle and support it securely on jackstands. Remove the splash guard from below the engine compartment **(see illustration)**.

4   Disconnect the exhaust pipes from the manifolds **(see illustration)**.

5   Remove the bolts and the heat shields from each manifold **(see illustrations)**.

6   Remove the self-locking nuts retaining the manifold/converter to the cylinder head and remove the manifold/converter **(see accompanying illustration and illustration 7.5b)**. Discard the self-locking nuts and obtain new ones for reassembly.

7   Carefully inspect the manifold for cracks and warpage. If the manifold is cracked or warped, replace it with a new one.

Installation

8   Use a scraper to remove any traces of old gasket material and carbon deposits from the manifold and cylinder head mating surfaces.

9   Position a new gasket over the cylinder head studs.

10   Install the manifold and thread the mounting nuts into place. Working from the center out, tighten the nuts to the torque listed in this Chapter's Specifications in three equal steps.

11   The remainder of the installation is the reverse of removal. Apply engine oil to the studs and install new self-locking nuts.

12   Run the engine and check for exhaust leaks.

8   Timing belt and sprockets - removal, inspection and installation

Caution: *The timing system is complex, and severe engine damage will occur if you make any mistakes. Do not attempt this procedure unless you are highly experienced with* this type of repair. If you are at all unsure of your abilities, be sure to consult an expert. Double-check all your work and be sure everything is correct before you attempt to start the engine.

Removal

Refer to illustrations 8.11a, 8.11b, 8.12, 8.13a, 8.13b, 8.14, 8.15, 8.16, 8.17, 8.18, 8.19 and 8.20

1   Disconnect the cable from the negative terminal of the battery (see Chapter 5, Section 1).

2   Place the transaxle in Park, apply the parking brake and block the rear wheels.

3   Remove the drivebelt(s) (see Chapter 1). **Note:** *On earlier models, the power steering pump and alternator each have their own drivebelts. Refer to Chapter 1 for belt removal.*

4   Remove the spark plugs to make it easier to turn the crankshaft (see Chapter 1), then position the number one piston at TDC (see Section 3).

5   Loosen the lug nuts on the right front wheel. Raise the front of the vehicle and support it securely on jackstands. Remove the right front wheel.

6   Remove the right front inner fender splash shield (see Chapter 11).

7   Remove the engine cover **(see illustration 6.2a and 6.2b)**.

8   Remove the one bolt and the oil dipstick tube. Discard the old O-ring and install a new one before installation.

9   Support the engine by placing a floor jack under the oil pan with a block of wood on the jack to protect the pan.

10   Remove the two bolts and the wiring harness retainer holding the passenger-side engine mount to the block, remove the through-bolt, and remove the mount (see Section 17). Remove the engine mount bracket.

11   Remove the upper timing belt covers **(see illustrations)**.

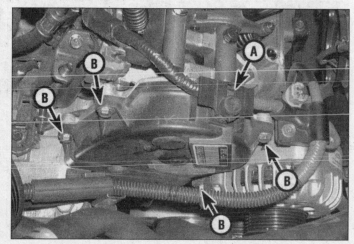

8.11a Detach the wiring harness from the retainer (A) and remove the bolts (B) from the upper timing belt cover (front cylinder bank)

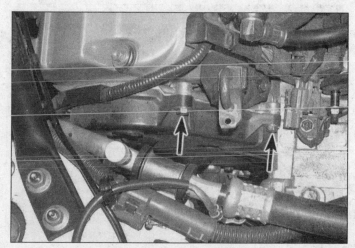

8.11b Remove the upper timing belt cover from the rear cylinder bank (arrows indicate two of the four bolts)

8.12 Mark the direction of rotation on the timing belt

8.13a Camshaft timing marks (front cylinder bank) - align the mark on the sprocket with the mark on the rear cover

8.13b Camshaft sprocket timing marks - rear cylinder bank

8.14 Use a long ratchet or breaker bar to loosen the crankshaft pulley bolt, as it can be *very* tight

12   If you intend to re-use the belt, mark the belt to indicate the direction of rotation **(see illustration)**.

13   Make sure the timing marks are properly aligned **(see illustrations)**.

14   Remove the torque converter cover, wedge a large screwdriver into the driveplate ring gear teeth, then have an assistant unscrew the crankshaft pulley bolt **(see illustration)**. **Note:** *When the crankshaft pulley bolt is loosened, the position of the timing marks on the crankshaft pulley and the camshafts may be disturbed. Check and align them again. Temporarily reinstall the crankshaft pulley bolt to turn the crankshaft.*

15   Remove the lower timing belt cover **(see illustration)**.

16   Slip the timing belt guide plate off the crankshaft sprocket, noting how it's installed. Also note the alignment of the crankshaft sprocket timing marks **(see illustration)**.

8.15 Remove the bolts and the lower timing belt cover - there are 7 bolts in all

8.16 Crankshaft sprocket timing marks

8.17 Thread the long battery hold-down bolt (A) into the boss as shown to hold the timing belt adjuster (B) in position

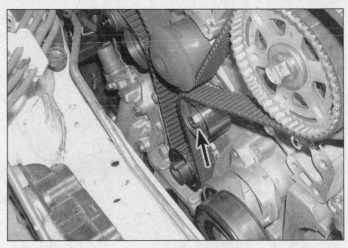

8.18 Loosen the timing belt idler, remove the idler pulley and the timing belt

17   Remove one of the long hold-down bolts from the battery tray and bevel the threaded end somewhat with a file or grinder. Thread the bolt into the boss so that it pushes against the timing belt adjuster - the bolt is used to hold the adjuster in position **(see illustration)**. Do not apply any more than hand pressure in tightening.

18   Remove the idler pulley bolt **(see illustration)**, then remove the timing belt. **Note:** *Discard the idler pulley bolt; a new one should be used upon installation.*

19   The camshaft sprockets can be removed at this point, if they are damaged or to replace the oil seals **(see illustration)**. Remove the keys from the shafts so they don't fall out and get lost. **Caution:** *Don't allow the camshaft(s) to turn.*

20 . If it's worn or damaged, or if you're replacing the crankshaft front oil seal, the crankshaft sprocket can now be removed **(see illustration)**. If it won't come off by hand, carefully pry it off. **Note:** *Before removing the sprocket, remove the Crankshaft Position (CKP) sensor (see Chapter 6).*

8.19 Use a two-pin spanner to prevent the camshaft from turning while you loosen the sprocket bolt

Inspection

21   Inspect the sprocket teeth for wear and damage. Check the timing belt for any cracks or oil residue. Also check the camshaft for excessive endplay (see Section 11).

Check the timing belt tensioner for smooth operation. Replace any worn parts with new ones.

22   Now that the timing belt is removed, inspect the water pump (see Chapter 3). **Note:** *Because of the work involved in getting at the water pump, it's a good idea to replace the water pump whenever the timing belt is removed.*

Installation

Refer to illustration 8.26

23   Remove all dirt and oil from the timing belt area. Clean the teeth of the sprockets with brake system cleaner.

24   If any of the timing belt sprockets were removed, install them now with their keys and tighten the bolts to the torque listed in this Chapter's Specifications.

25   Install the idler pulley using a new bolt, but don't tighten the bolt yet (just finger-tight).

26   Recheck the position of the timing marks **(see illustrations 8.13a, 8.13b and 8.16)**. Install the timing belt in a clockwise

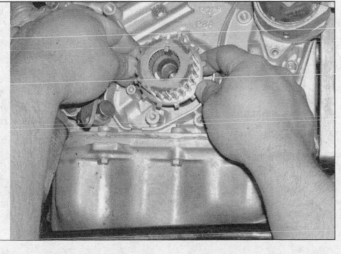

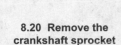

8.20 Remove the crankshaft sprocket

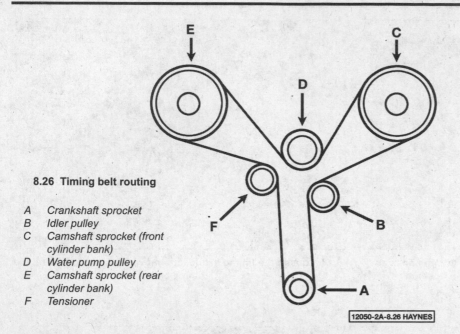

8.26 Timing belt routing

A   Crankshaft sprocket
B   Idler pulley
C   Camshaft sprocket (front cylinder bank)
D   Water pump pulley
E   Camshaft sprocket (rear cylinder bank)
F   Tensioner

12050-2A-8.26 HAYNES

8.37 Compress the tensioner by prying against the pulley (A) until the holes on the rod and tensioner body are in alignment, then insert a pin (B) with a diameter of 0.08 inch (2.0 mm), locking the tensioner in a retracted position

direction, starting at the crankshaft sprocket and tensioner pulley, then rear camshaft sprocket, water pump, front camshaft sprocket, and idler pulley **(see illustration)**. If you're re-using the original belt, the arrow you made in Step 12 should point in the normal direction of rotation. **Note:** *If you're installing a new timing belt, or if the tensioner piston has extended and you're unable to install the original timing belt, remove the tensioner and compress the piston as described in Steps 35 through 38.*

27   Install the outer timing belt guide over the crankshaft sprocket with the concave side facing away from the belt.

28   Tighten the idler pulley bolt to the torque listed in this Chapter's Specifications. Remove the battery hold-down bolt that was holding the tensioner pulley in position **(see illustration 8.17)**.

29   Turn the crankshaft slowly six revolutions clockwise using a socket and breaker bar on the crankshaft pulley bolt to seat the belt, then return to TDC. Recheck the alignment of cam and crank sprocket timing marks. **Caution:** *If you feel any resistance, back up and recheck the belt timing. Do not force the crankshaft to turn or engine damage will occur! If you feel any resistance, STOP! There is something wrong - most likely valves are contacting the pistons. You must find the problem before proceeding. Check your work and see if any updated repair information is available.*

30   Install the lower timing belt cover.

31   Install the crankshaft pulley, aligning the pulley keyway with the crankshaft key. Install the bolt and tighten it to the torque listed in this Chapter's Specifications. Use the method described in Step 14 to keep the crankshaft from turning.

32   Recheck the timing marks **(see illustrations 8.13a, 8.13b and 8.16)**. **Caution:**

If the timing marks are not aligned exactly as shown, repeat the timing belt installation procedure. DO NOT start the engine until you're absolutely certain that the timing belt is installed correctly. Serious and costly engine damage could occur if the belt is installed incorrectly.

33   The remainder of the installation is the reverse of removal.

34   Run the engine and check for coolant or oil leaks.

Tensioner retracting/replacement

Refer to illustration 8.37

35   The belt tensioner does not normally need to be removed for a timing belt replacement procedure, but there are other engine procedures (water pump replacement, etc.) that require the tensioner be removed. Once removed, the tensioner piston will extend in length. The following Steps apply only if the tensioner has been removed from the engine.

36   On 1999 models only, the tensioner has a bolt at the end nearest the mounting bolts. Clamp one of the mounting ears in a vise and remove the bolt, then use a flat-bladed screwdriver to turn the internal slot in the adjuster housing clockwise until the tensioner retracts enough to install a U-shaped clamp (available from Acura) that secures the tensioner in a retracted position.

37   On later models, compress the tensioner in a press until you can insert a drill bit or other pin (0.080-inch or 2 mm diameter) into the tensioner to hold it in the retracted position **(see illustration)**.

38   Install the tensioner, being careful not to dislodge the locating pin (or holding clamp on 1999 models), and tighten the mounting bolts

to the torque listed in this Chapter's Specifications. After completing the remainder of the timing belt installation procedure, remove the tensioner locating pin.

9   Crankshaft front oil seal - replacement

Refer to illustration 9.2

1   Remove the crankshaft position sensor (see Chapter 6), then remove the timing belt and crankshaft sprocket (see Section 8).

2   Carefully pry the seal out of the engine with a screwdriver or seal removal tool **(see illustration)**. If you use a screwdriver, don't scratch the housing bore or damage the crankshaft (if the crankshaft is scratched, the new seal will end up leaking).

3   Clean the oil seal bore and coat the outer edge of the new seal with a small amount of engine oil to ease installation. Apply multi-purpose grease to the seal lip.

9.2 Carefully pry out the oil seal

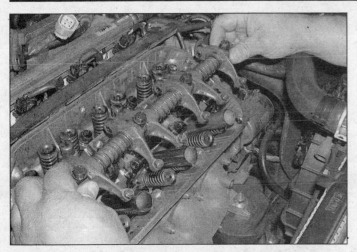

10.5 Leave the rocker assembly mounting bolts in place as you remove the assembly (this will keep the components in order on the shafts)

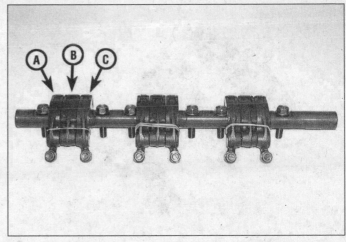

10.6 VTEC intake rocker arm components (note the rubber bands installed to hold the components together)

A   Primary intake rocker arm
B   Mid intake rocker arm
C   Secondary intake rocker arm

4   Using a seal driver or a socket with an outside diameter slightly smaller than the outside diameter of the seal, carefully drive the new seal into place with a hammer. Make sure it's installed squarely and driven in to the same depth as the original.

5   Reinstall the crankshaft sprocket and timing belt (see Section 8), and the crankshaft position sensor (see Chapter 6).

6   The remainder of the installation is the reverse of removal. Run the engine and check for oil leaks at the front seal.

10   Rocker arm assembly - removal, inspection and installation

Removal

Refer to illustration 10.5

1   Remove the valve cover (see Section 4).

2   Remove the timing belt (see Section 8).

3   Loosen the rocker arm adjusting screws **(see illustration 5.7)**.

4   Loosen the rocker shaft mounting bolts 1/4-turn at a time, in the reverse of the tightening sequence, until the spring pressure is relieved **(see illustration 10.12)**.

5   Lift the rocker arms and shaft assembly from the cylinder head **(see illustration)**. Do not remove the shaft mounting bolts; they will keep the rocker arm assembly components together.

Inspection

Refer to illustrations 10.6, 10.7, 10.8 and 10.9

6   If you wish to disassemble and inspect the rocker arm assembly - a good idea as long as you have them off - remove the mounting bolts and slip the rocker arms and springs off the shafts **(see illustration)**. Keep the parts

in order so you can reassemble them in the same positions. **Note:** *Keep the rocker arms for each cylinder together by wrapping them with a heavy rubber band.*

7   Thoroughly clean the parts and inspect them for wear and damage. Check the rocker arm faces that contact the camshaft and the rocker arm tips **(see illustration)**. Check the surfaces of the shafts that the rocker arms ride on, as well as the bearing surfaces inside the rocker arms, for scoring and excessive wear. Replace any parts that are damaged or excessively worn. Also, make sure the oil holes in the shafts are not plugged. Check the roller tips for wear and smoothness of operation.

8   Remove the lost motion assemblies from the cylinder head **(see illustration)**, and clean them. Check for smoothness of plunger operation by pushing down gently with your finger.

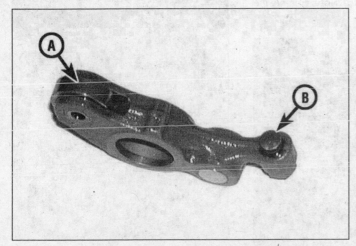

10.7 Inspect the rocker arms for wear and damage at the roller (A) and the valve stem end of the adjusters (B)

10.8 Push down on the plunger of each lost motion assembly - they should move smoothly

10.9 Check for smooth movement of the piston in each VTEC rocker arm

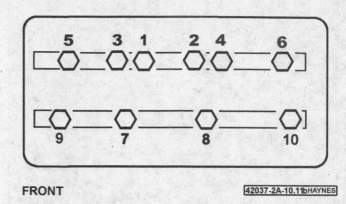

10.12 Rocker arm/shaft mounting bolts TIGHTENING sequence

9　Check the smoothness of operation of the VTEC pistons in each intake rocker arm **(see illustration)**.

Installation

Refer to illustration 10.12

10　Lubricate all components with engine oil and reassemble the shafts. When installing the rocker arms, shafts and springs, note the markings and the difference between the left and right side parts. **Note:** *Intake rocker arms are straight, while exhaust rockers are angled. Exhaust rockers are marked A and B (one of each in a cylinder's pair) and they angle towards each other at the valve adjustment ends.*

11　Coat the wear surfaces of the rocker arms with camshaft installation lubricant and install the rocker arm assembly.

12　Tighten the rocker shaft (or bridge) mounting bolts a little at a time, following the recommended tightening sequence, to the torque listed in this Chapter's Specifications **(see illustration)**.

13　Check the valve clearance and adjust to Specifications (see Section 5).

14　The remainder of the installation is the reverse of removal.

15　Run the engine and check for oil leaks and proper operation.

11 Camshafts - removal, inspection and installation

Warning: *Wait until the engine is completely cool before beginning this procedure.*

Removal

Refer to illustrations 11.7, 11.8 and 11.9

1　If you're going to remove the camshaft from the front cylinder head, drain the engine coolant and remove the left and right engine compartment covers (see Chapter 1).

2　Remove the valve covers (see Section 4) and the timing belt (see Section 8).

3　Remove the rocker arms/shafts as an assembly (see Section 10). **Note:** *Refer to the*

Inspection procedures below and check camshaft endplay before removing the camshafts.

4　Remove the camshaft sprockets (see Section 8).

5　If you're removing the camshaft from the front cylinder head, remove the battery and the battery tray (see Chapter 5).

6　If you're removing the camshaft from the front cylinder head, detach the upper radiator hose from the coolant passage (see Chapter 3). If you're removing the camshaft from the rear cylinder head, detach the brake lines from the master cylinder (see Chapter 9).

7　If you're removing the camshaft from the front cylinder head, remove the EGR valve to access the camshaft retainer plate **(see illustration)**.

8　Remove the camshaft retainer plate **(see illustration)**.

9　Carefully slide the camshaft out of the cylinder head, being careful not to nick the lobes or journals as you withdraw it **(see illustration)**.

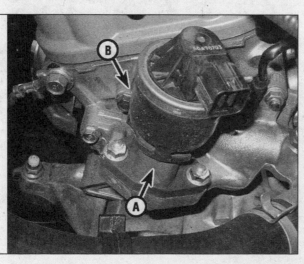

11.7 To access the retainer plate for the front camshaft, remove the EGR valve (A), then the two bolts on the plate (B) located behind the EGR valve

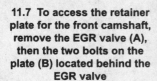

11.8 Remove the bolts and the camshaft retainer plate

11.9 Pull the camshaft straight out of the cylinder head, taking care not to nick the journals or bearings

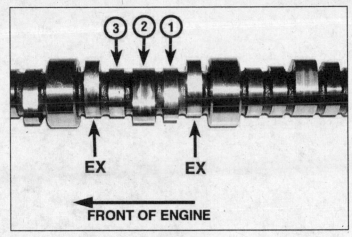

11.12a Arrangement of camshaft lobes on the left (front) cylinder bank camshaft

1   Primary intake lobe   3   Secondary intake lobe
2   Mid intake lobe

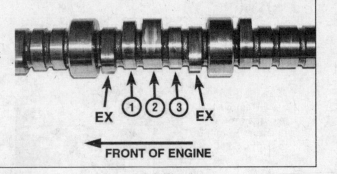

11.12b Arrangement of camshaft lobes on the right (rear) cylinder bank camshaft

1   Primary intake lobe
2   Mid intake lobe
3   Secondary intake lobe

Inspection

Refer to illustrations 11.12a and 11.12b

10   Keeping careful track of the location of the components (see illustration 10.6), remove the rocker arms and springs from the rocker shafts and bolt the bare rocker shafts (or bridge) to the cylinder head, tightening them to the torque listed in this Chapter's Specifications.

11   Mount a dial indicator so that it contacts the nose of the camshaft. Pry the camshaft forwards and back with a screwdriver, with the tip taped to prevent damage to the camshaft. Record the movement of the dial indicator and compare it to this Chapter's Specifications. If the endplay is excessive, install a new retainer plate and check the endplay again. If the endplay is still excessive, the camshaft must be replaced.

12   Remove the retainer plate and slide the camshaft out of the head. Measure the journal diameters and lobe heights on each camshaft, comparing your measurements to this Chapter's Specifications. Check also for visual signs of wear, scoring, pitting or overheating. Note: *The arrangement of lobes is different between the front and rear camshafts (see illustrations).*

Installation

Refer to illustration 11.13

13   The camshaft oil seal should be replaced whenever a camshaft is removed or replaced. Remove the timing belt rear covers from each cylinder head to access the camshaft seals (see illustration).

14   Pry the old seal out with a screwdriver or seal removal tool.

15   Lubricate the lip with engine oil, then install a new camshaft oil seal by driving it in squarely with a seal installation tool to the same depth as the original seal. A socket of the appropriate size will also work.

16   Clean the camshaft thoroughly with solvent, then lubricate the journals and lobes with camshaft installation lubricant and carefully install the camshaft into the cylinder head.

17   Lubricate and install a new O-ring on the camshaft retainer plate. Install the retainer plate and tighten the bolts to the torque listed in this Chapter's Specifications.

18   The remainder of the installation is the reverse of removal. Refer to Section 5 for the valve adjustment procedure. If the coolant was drained, refill the cooling system (see Chapter 1). If the brake lines were detached from the master cylinder, bleed the brake system (see Chapter 9).

19   Run the engine and check for oil leaks at the camshaft seals. Run the engine at low speed for five minutes to allow the air to bleed from the lost motion assemblies, then check for leaks and proper operation. Note: *There will be some tappet noise during the first few minutes of operation. If the noise continues, it may indicate a problem with one of the lost motion assemblies.*

11.13 Remove the two bolts and the timing belt rear cover from each cylinder head for access to the camshaft oil seals

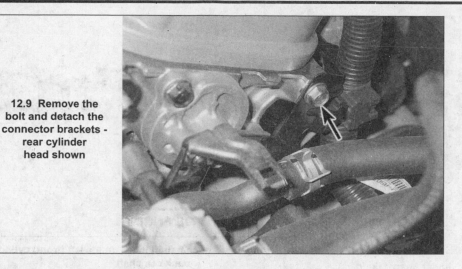

12.9 Remove the bolt and detach the connector brackets - rear cylinder head shown

12 Cylinder heads - removal and installation

Warning: *Allow the engine to cool completely before beginning this procedure.*

Removal

Refer to illustrations 12.9, 12.10a, 12.10b and 12.16

1   Relieve the fuel system pressure (see Chapter 4).

2   Disconnect the cable from the negative terminal of the battery (see Chapter 5, Section 1).

3   Drain the cooling system, including the cylinder block (see Chapter 1).

4   Remove the power steering pump and set it aside without disconnecting the power steering fluid lines (see Chapter 10).

5   If you're removing the front cylinder head, remove the alternator (see Chapter 5).

6   Remove the upper intake manifold (see Section 6).

7   Remove the exhaust manifolds or con-

verters (see Section 7).

8   Remove the timing belt and the camshaft sprockets (see Section 8). Remove the timing belt rear covers from each cylinder head **(see illustration 11.13)**.

12.10a Remove the harness ground connectors from the coolant passage

9   Remove the connector brackets from the transaxle side of the front and rear cylinder heads **(see illustration)**.

10   Remove the coolant passage from the cylinder heads **(see illustrations)**.

11   Remove the valve covers (see Section 4) and the rocker arms/shafts assembly (see Section 10).

12   If you're removing the rear cylinder head, remove the EVAP purge valve joint from its bracket on the rear cylinder head.

13   Remove the fuel rails and injectors (see Chapter 4).

14   Remove the lower intake manifolds (see Section 6).

15   Using a socket and breaker bar, loosen the cylinder head bolts in 1/4-turn increments until they can be removed by hand. Loosen them in a sequence opposite that of the tightening sequence **(see illustration 12.23)**

16   Lift the cylinder head off the engine block. If the head is stuck, pry against an external casting protrusion **(see illustration)**. **Caution:** *Don't pry between the head and block. The gasket surfaces may be damaged and leaks could result.*

12.10b Remove the coolant passage mounting bolts from both cylinder heads - lightly tap the passage with a soft-faced hammer to break the gasket seal and remove the coolant passage

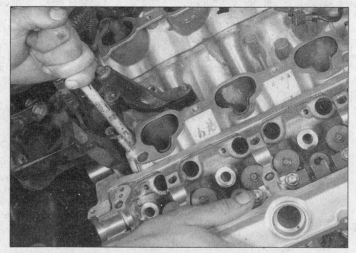

12.16 Pry up carefully on a casting protrusion

Installation

Refer to illustrations 12.20 and 12.23

17 The mating surfaces of the cylinder heads and block must be perfectly clean when the heads are installed. Use a plastic gasket scraper to remove all traces of carbon and old gasket material. Be careful not to gouge the delicate aluminum. Clean the mating surfaces with brake system cleaner. If there's oil on the mating surfaces when the head is installed, the gasket may not seal correctly and leaks could develop. When working on the block, stuff the cylinders with clean shop rags to keep out debris. Use a vacuum cleaner to remove material that falls into the cylinders.

18 Check the block and head mating surfaces for nicks, deep scratches and other damage. If damage is slight, it can be removed with a file; if it's excessive, machining may be the only alternative.

19 Use a tap of the correct size to chase the threads in the head bolt holes, then clean the holes with compressed air - make sure that nothing remains in the holes. **Warning:** *Wear eye protection when using compressed air!*

20 Mount each bolt in a vise and run a die down the threads to remove corrosion and restore the threads. Dirt, corrosion, sealant and damaged threads will affect torque readings. If you're working on an engine with 12-point cylinder head bolts, measure the diameter of the bolts at the indicated areas **(see illustration)**. Replace any bolt with a diameter less than the minimum allowable. **Note:** *It is suggested that new head bolts be used when the heads are installed, regardless of measurement or condition.*

21 Clean the oil control orifices thoroughly and reinstall them with new O-rings. Position the new gaskets over the oil control orifices and locating dowels in the block.

22 Carefully set the head on the block without disturbing the gasket.

23 Before installing the head bolts, apply a small amount of clean engine oil to the threads and under the bolt heads. Install the bolts and special washers and tighten them finger tight. Following the recommended sequence **(see illustration)**, tighten the bolts (in stages) to the torque listed in this Chapter's Specifications.

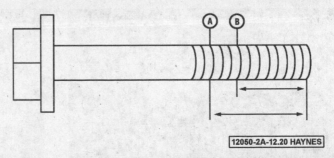

12.20 Measurement points for 12-point cylinder head bolts. Minimum diameter for either point is 0.42 inch (10.6 mm)

A   2.0 inches (50 mm)   B   1.8 inches (45 mm)

24 The remainder of the installation is the reverse of removal. Refill the cooling system, change the oil and filter (see Chapter 1), then run the engine and check for leaks. Run the engine at low speed for five minutes to allow the air to bleed from the lost motion assemblies, then check for leaks and proper operation. **Note:** *There will be some tappet noise during the first few minutes of operation. If the noise continues, it may indicate a problem with one of the lost motion assemblies.*

13 Oil pan - removal and installation

Note: *The following procedure requires removal of the front suspension subframe, and is considered a difficult procedure for the home mechanic. A means of supporting the vehicle safely with room enough to work underneath is required, as is a transmission jack and an engine support fixture, which can be rented.*

Removal

Refer to illustrations 13.17a, 13.17b and 13.17c

1 Disconnect the cable from the negative terminal of the battery (see Chapter 5, Section 1).

2 Block the rear wheels and set the parking brake. Remove the engine compartment covers (left and right) and the engine cover (see Chapter 1).

3 Remove the air cleaner and intake duct (see Chapter 4).

4 On models so equipped, remove the strut brace between the two shock towers in the engine compartment (see Chapter 10).

5 Remove the battery and battery tray (see Chapter 5).

6 Remove the power steering pump/reservoir and plug the hoses (see Chapter 10).

7 Install an engine support fixture and raise the engine just enough to take the weight off the engine mounts.

8 Raise the front of the vehicle and support it securely on jackstands.

9 Remove the engine underside splash shield **(see illustration 7.3)**.

10 Drain the engine oil and remove the oil filter (see Chapter 1).

11 Disconnect the power steering hoses from the steering gear.

12 On later models with automatic transmission, remove the bracket securing the shift cable to the front subframe.

13 Remove the front suspension subframe assembly (see Chapter 10).

14 Unbolt the exhaust pipes from the exhaust manifold/catalytic converter assemblies (see Section 7) and from the rear portion of the exhaust system (see Chapter 4). Remove the front portion of the exhaust system.

15 On models with automatic transmission, remove the lower transmission mount (see Chapter 7B). On manual transmission models, remove both lower transmission mounts and the rear engine damper.

16 Remove the through-bolts from the front and rear engine mounts (see Section 17).

17 Remove the torque converter cover, then remove the bolts **(see accompanying illustrations and illustration 13.22)** and lower the oil pan. The bolts at the timing belt end of the engine can be removed with a 1/4-inch drive flex-socket, extension and ratchet. If the pan is stuck, carefully pry at the tabs on the

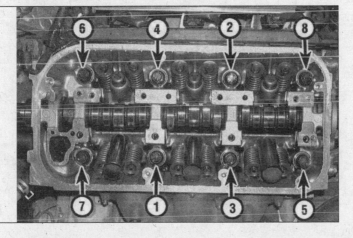

12.23 Cylinder head bolt TIGHTENING sequence

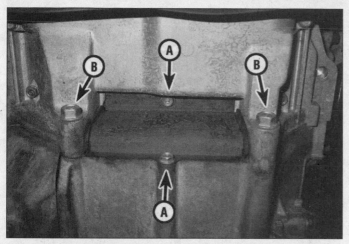

13.17a Remove the two bolts (A) securing the torque converter cover, then remove the two oil pan-to-transaxle bolts (B)

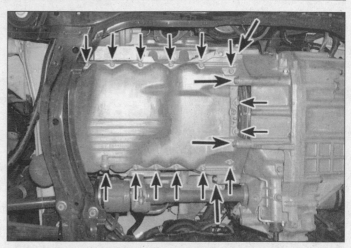

13.17b Remove the bolts from around the perimeter of the oil pan (not all bolts visible here)

13.17c Use a prybar or screwdriver to pry the pan loose at the casting tabs - DO NOT pry on the gasket surface

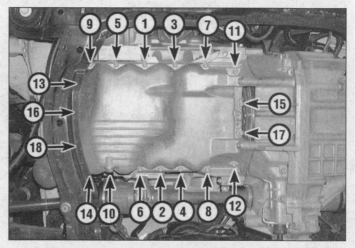

13.22 Oil pan bolt tightening sequence

casting corners **(see illustration)**. Don't damage the mating surfaces of the pan and block or oil leaks could develop.

Installation

Refer to illustration 13.22

18   Use a scraper to remove all traces of old sealant from the block and oil pan. Be careful not to gouge the delicate aluminum surfaces. Clean the mating surfaces with lacquer thinner or acetone.

19   Make sure the threaded bolt holes in the block are clean.

20   Inspect the oil pump pick-up screen assembly for damage or a blocked strainer (see Section 14).

21   Apply a bead of sealant to the mating surface of the oil pan. **Note:** *Install the oil pan within 4 minutes of sealant application.*

22   Carefully position the oil pan on the engine block and install the bolts. Follow the correct torque sequence **(see illustration)** and tighten them a little at a time to the torque listed in this Chapter's Specifications. After

the oil pan-to-block bolts have been tightened, tighten the pan-to-transaxle bolts to the torque listed in this Chapter's Specifications.

23   The remainder of installation is the reverse of removal. Be sure to add oil and install a new oil filter. **Note:** *Wait 30 minutes (to allow the sealant to cure) before adding oil.*

24   Run the engine and check for oil pressure and leaks.

14 Oil pump - removal, inspection and installation

Removal

Refer to illustrations 14.3 and 14.5

1   Remove the crankshaft position sensor (see Chapter 6).

2   Remove the timing belt, crankshaft sprocket and idler pulley (see Section 8).

3   Remove the oil pan (see Section 13) and oil pick-up screen **(see illustration)**. If

equipped, remove the oil level sensor.

4   Remove the oil filter adapter housing/ VTEC solenoid assembly from the front of the oil pump.

14.3 Oil pick-up screen bolt locations (early model shown, later models have larger, boxy screen assembly)

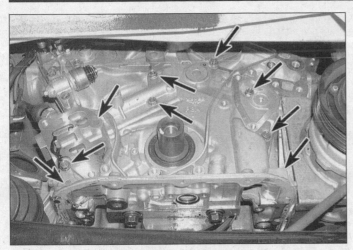

14.5 Oil pump housing bolt locations

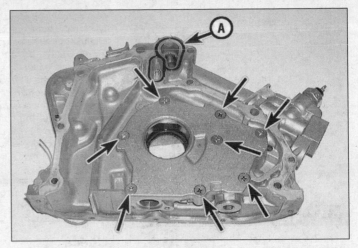

14.6 Remove the screws from the pump cover and replace the O-ring seal (A)

5 Remove the bolts and detach the oil pump housing from the engine (see illustration). You may have to pry carefully between the main bearing cap and the pump housing with a screwdriver.

Inspection

Refer to illustrations 14.6 and 14.7

6 Use a Phillips screwdriver to remove the screws holding the pump cover to the rear of the housing (see illustration).

7 Lift the cover off and inspect the pump rotors (see illustration). If any wear or damage is evident, replace the pump. Check the rotor clearances with feeler gauges and compare the readings to this Chapter's Specifications. If any of the clearances are beyond the Specifications, replace the entire oil pump assembly.

8 Use a plastic scraper to remove any traces of old sealant from the pump body and engine block, being careful not to damage the delicate aluminum.

Installation

9 Replace the old crankshaft oil seal (see Section 9). Apply engine oil or multi-purpose grease to the seal lip.

10 Pack the pump cavities with petroleum jelly and install the cover. Apply thread-locking compound to the threads and tighten the screws to the torque listed in this Chapter's Specifications following a criss-cross pattern.

11 Use brake system cleaner and a clean rag to remove all traces of oil from the gasket surfaces.

12 Apply a bead of liquid gasket to the oil pump flange and the threads of the mounting bolts. Avoid using an excessive amount of sealant, especially around oil passages and bolt holes. Parts must be assembled within five minutes of sealant application, otherwise the material must be removed and reapplied. Wherever O-rings are employed, use new ones.

13 Engage the flat surfaces on the oil pump drive rotor with the matching flats on the crankshaft and slide the pump into place.

14 Install the pump mounting bolts in their original locations and tighten them to the torque listed in this Chapter's Specifications in a criss-cross pattern.

15 Using a new O-ring, install the oil pick-up screen and tighten the fasteners to the torque listed in this Chapter's Specifications.

16 The remainder of the installation is the reverse of removal.

17 Wait 30 minutes to allow the sealant to cure, then add oil, start the engine and check for oil leaks and pressure.

18 Recheck the engine oil level after operating the engine.

15 Flywheel/driveplate - removal and installation

1 Remove the engine and transaxle (see Chapter 2B), then separate the transaxle from the engine (see Chapter 7).

2 If the vehicle is equipped with a manual transmission, remove the pressure plate and clutch disc (see Chapter 8). Now is a good time to check/replace the clutch components and pilot bearing if necessary. If the vehicle is equipped with an automatic transmission, now

would be a good time to check and replace the front pump seal/O-ring.

3 Use paint or a center-punch to make alignment marks on the flywheel/driveplate and crankshaft to ensure correct alignment during reinstallation.

4 Remove the bolts that secure the flywheel/driveplate to the crankshaft. If the crankshaft turns, hold the flywheel with a pry-bar or wedge a screwdriver into the ring gear teeth to jam the flywheel.

5 Remove the flywheel/driveplate from the crankshaft. Since the flywheel is fairly heavy, be sure to support it while removing the last bolt. Retrieve the washer on models with an automatic transaxle.

6 Clean the flywheel to remove grease and oil. Inspect the surface for cracks, rivet grooves, burned areas and score marks. Light scoring can be removed with emery cloth. Check for cracked and broken ring gear teeth or a loose ring gear. Lay the flywheel on a flat surface and use a straightedge to check for warpage.

7 Clean and inspect the mating surfaces of the flywheel/driveplate and the crankshaft. If the crankshaft rear seal is leaking, replace it before reinstalling the flywheel/driveplate (see Section 16).

14.7 Inspect the condition of the rotors and the inside of the cover - with feeler gauges, measure the clearances at (A) (outer rotor-to-housing) and (B) (inner rotor-to-outer rotor). Also lay a straightedge across the face of the pump housing and measure the housing-to-rotor axial clearance

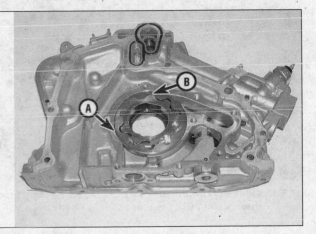

16.2 Carefully pry the rear main seal out - don't damage the surface of the crankshaft or the new seal will leak

8   Position the flywheel/driveplate against the crankshaft. Be sure to align the marks made during removal. Note that some engines have an alignment dowel or staggered bolt holes to ensure correct installation. Before installing the bolts, apply thread locking compound to the threads.

9   Wedge a screwdriver into the ring gear teeth to keep the flywheel/driveplate from turning as you tighten the bolts to the torque listed in this Chapter's Specifications.

10   The remainder of installation is the reverse of the removal.

16   Rear main oil seal - replacement

Refer to illustration 16.2

1   Remove the driveplate (see Section 15).
2   The seal can be replaced without removing the oil pan or removing the seal retainer. However, the lip of the seal is quite stiff and it's possible to cock the seal in the retainer bore or damage it during installation. Pry out the old

seal with a screwdriver **(see illustration)**.
3   Apply multi-purpose grease to the crankshaft seal journal and the lip of the new seal, then carefully drive the new seal into place with a seal driver. The lip is stiff, so carefully work it onto the seal journal of the crankshaft. Don't rush it or you may damage the seal. **Note:** *Drive the seal in squarely and only until it is flush with the back of the seal plate, no further. Make sure the spring side is facing in.*
4   The remainder of the installation is the reverse of removal.

17   Powertrain mounts - check and replacement

Check

Caution: *The front and rear mounts on some models are computer-controlled. The following check procedure does not apply to these mounts. Refer to Section 18 for the checking procedure for the Engine Mount Control system.*
1   There are three engine mounts on these models, plus an engine damper on later models. The transaxle has one upper and two lower mounts.
2   During the check, the engine must be raised slightly to remove the weight from the mounts.
3   Raise the vehicle and support it securely on jackstands, then position a floor jack under the engine oil pan. Place a large block of wood between the jack head and the oil pan, then carefully raise the engine just enough to take the weight off the mounts. **Warning:** DO NOT *place any part of your body under the engine when it's supported only by a jack!*
4   Check the mounts to see if the rubber is cracked, hardened or separated from the casing.
5   Check for relative movement between the mount plates and the engine or subframe. Use a large screwdriver or prybar to attempt to move the mounts. If movement is noted,

lower the engine and tighten the mount fasteners.
6   Apply the parking brake, block the rear wheels, raise the front of the vehicle and support it securely on jackstands (if not already done).

Replacement

Refer to illustrations 17.9, 17.13, 17.14, 17.17 and 17.23

Right (passenger-side) mounts

7   Disconnect the cable from the negative terminal of the battery (see Chapter 5, Section 1).
8   Use a floor jack under the engine to take the weight from the mount. Place a large block of wood between the jack head and the oil pan, then carefully raise the engine just enough to take the weight off the mount. **Warning:** DO NOT *place any part of your body under the engine when it's supported only by a jack!*
9   Remove the bolts holding the engine bracket in place, then the through-bolt from the mount. Remove the mount-to-body bolts and remove the mount **(see illustration)**.
10   Installation is the reverse of removal. **Note:** *Tighten the bolts securely only after the engine/transaxle weight is back onto the mounts and the jack is removed.*

Left (driver's-side) mounts

11   The two driver's-side transaxle lower mounts is between the bottom of the transaxle and the subframe, and the upper transaxle mount is between the transaxle and the body.
12   Use a floor jack under the transaxle to take the weight from the mount. Place a large block of wood between the jack head and the oil pan, then carefully raise the transaxle just enough to take the weight off the mounts.
13   To remove the lower mounts, remove the nuts securing the mounts to the subframe (A), then unbolt and remove the mount from the transaxle **(see illustration)**.

17.9 Remove the two top bracket bolts (A) on the right mount, the through-bolt (B), then the mount-to-body bolts (C)

17.13 Remove the nuts (A) securing each of the lower transaxle mounts to the subframe, then the two bolts (B, one shown here per mount) securing each mount to the engine

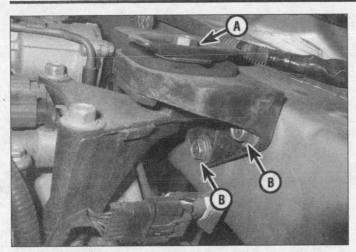

17.14 To remove the upper transaxle mount, remove the upper bolt (A), then the three mount-to-body bolts (B, two shown here)

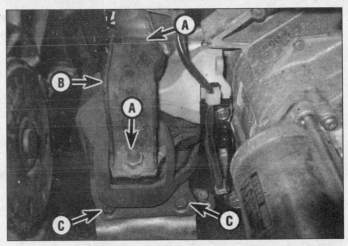

17.17 Remove the front mount bracket nuts (A), then the through-bolt (B, accessible once the bracket is removed), then the four mount base bolts (C, two shown here) at the subframe

14   To remove the upper transaxle mount, remove the top body-to-mount bolt, then remove the bolts securing the mount to the transaxle **(see illustration)**.

15   Installation is the reverse of removal. **Note:** *Tighten the bolts securely only after the engine/transaxle weight is back onto the mounts and the jack is removed.*

Front mount

16   The front mount is located between the engine and radiator. Disconnect the vacuum hose from the mount and plug it to prevent entry of dirt or moisture.

17   Remove the bolts securing the safety bracket, remove the through-bolt, then remove the four mount-to-subframe bolts **(see illustration)**.

18   Use a floor jack under the engine to take the weight from the mount. Place a large block of wood between the jack head and the oil pan, then carefully raise the engine just enough to take the weight off the mount. **Warning:** DO NOT *place any part of your body under the engine when it's supported only by a jack!*

19   Remove the four bolts securing the mount to the subframe.

20   Raise the engine slightly and remove the mount. Installation is the reverse of removal.

Rear mount

21   Raise the front of the vehicle and support it securely on jackstands.

22   Disconnect the vacuum hose from the mount and plug it to prevent entry of dirt or moisture.

23   Remove the bolt where the mount stud goes through the engine bracket **(see illustration)**.

24   Use a floor jack under the engine to take the weight from the mount. Place a large block of wood between the jack head and the oil pan, then carefully raise the engine just enough to take the weight off the mount. Remove the four bolts securing the mount to the chassis.

25   Raise the engine enough for the mount to clear the upper bracket and remove the mount.

26   The remainder of the installation is the reverse of removal. **Note:** *Tighten the bolts securely only after the engine/transaxle weight is back onto the mounts and the jack is removed.*

Rear engine damper

27   On later models, the damper, which looks like a small shock absorber, is located at the left/rear of the engine, near the bellhousing.

28   Remove the upper and lower mounting bolts and remove the damper.

29   Installation is the reverse of removal.

Final tightening, all mounts

30   To ensure maximum bushing life and prevent excessive noise and vibration, the vehicle should be level and the engine weight should be on the mounts during the final tightening stage. **Note:** *Use non-hardening thread locking compound on the nuts/bolts. Ensure that the bushings are not twisted or offset. If you have replaced more than one mount, or when you are installing the engine, tighten*

the mounts in the following order: front, rear, passenger-side and driver's-side.

---

18   Engine Mount Control System - description and check

Description

1   The covered Acura models have special front and rear engine mounts that are computer-controlled to reduce vibrations during idle. The interior of the liquid-filled mount has two chambers. When the engine is idling, the Powertrain Control Module (PCM) signals a control solenoid valve in the mount which induces a counter-vibration, to reduce normal vibrations. At engine speeds over 1,000 rpm, the solenoid is shut off and the engine mount changes to its normal mode.

Check

2   Aside from checking the mounts for loose vacuum lines and fluid leakage, testing of this system must be performed by a dealer service department or other qualified automotive repair facility.

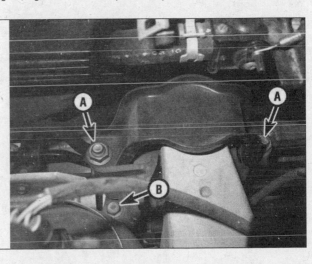

17.23 Remove the upper nuts (A) from the mount top bracket and remove the bracket for access to the through-bolt (not visible here), then the four mount base bolts (B, one seen here) at the subframe

Notes

Chapter 2 Part B
General engine overhaul procedures

Contents

Specifications

General

Bore (3.2L and 3.5L engines)	3.50 inches (89.0 mm)
Stroke	
3.2L	3.39 inches (86.0 mm)
3.5L	3.66 inches (93.0 mm)
Displacement	
3.2L	196 cubic inches (3.2 liters)
3.5L	212 cubic inches (3.5 liters)
Cylinder compression pressure	135 to 163 psi (930 to 1,130 kPa)
Oil pressure at 178-degrees F (80-degrees C)	
At curb idle	10 psi (78 kPa)
At 3,000 rpm	71 psi (490 kPa)

Torque specifications

Note: *One foot-pound (ft-lb) of torque is equivalent to 12 inch-pounds (in-lbs) of torque. Torque values below approximately 15 foot-pounds are expressed in inch-pounds, because most foot-pound torque wrenches are not accurate at these smaller values.*

	Ft-lbs (unless otherwise indicated)	Nm
Connecting rod bearing cap bolts		
Step 1	168 in-lbs	19
Step 2	Tighten an additional 1/4-turn (90-degrees)	
Main bearing caps **(see illustration 10.19)**		
Main bolts	56	76
Side bolts	36	49
Oil jet bolts	144 in-lbs	16

1.1 An engine block being bored. An engine rebuilder will use
special machinery to recondition the cylinder bores

1.2 If the cylinders are bored, the machine shop will normally
hone the engine on a machine like this

1   General information - engine overhaul

Refer to illustrations 1.1, 1.2, 1.3, 1.4, 1.5 and 1.6

Included in this portion of Chapter 2 are general information and diagnostic testing procedures for determining the overall mechanical condition of your engine.

The information ranges from advice concerning preparation for an overhaul and the purchase of replacement parts and/or components to detailed, step-by-step procedures covering removal and installation.

The following Sections have been written to help you determine whether your engine needs to be overhauled and how to remove and install it once you've determined it needs to be rebuilt. For information concerning in-vehicle engine repair, see Chapter 2A.

The Specifications included in this Part are general in nature and include only those

necessary for testing the oil pressure and checking the engine compression. Refer to Chapter 2A for additional engine Specifications.

It's not always easy to determine when, or if, an engine should be completely overhauled, because a number of factors must be considered.

High mileage is not necessarily an indication that an overhaul is needed, while low mileage doesn't preclude the need for an overhaul. Frequency of servicing is probably the most important consideration. An engine that's had regular and frequent oil and filter changes, as well as other required maintenance, will most likely give many thousands of miles of reliable service. Conversely, a neglected engine may require an overhaul very early in its service life.

Excessive oil consumption is an indication that piston rings, valve seals and/or valve guides are in need of attention. Make sure that oil leaks aren't responsible before decid-

ing that the rings and/or guides are bad. Perform a cylinder compression check to determine the extent of the work required (see Section 3). Also check the vacuum readings under various conditions (see Section 4).

Check the oil pressure with a gauge installed in place of the oil pressure sending unit and compare it to this Chapter's Specifications (see Section 2). If it's extremely low, the bearings and/or oil pump are probably worn out.

Loss of power, rough running, knocking or metallic engine noises, excessive valve train noise and high fuel consumption rates may also point to the need for an overhaul, especially if they're all present at the same time. If a complete tune-up doesn't remedy the situation, major mechanical work is the only solution.

An engine overhaul involves restoring the internal parts to the specifications of a new engine. During an overhaul, the piston rings are replaced and the cylinder walls are

1.3 A crankshaft having a main bearing journal ground

1.4 A machinist checks for a bent connecting rod, using specialized equipment

reconditioned (rebored and/or honed) **(see illustrations 1.1 and 1.2)**. If a rebore is done by an automotive machine shop, new oversize pistons will also be installed. The main bearings, connecting rod bearings and camshaft bearings are generally replaced with new ones and, if necessary, the crankshaft may be reground to restore the journals **(see illustration 1.3)**. Generally, the valves are serviced as well, since they're usually in less-than-perfect condition at this point. While the engine is being overhauled, other components, such as the distributor, starter and alternator, can be rebuilt as well. The end result should be similar to a new engine that will give many trouble free miles. **Note:** *Critical cooling system components such as the hoses, drivebelts, thermostat and water pump should be replaced with new parts when an engine is overhauled.* The radiator should be checked carefully to ensure that it isn't clogged or leaking (see Chapter 3). If you purchase a rebuilt engine or short block, some rebuilders will not warranty their engines unless the radiator has

been professionally flushed. Also, we don't recommend overhauling the oil pump - always install a new one when an engine is rebuilt.

Overhauling the internal components on today's engines is a difficult and time-consuming task which requires a significant amount of specialty tools and is best left to a professional engine rebuilder **(see illustrations 1.4, 1.5 and 1.6)**. A competent engine rebuilder will handle the inspection of your old parts and offer advice concerning the reconditioning or replacement of the original engine, never purchase parts or have machine work done on other components until the block has been thoroughly inspected by a professional machine shop. As a general rule, time is the primary cost of an overhaul, especially since the vehicle may be tied up for a minimum of two weeks or more. Be aware that some engine builders only have the capability to rebuild the engine you bring them while other rebuilders have a large inventory of rebuilt exchange engines in stock. Also be aware that many machine shops could take

as much as two weeks time to completely rebuild your engine depending on shop workload. Sometimes it makes more sense to simply exchange your engine for another engine that's already rebuilt to save time.

2 Oil pressure check

Refer to illustration 2.2

1 · Low engine oil pressure can be a sign of an engine in need of rebuilding. A low oil pressure indicator (often called an "idiot light") is not a test of the oiling system. Such indicators only come on when the oil pressure is dangerously low. Even a factory oil pressure gauge in the instrument panel is only a relative indication, although much better for driver information than a warning light. A better test is with a mechanical (not electrical) oil pressure gauge.

2   Locate the oil pressure indicator sending unit; it's located on the oil pump housing

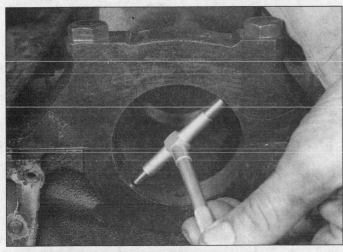

1.5 A bore gauge being used to check the main bearing bore

1.6 Uneven piston wear like this indicates a bent connecting rod

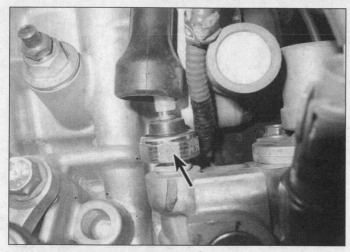

2.2 The oil pressure sending unit is located on top of the oil pump housing

3.6 Use a compression gauge with a threaded fitting for the spark plug hole, not the type that requires hand pressure to maintain the seal

above the oil filter adapter **(see illustration)**.

3   Unscrew and remove the oil pressure sending unit, then screw in the hose for your oil pressure gauge. If necessary, install an adapter fitting. Use Teflon tape or thread sealant on the threads of the adapter and/or the fitting on the end of your gauge's hose.

4   Connect an accurate tachometer to the engine, according to the tachometer manufacturer's instructions.

5   Check the oil pressure with the engine running (normal operating temperature) at the specified engine speed, and compare it to this Chapter's Specifications. If it's extremely low, the bearings and/or oil pump are probably worn out.

3   Cylinder compression check

Refer to illustration 3.6

1   A compression check will tell you what mechanical condition the upper end of your engine (pistons, rings, valves, head gaskets) is in. Specifically, it can tell you if the compression is down due to leakage caused by worn piston rings, defective valves and seats or a blown head gasket. **Note:** *The engine must be at normal operating temperature and the battery must be fully charged for this check.*

2   Begin by cleaning the area around the ignition coils before you remove the spark plugs (compressed air should be used, if available). The idea is to prevent dirt from getting into the cylinders as the compression check is being done.

3   Remove all of the spark plugs from the engine (see Chapter 1).

4   Block the throttle open. On models that have an accelerator cable connected to the throttle body, you can simply depress the accelerator pedal when the engine is cranked over. On models with the Electronic Throttle Control (ETC) system, remove the air intake

duct from the throttle body (see Chapter 4) and use a wood dowel or something similar to block the throttle plate open. **Caution:** *Be certain that whatever is used to block the throttle open doesn't scratch the throttle body bore or get sucked into the intake manifold.*

5   Disable the fuel system (see Chapter 4, Section 2).

6   Install a compression gauge in the spark plug hole **(see illustration)**.

7   Crank the engine over at least seven compression strokes and watch the gauge. The compression should build up quickly in a healthy engine. Low compression on the first stroke, followed by gradually increasing pressure on successive strokes, indicates worn piston rings. A low compression reading on the first stroke, which doesn't build up during successive strokes, indicates leaking valves or a blown head gasket (a cracked head could also be the cause). Deposits on the undersides of the valve heads can also cause low compression. Record the highest gauge reading obtained.

8   Repeat the procedure for the remaining cylinders and compare the results to this Chapter's Specifications.

9   Add some engine oil (about three squirts from a plunger-type oil can) to each cylinder, through the spark plug hole, and repeat the test.

10   If the compression increases after the oil is added, the piston rings are definitely worn. If the compression doesn't increase significantly, the leakage is occurring at the valves or head gasket. Leakage past the valves may be caused by burned valve seats and/or faces or warped, cracked or bent valves.

11   If two adjacent cylinders have equally low compression, there's a strong possibility that the head gasket between them is blown. The appearance of coolant in the combustion chambers or the crankcase would verify this condition.

12   If one cylinder is slightly lower than the others, and the engine has a slightly rough idle, a worn lobe on the camshaft could be the cause.

13   If the compression is unusually high, the combustion chambers are probably coated with carbon deposits. If that's the case, the cylinder heads should be removed and decarbonized.

14   If compression is way down or varies greatly between cylinders, it would be a good idea to have a leak-down test performed by an automotive repair shop. This test will pinpoint exactly where the leakage is occurring and how severe it is.

4   Vacuum gauge diagnostic checks

Refer to illustrations 4.4 and 4.6

1   A vacuum gauge provides inexpensive but valuable information about what is going on in the engine. You can check for worn rings or cylinder walls, leaking head or intake manifold gaskets, incorrect carburetor adjustments, restricted exhaust, stuck or burned valves, weak valve springs, improper ignition or valve timing and ignition problems.

2   Unfortunately, vacuum gauge readings are easy to misinterpret, so they should be used in conjunction with other tests to confirm the diagnosis.

3   Both the absolute readings and the rate of needle movement are important for accurate interpretation. Most gauges measure vacuum in inches of mercury (in-Hg). The following references to vacuum assume the diagnosis is being performed at sea level. As elevation increases (or atmospheric pressure decreases), the reading will decrease. For every 1,000 foot increase in elevation above approximately 2,000 feet, the gauge readings will decrease about one inch of mercury.

4.4 A simple vacuum gauge can be handy in diagnosing engine condition and performance

15 Check for a slow return after revving the engine by quickly snapping the throttle open until the engine reaches about 2,500 rpm and let it shut. Normally the reading should drop to near zero, rise above normal idle reading (about 5 in-Hg over), then return to the previous idle reading. If the vacuum returns slowly and doesn't peak when the throttle is snapped shut, the rings may be worn. If there is a long delay, look for a restricted exhaust system (often the muffler or catalytic converter). An easy way to check this is to temporarily disconnect the exhaust ahead of the suspected part and redo the test.

5 Engine rebuilding alternatives

The do-it-yourselfer is faced with a number of options when purchasing a rebuilt engine. The major considerations are cost, warranty, parts availability and the time required for the rebuilder to complete the project. The decision to replace the engine block, piston/connecting rod assemblies and crankshaft depends on the final inspection results of your engine. Only then can you make a cost effective decision whether to have your engine overhauled or simply purchase an

4 Connect the vacuum gauge directly to intake manifold vacuum, not to ported (throttle body) vacuum **(see illustration)**. Be sure no hoses are left disconnected during the test or false readings will result.

5 Before you begin the test, allow the engine to warm up completely. Block the wheels and set the parking brake. With the transaxle in Park, start the engine and allow it to run at normal idle speed. **Warning:** *Keep your hands and the vacuum gauge clear of the fans.*

6 Read the vacuum gauge; an average, healthy engine should normally produce about 17 to 22 in-Hg with a fairly steady needle **(see illustration)**. Refer to the following vacuum gauge readings and what they indicate about the engine's condition:

7 A low, steady reading usually indicates a leaking gasket between the intake manifold and cylinder head(s) or throttle body, a leaky vacuum hose, late ignition timing or incorrect camshaft timing. Check and eliminate all possible causes before you remove the timing belt cover to check the timing marks.

8 If the reading is three to eight inches below normal and it fluctuates at that low reading, suspect an intake manifold gasket leak at an intake port or a faulty fuel injector.

9 If the needle has regular drops of about two-to-four inches at a steady rate, the valves are probably leaking. Perform a compression check or leak-down test to confirm this.

10 An irregular drop or down-flick of the needle can be caused by a sticking valve or an ignition misfire. Perform a compression check or leak-down test and read the spark plugs.

11 A rapid vibration of about four in-Hg vibration at idle combined with exhaust smoke indicates worn valve guides. Perform a leak-down test to confirm this. If the rapid vibration occurs with an increase in engine speed, check for a leaking intake manifold gasket or head gasket, weak valve springs, burned valves or ignition misfire.

12 A slight fluctuation, say one inch up and down, may mean ignition problems. Check all the usual tune-up items and, if necessary, run

the engine on an ignition analyzer.

13 If there is a large fluctuation, perform a compression or leak-down test to look for a weak or dead cylinder or a blown head gasket.

14 If the needle moves slowly through a wide range, check for a clogged PCV system, incorrect idle fuel mixture, throttle body or intake manifold gasket leaks.

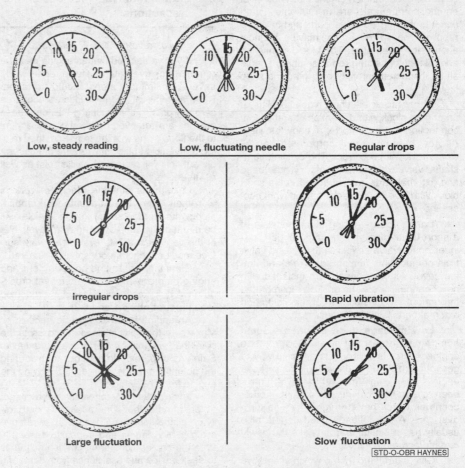

Low, steady reading

Low, fluctuating needle

Regular drops

irreguiar drops

Rapid vibration

Large fluctuation

Slow fluctuation

STD-O-OBR HAYNES

4.6 Typical vacuum gauge readings

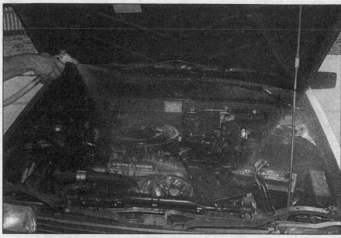

6.1 After tightly wrapping water-vulnerable components, use a spray cleaner on everything, with particular concentration on the greasiest areas, usually around the valve cover and lower edges of the block. If one section dries out, apply more cleaner

6.2 Depending on how dirty the engine is, let the cleaner soak in according to the directions, then hose off the grime and cleaner. Get the rinse water down into every area you can get at; then dry important components with a hair dryer or paper towels

exchange engine for your vehicle.

Some of the rebuilding alternatives include:

Individual parts - If the inspection procedures reveal that the engine block and most engine components are in reusable condition, purchasing individual parts and having a rebuilder rebuild your engine may be the most economical alternative. The block, crankshaft and piston/connecting rod assemblies should all be inspected carefully by a machine shop first.

Short block - A short block consists of an engine block with a crankshaft and piston/ connecting rod assemblies already installed. All new bearings are incorporated and all clearances will be correct. The existing camshafts, valve train components, cylinder head and external parts can be bolted to the short block with little or no machine shop work necessary.

Long block - A long block consists of a short block plus an oil pump, oil pan, cylinder head, valve cover, camshaft and valve train components, timing sprockets and timing cover. All components are installed with new bearings, seals and gaskets incorporated throughout. The installation of manifolds and external parts is all that's necessary.

Low mileage used engines - Some companies now offer low mileage used engines which is a very cost effective way to get your vehicle up and running again. These engines often come from vehicles which have been totaled in accidents or come from other countries which have a higher vehicle turnover rate. A low mileage used engine also usually has a similar warranty like the newly remanufactured engines.

Give careful thought to which alternative is best for you and discuss the situation with local automotive machine shops, auto parts

dealers and experienced rebuilders before ordering or purchasing replacement parts.

6   Engine removal - methods and precautions

Refer to illustrations 6.1, 6.2, and 6.3

If you've decided that an engine must be removed for overhaul or major repair work, several preliminary steps should be taken. Read all removal and installation procedures carefully prior to committing to this job. These engines are removed by lowering the engine to the floor, along with the transaxle, then raising the vehicle sufficiently to slide the assembly out; this will require a vehicle hoist as well as an engine hoist.

Locating a suitable place to work is extremely important. Adequate work space, along with storage space for the vehicle, will be needed. If a shop or garage isn't available, at the very least a flat, level, clean work surface made of concrete or asphalt is required.

Cleaning the engine compartment and engine before beginning the removal procedure will help keep tools clean and organized **(see illustrations 6.1 and 6.2)**.

An engine hoist will also be necessary. Make sure the hoist is rated in excess of the combined weight of the engine and transaxle. Safety is of primary importance, considering the potential hazards involved in removing the engine from the vehicle.

If you're a novice at engine removal, get at least one helper. One person cannot easily do all the things you need to do to remove a big heavy engine and transaxle assembly from the engine compartment. Also helpful is to seek advice and assistance from someone who's experienced in engine removal.

Plan the operation ahead of time. Arrange for or obtain all of the tools and equip-

6.3 Get an engine stand sturdy enough to firmly support the engine while you're working on it. Stay away from three-wheeled models; they have a tendency to tip over more easily, so get a four-wheeled unit

ment you'll need prior to beginning the job **(see illustration 6.3)**. Some of the equipment necessary to perform engine removal and installation safely and with relative ease are (in addition to a vehicle hoist and an engine hoist) a heavy duty floor jack (preferably fitted with a transmission jack head adapter), complete sets of wrenches and sockets as described in the front of this manual, wooden blocks, plenty of rags and cleaning solvent for mopping up spilled oil, coolant and gasoline.

Plan for the vehicle to be out of use for quite a while. A machine shop can do the work that is beyond the scope of the home mechanic. Machine shops often have a busy schedule, so before removing the engine,

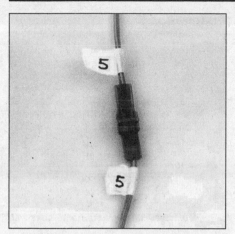

7.10 Label both ends of each wire or vacuum connection before disconnecting them

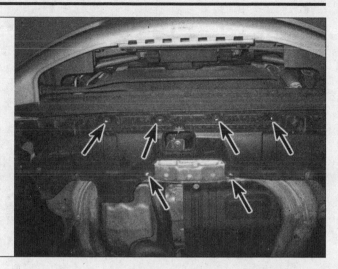

7.20 Location of the engine lower splash shield fasteners - some hidden from view

consult the shop for an estimate of how long it will take to rebuild or repair the components that may need work.

7 Engine - removal and installation

Warning 1: *Gasoline is extremely flammable, so take extra precautions when you work on any part of the fuel system. Don't smoke or allow open flames or bare light bulbs near the work area, and don't work in a garage where a gas-type appliance (such as a water heater or clothes dryer) is present. Since gasoline is carcinogenic, wear fuel-resistant gloves when there's a possibility of being exposed to fuel, and, if you spill any fuel on your skin, rinse it off immediately with soap and water. Mop up any spills immediately and do not store fuel-soaked rags where they could ignite. The fuel system is under constant pressure, so, if any fuel lines are to be disconnected, the fuel pressure in the system must be relieved first (see Chapter 4 for more information). When you perform any kind of work on the fuel system, wear safety glasses and have a Class B type fire extinguisher on hand.*

Warning 2: *The engine must be completely cool before beginning this procedure.*

Note 1: *Engine removal on these models is a difficult job, especially for the do-it-yourself mechanic working at home. Because of the vehicle's design, the manufacturer states that the engine and transaxle have to be removed as a unit from the bottom of the vehicle, not the top. With a floor jack and jackstands, the vehicle can't be raised high enough and supported safely enough for the engine/transaxle assembly to slide out from underneath. The manufacturer recommends that removal of the engine transaxle assembly only be performed on a frame-contact type vehicle hoist.*

Note 2: *Read through the entire Section before beginning this procedure. The engine and transaxle are removed as a unit from below, then separated outside the vehicle.*

Note 3: *Keep in mind that during this procedure you'll have to adjust the height of the vehicle to perform certain operations.*

Removal

Refer to illustrations 7.10, 7.20, 7.31a and 7.31b

1   Park the vehicle on a frame-contact type vehicle hoist, then engage the arms of the hoist with the jacking points of the vehicle. Raise the hoist arms until they contact the vehicle, but not so much that the wheels come off the ground.

2   With the help of an assistant, disconnect the hood struts from the ballstuds on the hood and raise the hood to the wide-open position, then thread the right-side ballstud into the lower hole in the hood. Attach the top of the hood strut to the ballstud. **Caution:** *Do not try to lower the hood while propped in this position or the hood could be damaged.*

3   Relieve the fuel system pressure (see Chapter 4), then disconnect the cable from the negative terminal of the battery (see Chapter 5, Section 1).

4   Remove the engine cover (see Chapter 2A, Section 6), and the left and right engine compartment covers.

5   Remove the air filter housing and the air intake duct (see Chapter 4).

6   Disconnect the accelerator cable and cruise control cable (if equipped) from the throttle body. On later models, disconnect the large connector at the throttle body, and the various hoses.

7   Remove the battery and the battery tray (see Chapter 5).

8   Disconnect the main engine harness connectors and release the harness clips at the firewall, so that the engine can be removed with its harness.

9   Disconnect the engine harness connectors near the battery tray and remove the ground cable, the harness bracket and the alternator cable. Position the components off to the side. Follow all wiring harnesses from the engine and transaxle and disconnect the electrical connectors leading to the vehicle wiring harnesses.

10   Clearly label and disconnect all vacuum lines, emissions hoses, and ground straps between the engine and the engine compartment. Masking tape and/or a touch up paint applicator work well for marking items **(see illustration)**. Take instant photos or sketch the locations of components and brackets.

11   Disconnect the fuel line(s) from the fuel rail (see Chapter 4).

12   Loosen the front wheel lug nuts, then raise the vehicle on the hoist. Remove the wheels, then loosen the driveaxle/hub nuts (see Chapter 8).

13   Remove the drivebelts (see Chapter 1).

14   Detach the power steering pressure hose from the power steering pump, then remove the power steering pump (see Chapter 10). Also remove the bracket securing the hose to the rear cylinder head.

15   Drain the cooling system (see Chapter 1).

16   Detach the heater hoses at the firewall and remove the upper and lower radiator hoses (see Chapter 3).

17   Remove the cooling fan(s) and radiator (see Chapter 3).

18   Remove the air conditioning compressor without disconnecting the hoses (see Chapter 3). Support the compressor with a piece of rope, tying it to prevent straining the hose connectors.

19   Working inside the driver's compartment, remove the driver's side lower trim panel and remove the pinch bolt from the intermediate shaft and steering gear input shaft connector (see Chapter 10). Be sure to paint a mark across the connector to insure correct alignment on reassembly.

20   Raise the vehicle and remove the engine lower splash shield **(see illustration)**.

21   Drain the engine oil and the automatic transaxle fluid (see Chapter 1).

22   Detach the stabilizer bar links from the stabilizer bar (see Chapter 10).

23   Detach the tie-rod ends from the steering knuckle arms (see Chapter 10).

24   Remove the driveaxles (see Chapter 8).

25   Disconnect the shift cable from the transaxle (see Chapter 7).

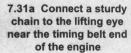

7.31a Connect a sturdy chain to the lifting eye near the timing belt end of the engine

26   Disconnect the power steering return hose from the pipe near the right steering gear boot. Follow the pipe along the subframe and detach the hose from its forward end, then free the hose clips from the subframe.

27   Unplug the electrical connector from the power steering pressure switch.

28   Detach the exhaust pipe from the exhaust manifold/catalytic converter assemblies and from the rear portion of the exhaust system, then remove the front portion of the exhaust system (see Chapter 4).

29   Disconnect the vacuum hoses, then remove the front and rear engine mounts (see Chapter 2A).

30   On models with an automatic transmission, remove the torque converter cover. Mark the position of the torque converter to the driveplate, then remove the torque converter bolts.

31   Support the engine from above with chains and a weight distributing bar. Attach one end of the chain to the lift bracket near the power steering pump **(see illustration)**. Attach the other end of the chain to a lift bracket bolted to the transaxle **(see illustration)**. Be sure the positioning of the chain will support the engine and transaxle in a balanced attitude. **Note:** *The sling or chain must be long enough to allow the engine hoist to lower the engine/transaxle assembly to the ground, without letting the hoist arm contact the vehicle.* **Warning:** *Never crawl under an engine supported only by a hoist!*

32   Roll the hoist into position and attach the chains to it. Take up the slack until there is slight tension on the hoist. **Note:** *Depending on the design of the engine hoist, it may be helpful to position the hoist from the side of the vehicle, so that when the engine/transaxle assembly is lowered, it will fit between the legs of the hoist.*

33   Unbolt the left (driver's side) transaxle mounts from the subframe (see Chapter 2A).

34   Unbolt the rear engine mount from the subframe, then remove the engine damper, if equipped (see Chapter 2A).

35   Carefully mark the position of the subframe in relation to the vehicle chassis.

36   Support the subframe with two floor

jacks (one on each side) and remove the subframe mounting bolts (see Chapter 10). Lower the subframe to the floor and remove it from under the vehicle.

37   Unbolt the passenger's side engine mount from the bracket on the engine (see Chapter 2A).

38   Recheck to be sure nothing is still connecting the engine or transaxle to the vehicle. Disconnect and label anything still remaining.

39   Slowly lower the engine/transaxle assembly to the floor.

40   Once the powertrain assembly is on the floor, disconnect the engine hoist and raise the vehicle using the vehicle hoist until it clears the powertrain assembly.

41   Reconnect the chain and raise the engine and transaxle. Support the engine with blocks of wood or another floor jack, while leaving the chain attached to the right-side mounting boss. Support the transaxle with another floor jack, preferably one with a transmission jack head adapter. At this point the transaxle can be unbolted and removed from the engine. Be very careful to ensure that the components are supported securely so they won't topple off their supports during disconnection.

42   Reconnect the lifting chain to the engine, then raise the engine and attach it to an engine stand.

Installation

43   Installation is the reverse of removal, noting the following points:

a) *Check the engine/transaxle mounts. If they're worn or damaged, replace them.*

b) *Attach the transaxle to the engine following the procedure described in Chapter 7.*

c) *Add coolant, engine oil, power steering and transmission fluids (see Chapter 1).*

d) *Align the subframe reference marks before tightening the bolts (see Chapter 10).*

e) *Tighten the subframe mounting bolts and bracket bolts (see Chapter 10). Note the locations and sizes of the various bolts. Replace all the large subframe bolts with new ones.*

f) *Reconnect the negative battery cable (see Chapter 5, Section 1).*

g) *Run the engine and check for proper operation and leaks. Shut off the engine and recheck fluid levels.*

8   Engine overhaul - disassembly sequence

1   It's much easier to remove the external components if the engine is mounted on a portable engine stand. A stand can often be rented quite cheaply from an equipment rental yard. Before the engine is mounted on a stand, the driveplate should be removed from the engine.

2   If a stand isn't available, it's possible to remove the external engine components with it blocked up on the floor. Be extra careful not to tip or drop the engine when working without a stand.

3   If you're going to obtain a rebuilt engine, all external components must come off first, to be transferred to the replacement engine. These components include:

Driveplate
Ignition system components
Emissions-related components
Engine mounts and mount brackets
Engine rear cover (spacer plate between driveplate and engine block)

7.31b Connect another chain to the lifting eye near the transaxle

9.1 Before you try to remove the pistons, use a ridge reamer to remove the raised material (ridge) from the top of the cylinders

9.3 Checking the connecting rod endplay (side clearance)

Intake/exhaust manifolds
Fuel injection components
Oil filter
Spark plugs
Thermostat and housing assembly
Water pump

Note: *When removing the external components from the engine, pay close attention to details that may be helpful or important during installation. Note the installed position of gaskets, seals, spacers, pins, brackets, washers, bolts and other small items.*

4   If you're going to obtain a short block (assembled engine block, crankshaft, pistons and connecting rods), then remove the timing belt, cylinder heads, oil pan, oil pump pick-up tube, oil pump and water pump from your engine so that you can turn in your old short block to the rebuilder as a core. See *Engine rebuilding alternatives* for additional information regarding the different possibilities to be considered.

9   Pistons and connecting rods - removal and installation

Removal

Refer to illustrations 9.1, 9.3 and 9.4

Note: *Prior to removing the piston/connecting rod assemblies, remove the cylinder heads and oil pan (see Chapter 2A).*

1   Use your fingernail to feel if a ridge has formed at the upper limit of ring travel (about 1/4-inch down from the top of each cylinder). If carbon deposits or cylinder wear have produced ridges, they must be completely removed with a special tool **(see illustration)**. Follow the manufacturer's instructions provided with the tool. Failure to remove the ridges before attempting to remove the piston/connecting rod assemblies may result in piston breakage.

2   After the cylinder ridges have been removed, turn the engine so the crankshaft is

facing up. Remove the baffle plate.

3   Before the connecting rods are removed, check the connecting rod endplay with feeler gauges. Slide them between the first connecting rod and the crankshaft throw until the play is removed **(see illustration)**. Repeat this procedure for each connecting rod. The endplay is equal to the thickness of the feeler gauge(s). Check with an automotive machine shop for the endplay service limit (a typical endplay should measure between 0.005 to 0.015 inch [0.127 to 0.396 mm]). If the play exceeds the service limit, new connecting rods will be required. If new rods (or a new crankshaft) are installed, the endplay may fall under the minimum allowable. If it does, the rods will have to be machined to restore it. If necessary, consult an automotive machine shop for advice.

4   Check the connecting rods and caps for identification marks. If they aren't plainly marked, use paint or marker **(see illustration)** to clearly identify each rod and cap (1, 2, 3, etc., depending on the cylinder they're associated with). **Caution:** *Do not use a punch and hammer to mark the connecting rods or they may be damaged.*

5   Loosen each of the connecting rod

cap bolts 1/2-turn at a time until they can be removed by hand. **Note:** *New connecting rod cap bolts must be used when reassembling the engine, but save the old bolts for use when checking the connecting rod bearing oil clearance.*

6   Remove the number one connecting rod cap and bearing insert. Don't drop the bearing insert out of the cap.

7   Remove the bearing insert and push the connecting rod/piston assembly out through the top of the engine. Use a wooden or plastic hammer handle to push on the upper bearing surface in the connecting rod. If resistance is felt, double-check to make sure that all of the ridge was removed from the cylinder.

8   Repeat the procedure for the remaining cylinders.

9   After removal, reassemble the connecting rod caps and bearing inserts in their respective connecting rods and install the cap bolts finger tight. Leaving the old bearing inserts in place until reassembly will help prevent the connecting rod bearing surfaces from being accidentally nicked or gouged.

10   The pistons and connecting rods are now ready for inspection and overhaul at an automotive machine shop.

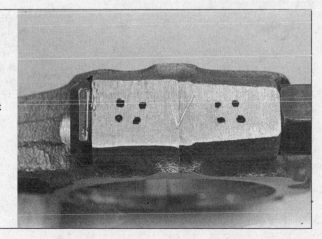

9.4 If the connecting rods or caps are not marked, use permanent ink or paint to mark the caps to the rods by cylinder number (for example, this would be number 4 cylinder connecting rod)

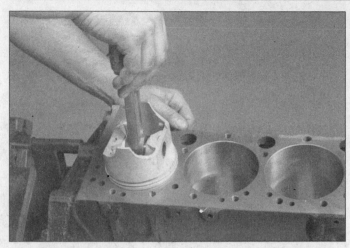

9.13 Install the piston ring into the cylinder, then push it down into position using a piston so the ring will be square in the cylinder

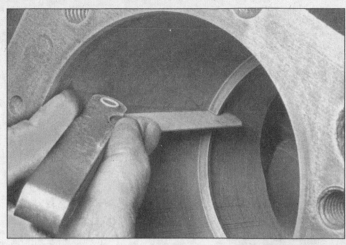

9.14 With the ring square in the cylinder, measure the ring end gap with a feeler gauge

Piston ring installation

Refer to illustrations 9.13, 9.14, 9.15, 9.19a, 9.19b and 9.22

11   Before installing the new piston rings, the ring end gaps must be checked. It's assumed that the piston ring side clearance has been checked and verified correct.

12   Lay out the piston/connecting rod assemblies and the new ring sets so the ring sets will be matched with the same piston and cylinder during the end gap measurement and engine assembly.

13   Insert the top (number one) compression ring into the first cylinder and square it up with the cylinder walls by pushing it in with the top of the piston **(see illustration)**. The ring should be near the bottom of the cylinder, at the lower limit of ring travel.

14   To measure the end gap, slip feeler gauges between the ends of the ring until a gauge equal to the gap width is found **(see illustration)**. The feeler gauge should slide between the ring ends with a slight amount of drag. A typical ring gap should fall between 0.010 and 0.020 inch (0.25 to 0.50 mm) for compression rings and up to 0.030 inch (0.76 mm) for the oil ring steel rails. If the gap is larger or smaller than specified, double-check to make sure you have the correct rings before proceeding.

15   If the gap is too small, it must be enlarged or the ring ends may come in contact with each other during engine operation, which can cause serious damage to the engine. If necessary, increase the end gaps by filing the ring ends very carefully with a fine file. Mount the file in a vise equipped with soft jaws, slip the ring over the file with the ends contacting the file face and slowly move the ring to remove material from the ends. When performing this operation, file only by pushing the ring from the outside end of the file towards the vise **(see illustration)**.

16   Excess end gap isn't critical unless it's greater than 0.040 inch (1.01 mm). Again, double-check to make sure you have the correct ring type.

17   Repeat the procedure for each ring that will be installed in the first cylinder and for each ring in the remaining cylinders. Remember to keep rings, pistons and cylinders matched up.

18   Once the ring end gaps have been checked/corrected, the rings can be installed on the pistons.

19   The oil control ring (lowest one on the piston) is usually installed first. It's composed of three separate components. Slip the spacer/expander into the groove **(see illustration)**. If an anti-rotation tang is used, make sure it's inserted into the drilled hole in the ring groove. Next, install the upper side rail in the same manner **(see illustration)**. Don't use a piston ring installation tool on the oil ring side rails, as they may be damaged. Instead, place one end of the side rail into the groove between the spacer/expander and the ring land, hold it firmly in place and slide a finger around the piston while pushing the rail into the groove. Finally, install the lower side rail.

20   After the three oil ring components have been installed, check to make sure that both

9.15 If the ring end gap is too small, clamp a file in a vise as shown and file the piston ring ends - be sure to remove all raised material

9.19a Installing the spacer/expander in the oil ring groove

9.19b DO NOT use a piston ring installation tool when installing the oil control side rails

9.22 Use a piston ring installation tool to install the number 2 and the number 1 (top) rings - be sure the directional mark on the piston ring(s) is facing toward the top of the piston

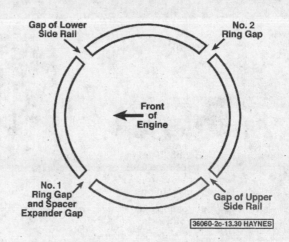

9.30 Location of the piston ring end gaps

the upper and lower side rails can be rotated smoothly inside the ring grooves.

21 The number two (middle) compression ring is installed next. It's usually stamped with a mark which must face up, toward the top of the piston. Do not mix up the top and middle rings, as they have different cross-sections. **Note:** *Always follow the instructions printed on the ring package or box - different manufacturers may require different approaches.*

22 Use a piston ring installation tool and make sure the identification mark is facing the top of the piston, then slip the ring into the middle groove on the piston **(see illustration)**. Don't expand the ring any more than necessary to slide it over the piston.

23 Install the number one (top) compression ring in the same manner. Make sure the mark is facing up. Be careful not to confuse the number one and number two compression rings.

24 Repeat the procedure for the remaining pistons and rings.

Installation

25 Before installing the piston/connecting rod assemblies, the cylinder walls must be perfectly clean, the top edge of each cylinder bore must be chamfered, and the crankshaft must be in place.

26 Remove the cap from the end of the number one connecting rod (refer to the marks made during removal). Remove the original bearing inserts and wipe the bearing surfaces of the connecting rod and cap with a clean, lint-free cloth. They must be kept spotlessly clean.

Connecting rod bearing oil clearance check

Refer to illustrations 9.30, 9.35, 9.37 and 9.41

27 Clean the back side of the new upper bearing insert, then lay it in place in the connecting rod.

28 Make sure the tab on the bearing fits into the recess in the rod. Don't hammer the bear-

ing insert into place and be very careful not to nick or gouge the bearing face. Don't lubricate the bearing at this time.

29 Clean the back side of the other bearing insert and install it in the rod cap. Again, make sure the tab on the bearing fits into the recess in the cap, and don't apply any lubricant. It's critically important that the mating surfaces of the bearing and connecting rod are perfectly clean and oil free when they're assembled.

30 Position the piston ring gaps at the specified intervals around the piston as shown **(see illustration)**.

31 Lubricate the piston and rings with clean engine oil and attach a piston ring compressor to the piston. Leave the skirt protruding about 1/4-inch to guide the piston into the cylinder. The rings must be compressed until they're flush with the piston.

32 Rotate the crankshaft until the number one connecting rod journal is at BDC (bottom dead center) and apply a liberal coat of engine oil to the cylinder walls.

33 With the arrow on the top of the piston crown facing the front (timing belt end) of the engine, gently insert the piston/connecting rod assembly into the number one cylinder bore

and rest the bottom edge of the ring compressor on the engine block. Install the pistons with the cavity mark(s) facing toward the timing belt.

34 Tap the top edge of the ring compressor to make sure it's contacting the block around its entire circumference.

35 Gently tap on the top of the piston with the end of a wooden or plastic hammer handle **(see illustration)** while guiding the end of the connecting rod into place on the crankshaft journal. The piston rings may try to pop out of the ring compressor just before entering the cylinder bore, so keep some downward pressure on the ring compressor. Work slowly, and if any resistance is felt as the piston enters the cylinder, stop immediately. Find out what's hanging up and fix it before proceeding. Do not, for any reason, force the piston into the cylinder - you might break a ring and/or the piston.

36 Once the piston/connecting rod assembly is installed, the connecting rod bearing oil clearance must be checked before the rod cap is permanently installed.

37 Cut a piece of the appropriate size Plastigage slightly shorter than the width of the connecting rod bearing and lay it in place on the

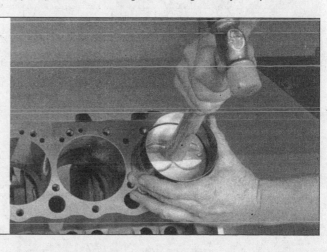

9.35 Use a plastic or wooden hammer handle to push the piston into the cylinder

ENGINE BEARING ANALYSIS

Debris

Babbitt bearing embedded with debris from machinings

Microscopic detail of debris

Microscopic detail of gouges

Overplated copper alloy bearing gouged by cast iron debris

Aluminum bearing embedded with glass beads

Microscopic detail of glass beads

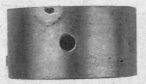

Damaged lining caused by dirt left on the bearing back

Misassembly

Result of a lower half assembled as an upper - blocking the oil flow

Excessive oil clearance is indicated by a short contact arc

Polished and oil-stained backs are a result of a poor fit in the housing bore

Result of a wrong, reversed, or shifted cap

Overloading

Damage from excessive idling which resulted in an oil film unable to support the load imposed

Damaged upper connecting rod bearings caused by engine lugging; the lower main bearings (not shown) were similarly affected

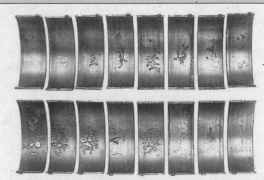

The damage shown in these upper and lower connecting rod bearings was caused by engine operation at a higher-than-rated speed under load

Misalignment

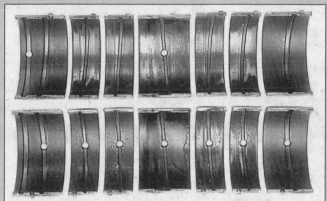

A poorly finished crankshaft caused the equally spaced scoring shown

A tapered housing bore caused the damage along one edge of this pair

A warped crankshaft caused this pattern of severe wear in the center, diminishing toward the ends

A bent connecting rod led to the damage in the "V" pattern

Lubrication

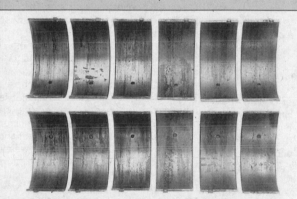

Result of dry start: The bearings on the left, farthest from the oil pump, show more damage

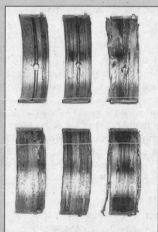

Result of a low oil supply or oil starvation

Severe wear as a result of inadequate oil clearance

Corrosion

Microscopic detail of corrosion

Corrosion is an acid attack on the bearing lining generally caused by inadequate maintenance, extremely hot or cold operation, or inferior oils or fuels

Microscopic detail of cavitation

Example of cavitation - a surface erosion caused by pressure changes in the oil film

Damage from excessive thrust or insufficient axial clearance

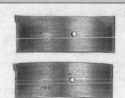

Bearing affected by oil dilution caused by excessive blow-by or a rich mixture

number one connecting rod journal, parallel with the journal axis **(see illustration)**.

38   Clean the connecting rod cap bearing face and install the rod cap. Make sure the mating mark on the cap is on the same side as the mark on the connecting rod **(see illustration 9.4)**.

39   Install the old rod bolts at this time, and tighten them to the torque listed in this Chapter's Specifications. **Note:** *Use a thin-wall socket to avoid erroneous torque readings that can result if the socket is wedged between the rod cap and the bolt. If the socket tends to wedge itself between the fastener and the cap, lift up on it slightly until it no longer contacts the cap.* DO NOT rotate the crankshaft at any time during this operation.

40   Remove the fasteners and detach the rod cap, being very careful not to disturb the Plastigage. Discard the cap bolts at this time as they cannot be reused. **Note:** *You MUST use new connecting rod cap bolts.*

41   Compare the width of the crushed Plastigage to the scale printed on the Plastigage envelope to obtain the oil clearance **(see illustration)**. The connecting rod oil clearance is usually about 0.001 to 0.002 inch. Consult an automotive machine shop for the clearance specified for the rod bearings on your engine.

42   If the clearance is not as specified, the bearing inserts may be the wrong size (which means different ones will be required). Before deciding that different inserts are needed, make sure that no dirt or oil was between the bearing inserts and the connecting rod or cap when the clearance was measured. Also, recheck the journal diameter. If the Plastigage was wider at one end than the other, the journal may be tapered. If the clearance still exceeds the limit specified, the bearing will have to be replaced with an undersize bearing. **Caution:** *When installing a new crankshaft, always use a standard size bearing.*

Final installation

43   Carefully scrape all traces of the Plastigage material off the rod journal and/or bearing face. Be very careful not to scratch the bearing - use your fingernail or the edge of a plastic card.

44   Make sure the bearing faces are perfectly clean, then apply a uniform layer of clean moly-base grease or engine assembly lube to both of them. You'll have to push the piston into the cylinder to expose the face of the bearing insert in the connecting rod.

45   Slide the connecting rod back into place on the journal, install the rod cap, install the **new** bolts and tighten them to the torque listed in this Chapter's Specifications. Again, work up to the torque in three steps.

46   Repeat the entire procedure for the remaining pistons/connecting rods.

47   The important points to remember are:

a)   *Keep the back sides of the bearing inserts and the insides of the connecting rods and caps perfectly clean when assembling them.*

9.37 Place Plastigage on each connecting rod bearing journal parallel to the crankshaft centerline

b)   *Make sure you have the correct piston/rod assembly for each cylinder.*
c)   *The mark on the piston must face the front (timing belt end) of the engine.*
d)   *Lubricate the cylinder walls liberally with clean oil.*
e)   *Lubricate the bearing faces when installing the rod caps after the oil clearance has been checked.*
f)   *Use new rod cap bolts.*

48   After all the piston/connecting rod assemblies have been correctly installed, rotate the crankshaft a number of times by hand to check for any obvious binding.

49   As a final step, check the connecting rod endplay again.

50   Compare the measured endplay to the tolerance listed in this Chapter's Specifications to make sure it's acceptable. If it was correct before disassembly and the original crankshaft and rods were reinstalled, it should still be correct. If new rods or a new crankshaft were installed, the endplay may be inadequate. If so, the rods will have to be removed and taken to an automotive machine shop for resizing.

10   Crankshaft - removal and installation

Removal

Refer to illustrations 10.1 and 10.3

Note: *The crankshaft can be removed only after the engine has been removed from the vehicle. It's assumed that the driveplate, crankshaft pulley, timing belt, oil pan, oil pump body, oil filter and piston/connecting rod assemblies have already been removed. The rear main oil seal retainer must be unbolted and separated from the block before proceeding with crankshaft removal.*

1   Before the crankshaft is removed, measure the endplay. Mount a dial indicator with the indicator in line with the crankshaft and touching the end of the crankshaft as shown **(see illustration)**.

9.41 Use the scale on the Plastigage package to determine the bearing oil clearance - be sure to measure the widest part of the Plastigage and use the correct scale; it comes with both standard and metric scales

2   Pry the crankshaft all the way to the rear and zero the dial indicator. Next, pry the crankshaft to the front as far as possible and check the reading on the dial indicator. The distance traveled is the endplay. A typical crankshaft endplay will fall between 0.003 to 0.010 inch (0.076 to 0.254 mm). If it is greater than that, check the crankshaft thrust surfaces for wear after it's removed. If no wear is evident, new main bearings should correct the endplay.

3   If a dial indicator isn't available, feeler gauges can be used. Gently pry the crankshaft all the way to the front of the engine. Slip feeler gauges between the crankshaft and the front face of the thrust bearing or washer to determine the clearance **(see illustration)**.

4   Loosen the side bearing cap bolts 1/4-turn at a time each, until they can be removed by hand, then do the same for the main cap bolts, following the reverse of the tightening sequence **(see illustration 10.19)**.

5   Gently tap the main bearing caps with a soft-face hammer. Pull the main bearing caps straight up and off the cylinder block. Try not to drop the bearing inserts if they come out with the caps.

6   Carefully lift the crankshaft out of the engine. It may be a good idea to have an assistant available, since the crankshaft is quite heavy and awkward to handle. With the bearing inserts in place inside the engine block and main bearing caps, reinstall the main bearing caps and tighten the bolts finger tight. Make sure you install the main bearing caps with the arrows facing the front (timing belt end) of the engine.

Installation

7   Crankshaft installation is the first step in engine reassembly. It's assumed at this point that the engine block and crankshaft have been cleaned, inspected and repaired or reconditioned.

8   Position the engine block with the bottom facing up.

9   Remove the main bearing caps.

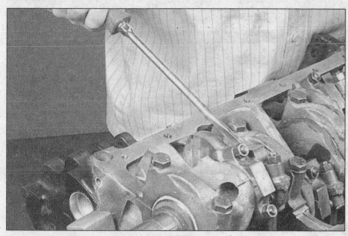

10.1 Checking crankshaft endplay with a dial indicator

10.3 Checking crankshaft endplay with feeler gauges at the thrust bearing journal

10   If they're still in place, remove the original bearing inserts from the block and from the main bearing caps. Wipe the bearing surfaces of the block and main bearing caps with a clean, lint-free cloth. They must be kept spotlessly clean. This is critical for determining the correct bearing oil clearance.

Main bearing oil clearance check

Refer to illustrations 10.17, 10.19 and 10.21

11   Without mixing them up, clean the back sides of the new upper main bearing inserts (with grooves and oil holes) and lay one in each main bearing saddle in the block. Each upper bearing has an oil groove and oil hole in it. **Caution:** *The oil holes in the block must line up with the oil holes in the upper bearing inserts.* The thrust washers must be installed in the number 3 crankshaft journal. Clean the back sides of the lower main bearing inserts and lay them in the corresponding main bearing caps. Make sure

the tab on the bearing insert fits into the recess in the block or main bearing cap assembly. The upper bearings with the oil holes are installed in the engine block while the lower bearings without the oil holes are installed in the main bearing caps. **Caution:** *DO NOT apply any lubrication at this time.*

12   Clean the faces of the bearing inserts in the block and the crankshaft main bearing journals with a clean, lint-free cloth.

13   Check or clean the oil holes in the crankshaft, as any dirt here can go only one way - straight through the new bearings.

14   Once you're certain the crankshaft is clean, carefully lay it in position in the cylinder block.

15   Before the crankshaft can be permanently installed, the main bearing oil clearance must be checked.

16   Cut several strips of the appropriate size of Plastigage. They must be slightly shorter than the width of the main bearing journal.

17   Place one piece on each crankshaft main bearing journal, parallel with the journal

axis as shown **(see illustration)**.

18   Clean the faces of the bearing inserts in the main bearing caps. Install the caps onto the crankshaft and cylinder block. DO NOT disturb the Plastigage. Make sure you install the main bearing caps with the arrows facing the front (timing belt end) of the engine.

19   Apply clean engine oil to all bolt threads prior to installation, then install all bolts finger-tight. Tighten the main bearing cap bolts (the 8 main bolts followed by the 8 side bolts) in the sequence shown **(see illustration)** progressing in steps, to the torque listed in this Chapter's Specifications. DO NOT rotate the crankshaft at any time during this operation.

20   Remove the bolts in the reverse order of the tightening sequence and carefully lift the main bearing caps straight up and off the block. Do not disturb the Plastigage or rotate the crankshaft. If the main bearing caps are difficult to remove, tap them gently from side-to-side with a soft-face hammer to loosen it.

10.17 Place the Plastigage onto the crankshaft bearing journal as shown

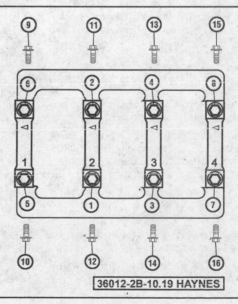

10.19 Main bearing cap bolt tightening sequence

36012-2B-10.19 HAYNES

COMMON ENGINE OVERHAUL TERMS

B

Backlash - The amount of play between two parts. Usually refers to how much one gear can be moved back and forth without moving the gear with which it's meshed.

Bearing Caps - The caps held in place by nuts or bolts which, in turn, hold the bearing surface. This space is for lubricating oil to enter.

Bearing clearance - The amount of space left between shaft and bearing surface. This space is for lubricating oil to enter.

Bearing crush - The additional height which is purposely manufactured into each bearing half to ensure complete contact of the bearing back with the housing bore when the engine is assembled.

Bearing knock - The noise created by movement of a part in a loose or worn bearing.

Blueprinting - Dismantling an engine and reassembling it to EXACT specifications.

Bore - An engine cylinder, or any cylindrical hole; also used to describe the process of enlarging or accurately refinishing a hole with a cutting tool, as to bore an engine cylinder. The bore size is the diameter of the hole.

Boring - Renewing the cylinders by cutting them out to a specified size. A boring bar is used to make the cut.

Bottom end - A term which refers collectively to the engine block, crankshaft, main bearings and the big ends of the connecting rods.

Break-in - The period of operation between installation of new or rebuilt parts and time in which parts are worn to the correct fit. Driving at reduced and varying speed for a specified mileage to permit parts to wear to the correct fit.

Bushing - A one-piece sleeve placed in a bore to serve as a bearing surface for shaft, piston pin, etc. Usually replaceable.

C

Camshaft - The shaft in the engine, on which a series of lobes are located for operating the valve mechanisms. The camshaft is driven by gears or sprockets and a timing chain. Usually referred to simply as the cam.

Carbon - Hard, or soft, black deposits found in combustion chamber, on plugs, under rings, on and under valve heads.

Cast iron - An alloy of iron and more than two percent carbon, used for engine blocks and heads because it's relatively inexpensive and easy to mold into complex shapes.

Chamfer - To bevel across (or a bevel on) the sharp edge of an object.

Chase - To repair damaged threads with a tap or die.

Combustion chamber - The space between the piston and the cylinder head, with the piston at top dead center, in which air-fuel mixture is burned.

Compression ratio - The relationship between cylinder volume (clearance volume) when the piston is at top dead center and cylinder volume when the piston is at bottom dead center.

Connecting rod - The rod that connects the crank on the crankshaft with the piston. Sometimes called a con rod.

Connecting rod cap - The part of the connecting rod assembly that attaches the rod to the crankpin.

Core plug - Soft metal plug used to plug the casting holes for the coolant passages in the block.

Crankcase - The lower part of the engine in which the crankshaft rotates; includes the lower section of the cylinder block and the oil pan.

Crank kit - A reground or reconditioned crankshaft and new main and connecting rod bearings.

Crankpin - The part of a crankshaft to which a connecting rod is attached.

Crankshaft - The main rotating member, or shaft, running the length of the crankcase, with offset throws to which the connecting rods are attached; changes the reciprocating motion of the pistons into rotating motion.

Cylinder sleeve - A replaceable sleeve, or liner, pressed into the cylinder block to form the cylinder bore.

D

Deburring - Removing the burrs (rough edges or areas) from a bearing.

Deglazer - A tool, rotated by an electric motor, used to remove glaze from cylinder walls so a new set of rings will seat.

E

Endplay - The amount of lengthwise movement between two parts. As applied to a crankshaft, the distance that the crankshaft can move forward and back in the cylinder block.

F

Face - A machinist's term that refers to removing metal from the end of a shaft or the face of a larger part, such as a flywheel.

Fatigue - A breakdown of material through a large number of loading and unloading cycles. The first signs are cracks followed shortly by breaks.

Feeler gauge - A thin strip of hardened steel, ground to an exact thickness, used to check clearances between parts.

Free height - The unloaded length or height of a spring.

Freeplay - The looseness in a linkage, or an assembly of parts, between the initial application of force and actual movement. Usually perceived as slop or slight delay.

Freeze plug - See Core plug.

G

Gallery - A large passage in the block that forms a reservoir for engine oil pressure.

Glaze - The very smooth, glassy finish that develops on cylinder walls while an engine is in service.

H

Heli-Coil - A rethreading device used when threads are worn or damaged. The device is installed in a retapped hole to reduce the thread size to the original size.

I

Installed height - The spring's measured length or height, as installed on the cylinder head. Installed height is measured from the spring seat to the underside of the spring retainer.

J

Journal - The surface of a rotating shaft which turns in a bearing.

K

Keeper - The split lock that holds the valve spring retainer in position on the valve stem.

Key - A small piece of metal inserted into matching grooves machined into two parts fitted together - such as a gear pressed onto a shaft - which prevents slippage between the two parts.

Knock - The heavy metallic engine sound, produced in the combustion chamber as a result of abnormal combustion - usually detonation. Knock is usually caused by a loose or worn bearing. Also referred to as detonation, pinging and spark knock. Connecting rod or main bearing knocks are created by too much oil clearance or insufficient lubrication.

L

Lands - The portions of metal between the piston ring grooves.

Lapping the valves - Grinding a valve face and its seat together with lapping compound.

Lash - The amount of free motion in a gear train, between gears, or in a mechanical assembly, that occurs before movement can begin. Usually refers to the lash in a valve train.

Lifter - The part that rides against the cam to transfer motion to the rest of the valve train.

M

Machining - The process of using a machine to remove metal from a metal part.

Main bearings - The plain, or babbit, bearings that support the crankshaft.

Main bearing caps - The cast iron caps, bolted to the bottom of the block, that support the main bearings.

O

O.D. - Outside diameter.

Oil gallery - A pipe or drilled passageway in the engine used to carry engine oil from one area to another.

Oil ring - The lower ring, or rings, of a piston; designed to prevent excessive amounts of oil from working up the cylinder walls and into the combustion chamber. Also called an oil-control ring.

Oil seal - A seal which keeps oil from leaking out of a compartment. Usually refers to a dynamic seal around a rotating shaft or other moving part.

O-ring - A type of sealing ring made of a special rubberlike material; in use, the O-ring is compressed into a groove to provide the sealing action.

Overhaul - To completely disassemble a unit, clean and inspect all parts, reassemble it with the original or new parts and make all adjustments necessary for proper operation.

P

Pilot bearing - A small bearing installed in the center of the flywheel (or the rear end of the crankshaft) to support the front end of the input shaft of the transmission.

Pip mark - A little dot or indentation which indicates the top side of a compression ring.

Piston - The cylindrical part, attached to the connecting rod, that moves up and down in the cylinder as the crankshaft rotates. When the fuel charge is fired, the piston transfers the force of the explosion to the connecting rod, then to the crankshaft.

Piston pin (or wrist pin) - The cylindrical and usually hollow steel pin that passes through the piston. The piston pin fastens the piston to the upper end of the connecting rod.

Piston ring - The split ring fitted to the groove in a piston. The ring contacts the sides of the ring groove and also rubs against the cylinder wall, thus sealing space between piston and wall. There are two types of rings: Compression rings seal the compression pressure in the combustion chamber; oil rings scrape excessive oil off the cylinder wall.

Piston ring groove - The slots or grooves cut in piston heads to hold piston rings in position.

Piston skirt - The portion of the piston below the rings and the piston pin hole.

Plastigage - A thin strip of plastic thread, available in different sizes, used for measuring clearances. For example, a strip of plastigage is laid across a bearing journal and mashed as parts are assembled. Then parts are disassembled and the width of the strip is measured to determine clearance between journal and bearing. Commonly used to measure crankshaft main-bearing and connecting rod bearing clearances.

Press-fit - A tight fit between two parts that requires pressure to force the parts together. Also referred to as drive, or force, fit.

Prussian blue - A blue pigment; in solution, useful in determining the area of contact between two surfaces. Prussian blue is commonly used to determine the width and location of the contact area between the valve face and the valve seat.

R

Race (bearing) - The inner or outer ring that provides a contact surface for balls or rollers in bearing.

Ream - To size, enlarge or smooth a hole by using a round cutting tool with fluted edges.

Ring job - The process of reconditioning the cylinders and installing new rings.

Runout - Wobble. The amount a shaft rotates out-of-true.

S

Saddle - The upper main bearing seat.

Scored - Scratched or grooved, as a cylinder wall may be scored by abrasive particles moved up and down by the piston rings.

Scuffing - A type of wear in which there's a transfer of material between parts moving against each other; shows up as pits or grooves in the mating surfaces.

Seat - The surface upon which another part rests or seats. For example, the valve seat is the matched surface upon which the valve face rests. Also used to refer to wearing into a good fit; for example, piston rings seat after a few miles of driving.

Short block - An engine block complete with crankshaft and piston and, usually, camshaft assemblies.

Static balance - The balance of an object while it's stationary.

Step - The wear on the lower portion of a ring land caused by excessive side and back-clearance. The height of the step indicates the ring's extra side clearance and the length of the step projecting from the back wall of the groove represents the ring's back clearance.

Stroke - The distance the piston moves when traveling from top dead center to bottom dead center, or from bottom dead center to top dead center.

Stud - A metal rod with threads on both ends.

T

Tang - A lip on the end of a plain bearing used to align the bearing during assembly.

Tap - To cut threads in a hole. Also refers to the fluted tool used to cut threads.

Taper - A gradual reduction in the width of a shaft or hole; in an engine cylinder, taper usually takes the form of uneven wear, more pronounced at the top than at the bottom.

Throws - The offset portions of the crankshaft to which the connecting rods are affixed.

Thrust bearing - The main bearing that has thrust faces to prevent excessive endplay, or forward and backward movement of the crankshaft.

Thrust washer - A bronze or hardened steel washer placed between two moving parts. The washer prevents longitudinal movement and provides a bearing surface for thrust surfaces of parts.

Tolerance - The amount of variation permitted from an exact size of measurement. Actual amount from smallest acceptable dimension to largest acceptable dimension.

U

Umbrella - An oil deflector placed near the valve tip to throw oil from the valve stem area.

Undercut - A machined groove below the normal surface.

Undersize bearings - Smaller diameter bearings used with re-ground crankshaft journals.

V

Valve grinding - Refacing a valve in a valve-refacing machine.

Valve train - The valve-operating mechanism of an engine; includes all components from the camshaft to the valve.

Vibration damper - A cylindrical weight attached to the front of the crankshaft to minimize torsional vibration (the twist-untwist actions of the crankshaft caused by the cylinder firing impulses). Also called a harmonic balancer.

W

Water jacket - The spaces around the cylinders, between the inner and outer shells of the cylinder block or head, through which coolant circulates.

Web - A supporting structure across a cavity.

Woodruff key - A key with a radiused backside (viewed from the side).

10.21 Use the scale on the Plastigage package to determine the bearing oil clearance - be sure to measure the widest part of the Plastigage and use the correct scale; it comes with both standard and metric scales

21   Compare the width of the crushed Plastigage on each journal to the scale printed on the Plastigage envelope to determine the main bearing oil clearance **(see illustration)**. A typical main bearing oil clearance should fall between 0.0015 and 0.0023-inch. Check with an automotive machine shop for the oil clearance for your engine.

22   If the clearance is not as specified, the bearing inserts may be the wrong size (which means different ones will be required). Before deciding if different inserts are needed, make sure that no dirt or oil was between the bearing inserts and the cap or block when the clearance was measured. If the Plastigage was wider at one end than the other, the crankshaft journal may be tapered. If the clearance still exceeds the limit specified, the bearing insert(s) will have to be replaced with an undersize bearing insert(s). **Caution:** *When installing a new crankshaft, always install a standard bearing insert set.*

23   Carefully scrape all traces of the Plastigage material off the main bearing journals and/or the bearing insert faces. Be sure to remove all residue from the oil holes. Use your fingernail or the edge of a plastic card - don't nick or scratch the bearing faces.

Final installation

24   Carefully lift the crankshaft out of the cylinder block. **Note:** *Install the oil jets and the oil jet bolts into the engine block and tighten*

them to the torque listed in this Chapter's Specifications.

25   Clean the bearing insert faces in the cylinder block, then apply a thin, uniform layer of moly-base grease or engine assembly lube to each of the bearing surfaces. Be sure to coat the thrust faces as well as the journal face of the thrust bearing.

26   Make sure the crankshaft journals are clean, then lay the crankshaft back in place in the cylinder block.

27   Clean the bearing insert faces and apply the same lubricant to them. Clean the engine block thoroughly. The surfaces must be free of oil residue.

28   Assemble the main bearing caps and bearings and install each main bearing cap onto the crankshaft and cylinder block. Make sure the arrows face the front (timing belt end) of the engine.

29   Prior to installation, apply clean engine oil to all bolt threads, wiping off any excess, then install all bolts finger-tight.

30   Torque the main bearing cap bolts followed by the side bolts in the correct sequence **(see illustration 10.19)**.

31   Recheck crankshaft endplay with a feeler gauge or a dial indicator. The endplay should be correct if the crankshaft thrust faces aren't worn or damaged and if new bearings have been installed.

32   Rotate the crankshaft a number of times by hand to check for any obvious binding. It should rotate with a running torque of 50 in-lbs or less. If the running torque is too high, correct the problem at this time.

33   Install a new rear main oil seal (see Chapter 2A).

11   Engine overhaul - reassembly sequence

1   Before beginning engine reassembly, make sure you have all the necessary new parts, gaskets and seals as well as the following items on hand:

Common hand tools
A 1/2-inch drive torque wrench
New engine oil
Gasket sealant
Thread locking compound

2   If you obtained a short block it will be necessary to install the cylinder heads, the oil pump and pick-up tube, the oil pan, the water pump, the timing belt and timing covers, and the valve covers (see Chapter 2A). In order to save time and avoid problems, the external

components must be installed in the following general order:

Thermostat and housing cover
Water pump
Intake and exhaust manifolds
Fuel injection components
Emission control components
Spark plugs
Ignition coils
Oil filter
Engine mounts and mount brackets
Driveplate

12   Initial start-up and break-in after overhaul

Warning: *Have a fire extinguisher handy when starting the engine for the first time.*

1   Once the engine has been installed in the vehicle, double-check the engine oil and coolant levels.

2   With the spark plugs out of the engine and the ignition system and fuel pump disabled (see Section 3), crank the engine until oil pressure registers on the gauge or the light goes out.

3   Install the spark plugs and ignition coils, then restore the fuel pump function.

4   Start the engine. It may take a few moments for the fuel system to build up pressure, but the engine should start without a great deal of effort.

5   After the engine starts, it should be allowed to warm up to normal operating temperature. While the engine is warming up, make a thorough check for fuel, oil and coolant leaks.

6   Shut the engine off and recheck the engine oil and coolant levels.

7   Drive the vehicle to an area with minimum traffic, accelerate from 30 to 50 mph, then allow the vehicle to slow to 30 mph with the throttle closed. Repeat the procedure 10 or 12 times. This will load the piston rings and cause them to seat properly against the cylinder walls. Check again for oil and coolant leaks.

8   Drive the vehicle gently for the first 500 miles (no sustained high speeds) and keep a constant check on the oil level. It is not unusual for an engine to use oil during the break-in period.

9   At approximately 500 to 600 miles, change the oil and filter.

10   For the next few hundred miles, drive the vehicle normally. Do not pamper it or abuse it.

11   After 2000 miles, change the oil and filter again and consider the engine broken in.

Chapter 3
Cooling, heating and air conditioning systems

Contents

Specifications

General

Radiator cap pressure rating	14 to 18 psi (93 to 123 kPa)
Thermostat rating (opening to fully open temperature range)	
1999 models.................	163 to 194 degrees F (73 to 90 degrees C)
2000 and later models.................	169 to 194 degrees F (76 to 90 degrees C)
Coolant type.................	See Chapter 1
Cooling system capacity.................	See Chapter 1
Refrigerant type.................	R-134a
Refrigerant capacity	
2003 and earlier models.................	21 to 23 ounces (600 to 650 grams)
2004 and later models.................	18 to 19 ounces (500 to 550 grams)

Torque specifications

Note: *One foot-pound (ft-lb) of torque is equivalent to 12 inch-pounds (in-lbs) of torque. Torque values below approximately 15 foot-pounds are expressed in inch-pounds, because most foot-pound torque wrenches are not accurate at these smaller values.*

	Ft-lbs (unless otherwise indicated)	Nm
Compressor line fitting nuts/bolts	86 in-lbs	10
Compressor mounting bolts.................	16	22
Condenser line fitting bolts.................	86 in-lbs	10
Condenser mounting bolts.................	86 in-lbs	10
Radiator bracket bolts		
2003 and earlier models.................	86 in-lbs	10
2004 and later models.................	104 in-lbs	12
Thermostat housing cover bolts	104 in-lbs	12
Water pump mounting bolts.................	104 in-lbs	12

1.1 Underhood engine cooling and air conditioning components (2004 model shown - other models similar)

1	Air conditioning line service port (high side)	3 Fuse and relay boxes
2	Air conditioning line service port (low side)	4 Thermostat housing (at the end of the lower radiator hose)
		5 Upper radiator hose
6	Radiator and radiator cap	
7	Coolant reservoir	
8	Radiator cover	

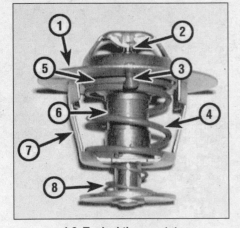

1.2 Typical thermostat:

1	Flange	5	Valve seat
2	Piston	6	Valve
3	Jiggle valve	7	Frame
4	Main coil spring	8	Secondary coil spring

1   General information

Engine cooling system

Refer to illustrations 1.1 and 1.2

All vehicles covered by this manual employ a pressurized engine cooling system with thermostatically controlled coolant circulation **(see illustration)**. An impeller-type water pump mounted on the engine block pumps coolant through the engine. The coolant flows around each cylinder and toward the rear of the engine. Cast-in coolant passages direct coolant around the intake and exhaust ports, near the spark plug areas and in close proximity to the exhaust valve guides.

A wax-pellet type thermostat controls engine coolant temperature. During warm up, the closed thermostat prevents coolant from circulating through the radiator. As the engine nears normal operating temperature, the thermostat opens and allows hot coolant to travel through the radiator, where it's cooled before returning to the engine **(see illustration)**.

The cooling system is sealed by a pressure-type radiator cap, which raises the boiling point of the coolant and increases the cooling efficiency of the radiator. If the system pressure exceeds the cap pressure relief value, the excess pressure in the system forces the spring-loaded valve inside the cap off its seat and allows the coolant to escape through the overflow tube into a coolant reservoir. When the system cools, the excess coolant is automatically drawn from the reservoir back into the radiator.

The coolant reservoir serves as both the point at which fresh coolant is added to the cooling system to maintain the proper fluid level and as a holding tank for overheated coolant.

This type of cooling system is known as a closed design because coolant that escapes past the pressure cap is saved and reused.

Engine cooling fans

All vehicles covered by this manual are equipped with two electric cooling fans: a

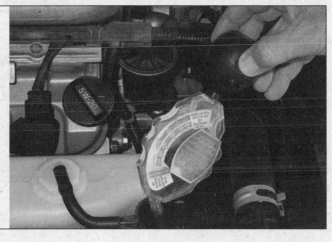

2.4 Use a hydrometer (available at most auto parts stores) to test the condition of your coolant

radiator fan and a condenser fan. The fans are controlled electronically. The radiator and condenser fan relays are located in fuse and relay boxes found in the engine compartment. 2003 and earlier models utilize a series of fan switches and a radiator fan control module to operate the fans. 2004 and later models utilize Engine Coolant Temperature (ECT) sensors and work with the onboard computer to operate the cooling fans.

Heating system

The heating system consists of a blower (fan) and heater core located in the heater box, the hoses connecting the heater core to the engine cooling system and the heater/air conditioning control head on the dashboard. Hot engine coolant is circulated through the heater core. When the heater is turned on by the controls, a flap door opens to expose the heater box to the passenger compartment. The blower forces air through the hot core and heats it. The hot air is directed to different parts of the passenger compartment through various vents and ducts.

Air conditioning system

The air conditioning system consists of a condenser mounted in front of the radiator, an evaporator mounted adjacent to the heater core, a compressor mounted on the engine, a receiver-drier next to the condenser and the plumbing connecting all of the above components.

A blower (fan) forces the warmer air of the passenger compartment through the evaporator core (sort of a radiator-in-reverse), transferring the heat from the air to the refrigerant. The liquid refrigerant boils off into low pressure vapor, taking the heat with it when it leaves the evaporator.

2 Antifreeze - general information

Refer to illustration 2.4

Warning: *Do not allow antifreeze to come in contact with your skin or painted surfaces of the vehicle. Rinse off spills immediately with plenty of water. Antifreeze is highly toxic if ingested. Never leave antifreeze lying around*

in an open container or in puddles on the floor; children and pets are attracted by its sweet smell and may drink it. Check with local authorities about disposing of used antifreeze. Many communities have collection centers which will see that antifreeze is disposed of safely. Never dump used antifreeze on the ground or pour it into drains.

The cooling system should be filled with a water/ethylene glycol based antifreeze solution, which will prevent freezing down to at least -20-degrees F (even lower in cold climates). It also provides protection against corrosion and increases the coolant boiling point. The engines in these vehicles have aluminum heads and blocks. The manufacturer recommends that the correct type of coolant be used and strongly urges that coolant types not be mixed (see the Chapter 1 Specifications).

Drain, flush and refill the cooling system at the intervals specified in the Chapter 1 Maintenance schedule. The use of antifreeze solutions for periods longer than recommended is likely to cause damage and encourage the formation of rust and scale in the system.

Before adding antifreeze to the system, inspect all hose connections. Antifreeze can leak through very minute openings.

Hydrometers are available at most auto parts stores to test the coolant **(see illustration)**. Use antifreeze that meets factory specifications (see Chapter 1).

3 Thermostat - check and replacement

Warning: *Do not remove the radiator cap, drain the coolant or replace the thermostat until the engine has cooled completely.*

Check

1   Before assuming the thermostat is to blame for a cooling system problem, check the coolant level, drivebelt and tensioner condition (see Chapter 1) and temperature gauge operation.

2   If the engine seems to be taking a long time to warm up, based on heater output or temperature gauge operation, the thermostat is probably stuck open. Replace the thermostat with a new one.

3   If the engine runs hot, use your hand to check the temperature of the lower radiator hose. If the hose isn't hot, but the engine is, the thermostat is probably stuck closed, preventing the coolant inside the engine from escaping to the radiator. Replace the thermostat. **Caution:** *Don't drive the vehicle without a thermostat. The computer may stay in open loop and emissions and fuel economy will suffer.*

4   If the lower radiator hose is hot, it means that the coolant is flowing and the thermostat is open. Consult the *Troubleshooting* Section at the front of this manual for cooling system diagnosis.

Replacement

Refer to illustrations 3.9 and 3.10

5   Remove the battery (see Chapter 5).

6   Drain the cooling system (see Chapter 1). If the coolant is relatively new or in good condition, save it and reuse it. Read the **Warning** in Section 2.

7   On 2003 and earlier models, remove the electrical connector from the thermostat housing.

8   On 2004 and later models, remove the ground wires attached to the housing.

9   Remove the thermostat housing cover bolts and cover. If the cover is stuck, tap it with a soft-face hammer to jar it loose. Be prepared for some coolant to spill as the seal is broken **(see illustration)**. **Note:** *The radia-*

3.9 Thermostat mounting details:

1   Ground wires and bolt
2   Thermostat housing cover mounting bolts (one hidden from view in this photo - vicinity given)

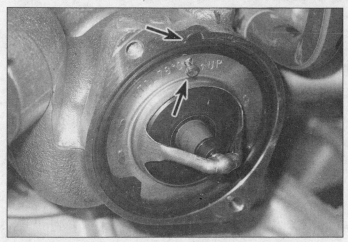

3.10 Note that the jiggle pin is at the 12 o'clock position along with the external tab on the seal. The spring end of the thermostat is inside the bore of the housing

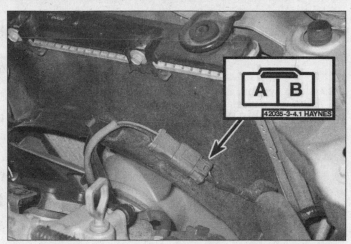

4.1a To test either fan motor, disconnect the electrical connector and use jumper wires to connect the fan directly to the battery (B) and ground (A) - if the fan still doesn't work, replace the motor. The location of the air conditioning condenser fan electrical connector is shown

4.1b Location of the radiator fan electrical connector

4.3 The location of the radiator fan relay (A), the condenser fan relay (B) and the fan control relay (C) (2004 model shown, other models similar)

tor hose can remain attached to the housing cover.

10   Take note of how the thermostat is installed and the position of the seal with the orientation of the jiggle pin, then remove it **(see illustration)**.

11   Remove all traces of the old seal from the mating surfaces of the thermostat housing cover and housing.

12   Install a new seal over the thermostat. Make sure the external tab on the seal is aligned correctly with the jiggle valve **(see illustration 3.10)**.

13   Install the new thermostat in the housing; no sealant is necessary. Make sure the jiggle pin is positioned correctly and the spring end is directed into the engine **(see illustration 3.10)**.

14   Install the thermostat housing cover, tightening the bolts to the torque listed in this Chapter's Specifications.

15   Reattach the hose and tighten the hose clamp securely. Reconnect the electrical connector or ground wires.

16   Refill the cooling system (see Chapter 1).
17   Reinstall the battery (see Chapter 5).
18   Start the engine and allow it to reach normal operating temperature, then check for leaks and proper thermostat operation (as described in Steps 2 through 4).

---

4   Engine cooling fans and component - check and replacement

---

Warning: *To avoid possible injury or damage, DO NOT operate the engine with a damaged fan. Do not attempt to repair fan blades - replace a damaged fan with a new one.*

Check

Refer to illustrations 4.1a, 4.1b, 4.3, 4.5a, 4.5b and 4.5c

1   If the engine temperature is excessive (overheating) and the cooling fan is not coming on, unplug the fan motor electrical connec-

tor **(see illustrations)**, then connect the motor directly to the battery with a fused jumper cable on terminal B. Use another jumper wire to ground terminal A. If the fan motor doesn't come on while applying battery power, replace the motor. These models are equipped with two fans. If the radiator fan motor (driver side) checks out okay, be sure to test the air conditioning condenser fan motor (passenger side) as well. **Caution:** *Do not apply battery power to the harness (power supply) side of the connector.*

2   If the radiator fan motor is okay, but it isn't coming on when the engine gets hot, the fan relay(s) might be defective.

3   Locate the fan relays in the engine compartment fuse/relay box **(see illustration)**. **Note:** *On 2007 and later models, an additional small relay box is on the right side of the engine compartment in the area behind the condenser fan.*

4   Test the relay(s) (see Chapter 12).

5   If the relays are okay, test the radiator fan switches. **Note:** *2003 and earlier model*

4.5a Location of the radiator fan switch A (2003 and earlier models only)

4.5b Location of the radiator fan switch B and the electrical connector (2003 and earlier models only)

years are the only models that utilize fan switches. On all other models, the Engine Coolant Temperature (ECT) sensor (two ECT sensors on 2007 and later models) replaces the fan switches (see Chapter 6). The radiator fan switches control the operation of the fans based on temperature. The fan switches are located in the thermostat housing (switch A), in the cylinder head behind the front camshaft pulley (switch B) or at the bottom of the radiator (switch C, S type only) **(see illustrations)**. The switches can be tested with an ohmmeter. Continuity will exist at certain temperatures. See the table for specifications **(see illustration)**. **Note:** *Although it is best to remove a switch and test it by placing the appropriate end in hot water and using a thermometer to monitor temperature, a preliminary test can*

be done with the switch installed and the engine warm, if it is accessible. Remove the switch and test it appropriately if you believe it is defective, but wait for the engine to cool first (see "Cooling fan switches" below).

6   If the relay(s) and the fan switch are okay, check all wiring and connections to the fan motors. Any further checking should be directed to a qualified repair facility.

Replacement

Warning: *Wait until the engine is completely cool before beginning this procedure.*

7   Disconnect the cable from the negative battery terminal (see Chapter 5, Section 1).

8   Set the parking brake, raise the front of the vehicle and support it securely on

jackstands. Remove the lower splash shield from under the radiator (see Chapter 2).

9   Drain the cooling system (see Chapter 1). If the coolant is relatively new or in good condition, save it and reuse it. Read the **Warning** in Section 2. **Note:** *This step is not necessary if you are only removing the air conditioning condenser fan (right side - passengers side).*

Cooling fans

Refer to illustrations 4.14a, 4.14b, 4.15 and 4.16b

10   Remove the radiator cover (see Chapter 11, Section 9).

11   Remove the coolant reservoir (see Section 5).

12   Detach the upper radiator hose from the

Cooling fan switch	Temperature	Continuity
Switch "A"	196 to 203 degrees F	Yes (on)
Switch "A"	5 to 15 degrees F below "ON" temperature	No (off)
Switch B	217 to 232 degrees F	Yes (on)
Switch B	5 to 23 degrees F below "ON" temperature	No (off)
Switch C	205 to 216 degrees F	Yes (on)
Switch C	5 to 23 degrees F below "ON" temperature	No (off)

12050-3-4.5C HAYNES

4.5c Fan switch continuity chart (2003 and earlier models only)

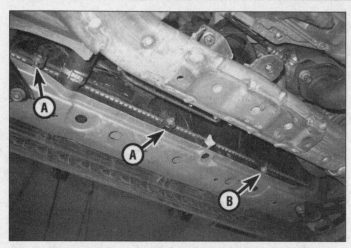

4.14a The lower radiator fan shroud mounting bolts (A) and the condenser fan shroud mounting bolt (B)

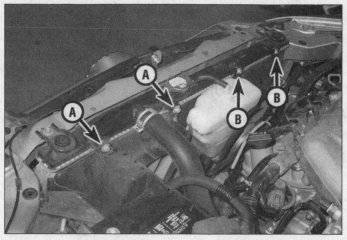

4.14b The upper radiator fan shroud mounting bolts (A) and condenser fan shroud mounting bolts (B)

4.15 To remove the fan, unscrew the nut in the center, then pull the fan blade from the motor shaft

remove the motor shaft nut **(see illustration)**.

16   To detach the fan motor from the shroud, remove the mounting screws **(see illustrations)**.

17   Installation is the reverse of removal.

18   Refill the cooling system (see Chapter 1).

19   Reconnect the battery (see Chapter 5, Section 1).

Cooling fan switches (2003 and earlier models)

Warning: *Wait until the engine is completely cool before beginning this procedure.*

20   For switches A, disconnect the electrical connector, then unscrew the switch from the thermostat housing cover **(see illustration 4.5a)**. For switch C (S type only), disconnect the electrical connector, then unscrew the switch from the radiator. For switch B, remove the front camshaft pulley, disconnect the electrical connector, and unbolt the switch from the cylinder head (see Chapter 2) **(see illustration 4.5b)**.

21   Installation is the reverse of removal, noting the following points:

radiator **(see illustration 6.6)**. **Note:** *This step is not necessary if you are removing the air conditioning condenser fan (right side - passenger's side)*.

13   Disconnect the fan electrical connectors and also any wiring harnesses secured to the

fan shroud assembly **(see illustrations 4.1a and 4.1b)**.

14   Unbolt the fan shroud assembly from the radiator and carefully lift it up and out of the engine compartment **(see illustrations)**.

15   To detach the radiator fan from the motor,

4.16a Radiator fan motor mounting screws

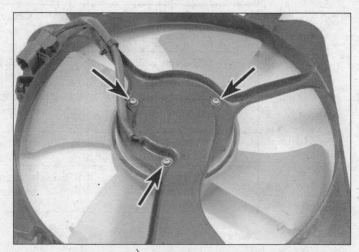

4.16b Condenser fan motor mounting screws

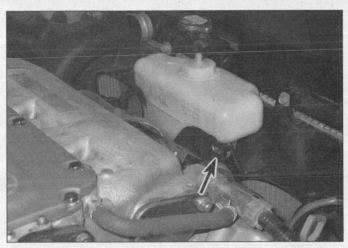

5.2 Location of the coolant reservoir mounting bolt (2004 model shown - other models similar)

6.5 Lower radiator mounting details (2004 model shown - other models similar)

1	Lower radiator hose	2	Rubber cushion locations

a) Use a new sealing ring and lubricate it with coolant when installing a switch.

b) Refill the cooling system (see Chapter 1).

c) Reconnect the battery (see Chapter 5, Section 1).

d) Start the engine and allow it to reach normal operating temperature, then verify proper fan operation.

5 Coolant reservoir - removal and installation

Refer to illustration 5.2
Warning: *Wait until the engine is completely cool before beginning this procedure.*

1 Disconnect the reservoir hose from the radiator filler neck. Plug the hose to prevent leakage.

2 On 2004 and later models, remove the mounting bolt **(see illustration)**.

3 Lift the reservoir out of the engine compartment. **Note:** *On 2003 and earlier models,* the reservoir is located at the left side of the radiator and is retained by a bracket.

4 Clean out the tank with soapy water and a brush to remove any deposits inside. Inspect the reservoir carefully for cracks. If you find a crack, replace the reservoir.

5 Installation is the reverse of removal.

6 Radiator - removal and installation

Warning: *Wait until the engine is completely cool before beginning this procedure.*

Removal

Refer to illustrations 6.5 and 6.6

1 Disconnect the cable from the negative battery terminal (see Chapter 5, Section 1).

2 Set the parking brake and block the rear wheels. Raise the front of the vehicle and support it securely on jackstands. Remove the front engine splash shield beneath the radiator (see Chapter 2).

3 Drain the cooling system (see Chapter 1). If the coolant is relatively new or in good condition, save it and reuse it. Read the **Warning** in Section 2.

4 Remove the radiator cover (see Chapter 11, Section 9) and the engine cooling fans (see Section 4).

5 Disconnect the lower radiator hose and the transaxle fluid lines, if equipped from the radiator **(see illustration)**. **Note:** *On models so equipped, also disconnect the radiator fan switch or Engine Coolant Temperature (ECT) sensor 2 electrical connector from the bottom-center of the radiator. The switch can be removed and installed in a replacement radiator if necessary. Replace the O-ring for the switch if it is removed.*

6 Disconnect the upper radiator hose and remove the radiator brackets **(see illustration)**.

7 Carefully lift out the radiator. Don't spill coolant on the vehicle or scratch the paint.

8 Inspect the radiator for leaks and damage. If it needs repair, have a radiator shop or dealer service department perform the work as special techniques are required.

9 Bugs and dirt can be removed from the radiator by spraying with a garden hose nozzle from the back side. The radiator should be flushed out with a garden hose before reinstallation.

10 Check the rubber cushions between the bottom of the radiator and the lower radiator support for deterioration and replace if necessary **(see illustration 6.5)**.

Installation

11 Installation is the reverse of the removal procedure. Guide the radiator into the mounts (cushions) until it seats completely into the lower radiator support.

12 Tighten the radiator bracket bolts to the torque listed in this Chapter's Specifications.

13 After installation, fill the cooling system with the proper coolant (see Chapter 1).

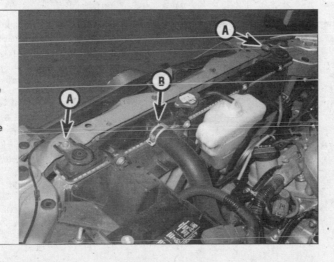

6.6 Radiator mounting bracket bolts (A) and the upper radiator hose (B). Use pliers on the hose clamp tabs to expand the hose clamp and slide it up the hose (away from the radiator); leave it on the hose and remove it later if necessary

7.2 A water pump weep hole below the pulley

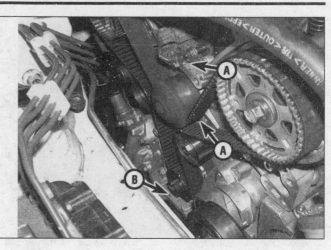

7.3 The weep holes (A) are located above and below the pulley - you'll need a flashlight and a small mirror to find them. The area below the crankshaft sprocket (B) should be checked for coolant

14   Reconnect the battery (see Chapter 5, Section 1).

15   Start the engine and check for leaks. Allow the engine to reach normal operating temperature, indicated by the upper radiator hose becoming hot. Recheck the coolant level and add more if required.

16   If any transaxle fluid lines were disconnected, check the fluid level and add fluid as needed (see Chapter 1).

7   Water pump - check

Refer to illustrations 7.2 and 7.3

1   A failure in the water pump can cause serious engine damage due to overheating.

2   If a failure occurs in the pump seal, coolant may leak at the bottom of the timing belt cover; originating from a weep hole on the water pump **(see illustration)**.

3   With the timing belt cover removed (and the belt, if necessary), look for leaks on the top and bottom of the water pump using a flashlight and a mirror **(see illustration)**.

4   If the water pump shaft bearings fail, there may be a howling sound near the water pump while it's running. Don't mistake drivebelt slippage, which causes a squeal-ing sound, for water pump bearing failure. Attempt to find the source of the noise with a mechanic's stethoscope.

5   A quick water pump performance check can be done by doing the following:

a) *Make certain that the coolant level in the system is full.*

b) *Start the vehicle and warm it up fully.*

c) *Turn the heater on in the passenger compartment.*

d) *Check for little or no heat output. If this is the case, the water pump may be failing because coolant flow does not appear to be going through the heater core.*

6   A water pump may still be due for replacement even if it's not leaking or making any noise. The only sure way to tell if replacement is necessary is to remove the pump and examine it closely. A loose or corroded impeller, a leaking shaft seal or a worn shaft bearing are all causes for replacement.

8   Water pump - replacement

Refer to illustration 8.5

Warning: *Wait until the engine is completely cool before beginning this procedure.*

1   Disconnect the cable from the negative battery terminal (see Chapter 5, Section 1).

2   Drain the cooling system (see Chapter 1). If the coolant is relatively new or in good condition, save it and reuse it. Read the **Warning** in Section 2.

3   Remove the drivebelt (see Chapter 1).

4   Remove the timing belt and the timing belt tensioner (see Chapter 2).

5   Remove the water pump mounting bolts and detach it from the engine **(see illustration)**. Check the impeller on the backside for evidence of corrosion or missing fins.

6   Make sure the bolt threads and the threaded holes in the engine are clear of corrosion.

7   Compare the new pump to the old one to make sure they're identical.

8   Remove all traces of the O-ring from the engine mounting surface.

9   Make sure that the mounting surfaces on the engine and water pump are clean.

10   Place a new O-ring into the groove of the new pump

11   Carefully attach the pump to the engine and thread the mounting bolts finger tight. Make sure that the dowel pins are in their original locations.

12   Tighten the bolts to the torque listed in this Chapter's Specifications in 1/4-turn increments. Don't overtighten the bolts or the pump may become distorted and leak.

13   Reinstall all parts removed for access to the pump.

14   Refill the cooling system and check the drivebelt tension (see Chapter 1).

15   Reconnect the battery (see Chapter 5, Section 1). Run the engine and check for leaks.

9   Coolant temperature sending unit - check and replacement

Warning: *Wait until the engine is completely cool before beginning this procedure.*

Note: *The 1999 model year vehicles are the only ones that utilize a coolant temperature sending unit. All other model years utilize Engine Coolant Temperature (ECT) sensors and the Powertrain Control Module (PCM) to operate the temperature gauge.*

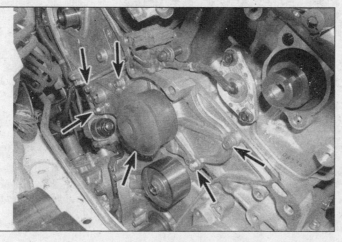

8.5 Water pump mounting bolts - check the bottom for an additional bolt that is out of view in this photo

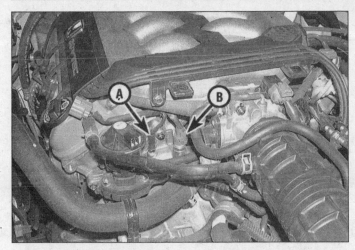

9.1 The temperature sending unit (A) is mounted in the water passage/thermostat housing near an Engine Coolant Temperature (ECT) sensor (B). The temperature sending unit has one wire in its connector; the ECT sensor has two (1999 models)

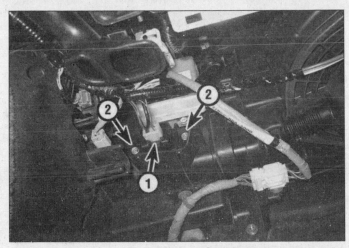

10.2 Blower motor power transistor details (2004 model shown - other models similar)

1   Power transistor electrical connector
2   Power transistor mounting screws

Check

Refer to illustration 9.1

1   The temperature gauge operation depends on a sending unit mounted in the water passage/thermostat housing on the engine **(see illustration)**. **Warning:** *This vehicle is equipped with electric cooling fans that can come on even when the engine is not running. Stay clear of the fan blades.*

2   If the temperature gauge reads HOT when the engine is cold, check the wiring between the temperature gauge and the sending unit for a short circuit (going to ground).

3   If the engine is warm but the temperature gauge reads COLD, test the gauge by briefly grounding the wire to the sending unit while the ignition is in the On position and the is engine OFF. The gauge should read HOT. If this is the case, then the gauge and circuit are working; test the sending unit (see Step 5).

4   If the gauge doesn't respond to the test outlined in Step 3, check for an open circuit in the gauge wiring.

5   To test the sending unit, disconnect the electrical connector and attach an ohmmeter from the pin on top of the sender to an engine ground. With the engine warm and the coolant close to 133 degrees F, the resistance should be around 137 ohms. When the engine is hot and the coolant temperature is between 185 to 212 degrees F, the resistance should drop between 46 to 30 ohms. Consider the sender faulty if it is considerably out of range from these specifications.

Replacement

6   Prepare the new sending unit for installation by applying a conductive sealant on the threads (not Teflon tape). Make sure the engine is cool before removing the defective sending unit.

7   Disconnect the electrical connector for the sending unit. Unscrew the unit from the engine and quickly install the replacement. Coolant will flow from the hole as the unit is removed, so be prepared to catch it. Check the coolant level after the replacement sending unit has been installed.

8   Reconnect the electrical connector and test the operation of the temperature gauge.

10   Blower motor power transistor and blower motor - replacement

Warning: *The models covered by this manual are equipped with Supplemental Restraint Systems (SRS), more commonly known as airbags. Always disable the airbag system before working in the vicinity of any airbag system component to avoid the possibility of accidental deployment of the airbag, which could cause personal injury (see Chapter 12).*

1   Working in the passenger compartment under the glove box, remove the insulating cover under the instrument panel (see Chapter 11, Section 25).

Blower motor power transistor

Refer to illustration 10.2

2   Disconnect the electrical connector from the blower motor power transistor **(see illustration)**.

3   Remove the blower motor power transistor mounting screws and remove the transistor.

4   Installation is the reverse of removal.

Blower motor

Refer to illustration 10.5

5   Disconnect the electrical connector from the blower motor **(see illustration)**.

6   Remove the blower motor mounting screws and remove the blower motor assembly.

10.5 Blower motor details (2004 model shown - other models similar)

1   Blower motor electrical connector
2   Blower motor mounting screws

7   Remove the circlip from the blower motor shaft to release the fan from the motor.

8   Installation is the reverse of removal.

11   Heater/air conditioning control assembly - removal and installation

1   The air conditioning controls for 2004 and later models are integrated with the audio and navigation display (if equipped). Refer to Chapter 12 for the removal and installation of the audio, navigation and air conditioning controls. Once removed, the display module (with the heater/air conditioning controls) can be replaced.

2   On 2003 and earlier models with navigation, the climate control assembly is mounted

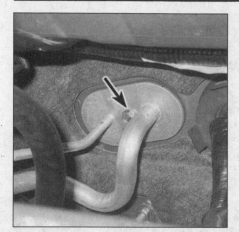

12.4a On 2004 and later models, remove this bolt to disconnect the air conditioning lines at the firewall

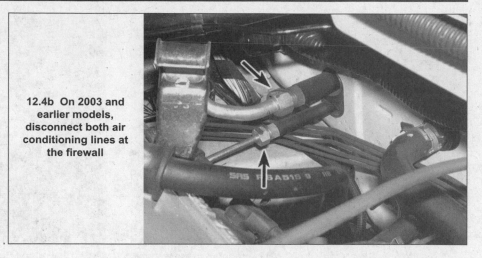

12.4b On 2003 and earlier models, disconnect both air conditioning lines at the firewall

in the instrument panel's center console along with the audio unit. Refer to Chapter 12 for the removal and installation of the audio, navigation and air conditioning controls. Once separated from the audio unit, the heater/air conditioning control assembly can be replaced.

3   On 2003 and earlier models without navigation, the climate control assembly is mounted in the instrument cluster trim panel assembly; refer to Chapter 11 for removal of this panel.

4   With the trim panel removed from the vehicle, simply remove the four mounting screws from the back of the heater/air conditioning control assembly, then remove it from the trim panel.

12   Heater core - replacement

Refer to illustrations 12.4a, 12.4b, 12.5, 12.6, 12.7a, 12.7b, 12.9a and 12.9b

Warning 1: *The models covered by this manual are equipped with Supplemental Restraint Systems (SRS), more commonly known as*

airbags. *Always disable the airbag system before working in the vicinity of any airbag system component to avoid the possibility of accidental deployment of the airbag, which could cause personal injury (see Chapter 12).*

Warning 2: *The air conditioning system is under high pressure. DO NOT loosen any fittings or remove any components until after the system has been discharged. Air conditioning refrigerant must be properly discharged into an EPA-approved container at a dealer service department or an automotive air conditioning repair facility. Always wear eye protection when disconnecting air conditioning system fittings.*

Warning 3: *Wait until the engine is completely cool before beginning this procedure.*

1   Have the air conditioning system refrigerant discharged and recovered by an air conditioning technician.

2   Disconnect the cable from the negative battery terminal (see Chapter 5, Section 1).

3   Drain the cooling system (see Chapter 1).

4   Disconnect the air conditioning evaporator lines at the firewall **(see illustrations)**.

5   Mark the heater control valve cable at the retaining clip so that it can be reinstalled in the same position. Release the clip and

detach the cable **(see illustration)**. **Note:** *Turn the heater valve arm counterclockwise (2004 and later models) or clockwise (2003 and earlier models) to the fully open position after the cable has been disconnected.*

6   Disconnect the heater hoses from the heater core at the firewall **(see illustration)**.

7   Remove the heater/air conditioning unit mounting nut from the firewall within the engine compartment **(see illustrations)**. **Note:** *Be careful not to damage any of the lines that are in front of the mounting nut.*

8   Remove the instrument panel (see Chapter 11).

9   Disconnect any electrical connectors to the unit and the heater valve control cable that is located on the left side **(see illustrations)**.

2004 and later models

Refer to illustrations 12.10, 12.11, 12.13 and 12.16

10   Remove the mounting fasteners, then lift the heater/air conditioning unit out of the vehicle **(see illustration)**. **Note:** *The two housings (the heater core housing and the blower motor housing) that make up the heater/air conditioning unit will separate when all of the mounting fasteners are removed.*

12.5 Mark the heater valve control cable before removal (A), then release the clip from the bottom (B)

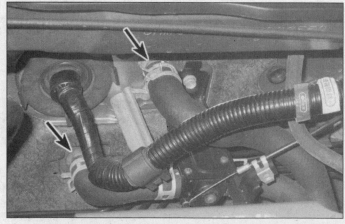

12.6 Disconnect the heater hoses from the heater core at the firewall (2004 model shown - other models similar)

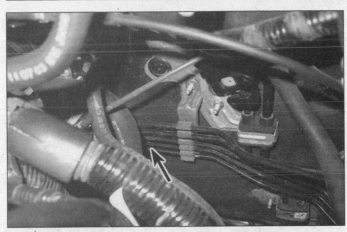

12.7a On 2004 and later models, the mounting nut for the heater/air conditioning unit is near the heater control valve and behind some brake lines at the firewall

12.7b On 2003 and earlier models, the mounting nut for the heater/air conditioning unit is near the heater control valve and above some brake lines at the firewall

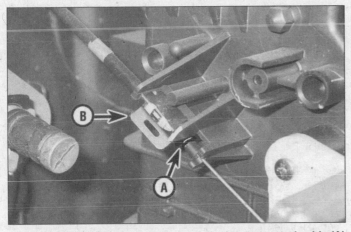

12.9a On 2004 and later models, mark the heater control cable (A) and lift the tab (B) to release it from the bracket, then remove the cable end from the unit

12.9b On 2003 and earlier models, the heater control cable is underneath the heater/air conditioning unit

11   Remove the mounting screws for the upper duct and pull it directly up to remove it (see illustration). Note: Be careful not to damage the evaporator temperature sensor while removing the upper duct. It is a small thin part that will come out along with the duct.

12   Remove the mounting screws for the lower duct, pull the A/C evaporator up about an inch and remove the lower duct. Note: The

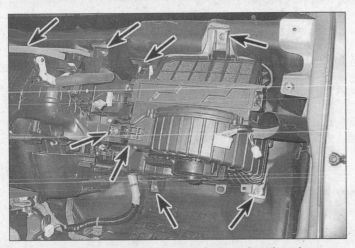

12.10 Heater/air conditioning unit fastener locations (some fasteners are hidden from view in this photo)

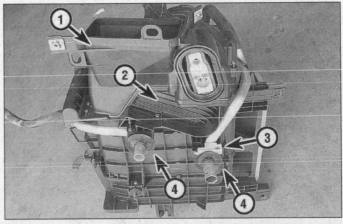

12.11 Heater/air conditioning unit details for heater core removal (mounted-side view)

1   Top duct   3   Line retainer
2   Lower duct   4   Sealing grommets

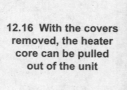

12.13 Heater/air conditioning unit details for heater core removal (cab-side view)

1   Harness
2   Heater outlet duct
3   Heater core cover

upper and lower duct cover the A/C evaporator and also secure the lines for the heater core.

13   Disconnect the electrical connectors and harness fasteners on the unit **(see illustration)**.

14   Remove the mounting screws for the heater outlet duct, then remove it.

15   Remove the mounting screws for the heater core cover, then remove it.

16   Remove the heater core **(see illustration)**.

2003 and earlier models

Refer to illustrations 12.17, 12.18 and 12.19

17   Remove the evaporator housing from heater/air conditioning unit **(see illustration)**. **Note:** The evaporator housing is one of three housings (the heater core housing, the evaporator housing and the blower motor housing) that make up the heater/air condi-

12.16 With the covers removed, the heater core can be pulled out of the unit

tioning unit. These housings are removed individually, but the evaporator housing must be removed before the heater core housing can be removed.

18   Remove the heater core housing from the firewall **(see illustration)**.

19   Remove the components and fasteners from the housing so that the housing can be divided **(see illustration)**.

20   With the housing divided, carefully lift out the heater core.

All models

21   Installation is the reverse of removal, noting the following points:

a) When reinstalling the heater/air conditioning unit or evaporator housing, make certain that the evaporator drain tube is placed correctly through the port that leads outside and that the refrigerant line fittings are connected properly with new O-rings seals of the correct type, if equipped.

b) Be sure to connect all electrical connectors on the heater/air conditioning unit before reinstalling the instrument panel.

c) Make sure that the heater control valve cable is placed back in the same position by noting the index marks created in Steps 5 and 9.

d) Reconnect the heater hoses within the engine compartment.

22   Reconnect the battery (see Chapter 5, Section 1).

23   Refill the cooling system (see Chapter 1).

24   Have the air conditioning system evacuated, recharged and leak tested by the shop that discharged it.

13   Air conditioning and heating system - check and maintenance

Refer to illustration 13.1

Warning: The air conditioning system is under high pressure. DO NOT loosen any fittings or remove any components until after the system has been discharged. Air conditioning refrigerant must be properly discharged into an EPA-approved container at a dealer service

12.17 Remove the mounting fasteners for the evaporator housing (some fasteners are hidden from view in this photo)

12.18 Remove the mounting fasteners for the heater core housing (some fasteners are hidden from view in this photo)

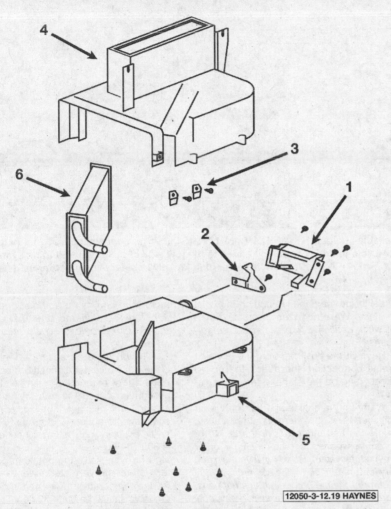

12.19 Heater core housing details:

1	Mode control motor	3	Heater core pipe	5	Lower housing
2	Mode control motor		brackets	6	Heater core
	linkage	4	Upper housing		

department or an automotive air conditioning repair facility. Always wear eye protection when disconnecting air conditioning system fittings.

1 The following maintenance checks should be performed on a regular basis to ensure the air conditioner continues to operate at peak efficiency.

a) *Check the drivebelt. If it's worn or deteriorated, replace it (see Chapter 1).*

b) *Check the system hoses. Look for cracks, bubbles, hard spots and deterioration. Inspect the hoses and all fittings for oil bubbles and seepage. If there's any evidence of wear, damage or leaks, replace the hose(s).*

c) *Inspect the condenser fins for leaves, bugs and other debris. Use a fin comb or compressed air to clean the condenser.*

d) *Make sure the system has the correct refrigerant charge.*

e) *Check the evaporator housing drain tube (see illustration) for blockage.*

2 It's a good idea to operate the system for

about 10 minutes at least once a month, particularly during the winter. Long term non-use can cause hardening, and subsequent failure, of the seals.

3 Because of the complexity of the air conditioning system and the special equipment necessary to service it, in-depth troubleshooting and repairs are not included in this manual (refer to the *Haynes Automotive Heating and Air Conditioning Repair Manual*). However, simple checks and component replacement procedures are provided in this Chapter.

4 The most common cause of poor cooling is simply a low system refrigerant charge. If a noticeable drop in cool air output occurs, the following quick check will help you determine if the refrigerant level is low.

Checking the refrigerant charge

5 Warm the engine up to normal operating temperature.

6 Place the air conditioning temperature selector at the coldest setting and the blower at the highest setting. Open the vehicle doors (to make sure the air conditioning system doesn't cycle off as soon as it cools the passenger compartment).

7 With the compressor engaged - the clutch will make an audible click and the center of the clutch will rotate - feel the evaporator inlet and outlet lines at the firewall **(see illustration 12.4a)**. The inlet (small diameter) line should feel somewhat warm and the outlet (large diameter) line should feel cold. If so, the system charge is probably adequate.

8 Place a thermometer in the dashboard vent nearest the evaporator and operate the system until the indicated temperature is around 40 to 45 degrees F. If the ambient (outside) air temperature is very high, say 110 degrees F, the duct air temperature may be as high as 60 degrees F, but generally the air conditioning is 30-40 degrees F cooler than the ambient air. **Note:** *Humidity of the ambient air also affects the cooling capacity of the system. Higher ambient humidity lowers the effectiveness of the air conditioning system.*

13.1 The end of the evaporator drain hose is located under the vehicle

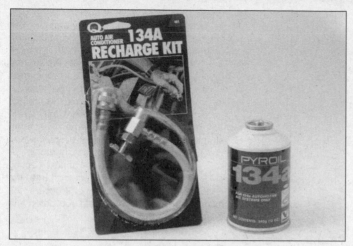

13.9 A basic charging kit for R-134a systems is available at most auto parts stores - it must say R-134a (not R-12) and so should the can of refrigerant

13.12a Cans of R-134a refrigerant (available at auto parts stores) can be added to the low side of the air conditioning system with a simple recharging kit (1999 model shown - other models similar)

Adding refrigerant

Refer to illustrations 13.9, 13.12a, 13.12b, 13.13 and 13.15

9   Buy an automotive charging kit at an auto parts store **(see illustration)**. A charging kit includes a can of refrigerant, a tap valve and a short section of hose that can be attached between the tap valve and the system low side service valve. **Caution:** *There are two types of refrigerant used in automotive systems; R-12 (which has been widely used on earlier models) and the more environmentally-friendly R-134a used in all models covered by this manual. These two refrigerants (and their appropriate refrigerant oils) are not compatible and must never be mixed or components will be damaged. Use only R-134a refrigerant in the models covered by this manual.*

10   Hook up the charging kit by following the manufacturer's instructions. **Warning:** *DO NOT hook the charging kit hose to the system high side! The fittings on the charging kit are designed to fit only on the low side of the system.*

11   Back off the valve handle on the charging kit and screw the kit onto the refrigerant can, making sure first that the O-ring or rub-ber seal inside the threaded portion of the kit is in place. **Warning:** *Wear protective eye-wear when dealing with pressurized refrigerant cans.*

12   Remove the dust cap from the low-side charging connection and attach the quick-connect fitting on the kit hose **(see illustrations)**.

13   Warm up the engine and turn on the air conditioner. Keep the charging kit hose away from the fan and other moving parts. **Note:** *The compressor needs to be running in order to charge the system. However, if your system is very low on refrigerant, the compressor may turn off or not come on at all. If this happens, disconnect the A/C pressure switch electrical connector and use a jumper wire between the two terminals on the harness (power supply) side of the connector* **(see illustration)**. *This will keep the compressor running.*

14   Turn the valve handle on the kit until the stem pierces the can, then back the handle out to release the refrigerant. You should be able to hear the rush of gas. Add refrigerant to the low side of the system until the temperature of the evaporator inlet and outlet lines is as described in Step 7. Allow stabilization time between each addition. **Caution:** *Never add*

more than one can of refrigerant to the system. If more refrigerant than that is required, the system should be evacuated and leak tested.

15   If you have an accurate thermometer, place it in the center air conditioning vent **(see illustration)** and note the temperature of the air coming out of the vent. A fully-charged system which is working correctly should cool down to about 40 degrees F. Generally, an air conditioning system will put out air that is 30 to 40 degrees F cooler than the ambient air. For example, if the ambient (outside) air temperature is very high (over 100 degrees F), the temperature of air coming out of the registers should be 60 to 70 degrees F.

16   When the can is empty, turn the valve handle to the closed position and release the connection from the low-side port. Replace the dust cap.

17   Remove the charging kit from the can and store the kit for future use with the piercing valve in the UP position, to prevent inadvertently piercing the can on the next use.

13.13 Disconnect the electrical connector for the air conditioning pressure switch and jump the two terminals on the harness connector

13.12b Location of the low side (suction) service port (A) and the high side (discharge) service port (B) (2004 model shown)

13.15 Insert a thermometer in the center vent, turn on the air conditioning system and wait for it to cool down; depending on the humidity, the output air should be 30 to 40 degrees cooler than the ambient air temperature

13.23 To disinfect the evaporator housing, insert the nozzle of the disinfectant can through the opening in the recirculation housing and point it toward the evaporator core (which is toward the left of the opening) - glove box removed for access

Heating systems

18   If the carpet under the heater core is damp, or if antifreeze vapor or steam is coming through the vents, the heater core is leaking. Remove it (see Section 12) and install a new unit (most radiator shops will not repair a leaking heater core).

19   If the air coming out of the heater vents isn't hot, the problem could stem from any of the following causes:

a) *The thermostat is stuck open, preventing the engine coolant from warming up enough to carry heat to the heater core. Replace the thermostat (see Section 3).*

b) *There is a blockage in the system, preventing the flow of coolant through the heater core. Feel both heater hoses at the firewall. They should be hot. If one of them is cold, there is an obstruction in one of the hoses or in the heater core, or the heater control valve is shut. Detach the hoses and back flush the heater core with a water hose. If the heater core is clear but circulation is impeded, remove the two hoses and flush them out with a water hose.*

c) *If flushing fails to remove the blockage from the heater core, the core must be replaced (see Section 12).*

Eliminating air conditioning odors

Refer to illustration 13.23

20   Unpleasant odors that often develop in air conditioning systems are caused by the growth of a fungus, usually on the surface of the evaporator core. The warm, humid environment there is a perfect breeding ground for mildew to develop.

21   The evaporator core on most vehicles is difficult to access, and factory dealerships have a lengthy, expensive process for eliminating the fungus by opening up the evaporator case and using a powerful disinfectant and rinse on the core until the fungus is gone. You can service your own system at home, but it takes something much stronger than basic household germ-killers or deodorizers.

22   Aerosol disinfectants for automotive air conditioning systems are available in most auto parts stores, but remember when shopping for them that the most effective treatments are also the most expensive. The basic procedure for using these sprays is to start by running the system in the RECIRC mode for ten minutes with the blower on its highest speed. Use the highest heat mode to dry out the system and keep the compressor from engaging by disconnecting the wiring connector at the compressor (see Section 14).

23   Make sure that the disinfectant can comes with a long spray hose. Work the nozzle through the opening in the heater/air conditioning recirculation housing so that it protrudes just inside the blower motor housing **(see illustration)**, then spray according to the manufacturer's recommendations. Follow the manufacturer's recommendations for the length of spray and waiting time between applications.

24   Once the evaporator has been cleaned, the best way to prevent the mildew from coming back again is to make sure your evaporator housing drain tube is clear **(see illustration 13.1)**.

14   Air conditioning compressor - removal and installation

Warning: *The air conditioning system is under high pressure. Do not loosen any hose fittings or remove any components until after the system has been discharged. Air conditioning refrigerant must be properly discharged into an EPA-approved recovery/recycling unit at a dealer service department or an automotive air conditioning repair facility. Always wear eye protection when disconnecting air conditioning system fittings.*

Caution: *When replacing entire components, additional refrigerant oil should be added equal to the amount that is removed with the component being replaced. Be sure to read the can before adding any oil to the system, to make sure it is compatible with the R-134a system.*

Note: *The receiver-drier should be replaced whenever the compressor is replaced.*

Removal

Refer to illustration 14.8

1   Have the air conditioning system refrigerant discharged and recovered by an air conditioning technician.

2   Disconnect the cable from the negative battery terminal (see Chapter 5, Section 1).

3   Remove the drivebelt (see Chapter 1).

4   Remove the condenser fan (see Section 4).

5   Remove the alternator (see Chapter 5).

6   Set the parking brake, raise the front of the vehicle and supporting it securely on jackstands.

7   Remove the splash shield from under the engine compartment (see Chapter 2).

8   Disconnect the compressor clutch electrical connector **(see illustration)**.

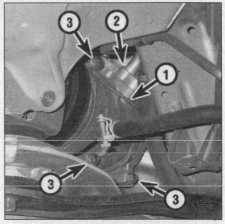

14.8 Compressor details (2004 model shown, other models similar):

1   *Clutch wire harness (follow to connector)*

2   *Low-pressure line fitting (the high-pressure line fitting is next to this one and just out of view in this photo)*

3   *Mounting bolt locations (one is out of view in this photo)*

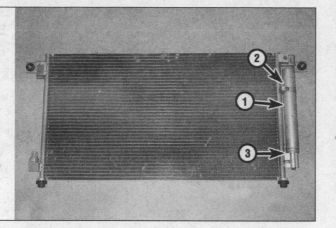

15.3 Air conditioning receiver-drier details (typical shown for 2004 and later models):

1   Receiver drier
2   Bracket bolt
3   Separate the receiver-drier from the condenser fitting at this point

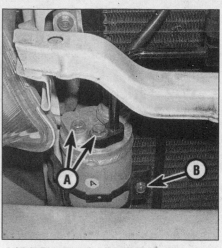

15.6 Remove the line fitting mounting bolts (A) and separate the refrigerant lines from the receiver-drier. Remove the mounting bracket bolt (B) to remove the receiver-drier (bumper cover removed for clarity)

9   Disconnect the refrigerant lines from the compressor. Plug or cap all openings immediately to prevent the entry of dirt and moisture.
10   Remove the compressor mounting bolts **(see illustration 14.8)**.
11   Carefully guide the compressor out of the engine compartment. **Note:** *Be careful not to damage the radiator fins during removal.*

Installation

12   If a new compressor is being installed, follow the directions with the compressor regarding the draining of excess oil prior to installation. Any refrigerant oil added must be compatible with R-134a refrigerant.
13   The clutch may have to be transferred from the original compressor to the new one.
14   Installation is the reverse of removal. Replace all O-rings with new ones specifically made for air conditioning system use and compatible with R-134a refrigerant. Lubricate them with refrigerant oil. Tighten the mounting fasteners and the line fitting nuts to the torque values listed in this Chapter's Specifications.
15   Reconnect the battery (see Chapter 5, Section 1).
16   Have the system evacuated, recharged and leak-tested by the shop that discharged it.

15   Air conditioning receiver-drier - removal and installation

Warning: *The air conditioning system is under high pressure. Do not loosen any hose fittings or remove any components until after the system has been discharged. Air conditioning refrigerant must be properly discharged into an EPA-approved recovery/recycling unit at a dealer service department or an automotive air conditioning repair facility. Always wear eye protection when disconnecting air conditioning system fittings.*
Caution: *When replacing entire components, additional refrigerant oil should be added equal to the amount that is removed with the component being replaced. Be sure to read the can before adding any oil to the system,*

to make sure it is compatible with the R-134a system.
1   Have the refrigerant discharged and recovered by an air conditioning technician.

2004 and later models

Refer to illustration 15.3
2   Remove the condenser (see Section 16).
3   Remove the bracket bolt that mounts the receiver-drier to the condenser **(see illustration)**.
4   Carefully separate the receiver-drier from the condenser.

2003 and earlier models

Refer to illustration 15.6
5   Remove the radiator cover (see Chapter 11).
6   Disconnect the line fittings from the top of the receiver-drier **(see illustration)**.
7   Detach the receiver-drier from the mounting bracket and carefully remove it **(see illustration 15.6)**.

All models

8   Installation is the reverse of removal. Be sure to install new O-rings onto the receiver-drier fittings and lightly coat them with refrigerant oil. **Note:** *Only use O-rings that are designed specifically for A/C system applications.* If you are replacing the receiver-drier, add 1/3-ounce of refrigerant oil to the new replacement.
9   Have the system evacuated, charged and leak tested by the shop that discharged it.

16   Air conditioning condenser - removal and installation

Warning: *The air conditioning system is under high pressure. Do not loosen any hose fittings or remove any components until after the system has been discharged. Air conditioning refrigerant must be properly discharged into*

an EPA-approved recovery/recycling unit at a dealer service department or an automotive air conditioning repair facility. Always wear eye protection when disconnecting air conditioning system fittings.
Caution: *When replacing entire components, additional refrigerant oil should be added equal to the amount that is removed with the component being replaced. Be sure to read the can before adding any oil to the system, to make sure it is compatible with the R-134a system.*

Removal

Refer to illustrations 16.8a, 16.8b, 16.8c, 16.9a and 16.9b
1   Have the refrigerant discharged and recovered by an air conditioning technician.
2   Disconnect the cable from the negative battery terminal (see Chapter 5, Section 1).
3   On 2004 and later models, remove the small cover over the air intake duct (see Chapter 4)
4   On 2004 and later models, remove the battery and battery tray (see Chapter 5).
5   Remove the radiator cover (see Chapter 11, Section 9).
6   Remove the radiator mounting brackets **(see illustration 6.6)**.
7   On 2004 and later models, disconnect the air conditioning pressure switch electrical connector.
8   Remove the line fitting bolts and disconnect the refrigerant lines from the condenser **(see illustrations)**. Cap all openings to prevent the entry of dirt or moisture.
9   Remove the condenser mounting bolts **(see illustrations)**.
10   Carefully lift the condenser straight up and out of the engine compartment. **Note:** *The radiator and condenser fins are very delicate and easily damaged.*

16.8a Refrigerant line connections to the condenser for 2004 and later models (bumper cover removed for clarity)

16.8b Upper refrigerant line connection to the condenser for 2003 and earlier models (bumper cover removed for clarity)

16.8c Lower refrigerant line connection to the condenser for 2003 and earlier models (bumper cover removed for clarity)

16.9a Location of the condenser mounting bolts for 2004 and later models

Installation

11   Installation is the reverse of removal. Assemble all connections with new O-rings, lightly lubricated with R-134a refrigerant oil.

Note: *Only use O-rings that are designed specifically for A/C system applications.* If the condenser is new, add 5/6-ounce of fresh refrigerant oil.

12   Reconnect the battery. Refer to Chapter 5, Section 1.

13   Have the system evacuated, charged and leak tested by the shop that discharged it.

17   Air conditioning pressure switch - replacement

Refer to illustration 17.3

Warning: *The air conditioning system is under high pressure. Do not loosen any hose fittings or remove any components until after the system has been discharged. Air conditioning refrigerant must be properly discharged into an EPA-approved recovery/recycling unit at a dealer service department or an automotive air conditioning repair facility. Always wear eye protection when disconnecting air conditioning system fittings.*

Note: *The air conditioning pressure switch detects low and high system pressure and shuts the system off if the pressure exceeds preset values.*

1   Have the refrigerant discharged and recovered by an air conditioning technician.

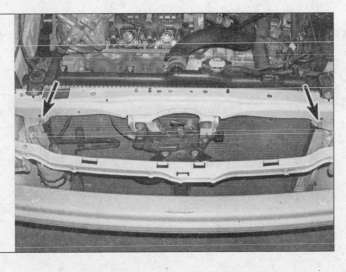

16.9b Location of the condenser mounting bolts for 2003 and earlier models

2   Remove the radiator cover (see Chapter 11, Section 9).

3   Unplug the electrical connector from the air conditioning pressure switch **(see illustration)**. **Note:** *On 2004 and later models, the switch is mounted to the condenser near the lower line fitting on the right (passenger's) side. On 2003 and earlier models, the switch is mounted to the top of the receiver-drier located in front of the condenser.*

4   Unscrew the pressure switch.

5   Lubricate the O-ring on the switch with clean refrigerant oil of the correct type.

6   Screw the new switch in place until hand tight, then tighten it securely.

7   Reconnect the electrical connector.

8   Have the system evacuated, charged and leak tested by the shop that discharged it.

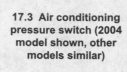

17.3 Air conditioning pressure switch (2004 model shown, other models similar)

Chapter 4
Fuel and exhaust systems

Contents

Specifications

Accelerator cable deflection	3/8 to 1/2-inch (10 to 12 mm)
Fuel system pressure	
1999 and 2000 models	
Pressure regulator vacuum hose disconnected	41 to 48 psi (280 to 330 kPa)
Pressure regulator vacuum hose connected	32 to 40 psi (220 to 270 kPa)
2001 through 2003 models	
Pressure regulator vacuum hose disconnected	48 to 55 psi (330 to 380 kPa)
Pressure regulator vacuum hose connected	40 to 46 psi (270 to 320 kPa)
2004 through 2006 models	57 to 64 psi (390 to 440 kPa)
2007 and later	55 to 63 psi (380 to 430 kPa)

Torque specifications

	Ft-lbs	Nm
Fuel pressure regulator (2000 through 2003 models only)	22	30
Fuel pulsation damper (2000 through 2003 models only)	16	22
Throttle body mounting bolts/nuts (all models)	16	22

1   General information

Air induction system

The air induction system consists of the air filter assembly, the air intake duct, the resonator(s), the throttle body and the intake manifold.

The throttle body contains a throttle plate, which regulates the amount of air entering the intake manifold. On 2003 and earlier models, the throttle plate is opened and closed by the accelerator cable. The throttle body is also the location of the Throttle Position (TP) sensor, a potentiometer that monitors the opening angle of the throttle plate and sends a variable voltage signal to the Powertrain Control Module (PCM). A Manifold Absolute Pressure (MAP) sensor is located on top of the throttle body.

On 2004 and later models, the throttle plate is electronically controlled by the Powertrain Control Module (PCM). Even on these models there is an "accelerator cable," but it connects the accelerator pedal to the Accelerator Pedal Position (APP) sensor (which is located on the firewall) not to the throttle body. On these models, the APP sensor relays the angle of the throttle link to the PCM, which processes this information and commands a small servo inside the throttle body to open or close the throttle plate. This setup allows the PCM to fine tune the position of the throttle plate in response to other inputs besides the position of the accelerator pedal, which means better fuel efficiency and lower emissions.

All of the air induction components (air filter housing, air intake duct, resonator and throttle body) are covered in this Chapter, except for the intake manifold, which is in Chapter 2A. The information sensors (APP and IAT sensors) and the PCM are in Chapter 6.

Fuel system

The fuel system consists of the fuel tank, an electric fuel pump (located in the fuel tank), the fuel rail and the fuel injectors. Programmed Fuel Injection (PGM-FI) is a sequential multiport system, which means that the fuel injectors deliver fuel directly into the intake ports of the cylinders in firing order sequence (1-4-2-5-3-6). Sequential multiport systems provide much better control of the air/fuel mixture ratio than earlier fuel injection systems, and are therefore able to produce more power, better mileage and lower emissions.

2003 and earlier models are equipped with a fuel pulsation damper and a vacuum-operated fuel pressure regulator. 2004 and later models don't use a fuel pulsation damper, and the fuel pressure regulator is an integral component of the fuel pump/fuel level sending unit module inside the fuel tank. On these later models, the pressure regulator is simply spring-loaded; it is not vacuum-operated.

For more information about the PGM-FI system, see Section 11. For more information about the PCM and the information sensors, refer to Chapter 6.

Exhaust system

The exhaust system consists of the exhaust manifolds, the "Y" pipe that connects both manifolds to the rest of the exhaust system, the muffler and the tailpipe. On 2003 and earlier models, the catalytic converter is located under the vehicle, just downstream from the Y-pipe coming from the exhaust manifolds. 2004 and later models use this same catalyst, but they're also equipped with a pair of warm-up catalysts, each of which also functions as an exhaust manifold; it is bolted directly to the cylinder head. The exhaust manifolds are covered in Chapter 2A, and the catalytic converter is covered in Chapter 6. The rest of the exhaust system is covered in this Chapter.

2   Fuel pressure relief procedure

Warning: *Gasoline is extremely flammable, so take extra precautions when you work on any part of the fuel system. Don't smoke or allow open flames or bare light bulbs near the work area, and don't work in a garage where a gas-type appliance (such as a water heater or clothes dryer) is present. Since gasoline is carcinogenic, wear latex gloves when there's a possibility of being exposed to fuel, and, if you spill any fuel on your skin, rinse it off immediately with soap and water. Mop up any spills immediately and do not store fuel-soaked rags where they could ignite. The fuel system is under constant pressure, so, if any fuel lines are to be disconnected, the fuel pressure in the system must be relieved first. When you perform any kind of work on the fuel system, wear safety glasses and have a Class B type fire extinguisher on hand.*

1   Remove the left kick panel to access the under-dash fuse and relay box (see Chapter 11).

2   On 2003 and earlier models, pull the No. 1 fuse from the under-dash fuse and relay box. **Note:** *The No. 1 fuse protects the circuit for the PGM-FI relay, which is difficult to access because it's up under the dash.*

3   On 2004 and later models, remove the left (driver's side) kick panel and pull the PGM-FI relay 2 from the under-dash fuse and relay box. There are three rows of fuses on the bottom part of the panel. The PGM-FI relay 2 is the relay on the left of the bottom row of relays located immediately above the top row of fuses.

4   Try to start the engine, which will either start and immediately stall or will crank but not start because the fuel pump has been disabled. Turn the ignition key to OFF.

5   The fuel pressure is now relieved, but there is still residual fuel in the lines, so be sure to have shop rags handy to soak up any spilled fuel when disconnecting fuel lines. **Warning:** *Be sure to disconnect the battery (see Chapter 5, Section 1) before disconnecting any fuel lines.*

3   Fuel pump/fuel pressure - check

Warning: *Gasoline is extremely flammable, so take extra precautions when you work on any part of the fuel system. See the* **Warning** *in Section 2.*

General checks

1   Verify that there is fuel in the fuel tank.

2   Verify that the fuel pump actually runs. Turn the ignition switch to ON - you should hear a brief whirring noise for about two seconds as the pump comes on and pressurizes the system. **Note:** *If you can't hear the pump from inside the vehicle, open the fuel filler neck cap, then have an assistant turn the ignition switch to ON while you listen to the pump through the fuel filler neck.*

Fuel pump/fuel pressure test
2003 and earlier models

Refer to illustrations 3.3, 3.5, 3.6 and 3.12

3   To measure the fuel pressure, you'll need a fuel pressure gauge **(see illustration)** capable of reading pressures in excess of 48 psi (330 kPa) for 1999 and 2000 models, and in excess of 55 psi (380 kPa) for 2001 through 2003 models. You will also need some fuel hose and a suitable double flare fitting and adapter nut.

4   Before disconnecting any fuel line fittings, relieve the fuel system pressure (see Section 2), then disconnect the cable from the negative terminal of the battery (see Chapter 5, Section 1).

5   Remove the fuel pulsation damper from the fuel rail **(see illustration)**.

6   Connect the fuel pressure gauge to the fuel system **(see illustration)**.

7   Reconnect the battery.

8   Turn the ignition switch to ON (don't start the engine yet) with the air conditioning off. The fuel pump should run for about two seconds, and pressure should register on the gauge and should hold steady.

9   Start the engine and let it warm up until it's idling at its normal operating temperature.

10   Disconnect the vacuum hose from the fuel pressure regulator (see Section 15). Note the indicated fuel pressure reading on the gauge and compare it with the operating range listed in this Chapter's Specifications. Reconnect the vacuum hose to the fuel pressure regulator, note the indicated fuel pressure and compare it with the range listed in this Chapter's Specifications. If both fuel pressure readings are within the specified range, the system is operating correctly.

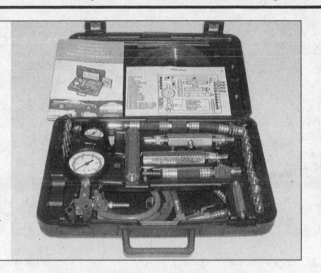

3.3 An aftermarket fuel pressure testing kit like this one should contain all the necessary fittings and adapters, along with the fuel pressure gauge, to test most systems

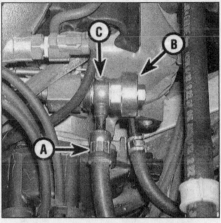

3.5 To tap into the fuel supply line (A) on 2003 and earlier models, unscrew the fuel pulsation damper (B) from the fuel supply line banjo fitting (C) and install the correct diameter banjo bolt (with the Schrader valve on the other end) from your fuel pressure testing kit. Hook up the appropriate test hose from the kit with the Schrader valve and connect the fuel pressure gauge to the other end of the test hose

11   Note that the operating fuel pressure range is slightly lower when the vacuum hose is connected to the fuel pressure regulator than when it's disconnected. This is because intake manifold vacuum is high at idle, so it raises the diaphragm inside the pressure regulator slightly, allowing fuel to return to the fuel tank, and lowering the pressure. But when you disconnect the vacuum hose from the regulator, the spring-loaded diaphragm seals off the return line, raising the pressure.

12   If the indicated fuel pressure doesn't go up when you disconnect the vacuum line from the regulator, apply vacuum to the pressure regulator with a hand-held vacuum pump **(see illustration)** and note what happens. If the fuel pressure drops, the regulator is okay, but there's probably a crack or tear in the vacuum hose. Replace the vacuum hose and retest.

13   If the indicated fuel pressure doesn't go down when you connect the vacuum hose to the regulator, inspect the vacuum hose. If it's torn or cracked, replace it and retest. If the pressure still doesn't go down with the new

vacuum hose connected, replace the regulator.

14   If the indicated fuel pressure is higher than the specified range with the vacuum hose connected, verify that the fuel pressure regulator is receiving a good vacuum signal by checking it with a vacuum gauge. Vacuum should fluctuate up and down in accordance with the increase or decrease in the engine rpm (at idle the vacuum is high, but as engine is revved-up, the vacuum signal drops, then builds up again). If vacuum is present, check for a kinked, pinched or clogged fuel return hose or line. If the return line is OK, replace the regulator.

15   If the indicated fuel pressure is lower than the specified range, start the engine and pinch off the return line. If the pressure now rises above the specified operating range, the regulator is not closing fully. Replace it (see Section 15).

16   If the indicated fuel pressure is still lower than the specified range, the fuel filter might

be clogged. Replace the filter (see Sections 5 and 6).

17   If the indicated fuel pressure is still lower than the specified range after replacing the filter, one or more of the fuel injectors or injector O-rings might be leaking (see Section 16), or the fuel pump might be faulty (see Sections 5 and 6). Replace the defective component(s) and retest.

18   After the test is complete, relieve the system fuel pressure (see Section 2), then disconnect the cable from the negative battery terminal.

19   Remove your fuel pressure testing rig,

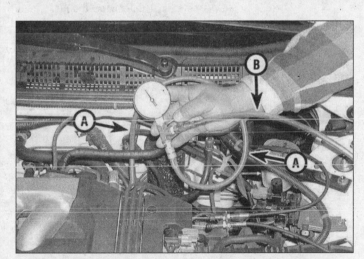

3.6 This setup shows the fuel pressure test hose (A) with an optional fuel pressure relief hose (B) that you can use to relieve fuel pressure by draining off residual fuel into an approved container when you're done with the test

3.12 If the indicated fuel pressure doesn't go up when you disconnect the vacuum line from the fuel pressure regulator, hook up a hand-held vacuum pump to the regulator and apply vacuum. If the fuel pressure now drops, the regulator wasn't receiving vacuum

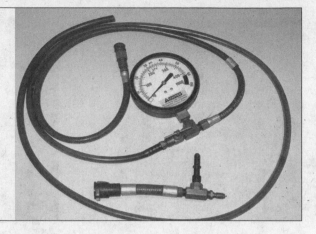

3.21 To check fuel pressure on 2004 and later models, you'll need a fuel pressure gauge and an adapter setup that will connect the gauge between the two halves of the quick-connect fitting between the fuel supply line and the fuel rail

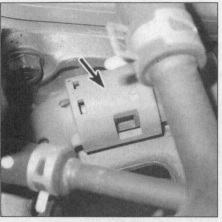

3.23a To remove the cover from the quick-connect fitting on 2004 and later models, simply pull it off

then reconnect the fuel supply line to the connection at the firewall.

20   Reconnect the cable to the negative battery terminal (see Chapter 5, Section 1). Start the engine and check for fuel leaks.

2004 and later models

Refer to illustrations 3.21, 3.23a, 3.23b, 3.23c and 3.24

21   To measure the fuel pressure, you'll need a fuel pressure gauge capable of reading in excess of 64 psi (440 kPa). To tee the gauge into the fuel system at the connection on the fuel rail, you'll need an adapter setup that will connect the gauge between the two halves of the quick-connect fitting **(see illustration)**.

22   Before disconnecting any fuel line fittings, relieve system fuel pressure (see Section 2), then disconnect the cable from the negative battery terminal (see Chapter 5, Section 1).

23   Remove the quick-connect fitting cover, open the clamp that secures the fuel supply line to its mounting bracket, then disconnect the fuel supply line quick-connect fitting at the fuel rail **(see illustrations)**.

24   Connect the fuel pressure gauge to the fuel system **(see illustration)**.

25   Reconnect the battery.

26   Turn the ignition switch to ON (don't start the engine yet) with the air conditioning off. The fuel pump should run for about two seconds, and pressure should register on the gauge and should hold steady.

27   Start the engine and let it warm up until it's idling at its normal operating temperature.

28   Note the indicated fuel pressure reading on the gauge and compare it with the operating range listed in this Chapter's Specifications.

29   If the indicated pressure is within the specified range, the system is operating correctly.

30   If the indicated pressure is lower than the specified range, the fuel filter might be clogged or the fuel pump or fuel pressure regulator might be defective (see Sections 5 and 6).

31   After the test is complete, relieve the system fuel pressure (see Section 2).

32   Disconnect the cable from the negative battery terminal.

33   Remove your fuel pressure testing rig, then reconnect the fuel supply line, using a new retainer.

34   Reconnect the cable to the negative battery terminal (see Chapter 5, Section 1). Start the engine and check for fuel leaks.

4   Fuel lines and fittings - general information

Refer to illustrations 4.2a and 4.2b

Warning: *Gasoline is extremely flammable, so take extra precautions when you work on any part of the fuel system. See the* **Warning** *in Section 2.*

1   Always relieve the fuel pressure before servicing fuel lines or fittings (see Section 2), then disconnect the cable from the negative battery terminal (see Chapter 5, Section 1) before proceeding.

2   The fuel supply and return lines connect the fuel pump in the fuel tank to the fuel rail on the engine. The Evaporative Emission (EVAP) system lines connect the fuel tank to

3.23b To open the clamp that secures the fuel supply line to its mounting bracket on 2004 and later models, use a small screwdriver to pry open the clamp, then swing back the upper half of the clamp

3.23c To disconnect the quick-connect fitting between the fuel supply line and the fuel rail on 2004 and later models, depress the two release tabs on the retainer and pull off the fitting

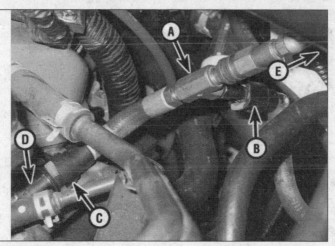

3.24 Fuel pressure gauge connection details - 2004 and later models

A   Tee-fitting/adapter
B   Supply line quick-connect fitting
C   Adapter quick-connect fitting
D   Fuel rail
E   Hose to pressure gauge

the EVAP canister and connect the canister to the intake manifold. All lines are secured to the underbody with small metal and/or plastic brackets that are bolted to the vehicle floor-pan **(see illustrations)**.

3   Whenever you're working under the vehicle, be sure to inspect all fuel and evaporative emission lines for leaks, kinks, dents and other damage. Always replace a damaged fuel or EVAP line immediately. Leaking fuel and EVAP lines will result in loss of fuel and excessive air pollution (the leaking raw fuel emits unburned hydrocarbon vapors into the atmosphere).

4   If you find signs of dirt in the lines during disassembly, disconnect all lines and blow them out with compressed air. Inspect the fuel strainer on the fuel pump pick-up unit (see Sections 5 and 6) for damage and deterioration. And inspect the fuel filter, which is an integral component of the fuel pump/fuel level sending unit module (see Sections 5 and 6).

Steel tubing

5   Because fuel lines used on fuel-injected vehicles are under fairly high pressure, it is critical that they be replaced with lines of equivalent specification. If you have to replace a fuel or EVAP line, use only steel tubing that meets the manufacturer's specifications. Don't use copper or aluminum tubing to replace steel tubing. These materials cannot withstand normal vehicle vibration.

6   Some steel fuel lines have threaded fittings. When loosening these fittings to service or replace components:

a) Always hold the stationary fitting with a wrench while turning the tube nut (this will prevent the line from twisting).

b) If you're going to replace one of these fittings, use original equipment parts or parts that meet original equipment standards.

Plastic tubing

7   Some fuel lines - between the fuel supply and return pipes of the fuel pump and the front of the fuel tank, for example - are plastic. If you ever have to replace either line, use only original equipment plastic tubing. **Caution:** *When removing or installing plastic fuel line tubing, be careful not to bend or*

twist it too much, which can damage it. And damaged fuel lines MUST be replaced! Also, be aware that the plastic fuel tubing is NOT heat resistant, so keep it away from excessive heat. Nor is it acid-proof, so don't wipe it off with a shop rag that has been used to wipe off battery electrolyte. If you accidentally spill or wipe electrolyte on plastic fuel tubing, replace the tubing.

Flexible hoses

Warning: *Use only original equipment replacement hoses or their equivalent. Unapproved hoses might fail when subjected to the high operating pressures of the fuel system.*

8   Don't route fuel hoses (or metal lines) within four inches of the exhaust system or within ten inches of the catalytic converter. Make sure that no rubber hoses are installed directly against the vehicle, particularly in places where there is any vibration. If allowed to touch some vibrating part of the vehicle, a hose can easily become chafed and it might start leaking. A good rule of thumb is to maintain a minimum of 1/4-inch clearance around a hose (or metal line) to prevent contact with the vehicle underbody.

Disconnecting and reconnecting fuel system fittings

9   Different fittings are used on Acura fuel systems, depending on the model year. Earlier models use a threaded banjo-type fitting at the fuel pulsation damper, and some models use conventional spring-type hose clamps to secure fuel hoses on the return (low-pressure) side of the system, between the fuel pressure regulator and the fuel tank. Quick-connect fittings are used to connect lines on the (high-pressure) supply side of the system, such as the connections at the fuel pump (supply and return line connections).

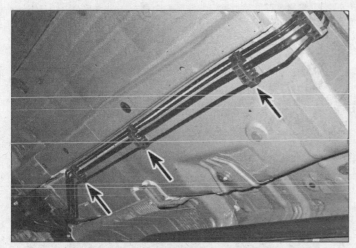

4.2a The fuel and EVAP lines are secured to the underside of the vehicle by a series of plastic brackets and clips similar to the ones that you see here

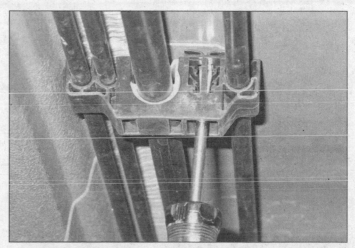

4.2b To release this type of fuel/EVAP line bracket from the underside of the vehicle, insert a screwdriver as shown and spread the teeth apart to release them from the mounting stud, then disengage the bracket from the fuel and EVAP lines

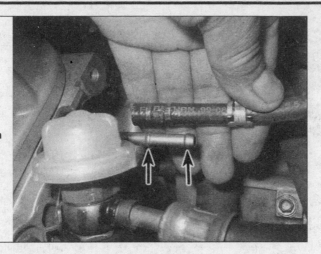

4.13 Slide the hose onto the metal line up to the second raised ridge on the line or pipe (left arrow), then center the clamp between the two ridges

hose clamp down the hose until it's centered between the two ridges **(see illustration)**.

14   Reconnect the cable to the negative battery terminal (see Chapter 5, Section 1).

15   Start the engine and verify that no fuel is leaking out at the connection you just reconnected. If there's a leak, either the clamp is weak or it's not centered correctly between the two raised ridges on the metal line or pipe to which you connected the fuel hose. Or the hose itself is leaking because it's cracked or torn where the clamp squeezes down on it.

Quick-connect fuel system fittings

Refer to illustrations 4.16, 4.18, 4.19, 4.20, 4.21, 4.22 and 4.23

Caution: *When disconnecting or reconnecting quick-connect fittings, be careful not to bend or twist them excessively, or they will be damaged and will have to be replaced. Also, be aware that the quick-connect fittings are NOT heat resistant, so keep them away from excessive heat. Nor are they acid-proof, so don't wipe them off with a shop rag that has been used to wipe off battery electrolyte. If you accidentally spill or wipe electrolyte on quick-connect fittings, replace them.*

Conventional spring-type hose clamps

Refer to illustration 4.13

10   Relieve the system fuel pressure (see Section 2), then disconnect the cable from the negative battery terminal (see Chapter 5, Section 1).

11   To disconnect a spring-type hose clamp, simply squeeze the two ends together with a pair of pliers to loosen the clamp, then slide

the clamp away from the pipe to which the hose is attached.

12   If a spring-type hose clamp feels easy to squeeze open, or if it's obviously not clamping the hose tightly against the metal pipe to which the hose is connected, replace the clamp.

13   When installing spring-type hose clamps, be sure to slide the hose onto the pipe to which you're connecting it up to the second raised ridge on the pipe, then slide the

Engine compartment	Tokai	Blue/green	0.3 in (8 mm)
Fuel pump: fuel feed line, fuel pump side	Tokai	Orange	0.4 in (9.5 mm)
Fuel pump: fuel feed line, fuel line side	Tokai	Green	0.2 in (6.3 mm)
EVAP canister: fuel vapor line	Tokai	Orange	0.4 in (9.5 mm)

4.16 Quick-connect fitting color code

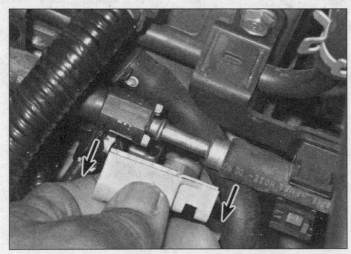

4.18 To remove the protective cover (if equipped) from a quick-connect fitting, simply pull it straight off

4.19 To disconnect a quick-connect fitting, squeeze the retainer tabs and pull the fitting off of the pipe

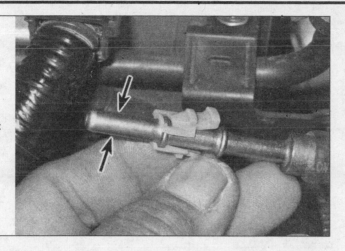

4.20 Spread apart the sides of the old retainer, remove it and discard it, then inspect the contact surface of the fuel line for dirt, damage and rust

4.21 Whenever you disconnect a quick-connect fitting, be sure to inspect the O-ring inside the fitting. If it's cracked, torn or damaged, replace it

16   There are quick-connect fittings at both ends of the fuel supply line: at the fuel pump and fuel rail, and at some EVAP line fittings as well. You MUST replace the quick-connect fitting retainers whenever you disconnect a quick-connect fitting. It is critical that you use the correct replacement retainer, which depends on the manufacturer of the tubing and the end of the tube (fuel pump end or fuel rail end) on which you're installing it, because the retainers are not all the same diameter. To help you identify the retainer(s) you're replacing, they are color-coded **(see illustration)**.

17   Relieve the system fuel pressure (see Section 2), then disconnect the cable from the negative battery terminal (see Chapter 5, Section 1).

18   Remove the quick-connect fitting cover **(see illustration)** if equipped.

19   Holding the black side of the fitting with one hand, squeeze the retainer tabs to release them, then pull the fitting off of the pipe **(see illustration)**. Cover the disconnected ends of the fitting with plastic bags to keep out dirt and moisture.

20   Remove the old retainer from the fitting and inspect the contact surface area on the fuel line for dirt and damage **(see illustration)**. If it's dirty, wipe it off with a clean shop rag. If it's rusty, remove and inspect the fuel lines, then remove and inspect the fuel pump (see Sections 5 and 6), the fuel pressure regulator (see Section 6 or 15) and the fuel filter (see Section 6). If any of these components are damaged, replace them (see Sections 5 and 6).

21   Inspect the old O-ring inside the bore of the fitting **(see illustration)**. If it's cracked, torn or otherwise damaged, replace it.

22   Insert a new retainer into the female side of the fitting **(see illustration)**. Be sure to align the locking pawls of the retainer with the windows in the sides of the connector.

23   Press the quick-connect fitting and pipe together until the locking pawls on both retainer tabs are locked into place by the ridge on the male end of the fuel pipe **(see illustration)**.

24   Verify that the quick-connect fitting is correctly reconnected by trying to pull the fitting off of the pipe.

25   Install any components that you had to remove to access the fuel line or EVAP line fitting(s).

26   Reconnect the cable to the negative battery terminal (see Chapter 5, Section 1).

27   Start the engine and check for leaks.

5   Fuel pump/fuel level sending unit module - removal and installation

1   Disconnect the cable from the negative battery terminal (see Chapter 5, Section 1).

2   Relieve the fuel system pressure (see Section 2).

3   Remove the back seat cushion (see Chapter 11).

2003 and earlier models

Refer to illustrations 5.4, 5.6 and 5.10

Warning: *Gasoline is extremely flammable, so take extra precautions when you work on any part of the fuel system. See the* **Warning** *in Section 2.*

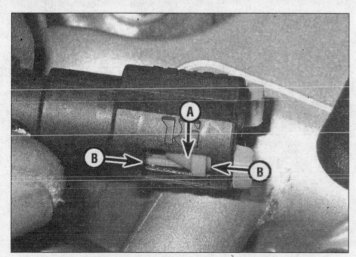

4.22 Insert a new retainer into the female side of the fitting and align the retainer's locking pawls (A) with the windows (B) in the connector

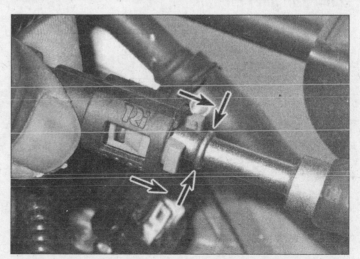

4.23 To reconnect a quick-connect fitting, push the female side of the fitting onto the male side until the locking pawls of the retainer snap into place on the raised ridge on the male pipe

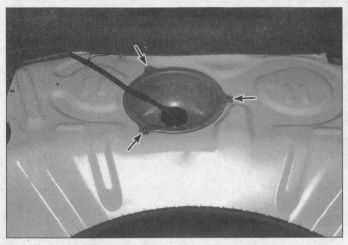

5.4 To detach the fuel pump cover from the floor, remove these three screws (2003 and earlier models)

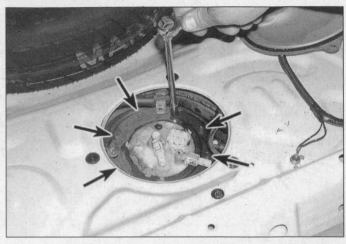

5.6 To detach the fuel pump/fuel level sending unit from the fuel tank, remove the eight retaining screws (two screws not visible) (2003 and earlier models)

4   Remove the screws that retain the fuel pump access cover **(see illustration)**.

5   Unplug the electrical connector from the fuel pump and detach the fuel lines (see Section 4, if necessary).

6   Remove the fuel pump assembly retaining screws **(see illustration)**.

7   Remove the fuel pump from the tank.

8   Remove the electrical connector from the fuel pump.

9   Squeeze the hose clamps with a pair of pliers - remove the upper clamp from the hose and slide the lower clamp half-way up the hose, off the fuel pump inlet.

10   Remove the sock (fuel inlet filter) from the end of the pump **(see illustration)**.

11   Separate the pump from the fuel pump bracket.

12   Installation is the reverse of removal. Be sure to use a new gasket on the pump flange.

2004 and later models

Refer to illustrations 5.14, 5.16a, 5.16b and 5.19

Warning: *Gasoline is extremely flammable,*

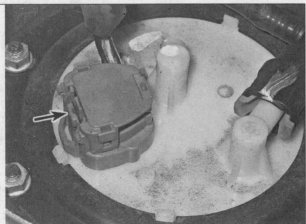

5.10 Pry off the retaining clip with a small screwdriver and detach the sock (fuel inlet filter) from the fuel pump (2003 and earlier models)

so take extra precautions when you work on any part of the fuel system. See the **Warning** *in Section 2.*

13   Remove the fuel pump access cover **(see illustration 5.4)**.

14   Disconnect the electrical connector from

the fuel pump/fuel gauge sending unit **(see illustration)**.

15   Disconnect the quick-connect fitting for the fuel supply line and set the supply line aside (see Section 4, if necessary).

16   Remove the fuel pump/fuel gauge sending unit locknut **(see illustrations)**.

17   Remove the fuel pump/fuel gauge sending unit from the tank; carefully angle it out to protect the float arm and float from damage. After removing the pump/fuel gauge sending unit, inspect the seal for cracks, tears and deterioration. If it's damaged, replace it.

18   Before installing the fuel pump/fuel gauge sending unit in the fuel tank, install a new gasket in the hole *first*. Don't try to install it with the fuel pump/fuel gauge sending unit, which might cause it to become pinched or distorted.

19   When installing the fuel pump/fuel gauge sending unit, be sure to align the index mark on top of the module between the two marks on the edge of the hole **(see illustration)**, then tighten the fuel pump/fuel gauge sending unit locknut securely.

20   Installation is the reverse of removal.

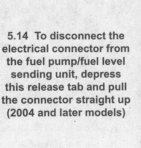

5.14 To disconnect the electrical connector from the fuel pump/fuel level sending unit, depress this release tab and pull the connector straight up (2004 and later models)

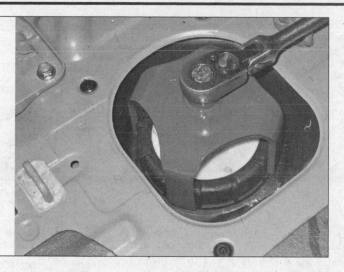

5.16a This is the special tool (available at most auto parts stores) for loosening and tightening the fuel pump/fuel level sending unit locknut (2004 and later models)

6 Fuel pump/fuel level sending unit module - component replacement

Warning: *Gasoline is extremely flammable, so take extra precautions when you work on any part of the fuel system. See the* **Warning** *in Section 2.*

1 Relieve the fuel system pressure (see Section 2).
2 Disconnect the cable from the negative battery terminal (see Chapter 5, Section 1).
3 Remove the fuel pump/fuel level sending unit from the fuel tank (see Section 5), then place the fuel pump/fuel level sending unit module on a clean workbench.

2003 and earlier models

Refer to illustration 6.6

Note: *On these models, the only components that you can replace separately are the fuel pump module assembly and the fuel level*

sending unit. Once you have removed the fuel level sending unit from the fuel pump module assembly, no further disassembly is possible.

If any component of the fuel pump module assembly is defective, you must replace the entire fuel pump module assembly.

4 Remove the fuel pump/fuel level sending unit from the fuel tank (see Section 5).
5 Disconnect the sending unit electrical connector from the base of the fuel pump/fuel level sending unit.
6 Separate the fuel level sending unit from the fuel pump bracket **(see illustration)**.
7 Installation is the reverse of removal.
8 Be sure to use a new gasket under the sealing flange.

2004 and later models

Refer to illustrations 6.9, 6.10, 6.11a, 6.11b, 6.13, 6.14a, 6.14b, 6.16a, 6.16b and 6.18

Note: *On these models, you can replace the fuel pump, fuel level sending unit, fuel filter and/or fuel pressure regulator separately.*

9 Disconnect the electrical connector for the fuel level sending unit, then detach the

5.16b If you're unable to obtain the special locknut tool, use a large pair of water pump pliers to loosen the locknut; just be careful not to damage it (2004 and later models)

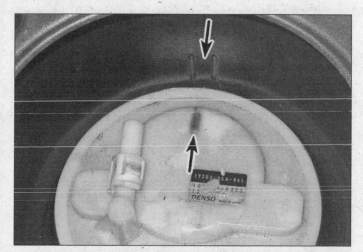

5.19 When installing the fuel pump/fuel level sending unit, make sure that the index mark on top of the fuel pump/fuel level sending unit is pointing between the two marks on the edge of the pump mounting hole (2004 and later models)

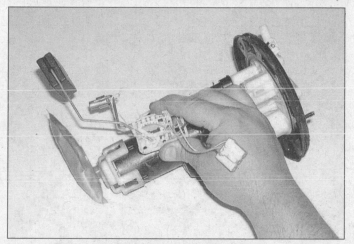

6.6 To separate the sending unit from the fuel pump assembly, push it down, toward the fuel pump inlet filter (2003 and earlier models)

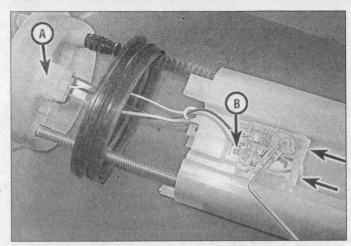

6.9 Depress the release tab (A) and disconnect the electrical connector, then depress the locking lug (B) with a screwdriver and push the sending unit toward the upper end of the housing with your thumbs (2004 and later models)

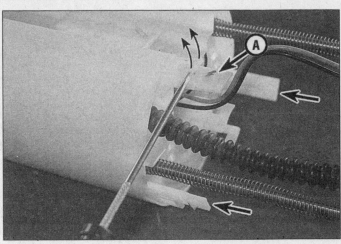

6.10 To disengage each lock tab from its locking lug (A), carefully pry the tab off the lug. When all three lock tabs are freed from their lugs, pull off the case (2004 and later models)

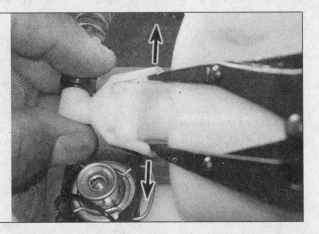

6.11a To disconnect the fuel supply line fitting from the fuel pump/fuel filter housing, spread these two locking tangs apart and pull off the fitting (2004 and later models)

fuel level sending unit from the fuel filter housing **(see illustration)**.

10   Remove the case from the fuel pump/fuel filter housing **(see illustration)**.

11   Disconnect the fuel supply line fitting from the fuel pump/fuel filter housing **(see illustration)**. Remove and discard the O-ring for the fuel supply line fitting **(see illustration)**. This

O-ring must be replaced when reassembling the pump module.

12   Disconnect the electrical connectors for the fuel pump wiring harness and detach the pump ground wire from the fuel pump/fuel filter housing.

13   Remove the fuel pressure regulator housing **(see illustration)**, then disconnect the fuel pump ground wire from the regulator housing.

14   Remove the fuel pressure regulator retaining clip and pull the regulator out of the housing **(see illustrations)**.

15   Remove and discard the fuel pressure regulator O-rings **(see illustration 6.14b)**. This O-ring must be replaced when reassembling the pump module. Inspect the condition of the spacer and the mesh filter screen. If either of these parts is damaged, replace it.

16   Remove the fuel pump **(see illustrations)**.

17   Remove and discard the fuel pump

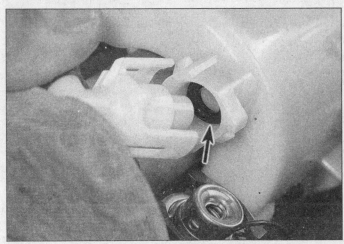

6.11b Inspect the fuel supply line fitting O-ring. Replace it if it's cracked, torn or deteriorated (2004 and later models)

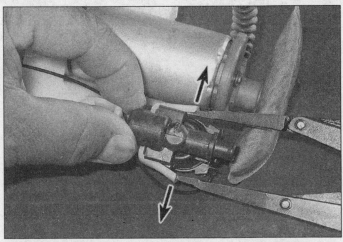

6.13 To remove the fuel pressure regulator housing from the fuel pump/fuel filter housing, spread these two locking tangs apart and pull out the housing (2004 and later models)

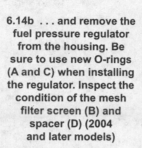

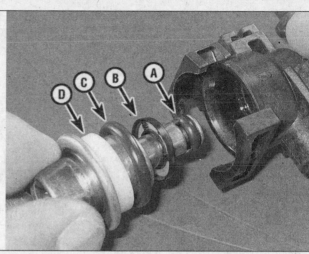

6.14b . . . and remove the fuel pressure regulator from the housing. Be sure to use new O-rings (A and C) when installing the regulator. Inspect the condition of the mesh filter screen (B) and spacer (D) (2004 and later models)

6.14a Remove the fuel pressure regulator retaining clip . . .

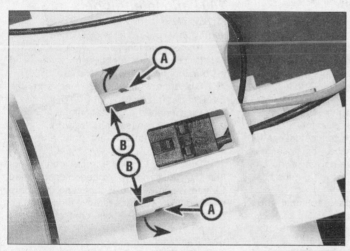

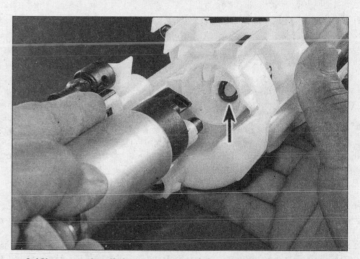

6.16a The fuel pump is secured to the pump/filter housing by a pair of locking lugs (A). To disengage the two slotted lock tabs (B) from the lugs, carefully pry them away from the pump . . .

6.16b . . . and pull the pump out of the housing. Remove and discard the pump O-ring inside the upper end of the pump recess. This O-ring must be replaced (2004 and later models)

O-ring inside the upper end of the pump recess **(see illustration 6.16b)**. This O-ring must be replaced when reassembling the pump module.

18   Remove the suction filter retainer clip **(see illustration)** and remove the suction fil-

ter from the fuel pump.
19   Before reassembling the fuel pump, fuel filter and fuel level sending unit, wash the fuel strainer thoroughly in clean solvent. If it's impossible to clean, replace it.
20   Reassembly is the reverse of disassem-

bly. Be sure to use new O-rings and a new retainer clip on the strainer during reassembly.
21   Before installing the fuel pump access cover, reconnect the cable to the negative battery terminal (see Chapter 5, Section 1), start the engine and check for fuel leaks at the pump fuel line connections.

7   Fuel tank - removal and installation

Warning: *Gasoline is extremely flammable, so take extra precautions when you work on any part of the fuel system. See the* **Warning** *in Section 2.*
Note: *The following procedure is much easier to perform if the fuel tank is empty. The tank has no drain plug, so the fuel must be siphoned from the tank with a siphoning kit, which is available at most auto parts stores. NEVER try to start the siphoning action with your mouth!*
1   Remove the fuel tank filler cap to relieve fuel tank pressure.

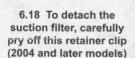

6.18 To detach the suction filter, carefully pry off this retainer clip (2004 and later models)

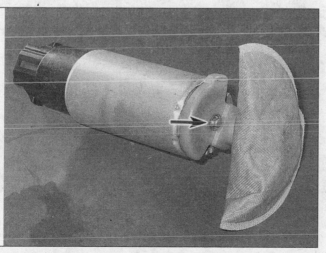

7.24 Loosen the clamps and detach the breather and fuel filler neck hoses from their pipes

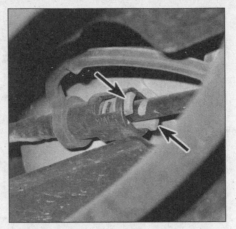

7.26 Squeeze the retainer tangs and disconnect the quick-connect fitting for the fuel supply line

2   Relieve the fuel system pressure (see Section 2).

3   Disconnect the cable from the negative battery terminal (see Chapter 5, Section 1).

4   Disconnect the electrical connector from the fuel pump/fuel level sending unit module (see Section 5).

5   If the fuel tank is empty or nearly empty, it's not necessary to siphon the remaining fuel from the tank. But if there is a lot of fuel in the tank, remove the fuel pump/fuel level sending unit (see Section 5) and siphon out the remaining fuel through the hole in the tank. **Warning:** *Always siphon fuel into an approved gasoline container.*

6   Raise the vehicle and place it securely on jackstands.

7   Remove the rear part of the exhaust system (see Section 17).

2003 and earlier models

8   Remove the fuel filler neck cover bolts and remove the cover.

9   Remove the fuel filler neck hose, the fuel tank EVAP recirculation hose and the fuel tank EVAP signal hose from the metal pipes. **Note:**

The fuel tank EVAP recirculation hose and the EVAP signal hose are both connected to the vapor control valve on top of the fuel tank.

10   Disconnect the quick-connect fittings for the fuel supply and return lines. The fuel supply and return line quick-connect fittings are located at the left side of the EVAP canister, which is located front of the fuel tank.

11   Disconnect the quick-connect fittings for the fuel tank EVAP vent hose. This hose goes to the vapor control valve on top of the fuel tank. Disengage the vent hose from the hose clip.

12   Disconnect the bypass solenoid valve hose from the vapor control valve hard line (the hard line can stay connected to the vapor control valve during tank removal).

13   Disconnect the EVAP hose from the two-way valve. The two-way valve is located in front of the EVAP canister, below the bypass solenoid valve.

14   Disconnect the electrical connectors from the ABS rear wheel speed sensors (see Chapter 9).

15   Remove the rear stabilizer bar (see Chapter 10).

16   Remove the heat shield.

17   Detach both parking brake cable brackets, remove the rear brake caliper bolts and hang the calipers from the coil springs with wire, then remove the parking brake cables (see Chapter 9).

18   Remove the bolts that secure the lower ends of the shock absorbers to the rear knuckles (see Chapter 10).

19   Support the rear suspension subframe/ fuel tank assembly with a floor jack, then remove the rear suspension subframe mounting bolts and lower the rear suspension subframe and fuel tank assembly.

20   Remove the four fuel tank strap bolts and remove the two straps.

21   Lift the fuel tank out of the rear suspension subframe.

22   Installation is the reverse of removal.

2004 and later models

Refer to illustrations 7.24, 7.26, 7.30a and 7.30b

23   Remove the fuel tank covers.

24   Disconnect the fuel filler neck hose and the breather hose **(see illustration)**.

25   Disconnect the EVAP hose from the EVAP canister (see Chapter 6).

26   Disconnect the quick-connect fitting for the fuel supply line **(see illustration)**.

27   Remove the exhaust pipe and heat shield.

28   Disconnect the electrical connectors from the ABS rear wheel speed sensors (see Chapter 9). Without disconnecting the brake hoses from the calipers, remove the rear brake calipers and the brake hose bracket bolts and hang the calipers from the coil springs with wire. Remove the brake pads from the caliper mounting brackets. Detach the parking brake cables from the parking brake shoes and backing plates (see Chapter 9).

29   Remove the bolts that secure the lower ends of the shock absorbers to the rear knuckles (see Chapter 10).

30   Support the rear suspension subframe/ fuel tank assembly. Remove the rear suspension subframe mounting bolts **(see illustra-**

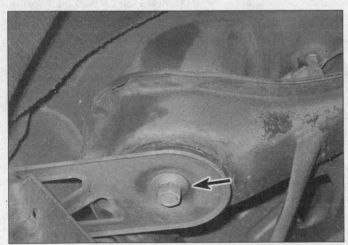

7.30a To detach the rear suspension subframe assembly, remove the two front bolts (left side shown) . . .

7.30b . . . and the two rear mounting bolts and bracket bolts (right side shown)

9.1 Air intake duct details (2004 model shown, other models similar):

1   *Mass Air Flow (MAF) sensor electrical connector*
2   *Clip*
3   *PCV fresh air inlet hose clamp*
4   *Spring clamp*
5   *Hose clamp*

9.11 To remove the radiator from the air filter housing on a 1999 model, remove this bolt, then lift up the end that's bolted and disengage the two locator pins from their insulator grommets at the other end of the radiator

tions), then carefully lower the rear suspension subframe and fuel tank assembly onto the floor.

31   Remove the four fuel tank strap bolts and remove the two straps.

32   Lift the fuel tank out of the rear suspension subframe assembly.

33   Installation is the reverse of removal.

8   Fuel tank cleaning and repair - general information

1   The fuel tanks installed in the vehicles covered by this manual are not repairable. If the fuel tank has been removed for cleaning, this is a job that should be left to a professional who has experience in this critical and potentially dangerous work. Even after cleaning and flushing of the fuel tank, explosive fumes can remain.

2   If the fuel tank is removed from the vehicle, it should not be placed in an area where sparks or open flames could ignite the fumes coming out of the tank. Be especially careful inside garages where a gas-type appliance is located, because it could cause an explosion.

9   Air filter housing - removal and installation

Air intake duct

Refer to illustration 9.1

1   Disconnect the PCV fresh air inlet hose **(see illustration)** from the air intake duct.

2   Clearly label any other hoses and/or cables that are attached or connected to the air intake duct, then detach or disconnect them and set them aside.

3   Loosen the hose clamps at each end of the air intake duct.

4   Remove the air intake duct.

5   Installation is the reverse of removal.

Air filter housing

1999 models

Refer to illustration 9.11

Warning: *Wait until the engine is completely cool before beginning this procedure.*

6   Drain the engine coolant (see Chapter 1).

7   Remove the air intake duct (see Steps 1 through 4).

8   Remove the air filter housing retaining bolts, lift up the air filter housing assembly, loosen the spring-type hose clamps and disconnect the inlet and outlet hoses from the underside of the filter housing.

9   Remove the four air filter housing cover

bolts and remove the filter housing cover.

10   Remove the air filter element (see Chapter 1).

11   Remove the radiator mounting bolt **(see illustration)** and remove the radiator from the air filter housing.

12   Inspect the condition of the air filter housing insulator(s). If an insulator is cracked, torn or otherwise deteriorated, replace it.

13   Installation is the reverse of removal. Refer to Chapter 1 and refill the engine coolant.

2000 and later models

Refer to illustrations 9.16a and 9.16b

14   Remove the air intake duct (see Steps 1 through 4).

15   Remove the air filter housing cover and remove the air filter element (see Chapter 1).

16   Remove the air filter housing retaining bolts **(see illustrations)** and remove the filter housing.

17   Inspect the condition of the air filter housing insulator(s). If an insulator is cracked, torn or otherwise deteriorated, replace it.

18   Installation is the reverse of removal.

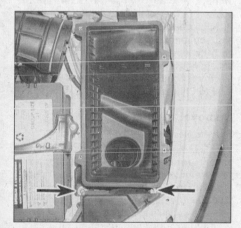

9.16a To detach the air filter housing on a 2000 through 2003 model, remove these three bolts

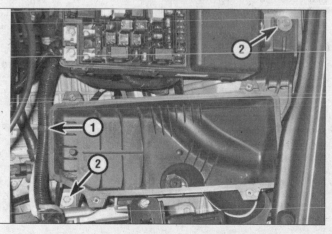

9.16b To detach the air filter housing on 2004 and later models, detach the battery cable clip (1), if applicable, and remove these two bolts (2)

10.2 To disengage the accelerator cable end (A) from the throttle lever cam, rotate the throttle cam until the cable is aligned with the slot (B) in the cam, then pull out the cable end (2003 and earlier models)

10.3 Loosen the accelerator cable locknut and disengage the cable from the cable bracket (2003 and earlier models)

10   Accelerator cable - removal, installation and adjustment

2003 and earlier models

Removal and installation

Refer to illustrations 10.2, 10.3, 10.5 and 10.6

1   Disconnect the cable from the negative battery terminal (see Chapter 5, Section 1).

2   Rotate the throttle lever cam until the cable is lined up with the slot in the cam, then disengage the cable end plug from the cam **(see illustration)**.

3   Using a pair of wrenches, loosen the accelerator cable locknut at the cable bracket **(see illustration)** and disengage the accelerator cable from its bracket.

4   Tracing the cable from the cable bracket back to the firewall, detach or disengage it from any clamps, clips or cable guides.

5   Using a flashlight so that you can see underneath the dash, locate the cable connection at the top of the accelerator pedal and disengage the cable from the pedal arm **(see illustration)**.

6   Remove the two nuts **(see illustration)** that secure the accelerator cable grommet and mounting flange to the firewall, then pull the cable through the firewall.

7   Installation is the reverse of removal.

Adjustment

Refer to illustration 10.8

8   Rotate the accelerator cable throttle cam toward the cable bracket until the small lever on the bottom of the cam contacts the throttle stop bracket, then measure the cable deflection **(see illustration)** and compare your measurement to the cable deflection listed in this Chapter's Specifications.

9   If the cable deflection is incorrect, loosen the cable locknut and turn the adjustment nut until the deflection is within the specified range.

10.5 Disengage the plastic retainer from the accelerator pedal arm by squeezing these two locking tabs together and pulling the cable to the rear, then separate the cable from the pedal arm by guiding the cable out the slot (2003 and earlier models)

2004 and later models

10   These models are equipped with an electronic throttle body that doesn't use a traditional accelerator cable that actuates the throttle plate. Instead, the throttle plate is opened and closed by an electric servo motor that is controlled by the Powertrain Control Module (PCM). However, these models are still equipped with an "accelerator cable," though it isn't an accelerator cable in the conventional sense (the cable that connects the accelerator pedal to the throttle plate linkage on the throttle body). Instead, this cable connects the accelerator pedal to the throttle linkage for the Accelerator Pedal Position (APP) sensor, which is located on the firewall. The APP sensor monitors the position (angle) of the throttle linkage and, like the Throttle Position (TP) sensor, produces an analog voltage

10.6 To detach the accelerator cable grommet and mounting flange from the firewall, remove these two nuts, then pull the cable through the firewall (2003 and earlier models)

output that the PCM uses to determine the position (angle) of the accelerator pedal. The PCM processes this information continuously, and commands the servo inside the throttle body to open and close the throttle plate accordingly. For more information about the electronic control system and the APP sensor, refer to Chapter 6.

Removal and installation

Refer to illustrations 10.12, 10.13 and 10.14

11   Disconnect the cable from the negative battery terminal (see Chapter 5, Section 1).

12   Remove the APP sensor cover bolts **(see illustration)** and remove the cover.

13   Using a pair of wrenches, loosen the accelerator cable locknut at the cable bracket **(see illustration)** and disengage the accelerator cable from its bracket.

14 .   Rotate the throttle lever cam counterclockwise to its fully open position so that the

10.8 Close the throttle cam fully and measure the cable deflection where indicated; if it is out of range, adjust it by loosening the locknut (A) and turning the adjustment nut (B) (2003 and earlier models)

10.12 To detach the cover from the APP sensor assembly, remove these two bolts (2004 and later models)

cable is lined up with the slot in the cam, then disengage the cable from the cam **(see illustration)**.

15   Using a flashlight so that you can see underneath the dash, locate the cable connection at the top of the accelerator pedal and disengage the cable from the pedal arm **(see illustration 10.5)**.

16   Remove the two nuts **(see illustration 10.6)** that secure the accelerator cable grommet and mounting flange to the firewall, then pull the cable through the firewall.

17   Installation is the reverse of removal. Be sure to check and, if necessary, adjust the accelerator cable before installing the cover.

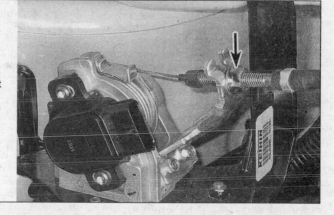

10.13 Loosen the accelerator cable locknut at the cable bracket and disengage the cable from the bracket (2004 and later models)

Adjustment

Refer to illustration 10.18

18   With the throttle cam in its closed position, deflect the accelerator cable between the cable bracket and the throttle cam and measure the amount of cable deflection **(see illustration)**. Compare your measurement to the cable deflection listed in this Chapter's Specifications.

19   If the cable deflection is incorrect, loosen

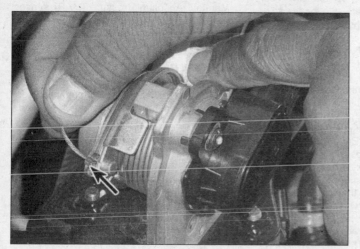

10.14 Rotate the cam counterclockwise until the cable is lined up with the slot, then slide out the cable end plug from its mounting hole in the cam (2004 and later models)

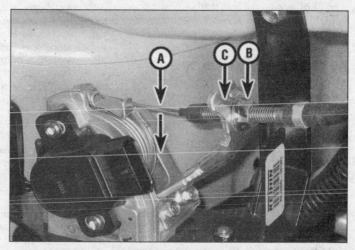

10.18 To check accelerator cable freeplay, deflect the cable downward at point A and measure the deflection. If the deflection is incorrect, loosen the cable locknut (B) and turn the adjuster nut (C) until the deflection is correct. Tighten the locknut when you're done (2004 and later models)

the cable locknut and turn the adjustment nut until the deflection is within the specified range.

20   Once you have adjusted the cable, have an assistant depress the accelerator pedal all the way until it stops, while you verify that the throttle cam is opening fully. Then, have your assistant release the accelerator pedal while you verify that the throttle cam returns to its idle (closed) position. If the throttle cam doesn't open all the way and close fully, readjust the cable. Install the cover when you're done.

11   Programmed Fuel Injection (PGM-FI) system - general information

The Programmed Fuel Injection (PGM-FI) system is a sequential multiport system. This means that there is a fuel injector in each intake port, and that these fuel injectors inject fuel into the intake ports in the cylinder firing order (1-4-2-5-3-6). The injectors are turned on and off by the Powertrain Control Module (PCM). When the engine is running, the PCM constantly monitors engine operating conditions with an array of information sensors, calculates the correct amount of fuel, then varies the interval of time during which the injectors are open. Sequential multiport systems provide much better control of the air/fuel mixture ratio than earlier fuel injection systems, and are therefore able to produce more power, better mileage and lower emissions.

The PGM-FI system uses the PCM and an array of information sensors to determine and deliver the correct air/fuel ratio under all operating conditions. The PGM-FI system consists of three sub-systems: air induction, electronic control and fuel delivery. The PGM-FI system is also closely interrelated with PCM-controlled emission control systems. For additional information about the PCM, the information sensors and the emission control systems, refer to Chapter 6.

Air induction system

The air induction system consists of the resonator, the air filter assembly, the air intake duct, the throttle body and the intake manifold.

2003 and earlier models

The single-barrel, side-draft, cast aluminum throttle body contains a throttle plate that regulates the amount of air entering the intake manifold. The throttle plate is opened and closed by the accelerator cable. The Throttle Position (TP) sensor is located on one end of the shaft for the throttle plate. A TP sensor is a potentiometer that monitors the opening angle of the throttle plate and sends a variable voltage signal to the Powertrain Control Module (PCM). The lower part of the throttle body is heated by engine coolant to prevent icing in cold weather.

A Manifold Absolute Pressure (MAP) sensor is located on top of the throttle body. The MAP sensor measures intake manifold pressure and vacuum and generates a variable voltage signal that's proportionate to the pressure or vacuum. The PCM uses this data to calculate the load on the engine. Another information sensor, the Intake Air Temperature (IAT) sensor, is located at the left rear corner of the intake manifold. The IAT sensor relays a voltage signal to the PCM that varies in accordance with the temperature of the incoming air in the manifold. The PCM uses this data to calculate how rich or lean the air/fuel mixture should be. All of the air induction components (air filter housing, air intake duct and throttle body) are covered in this Chapter, except for the intake manifold, which is covered in Chapter 2A, and the information sensors, which are covered in Chapter 6.

When the engine is idling, the Idle Air Control (IAC) system maintains the correct idle speed by regulating the amount of air that bypasses the (closed) throttle plate in response to a command from the Powertrain Control Module (PCM). The IAC system consists of the IAC valve (located on the throttle body), the PCM, and several information sensors, including the Engine Coolant Temperature (ECT) sensor, the Intake Air Temperature (IAT) sensor and the Manifold Absolute Pressure (MAP) sensor. The IAC valve is activated and controlled by the PCM in response to the running conditions of the engine (cold or warm running, power steering pressure high or low, air conditioning system on or off, etc.). As the PCM receives data from the information sensors (vehicle speed, coolant temperature, air conditioning and/or power steering load, etc.), it adjusts the idle according to the demands of the engine and driver.

2004 and later models

These models are equipped with an electronic throttle control system, which consists of the throttle actuator, the throttle actuator control module, the throttle actuator control relay, two Throttle Position (TP) sensors, the Accelerator Pedal Position (APP) sensor and the Powertrain Control Module (PCM). The single-barrel, side-draft, cast aluminum electronic throttle body contains a throttle plate that regulates the amount of air entering the intake manifold. The throttle plate is opened and closed by the integral throttle actuator (electric motor). The PCM-controlled throttle actuator opens and closes the throttle plate in response to the position of the accelerator pedal. The position (angle) of the accelerator pedal is determined by the Accelerator Pedal Position (APP) sensor, which is located on the firewall. The accelerator pedal is connected to the APP sensor by an accelerator cable. On 2007 Acura models, there is no cable because the APP sensor is an integral component of the accelerator pedal assembly. The throttle body is also the location of two Throttle Position (TP) sensors. A TP sensor is a potentiometer that monitors the opening angle of the

throttle plate and sends a variable voltage signal to the Powertrain Control Module (PCM). Both TP sensors are integral components of the electronic throttle body and cannot be serviced separately. The lower part of the electronic throttle body is heated by engine coolant to prevent icing in cold weather.

A Manifold Absolute Pressure (MAP) sensor is located on top of the throttle body. The MAP sensor measures intake manifold pressure and vacuum and generates a variable voltage signal that's proportionate to the pressure or vacuum. The PCM uses this data to calculate the load on the engine. Another information sensor, the Intake Air Temperature (IAT) sensor, monitors the temperature of the air entering the engine and sends a signal to the PCM that varies in accordance with the temperature of the incoming air in the manifold. The PCM uses this data to calculate how rich or lean the air/fuel mixture should be. On 2003 and earlier models, the IAT sensor is located at the left rear corner of the intake manifold. On 2004 through 2006 models, the IAT sensor is located at the left end of the intake manifold, on the front side of the mounting flange for the throttle body, between the throttle body and the manifold. On 2007 and later models, the IAT sensor is located on the left end of the intake manifold, just ahead of the throttle body mounting flange.

All of the air induction components (resonator, air filter housing, air intake duct and throttle body) are covered in this Chapter, except for the intake manifold, which is covered in Chapter 2A, and the information sensors, which are covered in Chapter 6.

These models are also equipped with an electronic idle control system. When the engine is idling, the PCM controls the idle speed by opening and closing the throttle plate as necessary in response to inputs from several information sensors, including the Engine Coolant Temperature (ECT) sensor, the Intake Air Temperature (IAT) sensor, the Manifold Absolute Pressure (MAP) sensor, the Power Steering Pressure (PSP) switch and the air conditioning ON switch.

Electronic control system

For more information about the electronic control system (the PCM), its information sensors and output actuators, refer to Chapter 6.

Fuel delivery system

The fuel delivery system consists of the fuel pump, the fuel filter, the fuel pressure regulator the fuel rail and fuel injectors, and the lines and fittings that carry fuel between all of these components. Earlier models are also equipped with a fuel pulsation damper (see below).

Fuel pump/fuel level sending unit module

The fuel pump module is an in-tank design, and it can be removed from the top of the fuel tank without removing the tank.

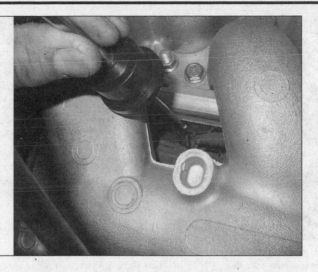

12.7 Use a stethoscope to listen to each injector; it should make a clicking sound that rises and falls with engine speed (2003 and earlier model shown; checking the middle injectors on 2004 and later models is difficult because the intake manifold obscures them)

Fuel is drawn through a sock (fuel pump inlet strainer) at the pump inlet, then pumped out the other end of the pump into an integral fuel filter (located in the same housing as the pump). After the pressurized fuel has been filtered, it's pumped through a supply line up to the fuel rail, which is located between the cylinder heads on the engine. The fuel pump module also includes a fuel level sending unit, which uses a float on the end of a float arm to operate a variable potentiometer, which sends a voltage signal to the PCM and to the fuel level gauge on the instrument cluster.

Fuel pressure regulator and pulsation damper - 2003 and earlier models

Right as the fuel reaches the fuel rail, it's pumped through a fuel pulsation damper, which is located at the connection for the fuel supply line. The pulsation damper attenuates the hydraulic and acoustic noise produced by the fuel pump when it's operating. A fuel pressure regulator, which is screwed into the fuel rail on 1999 models and screwed into the same junction block connection as the fuel supply line and the pulsation damper on 2000 through 2003 models, maintains the fuel pressure within the specified operating range.

Fuel pressure regulator - 2004 and later models

These models, which use a *returnless* fuel system, do not use a pulsation damper or a fuel return line. They have a pressure regulator, but it's an integral component of the fuel pump/fuel level sending unit module and is spring-loaded but not vacuum-controlled. When the fuel pressure rises beyond its normal operating range, the pressure regulator opens and fuel is diverted out of the fuel pump module and dumped directly back into the fuel tank.

Fuel rail and fuel injector assembly (all models)

The fuel rail assembly is simply of a pair of tubes that are bolted to the lower intake manifold alongside the inner wall of each cylinder head. The fuel rail houses the upper end of each fuel injector, and the lower end of each injector is inserted into the intake manifold. Each fuel injector is a solenoid-actuated, pintle-type design consisting of a solenoid, plunger, needle valve and housing. When the engine is running, there is always voltage on the hot side of each injector terminal. The PCM turns the injectors on and off by switching their ground paths on and off. When the ground path for an injector is closed by the PCM, current flows through the solenoid coil, the needle valve raises and pressurized fuel inside the injector housing squirts out the nozzle. The quantity of fuel injected each time an injector opens is determined by the pulse width, which is the interval of time during which the valve is open.

12 Programmed Fuel Injection (PGM-FI) system - check

Refer to illustration 12.7

Warning: *Gasoline is extremely flammable, so take extra precautions when you work on any part of the fuel system. See the* **Warning** *in Section 2.*

Note: *The following procedure is based on the assumption that the fuel pump is working and the fuel pressure is adequate (see Section 3).*

1 Check all electrical connectors that are related to the system. Check the ground wire connections for tightness. Loose connectors and poor grounds can cause many problems that resemble more serious malfunctions.

2 Verify that the battery is fully charged. The Powertrain Control Module (PCM), information sensors and output actuators (the fuel injectors are output actuators) depend on a stable voltage supply in order to meter fuel correctly.

3 Inspect the air filter element (see Chapter 1). A dirty or partially blocked filter will severely impede performance and economy.

4 Check all fuses related to the fuel system (see Chapter 12). If you find a blown fuse, replace it and see if it blows again. If it does, look for a wire shorted to ground in the circuit(s) protected by that fuse.

5 Check the air induction system between the throttle body and the intake manifold for air leaks, which will cause a lean air/fuel mixture ratio (when the mixture ratio becomes excessively lean, the engine will begin misfiring). Also inspect the condition of all vacuum hoses connected to the intake manifold and to the throttle body. A loose or broken vacuum hose will allow false (unmetered) air into the intake manifold. The Manifold Absolute Pressure (MAP) sensor and the PCM can compensate for some false air, but if it's excessive, especially at idle and during other high-intake-manifold-vacuum conditions, the engine will misfire.

6 Remove the air intake duct from the throttle body and look for dirt, carbon, varnish, or other residue in the throttle body, particularly around the throttle plate. If it's dirty, clean it with carburetor cleaner, a toothbrush and a clean shop towel.

7 With the engine running, place an automotive stethoscope against each injector, one at a time, and listen for a clicking sound that indicates operation **(see illustration)**. If you don't have a stethoscope, touch the tip of a long screwdriver against each injector and listen through the handle.

8 If you can hear the injectors operating, but the engine is misfiring, the electrical circuits are functioning correctly, but the injectors might be dirty or clogged. Try a commercial injector cleaning product (available at auto parts stores). If cleaning the injectors doesn't help, the injectors probably need to be cleaned professionally, or replaced.

9 If an injector is not operating (it makes no sound), disconnect the injector electrical connector and measure the resistance across the injector terminals with an ohmmeter. Compare your measurement with the resistance values of the other injectors. If the resistance of the non-operational injector is well outside the range of resistance of the other injectors, replace it.

10 If the injector is not operating, but the resistance reading is within the range of resistance of the other injectors, the PCM or the circuit between the PCM and the injector might be faulty.

13 Throttle body - removal and installation

Warning: *Wait until the engine is completely cool before beginning this procedure.*

1 Disconnect the cable from the negative battery terminal (see Chapter 5, Section 1).

2 Remove the air intake duct (see Section 9).

13.3 To detach the accelerator cable and cruise control cable bracket from the throttle body, remove these two screws (2003 and earlier models)

13.4 Disconnect the electrical connector from the Manifold Absolute Pressure (MAP) sensor (2003 and earlier models)

13.5 Disconnect the electrical connector from the Throttle Position (TP) sensor (2003 and earlier models)

cruise control cable from the throttle lever cam as described in Section 10.

4   Disconnect the electrical connector from the Manifold Absolute Pressure (MAP) sensor **(see illustration)**.

5   Disconnect the electrical connector from the Throttle Position (TP) sensor **(see illustration)**.

6   Clamp-off the coolant hoses to the bottom of the throttle body, then loosen and slide back the hose clamps and disconnect the hoses **(see illustration)**. Be prepared to soak up any coolant that spills out.

7   Disconnect the Evaporative Emissions (EVAP) purge valve hose from the throttle body **(see illustration)**.

8   Disconnect the electrical connector from the Idle Air Control (IAC) valve **(see illustration)**.

9   Remove the two bolts and two nuts that attach the throttle body to the intake manifold **(see illustration)** and remove the throttle body, the spacer and the two gaskets.

2003 and earlier models

Refer to illustrations 13.3, 13.4, 13.5, 13.6, 13.7, 13.8 and 13.9

3   Detach the cable bracket **(see illustration)** from the throttle body. **Note:** *By detaching the cable bracket from the throttle body, but leaving the accelerator and cruise control cables attached to the cable bracket, you won't disturb the adjustment of either cable.* Disconnect the accelerator cable and the

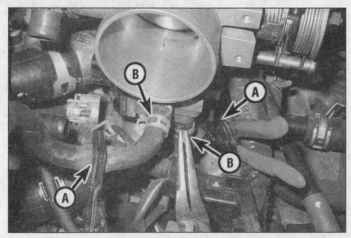

13.6 Pinch off the two coolant hoses connected to the throttle body, then loosen the hose clamps, slide them back and disconnect both coolant hoses from the throttle body (2003 and earlier models)

13.7 Loosen the hose clamp, slide it back and disconnect the Evaporative Emissions (EVAP) system purge valve hose from the throttle body (2003 and earlier models)

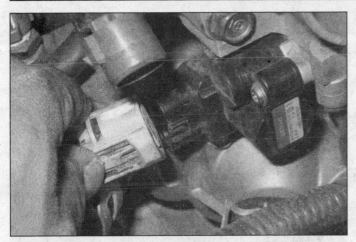

13.8 Disconnect the electrical connector from the Idle Air Control (IAC) valve, which is located underneath the throttle body (2003 and earlier models)

13.9 To detach the throttle body from the intake manifold, remove the two upper mounting nuts and the two lower mounting bolts (2003 and earlier models)

13.15 To disconnect the electrical connector from the MAP sensor, depress this release tab and pull off the connector (2004 and later models)

13.16 To disconnect the throttle body electrical connector, depress this release tab and pull off the connector (2004 and later models)

10   Remove all traces of old gasket material from the throttle body, the spacer and the intake manifold.

11   Installation is the reverse of removal. Be sure to use new gaskets and tighten the throttle body mounting bolts and nuts to the torque listed in this Chapter's Specifications.

12   Check the coolant level and add some, as necessary, to bring it to the appropriate level (see Chapter 1).

13   Check the accelerator cable adjustment and adjust it if necessary (see Section 10).

14   Reconnect the cable to the negative battery terminal (see Chapter 5, Section 1), then start the engine and check for air and coolant leaks.

2004 and later models

Refer to illustrations 13.15, 13.16, 13.17, 13.18 and 13.19

Warning: *Wait until the engine is completely cool before beginning this procedure.*

15   Disconnect the electrical connector from the MAP sensor **(see illustration)**.

16   Disconnect the throttle body electrical connector **(see illustration)**.

17   Clamp-off and disconnect the two coolant bypass hoses from the throttle body **(see illustration)**. Be prepared to soak up any coolant that spills out.

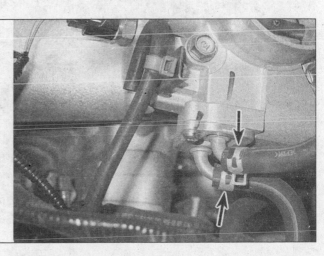

13.17 Pinch off the two coolant hoses connected to the throttle body, then loosen the hose clamps, slide them back and disconnect both coolant hoses from the throttle body (2004 and later models)

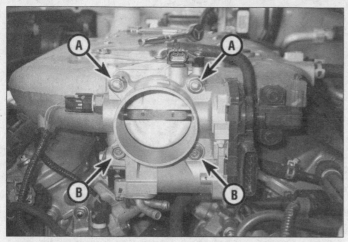

13.18   Remove the two nuts (A) and two bolts (B) securing the throttle body to the air intake plenum (2004 and later models)

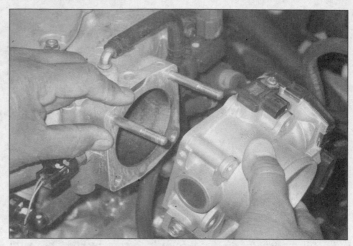

13.19   Remove the throttle body and its gasket (2004 and later models)

14.4   Remove this small black plastic ring from the fuel pulsation damper (2003 and earlier models)

18   Remove the two bolts and two nuts securing the throttle body to the air intake plenum **(see illustration)**.

19   Remove the throttle body and remove the throttle body gasket **(see illustration)**.

20   Installation is the reverse of removal. Be sure to tighten the throttle body mounting bolts and nuts to the torque listed in this Chapter's Specifications.

21   Check the coolant level and add some, as necessary, to bring it to the appropriate level (see Chapter 1).

14   Fuel pulsation damper (2003 and earlier models) - removal and installation

Refer to illustrations 14.4, 14.5a, 14.5b and 14.6

Warning: *Gasoline is extremely flammable, so take extra precautions when you work on*

any part of the fuel system. See the **Warning** *in Section 2.*

Note: *The pulsation damper is screwed into a junction block that's located at the left rear corner of the engine. The photos accompanying this Section depict the junction block on a 1999 model, which does not include the fuel pressure regulator. On 2000 through 2003 models, the fuel pressure regulator is screwed into the top of the junction block. However, the pulsation damper itself is the same unit on all models, so what you see here is typical.*

1   Relieve the fuel system pressure (see Section 2).

2   Disconnect the cable from the negative battery terminal (see Chapter 5, Section 1).

3   Remove the engine cover (see *Intake manifold - removal and installation* in Chapter 2A).

4   Remove the small black plastic ring from the fuel pulsation damper **(see illustration)**.

5   Remove the pulsation damper **(see illustrations)**.

14.5a   Using a back-up wrench on the fixed nut to protect the metal fuel line from kinking, loosen the fuel pulsation damper with another wrench . . .

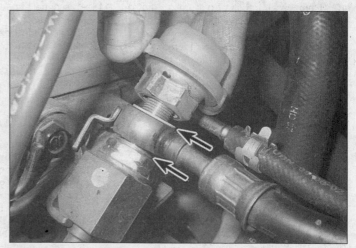

14.5b   . . . then remove the damper and discard the old sealing washers on each side of the banjo fitting (2003 and earlier models)

6   Use new sealing washers when installing the pulsation damper, and be sure to align the slot in the banjo fitting bracket with the locator pin on the junction block **(see illustration)**.

7   Tighten the fuel pulsation damper to the torque listed in this Chapter's Specifications.

8   Install the black plastic ring on the fixed nut. Make sure that the ridge on the inner bore of the ring is aligned with the notches in the nut.

9   Reconnect the cable to the negative battery terminal (see Chapter 5, Section 1).

10   Turn the ignition key to the On position and check for leaks around the pulsation damper.

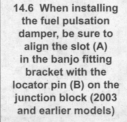
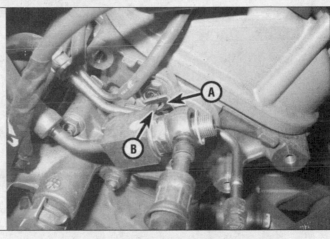

14.6 When installing the fuel pulsation damper, be sure to align the slot (A) in the banjo fitting bracket with the locator pin (B) on the junction block (2003 and earlier models)

15   Fuel pressure regulator - removal and installation

2003 and earlier models

Refer to illustrations 15.5, 15.6, 15.7a and 15.7b

Warning: *Gasoline is extremely flammable, so take extra precautions when you work on any part of the fuel system. See the* **Warning** *in Section 2.*

Note: *The photos accompanying this Section depict the fuel pressure regulator on a 1999 model, which is screwed into the fuel rail. On 2000 through 2003 models the regulator is screwed into the junction block at the left rear corner of the engine (the same junction block on which the pulsation damper is installed).*

1   Relieve the fuel system pressure (see Section 2).

2   Disconnect the cable from the negative battery terminal (see Chapter 5, Section 1).

3   On 1999 models, remove the intake manifold cover (see Chapter 2A). You can access the fuel pressure regulator without removing the cover on 2000 through 2003 models.

4   On 1999 models, remove the intake manifold (see Chapter 2A). You can access the fuel pressure regulator on 2000 through 2003 models without removing the intake manifold.

5   Disconnect the vacuum hose and the fuel return hose from the fuel pressure regulator **(see illustration)**. Before proceeding, note the orientation of the vacuum and fuel return hose pipes (make a sketch if necessary).

6   On 1999 models, remove the fuel pressure regulator from the fuel rail **(see illustration)**. On 2000 through 2003 models, remove the regulator from the junction block.

7   Be sure to use a new O-ring when installing the new pressure regulator. Even if you're planning to reinstall the *old* pressure regulator, be sure to remove and discard the old O-ring, then install a new O-ring and coat it with a little clean engine oil **(see illustrations)**.

8   When installing the fuel pressure regulator, be sure to orient it as it was before removal.

9   Installation is otherwise the reverse of removal. Be sure to tighten the fuel pressure regulator to the torque listed in this Chapter's Specifications.

10   When you're done, reconnect the cable to the negative battery terminal (see Chapter 5, Section 1), then turn the ignition key to the On position and check for fuel leaks around the fuel pressure regulator.

15.5 Disconnect the vacuum hose and fuel return hose from the fuel pressure regulator

15.6 To remove the fuel pressure regulator from the fuel rail, loosen the locknut with a wrench, then unscrew the regulator (1999 model shown)

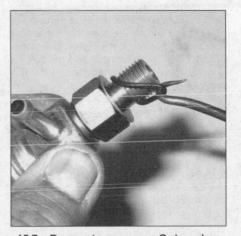

15.7a Be sure to use a new O-ring when installing the fuel pressure regulator; even if you're planning to reuse the old regulator, be sure to remove and discard the old O-ring and install a new one

15.7b Be sure to lubricate the new O-ring with a little clean engine oil before installing the fuel pressure regulator

16.6 To disconnect the electrical connector from a fuel injector, depress these two release tabs and pull off the connector

16.7a To disconnect the fuel supply hose from the front fuel rail on 2003 and earlier models, remove this nut

2004 and later models

11   The fuel pressure regulator is an integral component of the fuel pump/fuel level sending unit (see Section 6).

16   Fuel rail and injectors - removal and installation

1   Relieve the fuel system pressure (see Section 2).
2   Disconnect the cable from the negative battery terminal (see Chapter 5, Section 1).
3   Remove the engine or intake manifold cover (see Chapter 11).

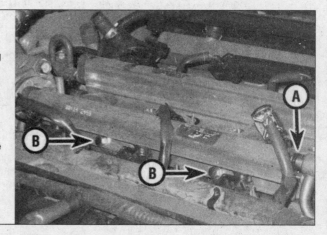

16.7b After disconnecting the fuel supply hose from the front fuel rail, replace this O-ring (A). To detach the fuel rail assembly, remove all four mounting bolts: two bolts on the front rail (B) and two more bolts (not shown) on the rear rail (2003 and earlier models)

2003 and earlier models

Removal

Refer to illustrations 16.6, 16.7a, 16.7b, 16.8, 16.9a, 16.9b and 16.9c

Warning: *Gasoline is extremely flammable, so take extra precautions when you work on any part of the fuel system. See the* **Warning** *in Section 2.*

4   Disconnect the vacuum hose from the fuel pressure regulator (see Section 15).
5   Remove the fuel pulsation damper (see Section 14) and disconnect the fuel supply line banjo fitting from the fuel rail (1999 models) or the junction block (2000 through 2003 models). Remove and discard the old fuel line banjo fitting sealing washers. Slide back the hose clamp and disconnect the fuel return hose from the fuel pressure regulator (see Section 15).
6   Disconnect the electrical connectors from the fuel injectors **(see illustration)**.
7   Disconnect the fuel supply hose from the front fuel rail **(see illustration)**, then remove and discard the old O-ring **(see illustration)**.

There's another similar hose that connects the right ends of the two fuel rails. This is the crossover hose. It's not necessary to disconnect the fuel crossover hose to remove the fuel rail and injectors. However, if the engine has a lot of miles on it, it's a good idea to disconnect the crossover hose and replace the O-rings where the hose connects to the fuel rails.

8   Remove the fuel rail mounting bolts **(see illustration 16.7b)**, then remove each fuel rail and its three injectors as a single assembly **(see illustration)**. If any of the injectors are difficult to extract from their bores, carefully pry them loose as shown.
9   Remove each injector from its bore in the fuel rail **(see illustration)**. Remove and discard the O-ring, the cushion ring and the seal rings **(see illustrations)**. Repeat this procedure for each injector. **Note:** *Even if you only removed the fuel rail assembly to replace a single injector or a leaking O-ring, it's a good idea to remove all of the injectors from the fuel rail and replace all of the O-rings at the same time.*

Installation

10   Install a new seal ring in each injector bore **(see illustration 16.9c)**. Apply a thin coat of clean engine oil to the inside of each seal ring.
11   Coat the new cushion rings and O-rings with clean engine oil and slide them into place on each of the fuel injectors.
12   Coat the outside surface of each O-ring and cushion ring with clean engine oil, then insert each injector into its corresponding bore in the fuel rail.
13   Install the injectors and fuel rail assembly on the intake manifold. Tighten the fuel rail mounting bolts securely.
14   The remainder of installation is the reverse of removal. Be sure to replace the O-ring on the fuel supply hose with a new one **(see illustration 16.7b)**.
15   When you're done reassembling everything, reconnect the cable to the negative battery terminal (see Chapter 5, Section 1). Turn the ignition switch to ON (but don't operate the starter). This activates the fuel pump for about two seconds, which builds up fuel pres-

16.8 To remove the fuel rails and the injectors, grasp each fuel rail firmly and pull up on the rails. If any of the injectors are difficult to extricate from their mounting bores in the intake manifold, carefully pry them out with a pair of angled needle-nose pliers (shown) or with some other suitable tool (2003 and earlier models)

16.9a To remove each injector from its bore in the fuel rail on 1999 through 2003 models, simply wiggle it from side to side and pull on it simultaneously (2003 and earlier models)

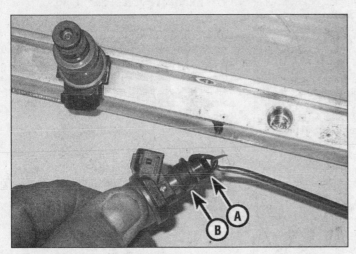

16.9b Carefully remove the O-ring (A) and the cushion ring (B) from the upper end of each injector and discard both of them. Whether you're installing the old injectors or new units, be sure to replace the O-ring and cushion ring on every injector (2003 and earlier models)

16.9c Carefully pry the seal ring from each of the six injector bores; be extremely careful not to damage the injector bores (2003 and earlier models)

sure in the fuel lines and the fuel rail. Repeat this step two or three times, then check the fuel lines, fuel rails and injectors for fuel leaks.

2004 and later models
Removal
Refer to illustrations 16.17, 16.18a, 16.18b, 16.19 and 16.20

16   Disconnect the electrical connectors from the fuel injectors (**see illustration 16.6**).
17   Disconnect the crossover hose from the front and rear fuel rails (**see illustration**) and set it aside.
18   Remove the four fuel rail mounting bolts

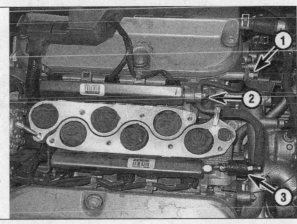

16.17 To disconnect the crossover hose from the fuel rail on 2004 and later models:

1   Remove the fuel supply line bracket mounting nut and pull the bracket off the stud on the rear cylinder head
2   Remove the nut from the stud on the rear fuel rail and pull off the fitting
3   Disconnect the quick-connect fitting from the front fuel rail (see Section 4)

16.18a To detach the fuel rail assembly from the intake manifold, remove the four mounting bolts: two on the front rail and two on the rear rail (2004 and later models)

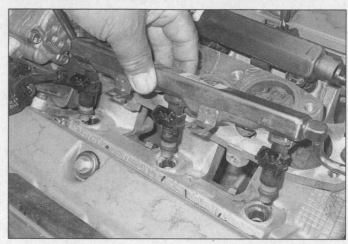

16.18b Remove each fuel rail and its three injectors as a single assembly (2004 and later models)

(see illustration), then remove each of the fuel rails and its three injectors as a single assembly (see illustration). If one of the injectors is difficult to extract from its bore in the intake manifold, carefully wriggle the fuel rail back and forth and side to side to work pry it loose.

19   To remove each injector from its bore in the fuel rail, remove the retainer, then carefully pull the injector straight out of the fuel rail (see illustration).

20   Remove and discard the upper and lower injector O-rings (see illustration). Repeat this procedure for each injector. **Note:** *Even if you only removed the fuel rail assembly to replace a single injector or a leaking O-ring, it's a good idea to remove all of the injectors from the fuel rail and replace all the O-rings at the same time.*

Installation

21   Coat the new upper and lower O-rings with clean engine oil and slide them into place on each of the fuel injectors.

22   Coat the outside surface of each upper and lower O-ring with clean engine oil, then insert each injector into its corresponding bore in the fuel rail. Install the injector retainers. Make sure that each retainer snaps into place.

23   Install the injectors and fuel rail assembly on the intake manifold. Tighten the fuel rail mounting bolts securely.

24   The remainder of installation is the reverse of removal. Be sure to replace the O-ring on the crossover hose fitting with a new one.

25   When you're done reassembling everything, reconnect the cable to the negative battery terminal (see Chapter 5, Section 1). Turn the ignition switch to ON (but don't operate the starter).This activates the fuel pump for about two seconds, which builds up fuel pressure in the fuel lines and the fuel rail. Repeat this step two or three times, then check the fuel lines, fuel rails and injectors for fuel leaks.

17 Exhaust system servicing - general information

Refer to illustrations 17.1a, 17.1b and 17.4
Warning: *Inspect and repair exhaust system components only after enough time has elapsed after driving the vehicle to allow the system components to cool completely. Also, when working under the vehicle, make sure it is securely supported on jackstands.*

1   The exhaust system consists of the exhaust manifolds, the catalytic converter(s), the muffler, the tailpipe and all connecting pipes, flanges and clamps. The exhaust system is isolated from the vehicle body and from chassis components by a series of rubber hangers (see illustrations). Periodically inspect these hangers for cracks or other signs of deterioration, replacing them as necessary.

16.19 To remove an injector from the fuel rail on a 2004 and later model, simply pull off the injector retainer with a pair of tweezers or small pliers, then carefully pull the injector straight out of its bore in the fuel rail

16.20 Remove and discard the upper and lower O-rings and replace them with new ones (2004 and later models)

17.1a Most exhaust system hangers look this one; to replace one of them, simply disengage it from the hooks

17.1b If the exhaust hanger is bolted to the underside of the vehicle, remove the mounting bolts to detach it

2   Conduct regular inspections of the exhaust system to keep it safe and quiet. Look for any damaged or bent parts, open seams, holes, loose connections, excessive corrosion or other defects which could allow exhaust fumes to enter the vehicle. Do not repair deteriorated exhaust system components; replace them with new parts.

3   If the exhaust system components are extremely corroded, or rusted together, you'll need welding equipment and a cutting torch to remove them. The convenient strategy at this point is to have a muffler repair shop remove the corroded sections with a cutting torch. If you want to save money by doing it yourself, but you don't have a welding outfit and cutting torch, simply cut off the old components with a hacksaw. If you have compressed air, there are special pneumatic cutting chisels (available from specialty tool manufacturers) that can also be used. If you decide to tackle the job at home, be sure to wear safety goggles to protect your eyes from metal chips and wear work gloves to protect your hands.

4   Here are some simple guidelines to follow when repairing the exhaust system:

a) *Work from the back to the front when removing exhaust system components.*

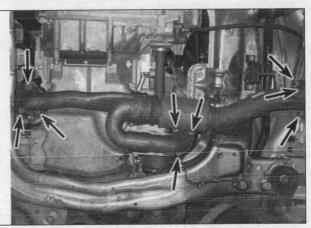

17.4 One place where the nuts and bolts are always in bad shape is at the flanges between the warm-up catalytic converters and the exhaust system (shown). Another spot where you'll find damaged fasteners further downstream is at the front and rear flanges for the under-floor catalytic converter

b) *Apply penetrating oil to the exhaust system component fasteners (see illustration) to make them easier to remove.*

c) *Use new gaskets, hangers and clamps when installing exhaust systems components.*

d) *Apply anti-seize compound to the threads of all exhaust system fasteners during reassembly.*

e) *Be sure to allow sufficient clearance between newly installed parts and all points on the underbody to avoid overheating the floor pan and possibly damaging the interior carpet and insulation. Pay particularly close attention to the catalytic converter and heat shield.*

Notes

Chapter 5
Engine electrical systems

Contents

Specifications

General

Battery voltage

Engine off .... 12 to 12.5 volts

Engine running .... 13.5 to 14.5 volts

Firing order 1-4-2-5-3-6

Torque specifications

	Ft-lbs	Nm
Starter motor mounting bolts		
Upper bolt	33	45
Lower bolt	47	64

1   General information, precautions and battery disconnection

The engine electrical systems include all ignition, charging and starting components. Because of their engine-related functions, these components are covered separately from body electrical devices such as the lights, the instruments, etc. (which you'll find in Chapter 12).

Precautions

Always observe the following precautions when working on the electrical system:

a) *Be extremely careful when servicing engine electrical components. They are easily damaged if checked, connected or handled improperly.*

b) *Never leave the ignition switched on for long periods of time when the engine is not running.*

c) *Never disconnect the battery cables while the engine is running.*

d) *Maintain correct polarity when connecting battery cables from another vehicle during jump starting - see the "Booster battery (jump) starting" Section at the front of this manual.*

e) *Always disconnect the cable from the negative battery terminal before working on the electrical system, but read the following battery disconnection procedure first.*

It's also a good idea to review the safety-related information regarding the engine electrical systems located in the "Safety first!" Section at the front of this manual, before beginning any operation included in this Chapter.

Battery disconnection

Some systems on the vehicle require battery power to be available at all times, either to maintain continuous operation (alarm system, power door locks, etc.), or to maintain control unit memory (radio station presets, Powertrain Control Module and other control units). When the battery is disconnected, the power that maintains these systems is cut. So, before you disconnect the battery, please note the following points to ensure that there are no unforeseen consequences of this action:

a) *The radio is equipped with an anti-theft system, so before disconnecting the battery, make sure that you have the correct anti-theft codes for the radio and, if equipped, for the navigation system. See your owner's manual for more information about the anti-theft codes.*

b) *When the battery is disconnected, the engine management system's Powertrain Control Module (PCM) will lose some data from its memory regarding the engine idle characteristics. It is imperative that you perform the PCM idle learn procedure (see procedure below) after disconnecting any of the components listed in the Sections below.*

c) *Remove the key from the ignition and keep it with you, so that it does not get locked inside in the event that the power door locks should engage accidentally when the battery is reconnected.*

Devices known as "memory-savers" can be used to avoid some of these problems. Precise details vary according to the device used. The typical memory saver is plugged into the cigarette lighter and is connected to a spare battery so that the vehicle battery can be disconnected from the electrical system. A memory saver will provide sufficient current to maintain audio unit anti-theft codes, PCM memory, etc. and will provide power to always-hot circuits such as the clock and radio memory circuits. **Warning 1:** *Some memory savers deliver a considerable amount of current in order to keep vehicle systems operational after the main battery is disconnected. If you're using a memory saver, make sure that the circuit concerned is actually open before servicing it.* **Warning 2:** *If you're going to work near any of the airbag system components, the battery MUST be disconnected and a memory saver must NOT be used. If a memory saver is used, power will be supplied to the airbag, which means that it could accidentally deploy and cause serious personal injury.*

To disconnect the battery for service procedures requiring power to be cut from the vehicle, loosen the cable clamp nut and disconnect the cable from the negative battery post. Isolate the cable end to prevent it from coming into accidental contact with the battery post.

Battery reconnection

After reconnecting the battery, you must:

a) *Enter the anti-theft code for the radio and navigation system (see your owner's manual)*

b) *Enter the radio station presets (see your owner's manual)*

c) *Reset the clock (see your owner's manual)*

d) *Reset the power window control unit*

e) *Perform all of the following procedures that apply to your vehicle.*

Powertrain Control Module (PCM) (2003 and earlier models only)

Caution: *Neither of the following procedures applies to the PCMs used on 2004 and later models. On those models you cannot do either of the following procedures at home because*

they can only be performed with special Acura diagnostic equipment.

Reset procedure

Turn the ignition switch to OFF, then remove the No. 13 CLOCK BACK-UP (7.5 amp) fuse from the passenger's under-dash fuse and relay box for 10 seconds. After resetting the PCM, perform the idle learn procedure as follows:

Idle learn procedure

1   Make sure that the PCM learns the engine idle characteristics after you do any of the following procedures:

a) *Disconnect the battery*

b) *Remove or reset the PCM (see above)*

c) *Remove or replace the driver's or passenger's under-dash fuse and relay box*

d) *Remove the BATTERY (120 amp) fuse from the under-dash fuse and relay box*

e) *Remove the BACK-UP, ACC (40 amp) fuse from the under-dash fuse and relay box*

f) *Remove the No. 13 CLOCK, BACK-UP (7.5 amp) fuse from the under-dash passenger's fuse and relay box*

g) *Remove the PGM-FI main relay*

h) *Disconnect the starter cable from its terminal on the engine compartment fuse and relay box*

i) *Disconnect the electrical connectors between the engine wiring harness and the left engine compartment wiring harness*

j) *Disconnect the electrical connectors between the two main dashboard wiring harnesses*

k) *Disconnect any of the main wiring harness grounds*

Note: *Erasing Diagnostic Trouble Codes (DTCs) does NOT require that you perform the idle learn procedure.*

2   Make sure that all electrical components (air conditioning system, lights, rear window defogger, sound system, etc.) are turned OFF.

3   Start the engine, bring it up to 3000 rpm and hold it there, with no load, in PARK or NEUTRAL, until the radiator fan comes on or until the engine coolant temperature reaches 194-degrees F (90 degrees C).

4   Allow the engine to idle for at least five minutes with the throttle fully closed and no load on the engine. **Note:** *If the radiator fan comes on during this five-minute period, don't include the time during which the fan runs as part of the five minutes.*

Resetting the power window control unit

2003 and earlier models

5   You must reset the power window control unit after you perform any of the following procedures:

a) *Disconnect the battery*

b) *Remove the No. 1 (20-amp) fuse from the driver's side under-dash fuse and relay box*

c) *Disconnect the 18-pin electrical connector from the power window control unit*

d) *Remove the window regulator, the window glass or the glass run channel*

6   Turn the ignition switch to OFF, then turn it to ON.

7   Remove the No. 1 (20-amp) fuse from the driver's side under-dash fuse and relay box.

8   Turn the ignition switch to ON for a few seconds, then turn it to OFF.

9   Reinstall the No. 1 (20-amp) fuse in the driver's under-dash fuse and relay box.

10   Turn the ignition switch to ON and verify that the driver's window does not work in AUTO.

11   Turn the ignition switch to ON and move the driver's window all the way down with the driver's switch.

12   Move the driver's window all the way up with the driver's switch.

13   When the window reaches the top, continue to depress the driver's switch for two seconds.

14   Verify that the window now works in AUTO.

15   If the window doesn't operate in AUTO, repeat this procedure.

2004 and later models

16   You must reset the power window control unit after you perform any of the following procedures:

a) *Remove or replace the power window regulator*

b) *Remove or replace the power window motor*

c) *Remove or replace the window run channel*

d) *Remove or replace the door glass*

e) *Remove power from the power window control unit while the power window timer is ON*

17   Turn the ignition switch to ON.

18   Move the driver's (or passenger's) window all the way down with the driver's (or passenger's) window DOWN switch.

19   Open the driver's (or passenger's) door. **Note:** *The next four steps must be performed within five seconds of each other.*

20   Turn the ignition switch to OFF.

21   Push and hold the driver's (or passenger's) window DOWN switch.

22   Turn the ignition switch to ON.

23   Release the driver's (or passenger's) window DOWN switch.

24   Repeat Steps 20 through 23 three more times. **Note:** *Don't forget that they must be performed within five seconds of each other.*

25   Wait one second.

26   Verify that AUTO UP and AUTO DOWN do *not* work. If AUTO UP and AUTO DOWN do work, go back to Step 17 and start over. If they don't work, proceed to the next Step.

27   Move the driver's (or passenger's) window all the way down with the driver's (or passenger's) window DOWN switch.

28   Pull up and hold the driver's (or passen-

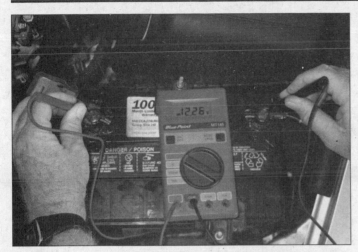

3.2 To test the open circuit voltage of the battery, touch the black probe of the voltmeter to the negative terminal and the red probe to the positive terminal of the battery; a fully charged battery should be about 12.6 volts

3.3 Some battery load testers are equipped with an ammeter that allows you to vary the amount of the load on the battery. Less expensive testers, like this one, only have a load switch that puts the battery under a fixed load

ger's) UP switch until the window reaches its fully closed position, then continue to hold the UP switch for one more second.

29   Verify that the power window control unit is correctly reset by using the driver's (or passenger's) window AUTO UP and AUTO DOWN switches.

30   If the window still does not work in AUTO, repeat this procedure several times. Make sure that you are completing Steps 20 through 23 within five seconds of each other.

31   If, after repeated attempts to reset the power window control unit, you are still unable to reset it, have it reset by a dealer service department.

2   Battery - emergency jump starting

Refer to the *Booster battery (jump) starting* procedure at the front of this manual.

3   Battery - check and replacement

Warning: *Always disconnect the cable from the negative battery terminal FIRST and hook it up LAST or the battery may be shorted by the tool being used to loosen the cable clamps.*

Check

Refer to illustrations 3.2 and 3.3

1   Remove the battery cover, disconnect the negative battery cable, then the positive cable from the battery.

2   First, check the battery state of charge by looking at the indicator window on the top of the battery and compare the color in the window to the label on the battery that explains the various colors. If the indicator window indi-

cates that the battery needs to be charged, do so before proceeding. Next perform an open voltage circuit test using a digital voltmeter. **Note:** *The battery's surface charge must be removed before accurate voltage measurements can be made. Turn on the high beams for ten seconds, then turn them off and let the vehicle stand for two minutes.* With the engine and all accessories Off, touch the negative probe of the voltmeter to the negative terminal of the battery and the positive probe to the positive terminal of the battery **(see illustration)**. The battery voltage should be 12.6 volts or slightly above. If the battery is less than the specified voltage, charge the battery before proceeding to the next test. Do not proceed with the battery load test unless the battery charge is correct.

3   Perform a battery load test. An accurate check of the battery condition can only be performed with a load tester (available at most auto parts stores). This test evaluates the ability of the battery to operate the starter and other accessories during periods of high current draw. Connect the load tester to the battery terminals **(see illustration)**. Load test the battery according to the tool manufac-

turer's instructions. Check to see that the battery voltage does not drop below 9.6 volts. If the battery condition is weak or defective, the tool will indicate this condition immediately. **Note:** *Cold temperatures will cause the minimum voltage reading to drop slightly. Follow the chart given in the manufacturer's instructions to compensate for cold climates. Minimum load voltage for freezing temperatures (32-degrees F) should be approximately 9.1 volts.*

Replacement

Refer to illustrations 3.5, 3.7, 3.8a, 3.8b and 3.9

4   Remove the left side engine compartment cover (see *Cowl and engine covers - removal and installation* in Chapter 11).

5   Disconnect the cable from the negative battery terminal first, then (and only then!) disconnect the cable from the positive battery terminal **(see illustration)**.

6   Remove the battery hold-down clamp nuts **(see illustration 3.5)** and remove the hold-down clamp.

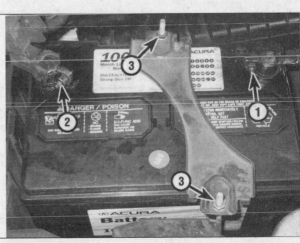

3.5 First, disconnect the cable from the negative terminal (1), then flip open the red plastic cover and disconnect the cable from the positive terminal (2). To remove the battery, unscrew the two hold-down clamp nuts (3) and remove the hold-down clamp

3.7 The battery is quite heavy and is mounted in a very tight space. The best way to protect yourself from injury when removing a battery is to use a special lifting strap like this one, available at most auto parts stores

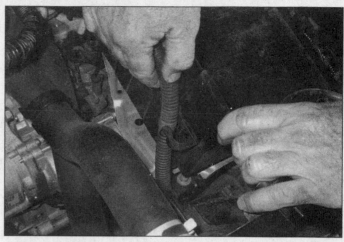

3.8a The plastic battery tray is not secured by any fasteners, but make sure that you detach any wiring harnesses before removing it

3.8b Once all harnesses are detached from the plastic battery tray, simply lift it out of the engine compartment

3.9 To remove the battery tray, remove these four bolts. Note any harnesses clipped or clamped to the battery tray mounting bolts and make sure that they're reattached when you install the tray

7   Lift out the battery (**see illustration**). Be careful - it's heavy. **Note:** *Battery straps and handlers are available at most auto parts stores for a reasonable price. They make it easier to remove and carry the battery.*

8   While the battery is out, remove the air intake duct cover, then remove the plastic battery box (**see illustrations**) and inspect it for corrosion. If there's corrosion on the plastic battery box, wash it with soap and water and rinse it off thoroughly.

9   While the plastic battery box is out, inspect the metal battery tray for corrosion. If there's corrosion on the battery tray, remove the tray's mounting bolts (**see illustration**) and remove the tray from the engine compartment. Clean the deposits from the metal to prevent the battery tray from further corrosion.

10   If you are replacing the battery, make sure you get one that's identical, with the same dimensions, amperage rating, cold cranking rating, etc.

11   Installation is the reverse of removal. Be sure to connect the positive cable first and the negative cable last (see Section 1).

4   Battery cables - check and replacement

Refer to illustrations 4.4a, 4.4b, 4.4c and 4.4d

1   Periodically inspect the entire length of each battery cable for damage, cracked or burned insulation and corrosion. Poor battery cable connections can cause starting problems and decreased engine performance.

2   Inspect the cable-to-terminal connections at the ends of the cables for cracks, loose wire strands and corrosion. The presence of white, fluffy deposits under the insulation at the cable terminal connection means that the cable is corroded and should be replaced. Also inspect the battery posts for distortion and corrosion. If they're corroded, clean them.

3   When removing the cables, always disconnect the cable from the negative battery terminal first and hook it up last, or you might accidentally short out the battery with the tool you're using to loosen the cable clamps. Even if you're only replacing the cable for the posi-

tive terminal, be sure to disconnect the negative cable from the battery first.

4   Disconnect the old cables from the battery, then trace each of them to their opposite ends and disconnect them (**see illustrations**). Be sure to note the routing of each cable before disconnecting it to ensure correct installation. There are battery positive cables at the engine compartment fuse and relay box, at the starter motor and at the alternator. There are many ground cables in the engine compartment; you'll find them on the walls of the engine compartment, on the engine block and even on the motor mount brackets. Raise the front of the vehicle and place it securely on jackstands, then use a flashlight to trace ground cables to their respective ground bolts.

5   If you are replacing any of the old cables, take them with you when buying new cables. It is vitally important that you replace the cables with identical parts.

4.4a The battery ground cable is bolted to the side of the engine compartment (battery removed for clarity)

4.4b To detach the positive cable from the starter B (battery) terminal, raise the vehicle and place it securely on jackstands, then peel back the rubber boot and remove this nut

6   Clean the threads of the solenoid or ground connection with a wire brush to remove rust and corrosion. Apply a light coat of battery terminal corrosion inhibitor or petroleum jelly to the threads to prevent future corrosion.

7   Attach the cable to the solenoid or ground connection and tighten the mounting nut/bolt securely.

8   Before connecting a new cable to the battery make sure that it reaches the battery post without having to be stretched.

9   Connect the cable to the positive battery terminal first, *then* connect the ground cables to the negative battery terminal (see Section 1).

5   Ignition system - general information

Warning: *Because of the high voltage generated by the ignition system, be extremely careful when performing any procedure involving ignition components.*

1   The electronic ignition system consists of the Powertrain Control Module (PCM), the ignition switch, the battery, the six ignition coils and the spark plugs.

2   The PCM alters ignition timing during warm-up, idle and warm running conditions. It controls ignition timing in accordance with the engine speed, the manifold absolute pressure and the engine coolant temperature. The PCM uses data from the Camshaft Position (Top Dead Center) [CMP (TDC)] sensors to determine ignition timing during start-ups, and anytime that the crank angle is abnormal. The PCM calculates engine speed based on the data that it receives from the Crankshaft Position (CKP) sensor. It uses a Manifold Absolute Pressure (MAP) sensor to determine manifold absolute pressure. For more information about the CMP (TDC), CKP and MAP sensors, refer to Chapter 6.

6   Ignition system - check

Refer to illustration 6.2

Warning: *Because of the high voltage generated by the ignition system, use extreme care when performing a procedure involving ignition components.*

1   If a malfunction occurs in the ignition system, check the following items first:

a) *Make sure that the cable clamps at the battery terminals are clean and tight.*

b) *Test the condition of the battery (see Section 3). If it doesn't pass all the tests, replace it.*

c) *Check the ignition coil connections.*

d) *Check any relevant fuses in the engine compartment fuse and relay box (see Chapter 12). If they're burned, determine the cause and repair the circuit.*

2   If the engine turns over but won't start, disconnect an ignition coil from a spark plug

4.4c To disconnect the battery positive cable harness from the engine compartment fuse and relay box, remove these two bolts

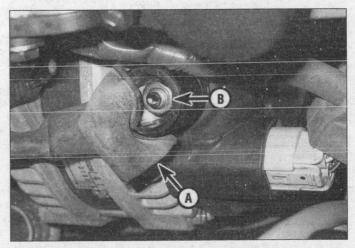

4.4d To disconnect the positive battery cable from the alternator, peel back the rubber boot (A) and remove this nut (B)

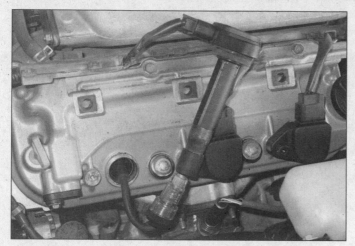

6.2 To use a spark tester, remove a coil and install the tester between the coil high-tension terminal and the spark plug, then crank the engine. If the coil is generating enough voltage to fire the plug, the tester will flash

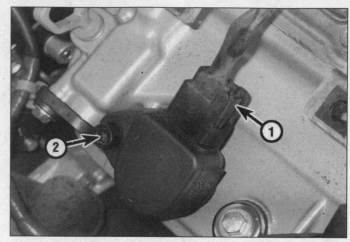

7.2 To disconnect the electrical connector from the ignition coil, depress the release tab (1) and pull off the connector. To detach an ignition coil from the valve cover, remove the coil retaining bolt (2)

(see Section 7), reconnect the electrical connector to the coil, then attach a spark tester between the ignition coil high-tension terminal and the spark plug (see illustration). Spark testers are available at most auto parts stores. Crank the engine and note whether or not the tester flashes.

3   If the tester flashes during cranking, the coil is delivering sufficient voltage to the spark plug to fire it. Repeat this test for each cylinder to verify that the other coils are OK.

4   If the tester doesn't flash, remove a coil from another cylinder and swap it for the one being tested. If the tester now flashes, you know that the original coil is bad. If the tester still doesn't flash, the PCM or wiring harness is probably defective. Have the PCM checked out by a dealer service department or other qualified repair shop (testing the PCM is beyond the scope of the do-it-yourselfer because it requires expensive special tools).

5   If the tester flashes during cranking but a misfire code (related to the cylinder being tested) has been stored, the spark plug could be fouled or defective.

7   Ignition coils - replacement

Refer to illustration 7.2

1   Remove the engine cover (see *Cowl and engine covers - removal and installation* in Chapter 11). On 2004 and later models, remove the right engine compartment cover, the left rear engine compartment cover and the right rear engine compartment cover.

2   Disconnect the electrical connector from the ignition coil (see illustration).

3   Remove the ignition coil mounting bolt (see illustration 7.2).

4   Grasp the coil firmly and pull it straight up to disengage it from the spark plug.

5   Installation is the reverse of removal.

8   Charging system - general information and precautions

The charging system includes the alternator (with an integral voltage regulator), a charge indicator light on the dash, the battery, an Electrical Load Detector (ELD), a 120-amp fuse and the wiring connecting all of these components. The charging system supplies electrical power for the ignition system, the lights, the radio, etc. The alternator is driven by a drivebelt at the one end of the engine. The alternator's voltage output is controlled by a conventional internal voltage regulator, which keeps charging output within a range of about 13.5 to 14.5 volts. The ELD, which is located in the engine compartment fuse and relay box, sends a variable voltage signal to the Powertrain Control Module (PCM) that varies in accordance with the total power demand imposed on the charging system by the electrical devices and systems in operation. The PCM uses this variable voltage signal to calculate the actual level of charging voltage needed and alters the charging voltage output accordingly.

The charging system doesn't ordinarily require periodic maintenance. However, the accessory drivebelt, battery and wires and connections should be inspected at the intervals outlined in Chapter 1.

The dashboard warning light should come on when the ignition key is turned to ON, but it should go off immediately after the engine is started. If it remains on, there is a malfunction in the charging system (see Section 9).

Be very careful when making electrical circuit connections to a vehicle equipped with an alternator and note the following:

a) *When reconnecting wires to the alternator from the battery, be sure to note the polarity.*

b) *Before using arc-welding equipment to repair any part of the vehicle, disconnect the wires from the alternator and the battery terminals.*

c) *Never start the engine with a battery charger connected.*

d) *Always disconnect both battery leads before using a battery charger.*

e) *The alternator is turned by an engine drivebelt that could cause serious injury if your hands, hair or clothes become entangled in it with the engine running.*

f) *Because the alternator is connected directly to the battery, it could arc or cause a fire if overloaded or shorted out.*

g) *Wrap a plastic bag over the alternator and secure it with rubber bands before steam cleaning the engine.*

9   Charging system - check

Refer to illustration 9.3

1   If a malfunction occurs in the charging circuit, do not immediately assume that the alternator is causing the problem. First, check the following items:

a) *Make sure the battery cable clamps, where they connect to the battery, are clean and tight.*

b) *Test the condition of the battery (see Section 3). If it does not pass all the tests, replace it with a new battery.*

c) *Check the external alternator wiring and connections.*

d) *Check the drivebelt condition and tension (see Chapter 1).*

e) *Check the alternator mounting bolts for tightness.*

f) *Run the engine and check the alternator for abnormal noise.*

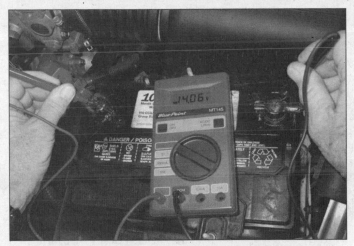

9.3 To check charging voltage, hook up a multimeter to the battery terminals and note the indicated voltage with the engine running (it should be 13.8 to 14.8 volts)

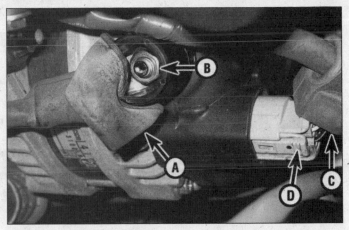

10.5 Peel back the rubber boot (A), remove the nut (B) from the B+ stud-type terminal and disconnect the output cable from the alternator, then peel back the other rubber weather boot (C), depress the release tab (D) and disconnect the electrical connector

g) *Check the 120-amp fuse in the engine compartment fuse and relay box (see Chapter 12). If it's burned, determine the cause and repair the circuit.*

h) *Check the charge light on the dash. It should illuminate when the ignition key is turned ON (engine not running). If it doesn't come on, disconnect the electrical connector and the ground wire from the alternator. The charge light should now come on (because by opening the charging circuit, you have eliminated all charging voltage). If the light still doesn't illuminate, check the fuse for the charging light circuit, in the left (driver's side) under-dash fuse and relay box. If the fuse is blown, troubleshoot and repair the charge light circuit, then replace the fuse. If the charge light still doesn't come on, check the bulb (see Chapter 12). If it's blown, replace it.*

i) *Make sure that the PCM hasn't stored any diagnostic trouble codes for the Electrical Load Detector (ELD) system (see Chapter 6 for more information about the ELD).*

2   With the ignition key turned to the OFF position, check battery voltage with all electrical accessories (blower fan, radio, cigarette lighter, cooling fan, etc.) turned off. It should be about 12.5 volts (it might be slightly higher if the engine has been turned off for less than an hour).

3   Check the charging voltage with the engine running. Start the engine, raise the engine rpm to 1500 and check the battery voltage again. It should now be approximately 13.8 to 14.8 volts **(see illustration)**.

4   Load the battery and observe the charging voltage. Turn on the high beam headlights, the A/C blower on HIGH, the windshield wipers and the radio. The voltage should drop and come back up as each accessory is selected. If the charging system is working properly the voltage should stay above 13.5 volts. If the voltage drops below 13 volts, the charging system is defective.

5   Lower the engine rpm back to idle and observe the charging voltage. The charging voltage should not drop below 13 volts with the decrease in engine rpm. Apply the brakes and observe the charging voltage at idle. It

should remain above 13 volts.

6   Turn off all the electrical loads (high beam headlights, the A/C blower on HIGH, the windshield wipers and the radio), run the engine at 1600 rpm and watch the charging voltage rise. It should not rise above 15 volts.

7   If the charging voltage does not exhibit distinct changes when engine rpm increases and accessory loads are added, the voltage regulator is defective. If the charging voltages are low and the drivebelts and battery are all in good condition, the alternator is defective. In this situation, replace the alternator and voltage regulator as a single unit.

10 Alternator - removal and installation

Refer to illustrations 10.5, 10.6 and 10.7

1   Disconnect the cable from the negative battery terminal (see Section 1).

2   Remove the intake manifold cover or engine cover (see *Cowl and engine covers - removal and installation* in Chapter 11).

3   Remove the drivebelt (see Chapter 1).

4   On 2004 and later models, disconnect the electrical connectors from the air conditioning condenser fan motor and from the air conditioning compressor clutch and remove the coolant reservoir. Remove the air conditioning condenser fan shroud assembly (see Chapter 3).

5   Remove the nut and disconnect the battery cable from the B+ terminal, then disconnect the four-pin electrical connector **(see illustration)**.

6   On 2004 and later models, the electrical harness is clamped to the alternator. Detach the harness from the small mounting bracket on the alternator and set the harness aside, then remove the bolt that secures the harness bracket to the alternator **(see illustration)** and set the harness aside.

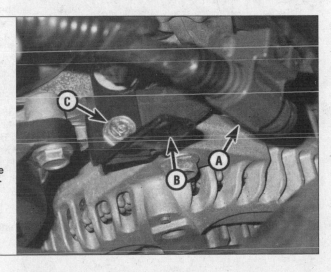

10.6 On 2004 and later models, detach the harness (A) from the bracket (B) on top of the alternator, then remove the bracket retaining bolt (C) and remove the bracket (you can leave the bracket on, but it's easier to remove the alternator with the bracket off)

10.7 Alternator upper (A) and lower (B) mounting bolts (2004 and later model shown, other models similar)

12.3 To use an inductive ammeter, simply hold the ammeter over the positive or negative battery cable (whichever cable has better clearance)

7   Remove the upper and lower alternator mounting bolts **(see illustration)** and remove the alternator.

8   If you're replacing the alternator, take the old one with you when purchasing the replacement unit. Make sure that the new/rebuilt unit looks identical to the old alternator. Look at the electrical terminals on the backside of the alternator. They should be the same in number, size and location as the terminals on the old alternator.

9   Many new/rebuilt alternators DO NOT have a pulley installed, so you might have to swap the pulley from the old unit to the new/rebuilt one. When buying an alternator, find out the store's policy regarding pulley swaps. Some stores perform this service free of charge. If your local auto parts store doesn't offer this service, you'll have to purchase a puller for removing the pulley and do it yourself.

10   Installation is the reverse of removal. Be sure to tighten the alternator mounting bolts securely. When you're done, reconnect the cable to the negative terminal of the battery (see Section 1). Check the charging voltage (see Section 9) to verify that the alternator is operating correctly.

11   Starting system - general information and precautions

The starting system consists of the battery, the starter motor, the starter solenoid and the wires connecting them. The solenoid is mounted directly on the starter motor. The solenoid/starter motor assembly is installed on the front of the transaxle bellhousing.

When the ignition key is turned to the START position, the starter solenoid is actuated through the starter control circuit. The starter solenoid then connects the battery to the starter. The battery supplies the electrical energy to the starter motor, which does the actual work of cranking the engine.

The starter can only be operated when the shift lever is in the PARK or NEUTRAL position.

Always observe the following precautions when working on the starting system:

a) *Excessive cranking of the starter motor can overheat it and cause serious damage. Never operate the starter motor for more than 15 seconds at a time without pausing to allow it to cool for at least two minutes.*

b) *The starter is connected directly to the battery and could arc or cause a fire if mishandled, overloaded or shorted out.*

c) *Always detach the cable from the negative terminal of the battery before working on the starting system.*

12   Starter motor and circuit - check

Refer to illustrations 12.3 and 12.4

1   If a malfunction occurs in the starting circuit, do not immediately assume that the starter is causing the problem. First, check the following items:

a) *Make sure the battery cable clamps, where they connect to the battery, are clean and tight.*

b) *Check the condition of the battery cables (see Section 4). Replace any defective battery cables.*

c) *Test the condition of the battery (see Section 3). If it does not pass all the tests, replace it with a new battery.*

d) *Check the starter solenoid wiring and connections. Refer to the wiring diagrams at the end of Chapter 12.*

e) *Check the starter mounting bolts for tightness.*

f) *Check the fuses in the engine compartment fuse and relay box (see Chapter 12). If they're burned, determine the cause and repair the circuit.*

g) *Check the operation of the gear position switch (automatic transaxle) or clutch start circuit (manual transaxle). Make sure the shift lever is in PARK or NEUTRAL (automatic transaxle) or the clutch pedal is pressed (manual transaxle).*

h) *Check the operation of the starter cut relay. The starter cut relay is located in*

the fuse/relay box under the dash on the driver's side. Refer to Chapter 12 for the testing procedure.

2   If the starter does not activate when the ignition switch is turned to the start position, check for battery voltage to the solenoid. This will determine if the solenoid is receiving the correct voltage signal from the ignition switch. Connect a voltmeter to the starter solenoid S terminal, then note the indicated voltage when an assistant turns the ignition switch to the START position. It should be about the same as battery voltage. If there's no voltage at the S terminal, refer to the wiring diagrams at the end of Chapter 12 and check the starting system fuses. Also check the starter cut relay for correct operation. Refer to Chapter 12 for help with testing relays. If voltage is available but the starter motor doesn't engage and spin the driveplate ring gear, remove the starter from the engine (see Section 13) and bench test the starter (see Step 4).

3   If the starter turns over slowly, check the starter cranking voltage and the current draw from the battery. This test must be performed with the starter assembly on the engine. Crank the engine over (for 10 seconds or less) and observe the battery voltage. It should not drop below 8.5 volts. Also, observe the current draw using an ammeter **(see illustration)**. It should not exceed 380 amps. If the starter motor exceeds these values, replace it. Several conditions might affect the starter's cranking power. The battery must be in good condition and the battery cold-cranking rating must not be under-rated for the application. Be sure to check the battery specifications carefully. The battery terminals and cables must be clean and not corroded. Also, in cases of extremely cold temperatures, make sure the battery and/or engine block is warmed before performing the tests.

4   If the starter is receiving voltage but does not activate, remove and check the starter/solenoid assembly on the bench. Most likely the solenoid is defective. In some rare cases,

the engine may be seized, so be sure to try and rotate the crankshaft pulley (see Chapter 2A) before proceeding. With the starter/solenoid assembly mounted in a vise on the workbench, connect one jumper cable from the negative terminal (-) to the body of the starter **(see illustration)**. Install another jumper cable from the positive terminal (+) on the battery to the B+ terminal on the starter. Install a starter switch and apply battery voltage to the solenoid S terminal (for 10 seconds or less) and observe the solenoid plunger, shift lever and overrunning clutch extend and rotate the pinion drive. If the pinion drive extends but does not rotate, the solenoid is operating but the starter motor is defective. If there is no movement but the solenoid clicks, the solenoid and/or the starter motor is defective. If the solenoid plunger extends and rotates the pinion drive, the starter/solenoid assembly is working properly.

13 Starter motor - removal and installation

Refer to illustrations 13.4, 13.5a and 13.5b

1 Disconnect the cable from the negative terminal of the battery (see Section 1).

2 On 2004 and later models, remove the battery and the battery tray (see Section 3).

3 On 1999 through 2001 models, detach the automatic transmission fluid cooler hose from the clamp on the starter motor. On 2004 and later models, detach the harness clamp from the starter motor.

4 Disconnect the cable and wire from the terminals on the starter solenoid **(see illustration)**.

5 Unscrew the starter motor mounting bolts **(see illustrations)** and remove the starter.

6 Installation is the reverse of removal. Be sure to tighten the starter mounting bolts to the torque listed in this Chapter's Specifications, then reconnect the cable to the negative terminal of the battery (see Section 1).

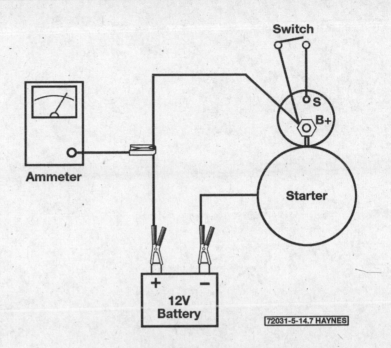

12.4 Starter motor bench testing details

13.4 Peel back the rubber boot (1) and pull off the electrical connector (2) from the solenoid S terminal, then peel back the other rubber boot (3) and remove the nut (4) from the B+ terminal

13.5a To detach the starter motor, remove the upper starter mounting bolt . . .

13.5b . . . and the lower starter mounting bolt

Notes

Chapter 6
Emissions and engine control systems

Contents

Specifications

IMRC cable adjustment (2003 and earlier models) .... 1/8 +/- 1/16-inch (3 +/- 1.5 mm)

Torque specifications

	Ft-lbs (unless otherwise noted)	Nm
Note: One foot-pound (ft-lb) of torque is equivalent to 12 inch-pounds (in-lbs) of torque. Torque values below approximately 15 foot-pounds are expressed in inch-pounds, because most foot-pound torque wrenches are not accurate at these smaller values.		
Engine Coolant Temperature (ECT) sensor	156 in-lbs	18
Intake Air Temperature (IAT) sensor	156 in-lbs	18
Knock sensor	23	31
Oxygen sensors	33	44
Transmission Range (TR) switch control shaft locknut (2007 on)	104 in-lbs	12

1 General information

Refer to illustration 1.4

To prevent pollution of the atmosphere from incompletely burned and evaporating gases, and to maintain good driveability and fuel economy, a number of emission control systems are incorporated. They include the:

Catalytic converter
Electrical Load Detector (ELD)
Evaporative Emissions Control (EVAP) system
Exhaust Gas Recirculation (EGR) system
On-Board Diagnostic-II (OBD-II) system
Positive Crankcase Ventilation (PCV) system
Programmed Fuel Injection (PGM-FI) system (electronic engine control system)
Variable Cylinder Management (VCM) system (2WD models)
Variable Valve Timing and Lift Electronic Control (VTEC) system (AWD models)

This Chapter includes general descriptions of these any other emissions-related devices and component replacement procedures (when possible) for each of the systems listed above. Before assuming that an emissions control system is malfunctioning, check the fuel and ignition systems carefully. The diagnosis of some emission control devices requires specialized tools, equipment and

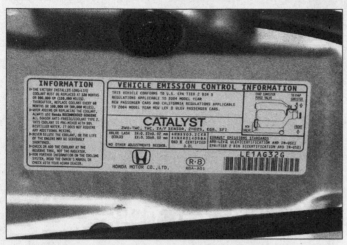

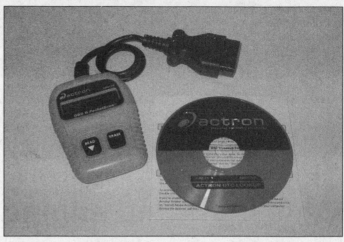

1.4 The Vehicle Emission Control Information (VECI) label is located in the engine compartment; the VECI label specifies the emission-control systems on your vehicle, and includes important tune-up specifications and a vacuum hose routing diagram

2.1 Simple code readers are an economical way to extract trouble codes when the CHECK ENGINE light comes on

training. If a procedure is beyond your ability, consult a dealer service department or other repair shop. Remember, the most frequent cause of emissions problems is simply a loose or broken wire or vacuum hose, so always check all hose and wiring connections first. **Note:** *Because of a federally mandated extended warranty which covers the emissions control system components, check with your dealer about warranty coverage before working on any emissions-related systems. Once the warranty has expired, you may wish to perform some of the component checks and/or replacement procedures in this Chapter to save money.*

Pay close attention to any special precautions outlined in this Chapter. It should be noted that the illustrations of the various systems might not exactly match the system installed on your vehicle because of annual changes made by the manufacturer during production and because of running changes made during a model year.

A Vehicle Emissions Control Information (VECI) label is attached to the underside of the hood **(see illustration)**. This label specifies the important emissions systems on the vehicle and it provides certain specifications for tune-ups. Part of the VECI label, the Vacuum Hose Routing Diagram, provides a vacuum hose schematic with emissions components identified. If there's a discrepancy between the information in this manual and the information on the VECI label, defer to the information on the VECI label. It contains the most up-to-date information about your vehicle, and might reflect some running change made to the vehicle after the manual was published.

2   On Board Diagnosis (OBD) system and trouble codes

Scan tool information
Refer to illustrations 2.1 and 2.2

1   Hand-held scanners are handy for analyzing the engine management systems used on late-model vehicles. Because extracting the Diagnostic Trouble Codes (DTCs) from an engine management system is now the first step in troubleshooting many computer-controlled systems and components, even the most basic generic code readers are capable of accessing a computer's DTCs **(see illustration)**. More powerful scan tools can also perform many of the diagnostics once associated with expensive factory scan tools. If you're planning to obtain a generic scan tool for your vehicle, make sure that it's compatible with OBD-II systems.

2   With the advent of the Federally mandated emission control system known as On-Board Diagnostics-II (OBD-II), specially designed scanners were developed. Several tool manufacturers have released OBD-II scan tools for the home mechanic **(see illustration)**. **Note:** *An aftermarket generic scanner should work with any model covered by this manual. Before purchasing a generic scan tool, verify that it will work properly with the OBD-II system you want to scan. If necessary, of course, you can always have the codes extracted by a dealer service department or an independent repair shop with a professional scan tool. Some auto parts stores even provide this service.*

OBD system general description

3   All models are equipped with the second generation OBD-II system. This system consists of an on-board computer known as the Powertrain Control Module (PCM), and information sensors, which monitor various functions of the engine and send data to the PCM. This system incorporates a series of diagnostic monitors that detect and identify fuel injection and emissions control systems faults and store the information in the computer memory. This updated system also tests sensors and output actuators, diagnoses drive cycles, freezes data and clears codes.

4   This powerful diagnostic computer must be accessed using an OBD-II scan tool, or OBD-II code reader, plugged into the 16-pin

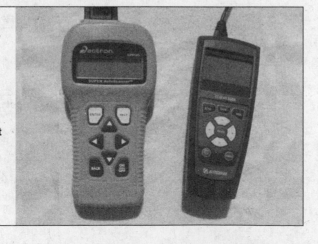

2.2 Scanners like these from Actron and AutoXray are powerful diagnostic aids - they can tell you just about anything that you want to know about your engine management system

Data Link Connector (DLC) located under the driver's dash area. The PCM is located below the center of the instrument panel, forward of the center console. The PCM is the brain of the electronically controlled fuel and emissions system. It receives data from a number of sensors and other electronic components (switches, relays, etc.). Based on the information it receives, the PCM generates output signals to control various relays, solenoids (fuel injectors) and other actuators. The PCM is specifically calibrated to optimize the emissions, fuel economy and driveability of the vehicle.

5   It isn't a good idea to attempt diagnosis or replacement of the PCM or emission control components at home while the vehicle is under warranty. Because of a federally mandated extended warranty that covers the emissions system components and because any owner-induced damage to the PCM, sensors and/or control devices might void this warranty, take the vehicle to a dealer service department if the PCM or a system component malfunctions.

Information sensors

6   **Accelerator Pedal Position (APP) sensor** - The APP sensor, which is part of the Electronic Throttle Control (ETC) system on 2004 and later models, is located on the firewall. These models use an electronic throttle body; there is no conventional accelerator cable between the accelerator pedal and the throttle plate inside the throttle body. There is, however, a throttle cable that connects the accelerator pedal to the APP sensor. The throttle plate inside the throttle body is electronically controlled by the PCM. The APP sensor is a potentiometer that receives a constant voltage input from the PCM and sends back a voltage signal that varies in relation to the position (angle) of the accelerator pedal. As you press the accelerator pedal, the APP sensor alters its voltage signal to the PCM in proportion to the angle of the pedal, and the PCM commands a motor inside the throttle body to open or close the throttle plate accordingly.

7   **Camshaft Position (CMP) sensor** - The CMP sensor produces a signal that the PCM uses to identify the number 1 cylinder and to time the firing sequence of the fuel injectors. On 1999 through 2003 models, there are two CMP sensors, one for the intake camshaft and one for the exhaust cam; on 2004 and later models, there is only one CMP sensor.

8   **Crankshaft Position (CKP) sensor** - The CKP sensor produces a signal that the PCM uses to determine the position of the crankshaft. The CKP sensor is located on the right (timing belt) end of the engine, down near the crankshaft timing belt sprocket.

9   **Electrical Load Detector (ELD)** - The ELD monitors the electrical load on the system and keeps the PCM informed. The PCM controls the voltage output of the alternator in response to the data conveyed by this signal.

The ELD is located inside the engine compartment fuse and relay box.

10   **Engine Coolant Temperature (ECT) sensor** - The ECT sensor is a thermistor (temperature-sensitive variable resistor) that sends a voltage signal to the PCM, which uses this data to determine the temperature of the engine coolant. The ECT sensor helps the PCM control the air/fuel mixture ratio and ignition timing, and it also helps the PCM determine when to turn the Exhaust Gas Recirculation (EGR) system on and off. The ECT sensor is located at the left end of the engine, below the throttle body, on the casting that carries coolant between the left ends of the cylinder heads. On 2007 and later models, an additional ECT sensor (ECT sensor 2) is located on the lower left rear side of the radiator.

11   **Fuel tank pressure sensor** - The fuel tank pressure sensor measures the fuel tank pressure when the PCM tests the EVAP system, and it's also used to control fuel tank pressure by signaling the EVAP system to purge the fuel tank vapors when the pressure becomes excessive. On 1999 through 2003 models, the fuel tank pressure sensor is located in front of the EVAP canister, and is integrated into the two-way valve/bypass solenoid valve/fuel tank pressure assembly. On 2004 and later models, the fuel tank pressure sensor is located on top of the EVAP canister.

12   **Fuel tank vapor control valve** - The fuel tank vapor control valve, which is used on 1999 through 2003 models, functions much like the fuel tank pressure sensor (see above). It is located on top of the fuel tank.

13   **Input shaft speed sensor** - The input shaft speed sensor is a magnetic pick-up coil located on the front of the transaxle.

14   **Intake Air Temperature (IAT) sensor** - The IAT sensor monitors the temperature of the air entering the engine and sends a signal to the PCM. On 1999 through 2003 models, the IAT sensor is located at the left rear corner of the intake manifold. On 2004 through 2006 models, the IAT sensor is located at the left end of the intake manifold, on the front side of the mounting flange for the throttle body, between the throttle body and the manifold. On 2007 and later models, the IAT sensor is located on the left end of the intake manifold, just ahead of the throttle body mounting flange.

15   **Knock sensor** - The knock sensor is a piezoelectric crystal that oscillates in proportion to engine vibration. (The term piezoelectric refers to the property of certain crystals that produce a proportional, repeatable voltage output when subjected to a certain level of mechanical stress.) The oscillation of the piezoelectric crystal produces a voltage output that is monitored by the PCM, which retards the ignition timing when the oscillation exceeds a certain threshold. When the engine is operating normally, the knock sensor oscillates consistently and its voltage signal is steady. When detonation occurs, engine vibration increases, and the oscillation of the knock sensor exceeds a design threshold.

(Detonation is an uncontrolled explosion, after the spark occurs at the spark plug, which spontaneously combusts the remaining air/fuel mixture, resulting in a pinging or slapping sound.) If allowed to continue, the engine could be damaged. The knock sensor is located below the intake manifold, in the valley between the cylinder heads, on top of the engine block. You have to remove the intake manifold to access the knock sensor.

16   **Manifold Absolute Pressure (MAP) sensor** - The MAP sensor, which is located on top of the throttle body, monitors the pressure or vacuum downstream from the throttle plate, inside the intake manifold. The MAP sensor measures intake manifold pressure and vacuum on the absolute scale - from zero instead of from sea-level atmospheric pressure (14.7 psi). The MAP sensor converts the absolute pressure into a variable voltage signal that changes with the pressure. The PCM uses this data to determine engine load so that it can alter the ignition advance and fuel enrichment.

17   **Output shaft speed sensor** - The output shaft speed sensor provides the Powertrain Control Module (PCM) with information about the rotational speed of the output shaft in the transmission. The PCM uses this information to control the torque converter and to calculate shift scheduling and the correct operating pressure for the transaxle.

18   **Oxygen sensors** - An oxygen sensor is a galvanic battery that generates a small variable voltage signal in proportion to the difference between the oxygen content in the exhaust stream and the oxygen content in the ambient air. The PCM uses the voltage signal from the upstream oxygen sensor to maintain a stoichiometric air/fuel ratio of 14.7:1 by constantly adjusting the on-time of the fuel injectors. On 1999 through 2003 models, there are two oxygen sensors: one upstream sensor (on the Y-pipe, ahead of the catalytic converter) and a downstream oxygen sensor (on the catalyst). On 2004 and later models, there is a warm-up catalytic converter for each cylinder head, so there are four oxygen sensors, one upstream and one downstream for each warm-up catalyst.

19   **Power Steering Pressure (PSP) switch** - The PSP switch monitors the pressure inside the power steering system. When the pressure exceeds a certain threshold at idle or during low speed maneuvers, the switch sends a voltage signal to the PCM, which raises the idle slightly to compensate for the extra load on the engine. The PSP switch is located on the power steering outlet (pressure) hose at the right end of the steering rack, right above the boot for the right tie-rod.

20   **Throttle Position (TP) sensor** - 1999 through 2003 models use a conventional, cable-actuated throttle body, which is equipped with a TP sensor. The TP sensor is a potentiometer that receives a constant voltage input from the PCM and sends back a voltage signal that varies in relation to the opening angle of the throttle plate inside the throttle body. This voltage signal tells the PCM

2.32 The Data Link Connector (DLC) is located under the lower left end of the dash

when the throttle is closed, half-open, wide open or anywhere in between. The PCM uses this data, along with information from other sensors, to calculate injector pulse width (the interval of time during which an injector solenoid is energized by the PCM). The TP sensor is located on the throttle body, on the end of the throttle plate shaft. If the TP sensor is defective on any of these models you must replace the throttle body. The TP sensor cannot be replaced separately.

21   **Transmission Range (TR) switch** - The TR switch is located at the manual lever on the left side of the transaxle. The TR switch functions like a conventional Park/Neutral Position (PNP) switch: it prevents the engine from starting in any gear other than Park or Neutral, and it closes the circuit for the back-up lights when the shift lever is moved to Reverse. The PCM also sends a voltage signal to the TR switch, which uses a series of step-down resistors that act as a voltage divider. The PCM monitors the voltage output signal from the switch, which corresponds to the position of the manual lever. Thus the PCM is able to determine the gear selected and is able to determine the correct pressure for the electronic pressure control system of the transaxle.

Powertrain Control Module (PCM)

22   The PCM is located inside the vehicle, under the instrument panel, at the forward end of the center console. The PCM is the brain of the engine management system. It receives information from all of the information sensors described above, processes all of this data, and issues commands to the output actuators. The PCM is a complex and expensive component, and new Acura PCMs must be programmed with a Honda Diagnostic Scan (HDS) tool before the car will run, so it's impossible to replace a PCM at home. If a Diagnostic Trouble Code (DTC) indicates a problem with the PCM (a very rare and unlikely occurrence), we recommend that you have the PCM serviced and, if necessary, replaced by an Acura dealer service department.

Output actuators

23   **EVAP canister purge valve** - The EVAP canister purge valve is normally closed, but when ordered to do so by the PCM, it allows the fuel vapors that are stored in the EVAP canister to be drawn into the intake manifold, where they're mixed with intake air, then burned along with the normal air/fuel mixture. The PCM-controlled purge valve also controls this vapor flow.

24   **EVAP canister vent shut valve** - The EVAP canister vent shut valve is located underneath the vehicle, on the EVAP canister. The canister vent shut valve is normally open, but it closes and seals off the EVAP system for inspection and maintenance tests and for OBD-II leak and pressure tests.

25   **Exhaust Gas Recirculation (EGR) valve** - When the engine is put under a load (hard acceleration, passing, going up a steep hill, pulling a trailer, etc.), combustion chamber temperature increases. When combustion chamber temperature exceeds 2500 degrees, excessive amounts of oxides of nitrogen (NOx) are produced. NOx is a precursor of photochemical smog. When combined with hydrocarbons (HC), other reactive organic compounds (ROCs) and sunlight, it forms ozone, nitrogen dioxide and nitrogen nitrate and other nasty stuff. The PCM-controlled EGR valve allows exhaust gases to be recirculated back to the intake manifold where they dilute the incoming air/fuel mixture, which lowers the combustion chamber temperature and decreases the amount of NOx produced during high-load conditions.

26   **Fuel injectors** - The fuel injectors, which spray a fine mist of fuel into the intake ports, where it is mixed with incoming air, are inductive coils under PCM control. For more information about the injectors, see Chapter 4.

27   **Idle Air Control (IAC) valve** - 1999 through 2003 models use a conventional, cable-operated throttle body, which is equipped with an Idle Air Control (IAC) valve. The IAC valve controls the amount of air allowed to bypass the throttle plate when the throttle plate is at its (nearly closed) idle position. The IAC valve is controlled by the PCM. When the engine is placed under an additional load at idle (high power steering pressure or running the air conditioning compres-

sor during low-speed maneuvers, for example), the engine can run roughly, stumble and even stall. To prevent this from happening, the PCM opens the IAC valve to increase the idle speed enough to overcome the extra load imposed on the engine. The IAC valve is mounted on the underside of the throttle body. On later models, the Powertrain Control Module and various information sensors such as the Power Steering Pressure (PSP) switch and the Brake Pedal Position (BPP) switch handle the idle function.

28   **Ignition coils** - The ignition coils are under the control of the Powertrain Control Module (PCM). There is no separate ignition control module. Instead, coil drivers inside the PCM turn the primary side of the coils on and off. The coils are located on top of the valve covers, directly above the spark plugs. For more information about the ignition coils, see Chapter 5.

29   **Two-way valve/bypass solenoid valve/ fuel tank pressure sensor** - On 1999 through 2003 models, the two-way valve, bypass solenoid and fuel tank pressure sensor are integrated into a single assembly that is located in front of the EVAP canister. The bypass solenoid valve opens (when commanded to do so by the PCM) to bypass the two-way valve when the PCM performs an EVAP system leak check.

Obtaining and clearing Diagnostic Trouble Codes (DTCs)

30   All models covered by this manual are equipped with on-board diagnostics. When the PCM recognizes a malfunction in a monitored emission control system, component or circuit, it turns on the Malfunction Indicator Light (MIL) on the dash. The PCM will continue to display the MIL until the problem is fixed and the Diagnostic Trouble Code (DTC) is cleared from the PCM's memory. You'll need a code reader or scan tool to access any DTCs stored in the PCM.

Accessing the DTCs

Refer to illustration 2.32

31   The Diagnostic Trouble Codes (DTCs) can only be accessed with a code reader or scan tool. Professional scan tools are expensive, but relatively inexpensive generic code readers and scan tools **(see illustrations 2.1 and 2.2)** are available at most auto parts stores.

32   Simply plug the connector of the tool into the diagnostic connector **(see illustration)**, which is located under the lower edge of the dash, to the left of the steering column. Then follow the instructions included with the tool to extract the DTCs.

33   Once you have extracted all of the stored DTCs, look them up on the accompanying DTC chart.

34   After troubleshooting the source of each DTC, make any necessary repairs or replace the defective component(s).

Clearing the DTCs

35   Clear the DTCs with the code reader or scan tool in accordance with the instructions provided by the tool's manufacturer.

Diagnostic Trouble Codes

36   The accompanying tables are a list of the Diagnostic Trouble Codes (DTCs) that can be accessed by a do-it-yourselfer working at home (there are many, many more DTCs available to professional mechanics with proprietary scan tools and software, but those codes cannot be accessed by a code reader or generic scan tool). If the problem persists after you have checked and repaired the connectors, wire harness and vacuum hoses (if applicable) for an emission-related system, component or circuit, have the vehicle checked by a dealer service department or other qualified repair shop.

OBD-II trouble codes

Note: *Not all trouble codes apply to all models.*

Code	Probable cause
P0107	Manifold Absolute Pressure (MAP) sensor circuit, low voltage
P0108	Manifold Absolute Pressure (MAP) sensor circuit, high voltage
P0111	Intake Air Temperature (IAT) sensor circuit, range or performance problem
P0112	Intake Air Temperature (IAT) sensor circuit, low voltage
P0113	Intake Air Temperature (IAT) sensor circuit, high voltage
P0116	Engine Coolant Temperature (ECT) sensor circuit, range or performance problem
P0117	Engine Coolant Temperature (ECT) sensor circuit, low voltage
P0118	Engine Coolant Temperature (ECT) sensor circuit, high voltage
P0122	Throttle Position (TP) sensor circuit, low voltage (2003 and earlier models)
P0122	Throttle Position (TP) sensor A circuit, low voltage (2004 and later models)
P0123	Throttle Position (TP) sensor circuit, high voltage (2003 and earlier models)
P0123	Throttle Position (TP) sensor A circuit, high voltage (2004 and later models)
P0125	Engine Coolant Temperature (ECT) sensor, malfunction or slow response (2006 and earlier models)
P0125	Engine Coolant Temperature (ECT) sensor 1, malfunction or slow response (2007 and later models)
P0128	Thermostat, range or performance problem (2003 and earlier models)
P0128	Cooling system malfunction (2004 and later models)
P0131	Upstream oxygen sensor circuit, low voltage
P0132	Upstream oxygen sensor circuit, high voltage
P0133	Upstream oxygen sensor circuit, slow response
P0133	Upstream oxygen sensor circuit (rear cylinder bank), slow response
P0134	Upstream oxygen sensor (rear cylinder bank), heater system malfunction

OBD-II trouble codes

Note: *Not all trouble codes apply to all models.*

Code	Probable cause
P0135	Upstream oxygen sensor circuit, heater circuit malfunction
P0135	Upstream oxygen sensor circuit (rear cylinder bank), heater circuit malfunction
P0137	Downstream oxygen sensor circuit, low voltage
P0137	Downstream oxygen sensor circuit (rear cylinder bank), low voltage
P0138	Downstream oxygen sensor circuit, high voltage
P0138	Downstream oxygen sensor circuit (rear cylinder bank), high voltage
P0139	Downstream oxygen sensor circuit, slow response
P0139	Downstream oxygen sensor circuit (rear cylinder bank), slow response
P0141	Downstream oxygen sensor, heater circuit malfunction
P0141	Downstream oxygen sensor (rear cylinder bank), heater circuit malfunction
P0153	Upstream oxygen sensor (front cylinder bank), slow response
P0154	Upstream oxygen sensor (front cylinder bank), heater system malfunction
P0155	Upstream oxygen sensor (front cylinder bank), heater circuit malfunction
P0157	Downstream oxygen sensor circuit (front cylinder bank), low voltage
P0158	Downstream oxygen sensor circuit (front cylinder bank), high voltage
P0159	Downstream oxygen sensor circuit (front cylinder bank), slow response
P0161	Downstream oxygen sensor circuit (front cylinder bank), heater circuit malfunction
P0171	Fuel system too lean
P0171	Fuel system too lean (rear cylinder bank)
P0172	Fuel system too rich
P0172	Fuel system too rich (rear cylinder bank)
P0174	Fuel system too lean (front cylinder bank)
P0175	Fuel system too rich (front cylinder bank)
P0222	Throttle Position (TP) sensor B circuit, low voltage (2004 and later models)
P0223	Throttle Position (TP) sensor B circuit, high voltage (2004 and later models)
P0300	Random misfire detected

Code	Probable cause
P0301	Cylinder no. 1 misfire detected
P0302	Cylinder no. 2 misfire detected
P0303	Cylinder no. 3 misfire detected
P0304	Cylinder no. 4 misfire detected
P0305	Cylinder No. 5 misfire detected
P0306	Cylinder No. 6 misfire detected
P0325	Knock sensor circuit malfunction
P0335	Crankshaft Position (CKP) sensor, no signal (2003 and earlier models)
P0335	Crankshaft Position (CKP) sensor A, no signal (2004 and later models)
P0336	Crankshaft Position (CKP) sensor, intermittent interruption (2003 and earlier models)
P0339	Crankshaft Position (CKP) sensor A, intermittent interruption (2004 and later models)
P0340	Camshaft Position (CMP) sensor, no signal
P0344	Camshaft Position (CMP) sensor, intermittent interruption
P0385	Crankshaft Position (CKP) sensor B, no signal
P0389	Crankshaft Position (CKP) sensor B, intermittent interruption
P0401	Exhaust Gas Recirculation (EGR) system, insufficient flow
P0404	Exhaust Gas Recirculation (EGR) control circuit, range or performance problem
P0406	Exhaust Gas Recirculation (EGR) valve position sensor circuit, high voltage
P0420	Catalyst system efficiency below threshold
P0420	Catalyst system efficiency below threshold (rear cylinder head)
P0430	Catalyst system efficiency below threshold (front cylinder head)
P0443	Evaporative Emission Control (EVAP) canister purge valve, circuit malfunction
P0451	Fuel Tank Pressure (FTP) sensor circuit, range or performance problem
P0452	Fuel Tank Pressure (FTP) sensor circuit, low voltage
P0453	Fuel Tank Pressure (FTP) sensor circuit, high voltage
P0455	Evaporative Emission Control (EVAP) system, very large leak detected
P0456	Evaporative Emission Control (EVAP) system, very small leak detected

OBD-II trouble codes

Note: *Not all trouble codes apply to all models.*

Code	Probable cause
P0457	Evaporative Emission Control (EVAP) system, leak detected/fuel cap loose or missing
P0461	Fuel level sensor (fuel gauge sending unit) circuit, range or performance problem
P0462	Fuel level sensor (fuel gauge sending unit) circuit, low voltage
P0463	Fuel level sensor (fuel gauge sending unit) circuit, high voltage
P0496	Evaporative Emission Control (EVAP), high purge flow
P0497	Evaporative Emission Control (EVAP), low purge flow
P0498	Evaporative Emission Control (EVAP) canister vent shut valve control circuit, low voltage
P0499	Evaporative Emission Control (EVAP) canister vent shut valve control circuit, high voltage
P0505	Idle control system malfunction
P0506	Idle control system, rpm lower than expected
P0507	Idle control system, rpm higher than expected
P0562	Charging system low voltage
P0563	Powertrain Control Module (PCM) power source circuit, unexpected voltage
P0602	Powertrain Control Module (PCM) programming error
P0603	Powertrain Control Module (PCM), Keep Alive Memory (KAM) error
P0615	Starter cut relay STRLD circuit malfunction
P0627	Fuel pump control module system malfunction
P062F	Powertrain Control Module (PCM) internal control module Keep Alive Memory (KAM) error
P0630	VIN not programmed or mismatch
P0685	Powertrain Control Module (PCM), internal circuit malfunction (power control circuit)

Automatic transaxle diagnostic trouble codes

Note: *Not all trouble codes apply to all models.*

Code	Probable cause
P0700	Automatic transmission control system malfunction
P0705	Transmission Range (TR) switch, multiple shift position input
P0706	Transmission Range (TR) switch, open circuit

Code	Probable cause
P0711	ATF temperature sensor, range or performance problem
P0712	ATF temperature sensor, short circuit
P0713	ATF temperature sensor, open circuit
P0715	Input shaft (mainshaft) speed sensor circuit malfunction (manual transaxle)
P0716	Input shaft (mainshaft) speed sensor, range or performance problem
P0717	Input shaft (mainshaft) speed sensor, no signal input
P0718	Input shaft (mainshaft) speed sensor, intermittent failure
P0720	Output shaft (countershaft) speed sensor circuit malfunction (manual transaxle)
P0721	Output shaft (countershaft) speed sensor, range or performance problem
P0722	Output shaft (countershaft) speed sensor, no signal input
P0723	Output shaft (countershaft) speed sensor, intermittent failure
P0730	Shift control system
P0731	1st gear, incorrect ratio
P0732	2nd gear, incorrect ratio
P0733	3rd gear, incorrect ratio
P0734	4th gear, incorrect ratio
P0735	5th gear, incorrect ratio
P0740	Lock-up control system
P0741	Torque converter clutch circuit, performance problem or stuck off
P0746	Automatic transaxle clutch pressure control solenoid valve A, stuck off
P0747	Automatic transaxle clutch pressure control solenoid valve A, stuck on
P0751	Shift solenoid valve A stuck off
P0752	Shift solenoid valve A stuck on
P0753	Shift control solenoid valve A
P0756	Shift solenoid valve B stuck off
P0757	Shift solenoid valve B stuck on
P0758	Shift control solenoid valve B

Automatic transaxle diagnostic trouble codes (continued)

Note: *Not all trouble codes apply to all models.*

Code	Probable cause
P0761	Shift solenoid valve C stuck off
P0762	Shift solenoid valve C stuck on
P0763	Shift control solenoid valve C
P0766	Shift solenoid valve D, stuck off
P0767	Shift solenoid valve D, stuck on
P0776	Automatic transaxle clutch pressure control solenoid valve B, stuck off
P0777	Automatic transaxle clutch pressure control solenoid valve B, stuck on
P0780	Shift control system
P0796	Automatic transaxle clutch pressure control solenoid valve C stuck off
P0797	Automatic transaxle clutch pressure control solenoid valve C stuck on
P0815	Transmission gear selection switch upshift switch, short or stuck on
P0816	Transmission gear selection switch downshift switch, short or stuck on
P0842	2nd clutch transmission fluid pressure switch, short or stuck on
P0843	2nd clutch transmission fluid pressure switch, open or stuck off
P0847	3rd clutch transmission fluid pressure switch, shorted or stuck on
P0848	3rd clutch transmission fluid pressure switch, open or stuck off
P0872	4th clutch transmission fluid pressure switch, shorted or stuck on
P0873	4th clutch transmission fluid pressure switch, open or stuck off
P0957	Transmission gear selection switch, shorted or stuck on
P0958	Transmission gear selection switch, shorted or stuck off
P0962	Automatic transaxle clutch pressure control solenoid valve A, open or short
P0963	Automatic transaxle clutch pressure control solenoid valve A
P0966	Automatic transaxle clutch pressure control solenoid valve B, open or short
P0967	Automatic transaxle clutch pressure control solenoid valve B
P0970	Automatic transaxle clutch pressure control solenoid valve C, open or short
P0971	Automatic transaxle clutch pressure control solenoid valve C

Code	Probable cause
P0973	Shift solenoid valve A, short
P0974	Shift solenoid valve A, open
P0976	Shift solenoid valve B, short
P0977	Shift solenoid valve B, open
P0979	Shift solenoid valve C, short
P0980	Shift solenoid valve C, open
P0982	Shift solenoid valve D, short
P0983	Shift solenoid valve D open

3   Accelerator Pedal Position (APP) sensor - replacement

Refer to illustrations 3.1, 3.4a and 3.4b

Note: *The APP sensor is located on the firewall, and is connected to the accelerator pedal by a cable.*

1   Disconnect the electrical connector from the APP sensor **(see illustration)**.
2   Remove the cover from the APP sensor **(see illustration 3.1)**.
3   Disconnect the accelerator cable from the APP sensor cam (see *Accelerator cable - removal, installation and adjustment* in Chapter 4).
4   Remove the APP sensor mounting bracket bolts **(see illustration)**, remove the sensor and bracket as a single assembly, then detach the sensor from the bracket **(see illustration)**.
5   Installation is the reverse of removal.

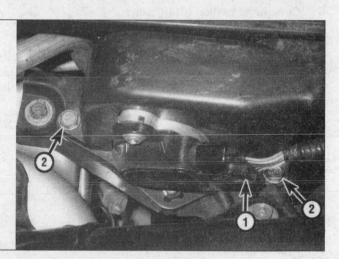

3.1 To disconnect the electrical connector from the APP sensor, depress the release tab (1). To detach the APP sensor cover, remove the two bolts (2) (2004 and later models)

After installing the APP sensor, be sure to check and, if necessary, adjust the accelera- tor cable (see *Accelerator cable - removal, installation and adjustment* in Chapter 4).

3.4a To detach the APP sensor mounting bracket, remove these two bolts

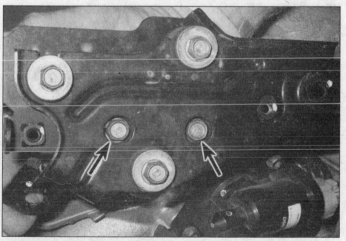

3.4b To detach the APP sensor from its mounting bracket, remove these two bolts

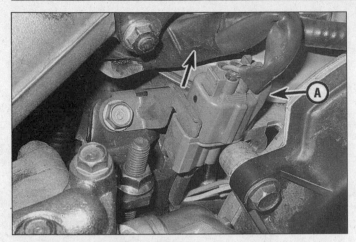

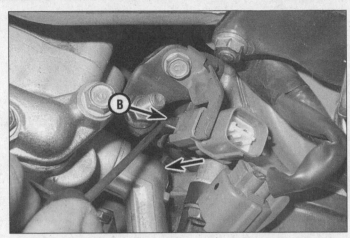

4.1a To disconnect the CMP (TDC) sensor electrical connector, depress the release button (A) and pull the upper half of the connector (the harness side) straight up . . .

4.1b . . . and to disengage the lower half of the connector (the sensor side) from its mounting bracket, depress the release button (B) and push the connector straight down (2001 and earlier models)

4   Camshaft Position (CMP) sensor - replacement

2001 and earlier models

Refer to illustrations 4.1a, 4.1b; 4.3 and 4.4

Note: *The CMP (TDC) sensors are located on the right (timing belt) end of the front cylinder head.*

1   Disconnect the CMP sensor electrical connector **(see illustrations)**.

2   Remove the timing belt cover and the timing belt, then remove the sprocket from the camshaft in the front cylinder head (see Chapter 2A).

3   Remove the rear timing belt cover mounting bolts **(see illustration)** and remove the cover.

4   Remove the CMP (TDC) sensor mounting bolts **(see illustration)** and remove the CMP (TDC) sensors.

5   Installation is the reverse of removal.

4.3 To detach the rear timing belt cover from the cylinder head, remove these two bolts (2001 and earlier models)

2002 and later models

Refer to illustrations 4.6, 4.8 and 4.9

Note: *The CMP sensor is located at the right (timing belt) end of the front cylinder head.*

6   Disconnect the electrical connector from the CMP sensor **(see illustration)**.

7   Remove the timing belt cover, the timing belt and the camshaft sprocket (see Chapter 2A).

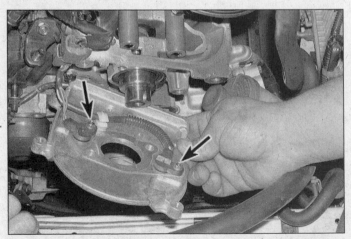

4.4 To detach the CMP (TDC) sensors from the rear timing belt cover, remove these mounting bolts (2001 and earlier models)

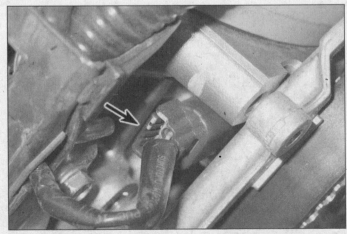

4.6 To disconnect the electrical connector from the CMP sensor, depress the release tab and pull off the connector (2002 and later models)

4.8 To detach the rear timing belt cover, remove these two bolts (2002 and later models)

4.9 To detach the CMP sensor from the rear timing belt cover, remove this mounting bolt (2002 and later Honda models)

5.2 The CKP sensor electrical connector is located behind the right end of the engine, above the timing belt tensioner (2003 and earlier models)

5.4 To detach the CKP sensor from the engine, remove this mounting bolt (2003 and earlier models)

8   Remove the rear timing belt cover mounting bolts **(see illustration)**, then remove the cover.
9   Remove the CMP sensor mounting bolt **(see illustration)** and remove the CMP sensor from the rear part of the timing belt cover.
10   Installation is the reverse of removal.

5   Crankshaft Position (CKP) sensor - replacement

Note: *The CKP sensor is located at the timing belt crankshaft sprocket.*

2003 and earlier models

Refer to illustrations 5.2 and 5.4

1   Raise the front of the vehicle and place it securely on jackstands. Remove the engine cover (see Chapter 2A).
2   Disconnect the CKP sensor electrical connector **(see illustration)**.
3   Remove the timing belt covers (see Chapter 2A).
4   Remove the CKP sensor mounting bolt

(see illustration) and remove the CKP sensor.
5   Installation is the reverse of removal.

2004 and later models

Refer to illustrations 5.8 and 5.9

6   Raise the front of the vehicle and place it securely on jackstands. Remove the engine

cover (see Chapter 2A).
7   Remove the crankshaft pulley and the upper and lower timing belt covers (see Chapter 2A).
8   Remove the two nuts that secure the shield for the CKP sensor wiring harness **(see illustration)** and remove the CKP sensor and the harness shield.

5.8 Remove the two nuts that secure the shield for the CKP sensor wiring harness shield, then remove the shield (2004 and later models)

5.9 To detach the CKP sensor from the engine block, remove the sensor mounting bolt (1), pull off the CKP sensor, depress the electrical connector release tab (2) and disconnect the connector from the sensor (2004 and later models)

6.3 The Electrical Load Detector (ELD) (1) is located inside the engine compartment fuse and relay box and is retained by two screws (2) (2003 and earlier models)

9   Remove the CKP sensor mounting bolt **(see illustration)**, remove the sensor from the engine block, disconnect the electrical connector from the sensor and remove the sensor.
10   Installation is the reverse of removal.

---

6   Electrical Load Detector (ELD) - replacement

2003 and earlier models

Refer to illustration 6.3

1   Disconnect the cable from the negative battery terminal (see Chapter 5, Section 1).
2   Remove the cover from the engine compartment fuse and relay box (see Chapter 12 if necessary).
3   Locate the ELD **(see illustration)** in the fuse and relay box.
4   Remove the two ELD mounting screws, then remove the ELD.
5   Installation is the reverse of removal. Reconnect the cable to the negative battery terminal (see Chapter 5, Section 1).

2004 and later models

6   The ELD is an integral component of the engine compartment fuse and relay box and cannot be removed separately. To replace the ELD you must replace the fuse and relay box.

---

7   Engine Coolant Temperature (ECT) sensor - replacement

ECT sensor (2006 and earlier models)/ECT sensor 1 (2007 and later models)

Refer to illustrations 7.3 and 7.5

Warning: *Wait until the engine has cooled completely before beginning this procedure.*
Note: *The ECT sensor (2006 and earlier*

7.3 The ECT sensor on 2006 and earlier models (and ECT sensor 1 on 2007 and later models) is located on the coolant passage that's routed underneath the throttle body. To remove it, disconnect the electrical connector, then unscrew the sensor with a wrench

models), or ECT sensor 1 (2007 and later models), is located on the coolant passage casting located under the throttle body.

1   Remove the engine cover.
2   Drain the engine coolant (see Chapter 1). **Note:** *If you don't drain the coolant, some coolant will run out of the coolant crossover when you remove the ECT sensor, so install the new sensor as quickly as possible.*
3   Disconnect the electrical connector from the ECT sensor **(see illustration)**.
4   Unscrew the ECT sensor with a wrench (most deep sockets won't fit over the ECT sensor). **Caution:** *If you're planning to reuse the old ECT sensor, handle it with care. Damage to the ECT sensor will adversely affect the operation of the PGM-FI system.*
5   Remove and discard the old ECT sensor O-ring **(see illustration)**. Whether you're plan-

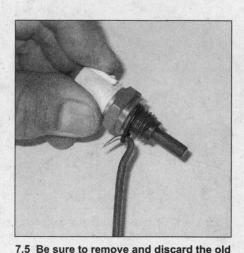

7.5 Be sure to remove and discard the old O-ring from the ECT sensor; always use a new O-ring when installing the ECT sensor

ning to reuse the old ECT sensor or install a new unit, be sure to use a new O-ring.
6   Installation is the reverse of removal. Be sure to tighten the ECT sensor to the torque listed in this Chapter's Specifications. Refill the cooling system (see Chapter 1).

ECT sensor 2 (2007 and later models)

Warning: *Wait until the engine has cooled completely before beginning this procedure.*
Note: *ECT sensor 2 is located on the lower left rear side of the radiator.*

7   Raise the front of the vehicle and place it securely on jackstands. Remove the engine splash shield.
8   Drain the engine coolant (see Chapter 1). If you don't drain the coolant, coolant will run out of the radiator when you remove the ECT sensor, so install the new sensor as quickly as possible.
9   Disconnect the electrical connector from the ECT sensor.

8.2a IAT sensor location (2003 and earlier models)

8.2b IAT sensor location (2004 through 2006 models). To disconnect the electrical connector from the IAT sensor, depress the release tab (A) and pull off the connector. On 2007 and later models, the IAT sensor is screwed into the left end of the intake manifold, in front of the throttle body mounting flange, at this location (B)

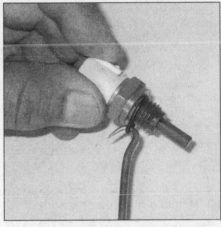

8.4a On 2003 and earlier models, be sure to remove and discard the old IAT sensor O-ring. Use a new O-ring when installing the IAT sensor, even if you're installing the old IAT sensor.

10   Unscrew the ECT sensor with a wrench (most deep sockets won't fit over the ECT sensor). **Caution:** *If you're planning to reuse the old ECT sensor, handle it with care. Damage to the ECT sensor will adversely affect the operation of the PGM-FI system.*

11   Remove and discard the old ECT sensor O-ring **(see illustration 7.5)**.

12   Install a new O-ring on the ECT sensor whether you're installing the old ECT sensor or a new unit.

13   Installation is the reverse of removal. Be sure to tighten the ECT sensor to the torque listed in this Chapter's Specifications. Refill the cooling system (see Chapter 1).

8   Intake Air Temperature (IAT) sensor - replacement

Refer to illustrations 8.2a, 8.2b, 8.4a and 8.4b
Note: *2003 and earlier models, the IAT sensor is located at the left rear corner of the intake manifold. On 2004 through 2006 models, the IAT sensor is located on the left end of the intake manifold, on the front side of the*
mounting flange for the throttle body, between the throttle body and the manifold. On 2007 and later models, the IAT sensor is located on the left end of the intake manifold, ahead of the throttle body flange.

1   Remove the engine or intake manifold cover (see Chapter 2A).

2   Disconnect the electrical connector from the IAT sensor **(see illustrations)**.

3   Unscrew and remove the IAT sensor.

4   Remove and discard the old IAT sensor O-ring **(see illustrations)**. Be sure to use a new O-ring, even if you're planning to reuse the old IAT sensor.

5   Installation is the reverse of removal. Be sure to use a new O-ring, and tighten the IAT sensor to the torque listed in this Chapter's Specifications.

9   Knock sensor - replacement

Refer to illustrations 9.4 and 9.5
Note: *The knock sensor is located under the intake manifold, on top of the engine block.*

1   Remove the intake manifold (see Chapter 2A).

2   Remove the fuel rail assembly (see Chapter 4).

3   Acura recommends removing the injector base (the lower intake manifold) to access the knock sensor. However, with the right tools (a deep socket and a flexible extension) we
have been able to access the knock sensor on a number of similar Honda and Acura V6 engines, so we recommend that you first try to replace the knock sensor without removing the lower intake manifold. If you're unable to do so, then remove the lower intake manifold (see Chapter 2A).

4   Disconnect the electrical connector from the knock sensor **(see illustration)**.

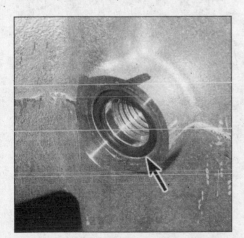

8.4b On 2004 and later models, the IAT sensor O-ring is countersunk into the intake manifold (2004 through 2006 model shown; 2007 and later models similar)

9.4 To disconnect the electrical connector from the knock sensor, depress this release button with the tip of a long slotted screwdriver and pull the connector straight up with a pair of long needle-nose pliers

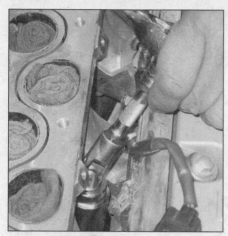

9.5 You'll need to use a deep socket, a universal joint and an extension to unscrew the knock sensor. If you're unable to replace the knock sensor this way, remove the lower intake manifold

5   Remove the knock sensor **(see illustration)**. If the sensor is equipped with an O-ring, remove and discard the old O-ring and install a new one.

6   Installation is the reverse of removal. Be sure to tighten the knock sensor to the torque listed in this Chapter's Specifications.

10 Manifold Absolute Pressure (MAP) sensor - replacement

Refer to illustrations 10.2a, 10.2b and 10.4
Note: *The MAP sensor is located on top of the throttle body.*

1   Remove the intake manifold cover or engine cover (see Chapter 2A).

2   Disconnect the electrical connector from

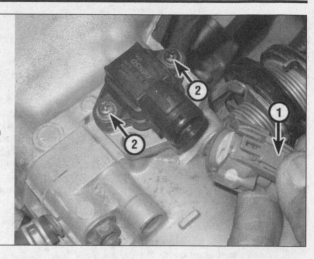

10.2a To disconnect the electrical connector from the MAP sensor, depress the release tab (1) and pull off the connector. To detach the MAP sensor from the throttle body, remove the two screws (2) (2003 and earlier models)

the MAP sensor **(see illustrations)**.

3   Remove the MAP sensor retaining screw(s) and remove the MAP sensor from the throttle body.

4   Remove the old MAP sensor O-ring **(see illustration)** and discard it.

5   Installation is the reverse of removal. Be sure to use a new O-ring and tighten the MAP sensor retaining screws securely.

11 Oxygen sensors - general precautions and replacement

General precautions

Note: *Because it is installed in the exhaust manifold or pipe, both of which contract when they cool off, an oxygen sensor might be very difficult to loosen when the engine is cold. Rather than risk damage to the sensor or its mounting threads, start and run the engine for a minute or two, then shut it off. Be careful not to burn yourself during the following procedure.*

1   Be particularly careful when servicing an oxygen sensor.

Oxygen sensors have a permanently attached pigtail and an electrical connector that cannot be removed. Damaging or removing the pigtail or electrical connector will render the sensor useless.

Keep grease, dirt and other contaminants away from the electrical connector and the louvered end of the sensor.

Do not use cleaning solvents of any kind on an oxygen sensor.

Oxygen sensors are extremely delicate. Do not drop a sensor, throw it around or handle it roughly.

Make sure that the silicone boot on the sensor is installed in the correct position. Otherwise, the boot might melt and prevent the sensor from operating correctly.

Replacement

2   Raise the vehicle and place it securely on jackstands.

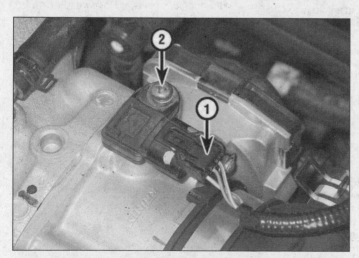

10.2b To remove the MAP sensor from the throttle body on 2004 and later models, depress the tab (1) and disconnect the electrical connector, then remove the sensor retaining screw (2) and pull the MAP sensor straight up (2004 and later models)

10.4 Be sure to remove and discard the old MAP sensor O-ring. Whether you're re-using the old MAP sensor or installing a new unit, always use a new O-ring (2003 and earlier models)

11.4 Use a wrench to remove the upstream oxygen sensor (there isn't room for an oxygen sensor socket) (2003 and earlier models)

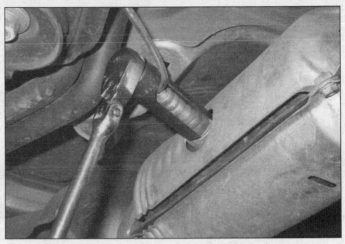

11.8 Use an oxygen sensor socket to remove the downstream oxygen sensor (use a wrench if you don't have an oxygen sensor socket) (2003 and earlier models)

2003 and earlier models

Note: *There are two oxygen sensors, one upstream and one downstream. Both oxygen sensors are located under the vehicle. The upstream oxygen sensor is located directly behind the exhaust pipe "Y" junction and ahead of the catalytic converter. The downstream sensor is screwed into the catalyst. You'll have to raise the vehicle to replace either sensor.*

Upstream oxygen sensor

Refer to illustration 11.4

3   After locating the upstream oxygen sensor, trace the sensor harness to the electrical connector and disconnect it.
4   Remove the upstream oxygen sensor **(see illustration)**.
5   If you're going to install the old sensor, apply anti-seize compound to the threads of the sensor to facilitate future removal. If you're going to install a new oxygen sensor, it's not necessary to apply anti-seize compound to the threads. The threads on new sensors already have anti-seize compound on them.
6   Installation is the reverse of removal. Be sure to tighten the oxygen sensor to the torque listed in this Chapter's Specifications.

Downstream oxygen sensor

Refer to illustration 11.8

7   After locating the downstream oxygen sensor, trace the sensor harness to the electrical connector and disconnect it.
8   Remove the upstream oxygen sensor **(see illustration)**.
9   If you're going to install the old sensor, apply anti-seize compound to the threads of the sensor to facilitate future removal. If you're going to install a new oxygen sensor, it's not necessary to apply anti-seize compound to the threads. The threads on new sensors already have anti-seize compound on them.
10   Installation is the reverse of removal. Be sure to tighten the oxygen sensor to the torque listed in this Chapter's Specifications.

11.12 The upstream oxygen sensors are located in the warm-up catalysts (2004 and later models)

2004 and later models

Upstream oxygen sensors

Refer to illustrations 11.12 and 11.13

Note: *The upstream oxygen sensors are located at the cylinder heads, at the top of the warm-up catalysts. This procedure applies to either upstream oxygen sensor.*

11   Remove the engine cover (see Chapter 2A).
12   After locating the upstream oxygen sensor **(see illustration)**, trace the sensor harness to the electrical connector and disconnect it.
13   Remove the upstream oxygen sensor with an oxygen sensor socket **(see illustration)**.
14   If you're going to install the old sensor, apply anti-seize compound to the threads of the sensor to facilitate future removal. If you're going to install a new oxygen sensor, it's not necessary to apply anti-seize compound to the threads. The threads on new sensors already have anti-seize compound on them.
15   Installation is the reverse of removal. Be sure to tighten the oxygen sensor to the torque listed in this Chapter's Specifications.

Downstream oxygen sensors

Refer to illustration 11.17

16   Raise the vehicle and place it securely on jackstands. Remove the engine under cover.

11.13 Use an oxygen sensor socket to remove the upstream oxygen sensor (2004 and later models)

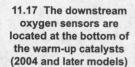

11.17 The downstream oxygen sensors are located at the bottom of the warm-up catalysts (2004 and later models)

12.3 Use two wrenches to remove the PSP switch: one to unscrew it and a back-up on the hex on the power steering fluid pressure line so you don't kink the line

17   Locate the downstream oxygen sensor **(see illustration)**, then trace the electrical lead up to the electrical connector and disconnect the connector.

18   Remove the upstream oxygen sensor with an oxygen sensor socket.

19   If you're going to install the old sensor, apply anti-seize compound to the threads of the sensor to facilitate future removal. If you're going to install a new oxygen sensor, it's not necessary to apply anti-seize compound to the threads. The threads on new sensors already have anti-seize compound on them.

20   Installation is the reverse of removal. Be sure to tighten the oxygen sensor to the torque listed in this Chapter's Specifications.

12   Power Steering Pressure (PSP) switch - replacement

Refer to illustration 12.3

Note: *The PSP switch is located on the power*

steering pressure hose, above the right end of the steering gear assembly.

1   Raise the front of the vehicle and place it securely on jackstands.

2   Disconnect the electrical connector from the PSP switch.

3   Using a wrench and a back-up wrench to protect the power steering line from kinking, unscrew the PSP switch **(see illustration)**. Have a pan ready to catch any power steering fluid that leaks out.

4   Installation is the reverse of removal.

5   Check the power steering fluid level, adding fluid of the proper type if necessary.

13   Throttle Position (TP) sensor - replacement

2003 and earlier models are equipped with a conventional, cable-operated throttle body that uses an externally mounted Throttle Position (TP) sensor. But the TP sensor is not available separately. If it's defective, you must replace the throttle body (see Chapter 4).

On 2004 and later models, which are equipped with electronic throttle bodies, the TP sensor is an integral component of the

throttle body assembly. Again, a defective TP sensor means the throttle body must be replaced.

14   Transmission range switch - replacement and adjustment

2006 and earlier models

Refer to illustrations 14.3, 14.4, 14.5, 14.6, 14.7a and 14.7b

1   Place the shift lever in NEUTRAL. Disconnect the cable from the negative terminal of the battery (see Chapter 5, Section 1).

2   Raise the vehicle and place it securely on jackstands.

3   Detach the transmission range switch electrical connector from its mounting bracket, then disconnect it **(see illustration)**.

4   Detach the wiring harness for the transmission range switch from the transaxle **(see illustration)**.

5   Remove the transmission range switch

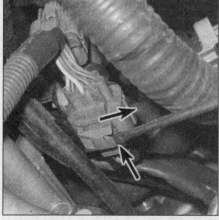

14.3 The electrical connector for the transmission range switch is secured to - and locked together by - a small metal bracket. To detach the connector from the bracket, insert a thin slotted screwdriver blade between the release lever and the connector, pry the release lever down and pull the connector off the bracket

14.4 To detach the wiring harness from the transaxle, remove this bolt (1), then squeeze the locator pins (2) together and push this clip out of its metal bracket

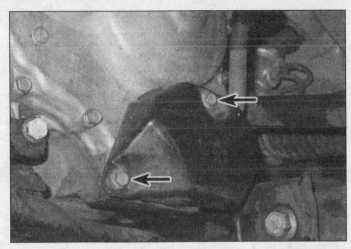

14.5 To detach the transmission range switch cover, remove these two bolts

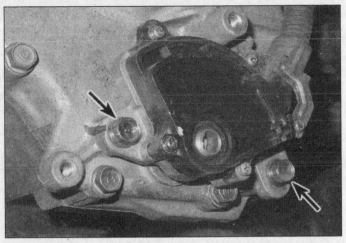

14.6 To detach the transmission range switch from the transaxle, remove these two bolts

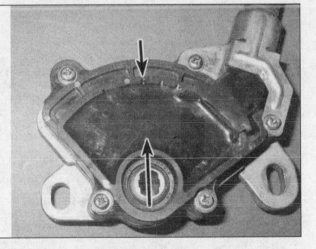

14.7a Before installing the transmission range switch, make sure that the switch is in the Neutral position: Rotate the moving part of the switch so that its longer inside diameter is aligned with the stationary Neutral index mark located on the upper part of the switch

cover bolts **(see illustration)** and remove the cover.

6   Remove the transmission range switch mounting bolts **(see illustration)** and remove the switch.

7   Before installing the transmission range switch, make sure that the switch is in the Neutral position **(see illustration)**. You'll hear/feel a click when you put the switch into Neutral. Also make sure that the control shaft is in the Neutral position before installing the transmission range switch. To do so, rotate the control shaft in a clockwise direction until it stops. As you rotate the shaft, it clicks into each gear position. Rotate it counterclockwise to the third gear position (third click), which is Neutral **(see illustration)**.

8   The remainder of installation is the reverse of removal. Be sure to tighten the transmission range switch mounting bolts securely. **Note:** *Be careful not to move the transmission range switch while tightening the switch mounting bolts.*

9   Turn the ignition switch to ON, move the shift lever through all the gears and verify that the transmission range switch is correctly synchronized with the gear position indica-tor on the instrument cluster. Then verify that the engine will NOT start in any gear position other than Park or Neutral, and that the back-up lights come on when the shift lever is in the Reverse position.

10   If the vehicle fails to meet any of these criteria, readjust the transmission range switch.

2007 and later models

Removal

11   Disconnect the cable from the negative terminal of the battery (see Chapter 5, Section 1).

12   Remove the battery and battery tray (see Chapter 5).

13   Remove the air intake duct and the air filter housing (see Chapter 4).

14   Remove the shift cable bracket nuts.

15   Remove the spring clip/washer and the control pin, then separate the end of the shift cable from the control lever.

16   Inspect the bushing in the end of the shift cable.

17   Disconnect the electrical connector from the transmission range switch.

18   On the control lever, pry open the lock washer lock tab and remove the nut, the lock washer, the spring washer and the control lever.

19   On the control shaft, pry open the lock washer lock tabs.

20   Hold the control shaft with a 6 mm wrench and loosen the locknut, then remove the locknut and the washer.

21   Remove the two switch mounting bolts and remove the switch.

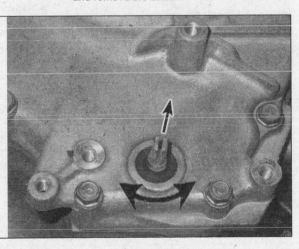

14.7b Make sure that the control shaft is also in the Neutral position before installing the transmission range switch. Rotate the shaft in a clockwise direction until it stops. As you rotate the shaft, it clicks into each gear position. Rotate it counterclockwise to the third gear position (third click), which is Neutral

15.2 The input shaft speed sensor is located at the left front corner of the transaxle. To remove it, depress the release tab and disconnect the electrical connector, then remove the bolt (2006 and earlier models)

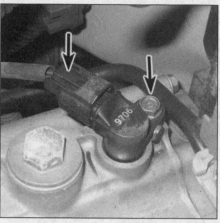

15.6 The output shaft speed sensor is located on top of the transaxle. To remove it, depress the release tab and disconnect the electrical connector, then remove the sensor mounting bolt (2006 and earlier models)

Installation

22   Before installing the switch, set the switch in the NEUTRAL position. The switch clicks into the NEUTRAL position, and the control shaft hole aligns with the NEUTRAL position line.
23   Turn the control shaft to the NEUTRAL position and install the switch on the control shaft.
24   Install a new lock washer on the control shaft and align the projection on the washer with the Neutral position line on the switch, then install the locknut.
25   Push the locknut against the transmission housing to set the switch onto the control shaft and tighten the locknut to the torque listed in this Chapter's Specifications.
26   While holding the shaft with a 6 mm wrench, bend the lock tabs of the new lock washer.
27   Installation is otherwise the reverse of removal. Use moly grease on the bushing on the end of the shift cable.

---

15   Transmission speed sensors - replacement

2006 and earlier models

Input shaft speed sensor

Refer to illustration 15.2
Note: *The input shaft speed sensor is located on the front left corner of the transaxle.*
1   Loosen the lug nuts for the left front wheel. Raise the vehicle and place it securely on jackstands. Remove the left front wheel.
2   Disconnect the electrical connector from the input shaft speed sensor **(see illustration)**.
3   Remove the input shaft speed sensor mounting bolt and remove the sensor.
4   Remove and discard the sensor O-ring.
5   Installation is the reverse of removal. Be sure to use a new O-ring and to tighten the sensor mounting bolt securely.

Output shaft speed sensor

Refer to illustration 15.6
Note: *The output shaft speed sensor is located on top of the transaxle.*
6   Disconnect the electrical connector from the output shaft speed sensor **(see illustration)**.
7   Remove the output shaft sensor mounting bolt and remove the sensor by pulling it straight up.
8   Remove and discard the sensor O-ring.
9   Installation is the reverse of removal. Be sure to use a new O-ring and to tighten the sensor mounting bolt securely.

2007 and later models

Note: *The input shaft speed sensor and output shaft speed sensor are located on the front of the transaxle.*
10   Raise the vehicle and place it securely on jackstands.
11   Remove the engine splash shield (see Chapter 2A).
12   Disconnect the electrical connector from the input shaft speed sensor or output shaft speed sensor.
13   Remove the input shaft speed sensor or output shaft speed sensor mounting bolt and remove the sensor.
14   Remove and discard the sensor O-ring.
15   Installation is the reverse of removal. Be sure to use a new O-ring and to tighten the sensor mounting bolt securely.

---

16   Powertrain Control Module (PCM) - removal and installation

The Powertrain Control Module (PCM) is the brain of the engine management system. It's located under the instrument panel, forward of the center console. It also controls a wide variety of other vehicle systems, including the immobilizer (vehicle security) system. If the PCM fails, the new immobilizer code must be programmed into the new PCM by a dealership service department before the engine will start. In order to program the new PCM, the dealer needs the vehicle, the new PCM unit and all of the vehicle keys. Additionally, there is no procedure in this repair manual that requires removal of the PCM, so we don't recommend that you do so.

---

17   Idle Air Control (IAC) valve - replacement

Refer to illustrations 17.2 and 17.3
Note: *On 2003 and earlier models, the IAC valve is located on the underside of the throttle body. 2004 and later models are equipped with an electronic throttle body, which doesn't have an IAC valve.*
1   Remove the throttle body from the intake manifold (see Chapter 4).
2   Remove the IAC valve mounting screws **(see illustration)** and remove the IAC valve.

17.2 To detach the IAC valve from the throttle body, remove these two screws

17.3 Remove and discard the old IAC valve gasket, and be sure to use a new gasket when installing the IAC valve

18.11 To detach the catalyst mounting flange from the exhaust system, remove these three nuts (2003 and earlier models)

3   Remove the old IAC valve gasket (**see illustration**) and discard it.
4   When installing the IAC valve, be sure to use a new gasket and tighten the IAC valve mounting screws securely.
5   Installation is otherwise the reverse of removal.

18 Catalytic converter – description, check and replacement

Note: *Because of a Federally mandated extended warranty which covers emissions-related components like the catalytic converter, check with a dealer service department before replacing the converter at your own expense.*

Description

1   A catalytic converter is an emission control device in the exhaust system that reduces certain pollutants in the exhaust gas stream. There are two types of converters: oxidation converters and reduction converters.
2   Oxidation converters contain a monolithic substrate (a ceramic honeycomb) coated with the semi-precious metals platinum and palladium. An oxidation catalyst reduces unburned hydrocarbons (HC) and carbon monoxide (CO) by adding oxygen to the exhaust stream as it passes through the substrate, which, in the presence of high temperature and the catalyst materials, converts the HC and CO to water vapor (H_2O) and carbon dioxide (CO_2).
3   Reduction converters contain a monolithic substrate coated with platinum and rhodium. A reduction catalyst reduces oxides of nitrogen (NOx) by removing oxygen, which, in the presence of high temperature and the catalyst material, produces nitrogen (N) and carbon dioxide (CO_2).
4   Catalytic converters that combine both types of catalysts in one assembly are known as "three-way catalysts" or TWCs. A TWC can

reduce all three pollutants. All models covered by this manual are equipped with three-way catalysts.
5   On 2003 and earlier models the catalytic converter is located in the exhaust pipe behind the junction of the outlet pipes of the exhaust manifolds. On 2004 and later models, there are two warm-up catalytic converters, one for each cylinder head; they're bolted directly to the cylinder heads. There are no separate exhaust manifolds; the "manifolds" are integral with the cylinder head castings.

Check

6   The test equipment for a catalytic converter (a loaded-mode dynamometer and a 5-gas analyzer) is expensive. If you suspect that the converter on your vehicle is malfunctioning, take it to a dealer or authorized emission inspection facility for diagnosis and repair.
7   Whenever you raise the vehicle to service underbody components, inspect the converter assembly for leaks, corrosion, dents and other damage. Carefully inspect the welds and/or flange bolts and nuts that attach the front and rear ends of the converter to the exhaust system. If you note any damage, replace the converter. **Warning:** *Inspect catalytic converters only after enough time has elapsed after driving the vehicle to allow the system components to cool completely. Also, when working under the vehicle, make sure that it is securely supported on jackstands.*
8   Although catalytic converters don't break too often, they can become clogged or even plugged up. The easiest way to check for a restricted converter is to use a vacuum gauge to diagnose the effect of a blocked exhaust on intake vacuum.
   a) *Connect a vacuum gauge to any intake manifold vacuum source (any pipe on the intake manifold with a vacuum hose connected to it will provide the necessary intake manifold vacuum).*

   b) *Warm the engine to operating temperature, place the transaxle in Park (automatic models) or Neutral (manual models) and apply the parking brake.*
   c) *Note the vacuum reading at idle and jot it down.*
   d) *Quickly open the throttle to near its wide-open position, then quickly get off the throttle and allow it to close. Note the vacuum reading and jot it down.*
   e) *Do this test three more times, recording your measurement after each test.*
   f) *If your fourth reading is more than one in-Hg lower than the reading that you noted at idle, the exhaust system might be restricted (the catalytic converter could be plugged, or an exhaust pipe or muffler could be restricted).*

Replacement

Warning: *Replace catalytic converters only after enough time has elapsed after driving the vehicle to allow the system components to cool completely. Also, when working under the vehicle, make sure it is securely supported on jackstands.*

2003 and earlier models

Refer to illustration 18.11

9   Raise the vehicle and place it securely on jackstands.
10   Disconnect the electrical connector from the downstream oxygen sensor and remove the sensor (see Section 11).
11   Remove the retaining nuts from the front and rear catalyst mounting flanges (**see illustration**).
12   Installation is the reverse of removal.
13   Be sure to replace any rusted or damaged fasteners and to tighten all fasteners securely.

18.16 To detach the upper end of the catalytic converter from the front cylinder head, remove these four nuts (2004 and later models)

18.20 To remove either warm-up catalyst, you'll have to remove the front exhaust pipe. Remove the three nuts from each lower catalyst flange and from the rear exhaust flange

2004 and later models

Warm-up catalytic converters

Refer to illustrations 18.16 and 18.20

Note: *There are two warm-up catalytic converters, one for each cylinder bank. Each converter is bolted directly to the cylinder head (there are no exhaust manifolds on these models).*

14   If you're removing the front catalytic converter, remove the condenser fan/shroud assembly (see Chapter 3).

15   Disconnect the electrical connector for the upstream oxygen sensor and remove the sensor (see Section 11).

16   Remove the nuts from the catalytic converter's upper mounting flange **(see illustration)**. **Note:** *Reinstall one nut loosely to prevent the converter from falling off the mounting studs when the lower end is detached from the exhaust system.*

17   Raise the vehicle and place it securely on jackstands.

18   Remove the engine splash shield (see Chapter 2A).

19   Disconnect the electrical connector for the downstream oxygen sensor and remove the sensor (see Section 11).

20   Remove the nuts from the lower mounting flanges of both warm-up catalysts and from the front exhaust pipe's rear flange **(see illustration)** and remove the front exhaust pipe.

21   Remove the catalytic converter and remove and discard the old mounting flange gaskets.

22   Be sure to use new gaskets and fasteners at both catalyst mounting flanges and tighten the flange nuts securely.

23   Install the front exhaust pipe using new gaskets and new fasteners and tighten all fasteners securely.

24   Install the upstream and downstream oxygen sensors, tighten them to the torque listed in this Chapter's Specifications and

reconnect the oxygen sensor electrical connectors (see Section 11). Installation is otherwise the reverse of removal.

Under-vehicle catalytic converter

Note: *In addition to the front and rear catalytic converters, these models have a third catalytic converter, under the vehicle, which is similar to the single converter used on 2003 and earlier models.*

25   Refer to Steps 9 through 13.

---

19   Evaporative Emissions Control (EVAP) system - description and component replacement

General description

1   The Evaporative Emissions Control (EVAP) system prevents fuel system vapors (which contain unburned hydrocarbons) from escaping into the atmosphere. On warm days, vapors trapped inside the fuel tank expand until the pressure reaches a certain threshold. Then the fuel vapors are routed from the fuel tank through the fuel vapor vent valve and the fuel vapor control valve to the EVAP canister, where they're stored temporarily until the next time the vehicle is operated. When the conditions are right (engine warmed up, vehicle up to speed, moderate or heavy load on the engine, etc.) the PCM opens the canister purge valve, which allows fuel vapors to be drawn from the canister into the intake manifold. Once in the intake manifold, the fuel vapors mix with incoming air before being drawn through the intake ports into the combustion chambers where they're burned up with the rest of the air/fuel mixture. The EVAP system is complex and virtually impossible to troubleshoot without the right tools and training. However, the following description should give you a good idea of how it works:

2   The **EVAP canister**, which contains

activated charcoal, is a repository for storing fuel vapors. You'll have to raise the vehicle to inspect or replace the canister, or any other part of the EVAP system, except for the canister purge valve (which is located in the engine compartment). But the canister is designed to be maintenance-free and should last the life of the vehicle. There are several other important components located on or near the canister: the canister filter, the canister vent shut valve, the two-way valve, the bypass solenoid valve and the fuel tank pressure sensor. The EVAP canister is located under the vehicle, ahead of the fuel tank.

3   When the canister is purged, fresh air is drawn through the filter before passing through the canister. The **EVAP canister filter** prevents dust and dirt particles from entering the EVAP canister and the EVAP system. The EVAP canister filter is located on the front side of the EVAP canister.

4   The **canister vent shut valve** is normally closed, but it opens to allow fresh air from the filter to enter the EVAP canister when the canister is being purged. The canister vent shut valve is located on the left end of the EVAP canister.

5   The **fuel tank pressure sensor** monitors the pressure inside the fuel tank, converts fuel tank absolute pressure into a variable voltage signal and transmits this data to the PCM. The fuel tank pressure sensor is located at the EVAP canister.

6   On 2003 and earlier models, when the pressure of the fuel vapors inside the fuel tank exceeds the preset value of the **two-way valve**, the valve opens and regulates the flow of excess vapors to the canister. The two-way valve also prevents excessive vacuum in the fuel tank by drawing in fresh air through the EVAP canister. The EVAP two-way valve is located in front of the EVAP canister. 2004 and later models do not use a two-way valve.

7   On 2003 and earlier models, the **bypass solenoid valve** opens to bypass the two-way

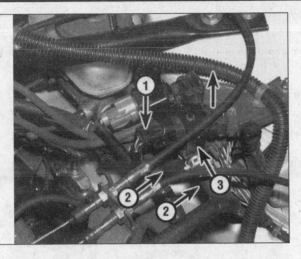

19.12 Depress the release tab (1) to disconnect the electrical connector, disconnect the two EVAP hoses (2), then slide the EVAP purge valve (3) straight up to disengage it from its rubber mounting insulator (1999 models)

valve when the PCM does an EVAP system leak check. The EVAP bypass solenoid valve is located behind the EVAP canister, below the fuel tank pressure sensor, to the right of the EVAP two-way valve. 2004 and later models do not use a bypass solenoid valve.

8   The **EVAP canister purge valve**, which is under the control of the Powertrain Control Module (PCM), regulates the flow of vapors being purged from the EVAP canister into the intake manifold. The canister purge valve is always closed when engine coolant temperature is below 147-degrees F (64-degrees C), which cuts off intake manifold vacuum to the EVAP canister. Above that threshold, the PCM opens or closes the purge solenoid valve in accordance with data from various information sensor inputs. The interval of time during which the purge valve is opened by the PCM is known as its "duty cycle." The purge valve is located in the engine compartment, to the left of the power brake booster.

General system checks

9   The most common symptom of a faulty EVAP system is a strong fuel odor (particularly during hot weather). If you smell fuel while driving or (more likely) right after you park the vehicle and turn off the engine, check the fuel filler cap first. Make sure that it's screwed onto

the fuel filler neck all the way. If the odor persists, inspect all EVAP hose connections, both in the engine compartment and under the vehicle. You'll have to raise the vehicle and place it securely on jackstands to inspect most of the EVAP system, since it's located under the vehicle. Be sure to inspect each hose attached to the canister for damage and leakage along its entire length. Repair or replace as necessary. Inspect the canister for damage and look for fuel leaking from the bottom. If fuel is leaking or the canister is otherwise damaged, replace it.

10   Poor idle, stalling, and poor driveability can be caused by a defective fuel vapor vent valve or canister purge valve, a damaged canister, cracked hoses, or hoses connected to the wrong tubes. Fuel loss or fuel odor can be caused by fuel leaking from fuel lines or hoses, a cracked or damaged canister, or a defective vapor valve.

11   To check for excessive fuel vapor pressure in the fuel tank, remove the gas cap and listen for the sound of pressure release. If the fuel tank emits a whooshing sound when you open the filler cap, fuel tank vapor pressure is excessive. Inspect the canister vapor hoses and the canister inlet port for blockage or collapsed hoses. Also inspect the vapor vent valve.

Component replacement

2003 and earlier models

EVAP canister purge valve

Refer to illustration 19.12

12   Disconnect the electrical connector from the purge control solenoid valve **(see illustration)**.
13   Disconnect the vacuum hoses from the purge control solenoid valve.
14   Remove the purge control solenoid valve.
15   Installation is the reverse of removal.

EVAP canister assembly

Note: *The EVAP canister assembly is located underneath the vehicle, in front of the fuel tank.*

16   To perform any of the following procedures, raise the vehicle and place it securely on jackstands.

EVAP canister

Refer to illustration 19.17

17   Disconnect the electrical connectors from the EVAP bypass solenoid valve and from the vent shut valve **(see illustration)**.
18   Clearly label the EVAP hoses connected to the EVAP canister, then disconnect them.
19   Remove the EVAP canister retaining bolt, lower the left end of the canister and disconnect the electrical connector from the fuel tank pressure sensor.
20   Pull the EVAP canister to the left to disengage the mounting slot in the right end of the canister from the mounting tab on the canister mounting bracket.
21   Installation is the reverse of removal.

EVAP canister vent shut valve

Refer to illustration 19.22

Note: *The EVAP canister vent shut valve is located on the left end of the EVAP canister.*

22   Disconnect the electrical connector and air filter hose from the vent shut valve **(see illustration)**.

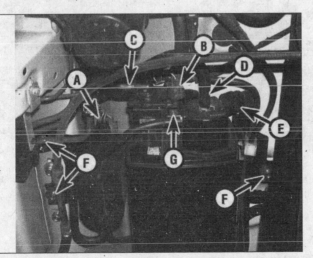

19.17 EVAP canister mounting details - 2003 and earlier models

A   *EVAP bypass solenoid valve electrical connectors*
B   *Vent shut valve electrical connector*
C   *EVAP hose to vent shut valve*
D   *EVAP hose from canister*
E   *Quick-connect fitting*
F   *EVAP canister mounting bracket bolts*
G   *EVAP canister mounting bolt*

19.22 Disconnect the electrical connector from the EVAP canister vent shut valve, then disconnect the hose that connects the canister air filter to the vent shut valve

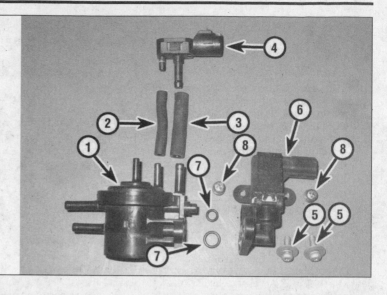

19.28 Two-way check valve/bypass solenoid valve/fuel tank pressure sensor assembly details

1 Two-way valve
2 Hose connecting fuel tank pressure sensor and two-way valve
3 Hose connecting fuel tank pressure sensor and bypass solenoid (tees into line between two-way valve and bypass solenoid valve)
4 Fuel tank pressure sensor
5 Bypass solenoid valve-to-two-way check valve retaining screws
6 Bypass solenoid valve
7 O-rings
8 Two-way check valve/bypass solenoid valve/fuel tank pressure sensor assembly retaining screws

23   Remove the EVAP canister retaining bolt and pull down the canister so that you can access the upper vent shut valve mounting screw.

24   Remove the vent shut valve mounting screws and remove the vent shut valve from the EVAP canister.

25   Remove and discard the vent shut valve O-ring. Using a new O-ring, install the vent shut valve and tighten the two mounting screws securely.

26   Installation is otherwise the reverse of removal.

EVAP two-way valve/bypass solenoid valve/fuel tank pressure sensor assembly

Refer to illustration 19.28
Note: *The EVAP two-way valve, bypass solenoid valve and Fuel Tank Pressure (FTP) sensor are all integrated into a single assembly*

and housed inside a two-piece plastic protective cover that's located right in front of the EVAP canister assembly.

27   Separate the two halves of the plastic cover that protects the two-way valve/bypass solenoid/FTP assembly.

28   Disconnect the various EVAP hoses and electrical connectors from the assembly and remove the assembly **(see illustration)**.

29   Separate the two-way valve/bypass solenoid valve/fuel tank pressure sensor assembly from the mounting bracket.

30   If you're replacing the two-way valve or the bypass solenoid valve, separate them from each other.

31   If you're replacing the fuel tank pressure sensor, disconnect it from the two vacuum hoses. Be sure to inspect both vacuum hoses for cracks, tears and deterioration. If either hose is damaged or deteriorated, replace it.

32   If you've separated the bypass solenoid valve from the two-way valve, be sure to remove and discard the old O-rings. Always use new O-rings when reattaching the two-way valve and the bypass solenoid valve.

33   Installation is the reverse of removal.

EVAP canister air filter

Refer to illustration 19.34
Note: *The EVAP canister air filter is located on a small bracket near the EVAP canister.*

34   Clearly label the hoses connected to the EVAP canister air filter **(see illustration)**, then disconnect them from the filter.

35   The canister air filter is secured to its mounting bracket by a pair of split-type locator pins. To detach the air filter from its mounting bracket, squeeze the two-halves of each locator pin together and pull the canister away from the bracket.

36   Installation is the reverse of removal.

19.34 Clearly label the three hoses connected to the EVAP canister air filter, then disconnect them (the orientation of the filter on your vehicle might differ, but the three hose connections are the same on all filters):

1 Fresh air inlet hose
2 Hose to EVAP two-way valve
3 Hose to EVAP canister vent shut valve

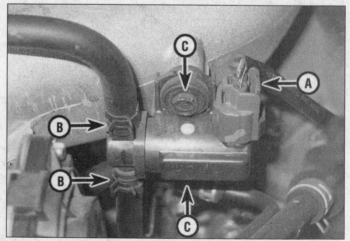

19.37 EVAP canister purge valve details on 2004 and later models:

A Electrical connector release tab
B Hose clamps
C Mounting bolts

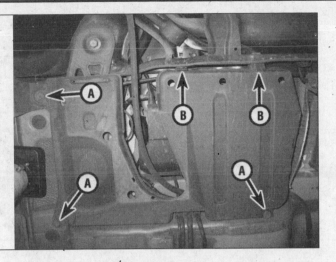

19.42 To remove the EVAP canister cover, remove these three bolts (A), then disengage these two tabs (B)

2004 and later models

EVAP canister purge valve

Refer to illustration 19.37

Note: *The EVAP canister purge valve is located in the engine compartment, at the left rear corner of the intake manifold.*

37   Disconnect the electrical connector from the EVAP canister purge valve **(see illustration)**.

38   Disconnect the vacuum hoses from the EVAP canister purge valve.

39   Remove the EVAP canister purge valve mounting bolts and remove the purge valve.

40   Installation is the reverse of removal.

EVAP canister assembly

Refer to illustrations 19.42, 19.43 and 19.44

Note: *The EVAP canister assembly is located under the left side of the vehicle, in front of the fuel tank. The EVAP canister assembly includes the canister vent shut valve, the Fuel Tank Pressure (FTP) sensor and the canister itself, all of which are located under the left side of the car, in front of the fuel tank.*

41   Raise the vehicle and place it securely on jackstands.

42   Remove the EVAP canister cover **(see illustration)**.

43   Disconnect the EVAP hoses and electrical connectors from the EVAP canister assembly **(see illustration)**.

44   Remove the three EVAP canister mounting bracket bolts **(see illustration)** and remove the canister and mounting bracket as a single assembly.

45   To separate the EVAP canister from its mounting bracket, remove the two retaining nuts.

46   Installation is the reverse of removal.

Fuel Tank Pressure (FTP) sensor

Refer to illustration 19.48

Note: *The FTP sensor is mounted on top of the EVAP canister.*

47   Remove the EVAP canister assembly.

48   Remove the FTP sensor retainer **(see illustration)**.

49   Pull the FTP sensor straight up, then remove and discard the old FTP sensor O-ring.

50   Be sure to use a new O-ring whether you're planning to install a new FTP sensor or the old unit. When installing the sensor retainer, push it in until the lugs on the ends of the retainer click into place. Make sure that the sensor retainer lugs on the retainer are properly engaged.

51   Installation is the reverse of removal.

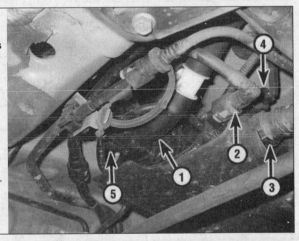

19.43 Typical 2004 and later EVAP canister assembly details (details may vary somewhat):

1   *Fresh air inlet hose from the inlet air filter*

2   *Quick-connect fitting for the EVAP hose that goes to the canister purge valve*

3   *Fitting for the EVAP hose coming from the fuel tank*

4   *Fuel Tank Pressure (FTP) sensor electrical connector*

5   *Canister vent shut valve electrical connector*

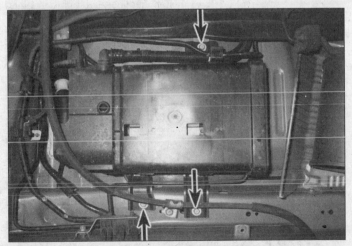

19.44 To detach the EVAP canister assembly from the underside of the vehicle, remove these three mounting bolts, then lower the canister and disconnect any remaining hoses and/or electrical connectors

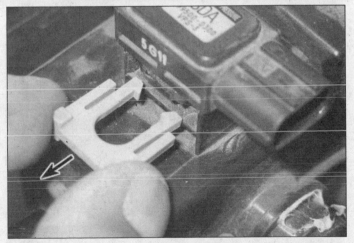

19.48 To remove the FTP sensor from the EVAP canister assembly, spread the two ends of the retainer apart and pull off the retainer, then pull out the FTP sensor

EVAP canister vent shut valve

Refer to illustration 19.53

Note: *The EVAP canister vent shut valve is mounted on the left end of the EVAP canister.*

52   Remove the EVAP canister assembly.

53   Pry open the four (two upper and two lower) lock tabs **(see illustration)** and pull out the canister vent shut valve.

54   Remove and discard the old vent shut valve O-ring.

55   Be sure to use a new O-ring whether you're planning to install a new canister vent shut valve or the old unit. And make sure that the shut valve is fully secured by all four lock tabs.

56   Installation is otherwise the reverse of removal.

EVAP canister air filter

Note: *The canister air filter is located on top of the EVAP canister mounting bracket.*

57   Remove the EVAP canister assembly.

58   Disconnect the hoses from the air filter.

59   Detach the filter from the canister mounting bracket.

60   Installation is the reverse of removal.

---

20 Exhaust Gas Recirculation (EGR) system - description and component replacement

Description

1   Oxides of nitrogen (or simply NOx) is a compound that is formed in the combustion chambers when the oxygen and nitrogen in the incoming air mix together. NOx is a natural byproduct of high combustion chamber temperatures. When NOx is emitted from the tailpipe, it mixes with reactive organic compounds (ROCs), hydrocarbons (HC) and sunlight to form ozone and photochemical smog. The EGR system reduces oxides of nitrogen by recirculating exhaust gases from the exhaust manifold, through the EGR valve and

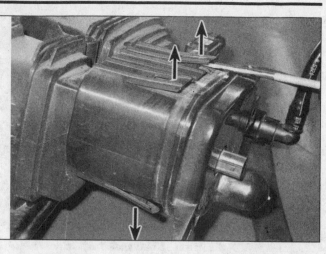

19.53 Pry open the four (two upper and two lower) lock tabs and pull out the canister vent shut valve

intake manifold, then back to the combustion chambers, where it mixes with the incoming air/fuel mixture before being consumed. These recirculated exhaust gases dilute the incoming air/fuel mixture, which cools the combustion chambers, thereby reducing NOx emissions.

2   The EGR system consists of the Powertrain Control Module (PCM), the EGR valve, the EGR valve position sensor and various other information sensors that the PCM uses to determine when to open the EGR valve. The degree to which the EGR valve is opened is referred to as "EGR valve lift." The PCM is programmed to produce the ideal EGR valve lift for varying operating conditions. The EGR valve position sensor, which is an integral part of the EGR valve, detects the amount of EGR valve lift and sends this information to the PCM. The PCM then compares it with the appropriate EGR valve lift for the operating conditions. The PCM increases current flow to the EGR valve to increase valve lift and reduces the current to reduce the amount of lift. If EGR flow is inappropriate to the operating conditions (idle, cold engine, etc.) the PCM simply cuts the current to the EGR valve and the valve closes.

EGR valve replacement

Refer to illustrations 20.4 and 20.6

3   Remove the engine cover (see Chapter 2A).

4   Disconnect the electrical connector from the EGR valve **(see illustration)**.

5   Remove the EGR valve mounting nuts **(see illustration 20.4)** and remove the EGR valve.

6   Remove and discard the old EGR valve gasket **(see illustration)**.

7   Installation is the reverse of removal. Be sure to use a new EGR valve gasket, and tighten the EGR valve mounting nuts securely.

---

21 Positive Crankcase Ventilation (PCV) system - description, check and component replacement

Description

1   The Positive Crankcase Ventilation (PCV) system reduces hydrocarbon emis-

20.4 To remove the EGR valve, depress this release tab (1) and disconnect the electrical connector from the EGR valve, then remove these two mounting nuts (2)

20.6 Be sure to remove all traces of old gasket material with a gasket scraper, and be extremely careful not to scratch or gouge the surfaces

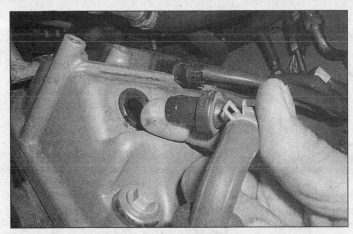

21.8 To check the PCV valve on 2003 and earlier models, plug it with your finger while the engine is idling and note whether you can feel the presence of intake manifold vacuum at the valve; if you can't, either the crankcase ventilation hose or the PCV valve is damaged or defective

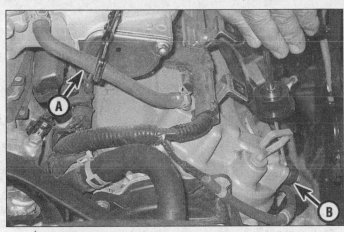

21.9 To check the PCV valve on 2004 and later models, pinch the PCV hose (A) while listening to the PCV valve (B) with a stethoscope. It should make a clicking sound each time that you pinch the hose

sions by scavenging crankcase vapors. It does this by circulating fresh air from the air intake duct into and through the crankcase, where it mixes with blow-by gases before being drawn by intake manifold vacuum through a PCV valve to the intake manifold. The PCV valve maintains idle quality by restricting the flow of crankcase vapors into the intake manifold when intake manifold vacuum is high, and allows full flow when intake manifold decreases. The main components of the PCV system are the PCV valve and a pair of vacuum hoses.

1999 models

2   On 1999 models, the PCV fresh air inlet hose connects the air intake duct to a pipe on the left end of the front valve cover. The crankcase ventilation hose (PCV hose) connects a pipe on the left end of the rear valve cover to a pipe on the intake mouth of the intake manifold (between the throttle body and the intake manifold). The PCV valve is located at the pipe in the left end of the rear valve cover.

2000 through 2003 models

3   On 2000 through 2003 models, the PCV fresh air inlet hose connects the air intake duct to a pipe on the left end of the front valve cover (same as 1999 models). The crankcase ventilation hose (PCV hose) runs along the top of the rear valve cover and connects to a pipe at the right rear corner of the intake manifold plenum. The PCV valve is in the left end of the rear valve cover. You have to remove the intake manifold cover to access the PCV valve and the crankcase ventilation hose (PCV hose).

2004 and later models

4   On 2004 and later models, the PCV fresh air inlet hose connects the air intake duct to a pipe on the left end of the rear valve cover. The crankcase ventilation hose (PCV hose) connects a pipe on the right end of the front valve cover to another pipe on the right

end of the intake manifold. The PCV valve is installed in the pipe (or just below it) in the right front corner of the front valve cover. You have to remove the engine cover to access the PCV valve and the crankcase ventilation hose (PCV hose).

Check

Refer to illustrations 21.8 and 21.9

5   On 2000 through 2006 models, remove the intake manifold cover; on 2007 and later models, remove the engine cover (see Chapter 2A).
6   Inspect the two PCV system hoses for cracks, tears or deterioration. If either hose is damaged or worn, replace it.
7   Start the engine and allow it to warm up until it's idling normally. Then leave it idling during the following test.
8   On 2003 and earlier models, pull out the PCV valve and cover the open end of the valve with your finger **(see illustration)**. You should feel intake vacuum at the PCV valve. If there is no vacuum at the valve, the crankcase ventilation hose is either clogged or it has a hole in it. Remove the crankcase ventilation hose (see *Component replacement* below), blow it out with compressed air, then inspect it for damage. If the hose is damaged or clogged, replace it, then retest the valve. If there is still no intake vacuum at the PCV valve, replace the valve. While the PCV valve is removed, inspect the PCV valve grommet for cracks, tears or deterioration. If the grommet is worn or damaged, replace it.
9   On 2004 and later models, pinch the PCV hose with your fingers or with pliers and listen to the PCV valve with a stethoscope **(see illustration)**. You should hear a clicking sound inside the PCV valve. Repeat this test several times. You should hear the clicking sound each time that you pinch the PCV hose. If there is no clicking sound, inspect the PCV valve grommet for cracks, tears or deterioration. If the grommet is damaged, replace

it and retest. If the grommet is okay, replace the PCV valve, then retest.
10   Install the intake manifold cover or engine cover.

Component replacement

2003 and earlier models

11   On 2000 through 2003 models, remove the intake manifold cover (see Chapter 2A).

Fresh air inlet hose

12   Loosen the hose clamp and disconnect the hose from the air intake duct.
13   Loosen the hose clamp and disconnect the hose from the pipe on the left end of the front valve cover.
14   Installation is the reverse of removal.

PCV valve and crankcase ventilation hose (PCV hose)

15   Disconnect the crankcase ventilation hose from the PCV valve.
16   Pull the PCV hose out of the left end of the rear valve cover **(see illustration 21.8)**.
17   Disconnect the crankcase ventilation hose from the intake manifold.
18   Inspect the PCV valve grommet for cracks, tears and other deterioration. If the grommet is worn or damaged, replace it.
19   Installation is the reverse of removal.

2004 and later models

20   Remove the intake manifold cover (2004 through 2006 models) or the engine cover (2007 and later models) (see Chapter 2A).

PCV fresh air inlet pipe and hose

21   To disconnect the fresh air inlet pipe from the air intake duct, loosen the spring type clamp and pull off the pipe.
22   Loosen and slide back the spring type clamps at both ends of the fresh air inlet hose, then pull the air inlet hose off the pipe on the left end of the rear valve cover and disconnect it from the fresh air inlet pipe.
23   Installation is the reverse of removal.

PCV valve

Refer to illustrations 21.24 and 21.25

Warning: *If the vehicle has been driven recently, make sure that the engine is cool before beginning this procedure.*

Note: *The PCV valve is located in the right end of the front valve cover.*

24   Remove the PCV valve retaining bolt **(see illustration)** and pull the PCV valve out of the valve cover.

25   Remove and discard the two old PCV O-rings **(see illustration)**.

26   Installation is the reverse of removal. Be sure to use new O-rings and tighten the PCV retaining bolt to the torque listed in this Chapter's Specifications.

Crankcase ventilation hose (PCV hose)

Refer to illustration 21.27

27   Loosen and slide back the two spring-type clamps **(see illustration)** and pull off the PCV hose.

28   Installation is the reverse of removal.

---

22   Variable Valve Timing and Lift Electronic Control (VTEC) system - description and component replacement

Description

1   A low-lift, short-duration camshaft intake lobe produces good torque, quick response, good fuel economy and low emissions at lower engine speeds, but can't deliver sufficient air/fuel mixture to the combustion chamber at higher engine speeds. A high-lift, long-duration intake cam lobe produces good power at high engine speeds, but produces a lumpy idle and poor driveability, wastes fuel and produces unacceptable emissions at lower engine speeds. That's why camshaft intake lobe profiles are always a compromise between economy and performance. But the **V**ariable Valve **T**iming and Lift **E**lectronic **C**ontrol (VTEC) system allows an engine to operate economically

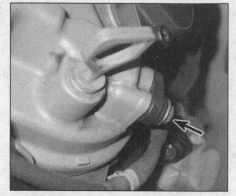

21.24 To remove the PCV valve, remove this bolt (2004 and later models)

and make good power at the same time.

2   The VTEC system is used on all models covered in this manual. The principal differences between VTEC and non-VTEC engines are in the cylinder head, the camshaft(s) and the rocker arms. The block, the lubrication and cooling systems and most other components are identical on VTEC and non-VTEC engines. For more information about the cylinder head, the camshaft(s) and the rocker arms, see Chapter 2. This Section is intended to familiarize you with how VTEC works and to show you how to replace the PCM-controlled components such as the VTEC solenoid valve and the VTEC oil pressure switch.

3   There are two cam lobes for each pair of intake valves on a VTEC engine. These primary and secondary lobe profiles differ in lift and duration: the secondary lobe has lower lift and less duration (it opens later and closes sooner), while the primary lobe has higher lift and more duration (opens sooner and closes later). Each lobe operates its own rocker arm, which in turn pushes on its own valve. At low speeds, the secondary camshaft lobe operates one intake valve and the primary cam lobe operates the other valve. The low-lift, short-duration lobe produces good low-end torque and responsiveness.

4   When more power is needed at higher engine speeds, the PCM activates the VTEC solenoid valve, which allows higher oil pressure to a hydraulically-operated, spring-loaded pin inside the primary rocker arm. When hydraulic pressure overcomes spring pressure, the pin slides sideways and locks the secondary rocker arm to the primary rocker arm. The two rocker arms are both activated by the primary cam lobe; the secondary rocker arm no longer contacts its own camshaft lobe again until the system is disengaged. So both valves are now opened by the primary camshaft lobe with its higher lift and longer duration, increasing performance.

5   The PCM turns the VTEC solenoid valve on and off in accordance with engine rpm, vehicle speed, throttle opening angle, engine load and coolant temperature. Although diagnosis of the VTEC system is beyond the scope of the home mechanic, it's not difficult to replace the VTEC solenoid valve or to clean the filter for the system, both of which are outlined below.

Component replacement

VTEC solenoid valve

Refer to illustrations 22.7a and 22.7b

Note: *The VTEC solenoid valve is located at the lower right corner of the backside of the engine block at the upper end of the oil filter housing, above the VTEC oil pressure switch.*

6   Raise the front of the vehicle and place it securely on jackstands.

7   Locate the VTEC solenoid valve **(see illustration)**, then trace the electrical lead up to the electrical connector **(see illustration)** and disconnect it.

8   Remove the two VTEC solenoid valve mounting bolts and remove the solenoid valve.

9   Remove and discard the VTEC solenoid valve O-ring.

10   Installation is the reverse of removal. Be sure to use a new O-ring and tighten the VTEC solenoid valve mounting bolts to the torque listed in this Chapter's Specifications.

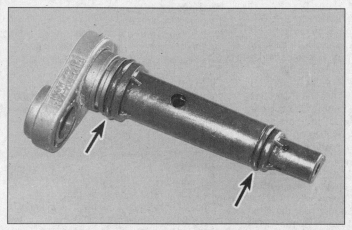

21.25 Remove and discard the two old PCV O-rings (2004 and later models)

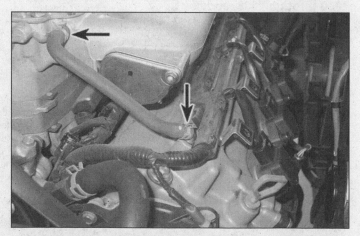

21.27 To remove the crankcase ventilation hose (PCV hose), loosen and slide back the two spring-type clamps and pull off the hose (2004 and later models)

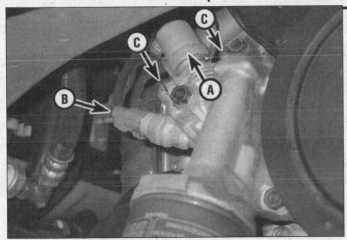

22.7a The VTEC solenoid valve (A) is located at the lower right rear corner of the engine, directly above the VTEC oil pressure switch (B). To detach the solenoid valve, simply remove the two mounting bolts (C)

22.7b To find the electrical connector for the VTEC solenoid valve, trace the electrical lead up to the connector. To disconnect the connector, depress the release tab (A) and pull the lower half of the connector out of the upper half (the upper half is fixed to a small metal support bracket)

VTEC oil pressure switch

Refer to illustrations 22.12 and 22.14

Note: *The VTEC oil pressure switch is located at the upper end of the oil filter housing, below the VTEC solenoid valve.*

11   Raise the front of the vehicle and place it securely on jackstands.

12   Disconnect the electrical connector from the VTEC oil pressure switch **(see illustration)**.

13   Unscrew and remove the VTEC oil pressure switch.

14   Remove and discard the old VTEC oil pressure switch O-ring **(see illustration)**.

15   Installation is the reverse of removal. Be sure to use a new O-ring and tighten the oil pressure switch to the torque listed in this Chapter's Specifications.

23 Intake Manifold Runner Control (IMRC) system - description, adjustment and component replacement

Note: *This system is used on 2003 and earlier models.*

Description

1   The Intake Manifold Runner Control (IMRC) system consists of the control module, the control actuator, the control cable and the two IMRC valves inside the intake manifold. When commanded to do so by the Powertrain Control Module (PCM), the control actuator opens or closes the IMRC valves via a short cable connected to a spring-loaded link on the right end of the shaft to which the valves are attached. You'll find the cable connection to this link at the right end of the intake manifold.

2   Basically, the control module closes the IMRC valves at low speed and opens them at high speed. When the IMRC valves are closed, they increase the effective length of the intake runners, which improves torque at low speed. When the valves are open, they shorten the effective length of the intake runners, which improves power at high speed. At idle and at low engine speeds, the air drawn into an engine with longer intake runners will have a higher velocity than one with shorter intake runners. However, at higher engine speeds, longer intake runners would prevent the cylinders from filling quickly enough and would therefore limit power. Most intake mani-

fold designs are a compromise between the conflicting demands of low and high engine speeds.

3   The IMRC system uses a specially designed intake manifold. Inside the manifold are a pair of long, rectangular-shaped valves mounted on a shaft that is controlled by the actuator. When the engine is idling or operating below a specified rpm, the two valves inside the manifold direct incoming air through a longer path. Directing incoming air through a longer intake path at low engine speeds promotes higher intake air velocities because the incoming air can move more quickly through the intake manifold to fill the cylinders. When engine speed reaches the specified rpm, the PCM energizes the actuator, which turns the shaft and the two valves, altering the intake pathway through the intake manifold. When the valves turn, they send the incoming air through a shorter intake path designed to handle a larger volume of air. At that point, the volume of air drawn into the cylinders is sufficient to promote good velocity even through the shorter intake path. The shorter intake path enhances performance during heavy acceleration or high cruising speeds.

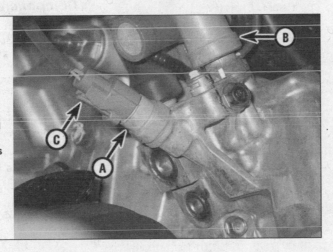

22.12 The VTEC oil pressure switch (A) is located below the VTEC solenoid valve (B). To disconnect the electrical connector from the oil pressure switch, depress the release tab (C) and pull off the connector

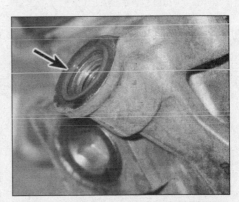

22.14 Always remove and discard the old VTEC oil pressure switch O-ring and install a new O-ring

24.5 To remove the IMT actuator from the intake manifold on 2004 and later models, depress the release tab (1) and disconnect the electrical connector, then remove the two actuator mounting bolts (2)

Control cable adjustment

4   Remove the engine cover (see Chapter 2A).

5   The IMRC valves are opened and closed by a short cable coming from the control actuator. The control cable is connected to a spring-loaded linkage cam on the right end of the intake manifold. When the IMRC valves are closed, there should be no clearance between the adjuster screw and the stop. Verify that there is no clearance here. If there is any clearance, adjust the control cable as follows.

6   Trace the cable to its other end at the control actuator on the backside of the intake manifold. The cable is connected to another cam link on the actuator. Freeplay is determined by the position of the adjuster nut and locknut on the threaded adjuster barrel at the end of the cable sheath. Check the cable freeplay between the cable bracket and the actuator cam and compare your measurement to the cable freeplay listed in this Chapter's Specifications. If the cable freeplay is outside the specified range, loosen the locknut and adjuster nut at the cable bracket and adjust the cable as necessary. When the freeplay is satisfactory, tighten the locknut and adjuster nut securely, then check the clearance again between the adjuster screw and the stop at the other end of the cable. Repeat, if necessary, until the cable freeplay produces zero clearance between the adjuster screw and the stop.

Component replacement

7   Remove the engine cover (see Chapter 2A).

IMRC control actuator

Note: *The IMRC control actuator is located on the backside of the intake manifold.*

8   Disconnect the electrical connector from the IMRC control actuator.

9   Remove the actuator mounting bolts and remove the actuator from the intake manifold.

10   Loosen the control cable locknut and adjuster nut and detach the cable from the cable bracket. To disengage the cable end plug from the cam link on the actuator, rotate the spring-loaded link cam counterclockwise and slide the end plug out of its slot in the cam.

11   Installation is the reverse of removal. Be sure to adjust control cable freeplay when you're done.

IMRC control cable

12   Remove the control actuator and disconnect the control cable from the actuator (see Steps 7 through 9).

13   At the IMRC valve end of the cable, loosen the control cable locknut and adjuster nut and detach the cable from the cable bracket. To disengage the cable end plug from the cam link on the IMRC valve shaft, rotate the spring-loaded link cam counterclockwise and slide the end plug out of its slot in the cam.

14   Installation is the reverse of removal

15   Be sure to adjust the control cable when you're done (see Steps 4 and 5).

IMRC control module

Note: *The IMRC control module is located under the instrument panel, on top of the center tunnel.*

16   Remove the passenger side center console trim (see Chapter 11).

17   Remove the IMRC control module retaining bolt.

18   Remove the IMRC control module from its mounting bracket, flip it upside down and disconnect the electrical connector from the module.

19   Installation is the reverse of removal.

Intake manifold

20   Refer to Chapter 2A.

24   Intake Manifold Tuning (IMT) system - description and component replacement

Note: *This system is used on 2004 and later models.*

Description

1   The Intake Manifold Tuning (IMT) system is a new and improved version of the previous Intake Manifold Runner Control (IMRC) system used on earlier models. The IMT system consists of the Powertrain Control Module (PCM), a tuning valve actuator with an integral position sensor, which is bolted onto the intake manifold, and the two IMT valves, which are located inside the intake manifold. The PCM uses the position sensor to monitor the position (angle) of the IMT valves. When the valves are closed, they improve torque at low speed by increasing the effective length of the intake runners. When the valves are open, they improve power at high speed by decreasing the effective length of the intake runners. At idle and at low engine speeds, the air drawn into an engine with longer intake runners will have a higher velocity than one with shorter intake runners. However, at higher engine speeds, longer intake runners would prevent the cylinders from filling quickly enough and would therefore limit power. Most intake manifold designs are a compromise between the conflicting demands of low and high engine speeds.

2   The IMT system helps to maintain a uniformly higher intake air velocity throughout the engine's operating range. Higher intake air velocity promotes better vaporization of the fuel sprayed into the stream of incoming air by the fuel injectors, which means more complete combustion, more power, better fuel economy and fewer emissions.

3   The IMT system uses a specially designed intake manifold. Inside the manifold are a pair of long, rectangular-shaped valves mounted on a shaft that is controlled by the actuator. When the engine is idling or operating below a specified rpm, the two valves inside the manifold direct incoming air through a longer path. Directing incoming air through a longer intake path at low engine speeds promotes higher intake air velocities because the incoming air can move more quickly through the intake manifold to fill the cylinders. When engine speed reaches the specified rpm, the PCM energizes the actuator, which turns the shaft and the two valves, altering the intake pathway through the intake manifold. When the valves turn, they send the incoming air through a shorter intake path designed to handle a larger volume of air. At that point, the volume of air drawn into the cylinders is sufficient to promote good velocity even through the shorter intake path. And the shorter intake path enhances performance during heavy acceleration or high cruising speeds.

Component replacement

IMT actuator

Refer to illustration 24.5

4   Remove the engine cover (see Chapter 2A).

5   Disconnect the electrical connector from the IMT actuator **(see illustration)**.

6   Remove the actuator mounting bolts and remove the actuator.

7   Remove and discard the actuator O-ring.

8   Installation is the reverse of removal. Be sure to use a new O-ring and tighten the actuator mounting bolts to the torque listed in this Chapter's Specifications.

Intake manifold

9   Refer to Chapter 2A.

Chapter 7 Part A
Manual transaxle

Contents

Specifications

Torque specifications

	Ft-lbs	Nm
Engine/transmission mount bolts/nuts	See Chapter 2A	
Subframe mounting bolts	See Chapter 10	
Transaxle-to-engine mounting bolts	54	73

1 General information

Vehicles covered by this manual are equipped with either a four-speed automatic transaxle (1999 models), five-speed automatic transaxle (2000 and later models) or six-speed manual transaxle.

All information on the manual transaxle is included in this Part of Chapter 7. Service procedures for the five-speed automatic transaxle can be found in Chapter 7, Part B. You'll also find certain procedures common to both transaxles - such as oil seal replacement - in this Chapter.

Depending on the expense involved in having a transaxle overhauled, it might be a better idea to consider replacing it with either a new or rebuilt unit. Your local dealer or transaxle shop should be able to supply information concerning cost, availability and exchange policy. Regardless of how you decide to remedy a transaxle problem, you can still save a lot of money by removing and installing the unit yourself.

2.4 Insert the tip of a large screwdriver or prybar behind the oil seal and very carefully pry it out

2.6 Using a seal driver or a large socket, drive the new seal squarely into the bore

2   Driveaxle oil seals - replacement

Refer to illustrations 2.4 and 2.6

1   Oil leaks frequently occur due to wear of the driveaxle oil seals. Replacement of these seals is relatively easy, since the repair can usually be performed without removing the transaxle from the vehicle.
2   Driveaxle oil seals are located at the sides of the transaxle, where the driveaxles are attached. If leakage at the seal is suspected, raise the vehicle and support it securely on jackstands. If the seal is leaking, lubricant will be found on the sides of the transaxle, below the seals.
3   Refer to Chapter 8 and remove the driveaxles.
4   Use a screwdriver or prybar to carefully pry the oil seal out of the transaxle bore **(see illustration)**.
5   If the oil seal cannot be removed with a screwdriver or prybar, a special oil seal removal tool (available at auto parts stores) will be required.
6   Using a seal driver or a large deep socket (slightly smaller than the outside diameter of the seal) as a drift, install the new oil seal **(see illustration)**. Drive it into the bore squarely and make sure it's completely seated. Coat the seal lip with transaxle lubricant.
7   Install the driveaxle(s). Be careful not to damage the lip of the new seal.

3   Shift cables - removal and installation

1   Remove the center console (see Chapter 11).
2   Remove the cotter pin and detach the cable end from the lock pins on the shift lever.
3   The shift cable is attached to the ball on the bottom of the shifter, where it is retained by a clip. The select cable is attached to a pin

on the right side of the shifter housing. Pry off the spring clips and detach the cables from the shift lever housing and the shift lever. Rotate the cables until the squared edge aligns with the slot in the shift lever housing cutout.
4   Pull back the carpet and dislodge the grommet from the floorpan.
5   Raise the front of the vehicle and support it securely on jackstands.
6   Unscrew the nut and detach the cable bracket from the floorpan.
7   Remove the cotter pins and washers and detach the cables from the shift levers on the transaxle.
8   Pry off the spring clip(s) and detach the cable(s) from the bracket on the transaxle.
9   Guide the cable(s) through the floorpan.
10   The remainder of the installation is the reverse of removal.

4   Back-up light switch - check and replacement

Check

1   Before testing the back-up light switch, check the fuse in the engine compartment fuse/relay box. Refer to the wiring diagrams at the end of Chapter 12.
2   Put the shift lever in Reverse and turn the ignition switch to the On position. The back-up lights should go on. Turn off the ignition switch.
3   If the back-up lights don't go on, check the back-up light bulbs in the tail light assembly.
4   If the fuse and bulbs are both okay, locate the back-up light switch on top of the transaxle, under the lifting hook. For access to the switch, remove the air intake duct and the air filter housing and resonator (see Chapter 4).
5   Remove the battery and the battery tray (see Chapter 5).
6   Trace the leads back to the back-up light

switch electrical connector, unplug the connector and hook up an ohmmeter or continuity tester across the terminals of the back-up light switch.
7   With the shift lever in Reverse, there should be continuity; with the shifter in any other gear, there should be no continuity.
8   If the switch fails this test, replace it (see below).
9   If the switch is OK, but the back-up lights aren't coming on, check for power to the switch. If voltage is not available, trace the circuit between the switch and the fuse block. If power is present, trace the circuit between the switch and the back-up lights for an open circuit condition.

Replacement

10   Unplug the back-up light switch electrical connector.
11   Unscrew the back-up light switch.
12   Using a new O-ring, install the new switch. **Note:** *Some models use RTV sealant to seal the switch. On these models, clean the threaded hole of old sealant, apply new sealant to the new switch, and install the switch within five minutes of applying the RTV.*
13   Plug in the connector.

5   Manual transaxle - removal and installation

Removal

1   Remove the air intake duct and the air filter housing and resonator (see Chapter 4).
2   Remove the engine compartment covers and the strut brace between the shock towers, if equipped (see Chapter 10).
3   Remove the battery and the battery tray (see Chapter 5).
4   Remove the clutch release cylinder and hydraulic line, without disconnecting any fittings. Support the cylinder out of the way with a length of wire or rope. **Caution:** *Don't*

depress the clutch pedal while the release cylinder is removed.

5   Clearly label and disconnect all vacuum lines, emissions hoses, electrical connectors and wiring harness clamps/brackets that may interfere with transaxle removal. Masking tape and/or a touch up paint applicator work well for marking items. Take instant photos or sketch the locations of components and brackets.

6   Remove the cover over the radiator (see Chapter 3).

7   Remove the upper transmission-to-engine bolts.

8   Support the engine with an engine support fixture or an engine hoist (an engine support fixture is recommended, as it doesn't have legs that extend under the vehicle that would get in the way). Connect the sling or chain to the left end (driver's side) of the engine, not to the lifting eye on the transaxle. Use the threaded hole(s) in the left end (driver's side) of the cylinder heads to attach the sling or chain.

9   Unstake and loosen the driveaxle/hub nuts (see Chapter 8). Loosen the front wheel lug nuts, then raise the vehicle and support it securely on jackstands. Remove the wheels.

10   Remove the engine splash shield (see Chapter 2A) and the inner fender splash shields (see Chapter 11). Cover the fenders and cowl using special pads. An old bedspread or blanket will also work.

11   Drain the transaxle fluid (see Chapter 1).

12   Remove the front section of the exhaust pipe, between the exhaust manifold(s) and the downstream catalytic converter.

13   Remove the driveaxles and the intermediate shaft (see Chapter 8).

14   Disconnect the shift cables from the transaxle.

15   Remove all of the powertrain mounts except the right side (drivebelt end) mount (see Chapter 2A).

16   Remove the subframe (see Chapter 10).

17   Support the transaxle with a jack, preferably one made for this purpose. Secure the transaxle to the jack with straps or chains.

18   Remove the lower transaxle-to-engine bolts.

19   Move the transaxle away from the engine to disengage the transaxle input shaft from the clutch disc, and far enough to clear the pressure plate. Lower the transaxle from the vehicle. **Note:** *It may be necessary to slowly lower the engine a slight amount while the jack supporting the transaxle is being lowered. This will provide more clearance between the transaxle and the body.*

Installation

20   If removed, install the clutch components (see Chapter 8).

21   Make sure the two dowel pins are installed. With the transaxle secured to the jack with a chain, raise it into position behind the engine, then carefully slide it forward, engaging the two dowel pins on the transaxle with the corresponding holes in the block and the input shaft with the clutch plate hub splines. Do not use excessive force to install the transaxle - if the input shaft does not slide into place, readjust the angle of the transaxle so it is level and/or turn the input shaft so the splines engage properly with the clutch plate hub.

22   Install the transaxle-to-engine bolts and tighten them to the torque listed in this Chapter's Specifications.

23   The remainder of installation is the reverse of removal, noting the following points:

a) *Refill the transaxle with the specified type of lubricant (see Chapter 1).*

b) *Tighten the driveaxle/hub nuts to the torque listed in the Chapter 8 Specifications, then stake them.*

c) *Tighten the wheel lug nuts to the torque listed in the Chapter 1 Specifications.*

d) *Road test the vehicle for proper operation and check for leaks.*

6   Manual transaxle overhaul - general information

1   Overhauling a manual transaxle is a difficult job for the do-it-yourselfer. It involves the disassembly and reassembly of many small parts. Numerous clearances must be precisely measured and, if necessary, changed with select-fit spacers and snap-rings. As a result, if transaxle problems arise, it can be removed and installed by a competent do-it-yourselfer, but overhaul should be left to a transaxle repair shop. Rebuilt transaxles may be available - check with your dealer parts department and auto parts stores. At any rate, the time and money involved in an overhaul is almost sure to exceed the cost of a rebuilt unit.

2   Nevertheless, it's not impossible for an inexperienced mechanic to rebuild a transaxle if the special tools are available and the job is done in a deliberate step-by-step manner so nothing is overlooked.

3   The tools necessary for an overhaul include internal and external snap-ring pliers, a bearing puller, a slide hammer, a set of pin punches, a dial indicator and possibly a hydraulic press. In addition, a large, sturdy workbench and a vise or transaxle stand will be required.

4   During disassembly of the transaxle, make careful notes of how each piece comes off, where it fits in relation to other pieces and what holds it in place. Noting how the parts are installed when you remove them will make it much easier to get the transaxle back together.

5   Before taking the transaxle apart for repair, it will help if you have some idea what area of the transaxle is malfunctioning. Certain problems can be closely tied to specific areas in the transaxle, which can make component examination and replacement easier. Refer to the *Troubleshooting* Section at the front of this manual for information regarding possible sources of trouble.

Notes

Chapter 7 Part B
Automatic transaxle

Contents

Specifications

General

Fluid type and capacity.. See Chapter 1

Torque specifications

	Ft-lbs (unless otherwise indicated)	Nm

Note: One foot-pound (ft-lb) of torque is equivalent to 12 inch-pounds (in-lbs) of torque. Torque values below approximately 15 ft-lbs are expressed in inch-pounds, since most foot-pound torque wrenches are not accurate at these smaller values.

	Ft-lbs	Nm
Engine-to-transaxle (lower 2 bolts from engine side)	28	38
Transaxle-to-engine mounting bolts	47	64
Torque converter-to-driveplate bolts	104 in-lbs	12
Torque converter cover bolts	104 in-lbs	12

1 General information

The automatic transaxle is an electronically controlled 4-speed unit in the 1999 model year, and a 5-speed model in 2000 and later models. The transaxle identification number is stamped onto a plate on the transaxle.

Due to the complexity of the clutches and the hydraulic control system, and because of the special tools and expertise required to perform an automatic transaxle overhaul, it should not be undertaken by the home mechanic. Therefore, the procedures in this Chapter are limited to general diagnosis, shift cable adjustment, certain component replacement procedures and transaxle removal and installation.

If the transaxle requires major repair work, it should be left to a dealer service department or an automotive or transaxle repair shop. You can, however, remove and install the transaxle yourself and save the expense, even if the repair work is done by a transaxle shop (but be sure a proper diagnosis has been made before removing the transaxle).

2 Diagnosis - general

Note: Automatic transaxle malfunctions may be caused by five general conditions: poor engine performance, improper adjustments, hydraulic malfunctions, mechanical malfunctions or malfunctions in the computer or its signal network. Diagnosis of these problems should always begin with a check of the easily repaired items: fluid level and condition (see Chapter 1), shift cable adjustment and transmission range switch adjustment. Next, perform a road test to determine if the problem has been corrected or if more diagnosis is necessary. If the problem persists after the preliminary tests and corrections are completed, additional diagnosis should be done by a dealer service department or transaxle repair shop. Refer to the Troubleshooting Section at the front of this manual for information on symptoms of transaxle problems.

3.2 Remove the locking nut from the shift lever pin (A), then detach the cable end (B) from its bracket

3.6 Remove the shift cable guide bracket from the floorpan

Preliminary checks

1   Drive the vehicle to warm the transaxle to normal operating temperature.

2   Check the fluid level as described in Chapter 1:

a) If the fluid level is unusually low, add enough fluid to bring the level within the designated area of the dipstick, then check for external leaks (see "Fluid leak diagnosis" below).

b) If the fluid level is abnormally high, drain off the excess, then check the drained fluid for contamination by coolant. The presence of engine coolant in the automatic transaxle fluid indicates that a failure has occurred in the internal radiator walls that separate the coolant from the transaxle fluid (see Chapter 3).

c) If the fluid is foaming, drain it and refill the transaxle, then check for coolant in the fluid, or a high fluid level.

3   Check for any stored trouble codes related to the transaxle (see Chapter 6). **Note:** *If the engine is malfunctioning, do not proceed with the preliminary checks until it has been repaired and runs normally.*

4   Inspect the shift cable linkage (see Section 3). Make sure that it's properly adjusted and that it operates smoothly.

Fluid leak diagnosis

5   Most fluid leaks are easy to locate visually. Repair usually consists of replacing a seal or gasket. If a leak is difficult to find, the following procedure may help.

6   Identify the fluid. Make sure it's transaxle fluid and not engine oil or brake fluid (automatic transaxle fluid is a deep red color).

7   Try to pinpoint the source of the leak. Drive the vehicle several miles, then park it over a large sheet of cardboard. After a minute or two, you should be able to locate the leak by determining the source of the fluid dripping onto the cardboard.

8   Make a careful visual inspection of the suspected component and the area immediately around it. Pay particular attention to gasket mating surfaces. A mirror is often helpful for finding leaks in areas that are hard to see.

9   If the leak still cannot be found, clean the suspected area thoroughly with a degreaser or solvent, then dry the area.

10   Drive the vehicle for several miles at normal operating temperature and varying speeds. After driving the vehicle, visually inspect the suspected component again.

11   Before attempting to repair a leak, check to make sure that the following conditions are corrected or they may cause another leak. **Note:** *Some of the following conditions cannot be fixed without highly specialized tools and expertise. Such problems must be referred to a transmission shop or a dealer service department.*

Seal leaks

12   If a transaxle seal is leaking, the fluid level may be too high, the vent may be plugged, the seal bore may be damaged, the seal itself may be damaged or improperly installed, the surface of the shaft protruding through the seal may be damaged or a loose bearing may be causing excessive shaft movement.

13   Make sure the dipstick tube seal is in good condition and the tube is properly seated. Periodically check the area around the sensors for leakage. If transaxle fluid is evident, check the O-ring for damage.

Case leaks

14   If the case itself appears to be leaking, the casting is porous and will have to be repaired or replaced.

15   Make sure the oil cooler hose fittings are tight and in good condition.

Fluid comes out vent pipe or fill tube

16   If this condition occurs, the transaxle is overfilled, there is coolant in the fluid, the case is porous, the dipstick is incorrect, the vent is plugged or the drain-back holes are plugged.

3   Shift cable - removal, installation and adjustment

Warning: *The models covered by this manual are equipped with Supplemental Restraint Systems (SRS), more commonly known as airbags. Always disable the airbag system before working in the vicinity of any airbag system component to avoid the possibility of accidental deployment of the airbag, which could cause personal injury (see Chapter 12). Do not use a memory saving device to preserve the PCM's memory when working on or near airbag system components.*

Removal

Refer to illustrations 3.2, 3.6, 3.7 and 3.9

1   If you're working on a 2007 and later model, remove the air intake duct and air filter housing (see Chapter 4), the battery and the battery tray (see Chapter 5).

2   Remove the center console (see Chapter 11). Position the shift lever in R. Remove the locking nut from the pin on the shift lever **(see illustration)**.

3   On 2006 and earlier models, twist the cable housing end one-quarter turn, until the shift cable end can be withdrawn from the shift cable bracket **(see illustration 3.2)**. On 2007 and later models, push down the button at the outside top of the cable end and withdraw the cable end straight out from the bracket.

4   Pry the rubber boot loose where the cable passes through the floorpan.

5   Raise the vehicle and support it securely on jackstands.

6   Working under the vehicle near the console, remove the shift cable guide bracket and grommet from the body **(see illustration)**.

7   Remove the bolts securing the shift cable

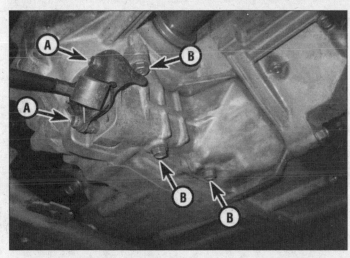

3.7 Remove the bolts (A) from the shift cable cover, then remove the shift cable cover mounting bolts (B) providing access to the cable end and shift arm

3.9 Bend the special washer's tang up and remove the lock-bolt and washer at the transaxle shifting shaft (2006 and earlier models)

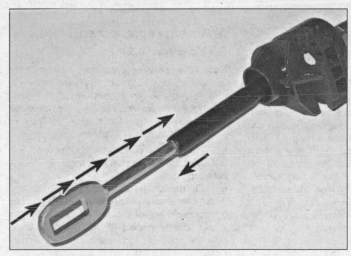

3.16 Push the shift cable until it stops, then back one click into the Reverse position

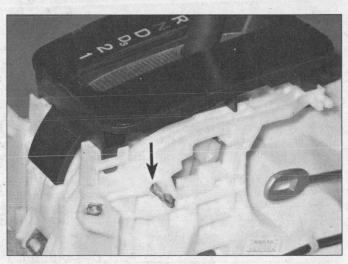

3.17 Install a 0.24 inch (6 mm) pin (here a 15/64-inch drill bit is being used) into the alignment hole on the shift lever bracket base and into the alignment hole in the shift lever

holder to the shift cable cover **(see illustration)**.

8 Remove the bolts from the shift cable cover and separate it from the transaxle.

9 On 2006 and earlier models, remove the locking bolt securing the shift arm to the shaft on the transaxle **(see illustration)**. On 2007 and later models, remove the two nuts securing the cable bracket to the transaxle, then remove the spring clip and pin to disconnect the shift cable end from the shift arm on the transaxle.

10 Remove the shift cable assembly. On 2007 and later models only, you will have to remove a bolt securing the cable to the subframe.

Installation and adjustment

Refer to illustrations 3.16 and 3.17

11 Installation is the reverse of the removal procedure, however, don't connect the cable to the shift lever bracket or lever inside the vehicle yet.

12 Make sure the shift lever is still in the Reverse position and the ignition is Off.

13 Reinstall the arm on the transaxle, making sure it is still in the reverse position. On 2006 and earlier models, attach the cable end with the lockbolt and a new special washer. Once the bolt is tightened, bend down the tab on the washer. On 2007 and later models, inspect the bushing on the transmission end of the cable and replace it if necessary, then install the pin and spring clip to attach the cable end to the arm on the transaxle. Install the nuts securing the cable housing to the transaxle.

14 Install the shift cable cover to the transaxle, then install the shift cable bracket to the cover. **Note:** *Try not to bend the cable any more than is necessary during installation.*

15 From inside the vehicle, turn the ignition to ON and make sure the R position is indicated at the shifter assembly. Turn the ignition to Off.

16 Push the shift cable all the way in until it stops, then back one click into the reverse position **(see illustration)**.

17 Install a 0.24-inch (6 mm) pin into the positioning hole on the shift lever bracket base and into the alignment hole on the shift lever **(see illustration)**. A drill bit with the correct diameter will also work.

18 Align the socket holder on the shift cable with the slot on the bracket base **(see illustration 3.2)**. Twist the cable end into the bracket base until it snaps into place with the square lug in the square slot.

19 Install the shift cable end onto the shift lever pin, making sure it fits over the square shank on the pin. **Note:** *The cable end is properly installed over the square lug only when the cable is snug against the stop; if there is a gap there when viewed from above,*

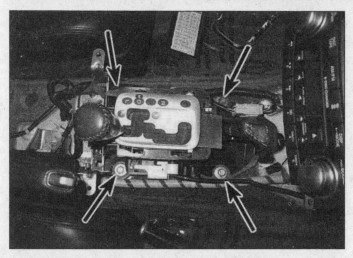

4.4 Shift lever assembly mounting bolts

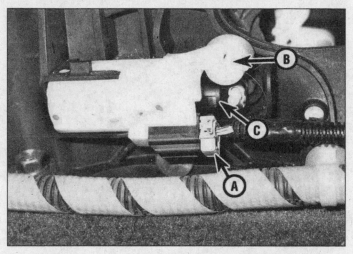

5.6 Disconnect the interlock solenoid connector (A), then lift up the locking lever (B) to release the solenoid (C, 2004 and later models)

the end is not aligned properly.
20   Install the nut on the shift lever pin and tighten it securely.
21   Remove the alignment pin or drill bit from the alignment hole.
22   Turn the ignition key to On (don't start the engine), move the shift lever to each gear position and verify that the gear position indicator light comes on in each position. Make sure the engine only starts in Park and Neutral.
23   The remainder of installation is the reverse of removal.

---

4   Shift lever assembly - removal and installation

Refer to illustration 4.4
Warning: *The models covered by this manual are equipped with Supplemental Restraint Systems (SRS), more commonly known as airbags. Always disable the airbag system before working in the vicinity of any airbag system component to avoid the possibility of accidental deployment of the airbag, which could cause personal injury (see Chapter 12). Do not use a memory saving device to preserve the PCM's memory when working on or near airbag system components.*
1   Remove the center console (see Chapter 11).
2   Disconnect the shift cable from the shift lever assembly (see Section 3).
3   Tag and disconnect all electrical connectors at the shifter housing.
4   Remove the four mounting bolts from the shift lever bracket base and remove the shifter assembly **(see illustration).**
5   Installation is the reverse of removal. Be sure to adjust the shift cable (see Section 3).

5   Shift interlock system - description and solenoid replacement

Warning: *The models covered by this manual are equipped with Supplemental Restraint Systems (SRS), more commonly known as airbags. Always disable the airbag system before working in the vicinity of any airbag system component to avoid the possibility of accidental deployment of the airbag, which could cause personal injury (see Chapter 12). Do not use a memory saving device to preserve the PCM's memory when working on or near airbag system components.*

Description
1   Vehicles equipped with an automatic transaxle have an interlock system to prevent the shifter from being moved out of the Park position unless the brake is applied. It also prevents the key from being removed from the ignition lock cylinder unless the shifter is placed in the Park position. The interlock system consists of two subsystems: a shift lock system and a key interlock system.

Key interlock system
2   The key interlock system prevents the ignition key from being removed from the ignition switch unless the shift lever is in the Park position.

Shift lock system
3   The shift lock system prevents the shift lever from moving from the Park position unless the brake pedal is depressed. Nor can the shift lever be shifted when the brake pedal and the accelerator pedal are depressed at the same time. In the event of a system malfunction, you can release the shift lever by inserting the ignition key or a screwdriver into the release slot near the shift lever.

Solenoid replacement
Refer to illustration 5.6
Note: *The following procedure pertains only to the shift lock solenoid. For information on how to replace the key interlock solenoid, refer to the "Ignition switch/key lock cylinder replacement" Section in Chapter 12. The key interlock solenoid isn't available separately.*
4   Remove the console (see Chapter 11).
5   Disconnect the shift lock solenoid electrical connector.
6   On models through 2003, pry open the metal clamp to free the solenoid, then slide the solenoid out of the shifter assembly. On 2004 and later models, lift up the locking lever over the solenoid to release it **(see illustration).**
7   Install the original plunger and plunger spring into the new shift lock solenoid.
8   Engage the hole in the end of the plunger with the post of the shift lock stop.
9   Push the new solenoid into the metal clamp on models through 2003, or push down the plastic locking lever on 2004 and later models.
10   Connect the shift lock solenoid electrical connector.
11   The remainder of installation is the reverse of removal.

---

6   Automatic transaxle - removal and installation

Refer to illustrations 6.8, 6.17 and 6.19

Removal
1   Open the hood and cover the fenders and cowl using special pads. An old bedspread or blanket will also work. With the help of an assistant, disconnect the hood struts from the ballstuds on the hood and raise the

6.8 Remove the bolts and set the ATF warmer aside with the hose connected (2006 and earlier models)

6.17 Remove the bolts (A) and the converter cover. Also remove the two engine-to-transaxle bolts (B)

hood to the wide-open position, then thread the right-side ballstud into the lower hole in the hood. Attach the top of the hood strut to the ballstud. **Caution:** *Do not try to lower the hood while it is propped in this position or the hood could be damaged.*

2   Remove the engine compartment covers (see Chapter 1). Remove the air intake duct and the air filter housing (see Chapter 4).

3   Remove the battery and the battery tray (see Chapter 5).

4   On 2007 and later models, remove the underhood fuse/relay box (see Chapter 12).

5   Remove the starter (see Chapter 5).

6   Clearly label and disconnect all vacuum lines, emissions hoses, electrical connectors and wiring harness clamps/brackets that may interfere with transaxle removal. Masking tape and/or a touch up paint applicator work well for marking items. Take instant photos or sketch the locations of components and brackets.

7   Release the transmission fluid lines from the clamps on the transaxle.

8   On 2006 and earlier models, unbolt and set aside the ATF warmer from the transaxle **(see illustration)**. **Note:** *Place rags around the warmer to catch the fluid that will spill.*

9   Disconnect the automatic transaxle fluid cooler lines from the transaxle. Be sure to position a pan to catch excess fluid. Plug the lines to prevent leakage.

10   Support the engine with an engine support fixture or an engine hoist (an engine support fixture is recommended, as it doesn't have legs that extend under the vehicle that would get in the way). Connect the sling or chain to the left end (driver's side) of the engine, not to the lifting eye on the transaxle. Use the threaded hole(s) in the left end (driver's side) of the cylinder head(s) to attach the sling or chain.

11   Unstake and loosen the driveaxle/hub nuts (see Chapter 8). Loosen the front wheel lug nuts, then raise the vehicle and support it securely on jackstands. Remove the wheels.

6.19 Rotate the driveplate to gain access to all the torque converter bolts

12   Remove the engine splash shield (see Chapter 2A).

13   Disconnect the shift control cable from the transaxle (see Section 3).

14   Drain the transaxle fluid (see Chapter 1). Be sure to use a new sealing washer when you reinstall the drain plug.

15   Remove the front section of the exhaust pipe, between the exhaust manifold(s) and the downstream catalytic converter.

16   Remove the driveaxles and the intermediate shaft (see Chapter 8).

17   Remove the torque converter cover and the two engine-to-transmission bolts nearby **(see illustration)**.

18   Mark the relationship of the torque converter to the driveplate so that they can be reinstalled in the same relationship to one another.

19   Remove the torque converter-to-driveplate bolts **(see illustration)** one at a time by rotating the crankshaft pulley for access to each bolt.

20   Remove all of the powertrain mounts except the right side (drivebelt end) mount (see Chapter 2A).

21   Remove the subframe (see Chapter 10).

22   Support the transaxle with a jack, preferably one made for this purpose. Secure the transaxle to the jack with straps or chains.

23   Remove the transaxle-to-engine bolts.

24   Move the transaxle back to disengage it from the engine block dowel pins and make sure the torque converter is detached from the driveplate. Secure the torque converter to the transaxle so it will not fall out during removal. Lower the transaxle from the vehicle. **Note:** *It may be necessary to slowly lower the engine a slight amount while the jack supporting the transaxle is being lowered. This will provide more clearance between the transaxle and the body.*

Installation

25   The manufacturer recommends flushing the transaxle cooler and the cooler hoses and lines with solvent whenever the transaxle is removed from the vehicle. Flush the lines and fluid cooler thoroughly and make sure no solvent remains in the lines or cooler after flushing. It's a good idea to repeat the flushing

procedure with clean automatic transaxle fluid to ensure that no solvent remains in the lines or cooler.

26   On 2006 and earlier models, it is recommended that the ATF fluid warmer be replaced if the transaxle is rebuilt or replaced. Also, when installing the fluid warmer, use new O-rings.

27   Prior to installation, make sure that the torque converter hub is securely engaged in the transaxle pump. **Note:** *If the torque converter was removed from the transaxle, be sure to replace the O-ring on the back side of the torque converter with a new one. With the transaxle secured to the jack, raise it into position. Be sure to keep it level so the torque converter does not slide out.*

28   Line-up the marks you made on the torque converter and driveplate.

29   Make sure the dowel pins are still installed, then move the transaxle forward carefully until the dowel pins are engaged with the holes in the engine block.

30   Install the transaxle-to-engine bolts and tighten them to the torque listed in this Chapter's Specifications. **Caution:** *Don't use the bolts to force the transaxle and engine together. If the transaxle doesn't slide easily up against the engine, find out why before you tighten the bolts*

31   The remainder of installation is the reverse of the removal procedure, noting the following points:

a) *Install all of the driveplate bolts before tightening any of them. Tighten the driveplate bolts to the torque listed in this Chapter's Specifications.*

b) *Tighten the subframe mounting bolts to the torque listed in the Chapter 10 Specifications.*

c) *Tighten the new driveaxle/hub nuts to the torque listed in the Chapter 8 Specifications, then stake the collars of the nuts to the grooves in the driveaxles.*

d) *Tighten the wheel lug nuts to the torque listed in the Chapter 1 Specifications.*

e) *Refill the transaxle with the specified type and amount of lubricant (see Chapter 1). Note that the transaxle may require more fluid than in a normal fluid and filter change, since the torque converter may be empty (the converter is not drained during a fluid change).*

f) *Start the engine, set the parking brake and shift the transaxle through all gears three times. Make sure the shift cable is adjusted properly (see Section 4).*

g) *Allow the engine to reach its proper operating temperature with the transaxle in Park or Neutral, then turn it off and check the fluid level again.*

h) *Road test the vehicle and check for fluid leaks.*

Chapter 8
Clutch and driveline

Contents

Specifications

General
Clutch fluid type .... See Chapter 1

Clutch pedal
Height .... 7.52 inches (191 mm)
Freeplay .... 0.39 to 0.71 inch (10 to 18 mm)

Torque specifications

Note: *One foot-pound (ft-lb) of torque is equivalent to 12 inch-pounds (in-lbs) of torque. Torque values below approximately 15 ft-lbs are expressed in inch-pounds, since most foot-pound torque wrenches are not accurate at these smaller values.*

	Ft-lbs (unless otherwise indicated)	Nm
Clutch master cylinder mounting nuts	112 in-lbs	13
Clutch pressure plate-to-flywheel bolts	19	26
Clutch release cylinder mounting fasteners	16	22
Driveaxle hub/nut*	181	245
Intermediate shaft bearing support mounting bolts	29	39
Wheel lug nuts	See Chapter 1	

*Replace with new nut

1 General information

The information in this Chapter deals with the components from the rear of the engine to the front wheels, except for the transaxle, which is dealt with in the previous Chapter. For the purposes of this Chapter, these components are grouped into two categories - clutch and driveaxles. Separate Sections within this Chapter offer general descriptions and checking procedures for components in each of the two groups.

Since nearly all the procedures covered in this Chapter involve working under the vehicle, make sure it's securely supported on sturdy jackstands or on a hoist where the vehicle can be easily raised and lowered.

2 Clutch - description and check

1   All vehicles with a manual transaxle use a single dry-plate, diaphragm-spring type clutch. The clutch disc has a splined hub which allows it to slide along the splines of the transaxle input shaft. The clutch and pressure plate are held in contact by spring pres-

sure exerted by the diaphragm in the pressure plate. The clutch is designed with a self adjusting system. The clutch pedal load does NOT decrease even when the disc wears. The fulcrum of the diaphragm spring is automatically adjusted as the clutch material wears.

2   The clutch release system is operated by hydraulic pressure. The hydraulic release system consists of the clutch pedal, a master cylinder and fluid reservoir, the hydraulic line, a release (or slave) cylinder which actuates the clutch release lever and the clutch release (or throwout) bearing.

3   When pressure is applied to the clutch pedal to release the clutch, hydraulic pressure is exerted against the outer end of the clutch release lever. As the lever pivots, the shaft fingers push against the release bearing. The bearing pushes against the fingers of the diaphragm spring of the pressure plate assembly, which in turn releases the clutch plate.

4   Terminology can be a problem when discussing the clutch components because common names are in some cases different from those used by the manufacturer. For example, the driven plate is also called the clutch plate or disc, the clutch release bearing is sometimes called a throwout bearing, the release cylinder is sometimes called the operating or slave cylinder.

5   Other than to replace components with obvious damage, some preliminary checks should be performed to diagnose clutch problems. These checks assume that the transaxle is in good working condition.

a) *The first check should be of the fluid level in the clutch master cylinder (see Chapter 1). If the fluid level is low, add fluid as necessary and inspect the hydraulic system for leaks. If the master cylinder reservoir has run dry, bleed the system as described in Section 5 and retest the clutch operation.*

b) *To check clutch spin-down time, run the engine at normal idle speed with the transaxle in Neutral (clutch pedal up - engaged). Disengage the clutch (pedal down), wait several seconds and shift the transaxle into Reverse. No grinding noise should be heard. A grinding noise would most likely indicate a problem in the pressure plate or the clutch disc.*

c) *To check for complete clutch release, run the engine (with the parking brake applied to prevent movement) and hold the clutch pedal approximately 1/2-inch from the floor. Shift the transaxle between 1st gear and Reverse several times. If the shift is rough, component failure is indicated. Check the release cylinder pushrod travel. With the clutch pedal depressed completely, the release cylinder pushrod should extend substantially. If it doesn't, check the fluid level in the clutch master cylinder.*

d) *Visually inspect the pivot bushing at the top of the clutch pedal to make sure there is no binding or excessive play.*

e) *Crawl under the vehicle and make sure the clutch release lever is solidly mounted on the ballstud.*

---

3   Clutch master cylinder - removal and installation

1   Remove the left side engine compartment cover and the front bulkhead cover (see Chapter 11).

2   Remove the air filter housing (see Chapter 4).

3   Remove the battery and battery tray (see Chapter 5).

4   Remove the two mounting bolts from the fuse/relay box and position the assembly off to the side (see Chapter 12).

5   Remove the clutch line mounting bracket and two clutch line clamps.

6   Clamp a pair of locking pliers onto the clutch fluid feed hose, a couple of inches downstream of the reservoir. The pliers should be just tight enough to prevent fluid flow when the hose is disconnected.

7   Remove the clutch fluid reservoir mounting bolt and position the assembly off to the side.

8   Disconnect the hydraulic line at the clutch master cylinder. Remove the retaining clip and separate the line from the cylinder. Have rags handy as some fluid will be lost as the line is removed. Cap or plug the ends of the lines (and/or hose) to prevent fluid leakage and the entry of contaminants. **Caution:** *Don't allow brake fluid to come into contact with the paint as it will damage the finish.*

9   Working inside the passenger compartment, remove the knee bolster and the trim panel from the driver's side (see Chapter 11).

10   Working under the dashboard, remove the cotter pin or spring clip from the master cylinder pushrod clevis. Pull out the clevis pin to disconnect the pushrod from the pedal. Unscrew the two clutch master cylinder retaining nuts and remove the cylinder.

11   Installation is the reverse of removal, noting the following points:

a) *Use new gasket between the master cylinder and the firewall. Tighten the master cylinder mounting nuts to the torque listed in this Chapter's Specifications.*

b) *Install a new O-ring seal on the hydraulic line fitting at the master cylinder.*

c) *Pry the tip of the retaining clip apart to prevent the clip from working its way off the master cylinder pushrod clevis.*

d) *Fill the clutch master cylinder reservoir with brake fluid conforming to DOT 3 specifications and bleed the clutch system as outlined in Section 5.*

---

4   Clutch release cylinder - removal and installation

Removal

1   Remove the left side engine compartment cover and the front bulkhead cover (see Chapter 11).

2   Remove the air filter housing (see Chapter 4).

3   Remove the battery and battery tray (see Chapter 5).

4   Remove the two mounting bolts from the fuse/relay box and position the assembly off to the side (see Chapter 12).

5   Disconnect the hydraulic line mounting bracket.

6   Remove the roll pins securing the hydraulic line to the release cylinder, then disconnect the line. Have a small can and rags handy - some fluid will be spilled as the line is removed. Plug the line to prevent excessive fluid loss.

7   Remove the two release cylinder mounting bolts and remove the release cylinder.

Installation

8   Lightly lubricate the release cylinder pushrod and the release fork pocket with high temperature grease. Install the release cylinder on the clutch housing. Make sure the pushrod is seated in the release fork pocket, then tighten the mounting bolts to the torque listed in this Chapter's Specifications.

9   Install a new O-ring on the hydraulic line, then connect the hydraulic line to the release cylinder and install the roll pins.

10   The remainder of installation is the reverse of removal, noting the following points:

a) *Fill the clutch master cylinder with brake fluid conforming to DOT 3 specifications.*

b) *Bleed the system as described in Section 5.*

---

5   Clutch hydraulic system - bleeding

1   Bleed the hydraulic system whenever any part of the system has been removed or the fluid level has fallen so low that air has been drawn into the master cylinder. The bleeding procedure is very similar to bleeding a brake system.

2   Fill the master cylinder with new brake fluid conforming to DOT 3 specifications. **Caution:** *Do not re-use any of the fluid coming from the system during the bleeding operation or use fluid which has been inside an open container for an extended period of time.*

3   Remove the dust cap from the bleeder valve and push a length of plastic hose over the valve. Place the other end of the hose into a clear container with about two inches of brake fluid. The hose end must be in the fluid at the bottom of the container.

4   Have an assistant depress the clutch pedal and hold it. Open the bleeder valve on the release cylinder, allowing fluid to flow through the hose. Close the bleeder valve when the flow of fluid (and bubbles) ceases. Once closed, have your assistant release the pedal.

5   Continue this process until all air is evacuated from the system, indicated by a

solid stream of fluid being ejected from the bleeder valve each time with no air bubbles in the hose or container. Keep a close watch on the fluid level inside the clutch master cylinder reservoir - if the level drops too far, air will get into the system and you'll have to start all over again.

6   Check carefully for proper operation before placing the vehicle into normal service.

6   Clutch components - removal, inspection and installation

Warning: *Dust produced by clutch wear is hazardous to your health. DO NOT blow it out with compressed air and DO NOT inhale it. DO NOT use gasoline or petroleum-based solvents to remove the dust. Brake system cleaner should be used to flush the dust into a drain pan. After the clutch components are wiped clean with a rag, dispose of the contaminated rags and cleaner in a covered, marked container.*

Caution: *A special tool setup is required to compress the clutch pressure plate during clutch removal and installation. Do not attempt this procedure without the special tools. If the special tools are not available, have the clutch components installed by a repair facility that has the proper tools.*

Removal

Refer to illustrations 6.5 and 6.6

1   Access to the clutch components is normally accomplished by removing the transaxle, leaving the engine in the vehicle.

2   If the engine is being removed for major overhaul, check the clutch for wear and replace worn components as necessary. However, the relatively low cost of the clutch components compared to the time and trouble spent gaining access to them warrants their replacement anytime the engine or transaxle

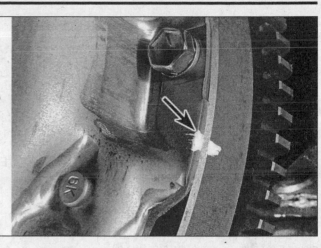

6.5 Mark the relationship of the pressure plate to the flywheel (if you're planning to re-use the old pressure plate)

is removed, unless they are new or in near-perfect condition. The following procedures are based on the assumption the engine will stay in place.

3   Remove the transaxle from the vehicle (see Chapter 7, Part A). Support the engine while the transaxle is out. Preferably, an engine support fixture or a hoist should be used to support it from above.

4   The clutch fork and release bearing can remain attached to the transaxle housing for the time being.

5   Carefully inspect the flywheel and pressure plate for indexing marks. The marks are usually an X, an O or a white letter. If they cannot be found, scribe or paint marks yourself so the pressure plate and the flywheel will be in the same alignment during installation **(see illustration).**

6   Install the special factory tool assembly or equivalent according to the tool manufacturer's instructions, tighten it to compress the diaphragm spring, then loosen the pressure plate-to-flywheel bolts in the pattern shown **(see illustration). Caution:** *The use of this tool is necessary to remove and install the pressure plate without damaging it. The tool compresses the diaphragm spring and takes the pressure off of the clutch cover while the bolts are removed and installed. It also incorporates an alignment tool to center the clutch disc in the pressure plate.*

7   Turning each bolt a little at a time, hold the pressure plate securely and completely remove the bolts, followed by the pressure plate and clutch disc.

Inspection

Refer to illustrations 6.10, 6.12a and 6.12b

8   Ordinarily, when a problem occurs in the clutch, it can be attributed to wear of the clutch driven plate assembly (clutch disc). However, all components should be inspected at this time.

9   Inspect the flywheel for cracks, heat checking, grooves and other obvious defects. If the imperfections are slight, a machine shop can machine the surface flat and smooth, which is highly recommended regardless of the surface appearance. Refer to Chapter 2 for the flywheel removal and installation procedure.

10   Inspect the lining on the clutch disc. There should be at least 1/16-inch of lining above the rivet heads. Check for loose rivets, distortion, cracks, broken springs and other obvious damage **(see illustration).** As mentioned above, ordinarily the clutch disc is routinely replaced, so if in doubt about the condition, replace it with a new one.

11   The release bearing should also be replaced along with the clutch disc (see Section 7).

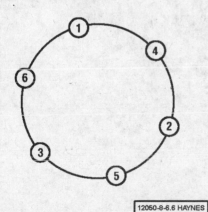

`12050-8-6.6 HAYNES`

6.6 Loosen the pressure plate mounting bolts in this sequence

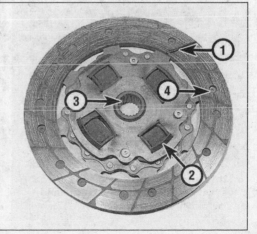

6.10 The clutch disc

1   ***Lining*** *- this will wear down in use*
2   ***Springs or dampers*** *- check for cracking and deformation*
3   ***Splined hub*** *- the splines must not be worn and should slide smoothly on the transaxle input shaft splines*
4   ***Rivets*** *- these secure the lining and will damage the flywheel or pressure plate if allowed to contact the surfaces*

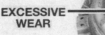

NORMAL FINGER WEAR   **EXCESSIVE FINGER WEAR**   **BROKEN OR BENT FINGERS**

6.12a Replace the pressure plate if excessive wear or damage are noted

12   Check the machined surfaces and the diaphragm spring fingers of the pressure plate **(see illustrations)**. If the surface is grooved or otherwise damaged, replace the pressure plate. Also check for obvious damage, distortion, cracking, etc. Light glazing can be removed with emery cloth or sandpaper. If a new pressure plate is required, new and re-manufactured units are available.

Installation

13   Before installation, clean the flywheel and pressure plate machined surfaces with brake cleaner. It's important that no oil or grease is on these surfaces or the lining of the clutch disc. Handle the parts only with clean hands.
14   Position the clutch disc against the flywheel with the longer portion of the hub facing the flywheel, and the mark on the other side of the hub aligned with the mark on the outer edge of the flywheel.
15   Insert the clutch portion of the special tool through the clutch disc and into the pilot bearing in the flywheel.
16   Install the compressor portion of the tool over the center portion (which is holding the clutch disc) and bolt it to the engine block. Tighten the center screw of the tool to compress the diaphragm spring of the pressure plate, then tighten the pressure plate-

to-flywheel bolts, a little at a time, in the pattern shown in **illustration 6.6**, until the torque listed in this Chapter's Specifications is reached. Remove the special tool.
17   Using high-temperature grease, lubricate the inner groove of the release bearing (see Section 7). Also place a small amount of grease on the release lever contact areas and the transaxle input shaft bearing retainer.
18   Install the clutch release bearing (see Section 7).

Pilot bearing replacement

2006 and earlier models

19   Remove the flywheel (see Chapter 2A).
20   Using a hammer and drift, drive the pilot bearing out of the flywheel, from the friction surface side toward the crankshaft side.
21   Lubricate the outer surface of the new pilot bearing with clean engine oil, then drive it into the flywheel (from the crankshaft side) - using a bearing driver or a socket with a diameter slightly smaller than that of the bearing - until it seats.
22   Install the flywheel (see Chapter 2A).

2007 and later models

Refer to illustrations 6.23 and 6.24
23   Remove the pilot bearing using a slide

hammer and puller attachment **(see illustration)**, which are available at most auto parts stores or tool rental yards.
24   To install a new pilot bearing, lightly lubricate the outside surface with grease, then drive it into the recess with a bearing driver or a socket **(see illustration)**. **Note:** *The seal end of the bearing must be facing toward the transmission.*

---

7   Clutch release bearing and lever - removal, inspection and installation

Warning: *Dust produced by clutch wear is hazardous to your health. DO NOT blow it out with compressed air and DO NOT inhale it. DO NOT use gasoline or petroleum-based solvents to remove the dust. Brake system cleaner should be used to flush the dust into a drain pan. After the clutch components are wiped clean with a rag, dispose of the contaminated rags and cleaner in a covered, marked container.*

Removal

1   Remove the transaxle (see Chapter 7A).
2   Pull the clutch release fork off the ball-stud and slide the release bearing off the input

6.12b Inspect the pressure plate surface for excessive score marks, cracks and signs of overheating

6.23 A small slide hammer is handy for removing a pilot bearing (2007 and later models)

6.24 Tap the bearing into place with a bearing driver or a socket that is slightly smaller than the outside diameter of the bearing (2007 and later models)

7.4 Hold the bearing by the outer race and rotate the inner race while applying pressure - if the bearing doesn't turn smoothly or if it's noisy, replace the bearing

8.1 Pedal height is the distance between the pedal and the floor (with the carpet pulled back)

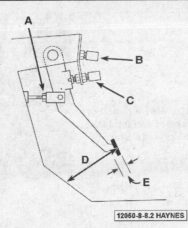

12050-8-8.2 HAYNES

8.2 Clutch pedal adjustment details

A   Clutch pushrod locknut
B   Clutch start (interlock) switch
C   Clutch pedal position switch
D   Pedal height
E   Pedal freeplay

shaft along with the release fork.

Inspection

Refer to illustration 7.4

3   Wipe off the bearing with a clean rag and inspect it for damage, wear and cracks. Don't immerse the bearing in solvent - it's sealed for life and immersion in solvent will ruin it.
4   Hold the center of the bearing and rotate the outer portion while applying pressure **(see illustration)**. If the bearing doesn't turn smoothly or if it's noisy or rough, replace it. **Note:** *Considering the difficulty involved with replacing the release bearing, we recommend replacing the release bearing whenever the clutch components are replaced.*

Installation

5   Lightly lubricate the friction surfaces of the release bearing, ballstud and the sleeve of the input shaft bearing retainer with high-temperature grease.
6   Install the release lever and bearing onto the input shaft.
7   The remainder of installation is the reverse of removal.

8   Clutch pedal adjustment

Refer to illustrations 8.1, 8.2 and 8.5
1   The height of the clutch pedal is the distance the pedal sits off the floor with the carpet pulled back **(see illustration)**. If the pedal height is not within the specified range, it must be adjusted.
2   To adjust the clutch pedal, loosen the locknut on the clutch pedal position switch and back the switch out until it no longer touches the pedal, then loosen the locknut on the clutch pushrod **(see illustration)**. Turn the pushrod to adjust the pedal height, then tighten the locknut.
3   Turn the clutch pedal position switch

clockwise until it just contacts the pedal arm, then turn it in an additional 3/4 to 1 turn. Tighten the locknut.
4   Adjust the clutch start switch as described in Section 9.
5   The freeplay is the pedal slack, or the distance the pedal can be depressed before it begins to have any effect on the clutch system **(see illustration)**. If the pedal freeplay is not within the specified range, but the pedal height is correct, there could be a problem with the self-adjusting clutch pressure plate.

9   Clutch start switch - check and replacement

Note: *The clutch start switch is also known as the clutch interlock switch.*

Check

1   Verify that the engine will not start when the clutch pedal is released.
2   Verify that the engine will start when the clutch pedal is depressed all the way.
3   If the engine won't start with the pedal depressed, or starts with the pedal released,

unplug the electrical connector from the switch. The clutch start switch is located near the top of the clutch pedal bracket **(see illustration 8.2)**. Check continuity between the connector terminals with the clutch pedal depressed.
4   If there's continuity between the terminals with the pedal depressed, the switch is okay; if there's no continuity between the terminals with the pedal depressed, replace the switch. If there's continuity between the terminals when the clutch pedal is released, replace the switch.

Replacement

5   Unplug the switch electrical connector, if you haven't already done so.
6   Loosen the locknut and unscrew the switch from the clutch pedal bracket.
7   Installation is the reverse of removal. To adjust the switch, loosen the locknut and turn the switch in or out, as necessary, to provide continuity through the switch when the clutch pedal is raised 1/8 to 5/16 inch (3 to 8 mm) from the fully depressed position.

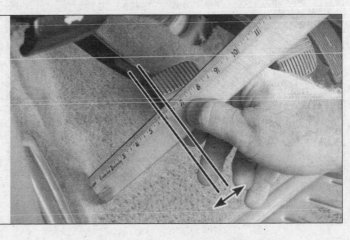

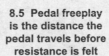

8.5 Pedal freeplay is the distance the pedal travels before resistance is felt

10.2 Use a punch or chisel and unstake the driveaxle/hub nut

10.3 To prevent the hub from turning while you're loosening the driveaxle/hub nut, wedge a prybar between two of the wheel studs

10 Driveaxle - removal and installation

Removal

Refer to illustrations 10.2, 10.3, 10.8a and 10.8b

1   Loosen the front wheel lug nuts, raise the vehicle and support it securely on jackstands. Remove the wheel.
2   Unstake the driveaxle/hub nut with a punch or chisel **(see illustration)**.
3   Loosen the driveaxle/hub nut with a large socket and breaker bar **(see illustration)**, then remove the driveaxle/hub nut from the axle and discard it.
4   Remove the inner fender splash shield (see Chapter 11).
5   Remove the damper fork from the lower control arm and shock absorber, then separate the lower control arm from the steering knuckle (see Chapter 10). On 2004 and later models, disconnect the stabilizer bar link from the lower control arm (see Chapter 10).
6   If you're removing the right-side drive-axle, remove the front portion of the exhaust system (see Chapter 4).
7   Swing the knuckle/hub assembly out (away from the vehicle) until the end of the driveaxle is free of the hub. **Note:** *If the drive-axle splines stick in the hub, tap on the end of the driveaxle with a plastic hammer. Support the outer end of the driveaxle with a piece of wire to avoid unnecessary strain on the inner CV joint.*
8   Place a drain pan under the transaxle, then pry the inner CV joint out of the transaxle (or, on models so equipped, off of the intermediate shaft) using a large screwdriver or prybar **(see illustrations)**. Support the CV joints and carefully remove the driveaxle from the vehicle. To prevent damage to the intermediate shaft seal or the differential seal, hold the inner CV joint horizontal until the driveaxle is clear of the intermediate shaft or transaxle.

Installation

Refer to illustrations 10.9a and 10.9b

9   Pry the old spring clip from the inner end of the driveaxle and install a new one **(see illustrations)**. Lubricate the differential or intermediate shaft seal with multi-purpose grease and raise the driveaxle into position while supporting the CV joints.
10   Insert the splined end of the inner CV joint into the differential side gear or inter-mediate shaft and make sure the spring clip locks in its groove. Grasp the inner CV joint housing (not the driveaxle) and pull out to make sure the driveaxle has seated securely in the transaxle.
11   Apply a light coat of multi-purpose grease to the outer CV joint splines, pull out on the strut/steering knuckle assembly and install the stub axle into the hub.
12   Insert the stud of the steering knuckle balljoint into the lower control arm and tighten the nut (see the torque specifications in Chapter 10). Be sure to use a new cotter pin. Install the damper fork (see Chapter 10).
13   Install the stabilizer link to the lower control arm (see Chapter 10).
14   Install a *new* driveaxle/hub nut, tight-

10.8a Use a large screwdriver or prybar to pop the inner end of the driveaxle from the transaxle . . .

10.8b . . . or, if you're removing a driveaxle from a vehicle equipped with an intermediate shaft, insert the prybar between the intermediate shaft bearing and the driveaxle to pop it loose

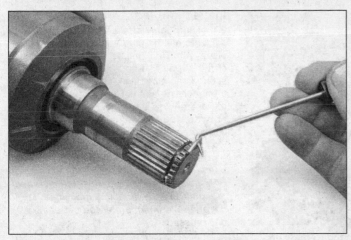

10.9a Pry the old spring clip from the inner end of the driveaxle with a small screwdriver or awl

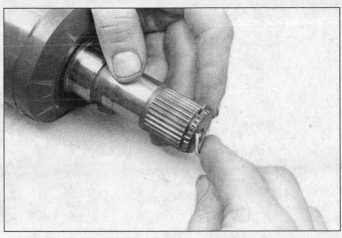

10.9b To install the new spring clip, start one end in the groove and work the clip over the shaft end, into the groove

ening it to the torque listed in this Chapter's Specifications. Using a hammer and a punch, stake the collar of the nut into the slot in the driveaxle.

15   Install the wheel and lug nuts, then lower the vehicle. Tighten the lug nuts to the torque listed in the Chapter 1 Specifications.

16   Check the transaxle lubricant, adding as necessary to bring it to the appropriate level (see Chapter 1).

11   Intermediate shaft - removal and installation

Removal

1   Remove the front portion of the exhaust system (see Chapter 4), then remove the right driveaxle (see Section 10).

2   Remove the exhaust pipe heat shield and mounting bracket.

3   Remove the three bearing support-to-engine block bolts and slide the intermediate shaft out of the transaxle. Be careful not to damage the transaxle seal when pulling the shaft out.

4   Check the support bearing for smooth operation by turning the shaft while holding the bearing. If it feels rough or sticky it should

be replaced. Take it to a dealer service department or other repair shop, as special tools are needed to perform this job.

Installation

5   Lubricate the lips of the transaxle seal with multi-purpose grease. Carefully guide the intermediate shaft into the transaxle side gear, then install the mounting bolts through the bearing support. Tighten the bolts to the torque listed in this Chapter's Specifications.

6   The remainder of installation is the reverse of the removal procedure.

12   Driveaxle boot - replacement

Note: *If the CV joints are worn, indicating the need for an overhaul (usually due to torn boots), explore all options before beginning the job. Complete rebuilt driveaxles are available on an exchange basis, which eliminates much time and work. If you decide to rebuild a CV joint, check on the cost and availability of parts before disassembling the driveaxle.*

Inner CV joint

1   Remove the driveaxle (see Section 10).

2   Mount the driveaxle in a vise with wood-lined jaws, to prevent damage to the axleshaft.

Check the CV joints for excessive play in the radial direction, which indicates worn parts. Check for smooth operation throughout the full range of motion for each CV joint. If a boot is torn, the recommended procedure is to disassemble the joint, clean the components and inspect for damage due to loss of lubrication and possible contamination by foreign matter. If the CV joint is in good condition, lubricate it with CV joint grease and install a new boot.

Disassembly

Refer to illustrations 12.4a, 12.4b, 12.5, 12.6 and 12.7

3   Cut the boot clamps with side-cutters, then remove and discard them.

4   Using a screwdriver, carefully pry up on the edge of the CV boot, pull it off the CV joint housing and slide it down the axleshaft, exposing the tri-pod assembly. Mark the relationship of the joint housing to the tri-pod **(see illustration).** To separate the axleshaft and tri-pod assembly from the inner joint housing, simply pull the housing straight off **(see illustration).** **Note:** *When removing the housing, hold the rollers in place on the tri-pod to pre-*

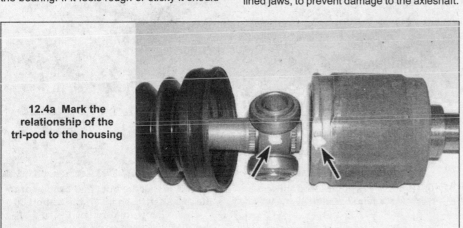

12.4a Mark the relationship of the tri-pod to the housing

12.4b Remove the boot from the inner CV joint and slide the joint housing from the tri-pod

12.5 Remove the snap-ring with a pair of snap-ring pliers

12.6 Make marks on the tri-pod and the driveaxle to ensure that they are reassembled properly

Inspection

9   Thoroughly clean all components with solvent until the old CV joint grease is completely removed. Inspect the bearing surfaces of the tri-pod and housing for cracks, pitting, scoring and other signs of wear. If any part of the inner CV joint is worn, you must replace the entire joint. Depending on the availability of parts, you may even have to purchase a complete driveaxle assembly. **Note:** *If you're working on a right-side driveaxle on a manual transaxle model, check the intermediate shaft bearing for smooth operation. If it feels rough or is noisy when rotated, take the intermediate shaft to an automotive machine shop to have the old bearing pressed out and a new one pressed in.*

Reassembly

Refer to illustrations 12.10a, 12.10b, 12.10c, 12.13, 12.15a, 12.15b, 12.15c, 12.15d and 12.15e

vent the rollers and the needle bearings from falling free.

5   Remove the tri-pod assembly snap-ring with a pair of snap-ring pliers **(see illustration)**.

6   Mark the tri-pod to the axleshaft to ensure that they are reassembled properly **(see illustration)**.

7   Use a hammer and a brass drift to drive the tri-pod assembly from the axleshaft **(see illustration)**.

8   Slide the boot off the shaft.

10   Wrap the splines on the inner end of the axleshaft with electrical or duct tape to protect the boots from the sharp edges of the splines and slide the clamps and boot onto the axleshaft **(see illustration 12.18g)**. Remove the tape and place the tri-pod on the axleshaft with the recessed portion of the splines toward the shaft **(see illustration)**. Tap the tri-pod onto the shaft with a brass drift until it's seated and install the snap-ring. Apply grease to the tri-pod assembly and inside the housing **(see illustration)**. Insert the tri-pod into the housing and pack the remainder of the grease around the tri-pod **(see illustration)**.

11   Slide the boot into place, making sure the raised bead on the inside of the seal boot is positioned in the groove on the interconnecting shaft. If the driveaxle has multiple locating grooves on the shaft, position the boot so only one of the grooves (the thinnest) is exposed.

12   Position the sealing boot into the groove on the housing retaining groove.

13   Position the CV joint mid-way through its travel, then equalize the pressure inside the

12.7 Drive the tri-pod joint from the driveaxle with a brass punch and hammer (be careful not to damage the bearing surfaces or the splines on the shaft)

12.10a Install the tri-pod with the recessed portion of the splines facing the axleshaft

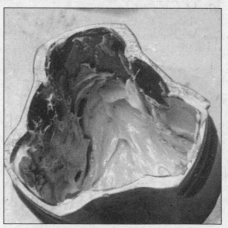

12.10b Place grease at the bottom of the CV joint housing

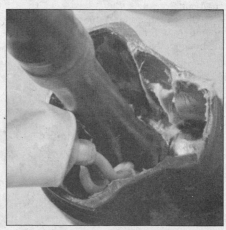

12.10c Install the boot and clamps onto the axleshaft, then insert the tri-pod into the housing, followed by the rest of the grease

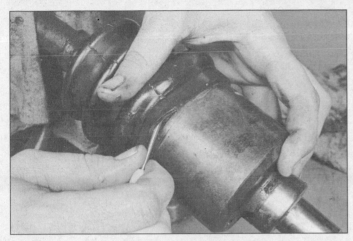

12.13 With the CV joint set mid-way through its travel, equalize the pressure inside the boot by inserting a small, dull screwdriver between the boot and the outer race

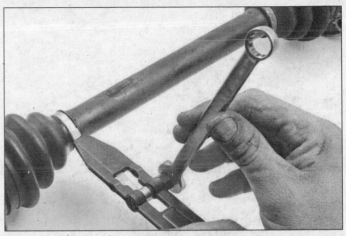

12.15a You'll need a special tightening tool to install band-type boot clamps: install the band with its end pointing in the direction of axle rotation and tighten it securely . . .

12.15b . . . then bend down the end of the clamp back and cut off the excess

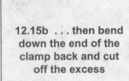

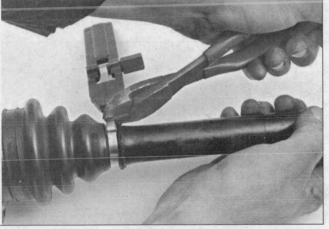

12.15c If you're installing crimp-type boot clamps, you'll need a pair of special crimping pliers (available at most auto parts stores)

boot by inserting a small, dull, flat screwdriver tip between the boot and the CV joint housing **(see illustration).**

14 Make sure each end of the boot is seated properly, and check that the boot is not distorted.

15 Install the boot clamps. There are three types of clamps you're likely to encounter: the band type, which requires a special tightening tool, the crimp type (which also requires a special tool), or the fold-over type **(see illustrations).**

16 The driveaxle is now ready for installation (see Section 10).

12.15d To install fold-over type boot clamps, bend the tang down . . .

12.15e . . . then tap the tabs over to hold it in place

12.18a Cut off the band retaining the boot to the shaft, then slide the boot toward the center of the shaft

12.18b Clean all grease off the axleshaft and paint a mark on the shaft, then measure the distance from your mark to the face of the inner race and record this measurement; the inner race must be installed on the axleshaft in exactly the same position in which it was installed prior to removal

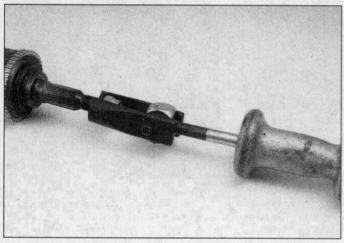

12.18c Outer CV joints can be removed with a slide hammer; you'll need an adapter and a slide hammer setup such as the one shown here

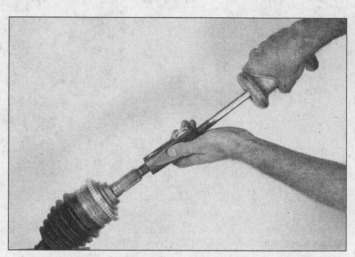

12.18d With the axleshaft firmly clamped down in a bench vise and the adapter gripping the driveaxle/hub nut, carefully extract the outer CV joint from the axleshaft

Outer CV joint

Refer to illustrations 12.18a through 12.18l

17   Remove the driveaxle (see Section 10).
18   Refer to the accompanying illustrations and perform the outer CV joint boot replacement procedure (see illustrations 12.18a through 12.18l).

12.18e After the old grease has been rinsed away, move the inner race through its full range of motion and inspect the bearing surfaces for wear or damage

12.18f Apply CV joint grease through the splined hole, then insert a wooden dowel (slightly smaller in diameter than the hole) into the hole and push down - the dowel will force the grease into the joint. Repeat this until the joint is packed

12.18g Wrap the splined area of the axleshaft with tape to prevent damage to the boot when installing it

12.18h Install the small clamp and the boot on the driveaxle and apply grease to the inside of the axle boot . . .

12.18i . . . until the level is up to the end of the axle

12.18j Install a new circlip into the groove at the end of the driveaxle. Position the CV joint assembly on the driveaxle, aligning the splines . . .

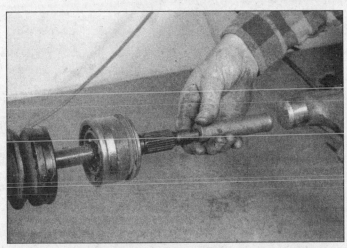

12.18k . . . then use a hammer and brass punch to carefully drive the joint onto the driveaxle to the same spot it was in before disassembly (see illustration 12.18b)

12.18l Seat the inner end of the boot in the groove and install the retaining clamp, then do the same on the other end of the boot - tighten boot clamps with the special tool

Notes

Chapter 9   Brakes

Contents

Specifications

General

Brake fluid type	See Chapter 1
Brake pedal	
Height (with carpet removed)	
2003 and earlier	6-21/32 inches (169 mm)
2004 and later	
Manual transaxle models	6-3/4 inches (171 mm)
Automatic transaxle models	6-11/16 inches (170 mm)
Freeplay	1/16 to 3/16 inch (1 to 5 mm)

Parking brake

Pedal or lever travel	
Pedal	2 to 4 clicks
Lever	
2006 and earlier	6 to 10 clicks
2007	6 to 8 clicks
Shoe lining minimum thickness	0.040 inch (1 mm)
Maximum drum diameter	Cast into drum

Disc brakes

Brake pad minimum thickness	See Chapter 1
Disc lateral runout limit	0.004 inch (0.10 mm)
Disc minimum thickness	Cast into disc
Parallelism (thickness variation) limit	0.0006 inch (0.015 mm)

Torque specifications

Note: *One foot-pound (ft-lb) of torque is equivalent to 12 inch-pounds (in-lbs) of torque. Torque values below approximately 15 foot-pounds are expressed in inch-pounds, because most foot-pound torque wrenches are not accurate at these smaller values.*

	Ft-lbs (unless otherwise indicated)	Nm
Brake hose banjo fitting bolt	25	34
Brake hose line fitting (S-type)	132 in-lbs	15
Caliper mounting bracket bolts (floating calipers only)		
Front	80	108
Rear	41	55
Caliper mounting bolts		
Front		
Fixed (S-type only)	125	170
Floating (typical)		
2003 and earlier	36	49
2004 and later	37	50
Rear	17	23
Master cylinder mounting nuts	11	15
Power brake booster mounting nuts	115 in-lbs	13
Wheel speed sensor mounting bolt	86 in-lbs	9.8
Wheel lug nuts	See Chapter 1	

1   General information

The vehicles covered by this manual are equipped with hydraulically operated front and rear brake systems. All brake systems are disc type.

The front and rear disc brakes are self-adjusting and automatically compensate for pad wear.

Hydraulic system

The hydraulic system is a split design, meaning there are two separate circuits that control the brakes. If one circuit fails, the other circuit will remain functional and a warning indicator will light up on the dashboard when a substantial amount of brake fluid is lost, showing that a failure has occurred.

Power brake booster

The power brake booster - which utilizes engine manifold vacuum and atmospheric pressure to provide assistance to the hydraulically operated brakes - is mounted on the firewall in the engine compartment.

Parking brake

A parking brake pedal or lever in the center console operates a series of cables attached to each rear brake. The cables pull on linkage that expand parking brake shoes in the center portion (drum) of the rear brake disc.

Service

After completing any operation involving disassembly of any part of the brake system, always test drive the vehicle to check for proper braking performance before resuming normal driving. When testing the brakes, perform the tests on a clean, dry, flat surface. Conditions other than these can lead to inaccurate test results.

Test the brakes at various speeds with both light and heavy pedal pressure. The vehicle should stop evenly without pulling to one side or the other. Avoid locking the brakes, because this slides the tires and diminishes braking efficiency and control of the vehicle.

Tires, vehicle load and wheel alignment are factors which also affect braking performance.

Precautions

There are some general cautions and warnings involving the brake system on this vehicle:

a) *Use only brake fluid conforming to DOT 3 specifications.*

b) *The brake pads and linings contain fibers which are hazardous to your health if inhaled. Whenever you work on brake system components, clean all parts with brake system cleaner. Do not allow the fine dust to become airborne. Also, wear an approved filtering mask.*

c) *Safety should be paramount whenever any servicing of the brake components is performed. Do not use parts or fasteners which are not in perfect condition, and be sure that all clearances and torque specifications are adhered to. If you are at all unsure about a certain procedure, seek professional advice. Upon completion of any brake system work, test the brakes carefully in a controlled area before putting the vehicle into normal service. If a problem is suspected in the brake system, don't drive the vehicle until it's fixed.*

d) *Used brake fluid is considered a hazardous waste and it must be disposed of in accordance with federal, state and local laws.* **DO NOT pour it down the sink, into septic tanks or storm drains, or on the ground.**

e) *Clean up any spilled brake fluid immediately and wash the area with large amounts of water. This is especially true for any finished or painted surfaces.*

2   Anti-lock Brake System (ABS) and Vehicle Stability Assist (VSA) - general information

1   The Anti-lock Brake (ABS) and Vehicle Stability Assist (VSA) systems are designed to help maintain vehicle steerability, directional stability and optimum deceleration under severe braking conditions on most road surfaces. The ABS system is primarily designed to prevent wheel lockup during heavy or panic braking situations. It works by monitoring the rotational speed of each wheel and controlling the brake line pressure to each wheel when engaged. Data provided by the ABS wheel speed sensors is also shared with the Vehicle Stability Assist feature. This system is designed to assist in correcting over/under steering. Another system integrated with the ABS and VSA systems is the Traction Control System (TCS). This system is designed to keep wheels from spinning during vehicle acceleration when road conditions are slick. Overall, these very sophisticated systems help maintain vehicle control when conditions are less than ideal.

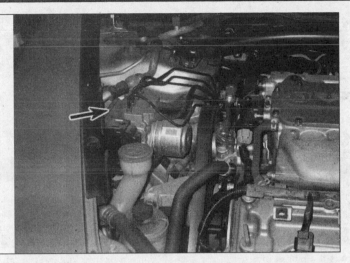

2.2 Location of the modulator unit used for ABS, TCS and VSA operation

Components

Modulator unit

Refer to illustration 2.2

2   The modulator unit is mounted in the engine compartment and consists of an electric hydraulic pump and solenoid valves **(see illustration)**.

a) *The electric pump provides hydraulic pressure to charge the reservoirs in the unit, which supplies pressure to the braking system. The pump and reservoirs are housed in the unit.*

b) *The solenoid valves modulate brake line pressure during ABS, TCS and VSA operation.*

Wheel speed sensors

3   Generally, there is a wheel speed sensor designated for each wheel. Each sensor generates a signal in the form of a low-voltage electrical current or a frequency when the wheel is turning. A variable signal is generated as a result of a square-toothed ring (tone-ring, exciter-ring, reluctor, etc.) that rotates very close to the sensor. The signal is directly proportional to the wheel speed and is interpreted by an electronic module (computer).

4   The front sensors are mounted in the steering knuckles. The tone-rings are located at the back of the wheel hubs (1999 through 2003 models) or integral with the hub bearings (2004 and later models, in which case they're called "encoders").

5   The rear sensors are mounted in the rear suspension knuckles. The tone-rings (1999 through 2003) or pulsers (2004 and later) are mounted similar to the front.

ABS/VSA computer

6   The ABS/VSA computer is mounted with the modulator and is the brain for these systems. The function of the computer is to accept and process information received from the various sensors to control the hydraulic line pressure, avoiding wheel lock up or wheel spin. The computer constantly monitors these systems for faults.

Diagnosis and repair

7   If a dashboard warning light comes on and stays on while the vehicle is in operation, the ABS/VSA system requires attention. Although special electronic ABS diagnostic testing tools are necessary to properly diagnose the system, you can perform a few preliminary checks before taking the vehicle to a dealer service department.

a) *Check the brake fluid level in the reservoir.*

b) *Verify that the computer electrical connectors are securely connected.*

c) *Check the electrical connectors at the hydraulic control unit.*

d) *Check the fuses.*

e) *Follow the wiring harness to each wheel and verify that all connections are secure and that the wiring is undamaged.*

8   If the above preliminary checks do not rectify the problem, the vehicle should be diagnosed by a dealer service department or other qualified repair shop. Due to the complexity of this system, all actual repair work must be done by a qualified automotive technician. **Warning:** *Do NOT try to repair an ABS/VSA wiring harness. These systems are sensitive to even the smallest changes in resistance. Repairing the harness could alter resistance values and cause the system to malfunction. If the wiring harness is damaged in any way, it must be replaced.* **Caution:** *Make sure the ignition is turned off before unplugging or reattaching any electrical connections.*

Wheel speed sensor - removal and installation

Refer to illustrations 2.11a and 2.11b

9   Loosen the wheel bolts, raise the vehicle and support it securely on jackstands. Remove the wheel.

10   Make sure the ignition key is turned to the Off position.

11   Trace the wiring back from the sensor, detaching all brackets and clips while noting its correct routing, then disconnect the electrical connector **(see illustrations)**.

12   Remove the mounting bolt and carefully pull the sensor out from the knuckle.

13   Installation is the reverse of the removal procedure. Tighten the mounting fastener securely.

14   Install the wheel and lug nuts, tightening them securely. Lower the vehicle and tighten the lug nuts to the torque listed in the Chapter 1 Specifications.

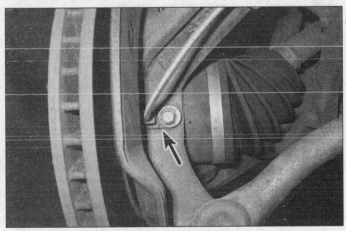

2.11a The front wheel speed sensors are located on the steering knuckles

2.11b The rear wheel speed sensors are located on the rear knuckles

3.5 Before removing the caliper, slowly depress the piston into the caliper bore by using a large C-clamp between the outer brake pad and the back of the caliper

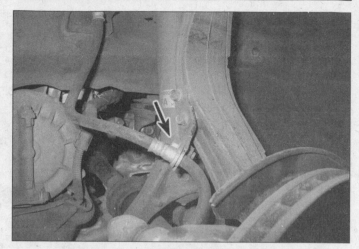

3.6a On front brakes, detach the brake hose from the steering knuckle

3.6b On rear brakes, detach the brake hose from the bracket below the shock absorber

3.6c Before removing anything else, clean the brake assembly with brake cleaner and allow it to dry - position a drain pan under the brake assembly to catch the residue - DO NOT USE COMPRESSED AIR TO BLOW BRAKE DUST OFF THE PARTS!

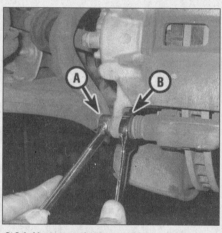

3.6d Unscrew the lower caliper mounting bolt (A) while holding the caliper pin (B) . . .

3.6e . . . then slowly swing the caliper up, being careful not to tear the upper caliper pin boot, and secure it to the strut with a piece of wire

3   Disc brake pads - replacement

Warning: *Disc brake pads must be replaced on both front or both rear wheels at the same time - never replace the pads on only one side. Also, the dust created by the brake system is harmful to your health. Never blow it out with compressed air and don't inhale any of it. An approved filtering mask should be worn when working on the brakes. Do not, under any circumstances, use petroleum-based solvents to clean brake parts. Use brake system cleaner only!*

1   Remove the cap from the brake fluid reservoir.

2   Loosen the wheel lug nuts, raise the front or rear of the vehicle and support it securely on jackstands.

3   Remove the front or rear wheels. Work on one brake assembly at a time, using the assembled brake for reference if necessary.

4   Inspect the brake disc carefully as outlined in Section 5. If machining is necessary, follow the information in that Section to remove the disc, at which time the calipers and pads can be removed as well.

Floating calipers (front and rear)

Refer to illustrations 3.5 and 3.6a through 3.6q

5   Push the piston back into the bore to provide room for the new brake pads. A C-clamp can be used to accomplish this **(see illustration)**. As the piston is depressed to the bottom of the caliper bore, the fluid in the master cylinder will rise. Make sure it doesn't overflow. If necessary, remove some of the fluid.

6   Follow the accompanying illustrations beginning with **illustration 3.6a**, for the actual

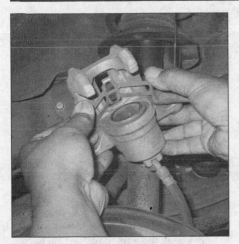

3.6f On rear calipers, check the condition of the pad spring

3.6g Remove the outer brake pad along with any shims

3.6h Remove the inner brake pad along with any shims

3.6i Remove the upper and lower pad retaining clips; make sure they are a tight fit and aren't worn. Clean and inspect them; replace them if necessary

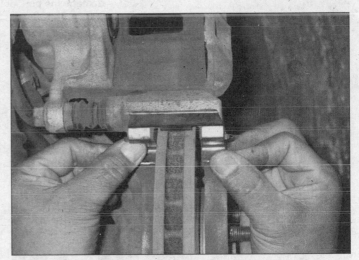

3.6j Install the upper and lower pad retaining clips

3.6k Remove the shim(s) from each brake pad, noting the order and position. Apply a thin film of disc brake grease in between the shim(s) and the back of each replacement brake pad

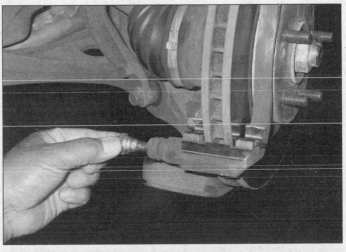

3.6l Pull out the lower sliding pin and clean it. Be careful not to damage the pin boot when removing the pin. SLIDING PINS ARE NOT INTERCHANGABLE – DO NOT MIX THEM UP

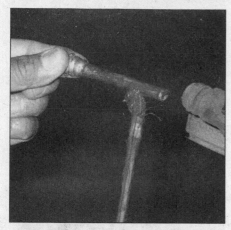

3.6m Apply a coat of high-temperature grease to the pin and reinstall it. Replace any boots that are worn or damaged

3.6n To clean and lubricate the upper sliding pin, pull the caliper away from the caliper mounting bracket while slowly withdrawing the pin. Be careful not to damage the pin boot. Reinstall the sliding pin with the caliper attached

3.6o Install the inner pad, making sure the ends are seated correctly on the pad support plates and any wear indicators are in their original positions

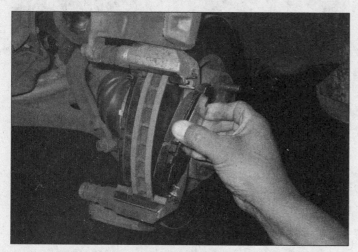

3.6p Install the outer pad, making sure the ends are seated correctly on the pad support plates

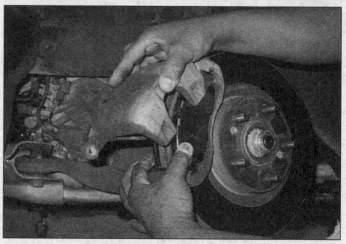

3.6q Position the caliper back over the pads, install the caliper mounting bolt and tighten it to the torque listed in this Chapter's Specifications

3.7 The pad pins hold the pads in the caliper. They are driven from the caliper in the direction of the arrows (typical shown)

pad replacement procedure. Be sure to stay in order and read the caption under each illustration. Once you have installed the new pads, proceed to Step 19.

Fixed calipers (S-Type, front only)

Refer to illustrations 3.7 and 3.12

7   From the large opening on the caliper, locate the two horizontal pad pins that go through the caliper and the brake pad backing plates (see illustration).

8   Locate the cross-spring in the center of the caliper opening that contacts both pad pins.

9   Use a small drift or punch to remove the pad pins; driving them from the outside of the caliper inwards (towards the engine). Remove the cross-spring. **Caution:** *Be sure to note the*

direction of the pad pins as they are removed. They must be installed in the same position and from the same side that they were removed.

10   Using needle-nose pliers, pull the inboard (inner) brake pad from the caliper. **Note:** *Remove only one pad during this step.*

11   Using a small pry tool or screwdriver, slowly push the caliper pistons into the bores on the inboard side. There are two pistons on each side of the caliper for a total of four. **Caution:** *One piston can be forced out of the caliper bore while the other is being pushed in on the same side. Use a small piece of wood or another tool to keep one piston from coming out while the other is being pushed in. As a piston is depressed to the bottom of the caliper bore, the fluid in the master cylinder reservoir will rise. Remove enough brake fluid so that the reservoir is about half full. Continue to*

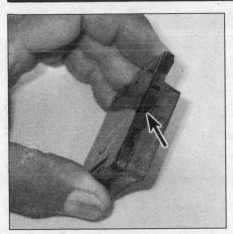

3.12 Lubricate each brake pad plate on both sides (edges) with copper-based brake paste. DO NOT get any lubricant on the pad lining (typical shown)

make sure that it doesn't overflow while pushing on all of the caliper pistons. **Note:** *If the caliper is going to be removed for disc service, remove the outboard pad.*

12   Prepare each new brake pad by using a very small amount of copper-based brake paste on the edges of the pad's metal back plate that contact the caliper **(see illustration)**. **Warning:** *Do not get any lubricant on the pad material.*

13   Position the new inboard brake pad into the caliper. **Note:** *The pad equipped with the wear indicator is used for the outboard position. Do not install a pad equipped with a wear indicator in the inboard position.*

14   Using needle-nose pliers, pull the outboard (outer) brake pad from the caliper.

15   Repeat Step 11 on the outboard side of the caliper.

16   Position the new outboard brake pad into the caliper. **Note:** *On 2006 and earlier models, the wear indicator faces down. On 2007 and later models, the wear indicator faces up.*

17   Install the top pad pin and place the cross-spring in position.

18   Press the bottom end of the cross-spring and install the bottom pad pin.

All calipers

19   Install the wheel and lug nuts, lower the vehicle and tighten the lug nuts to the torque listed in the Chapter 1 Specifications.

20   Before moving the vehicle, apply and release the brake pedal several times to bring the pads into contact with the brake discs.

21   Check the brake fluid level and add fluid, if necessary (see Chapter 1). Check the operation of the brakes in an isolated area before driving the vehicle in traffic.

---

4   Disc brake caliper - removal and installation

Warning: *The dust created by the brake system is harmful to your health. Never blow it out with compressed air and don't inhale any of it. An approved filtering mask should be worn when working on the brakes. Do not, under any circumstances, use petroleum-based solvents to clean brake parts. Use brake system cleaner only!*
Note: *Always replace calipers in pairs (front/front, rear/rear) - never replace just one of them.*

Removal

Refer to illustrations 4.2a and 4.2b

1   Loosen the wheel lug nuts, raise the vehicle and support it securely on jackstands. Remove the wheels.

2   Detach the brake hose bracket from the steering knuckle. Remove the banjo bolt for the brake hose fitting (or line fitting on front S-type calipers) and disconnect it from the caliper. Plug the openings immediately to keep contaminants out of the brake system and to minimize brake fluid loss **(see illustrations)**. **Note:** *If you're simply removing the caliper for access to other components, don't disconnect the hose.*

3   Remove the caliper mounting bolts.

4   Remove the caliper. If necessary, remove the caliper bracket from the steering knuckle or rear knuckle **(see illustration 5.2)**. **Note:** *On S-type models, there is no caliper mounting bracket for the front brakes. Remove the front caliper from the steering knuckle directly.*

Installation

5   Install the caliper by reversing the removal procedure. Tighten the caliper mounting bolts (and bracket bolts, if removed) to the torque values listed in this Chapter's Specifications. Install *new* sealing washers on both sides of the brake hose banjo fitting, then tighten the banjo bolt to the torque listed in this Chapter's Specifications. On S-type fixed calipers, tighten the line fitting securely. Reattach the brake hoses to the brackets and tighten the bolts securely.

6   Bleed the brake system (see Section 10).

7   Install the wheels and lug nuts. Lower the vehicle and tighten the lug nuts to the torque listed in the Chapter 1 Specifications.

---

5   Brake disc - inspection, removal and installation

Warning: *The dust created by the brake system is harmful to your health. Never blow it out with compressed air and don't inhale any of it. An approved filtering mask should be worn when working on the brakes. Do not, under any circumstances, use petroleum-based solvents to clean brake parts. Use brake system cleaner only!*

Inspection

Refer to illustrations 5.2, 5.3, 5.4a, 5.4b, 5.5a and 5.5b

1   Loosen the wheel lug nuts, raise the vehicle and support it securely on jackstands. Remove the wheel and install the lug nuts to hold the disc in place against the hub flange. **Note:** *If the lug nuts don't contact the disc when screwed on all the way, install washers under them. If you're checking the rear disc, release the parking brake.*

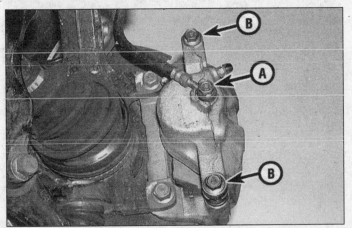

4.2a Remove the brake hose banjo bolt (A), then unscrew the caliper mounting bolts (B) - floating caliper shown

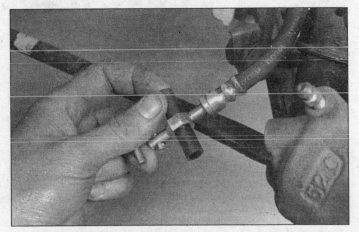

4.2b Using a short piece of rubber hose of the appropriate diameter, plug the brake line banjo fitting

5.2 Caliper mounting bracket-to-knuckle bolts
(front shown - rear similar)

5.3 The brake pads on this vehicle were obviously neglected, as
they wore down completely and cut deep grooves into the disc -
wear this severe means the disc must be replaced

2   Remove the brake caliper as outlined in Section 4 leaving the brake hose connected. Suspend the caliper out of the way with a piece of wire. Remove the two caliper mounting bracket-to-knuckle bolts as equipped **(see illustration)**. **Note:** *On S-type models (with fixed front calipers), no caliper mounting brackets are used; the front calipers mount directly to the steering knuckle.*

3   Visually check the disc surface for score marks, cracks and other damage. Light scratches and shallow grooves are normal after use and may not always be detrimental to brake operation. Deep score marks may require disc refinishing by an automotive machine shop or disc replacement **(see illustration)**. Be sure to check both sides of the disc. If pulsating has been noticed during application of the brakes, suspect disc runout. **Note:** *The most common symptoms of damaged or worn brake discs are pulsation in the brake pedal when the brakes are applied or loud grinding noises caused from severely worn brake pads. If these symptoms are extreme, it is very likely that the discs will need to be replaced.*

4   To check disc runout, place a dial indicator at a point about 1/2-inch from the outer edge of the disc **(see illustration)**. Set the indicator to zero and turn the disc. The indicator reading should not exceed the specified allowable runout limit. If it does, the disc should be refinished by an automotive machine shop. **Note:** *If disc refinishing or replacement is not necessary, you can deglaze the brake pad surface on the disc with emery cloth or sandpaper (use a swirling motion to ensure a non-directional finish)* **(see illustration)**.

5   It's absolutely critical that the disc not be machined to a thickness under the specified minimum thickness. The minimum (or discard) thickness is cast or stamped into the disc **(see illustration)**. The disc thickness can be checked with a micrometer **(see illustration)**.

Removal

Refer to illustrations 5.6a, 5.6b and 5.7

6   Remove the lug nuts which were installed to hold the disc in place, or remove the two disc retaining screws **(see illustration)** and remove the disc from the hub. If the disc is stuck to the hub and won't come off, thread two bolts into the holes provided **(see illustration)** and tighten them. Alternate between the bolts, turning them a couple of turns at a time, until the disc is free. Remove the disc from the hub.

7   On rear discs, make sure that the parking brake is released. If necessary, move the parking brake shoes away from the drum portion of the disc by turning the star-wheel adjuster **(see the accompanying illustration and illustration 6.5s)**.

Installation

8   Place the disc onto the flange. Install the disc retaining screws and tighten them

5.4a To check disc runout, mount a dial indicator as shown and
rotate the disc

5.4b Using a swirling motion, remove the glaze from the disc
surface with sandpaper or emery cloth

5.5a Use a micrometer to measure disc thickness

5.5b The minimum thickness specification is cast in the disc (A).
For rear discs (shown) the maximum diameter specification for
the drum portion is provided also (B) (typical shown)

5.6a If the disc retaining screws are stuck, use an impact
screwdriver to loosen them

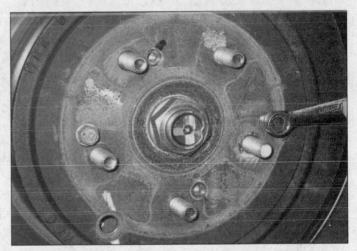

5.6b If the disc is stuck, thread two 8 mm bolts into the threaded
holes in the disc and tighten them to force the disc off the hub

securely. **Note:** *If there is any rust on the
face of the hub flange or on the disc where
it mounts to the flange, clean these surfaces
and lightly coat them with anti-seize lubricant
before installing the disc.*

9   On rear discs, adjust the parking brake
shoes (see Section 7).

10   Install the caliper mounting bracket (if
equipped) and caliper, tightening the bolts
to the torque values listed in this Chapter's
Specifications.

11   Install the wheel and lug nuts, then lower
the vehicle to the ground. Tighten the lug nuts
to the torque listed in the Chapter 1 Specifi-

cations. Depress the brake pedal a few times
to bring the brake pads into contact with the
disc. Bleeding won't be necessary unless the
brake hose was disconnected from the caliper. Check the operation of the brakes carefully before driving the vehicle.

6   Parking brake shoes -
replacement

Refer to illustrations 6.4 and 6.5a through 6.5x

Warning 1: *Dust created by the brake system
is hazardous to your health. Never blow it out
with compressed air and don't inhale any of
it. An approved filtering mask should be worn
when working on the brakes. Do not, under
any circumstances, use petroleum-based solvents to clean brake parts. Use brake system
cleaner only!*

Warning 2: *Parking brake shoes must be
replaced on both wheels - never replace the
shoes on only one wheel.*

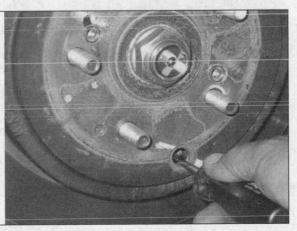

5.7 Remove the rubber plug
covering the access hole to
the parking brake adjuster
and rotate the disc to the six
o'clock position. Use a flat-
blade screw driver and turn
the star adjuster by rotating
it up or down

6.4 Before removing anything, clean the brake assembly with brake cleaner and allow it to dry - position a drain pan under the brake assembly to catch the residue - DO NOT USE COMPRESSED AIR TO BLOW BRAKE DUST OFF THE PARTS!

6.5a Remove the rear parking brake shoe upper return spring from the anchor and unhook it from the shoe

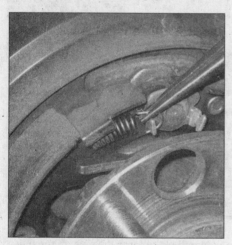

6.5b Remove the front parking brake shoe upper return spring from the anchor and unhook it from the shoe. . .

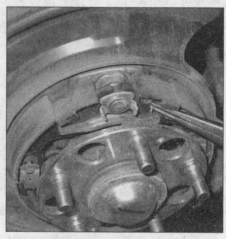

6.5c Remove the connecting rod spring from the rod and unhook it from the rear shoe

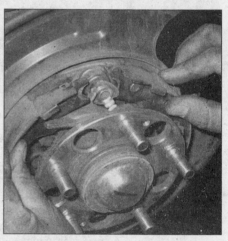

6.5d Spread the upper ends of the shoes apart and remove the connecting rod

6.5e Remove the lower return spring and front shoe

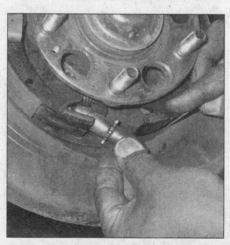

6.5f Remove the adjuster assembly

Replacement

1   Remove the rear brake discs (see Section 5).

2   Measure the thickness of the lining material on the shoes and compare it to the value in this Chapter's Specifications. If the lining has worn down below specification or has cracks, the shoes must be replaced.

3   Inspect the drum portion of the disc for scoring, grooves or cracks due to heat. If any of these conditions exist or there is significant wear to the drum, the disc must be replaced.

4   Wash off the brake parts with brake system cleaner (see illustration).

5   Follow the accompanying illustrations for the brake shoe replacement procedure (see illustrations 6.5a through 6.5x). Be sure to stay in order and read the caption under each illustration. It is best to disassemble one side at a time so that the assembled side can be used for reference.

6.5g Remove the front shoe hold-down spring and retaining pin by pressing on the spring and turning the pin

6.5h Remove the rear shoe hold-down spring and pin

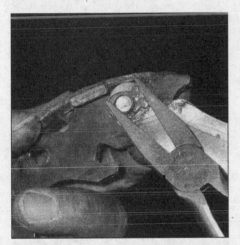

6.5i Pop the U-clip off the pivot pin on the back of the rear shoe . . .

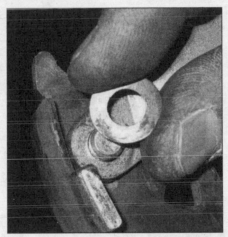

6.5j . . . be careful not to lose or damage the wave washer beneath it . . .

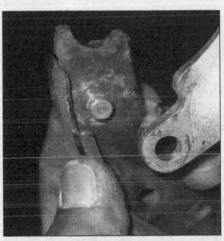

6.5k . . . and pull the parking brake lever off the pivot pin

6.5l Apply a thin coat of high-temperature grease to the contact surfaces of the backing plate and where the shoes meet the anchor (some areas are hidden from view in this photo)

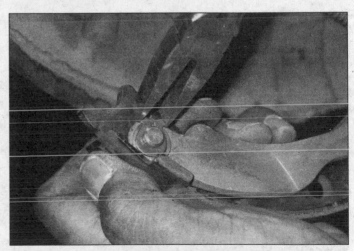

6.5m Apply a very small amount high-temperature grease to the pivot pin on the new brake shoe, then slide the parking brake lever onto the pin. Install the wave washer and a new U-clip

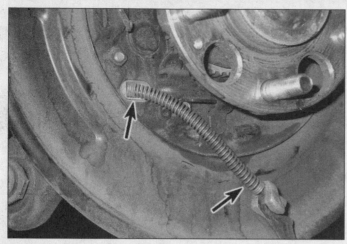

6.5n Lubricate the brake cable where it enters the backing plate and at the brake lever

6.5o Lubricate these areas of the adjuster with high-temperature grease

6.5p The hold-down pins are installed so that the arc in the pins point towards the shoe lining as shown

6.5q Install the rear shoe hold-down spring and pin

6.5r Install the front shoe hold-down spring and pin

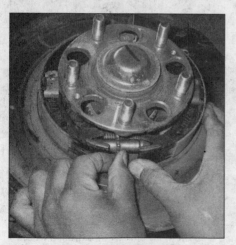

6.5s Install the adjuster

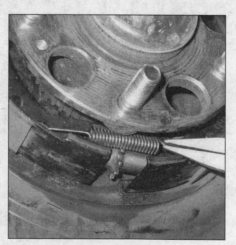

6.5t Install the lower return spring

6.5u Lubricate the ends of the connecting rod where it contacts the shoes with high-temperature grease, then install the rod

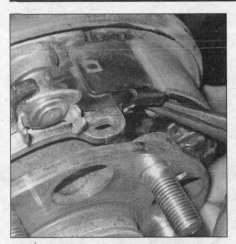

6.5v Install the connecting rod spring

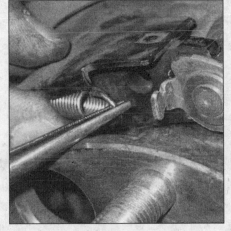

6.5w Install the front shoe upper return spring . . .

6.5x . . . and the rear shoe upper return spring

6   Install the brake disc and the disc retaining screws.

7   Adjust the rear parking brake shoes (see Section 7).

8   Install the caliper bracket **(see illustration 5.2)** and brake caliper (see Section 4). Be sure to tighten the fasteners to the torque values listed in this Chapter's Specifications.

9   Install the wheel and tighten the lug nuts to the torque specified in Chapter 1.

Shoe break-in

10   Break in the new shoes by performing the following procedure for your type of mechanism:

Parking brake lever

a) *Set and release the parking brake a few times.*

b) *Drive the vehicle one-quarter mile while pulling the parking brake lever up. Keep the release button pressed in. Exert about 20 pounds of pulling force on the lever.*

c) *Drive for another 10 seconds with about 30 pounds of pulling force on the lever.*

d) *RELEASE THE PARKING BRAKE LEVER. Stop the vehicle and allow the parking brake shoes and disc/drum to cool for 10 minutes.*

Parking brake pedal

a) *Set and release the parking brake a few times.*

b) *Set the parking brake pedal at one click.*

c) *Drive the vehicle one-quarter mile at about 30 miles per hour.*

d) *Stop the vehicle and RELEASE THE PARKING BRAKE IMMEDIATELY. Allow the parking brake shoes and disc/drum to cool for 10 minutes.*

e) *Repeat Steps b through d once more.*

11   Set the parking brake (lever or pedal) and count the number of clicks that it travels. Compare the number of clicks to the value in this Chapters Specifications. Adjust the parking brake if necessary (see Section 7).

7   Parking brake - adjustment

Refer to illustrations 7.6, 7.7a and 7.7b

Note: *If the parking brake shoe clearance or cable adjusting nut require a significant amount of adjustment, it is advisable to inspect the brake shoe lining thickness (see Section 6).*

1   The parking brake pedal or lever, when properly adjusted, should travel a specified number clicks when set. If it travels less than specified, there's a chance the parking brake might not be releasing completely and the parking brake shoes might be dragging on the drum. If the pedal travels more than specified, the parking brake may not hold the vehicle adequately on an incline, allowing the car to roll.

2   There are two areas of adjustment for the parking brake: the star-wheel adjuster at the bottom of the shoes for each rear wheel and the adjusting nut on the brake cable at the parking brake pedal or hand lever assembly. Adjustment at the shoes is performed first when the shoes have been replaced or when the number of clicks is greater than two when the parking brake is set.

3   Block the front wheels, raise the rear of the vehicle and support it securely on jackstands. Remove the rear wheels.

4   Use the access hole in the disc to adjust the parking brake shoe clearance **(see illustration 5.7)**. Turn the star-wheel adjuster until the disc cannot be rotated and then reverse the adjuster eight notches. Reinstall the rubber plug that covers the access hole..

5   Set the parking brake and count the number of clicks that it travels. Compare the number of clicks to the value in this Chapters Specifications If further adjustment is needed, move on to the next adjustment at the parking brake pedal or lever assembly.

6   Locate the adjusting nut at the pedal and either tighten or loosen it to achieve the proper number of clicks for setting the parking brake **(see illustration)**. Tightening the nut (turning it clockwise) decreases the number of clicks, while the opposite is achieved by loosening the nut (turning it counterclockwise).

7   For hand lever operated parking brakes, open the center console and remove the mat at the bottom. Open the lid to the parking brake equalizer and turn the adjusting nut in

7.6 Adjusting nut at the parking brake pedal (typical shown)

7.7a Open the lid in the center console to access the adjusting nut for the parking brake lever. A deep socket will reach the nut from the opening

7.7b The adjusting nut is located at the brake cable equalizer (center console removed for clarity)

8.3 On 2004 and later models, remove the mounting bolts for the engine compartment fuse/relay box and move it aside for clearance

6   Use a flare nut wrench to loosen the fittings at the ends of the brake lines where they enter the master cylinder (**see illustration 8.4**). Pull the brake lines slightly away from the master cylinder and plug the ends to prevent contamination.

7   Remove the master cylinder mounting nuts and pull the master cylinder off the studs and out of the engine compartment. Again, be careful not to spill the fluid as this is done.

8   If a new master cylinder is being installed, remove the reservoir from the master cylinder and transfer it to the new master cylinder, if necessary. **Note:** *Be sure to use new reservoir-to-master cylinder seals when transferring the reservoir.*

Installation

Refer to illustrations 8.10 and 8.19

9   Bench bleed the new master cylinder before installing it. Mount the master cylinder in a vise, with the jaws of the vise clamping on the mounting flange.

10   Attach a pair of master cylinder bleeder

the same manner as defined in the previous step (**see illustrations**).

8   Set and release the parking brake and confirm that the number of clicks for setting it is within specification.

never again use it for the preparation of food.

5   Place rags under the fluid fittings and prepare caps or plastic bags to cover the ends of the lines once they are disconnected. **Caution:** *Brake fluid will damage paint. Cover all body parts and be careful not to spill fluid during this procedure.*

8   Master cylinder - removal and installation

Removal

Refer to illustrations 8.3 and 8.4

1   Remove all engine and cowl covers as equipped (see Chapter 11).

2   Remove the strut brace (see Chapter 2).

3   On 2004 and later models, remove the mounting bolts for the fuse/relay box in the engine compartment and move it aside (**see illustration**).

4   Disconnect the electrical connector for the fluid level sensor and remove as much fluid as you can from the reservoir with a syringe, such as an old turkey baster (**see illustration**). **Warning:** *If a baster is used,*

8.4 Master cylinder mounting details

1   *Electrical connector*
2   *Mounting nut (one hidden from view on opposite side)*
3   *Brake line fittings*

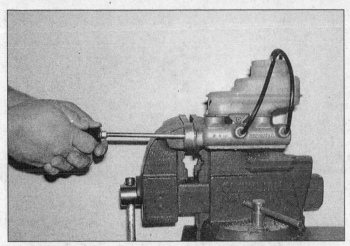

8.10 The best way to bleed air from the master cylinder before installing it on the vehicle is with a pair of bleeder tubes that direct brake fluid into the reservoir during bleeding

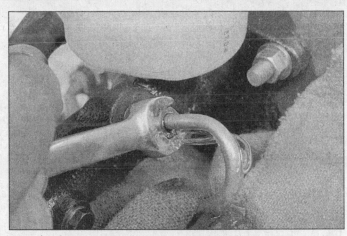

8.19 Have an assistant depress the brake pedal and hold it down. Loosen the fitting nut briefly and allow air and fluid to escape, then close the fitting nut quickly. Repeat these steps on both fittings until the fluid is clear of air bubbles

tubes to the outlet ports of the master cylinder **(see illustration)**.

11   Fill the reservoir with brake fluid of the recommended type (see Chapter 1).

12   Slowly push the pistons into the master cylinder (a large Phillips screwdriver can be used for this) - air will be expelled from the pressure chambers and into the reservoir. Because the tubes are submerged in fluid, air can't be drawn back into the master cylinder when you release the pistons.

13   Repeat the procedure until no more air bubbles are present.

14   Remove the bleed tubes, one at a time, and install plugs in the open ports to prevent fluid leakage and air from entering. Install the reservoir cap.

15   Install a new rod seal onto the master cylinder. Apply silicone grease to the inner and outer circumference of the seal and place the grooved side of the seal towards the master cylinder. **Note:** *The seal must be replaced every time the master cylinder is removed.*

16   Install the master cylinder over the studs on the power brake booster and tighten the

attaching nuts only finger tight at this time. **Note:** *On 2003 and earlier models, measure the distance from the piston pocket to the end of the master cylinder on the old master cylinder (see illustration 11.18c). Do the same measurement on the replacement master cylinder. If the measurements are not the same, refer to Step 18 in Section 11 of this Chapter to adjust the pushrod length on the power booster before installing the replacement master cylinder.*

17   Thread the brake line fittings into the master cylinder. Since the master cylinder is still a bit loose, it can be moved slightly in order for the fittings to thread in easily. Do not strip the threads as the fittings are tightened.

18   Fully tighten the mounting nuts, then the brake line fittings securely. Tighten the nuts to the torque listed in this Chapter's Specifications.

19   Fill the master cylinder reservoir with fluid, then bleed the master cylinder and the brake system as described in Section 10. To bleed the cylinder on the vehicle, have an assistant depress the brake pedal and hold

the pedal to the floor. Loosen the fitting to allow air and fluid to escape. Repeat this procedure on both fittings until the fluid is clear of air bubbles **(see illustration)**. **Caution:** *Have plenty of rags on hand to catch the fluid - brake fluid will ruin painted surfaces. After the bleeding procedure is completed, rinse the area under the master cylinder with clean water.*

20   The remainder of installation is the reverse of removal. Test the operation of the brake system carefully before placing the vehicle into normal service. **Warning:** *Do not operate the vehicle if you are in doubt about the effectiveness of the brake system. If the pedal continues to feel spongy after repeated bleedings or the BRAKE or ANTI-LOCK light stays on, have the vehicle towed to a dealer service department or other qualified shop to be bled.*

9   Brake hoses and lines - inspection and replacement

1   About every six months, with the vehicle raised and placed securely on jackstands, the flexible hoses which connect the steel brake lines with the front and rear brake assemblies should be inspected for cracks, chafing of the outer cover, leaks, blisters and other damage. These are important and vulnerable parts of the brake system and inspection should be complete. A light and mirror will be needed for a thorough check. If a hose exhibits any of the above defects, replace it with a new one.

Flexible hoses

Refer to illustration 9.3

2   Clean all dirt away from the ends of the hose.

3   Detach the brake hose from any brackets or mounting points between the brake line and hose junction and the caliper **(see illustration)**.

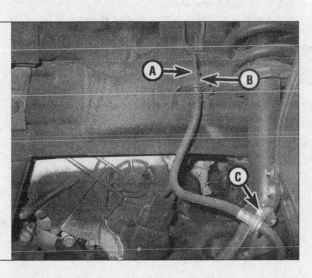

9.3 Unscrew the brake line threaded fitting with a flare-nut wrench to protect the fitting corners from being rounded off (A), then pull off the U-clip (B) with a pair of pliers and remove the brake line mounting bolt (C)

4   To disconnect a brake hose from the brake line, unscrew the metal tube nut with a flare nut wrench, then remove the U-clip from the female fitting at the bracket and remove the hose from the bracket.

5   Disconnect the hose from the caliper, discarding the sealing washers on either side of the fitting. **Note:** *On S-type models, loosen the tube nut fitting, with a flare-nut wrench (also known as a line wrench), at the caliper.*

6   Using new sealing washers, attach the new brake hose to the caliper. Tighten the brake hose banjo bolt to the torque listed in this Chapter's Specifications.

7   To reattach a brake hose to the metal line, insert the end of the hose through the frame bracket, make sure the hose isn't twisted, then attach the metal line by tightening the tube nut fitting securely. Install the U-clip at the frame bracket.

8   Carefully check to make sure the suspension or steering components don't make contact with the hose. Have an assistant push down on the vehicle and also turn the steering wheel lock-to-lock during inspection.

9   Bleed the brake system (see Section 10).

Metal brake lines

10   When replacing brake lines, be sure to use the correct parts. Don't use copper tubing for any brake system components. Purchase steel brake lines from a dealer parts department or auto parts store.

11   Prefabricated brake line, with the tube ends already flared and fittings installed, is available at auto parts stores and dealer parts departments. These lines can be bent to the proper shapes using a tubing bender.

12   When installing the new line, make sure it's well supported in the brackets and has plenty of clearance between moving or hot components.

13   After installation, check the master cylinder fluid level and add fluid as necessary. Bleed the brake system as outlined in Section 10 and test the brakes carefully before placing the vehicle into normal operation.

10   Brake hydraulic system - bleeding

Refer to illustration 10.8

Warning: *Wear eye protection when bleeding the brake system. If the fluid comes in contact with your eyes, immediately rinse them with water and seek medical attention.*

Note: *Bleeding the brake system is necessary to remove any air that's trapped in the system when it's opened during removal and installation of a hose, line, caliper, wheel cylinder or master cylinder.*

1   It will probably be necessary to bleed the system at all four brakes if air has entered the system due to low fluid level, or if the brake lines have been disconnected at the master cylinder.

2   If a brake line was disconnected only at

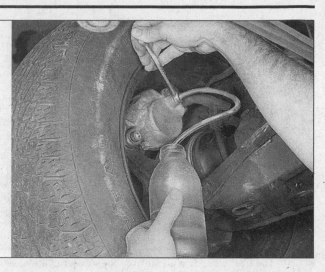

10.8 When bleeding the brakes, a hose is connected to the bleed screw at the caliper and submerged in brake fluid - air will be seen as bubbles in the tube and container (all air must be expelled before moving to the next wheel)

a wheel, then only that caliper or wheel cylinder must be bled.

3   If a brake line is disconnected at a fitting located between the master cylinder and any of the brakes, that part of the system served by the disconnected line must be bled.

4   Remove any residual vacuum from the brake power booster by applying the brake several times with the engine off.

5   Remove the master cylinder reservoir cap and fill the reservoir with brake fluid. Reinstall the cap. **Note:** *Check the fluid level often during the bleeding operation and add fluid as necessary to prevent the fluid level from falling low enough to allow air bubbles into the master cylinder.*

6   Have an assistant on hand, as well as a supply of new brake fluid, an empty clear plastic container, a length of plastic, rubber or vinyl tubing to fit over the bleeder valve and a wrench to open and close the bleeder valve.

7   Beginning at the front left wheel, loosen the bleeder screw slightly, then tighten it to a point where it's snug but can still be loosened quickly and easily. **Note:** *On S-type fixed calipers (front only), there are two bleeder valves; one for each side of the caliper. Bleed the outside of the caliper first, then the inside before moving on to the next wheel.*

8   Place one end of the tubing over the bleeder screw fitting and submerge the other end in brake fluid in the container **(see illustration).**

9   Have the assistant slowly depress the brake pedal and hold it in the depressed position.

10   While the pedal is held depressed, open the bleeder screw just enough to allow a flow of fluid to leave the valve. Watch for air bubbles to exit the submerged end of the tube. When the fluid flow slows after a couple of seconds, tighten the screw and have your assistant release the pedal.

11   Repeat Steps 9 and 10 until no more air is seen leaving the tube, then tighten the bleeder screw and proceed to the right front wheel, the right rear wheel and the left rear wheel, in that order, and perform the same

procedure. Be sure to check the fluid in the master cylinder reservoir frequently.

12   Never use old brake fluid. It contains moisture which can boil, rendering the brake system inoperative.

13   Refill the master cylinder with fluid at the end of the operation.

14   Check the operation of the brakes. The pedal should feel solid when depressed, with no sponginess. If necessary, repeat the entire process. **Warning:** *Do not operate the vehicle if you are in doubt about the effectiveness of the brake system. If the pedal continues to feel spongy after repeated bleedings or the BRAKE or ANTI-LOCK light stays on, have the vehicle towed to a dealer service department or other qualified shop to be bled.*

11   Power brake booster - removal and installation

Operating check

1   Depress the brake pedal several times with the engine off and make sure there is no change in the pedal reserve distance.

2   Depress the pedal and start the engine. If the pedal goes down slightly, operation is normal.

Airtightness check

3   Start the engine and turn it off after one or two minutes. Depress the brake pedal several times slowly. If the pedal goes down farther the first time but gradually rises after the second or third depression, the booster is airtight.

4   Depress the brake pedal while the engine is running, then stop the engine with the pedal depressed. If there is no change in the pedal reserve travel after holding the pedal for 30 seconds, the booster is airtight.

Removal

5   Disassembly of the power unit requires special tools and is not ordinarily performed by the home mechanic. If a problem develops, it's recommended that a new or factory

11.12 Unclip the top two brake lines (for the master cylinder) from the bracket against the firewall

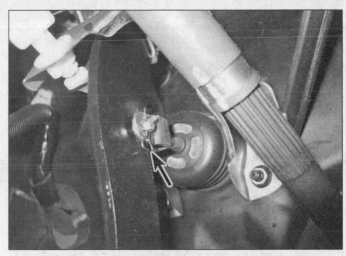

11.13 Remove the lock-pin and clevis pin to disconnect the pushrod from the pedal

rebuilt unit be installed.

6   To remove the booster, first remove the brake master cylinder as described in Section 8.

7   Disconnect the hose leading from the engine to the booster. Be careful not to damage the hose when removing it from the booster fitting.

2003 and earlier models

8   Remove the two mounting bolts for the bracket that secures the fuel line that is above the booster and to the left.

9   Remove the starter cable retainer (above the fuel line bracket in the previous Step) and move the cable aside for clearance.

10   Remove the mounting bolt for the bracket that secures the windshield wiper (intermittent) relay that is above the booster.

2004 and later models

Refer to illustration 11.12

11   Remove the air filter housing (see Chapter 4).

12   Detach the brake lines from the clip against the firewall **(see illustration)**.

All models

Refer to illustrations 11.13 and 11.14

13   Working inside the vehicle, locate the pushrod clevis pin connecting the booster to the brake pedal **(see illustration)**. Remove the lock-pin from the clevis pin with pliers, then remove the clevis pin.

14   Remove the four nuts **(see illustration)** holding the brake booster to the firewall.

15   Working outside the vehicle, carefully guide the booster out until the studs and pushrod clevis clear the holes in the firewall, then

remove the booster from the engine compartment. Be careful not to bend any of the brake lines or damage the booster studs while pulling it out.

Installation

2003 and earlier models

Refer to illustrations 11.16, 11.17a, 11.17b, 11.17c and 11.18

16   If a new power brake booster unit is being installed, measure the length of the pushrod from the center of the clevis hole to the booster's mounting surface. Include the gasket in the measurement and keep in mind that it will compress a bit. Compare the measurement with the value listed in this Chapter's Specifications **(see illustration)**. **Note:** *This Step is only necessary if the previous setting was changed or the booster is being replaced.*

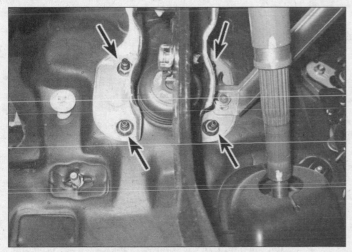

11.14 Remove the four booster mounting nuts

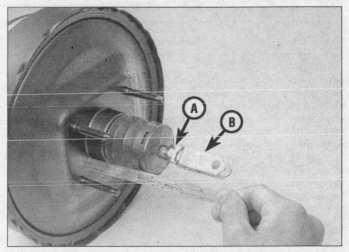

11.16 With the booster out of the vehicle, measure the pushrod length to the center of the clevis hole. To adjust the length, loosen the locknut on the pushrod (A) and turn the clevis (B)

11.17a Measure the distance that the booster pushrod protrudes from the face of the power booster (typical shown)

11.17b Measure the distance from the mounting flange to the end of the master cylinder (typical shown)

17   Check and adjust the booster pushrod-to-master cylinder clearance - if there is interference between the two, the brakes may drag; if there is too much clearance, there will be excessive brake pedal travel. Check the pushrod clearance as follows:

a) *Using a hand-held vacuum pump, apply a vacuum of 30 in-Hg to the booster. Measure the distance that the pushrod protrudes from the master cylinder mounting surface on the front of the power brake booster. Write down this measurement (see illustration). This is "dimension A."*

b) *Measure the distance from the mounting flange to the end of the master cylinder (see illustration). Write down this measurement. This is "dimension B."*

c) *Measure the distance from the end of the master cylinder to the bottom of the pocket in the piston (see illustration).*

Write down this measurement. This is "dimension C."

d) *Subtract measurement B from measurement C, then subtract measurement A from the difference between B and C. This the pushrod clearance.*

e) *The pushrod clearance should be at zero. If necessary, adjust the pushrod length to achieve the correct clearance (see the next Step).*

18   Use the adjuster on the clevis end (brake pedal side) of the power booster pushrod to obtain the correct clearance **(see illustration)**. Recheck the clearance and repeat this Step as often as necessary until a zero clearance is met. **Note:** *Maintain the correct amount of vacuum during this procedure; refer to the previous Step.*

2004 and later models

19   To install the booster, place it into position and tighten the retaining nuts to the

torque listed in this Chapter's Specifications. Connect the pushrod to the brake pedal and use a new lock-pin for the clevis pin. **Note:** *Apply some all-purpose grease to the clevis pin during installation.*

All models

20   Install of the master cylinder and brake hoses and lines, adjust the brake pedal free-play (see Section 13) and then bleed the brakes as described in Section 10.

21   The remainder of the Installation is the reverse of removal. Tighten the booster mounting nuts to the torque listed in this Chapter's Specifications. Also, be sure to use a new lock-pin for the clevis pin. **Note:** *Apply some all-purpose grease to the clevis pin during installation.*

22   Check and adjust the brake pedal height (see Section 13).

23   Carefully test the operation of the brakes before placing the vehicle into normal service.

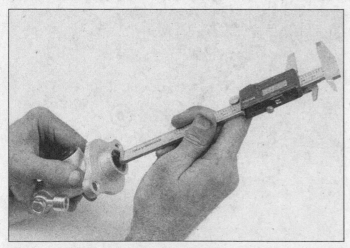

11.17c Measure the distance from the piston pocket to the end of the master cylinder

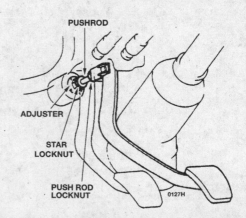

11.18 To adjust the length of the booster pushrod, loosen the star locknut and turn the adjuster in or out while holding the clevis. Be sure to tighten the star locknut after the correct pushrod clearance is achieved

12.1 Brake light switch electrical connector

13.2 With the brake pedal fully released, measure the distance from the top center of the pedal pad to the floor

12 Brake light switch/Brake Pedal Position switch - replacement

Refer to illustration 12.1

1   Disconnect the electrical connector from the brake light switch **(see illustration)**.

2   Rotate the switch counterclockwise slightly, so it unlocks from its holder, then pull it out of the holder.

3   To install the switch, insert it into its holder and push it in until the switch body contacts the rubber stop on the brake pedal bracket. Rotate the switch 45-degrees clockwise to lock it into place. It will achieve the proper clearance to the rubber stop automatically.

4   Plug the electrical connector into the switch.

5   Confirm that the brake lights work properly before placing the vehicle into normal service.

13 Brake pedal - adjustment

Brake pedal height

Refer to illustration 13.2

1   Disconnect the brake light switch elec-trical connector, then remove the brake light switch (see Section 12).

2   Pull the carpet back and find the insulator cutout, then with the brake pedal fully released, measure the distance from the top of the pad to the floor **(see illustration)**.

3   If the height is not as listed in this Chapter's Specifications, it must be adjusted.

4   Loosen the locknut just in front of the clevis on the power brake booster pushrod.

5   Turn the booster pushrod until the pedal height is correct.

6   Tighten the locknut securely.

7   After adjusting the pedal height, check the freeplay, then install the brake light switch (see Section 12).

Brake pedal freeplay

Refer to illustration 13.8

8   Press down lightly on the brake pedal and measure the distance that it moves freely before resistance is felt **(see illustration)**. The freeplay should be within the values listed in this Chapter's Specifications. If it isn't, check the clevis, clevis pin and the hole in the brake pedal arm for excessive wear.

9   Remove and install the brake light switch (see Section 12).

10   Re-adjust the brake pedal height and

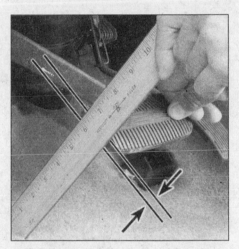

13.8 To measure brake pedal freeplay, press down lightly on the pedal and measure the distance that it moves freely before resistance is felt

check the freeplay once again. The proper amount of freeplay must occur to ensure that the brakes are not dragging.

Notes

Chapter 10
Suspension and steering systems

Contents

Specifications

General

Power steering fluid type .... See Chapter 1

Torque specifications

Ft-lbs (unless otherwise indicated) **Nm**

Note: *One foot-pound (ft-lb) of torque is equivalent to 12 inch-pounds (in-lbs) of torque. Torque values below approximately 15 foot-pounds are expressed in inch-pounds, because most foot-pound torque wrenches are not accurate at these smaller values.*

Front suspension

	Ft-lbs	Nm
Damper fork pinch bolt	32	43
Damper fork-to-lower control arm through-bolt/nut	47	64
Lower control arm inner pivot (horizontal) bolt	47	64
Lower control arm mounting bolt (vertical - 2004 and later models only)	76	103
Shock absorber-to-body mounting nuts		
2003 and earlier models		
8 x 1.25	12	16
10 x 1.25	37	50
2004 models		
8 x 1.25	16	22
10 x 1.25	37	50
2005 through 2006 models		
8 x 1.25	16	22
10 x 1.25	44	60
2007 and later models		
8 x 1.25	21	28
10 x 1.25	44	60
Damper shaft nut	22	30
Radius rod		
Rod-to-lower control arm bolts	119	162
Rod-to-subframe nut	40	54

Torque specifications

Ft-lbs (unless otherwise indicated) **Nm**

Note: *One foot-pound (ft-lb) of torque is equivalent to 12 inch-pounds (in-lbs) of torque. Torque values below approximately 15 foot-pounds are expressed in inch-pounds, because most foot-pound torque wrenches are not accurate at these smaller values.*

Front suspension (continued)

	Ft-lbs	Nm
Stabilizer bar link nut		
2003 and earlier models	29	39
2004 through 2006 models	22	30
2007 and later models	58	78
Stabilizer bar bracket bolts	33	44
Subframe mounting bolts		
Large bolts (A)	76	103
Front bracket bolts (B)	40	54
Rear bracket bolts (C)	69	93
Lower balljoint nut		
2003 and earlier models	36 to 43	49 to 58
2004 and later models	54 to 61	73 to 83
Upper balljoint nut	29 to 35	39 to 47
Upper control arm pivot bolts		
2003 and earlier models	47	64
2004 and later models	23	31

Rear suspension

	Ft-lbs	Nm
Anchor bolt mounting nut (for rear parking brakes)	103	140
Backing plate mounting nuts	28	38
Brake hose frame bracket		
2003 and earlier models	86 in-lbs	10
2004 and later models	16	22
Lower arm inner pivot bolt	43	58
Lower arm-to-knuckle bolt/nut	43	58
Control arm inner pivot bolt/nut	43	58
Control arm-to-knuckle nut	43	58
Trailing arm-to-chassis bolt	43	58
Trailing arm-to-knuckle bolt	43	58
Leading arm inner pivot bolt	43	58
Leading arm-to-knuckle bolt	43	58
Upper arm inner pivot bolt	43	58
Upper arm-to-knuckle castle nut	36 to 43	49 to 58
Hub nut	134	181
Damper shaft nut	22	30
Stabilizer bar link nut	29	39
Stabilizer bar bracket bolts	16	22
Shock absorber-to-knuckle bolt	43	58
Shock absorber upper mounting nuts	37	50

Airbag system

	Ft-lbs	Nm
Airbag module Torx bolts	86 in-lbs	10

Steering system

	Ft-lbs	Nm
U-joint pinch bolt(s)		
2003 and earlier models	17	23
2004 and later models	21	28
Power steering pump mounting fasteners		
2003 and earlier models	17	23
2004 and later models	16	22
Power steering pressure line fitting bolts	96 in-lbs	11
Steering column mounting fasteners		
2003 and earlier models		
Lower bolts	17	23
Upper nuts	12	16
2004 and later models	12	16
Steering wheel bolt	29	39
Steering gear mounting bolts		
2003 and earlier models		
Left side (through stiffeners)	32	43
Right side (clamp bolts)	28	38
2004 and later models		
Left side	43	58
Right side (clamp bolts)	28	38
Stiffener plate bolts	28	38
Tie-rod end-to-steering knuckle nut		
2003 and earlier models	32	43
2004 and later models	40	54

1.1a Front suspension components on 2004 and later models

1	Stabilizer bar	4	Lower control arm	6	Damper fork
2	Subframe	5	Lower balljoint	7	Tie-rod end
3	Shock absorber/coil spring assembly				

1   General information

Refer to illustrations 1.1a, 1.1b and 1.2

The front suspension is a fully independent design with upper and lower control arms, shock absorber/coil spring assemblies and a stabilizer bar **(see illustrations)**.

Each side of the rear suspension uses a trailing arm, a leading arm, two unequal length lower control arms (one is called a lower arm, the other is called the control arm), an upper control arm and a shock absorber/coil spring unit **(see illustration)**. A stabilizer bar connects the suspension on each side, to reduce body roll.

All models use a power-assisted rack-and-pinion steering gear. The power steering system employs an engine-driven pump connected by hoses to the steering gear.

Frequently, when working on the suspension or steering system components, you may come across fasteners which seem impossible to loosen. These fasteners on the under-

1.1b Front suspension components on 2003 and earlier models

1	Radius rod	3	Lower balljoint	6	Stabilizer bar
2	Shock absorber/coil spring assembly	4	Lower control arm	7	Steering gear
	Subframe	5	Tie-rod end		

side of the vehicle are continually subjected to water, road grime, mud, etc., and can become rusted or frozen, making them extremely difficult to remove. In order to unscrew these stubborn fasteners without damaging them (or other components), be sure to use lots of penetrating oil and allow it to soak in for a while. Using a wire brush to clean exposed threads will also ease removal of the nut or bolt and prevent damage to the threads. Sometimes a sharp blow with a hammer and punch is effective in breaking the bond between a nut and bolt threads, but care must be taken to prevent the punch from slipping off the fastener and ruining the threads. Heating the stuck fastener and surrounding area with a torch sometimes helps too, but isn't recommended because of the obvious dangers associated with fire. Long breaker bars and extension, or cheater, pipes will increase leverage, but never use an extension pipe on a ratchet - the ratcheting mechanism could be damaged. Sometimes, turning the nut or bolt in the tightening (clockwise) direction first will

1.2 Rear suspension components (2003 and earlier model shown - other models are similar)

1 Stabilizer bar	4 Upper arm
2 Leading arm	5 Shock absorber/coil spring assembly
3 Control arm	

6 Lower arm	
7 Trailing arm	

help to break it loose. Fasteners that require drastic measures to unscrew should always be replaced with new ones.

Since most of the procedures that are dealt with in this Chapter involve jacking up the vehicle and working underneath it, a good pair of jackstands will be needed. A hydraulic floor jack is the preferred type of jack to lift the vehicle, and it can also be used to support certain components during various operations. **Warning:** *Never, under any circumstances, rely on a jack to support the vehicle while working on it. Whenever any of the suspension or steering fasteners are loosened or removed they must be inspected and, if necessary, be replaced with new ones of the* same part number or of original equipment quality and design. Torque specifications must be followed for proper reassembly and component retention. Never attempt to heat or straighten any suspension or steering component. Instead, replace any bent or damaged part with a new one.

2.4 Damper fork fasteners

2.6 Front shock absorber mounting nuts (2003 and earlier model shown - other models similar)

1	10 x 1.25 nuts	2	8 x 1.25 nuts

2   Shock absorber/coil spring assembly (front) - removal and installation

Removal

Refer to illustrations 2.4 and 2.6

1   On 2004 and later models, remove the right-side engine cover, the right and left rear engine covers and the strut brace (see Chapters 2 and 11). **Note:** *Keep the vehicle on the ground during this Step.*

2   Loosen the wheel lug nuts, raise the vehicle and support it securely on jackstands. Remove the wheel.

3   Place a floor jack under the lower control arm to support it.

4   Remove the damper fork-to-shock absorber pinch bolt **(see illustration)**.

5   Remove the damper fork-to-lower control arm bolt and remove the fork. It may be necessary to gently tap the fork from the shock absorber.

6   Have an assistant support the shock absorber and coil spring assembly while removing the upper mounting nuts **(see illustration)**. Carefully remove the unit from the fenderwell.

Installation

7   With the aid of an assistant, guide the shock absorber assembly up into the fenderwell and insert the upper mounting studs through the holes in the body. Once the studs protrude from the holes, loosely install the nuts to keep the assembly in place.

8   Insert the lower end of the shock absorber into the damper fork, making sure the aligning tab on the back of the shock body enters the slot in the damper fork.

9   Connect the damper fork to the lower control arm, using a new nut on the damper fork bolt. Raise the lower control arm with

a floor jack to simulate normal ride height, then tighten the damper fork pinch bolt and damper fork-to-lower control arm bolt/nut to the torque listed in this Chapter's Specifications.

10   Remove the floor jack from the lower control arm.

11   Install the wheel and lug nuts, lower the vehicle and tighten the lug nuts to the torque listed in the Chapter 1 Specifications.

12   Tighten the upper mounting nuts to the torque listed in this Chapter's Specifications.

13   On 2004 and later models, install the strut brace and engine covers (see Chapters 2 and 11).

3   Shock absorber or coil spring - component replacement

Refer to illustrations 3.3 and 3.5

Warning: *Disassembling a shock/coil spring is potentially dangerous and utmost attention must be directed to the job, or serious injury may result. Use only a high-quality spring compressor and carefully follow the manufacturer's instructions furnished with the tool. After removing the coil spring from the shock assembly, set it aside in a safe, isolated area.* **Note:** *If the shocks or coil springs exhibit the telltale signs of wear (leaking fluid, loss of damping capability, chipped, sagging or cracked coil springs), explore all options before beginning any work. The shock absorbers or coil springs are not serviceable individually and must be replaced if a problem develops. However, complete assemblies may be available on an exchange basis, which eliminates much time and work. Whichever route you choose to take, check on the cost and availability of parts before disassembling your vehicle.*

1   Remove the shock absorber/coil spring assembly (see Section 2 or 10). **Note:** *Work*

on one assembly at a time so parts do not get mixed.

2   Mount the shock/coil spring assembly in a vise. Line the vise jaws with wood or rags to prevent damage to the unit and don't tighten the vise excessively.

3   Following the tool manufacturer's instructions, install the spring compressor (which can be obtained at most auto parts stores or equipment yards on a daily rental basis) on the spring and compress it sufficiently to relieve all pressure from the upper spring seat. This can be verified by wiggling the spring **(see illustration)**. **Note:** *Mark the orientation of the upper mount in relation to the spring or damper unit so it can be installed in the same position.*

3.3 Install the spring compressor following the tool manufacturer's instructions; compress the spring until all pressure is relieved from the upper spring seat (you can verify that the spring is loose by wiggling it)

4 Hold the shock damper rod with an Allen wrench and unscrew the self-locking retaining nut with a box-end wrench.

5 Disassemble the parts from the damper, taking care to lay the parts out in the exact order in which they are removed **(see illustration)**. **Warning:** *When removing the compressed spring, lift it off carefully and set it in a safe place. Keep the ends of the spring away from your body.*

6 Reassembly is the reverse of removal, noting the following points:

a) *Carefully place the spring onto the shock absorber body, with the end of the spring resting in the lowest part of the seat.*

b) *Use a new self-locking nut, then tighten the nut to the torque listed in this Chapter's Specifications.*

c) *Before releasing the spring compressor, make sure the upper mount is oriented as it was originally before removal in Step 3.*

7 After removing the spring compressor tool, the assembly is ready for installation (see Section 2 or 10).

---

4 Steering knuckle and hub - removal and installation

Warning: *Dust created by the brake system is harmful to your health. Never blow it out with compressed air and don't inhale any of it. Do not, under any circumstances, use petroleum-based solvents to clean brake parts. Use brake system cleaner only.*

Removal

1 Loosen the wheel lug nuts, raise the front of the vehicle and support it securely on jackstands, then remove the wheels.

2 Remove the driveaxle/hub nut (see Chapter 8).

3 Detach the brake hose bracket from the steering knuckle. Remove the brake caliper, hang it out of the way with a piece of wire, then remove the caliper mounting bracket, if equipped (see Chapter 9).

4 Remove the two mounting screws that retain the brake disc to the hub, then remove the brake disc (see Chapter 9).

5 Remove the ABS wheel speed sensor (see Chapter 9).

6 Disconnect the tie-rod end from the steering knuckle (see Section 15).

7 Separate the lower control arm from the balljoint in the bottom of the steering knuckle (see Section 8).

8 Separate the upper end of the knuckle from the upper control arm balljoint and keep it supported (see Section 9).

9 Carefully pull the knuckle and hub assembly off the driveaxle. If necessary, tap on the end of the driveaxle with a soft-face hammer. Support the driveaxle with a piece of wire to prevent damage to the inner CV joint. **Caution:** *Be careful not to overextend the inner CV joint while removing the knuckle.*

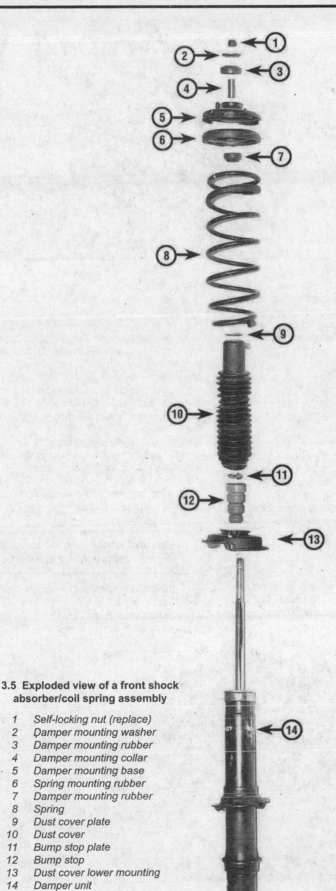

3.5 Exploded view of a front shock absorber/coil spring assembly

1 *Self-locking nut (replace)*
2 *Damper mounting washer*
3 *Damper mounting rubber*
4 *Damper mounting collar*
5 *Damper mounting base*
6 *Spring mounting rubber*
7 *Damper mounting rubber*
8 *Spring*
9 *Dust cover plate*
10 *Dust cover*
11 *Bump stop plate*
12 *Bump stop*
13 *Dust cover lower mounting*
14 *Damper unit*

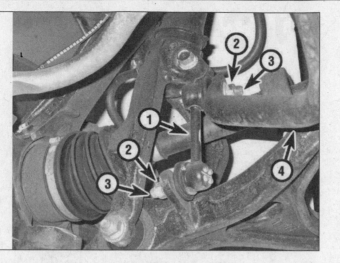

6.2 Remove the upper or lower link nut; if you're replacing the link, remove both nuts

1   *Stabilizer bar link*
2   *Link nut*
3   *Ballstud (hold with Allen wrench)*
4   *Front stabilizer bar*

10   If the wheel bearing is in need of replacement, take the steering knuckle/hub assembly to an automotive machine shop or other qualified repair facility to have the old wheel bearing pressed out and a new one pressed in.

Installation

11   Apply a light coat of wheel bearing grease to the driveaxle splines. Insert the driveaxle through the splined bore of the hub while guiding the steering knuckle into position.
12   Connect the upper end of the knuckle to the upper control arm balljoint (see Section 9). Tighten the balljoint stud nut to the torque listed in this Chapter's Specifications. Install a new cotter pin. **Note:** *Tighten the nut to the lower torque value given in the Specifications, then, if necessary, tighten it an additional amount to line up the slots in the nut with the hole in the balljoint stud to allow cotter pin insertion. Insert the pin from front to rear.*
13   Connect the balljoint on the bottom of the knuckle to the lower control arm (see Section 8). Tighten the nut to the torque listed in this Chapter's Specifications. Install a new cotter pin (see the **Note** in the previous Step).

14   Attach the brake disc to the hub, install the disc retaining screws and tighten them securely.
15   Install the caliper mounting bracket (if equipped) and caliper, tightening the bolts to the proper torque (see Chapter 9). Attach the brake hose bracket to the knuckle, tightening the bolts securely.
16   Install the driveaxle/hub nut and tighten it to the torque listed in the Chapter 8 Specifications. Re-stake it with a punch or blunt chisel (see Chapter 8).
17   Install the wheel and lug nuts, lower the vehicle and tighten the lug nuts to the torque listed in the Chapter 1 Specifications.
18   Install the lug nuts, lower the vehicle and tighten the lug nuts to the torque listed in the Chapter 1 Specifications.

5   Hub and wheel bearing assembly (front) - removal and installation

Due to the special tools and expertise required to press the hub and bearing from the steering knuckle, this job should be left to a professional mechanic. However, the steer-

ing knuckle and hub may be removed and the assembly taken to an automotive machine shop or other qualified repair facility equipped with the necessary tools. See Section 4 for the steering knuckle and hub removal procedure.

6   Stabilizer bar and bushings (front) - removal, inspection and installation

Removal

Refer to illustrations 6.2, 6.3a and 6.3b
1   On 2004 and later models, lower the front subframe (see Section 24). **Note:** *It is important to mention that the need to remove the stabilizer bar from the vehicle is usually due to damage from an accident. If this is the case, it is highly likely that other major components (such as the subframe itself) have also been damaged. We recommend having the vehicle inspected by a qualified body repair shop before replacing the stabilizer bar. However, the links and bushings can be replaced without removing the stabilizer bar.*
2   Remove the link nuts to separate the stabilizer bar link assemblies from the stabilizer bar **(see illustration)**. **Note:** *Use an Allen wrench to prevent the ballstud from turning when removing the link nut.*
3   Remove the stabilizer bar bushing bracket bolts **(see illustrations)**. Note which way the slits in the bushings are facing.
4   Remove the stabilizer bar from the vehicle.

Inspection

5   Inspect for cracked, torn, or distorted stabilizer bar bushings, bushing brackets, and worn or damaged stabilizer bar links.
6   To replace damaged stabilizer bar bushings, remove the bracket, open the bushing slit and peel the bushing from the stabilizer bar. **Caution:** *Install the new bushings with the slits facing the same way that the original bushing slits faced.*

6.3a Stabilizer bar bushing bracket and bolts (2004 and later models)

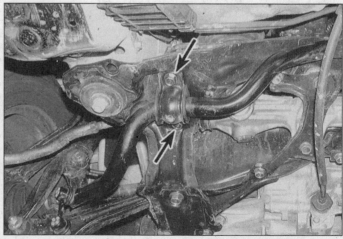

6.3b Stabilizer bar bushing bracket and bolts (2003 and earlier models)

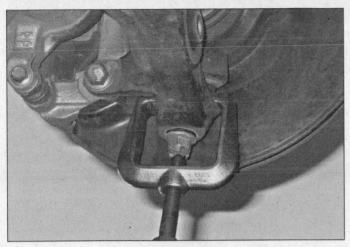

8.4 Use a small puller to separate the lower control arm from the balljoint (typical shown)

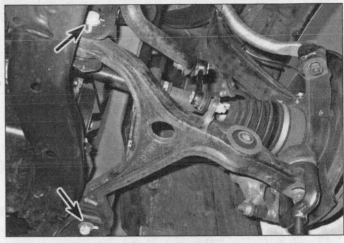

8.5 Lower control arm mounting and pivot bolt locations (2004 and later models)

Installation

7   Guide the stabilizer bar into position, if removed. Install the bushings, brackets and bolts. Tighten the bolts to the torque listed in this Chapter's Specifications.

8   Install the subframe, if removed.

9   Connect the stabilizer bar to the links. Tighten the nuts to the torque listed in this Chapter's Specifications. **Note:** *Use new self-locking nuts to attach the stabilizer bar links.*

10   Install the wheels and lug nuts. Lower the vehicle and tighten the lug nuts to the torque listed in the Chapter 1 Specifications.

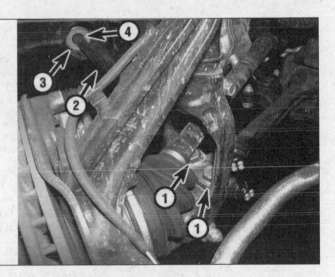

8.6a Lower control arm mounting details (2003 and earlier models)

1   *Radius rod-to-lower control arm bolts*
2   *Radius rod*
3   *Large washer*
4   *Adjusting shim location*

7   Balljoints - replacement

The front suspension uses two balljoints; the upper balljoint is mounted in the upper control arm, and the lower balljoint is mounted in the steering knuckle. The rear suspension uses one balljoint, on the outer end of the upper arm. At the time of writing, the balljoints are not serviceable separately and require replacement of the upper control arm or the steering knuckle in the event of balljoint failure. Check with your local auto parts store or a dealer parts department on the availability of parts before disassembling your vehicle.

The balljoint boots, however, are replaceable. They are secured by a wire set ring and are easily replaced after the components have been separated.

8   Lower control arm and radius rod (front) - removal and installation

Refer to illustrations 8.4, 8.5, 8.6a, 8.6b and 8.7

Note 1: *Only 2003 and earlier models are equipped with a radius rod.*

Note 2: *On 2004 and later models, the manu-* facturer states to replace the control arm-to-subframe mounting fasteners when they are removed.

1   Loosen the front wheel lug nuts, raise the vehicle, place it securely on jackstands and remove the wheel.

2   Remove the through-bolt and detach the damper fork from the lower control arm (see Section 2).

3   Detach the stabilizer bar link from the lower control arm (see Section 6).

4   Remove the cotter pin from the castle nut on the lower balljoint stud. Loosen the nut approximately one-quarter inch; don't remove it yet (this will prevent the components from separating uncontrollably when the parts suddenly pop loose). Using a two-jaw puller or equivalent, separate the lower control arm from the balljoint in the steering knuckle **(see illustration)**. Remove the nut.

5   On 2004 and later models, remove the pivot and mounting bolts from the inner end of the lower control arm, then remove the arm **(see illustration)**.

6   On 2003 and earlier models, remove the two radius rod bolts that fasten the radius rod to the control arm, then remove the pivot bolt from the inner end of the control arm and remove the arm **(see illustrations)**.

8.6b Location of the lower control arm mount fasteners (2003 and earlier models)

8.7 The location of the radius rod mounting nut at the rear of the subframe (2003 and earlier models)

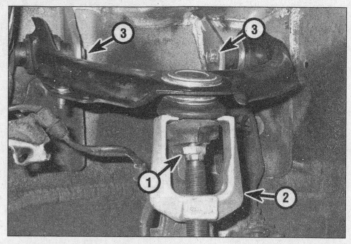

9.3 Use a two-jaw puller, or equivalent, to separate the balljoint from the steering knuckle

1	*Castle nut (loosened)*	*3*	*Upper control arm*
2	*Two-jaw puller*		*pivot bolts*

7   To remove the radius rod completely, remove the mounting nut at the subframe **(see illustration)**. While slowly guiding the radius rod out of the large washers and bushings, look for a smaller washer that is farthest from the end of the rod **(see illustration 8.6a)**. This small washer (if equipped) is a shim that is used to adjust the caster angle for the front wheel alignment. Return the shim to the same position upon installation to preserve the wheel alignment. **Note:** *Hold the other end of the radius rod with a wrench if it rotates while removing the mounting nut.*

8   Installation is the reverse of removal, noting the following points:

a) *Raise the outer end of the control arm with a floor jack to simulate normal ride height before tightening the pivot bolt and mounting bolt for the control arm.*
b) *Be sure to install a new cotter pin and read the* **Note** *in Section 4, Step 12.*
c) *Be sure to use new control arm mounting fasteners on 2004 and later models.*
d) *Tighten all fasteners to the torque values listed in this Chapter's Specifications.*

e) *Use a new self-locking nut for installing the radius rod to the subframe (if removed).*
f) *Tighten the wheel lug nuts to the torque listed in the Chapter 1 Specifications.*
g) *Test-drive the vehicle. If there are any concerns regarding vehicle handling and wheel alignment, have the front end alignment checked and, if necessary, adjusted.*

9   Upper control arm (front) - removal and installation

Refer to illustrations 9.3 and 9.6
Note: *On 2004 and later models, a 6mm x 300mm rod will be needed for upper control arm installation.*

1   Loosen the front wheel lug nuts, raise the vehicle, place it securely on jackstands and remove the wheel. Support the lower control arm with a floor jack.

2   Remove the shock absorber/coil spring

assembly (see Section 2). Remove the ABS wheel speed sensor harness bracket from the upper control arm.

3   Remove the cotter pin, then loosen, but do not remove, the castle nut from the upper balljoint stud **(see illustration)**. The nut will prevent the upper control arm and the steering knuckle from separating uncontrollably when the parts suddenly pop loose in the next step.

4   Separate the upper control arm from the steering knuckle with a two-jaw puller, then remove the nut. Don't let the top of the steering knuckle fall outward. If necessary, secure it with a piece of wire.

5   Remove the upper control arm mounting bolts **(see illustration 9.3)**, then the upper control arm. **Note:** *On 2003 and earlier models, before removing the mounting bolts, mark the relationship of the upper control arm to the frame for installation.*

6   Installation is the reverse of removal, noting the following points:

a) *On 2004 and later models, make a rod that's 6mm x 300mm and place it in the holes provided in the frame to position the upper control arm* **(see illustration)**. *With the tool in place, install the control arm mounting bolts and tighten them to the torque values listed in this Chapter's Specifications*
b) *On 2003 and earlier models, use the reference marks made in Step 5 and tighten the mounting bolts to the torque values listed in this Chapter's Specifications, while holding the control arm at the proper angle.*
c) *Be sure to install the ABS wheel speed sensor harness bracket and tighten the fasteners securely.*
d) *Install a new cotter pin after reconnecting the ballstud to the steering knuckle and read the* **Note** *in Section 4, Step 12.*

9.6 The tool holds the upper control arm in the correct position while the arm fasteners are tightened

10.3 Remove the shock absorber upper mounting nuts

10.5 Rear shock absorber lower mounting bolt

10   Shock absorber/coil spring assembly (rear) - removal and installation

Refer to illustrations 10.3 and 10.5

1   Loosen the rear wheel lug nuts, raise the vehicle, place it securely on jackstands and remove the rear wheels.

2   Remove the rear shelf (see Chapter 11).

3   Remove the shock absorber upper mounting nuts **(see illustration).**

4   Remove the nut from the upper end of the stabilizer bar link (see Section 13).

5   Remove the shock absorber lower mounting bolt **(see illustration).**

6   Pull the rear knuckle down and remove the shock absorber/coil spring assembly.

7   To inspect or replace the shock absorber or coil spring, see Section 3.

8   Installation is the reverse of removal, noting the following points:

a) *Raise the rear knuckle with a floor jack to simulate normal ride height, then tighten the shock absorber lower mounting bolt to the torque listed in this Chapter's Specifications.*

b) *Tighten the upper mounting nuts to the torque listed in this Chapter's Specifications.*

c) *Tighten the wheel lug nuts to the torque listed in the Chapter 1 Specifications.*

11   Rear knuckle - removal and installation

Removal

Refer to illustration 11.5

1   Loosen the rear wheel lug nuts, raise the rear of the vehicle and support it securely on jackstands. Remove the wheel.

2   Unbolt the brake hose bracket from the knuckle. Unbolt the brake caliper, hang it out of the way with a piece of wire, then remove the caliper mounting bracket (see Chapter 9).

3   Remove the two mounting bolts that retain the brake disc to the hub. Remove the brake disc (see Chapter 9).

4   Remove the hub and bearing assembly from the knuckle (see Section 12).

5   Remove the backing plate for the parking brakes **(see illustration)**. Hang the backing plate/parking brake shoe assembly with wire or rope - don't let it hang by the parking brake cable.

6   Detach the upper end of the stabilizer bar link from its mount (see Section 13).

7   Detach the lower end of the shock absorber assembly from the knuckle (see Section 10).

8   Unbolt the suspension arms from the knuckle (see Section 14).

9   Remove the knuckle from the suspension arms.

Installation

10   Connect the suspension arms to the knuckle, but don't tighten the fasteners yet (see Section 14).

11   Connect the lower end of the shock absorber to the knuckle, but don't tighten the bolt yet (see Section 10).

12   Attach the stabilizer bar link to its bracket on the knuckle (see Section 13).

13   Install the hub and bearing assembly (see Section 12).

14   Install the brake components (see Chapter 9).

15   Raise the rear suspension with a floor jack to simulate normal ride height, then tighten the fasteners to the torque values listed in this Chapter's Specifications.

16   Install the wheel and lug nuts, lower the vehicle and tighten the lug nuts to the torque listed in the Chapter 1 Specifications.

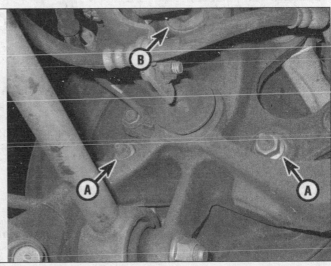

11.5 Remove the backing plate mounting nuts (A) and anchor bolt mounting nut (B)

12.3a Using a hammer and chisel, remove the dust cover

12.3b Unstake the hub nut with a suitable punch

12.5 Stake the new hub nut in place with a suitable punch

13.2 Remove the upper or lower link nut; if you're replacing the link, remove both nuts

1	Stabilizer bar link	3	Ballstud (hold with Allen wrench)
2	Link nut	4	Rear stabilizer bar

12 Hub and wheel bearing assembly (rear) - removal and installation

Refer to illustrations 12.3a, 12.3b and 12.5

Warning: *Dust created by the brake system is harmful to your health. Never blow it out with compressed air and don't inhale any of it. Do not, under any circumstances, use petroleum-based solvents to clean brake parts. Use brake system cleaner only.*

Note: *The rear hub and bearing are combined into a single assembly. The bearing is sealed for life and requires no lubrication or attention. If the bearing is worn or damaged, replace the entire hub and bearing assembly.*

1   Loosen the rear wheel lug nuts, raise the rear of the vehicle and support it securely on jackstands. Block the front wheels to prevent the vehicle from rolling. Remove the wheels.

2   Remove the brake disc (see Chapter 9).
3   Remove the dust cover, then unstake and remove the hub retaining nut **(see illustrations)**.
4   Remove the hub and bearing assembly from the spindle.
5   Installation is the reverse of removal, noting the following points:

a) *Install a new hub retaining nut and tighten it to the torque listed in this Chapter's Specifications. Stake the new hub nut in place* **(see illustration)**. **Note:** *Apply a little clean engine oil to the seating surface of the hub retaining nut before installing it.*
b) *Install the dust cover by tapping lightly around the edge until it is seated.*
c) *Tighten all brake related fasteners to the torque values listed in the Chapter 9 Specifications.*

d) *Install the wheel and lug nuts. Lower the vehicle and tighten the lug nuts to the torque listed in the Chapter 1 Specifications.*

13 Stabilizer bar and bushings (rear) - removal and installation

Refer to illustrations 13.2 and 13.3

1   Loosen the rear wheel lug nuts, raise the rear of the vehicle, place it securely on jackstands and remove the rear wheels.
2   Remove the stabilizer bar-to-link nuts **(see illustration)**. **Note:** *Use an Allen wrench to prevent the ballstud from turning when removing the link nut. To remove the link entirely, simply remove the nuts at each end of the link.*

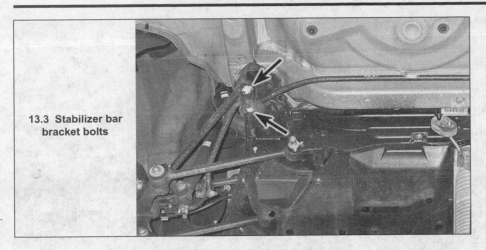

13.3 Stabilizer bar bracket bolts

3   Unbolt the bushing bracket from each side of the stabilizer bar **(see illustration)** and then remove the bar.

4   Pull the retainers off the bar and inspect the bushings for cracks, breaks and other signs of deterioration (see Section 6). If the bushings are damaged, replace them. Also check the stabilizer bar links for loose balljoints and other damage, replacing them if necessary.

5   Installation is the reverse of removal. **Note:** *Use new self-locking nuts to attach the stabilizer bar links.*

14   Rear suspension arms - removal and installation

Warning: *When loading the suspension with a floor jack, be extremely careful not to lift the vehicle from the jackstands or make the vehicle unstable.*

Note 1: *When installing any of the following components, it is recommended that new self-locking nuts, bolts and locking pins are used.*

Note 2: *Install components by lightly tightening the fasteners at first. Once installed, load the suspension with the vehicle's weight by placing a floor jack securely under the knuckle and raising it just enough to simulate normal ride height. Then tighten the fasteners to the values in this Chapter's Specifications.*

1   Loosen the rear wheel lug nuts, raise the vehicle, place it securely on jackstands and remove the wheel.

Upper arm

Refer to illustrations 14.2. 14.4a and 14.4b

2   Remove the brake hose bracket bolts but leave the hose/hydraulic line connected **(see illustration)**. **Caution:** *Do not kink or bend the metal brake line by moving it too much.*

3   Separate the wheel speed sensor wire harness from the rear knuckle and remove its bracket from the subframe.

4   To disconnect the upper arm balljoint from the knuckle, remove the lock pin (or cotter pin) and loosen the castle nut on the ballstud about one-quarter inch. Install a balljoint separator tool to unseat the ballstud from the knuckle **(see illustrations)**. Once the ballstud is loose, remove the castle nut and separate the arm from the knuckle entirely. **Caution:** *Take note of the direction of the castle nut lock pin; It is critical for proper installation.*

5   Remove the pivot bolt that attaches the inner end of the upper arm to the chassis.

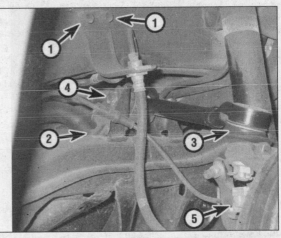

14.2 Upper arm mounting details:

1   *Brake hose/line frame bracket mounting bolts*
2   *Wheel speed wiring harness bracket at the subframe*
3   *Upper arm balljoint*
4   *Upper arm pivot bolt*
5   *Wheel speed wiring harness bracket at the rear knuckle*

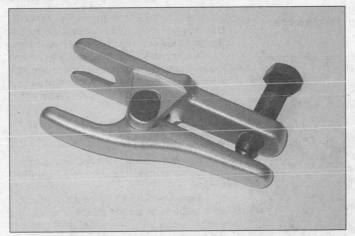

14.4a A balljoint separator tool like this one is available at most automotive parts stores and will not damage the balljoint boot when used correctly. Apply grease to the area of the tool that contacts the boot before installing it

14.4b Using a low-profile balljoint separator tool to separate the upper arm balljoint from the rear knuckle

14.8 Remove the nut and bolt from the lower arm at the knuckle and the bolt at the inner end of the arm

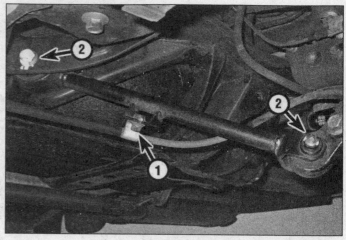

14.13 Trailing arm mounting details:

1   *Bracket and mounting bolts for the parking brake cable*
2   *Trailing arm mounting bolts (replace)*

6   Remove the upper arm. Inspect the bushing for cracks and deterioration and the balljoint for looseness and other signs of wear. If any undesirable conditions exist, replace the arm.

7   Installation is the reverse of removal. Be sure to tighten all fasteners to the torque values listed in this Chapter's Specifications after raising the rear knuckle with a floor jack to simulate normal ride height. Install a new lock pin on the castle nut. **Note 1:** *Although the position of the lock pin may vary a little, install it with the closed end of the pin pointed towards the front of the vehicle.* **Note 2:** *See* **Notes** *and* **Warning** *at the beginning of this Section.*

Lower arm

Refer to illustration 14.8

8   Remove the nut and bolt that attaches the lower arm to the knuckle and discard them **(see illustration)**.

9   Remove the pivot bolt that attaches the inner end of the lower arm to the chassis.

10   Remove the lower arm.

11   Inspect the lower arm bushings for cracks and deterioration. If either of them are worn, replace the arm.

12   Installation is the reverse of removal. Use new fasteners for attaching the lower arm to the rear knuckle. Be sure to tighten all fasteners to the torque values listed in this Chapter's Specifications after raising the rear knuckle with a floor jack to simulate normal ride height. **Note:** *See* **Notes** *and* **Warning** *at the beginning of this Section.*

Trailing arm

Refer to illustration 14.13

13   Disconnect the parking brake cable bracket from the trailing arm **(see illustration)**.

14   Remove the bolt that attaches the trailing arm to the knuckle and discard it.

15   Remove the bolt that attaches the trailing arm to the subframe and discard it.

16   Remove the trailing arm.

17   Inspect the bushing at the forward end of the arm. If it's cracked or deteriorated, replace the arm.

18   Installation is the reverse of removal. Use new fasteners for installation. Be sure to tighten all fasteners to the torque values listed in this Chapter's Specifications after raising the rear knuckle with a floor jack to simulate normal ride height. **Note:** *See* **Notes** *and* **Warning** *at the beginning of this Section.*

Leading arm

Refer to illustration 14.19

19   Remove the bolt that attaches the leading arm to the knuckle and discard it **(see illustration)**.

20   Remove the bolt that attaches the leading arm to the subframe and discard it.

21   Remove the leading arm.

22   Inspect the bushing at the inner end of the arm. If it's cracked or deteriorated, replace the arm.

23   Installation is the reverse of removal. Use new fasteners for installation. Be sure to tighten all fasteners to the torque values listed in this Chapter's Specifications after raising the rear knuckle with a floor jack to simulate normal ride height. **Note:** *See* **Notes** *and* **Warning** *at the beginning of this Section.*

Control arm

Refer to illustration 14.24

24   Remove the nut that attaches the control arm to the knuckle and discard it **(see illustration)**.

25   Mark the relationship of the adjustment cam to the subframe at the inner end of the arm. Remove the nut and bolt that attaches the inner end of the control arm to the subframe and discard them.

26   Remove the control arm.

27   Inspect the control arm bushings for cracks and deterioration. If either of them are

14.19 Leading arm bolt locations

14.24 Control arm bolt locations (A) with a mark on the adjusting cam (B)

15.2 Using a back-up wrench to prevent the tie-rod end from turning, loosen the jam nut

worn, replace the arm.

28   Installation is the reverse of removal. Use new fasteners for installation. Be sure to tighten all fasteners to the torque values listed in this Chapter's Specifications after raising the rear knuckle with a floor jack to simulate normal ride height. Also, be sure to align the marks you made on the adjustment cam and subframe. **Note:** *See* **Notes** *and* **Warning** *at the beginning of this Section.*

15   Tie-rod ends - removal and installation

Removal

Refer to illustrations 15.2, 15.3 and 15.4

1   Loosen the wheel lug nuts, raise the front of the vehicle and support it securely on jackstands. Apply the parking brake and block the rear wheels to keep the vehicle from rolling off the jackstands. Remove the wheel.

2   Loosen the tie-rod end jam nut **(see illustration)**.

3   Mark the relationship of the tie-rod end to the threaded portion of the tie-rod. This will ensure that the toe-in setting is restored upon reassembly **(see illustration)**.

4   Remove the cotter pin and loosen the nut from the tie-rod end ballstud a few turns. Disconnect the tie-rod end ballstud from the steering arm with a puller or a balljoint separator tool **(see illustration)**.

5   Remove the nut from the ballstud, separate the tie-rod end from the steering knuckle, and unscrew the tie-rod end from the tie-rod.

Installation

6   Thread the tie-rod end onto the tie-rod to the marked position and connect the tie-rod end to the steering arm. Install the nut onto the ballstud and tighten it to the torque listed in this Chapter's Specifications. Install a new cotter pin. **Note:** *If necessary, tighten the nut a little more to allow insertion of the cotter pin. Never loosen the nut to align the cotter pin holes.*

7   Tighten the jam nut securely and install the wheel. Lower the vehicle and tighten the

lug nuts to the torque listed in the Chapter 1 Specifications.

8   Have the front end alignment checked and, if necessary, adjusted.

16   Steering wheel - removal and installation

Warning 1: *These models are equipped with a Supplemental Restraint System (SRS), more commonly known as airbags. Always disable the airbag system before working in the vicinity of any airbag system component to avoid the possibility of accidental deployment of the airbag(s), which could cause personal injury (see Chapter 12).*

Warning 2: *Do not use a memory saving device to preserve the PCM or radio memory when working on or near airbag system components.*

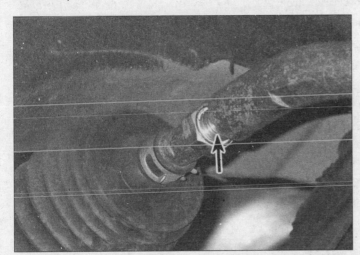

15.3 Make an alignment mark on the exposed threads, along the edge of the tie-rod end, so the new tie-rod end will be installed in the exact same position

15.4 Use a two-jaw puller, or equivalent, to separate the tie-rod end from the steering knuckle arm

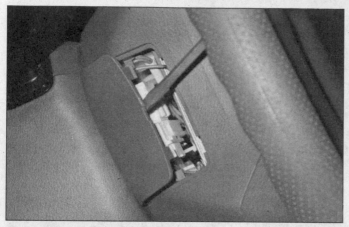

16.2 Remove the connector access panel from the underside of the steering wheel

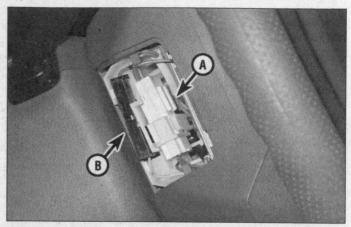

16.3a Remove and disconnect the electrical connectors for the airbag module (A) and the horn (B)

Removal

Refer to illustrations 16.2, 16.3a, 16.3b, 16.4, 16.6, 16.8, 16.10, 16.11, 16.13a and 16.13b

1   Make sure the front wheels are pointed straight ahead, then disconnect the cable from the negative terminal of the battery (see Chapter 5, Section 1). Wait at least three minutes before proceeding.

2   Remove the access panel from the bottom of the steering wheel for the airbag module and horn connectors **(see illustration)**.

3   Pull the connectors from their brackets and unplug them **(see illustrations)**.

4   Remove the airbag module fasteners from each side of the steering wheel **(see illustration)**. **Note:** *Some models may have covers over the fasteners; simply pry them off to get to the fasteners.*

5   Pull the airbag module out and carefully set it in a safe location. **Warning:** *Carry the airbag module with the trim side facing away from you, and set the airbag module down with the trim side facing up. Don't place anything on top of the airbag module.*

6   Disconnect the steering wheel switches **(see illustration)**. **Note:** *Disconnect audio control, navigation guide, cruise control or any*

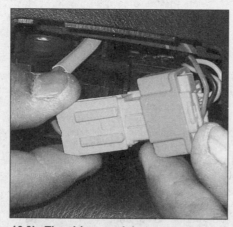

16.3b The airbag module connector has a sliding spring lock that must be moved to separate the connector

other switches, as equipped.

7   Remove the steering wheel retaining bolt, mark the relationship of the steering wheel to the hub at the 12 o'clock position, then reinstall the bolt until about 1/2-inch of the threads are showing between the bolt head and the

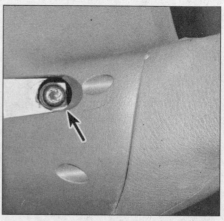

16.4 Remove the airbag fasteners from each side of the steering wheel

steering wheel.

8   Remove the steering wheel using a steering wheel puller **(see illustration)**. **Caution:** *Don't thread the bolts of the puller into the steering wheel hub more than five turns, as they could contact the airbag clockspring and damage it.* Once the steering wheel is

16.6 Disconnect the cruise control switch at either of these connectors (2004 model shown - other models are similar)

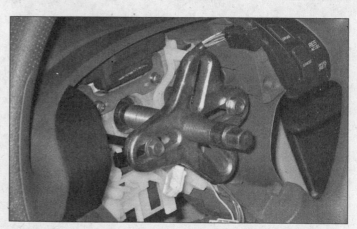

16.8 Use a steering wheel puller to remove the steering wheel

16.10 Release the clockspring lock tabs for removal (2002 and later models)

16.11 Remove the mounting screws for the clockspring (2001 and earlier models)

released from the shaft, remove the puller and retaining bolt, then pull the steering wheel off the shaft. **Caution:** *DO NOT turn the steering shaft or change the direction of the front wheels while the steering wheel is detached; damage to the airbag clockspring could occur if the steering components are not aligned properly during reassembly.*

9   If it is necessary to remove the clockspring, remove the steering column covers (see Chapter 11).

10   On 2002 and later models, unplug the clockspring electrical connectors, then carefully release the locking tabs and detach the clockspring from the combination switch assembly **(see illustration)**. **Note:** *Follow the wiring harnesses from the back of the clockspring. The electrical connectors are attached to a bracket on the bottom of the steering column assembly. On 2004 and later models, there is a connector on the back of the clockspring.*

11   On 2001 and earlier models, unplug the clockspring electrical connector and remove the three mounting fasteners to detach the clockspring from the combination switch assembly **(see illustration)**. **Note:** *Follow the wiring harness from the back of the clockspring. The electrical connector is attached to a bracket on the bottom of the steering column assembly.*

Installation

12   With the front wheels pointed straight ahead, make sure that the airbag clockspring is centered with the arrow on the clockspring pointing up. This shouldn't be a problem as long as you have not turned the steering shaft while the wheel was removed. If for some reason the shaft was turned, re-center the front wheels (the steering shaft mark should now be pointing at 12 o'clock) and center clockspring as follows:

a) *Rotate the clockspring clockwise until it stops.*
b) *Rotate the clockspring counterclockwise about two and a half to three turns, until the arrow on the clockspring points straight up.*

13   Be sure to align the index mark on the steering wheel hub with the mark on the shaft when you slip the wheel onto the shaft (the marks should be at the 12 o'clock position). Make sure the locating pins on the clockspring engage with the holes in the backside of the steering wheel, and the notches in the steering wheel hub engage with the lugs on the turn signal canceling cam (the lugs and notches should be in the 12 and 6 o'clock positions). Install the steering wheel bolt and tighten it to the torque listed in this Chapter's Specifications **(see illustrations)**.

14   Connect all of the steering wheel switch connectors that were disconnected during removal.

15   Reattach the airbag module using NEW fasteners and tighten them to the torque listed in this Chapter's Specifications.

16   Reconnect and secure the electrical connectors for the airbag module and the horn.

17   Reconnect the negative battery cable (see Chapter 5, Section 1).

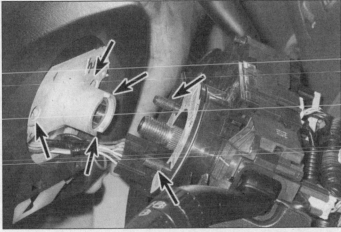

16.13a Match the locating pins and notches to properly install the steering wheel

16.13b Lugs on the signal canceling cam must be positioned in the 12 and 6 o'clock positions

17   Steering column - removal and installation

Warning 1: *These models are equipped with a Supplemental Restraint System (SRS), more commonly known as airbags. Always disable the airbag system before working in the vicinity of any airbag system component to avoid the possibility of accidental deployment of the airbag(s), which could cause personal injury (see Chapter 12).*

Warning 2: *Do not use a memory saving device to preserve the PCM or radio memory when working on or near airbag system components.*

Removal

Refer to illustrations 17.5a, 17.5b, 17.6, 17.7, 17.8, 17.9a, 17.9b and 17.9c

1   Park the vehicle with the wheels pointing straight ahead. Disconnect the cable from the negative terminal of the battery (see Chapter 5, Section 1).

2   Adjust the steering wheel so that it's tilted to its uppermost position and fully extended telescopically.

17.5a   Mounting screw locations for the combination switch assembly (2002 and later models)

17.5b   Mounting screw locations for the combination switch assembly (2001 and earlier models)

3   Remove the steering wheel (see Section 16). **Caution:** *Do not rotate the steering shaft or airbag clockspring. Also, do not change the angle of the front wheels without the steering wheel completely installed. If any of these things occur, the steering shaft and clockspring will need re-centering to* avoid damage to the airbag clockspring.

4   Remove the steering column covers and the driver's knee bolster (see Chapter 11).

5   Remove the combination switch assembly **(see illustrations). Note:** *Make sure to disconnect the electrical connectors to the assembly.* **Caution:** *Do not rotate the clockspring; it could be damaged if re-installed incorrectly. Use tape to keep it centered. Refer to Section 16 to re-center the clockspring if necessary.*

6   From inside the vehicle under the instrument panel, remove the steering shaft U-joint cover **(see illustration). Note:** *On 2003 and earlier models, remove the two round clips holding the cover to the steering column.*

7   On 2004 and later models, mark the relationship of both parts of the slider shaft to each other **(see illustration)**.

8   Mark the relationship of the U-joint to the steering gear's input shaft. Remove the pinch bolt from the U-joint and separate it from the input shaft **(see illustration). Note 1:** *On 2004 and later models, the slider shaft will separate if it is not held together. One technique is to loop wire through the U-joints on*

17.6   Pull up on the cover's edges near the fasteners to remove it

17.7   Mark the relationship of both sections of the slider shaft just in case they become separated during removal

17.8   Mark the relationship of the U-joint to the steering gear input shaft (A) then remove the U-joint pinch bolt (B)

17.9a Steering column fasteners - left side (2004 and later models)

17.9b Steering column fasteners - right side (2004 and later models)

each end and of the shaft tighten it enough to hold the two parts together. **Note 2:** *On 2003 and earlier models, remove both pinch bolts for the steering shaft U-joint if necessary.*

9   Remove the steering column mounting fasteners and slowly lower the column while making sure all wire harnesses have been detached, then remove the column from the vehicle **(see illustrations)**.

Installation

10   Guide the steering column into position while connecting the U-joint to the steering input shaft (remember to use the index marks made in Step 8). Install the steering column mounting fasteners and tighten them to the torque listed in this Chapter's Specifications.

11   Install the U-joint pinch bolt through the joint and the groove in the steering input shaft, then tighten it to the torque listed in this Chapter's Specifications.

12   The remainder of installation is the reverse of removal. Reconnect the negative battery cable (see Chapter 5, Section 1).

18   Steering gear boots - replacement

Refer to illustration 18.3

1   Loosen the lug nuts, raise the front of the vehicle and support it securely on jackstands. Remove the wheel.

2   Remove the tie-rod end and jam nut (see Section 15).

3   Remove the steering gear boot clamps and slide off the boot **(see illustration)**.

4   Before installing the new boot, wrap the threads on the end of the tie-rod with a layer of tape so the small end of the new boot isn't damaged when putting it on.

5   Slide the new boot into position on the steering gear until each end seats in its groove, then install and tighten the new clamps. See Chapter 8 for information on

17.9c Steering column fasteners (2003 and earlier models)

installing the inner boot clamp.

6   Remove the tape and install the tie-rod end (see Section 15).

7   Install the wheel and lug nuts. Lower the vehicle and tighten the lug nuts to the torque listed in the Chapter 1 Specifications.

19   Steering gear - removal and installation

Removal

1   Point the front wheels straight ahead. On 2004 and later models, remove the right-side engine cover and the left and right rear engine covers (see Chapter 11).

2   Disconnect the cable from the negative battery terminal (see Chapter 5, Section 1).

3   Remove the power steering fluid from the reservoir. This can be accomplished with a suction tool or large syringe, or by disconnecting the fluid hose and draining the fluid into a container.

4   Loosen the front wheel lug nuts, raise the

18.3 Steering gear boot clamp locations. The outer clamp can be loosened like a hose clamp, but the inner one must be cut off

vehicle and support it securely on jackstands. Remove both front wheels. **Note:** *On 2004 and later models, the jackstands must be behind the front suspension subframe, not supporting the vehicle by the subframe.*

5   Remove the engine splash shields and under cover (see Chapter 2).

6   From inside the vehicle under the instrument panel, remove the cover over the steering shaft U-joint **(see illustration 17.6)**

2004 and later

Refer to illustrations 19.8, 19.11, 19.16, 19.17, 19.18, 19.19 and 19.20

Warning: *Make sure the steering wheel is not turned while the steering gear is removed. This could result in damage to the airbag clockspring. To prevent the steering wheel from turning, place the ignition key in the LOCK position or thread the seat belt through the steering wheel and clip it into place.*

Note: *This procedure requires lowering the rear part of the subframe about 2 inches (50 mm).*

19.8 Fastener locations for the lower U-joint cover

19.11 The power steering pressure sensor is located along a pressure line between the power steering pump and the steering gear

7   Mark the relationship of the U-joint to the steering gear input shaft **(see illustration 17.8)**. Remove the pinch bolt from the U-joint, then separate it from the input shaft. Remove the small plastic center guide located on the steering gear input shaft and discard it, if equipped. **Note:** *Loop wire through the U-joints on each end of the sliding shaft and tighten it to hold the two sections of the shaft together. If they become separated, look for index marks on each section of the shaft to match them up again.*

8   Remove the lower cover that protects the steering shaft U-joint **(see illustration)**. **Note:** *On 2003 and earlier models, remove the two round clips holding the cover to the steering column.*

9   Support the engine from above with an engine support fixture or hoist (see Chapter 2).

10   Detach the tie-rod ends from the steering knuckles (see Section 15).

11   Disconnect the electrical connector on the power steering pressure switch located on the pressure line between the power steer-

ing pump and the steering gear **(see illustration)**.

12   Remove the engine splash shield and the engine under cover (see Chapter 2).

13   Using two floor jacks, support the subframe. Position one jack on each side of the subframe, midway between the front and rear corners **(see illustration 24.15)**.

14   Remove the rear engine mount-to-subframe mounting bolts and discard them (see Chapter 2).

15   Remove the middle subframe mounts on each side of the subframe **(see illustration 24.7)**.

16   Loosen the front subframe bracket and subframe mounting bolts 1-3/16 inches (30 mm). Do not remove the bolts **(see illustration)**.

17   Mark the relationship of the subframe to the unibody. Loosen the rear subframe bracket and subframe mounting bolts 1-15/16 inches (50 mm). Do not remove the bolts **(see illustration)**. **Note:** *There are holes in the subframe bracket, subframe and unibody that*

are used to align the subframe with the unibody during installation.

18   Carefully lower the jacks until the subframe contacts the loosened bolts **(see illustration)**. **Warning:** *Do not remove the jacks. They must continue to support the subframe.*

19   Remove the heat shield **(see illustration)**.

20   Remove the return hose and feed line brackets from the subframe and steering gear bracket **(see illustration 19.19 and the accompanying illustration)**.

21   Using a flare nut wrench, remove the return and feed (pressure) lines from the steering gear. Cap or plug all openings. **Note:** *Placing shop towels under the line connections will help protect surrounding parts from spilled fluid.*

22   Remove the mounting bolts on the left side of the steering gear **(see illustration 19.20)**.

23   Remove the two mounting bolts and bracket on the right side of the steering gear **(see illustration 19.19)**.

19.16 Loosen the front subframe bracket and subframe bolts so that the frame can be lowered in the front (one side shown - loosen both sides at the front)

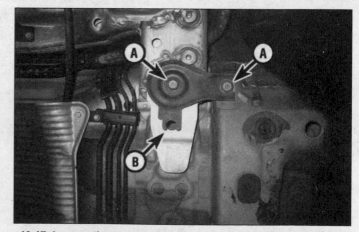

19.17 Loosen the rear subframe bracket and subframe bolts (A) so that the frame can be lowered in the rear. The alignment hole (B) can be seen through the bracket, subframe and unibody (one side shown - loosen both sides at the rear)

19.18 The subframe is lowered down to the loosened bolts. The floor jacks must continue to support the subframe. DO NOT rely on these bolts to support the subframe (rear corner shown)

19.19 Steering gear mounting details (right side):

1   Heat shield fasteners (vicinity shown for lower right fastener)
2   Feed (pressure) line clamp bolt
3   Return hose retainer
4   Steering gear mounting bolts (right side)

24   Carefully move the steering gear forward and remove the rubber grommet from around the steering gear input shaft. **Note:** Note the locating lug on the steering gear which fits into a slot on the grommet.

25   Apply tape around the input shaft to protect it (and other components) during removal.

26   Guide the steering gear assembly through the left wheel opening and remove it from the vehicle. Be careful not to damage the brake lines above the steering gear as it is removed.

2003 and earlier

Refer to illustrations 19.34 and 19.35

27   Remove the steering wheel and tape the clockspring in the centered position (see Section 16).

28   Mark the relationship of the U-joint to the steering gear input shaft **(see illustration 17.8)**. Remove both pinch bolts from the U-joint, then separate it from the input shaft.

29   Detach the tie-rods from the steering knuckles. Pull the right tie-rod to the extreme right position, then remove both tie-rods from the steering gear (see Section 15).

30   Remove the exhaust pipe between the warm-up catalytic converters at the exhaust manifolds and downstream catalytic converter at the bottom of the vehicle (see Chapter 4).

31   On vehicles equipped with an automatic transaxle, disconnect the shift cable from the transaxle (see Chapter 7).

32   Disconnect the power steering fluid pressure and return lines **(see illustration 19.20)**.

Note: On vehicle models equipped with premium options (navigation, etc.), there are additional fluid lines connected to the valve body of the power steering gear that lead to a sensor mounted in the transaxle. The sensor is referred to as a power steering speed sensor. These lines need to be detached from the steering gear for removal. The two metal lines that run along the top of the steering gear (pressure cylinder) and connect to the valve body STAY CONNECTED. Disconnect all other lines from the valve body to remove the steering gear.

33   Cap or plug all openings to prevent fluid loss and prevent contamination.

34   Remove the stiffener plates and mounting brackets from the subframe and steering gear **(see illustration)**.

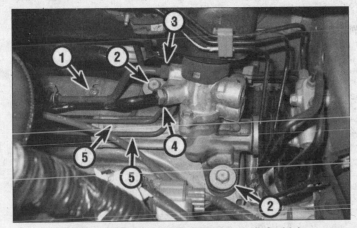

19.20 Steering gear mounting details (left side):

1   The location for the return line bracket at the subframe (removed)
2   Steering gear mounting bolts (left side)
3   Return line fitting at the valve body
4   Feed (pressure) line fitting at the valve body
5   Cylinder lines (do not remove from valve body)

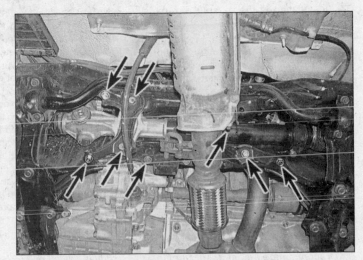

19.34 Locations of the stiffener plate and steering gear mounting bracket fasteners

19.35 Location of the steering gear mounting fasteners on the left side of the steering gear

20.3 Power steering pump details:

1	Pressure line	3	Mounting bolt locations (vicinity given for lower-right mounting bolt)
2	Feed line		

35   Support the steering gear and remove the mounting bolts **(see illustration)**. Lower the unit until the steering gear input shaft clears the opening through the firewall. Wrap electrical tape around the input shaft for protection.

36   Move the steering gear towards the passengers side, then guide the other end (driver's side) downward while moving it around the subframe. Remove the steering gear out towards the driver's side of the vehicle.

Installation

All models

37   Installation is the reverse of removal, noting the following points:

a) *Tighten the steering gear mounting bolts to the torque listed in this Chapter's Specifications.*

b) *With the jacks supporting the subframe to the unibody, replace the main subframe bolts with new ones. Align the subframe to its original position, then tighten the subframe mounting bolts to the torque listed in this Chapter's Specifications.*

c) *Do not connect the steering shaft (from the steering column) to the steering gear input shaft until the steering gear is mounted and the tie-rod ends are attached to the steering knuckles with the front wheels pointing straight forward.*

d) *Fill the power steering pump with the recommended fluid (see Chapter 1) and bleed the system (see Section 21.) Check for leaks and recheck the fluid level.*

e) *Reconnect the negative battery cable (see Chapter 5, Section 1).*

f) *Run the engine and check for proper operation and leaks. Shut off the engine and recheck the fluid level.*

g) *Have the front end alignment checked and adjusted.*

20   Power steering pump - removal and installation

Refer to illustration 20.3

Note: *Use shop towels to protect engine components from spilled fluid during this procedure. Clean any spilled fluid immediately.*

1   On 2004 and later models, remove the right-side engine cover (see Chapter 11) and engine mount bracket on the right side of the engine (see Chapter 2).

2   Remove the drivebelt (see Chapter 1).

3   Place a clamp on the power steering feed hose to minimize fluid loss when the hose is disconnected, then disconnect the fluid hoses at the pump **(see illustration)**. The return hose is held to the pump with a spring type clamp and the pressure line has two bolts holding it to the pump body. Cap or plug both hoses to prevent leakage or contamination. Install a new O-ring on the end of the pressure line. **Note:** *It's a good idea to remove the fluid from the power steering pump reservoir and replace it with new fluid before installing a replacement pump.*

4   Remove the pump mounting bolts and remove the pump from the engine.

5   Installation is the reverse of removal. Be sure to bleed the power steering system (see Section 21).

21   Power steering system - bleeding

1   Following any operation in which the power steering fluid lines have been disconnected, the power steering system must be bled to remove all air and obtain proper steering performance.

2   With the front wheels in the straight ahead position, check the power steering fluid level (see Chapter 1). If it's low, add fluid until it reaches the lower mark on the reservoir.

3   Start the engine and allow it to run at fast idle. Recheck the fluid level and add more if necessary to reach the lower mark on the reservoir. Make sure that there are no fluid leaks at any of the hose or line connections or in the system.

4   Bleed the system by turning the wheels from side-to-side, without hitting the stops. This will work the air out of the system. Make sure that there is fluid in the reservoir as this is done.

5   When the air is worked out of the system, return the wheels to the straight ahead position and leave the vehicle running for several more minutes before shutting it off.

6   Road test the vehicle to be sure the steering system is functioning normally and noise free.

7   Recheck the fluid level to be sure it is at the proper level while the engine is at normal operating temperature. Add fluid if necessary (see Chapter 1).

22 Wheels and tires - general information

Refer to illustration 22.1

1   All vehicles covered by this manual are equipped with metric-sized fiberglass or steel belted radial tires **(see illustration)**. Use of other size or type of tires may affect the ride and handling of the vehicle. Don't mix different types of tires, such as radials and bias belted, on the same vehicle as handling may be seriously affected. It's recommended that tires be replaced in pairs on the same axle, but if only one tire is being replaced, be sure it's the same size, structure and tread design as the other.

2   Because tire pressure has a substantial effect on handling and wear, the pressure on all tires should be checked at least once a month or before any extended trips (see Chapter 1).

3   Wheels must be replaced if they are bent, dented, leak air, have elongated bolt holes, are heavily rusted, out of vertical symmetry or if the lug nuts won't stay tight. Wheel repairs that use welding or peening are not recommended.

4   Tire and wheel balance is important to the overall handling, braking and performance of the vehicle. Unbalanced wheels can adversely affect handling and ride characteristics as well as tire life. Whenever a tire is installed on a wheel, the tire and wheel should be balanced by a shop with the proper equipment.

23 Wheel alignment - general information

Refer to illustration 23.1

1   A wheel alignment refers to the adjustments made to the wheels so they are in proper angular relationship to the suspension and the ground. Wheels that are out of proper alignment not only affect steering control, but also increase tire wear. Toe-in can be adjusted on the front and rear wheels. The front and rear camber angles and front caster angles should be checked to determine if any of the suspension components are worn out, bent or damaged **(see illustration)**.

2   Getting the proper wheel alignment is a very exacting process, one in which complicated and expensive machines are necessary to perform the job properly. Because of this, you should have a technician with the proper equipment perform these tasks. We will, however, use this space to give you a basic idea of what is involved with wheel alignment so you can better understand the process and deal intelligently with the shop that does the work.

3   Toe-in is the turning in of the wheels. The purpose of a toe specification is to ensure parallel rolling of the wheels. In a vehicle with zero toe-in, the distance between the front edges of the wheels will be the same as the dis-

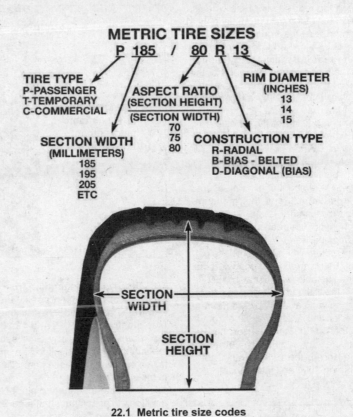

22.1 Metric tire size codes

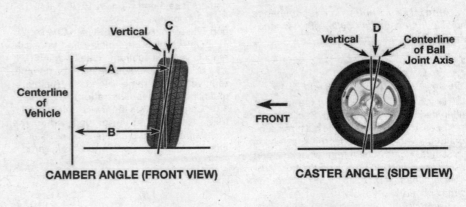

CAMBER ANGLE (FRONT VIEW)   CASTER ANGLE (SIDE VIEW)

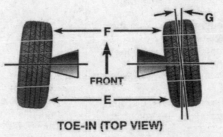

TOE-IN (TOP VIEW)

23.1 Camber, caster and toe-in angles

1   *A minus B = C (degrees camber)*   3   *E minus F = toe-in (measured in inches)*
2   *D = degrees caster*   4   *G = toe-in (expressed in degrees)*

tance between the rear edges of the wheels. The actual amount of toe-in is normally only a fraction of an inch. At the front end, toe-in is controlled by the tie-rod end position on the tie-rod. At the rear it is adjusted by turning an adjusting cam bolt on the inner end of the rear control arm. Incorrect toe-in will cause the tires to wear improperly by making them scrub against the road surface.

4   Camber is the tilting of the wheels from the vertical when viewed from the front or rear of the vehicle. When the wheels tilt out at the top, the camber is said to be positive (+). When the wheels tilt in at the top the camber is negative (-). The amount of tilt is measured in degrees from vertical and this measurement is called the camber angle. This angle affects the amount of tire tread which contacts the road and compensates for changes in the suspension geometry when the vehicle is cornering or traveling over an undulating surface. Camber isn't adjustable on these vehicles.

5   Caster is the tilting of the top of the steering axis from the vertical. A tilt toward the rear is positive caster and a tilt toward the front is negative caster. On 2003 and earlier models, caster is adjusted by adding or subtracting shims on the end of the radius rod. Caster isn't adjustable on 2004 and later models.

24   Subframe (front) - removal and installation

Warning: *The manufacturer recommends replacing the subframe bolts with new ones whenever they are removed.*

Removal

Refer to illustrations 24.7, 24.8 and 24.15

1   Disconnect the cable from the negative battery terminal (see Chapter 5, Section 1).
2   Loosen the front wheel lug nuts, raise the front of the vehicle and support it securely on jackstands. Remove both front wheels. **Note:** *The jackstands must be behind the front suspension subframe, not supporting the vehicle by the subframe.*
3   Remove the engine splash shield and engine under cover (see Chapter 2).
4   Remove the exhaust pipe between the warm-up catalytic converters at the exhaust manifolds and downstream catalytic converter at the bottom of the vehicle (see Chapter 4).
5   Remove the lower control arms (see Section 8).
6   On automatic transaxle models, disconnect the shift control cable from the transaxle (see Chapter 7B).
7   Remove the subframe middle mounts **(see illustration)**.
8   On automatic transaxle models, remove the transaxle oil cooler hose brackets from the subframe near the front engine mount, if equipped **(see illustration)**.
9   Remove the return and feed lines from the steering gear **(see illustration 19.20)**. Plug the lines to prevent fluid leakage.

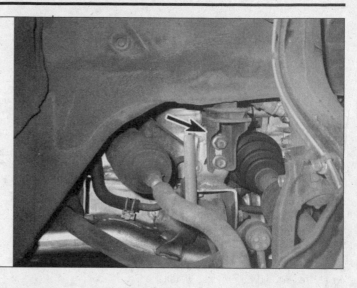

24.7 Mounting bolts for the subframe middle mount (right-side shown)

10   Remove the return line from under the right end of the steering gear, then remove it from the anchor attached to the subframe **(see illustrations 19.19 and 19.20)**. Release the return line from any clips securing it to the subframe. Also check to see that no other hoses or wiring harnesses are still connected to the subframe.
11   Separate the steering shaft U-joint from the steering gear input shaft (see Section 19).
12   Using two floor jacks, support the subframe. Position one jack on each side of the subframe, midway between the front and rear corners **(see illustration 24.15)**.
13   Support the engine with an engine support fixture or an engine hoist (see Chapter 2).
14   Detach all of the engine and transaxle mounts from the subframe (see Chapter 2).
15   With the jacks supporting the subframe, remove all subframe-to-chassis (unibody) mounting bolts **(see illustration)**.
16   Carefully lower the jacks until the subframe is resting on the ground. **Note:** *The steering gear and stabilizer bar will still be attached to the subframe when it is lowered.*

Installation

17   Installation is the reverse of removal, noting the following points:

a)   *Replace the subframe bolts with new ones. Align the subframe and tighten the subframe mounting bolts to the torque listed in this Chapter's Specifications.* **Note:** *Use a long drift tool (or equivalent) in the alignment holes in the rear corners of the subframe, subframe brackets and unibody to aid alignment* **(see Illustration 19.17)**.
b)   *Check the power steering fluid and automatic transaxle (if equipped) fluid levels, adding as necessary (see Chapter 1).*
c)   *Tighten all other suspension and steering fasteners to the torque listed in this Chapter's Specifications.*
d)   *Reconnect the negative battery cable (see Chapter 5, Section 1).*
e)   *Have the front end alignment checked and, if necessary, adjusted.*

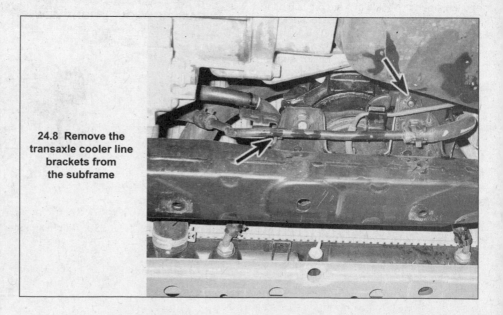

24.8 Remove the transaxle cooler line brackets from the subframe

24.15 Subframe mounting bolts (A), subframe front bracket bolts (B), subframe rear bracket bolts (C) and the area where the floor jacks should be placed (D)

Notes

Chapter 11 Body

Contents

1 General information

These models feature a unibody layout, using a floor pan with front and rear frame side rails which support the body components, and front and rear subframes which support suspension systems and other mechanical components.

Certain components are particularly vulnerable to accident damage and can be unbolted and repaired or replaced. Among these parts are the body moldings, bumpers, front fenders, the hood and trunk lid and all glass.

Only general body maintenance practices and body panel repair procedures within the scope of the do-it-yourselfer are included in this Chapter.

2 Body - maintenance

1   The condition of your vehicle's body is very important, because the resale value depends a great deal on it. It's much more difficult to repair a neglected or damaged body than it is to repair mechanical components. The hidden areas of the body, such as the wheel wells, the frame and the engine compartment, are equally important, although they don't require as frequent attention as the rest of the body.

2   Once a year, or every 12,000 miles, it's a good idea to have the underside of the body steam cleaned. All traces of dirt and oil will be removed and the area can then be inspected carefully for rust, damaged brake lines, frayed electrical wires, damaged cables and other problems.

3   At the same time, clean the engine and the engine compartment with a steam cleaner or water soluble degreaser.

4   The wheel wells should be given close attention, since undercoating can peel away and stones and dirt thrown up by the tires can cause the paint to chip and flake, allowing rust to set in. If rust is found, clean down to the bare metal and apply an anti-rust paint.

5   The body should be washed about once a week. Wet the vehicle thoroughly to soften the dirt, then wash it down with a soft sponge and plenty of clean soapy water. If the surplus dirt is not washed off very carefully, it can wear down the paint.

6   Spots of tar or asphalt thrown up from the road should be removed with a cloth soaked in solvent.

7   Once every six months, wax the body

and chrome trim. If a chrome cleaner is used to remove rust from any of the vehicle's plated parts, remember that the cleaner also removes part of the chrome, so use it sparingly.

3   Vinyl trim - maintenance

Don't clean vinyl trim with detergents, caustic soap or petroleum based cleaners. Plain soap and water works just fine, with a soft brush to clean dirt that may be ingrained. Wash the vinyl as frequently as the rest of the vehicle.

After cleaning, application of a high quality rubber and vinyl protectant will help prevent oxidation and cracks. The protectant can also be applied to weather-stripping, vacuum lines and rubber hoses, which often fail as a result of chemical degradation, and to the tires.

4   Upholstery and carpets - maintenance

1   Every three months remove the carpets or mats and clean the interior of the vehicle (more frequently if necessary). Vacuum the upholstery and carpets to remove loose dirt and dust.
2   Leather upholstery requires special care. Stains should be removed with warm water and a very mild soap solution. Use a clean, damp cloth to remove the soap, then wipe again with a dry cloth. Never use alcohol, gasoline, nail polish remover or thinner to clean leather upholstery.
3   After cleaning, regularly treat leather upholstery with a leather wax. Never use car wax on leather upholstery.
4   In areas where the interior of the vehicle is subject to bright sunlight, cover leather seats with a sheet if the vehicle is to be left out for any length of time.

5   Body repair - minor damage

Plastic body panels

The following repair procedures are for minor scratches and gouges. Repair of more serious damage should be left to a dealer service department or qualified auto body shop. Below is a list of the equipment and materials necessary to perform the following repair procedures on plastic body panels. Although a specific brand of material may be mentioned, it should be noted that equivalent products from other manufacturers may be used instead.

Wax, grease and silicone removing solvent
Cloth-backed body tape
Sanding discs
Drill motor with three-inch disc holder
Hand sanding block

Rubber squeegees
Sandpaper
Non-porous mixing palette
Wood paddle or putty knife
Curved tooth body file
Flexible parts repair material

Flexible panels (front and rear bumper covers)

1   Remove the damaged panel, if necessary or desirable. In most cases, repairs can be carried out with the panel installed.
2   Clean the area(s) to be repaired with a wax, grease and silicone removing solvent applied with a water-dampened cloth.
3   If the damage is structural, that is, if it extends through the panel, clean the backside of the panel area to be repaired as well. Wipe dry.
4   Sand the rear surface about 1-1/2 inches beyond the break.
5   Cut two pieces of fiberglass cloth large enough to overlap the break by about 1-1/2 inches. Cut only to the required length.
6   Mix the adhesive from the repair kit according to the instructions included with the kit, and apply a layer of the mixture approximately 1/8-inch thick on the backside of the panel. Overlap the break by at least 1-1/2 inches.
7   Apply one piece of fiberglass cloth to the adhesive and cover the cloth with additional adhesive. Apply a second piece of fiberglass cloth to the adhesive and immediately cover the cloth with additional adhesive in sufficient quantity to fill the weave.
8   Allow the repair to cure for 20 to 30 minutes at 60-degrees to 80-degrees F.
9   If necessary, trim the excess repair material at the edge.
10   Remove all of the paint film over and around the area(s) to be repaired. The repair material should not overlap the painted surface.
11   With a drill motor and a sanding disc (or a rotary file), cut a "V" along the break line approximately 1/2-inch wide. Remove all dust and loose particles from the repair area.
12   Mix and apply the repair material. Apply a light coat first over the damaged area; then continue applying material until it reaches a level slightly higher than the surrounding finish.
13   Cure the mixture for 20 to 30 minutes at 60-degrees to 80-degrees F.
14   Roughly establish the contour of the area being repaired with a body file. If low areas or pits remain, mix and apply additional adhesive.
15   Block sand the damaged area with sandpaper to establish the actual contour of the surrounding surface.
16   If desired, the repaired area can be temporarily protected with several light coats of primer. Because of the special paints and techniques required for flexible body panels, it is recommended that the vehicle be taken to a paint shop for completion of the body repair.

Steel body panels

See photo sequence

Repair of minor scratches

17   If the scratch is superficial and does not penetrate to the metal of the body, repair is very simple. Lightly rub the scratched area with a fine rubbing compound to remove loose paint and built-up wax. Rinse the area with clean water.
18   Apply touch-up paint to the scratch, using a small brush. Continue to apply thin layers of paint until the surface of the paint in the scratch is level with the surrounding paint. Allow the new paint at least two weeks to harden, then blend it into the surrounding paint by rubbing with a very fine rubbing compound. Finally, apply a coat of wax to the scratch area.
19   If the scratch has penetrated the paint and exposed the metal of the body, causing the metal to rust, a different repair technique is required. Remove all loose rust from the bottom of the scratch with a pocket knife, then apply rust inhibiting paint to prevent the formation of rust in the future. Using a rubber or nylon applicator, coat the scratched area with glaze-type filler. If required, the filler can be mixed with thinner to provide a very thin paste, which is ideal for filling narrow scratches. Before the glaze filler in the scratch hardens, wrap a piece of smooth cotton cloth around the tip of a finger. Dip the cloth in thinner, then quickly wipe it along the surface of the scratch. This will ensure that the surface of the filler is slightly hollow. The scratch can now be painted over as described earlier in this section.

Repair of dents

20   When repairing dents, the first job is to pull the dent out until the affected area is as close as possible to its original shape. There is no point in trying to restore the original shape completely as the metal in the damaged area will have stretched on impact and cannot be restored to its original contours. It is better to bring the level of the dent up to a point which is about 1/8-inch below the level of the surrounding metal. In cases where the dent is very shallow, it is not worth trying to pull it out at all.
21   If the back side of the dent is accessible, it can be hammered out gently from behind using a soft-face hammer. While doing this, hold a block of wood firmly against the opposite side of the metal to absorb the hammer blows and prevent the metal from being stretched.
22   If the dent is in a section of the body which has double layers, or some other factor makes it inaccessible from behind, a different technique is required. Drill several small holes through the metal inside the damaged area, particularly in the deeper sections. Screw long, self-tapping screws into the holes just enough for them to get a good grip in the metal. Now the dent can be pulled out by pulling on the protruding heads of the screws with locking pliers.

23 The next stage of repair is the removal of paint from the damaged area and from an inch or so of the surrounding metal. This is done with a wire brush or sanding disk in a drill motor, although it can be done just as effectively by hand with sandpaper. To complete the preparation for filling, score the surface of the bare metal with a screwdriver or the tang of a file, or drill small holes in the affected area. This will provide a good grip for the filler material. To complete the repair, see the subsection on filling and painting later in this Section.

Repair of rust holes or gashes

24 Remove all paint from the affected area and from an inch or so of the surrounding metal using a sanding disk or wire brush mounted in a drill motor. If these are not available, a few sheets of sandpaper will do the job just as effectively.

25 With the paint removed, you will be able to determine the severity of the corrosion and decide whether to replace the whole panel, if possible, or repair the affected area. New body panels are not as expensive as most people think and it is often quicker to install a new panel than to repair large areas of rust.

26 Remove all trim pieces from the affected area except those which will act as a guide to the original shape of the damaged body, such as headlight shells, etc. Using metal snips or a hacksaw blade, remove all loose metal and any other metal that is badly affected by rust. Hammer the edges of the hole in to create a slight depression for the filler material.

27 Wire brush the affected area to remove the powdery rust from the surface of the metal. If the back of the rusted area is accessible, treat it with rust inhibiting paint.

28 Before filling is done, block the hole in some way. This can be done with sheet metal riveted or screwed into place, or by stuffing the hole with wire mesh.

29 Once the hole is blocked off, the affected area can be filled and painted. See the following subsection on filling and painting.

Filling and painting

30 Many types of body fillers are available, but generally speaking, body repair kits which contain filler paste and a tube of resin hardener are best for this type of repair work. A wide, flexible plastic or nylon applicator will be necessary for imparting a smooth and contoured finish to the surface of the filler material. Mix up a small amount of filler on a clean piece of wood or cardboard (use the hardener sparingly). Follow the manufacturer's instructions on the package, otherwise the filler will set incorrectly.

31 Using the applicator, apply the filler paste to the prepared area. Draw the applicator across the surface of the filler to achieve the desired contour and to level the filler surface. As soon as a contour that approximates the original one is achieved, stop working the paste. If you continue, the paste will begin to stick to the applicator. Continue to add thin layers of paste at 20-minute intervals until the level of the filler is just above the surrounding metal.

32 Once the filler has hardened, the excess can be removed with a body file. From then on, progressively finer grades of sandpaper should be used, starting with a 180-grit paper and finishing with 600-grit wet-or-dry paper. Always wrap the sandpaper around a flat rubber or wooden block, otherwise the surface of the filler will not be completely flat. During the sanding of the filler surface, the wet-or-dry paper should be periodically rinsed in water. This will ensure that a very smooth finish is produced in the final stage.

33 At this point, the repair area should be surrounded by a ring of bare metal, which in turn should be encircled by the finely feathered edge of good paint. Rinse the repair area with clean water until all of the dust produced by the sanding operation is gone.

34 Spray the entire area with a light coat of primer. This will reveal any imperfections in the surface of the filler. Repair the imperfections with fresh filler paste or glaze filler and once more smooth the surface with sandpaper. Repeat this spray-and-repair procedure until you are satisfied that the surface of the filler and the feathered edge of the paint are perfect. Rinse the area with clean water and allow it to dry completely.

35 The repair area is now ready for painting. Spray painting must be carried out in a warm, dry, windless and dust free atmosphere. These conditions can be created if you have access to a large indoor work area, but if you are forced to work in the open, you will have to pick the day very carefully. If you are working indoors, dousing the floor in the work area with water will help settle the dust, which would otherwise be in the air. If the repair area is confined to one body panel, mask off the surrounding panels. This will help minimize the effects of a slight mismatch in paint color. Trim pieces such as chrome strips, door handles, etc., will also need to be masked off or removed. Use masking tape and several thickness of newspaper for the masking operations.

36 Before spraying, shake the paint can thoroughly, then spray a test area until the spray painting technique is mastered. Cover the repair area with a thick coat of primer. The thickness should be built up using several thin layers of primer rather than one thick one. Using 600-grit wet-or-dry sandpaper, rub down the surface of the primer until it is very smooth. While doing this, the work area should be thoroughly rinsed with water and the wet-or-dry sandpaper periodically rinsed as well. Allow the primer to dry before spraying additional coats.

37 Spray on the top coat, again building up the thickness by using several thin layers of paint. Begin spraying in the center of the repair area, then, using a circular motion, work out until the whole repair area and about two inches of the surrounding original paint is covered. Remove all masking material 10 to 15 minutes after spraying on the final coat of paint. Allow the new paint at least two weeks to harden, then use a very fine rubbing compound to blend the edges of the new paint into the existing paint. Finally, apply a coat of wax.

6   Body repair - major damage

1 Major damage must be repaired by an auto body shop specifically equipped to perform unibody repairs. These shops have the specialized equipment required to do the job properly.

2 If the damage is extensive, the body must be checked for proper alignment or the vehicle's handling characteristics may be adversely affected and other components may wear at an accelerated rate.

3 Due to the fact that all of the major body components (hood, fenders, etc.) are separate and replaceable units, any seriously damaged components should be replaced rather than repaired. Sometimes the components can be found in a wrecking yard that specializes in used vehicle components, often at considerable savings over the cost of new parts.

7   Hinges and locks - maintenance

Once every 3000 miles, or every three months, the hinges and latch assemblies on the doors, hood and trunk should be given a few drops of light oil or lock lubricant. The door latch strikers should also be lubricated with a thin coat of grease to reduce wear and ensure free movement. Lubricate the door and trunk locks with spray-on graphite lubricant.

8   Windshield and fixed glass - replacement

Replacement of the windshield and fixed glass requires the use of special fast-setting adhesive/caulk materials and some specialized tools and techniques. These operations should be left to a dealer service department or a shop specializing in glass work.

9   Cowl and engine covers - removal and installation

2003 and earlier models
Cowl cover

1 Remove the windshield wiper arms (see Chapter 12), then remove the three push fastener clips and remove the cowl cover.

2 Installation is the reverse of removal.

Bulkhead cover (radiator cover)

3 Using a trim removal tool, pop up the 10 push fasteners and remove the cover. Installation is the reverse of removal.

These photos illustrate a method of repairing simple dents. They are intended to supplement *Body repair - minor damage* in this Chapter and should not be used as the sole instructions for body repair on these vehicles.

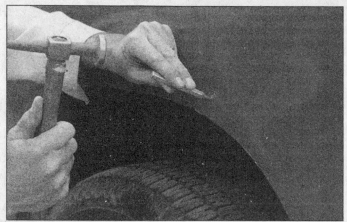

1 If you can't access the backside of the body panel to hammer out the dent, pull it out with a slide-hammer-type dent puller. In the deepest portion of the dent or along the crease line, drill or punch hole(s) at least one inch apart . . .

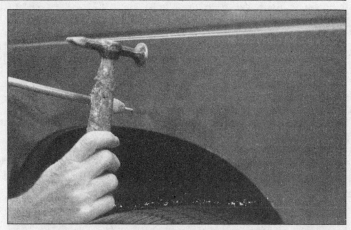

2 . . . then screw the slide-hammer into the hole and operate it. Tap with a hammer near the edge of the dent to help 'pop' the metal back to its original shape. When you're finished, the dent area should be close to its original contour and about 1/8-inch below the surface of the surrounding metal

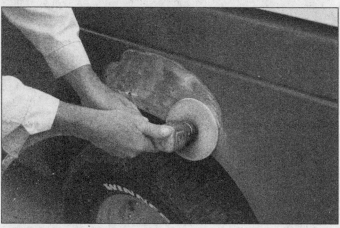

3 Using coarse-grit sandpaper, remove the paint down to the bare metal. Hand sanding works fine, but the disc sander shown here makes the job faster. Use finer (about 320-grit) sandpaper to feather-edge the paint at least one inch around the dent area

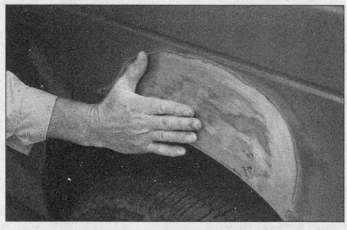

4 When the paint is removed, touch will probably be more helpful than sight for telling if the metal is straight. Hammer down the high spots or raise the low spots as necessary. Clean the repair area with wax/silicone remover

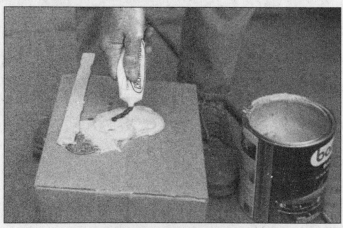

5 Following label instructions, mix up a batch of plastic filler and hardener. The ratio of filler to hardener is critical, and, if you mix it incorrectly, it will either not cure properly or cure too quickly (you won't have time to file and sand it into shape)

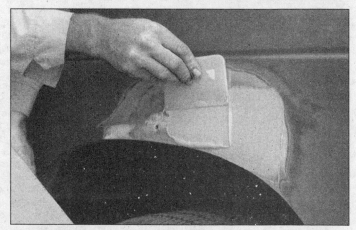

6 Working quickly so the filler doesn't harden, use a plastic applicator to press the body filler firmly into the metal, assuring it bonds completely. Work the filler until it matches the original contour and is slightly above the surrounding metal

7 Let the filler harden until you can just dent it with your fingernail. Use a body file or Surform tool (shown here) to rough-shape the filler

8 Use coarse-grit sandpaper and a sanding board or block to work the filler down until it's smooth and even. Work down to finer grits of sandpaper - always using a board or block - ending up with 360 or 400 grit

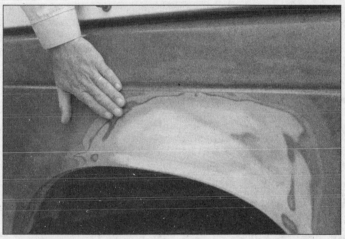

9 You shouldn't be able to feel any ridge at the transition from the filler to the bare metal or from the bare metal to the old paint. As soon as the repair is flat and uniform, remove the dust and mask off the adjacent panels or trim pieces

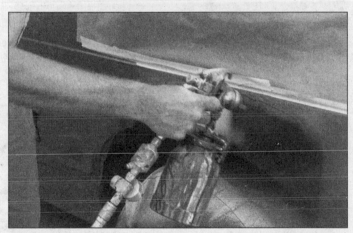

10 Apply several layers of primer to the area. Don't spray the primer on too heavy, so it sags or runs, and make sure each coat is dry before you spray on the next one. A professional-type spray gun is being used here, but aerosol spray primer is available inexpensively from auto parts stores

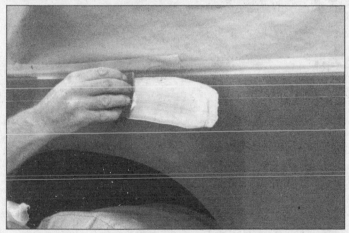

11 The primer will help reveal imperfections or scratches. Fill these with glazing compound. Follow the label instructions and sand it with 360 or 400-grit sandpaper until it's smooth. Repeat the glazing, sanding and respraying until the primer reveals a perfectly smooth surface

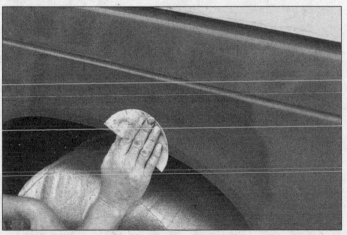

12 Finish sand the primer with very fine sandpaper (400 or 600-grit) to remove the primer overspray. Clean the area with water and allow it to dry. Use a tack rag to remove any dust, then apply the finish coat. Don't attempt to rub out or wax the repair area until the paint has dried completely (at least two weeks)

9.4 To remove the left side engine compartment cover, release the two hooks (one on each side) and disengage the two locator pins at the front of the cover (2004 and later models)

9.5 To remove the left rear engine cover, grasp it firmly and lift it straight up to disengage it from the three hooks (2004 and later models)

2004 and later models

Engine compartment covers

Refer to illustrations 9.4, 9.5, 9.6 and 9.7

Note: *The left side engine compartment cover can be removed independently of the other engine compartment covers. But the right side, left rear and right rear engine compartment covers must be removed in the sequence indicated below because of the way that they overlap. They must be installed in the reverse order of this sequence.*

4   Release the two hooks (one on each side), disconnect the two locator pins at the front of the cover, then remove the left side engine compartment cover **(see illustration)**.

5   Remove the cap from the windshield washer reservoir, then release the two hooks on the outer edge of the cover and three locator pins (one at the front end, two at the rear end of the cover). Remove the right side engine compartment cover **(see illustration)**.

6   Release the three hooks, then remove the left rear engine compartment cover **(see illustration)**.

7   Release the two hooks, then remove the right rear engine compartment cover **(see illustration)**.

Front bulkhead cover (radiator cover)

Refer to illustration 9.9

8   Remove the left side and right side engine compartment covers (see Steps 4 and 5 above)

9   The radiator cover is secured by five push fasteners **(see illustration)**. Pry up each push fastener, then grasp the cover firmly and pull it up.

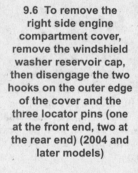

9.6 To remove the right side engine compartment cover, remove the windshield washer reservoir cap, then disengage the two hooks on the outer edge of the cover and the three locator pins (one at the front end, two at the rear end) (2004 and later models)

9.7 To remove the right rear engine compartment cover, release the two hooks, then disengage the cover from the three clips underneath (2004 and later models)

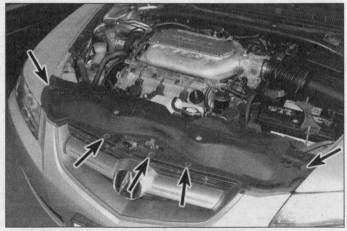

9.9 To detach the front bulkhead cover (radiator cover), pop up these five push fasteners (2004 and later models)

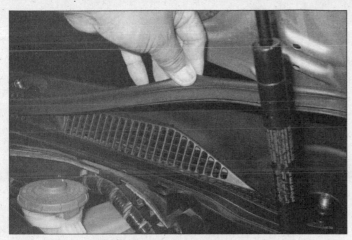

9.13 To remove the hood seal, simply pull it off
(2004 and later models)

9.14a To detach the right cowl cover, remove the pop fasteners
with a trim removal tool . . .

10   Make sure that all five push fasteners and the grommets for the locator pins are in good shape. If they're not, replace them. Installation is otherwise the reverse of removal.

Cowl covers

Refer to illustrations 9.13, 9.14a, 9.14b and 9.15

11   Remove the windshield wiper arms (see *Windshield wiper motor - removal and installation* in Chapter 12).

12   Remove the right side, left rear and right rear engine compartment covers (see Steps 5, 6 and 7).

13   Remove the hood rear seal **(see illustration)**.

14   Using a trim panel removal tool, pop up the push fasteners from the right cowl cover, lift up the cover, disconnect the windshield washer fluid line **(see illustrations)** and remove the right cowl cover.

15   Using a trim panel removal tool, pop up the push fastener **(see illustration)** from the left cowl cover and remove the cover.

16   Installation is the reverse of removal.

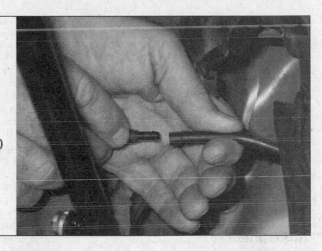

9.14b . . . then lift up the cover and disconnect the windshield washer fluid line (2004 and later models)

10   Hood - removal, installation and adjustment

Removal and installation

Refer to illustrations 10.2 and 10.4
Note: *The hood is heavy and somewhat awk-*

ward to remove and install - at least two people should perform this procedure.

1   Use blankets or pads to cover the fenders and cowl areas. This will protect the body and paint as the hood is lifted off.

2   Scribe or draw alignment marks around the bolt heads to ensure proper alignment during installation **(see illustration)**.

9.15 To detach the left cowl cover, remove the pop fastener with a trim removal tool (2004 and later models)

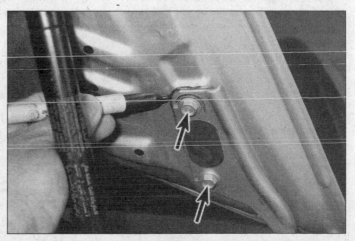

10.2 Scribe or draw alignment marks around the hood hinges to ensure proper alignment of the hood when it's reinstalled

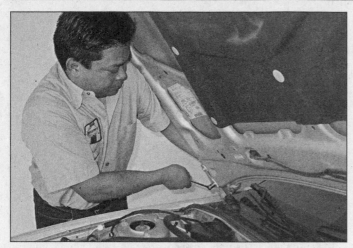

10.4 Support the hood with your shoulder while removing the hood bolts

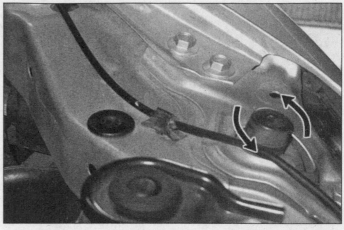

10.11 To adjust the vertical height of the leading edge of the hood so it's flush with the fenders, turn each edge cushion clockwise (to lower the hood) or counterclockwise (to raise the hood)

3   Disconnect any cables or wire harnesses which will interfere with removal, then unbolt the hood support strut from the hood.
4   Have an assistant help you support the weight of the hood. Remove the hinge-to-hood bolts, then lift off the hood **(see illustration)**.
5   Installation is the reverse of removal. If you position the hood so that the hinges fit within the scribe marks you made before loosening the bolts, in the same location they were in prior to removal, then the hood should still be aligned.
6   If you're installing a new hood, or didn't scribe the hinge positions, then you'll need to readjust the hood position.

Adjustment

Refer to illustration 10.11

7   You can adjust the hood fore-and-aft and right-and-left by means of the elongated holes in the hinges.
8   Scribe a line around the entire hinge plate so you can judge the amount of movement.
9   Loosen the bolts and move the hood into correct alignment. Move it only a little at a time. Tighten the hinge bolts or nuts and carefully lower the hood to check the alignment.

10   If necessary after installation, the entire hood latch assembly can be adjusted up-and-down as well as from side-to-side on the upper radiator support so the hood closes securely and is flush with the fenders. To do this, scribe a line around the hood latch mounting bolts to provide a reference point. Then loosen the bolts and reposition the latch assembly as necessary. Following adjustment, retighten the mounting bolts.
11   Adjust the vertical height of the leading edge of the hood by screwing the edge cushions in or out so that the hood, when closed, is flush with the fenders **(see illustration)**.
12   The hood latch assembly, as well as the hinges, should be periodically lubricated with white lithium-base grease to prevent sticking and wear.

11   Hood latch - removal and installation

Refer to illustrations 11.4 and 11.5

1   On 2001 and earlier models, pop up the 10 push fasteners with a trim removal tool and remove the front bulkhead cover (radiator cover).

2   On 2002 and later models, remove the front bumper cover (see Section 12).
3   Remove the hood latch cover. On most covers, simply pull the cover toward you, then pull it down, to remove it.
4   Using a marking pen, make a line around the latch to ensure correct alignment during reassembly. Remove the latch retaining bolts from the radiator support and remove the latch **(see illustration)**.
5   Disconnect the hood release cable by disengaging the cable from the latch assembly **(see illustration)**.
6   Installation is reverse of the removal.
Note: *Adjust the latch as necessary so that the hood engages securely when closed and the hood bumpers are slightly compressed.*

12   Bumper covers - removal and installation

Front bumper cover

1   Raise the vehicle and support it securely on jackstands.

11.4 Use a marking pen to mark the position of the hood latch, then remove the latch mounting bolts

11.5 Disengage the end of the hood release cable from the latch mechanism and remove the latch

2001 and earlier models

2   Working under the vehicle, remove the two bolts and two screws that secure the underside of the bumper cover to the fenders.

3   Remove the three clips that secure the upper part of the bumper cover directly below the grille.

4   Remove the six lower clips that secure the underside of the bumper cover to the left and right inner fender splash shields and to the engine under cover. Remove the bumper cover.

5   Installation is the reverse of removal.

2002 and 2003 models

6   Remove the 10 clips that secure the front bulkhead cover and remove the bulkhead cover (the black plastic trim piece that covers the upper radiator crossmember).

7   Remove the two clips that secure the grille to the upper radiator crossmember.

8   Working under the vehicle, remove the two bolts and two screws that secure the underside of the bumper cover to the fenders.

9   Remove the six lower clips that secure the underside of the bumper cover to the left and right inner fender splash shields and to

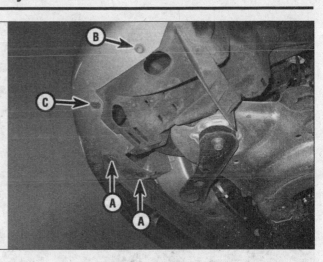

12.12 To remove each strake, remove these two bolts (A) (left side shown). To detach the front left corner of the front bumper cover, remove bolt (B) and push fastener (C) (2004 and later models)

the engine under cover. Remove the bumper cover.

10   Installation is the reverse of removal.

2004 and later models

Refer to illustrations 12.12, 12.14a, 12.14b and 12.16

11   Remove the left side engine compartment cover, the right side engine compartment cover and the front bulkhead cover (see Section 9).

12   Working underneath the front bumper cover, remove the two left strake mounting bolts (**see illustration**), disengage the strake mounting tab from the slot in the left end of the front air guide plate and remove the left strake. Remove the right strake the same way.

13   Remove the lower mounting fasteners from the left and right corners of the bumper cover (**see illustration 12.12**).

14   Remove the two lower push fasteners from the middle part of the underside of the bumper cover and remove the two upper push fasteners from each side of the grille (**see illustrations**).

15   Remove the two push fasteners that secure the front end of each inner fender splash shield (see Section 14) and pull back the splash shields to provide access to the voids behind the left and right corners of the front bumper cover.

16   Working inside the void behind each corner of the front bumper cover, remove the left and right bumper cover mounting screws (**see illustration**).

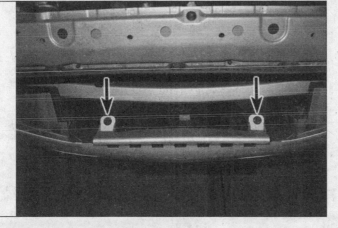

12.14a To detach the lower center part of the front bumper cover, remove these two push fasteners (2004 and later models)

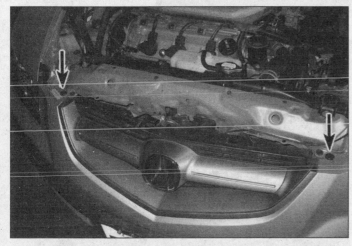

12.14b To detach the upper central part of the front bumper cover, remove these two push fasteners (2004 and later models)

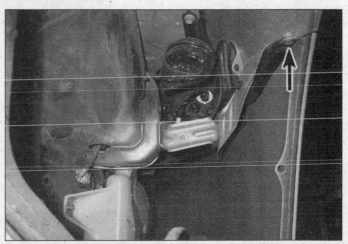

12.16 Working inside the void at each corner of the front bumper cover, remove this bumper cover mounting screw (2004 and later models)

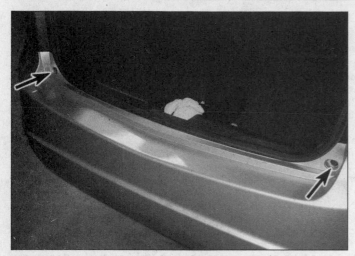

12.28 Carefully pry off the trim caps and remove the fasteners (2004 and later models)

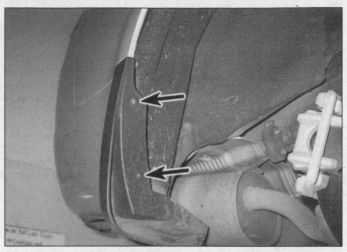

12.29a Remove these two screws and remove the mud flap . . .

17   Pull on the front bumper cover at the wheel arch areas to disengage the slots on the trailing edge of the bumper cover from the tabs on the side spacers. With the help of an assistant, pull each wheel arch part of the bumper cover away from the side spacer, while simultaneously pulling the bumper cover forward to disengage the bumper cover slots from the tabs on the corner upper beam.

18   Disconnect the fog light electrical connectors, if equipped, and remove the front bumper cover.

19   Installation is the reverse of removal.

Rear bumper cover

20   Raise the vehicle and support it securely on jackstands.

2003 and earlier models

21   Open the trunk lid. There are five clips located on top of the bumper cover, directly below the trunk and just above the license plate area. Remove these five clips.

22   There are two more clips located on the underside of the rear bumper cover, below the license plate area. Remove these two clips.

23   There are two more clips (one on the left and one on the right) located on the forward edges of the bumper cover, at the wheel arches. Remove these two clips.

24   There are two screws (one on the left and one on the right) located at the upper front corners of the bumper cover, in the underside of the wheel arches. Remove these two screws.

25   The rear bumper cover is also secured by hooks located on the mounting flange, to which the upper edge of the bumper cover is attached. To disengage the bumper cover from these hooks, carefully pull up on the upper edges of the cover and pull it off.

26   Disconnect the license plate light electrical connector and remove the rear bumper cover.

27   Installation is the reverse of removal.

2004 and later models

Refer to illustrations 12.28, 12.29a, 12.29b and 12.30

28   Open the trunk lid. Remove the fasteners securing the upper portion of the bumper cover **(see illustration)**.

29   Remove the screws at the forward edges of the bumper cover, at the wheel arches **(see illustrations)**.

30   There are eight push fasteners located on the underside of the bumper cover **(see illustration)**. Carefully pop out all eight push fasteners.

31   The rear bumper cover is also secured by hooks. To disengage the bumper cover from these hooks, carefully pull up on the upper edges of the cover and pull it off.

32   Installation is the reverse of removal.

12.29b . . . then remove this screw (right rear wheel well shown, left rear wheel well identical) (2004 and later models)

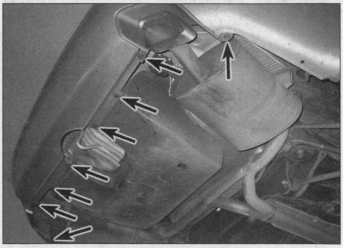

12.30 Carefully pry out the push fasteners with a trim removal tool (2004 and later models)

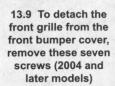

13.9 To detach the front grille from the front bumper cover, remove these seven screws (2004 and later models)

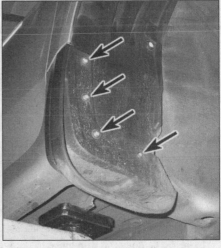

14.4a To remove the mud flap, remove these four screws (2004 and later models)

13 Front grille - removal and installation

2001 and earlier models

1   Remove the five grille mounting nuts: two on top of the grille, one at each end, and three along the bottom.
2   Detach the clips, on the backside of the upper front edge of the grille by carefully pulling off the grille.
3   Installation is the reverse of removal.

2002 and 2003 models

4   Remove the front bumper cover (see Section 12).
5   Remove the three clips, which are located on the inside of the bumper cover, adjacent to the underside of the grille.
6   To detach the grille from the bumper cover, disengage the three hooks located along the underside of the grille.
7   Installation is the reverse of removal.

2004 and later models

Refer to illustration 13.9

8   Remove the front bumper cover (see Section 12).
9   Remove the seven grille retaining screws **(see illustration)** to remove the grille cover and center molding.
10   Installation is the reverse of removal.

14 Front fender - removal and installation

Refer to illustrations 14.4a, 14.4b, 14.5, 14.6a, 14.6b, 14.6c, 14.7, 14.8 and 14.10

Note: *The photos accompanying this Section depict the front fender used on 2004 and later*

models. *The bolt locations on earlier fenders are slightly different, but the procedure you see here is typical, and similar to earlier models.*

1   Loosen the wheel lug nuts, raise the front of the vehicle and support it securely on jackstands. Remove the front wheel from the side on which you want to remove the front fender.
2   Remove the front bumper cover (see Section 12).
3   Remove the headlight housing (see Chapter 12).
4   Remove the mud flap, then remove the two bolts and seven push fasteners that secure the inner fender splash shield **(see illustrations)** and detach the shield.
5   Disconnect the electrical connector from the front sidemarker light and remove the foam insulator block **(see illustration)**.

14.4b To remove the inner fender splash shield, remove the push fasteners (A), then remove the bolts (B) (2004 and later models)

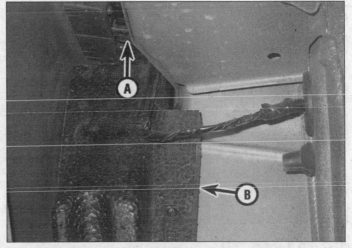

14.5 After removing the splash shield, depress the release tab (A) and disconnect the electrical connector from the front sidemarker light, then carefully pull out this piece of insulator foam (B) (2004 and later models)

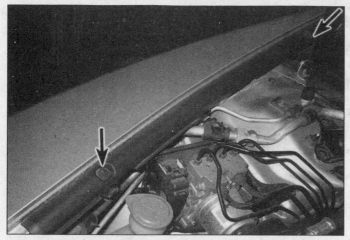

14.6a To remove the trim piece that covers the upper fender bolts, pry up these two push fasteners (2004 and later models)

14.6b Remove these three upper fender mounting bolts . . .

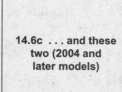

14.6c . . . and these two (2004 and later models)

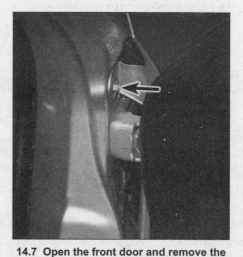

14.7 Open the front door and remove the upper rear fender mounting bolt (2004 and later models)

6   Remove the trim piece that covers the upper fender mounting bolts, then remove the upper fender mounting bolts **(see illustrations)**.

7   Remove the upper rear fender mounting bolt **(see illustration)**.

8   Pull out the front side sill **(see illustration)** and remove the lower rear fender mounting bolt.

9   Remove the headlight housing (see Chapter 12).

10   Remove the front fender mounting bolt **(see illustration)** and remove the fender. It's a good idea to have an assistant support the fender while it's being moved·away from the

vehicle to prevent damage to the surrounding body panels.

11   If you're replacing the fender, remove the front sidemarker light housing.

12   Installation is the reverse of removal.

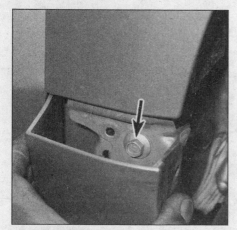

14.8 Pull out the forward end of the front side sill plate and remove the lower rear fender mounting bolt (2004 and later models)

14.10 After removing the headlight housing, remove this fender bracket bolt and remove the fender (2004 and later models)

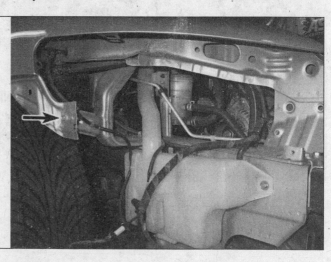

15.1a Each trunk lid hinge is covered by a two-piece plastic cover. The two pieces are snapped together. Pull the two halves apart and remove the cover from each hinge

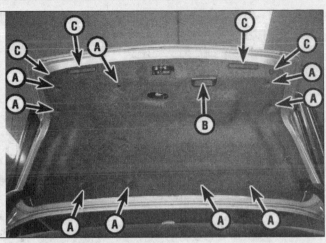

15.1b The trunk lid trim panel is secured to the underside of the trunk lid by push fasteners (A) and a screw in the trunk lid handle (B). You'll also have to remove the cushions (C)

15 Trunk lid - removal and installation

Note: *The trunk lid is heavy and somewhat awkward to remove and install. At least two people should perform this procedure.*

Removal and installation

Refer to illustrations 15.1a, 15.1b, 15.1c and 15.3

1 Open the trunk lid and remove the trunk lid trim panel **(see illustrations)**.

2 Unplug the electrical connector for the trunk lid latch and disconnect the trunk lid release cable from the latch (see Section 16). Remove the wire harness and trunk release cable from the trunk lid. Tie string or wire to the harness and release cable before pulling them out of the trunk lid to ensure that they're routed correctly when installing the trunk lid.

3 Scribe or draw alignment marks around the trunk hinges, then remove the hinge-to-trunk lid bolts from both sides **(see illustration)**. **Note:** *It's a good idea to have an assistant support the trunk lid while you're removing the bolts.*

4 Lift off the trunk lid.

5 Installation is the reverse of removal. Be sure to align the hinge flanges with the marks made on the trunk lid during removal. Do not install the trunk trim panel until you have verified that the trunk lid is correctly aligned.

Adjustment

Refer to illustration 15.9

6 After installation, close the lid and verify that it's correctly aligned with the adjacent body surfaces.

7 If you haven't just installed the trunk lid, then you'll need to remove the trunk lid trim panel **(see illustrations 15.1a, 15.1b and 15.1c)** and remove the rear shelf (see Section 28).

8 Fore-and-aft and side-to-side adjustments of the lid are controlled by the position of the hinge bolts in the slotted holes in the hinge plates. To adjust it, loosen the hinge bolts, reposition the lid and retighten the bolts.

9 To adjust the height of the closed trunk lid in relation to the surrounding body panels, move the striker up/down or left/right **(see illustration)**, then re-tighten the bolts. **Note:** *Make a reference mark around the striker before making adjustments.*

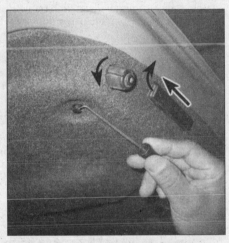

15.1c To remove the push fasteners, simply pull out the center section. To remove the cylindrical cushions, unscrew them. To remove the rectangular cushions, slide them toward the outside edge of the trunk lid and pull out the outer end

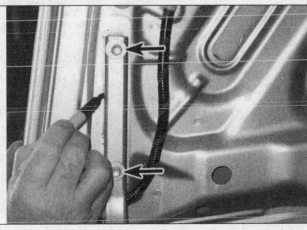

15.3 Mark the position of the trunk lid hinges with a marking pen, then remove the two bolts from each hinge

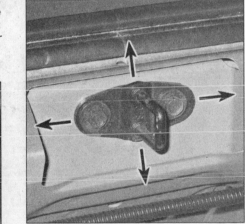

15.9 To adjust the height of the trunk lid in relation to the surrounding body panels, loosen the striker mounting bolts, move the striker up/down or left/right as necessary, then retighten the bolts

16.3 Disconnect the electrical connector (1) from the trunk lid latch, then remove the two latch retaining bolts (2) (one bolt not visible in this photo)

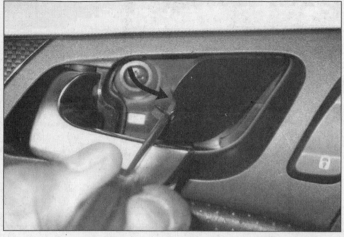

17.5a Carefully pry out the small trim cover with a small screwdriver or trim removal tool . . .

10   You can also fine-tune the height of the trailing edge of the trunk lid by turning the trunk lid edge cushions - small round rubber bumpers located on the lower edge of the trunk lid - in or out to lower or raise the trunk as necessary **(see illustration 15.1c)**.

16   Trunk lid latch - removal and installation

Refer to illustration 16.3

1   Open the trunk and remove the trunk lid trim panel **(see illustrations 15.1a, 15.1b and 15.1c)**.
2   Scribe a line around the trunk lid latch assembly for a reference point to aid the installation procedure.
3   Disconnect the electrical connector from the latch **(see illustration)**.
4   Remove the latch mounting bolts **(see illustration 16.3)** and remove the latch.
5   Disconnect the trunk lid release cable from the latch.
6   Installation is the reverse of removal.

17   Door trim panels - removal and installation

Refer to illustrations 17.5a, 17.5b, 17.6a, 17.6b, 17.7, 18.8a, 18.8b, 17.9a and 17.9b

1   Lower the window completely in the door, then disconnect the cable from the negative battery terminal (see Chapter 5, Section 1).
2   On 2003 and earlier models, carefully pry off and remove the mirror mounting trim cover (see Section 22).
3   Using a small screwdriver, pry off the trim cap and remove the screw that secures the door handle trim cover.
4   On 2003 and earlier models, pull out the door handle trim cover, disconnect the inner handle rod, then disconnect the electrical connector(s).
5   Using a small screwdriver or a small trim removal tool on 2004 and later models, push on the rear part of the small trim cover - there's a hook here on the backside of the cover - and pop out the mounting tab at the other end of the cover **(see illustration)**. Remove the two screws that secure the inner part of the handle trim cover **(see illustration)**.

17.5b . . . and remove these two screws (2004 and later models)

6   On 2003 and earlier models, remove the retaining screw from the armrest. On 2004 and later models, remove the trim panel retaining screw and the screw in the armrest **(see illustrations)**.

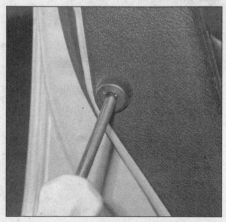

17.6a On 2004 and later models, remove the door trim panel retaining screw . . .

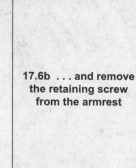

17.6b . . . and remove the retaining screw from the armrest

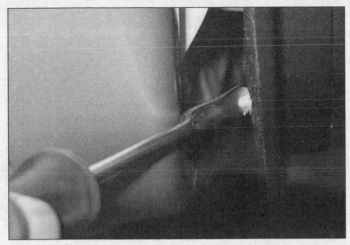

17.7 Using a trim panel removal tool, carefully pry the clips free from the perimeter of the door trim panel

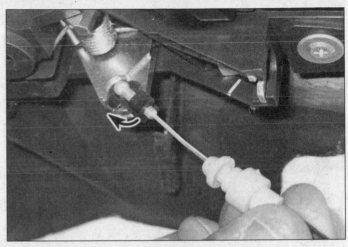

17.8a To disconnect the outside door handle cable from the inside door handle, flip open the plastic lock . . .

7   Remove the door trim panel using a door panel removal tool. Start from the bottom of the trim panel and work around the perimeter until all the fasteners have been released from the door **(see illustration)**.

8   To remove the door trim panel, pull it up, then disconnect all electrical connectors (all of the connectors are different sizes, so there is no possibility that you will mix up connectors during reassembly). Also disconnect the outside door handle cable from the inside door handle **(see illustrations)**.

9   For access to the outside door handle, the key lock cylinder or the door window regulator, raise the window fully, then remove the two alignment plugs **(see illustrations)** and carefully peel back the plastic watershield.

10   Installation is the reverse of removal.

18   Door - removal and installation

Refer to illustrations 18.4, 18.6, and 18.8

Note: *The door is heavy and somewhat awkward to remove and install - at least two peo-*

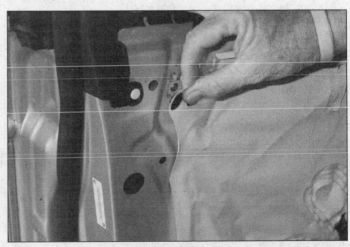

17.8b . . . and pull the cable end out of the bushing

ple should perform this procedure.

1   Lower the window completely in the door, then disconnect the cable from the negative battery terminal (see Chapter 5, Section 1).

2   Open the door all the way and support it on jacks or blocks covered with rags to prevent damaging the paint.

3   Remove the door trim panel and watershield (see Section 17).

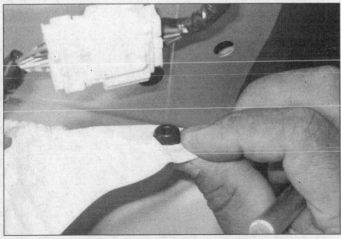

17.9a Before peeling off the watershield, remove the front alignment plug from the door . . .

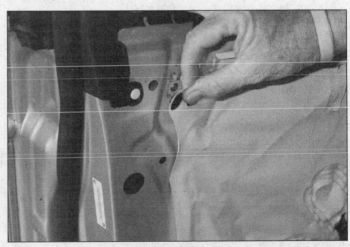

17.9b . . . and remove the rear alignment plug (the plugs ensure correct alignment of the watershield during installation)

18.4 To detach the door strut from the vehicle body, remove this bolt

18.6 Peel back the rubber conduit, then disconnect the electrical connectors

4 Remove the door stop strut **(see illustration)**.
5 Disconnect all electrical connections and ground wires inside the door, then detach all electrical harness retaining clips from the door.
6 Locate the protective rubber conduit through which the harness is routed between the body and the door. Disconnect the conduit from the door **(see illustration)**, disconnect all electrical connectors and pull the wiring harness through the conduit mounting hole.
7 To facilitate realignment during reassembly, mark the position of the door hinges with a marking pen.
8 With an assistant holding the door, remove the hinge-to-door bolts **(see illustration)** and lift off the door.
9 Installation is the reverse of removal.

19 Lock cylinder, door handle and latch - removal and installation

Warning: *Wear gloves when working inside the door openings to protect against cuts from sharp metal edges.*

2003 and earlier models
Key lock cylinder and outside door handle

1 Raise the window, then remove the door trim panel and watershield (see Section 17).
2 Working through the large access hole, remove the glass run channel. On 1999 models, pull the glass run channel away as necessary and remove the bolt, then remove the center lower channel by pulling it downward. On 2000 through 2003 models, simply remove the center lower channel with the lower glass run channel.
3 Using a small screwdriver, pry off the retainer lock cylinder retainer clip then pull out the lock cylinder and disconnect the lock cylinder actuator rod.

4 If you're replacing the lock cylinder, remove the retaining screw and separate the lock cylinder and lock cylinder switch.
5 Disconnect the lock cylinder switch electrical connector and detach the lock cylinder switch harness clips.
6 Remove the O-ring weather seal from the lock cylinder hole.
7 Remove the bolts that secure the outside handle protector. Remove the outside handle and protector as a single assembly.
8 Disengage the locator tab that secures the protector to the outside handle and separate the two components.
9 Detach the harness clip from the outside handle protector.
10 Note the distance that the outside handle actuator rod protrudes through the junction block, then pull out the outside handle and pry the outside handle actuator rod out of the junction block.
11 Installation is the reverse of removal.

Door latch

12 Raise the window, then remove the door trim panel and watershield (see Section 17).

13 Remove the outside handle.
14 Detach the harness clip and disconnect the actuator rod to the inside handle, then disconnect the electrical connectors.
15 Remove the latch mounting bolts and remove the latch through the hole in the door.
16 Installation is the reverse of removal.

2004 and later models
Key lock cylinder and outside door handle

Refer to illustrations 19.18, 19.19, 19.20a, 19.20b, 19.20c and 19.24

17 Raise the window, then remove the door trim panel and watershield (see Section 17).
18 Remove the center lower channel retaining bolt **(see illustration)** and remove the center lower channel.
19 Disconnect the outside handle actuator rod from the bushing **(see illustration)**.
20 Remove the maintenance hole seal from the door **(see illustration)**. If you're working on the driver's door, loosen the bolt that secures the lock cylinder **(see illustration)** and disconnect the lock cylinder actuator rod

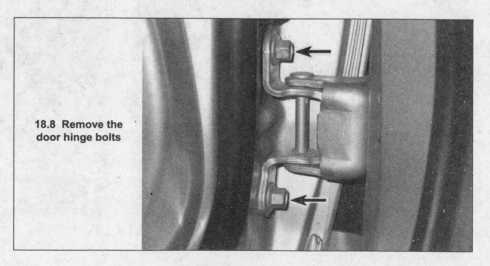

18.8 Remove the door hinge bolts

19.18 To detach the center lower channel from the door, remove this bolt

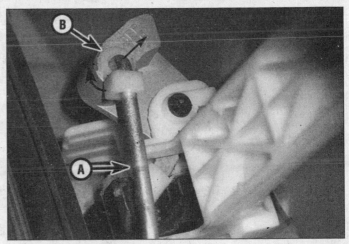

19.19 To disconnect the outside handle actuator rod (A) from the bushing (B), swing the plastic lock out of the way as shown, then pull the end of the actuator rod out of the bushing

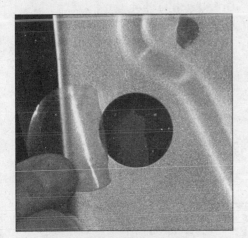

19.20a Carefully peel off the clear plastic seal from this maintenance hole

19.20b If you're working on the left (driver's side) door, loosen the bolt that secures the lock cylinder (or the outer handle cover on the passenger's side door)

19.20c To disconnect the lock cylinder rod (driver's door only) from the bushing, swing the plastic lock out of the way and pull the end of the rod out of the bushing

from the bushing **(see illustration)**. If you're working on the passenger's door, remove the maintenance hole ring from the passenger's door and loosen the bolt that secures the outside handle cover.

21 Disconnect the lock cylinder switch electrical connector and detach the harness clip. Remove the lock cylinder and lock cylinder switch as a single assembly from the driver's door.

22 To detach the switch from the lock cylinder, remove the lock cylinder switch retaining screw.

23 Pry loose the retaining tab and remove the outside handle cover.

24 Locate the pin in the outside handle base **(see illustration)**, pinch the lower end and pull it up.

25 Loosen the outside handle base retaining nut, disengage the base mounting tab and slide the base forward.

26 Disconnect the outside handle rod from the outside handle base.

27 Installation is the reverse of removal.

Door latch

Refer to illustrations 19.30 and 19.33

28 Raise the window glass all the way, then remove the door trim panel and watershield

(see Section 17). Remove the center lower channel **(see illustration 19.18)**.

29 Disconnect the outside handle rod from the outside handle **(see illustration 19.19)** and disconnect the lock cylinder rod from the

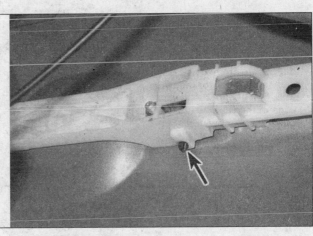

19.24 To remove the pin that retains the outside handle mounting base, squeeze the lower end of the pin and push the pin straight up

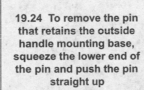

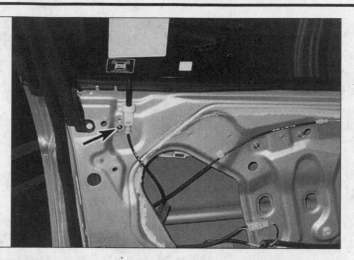

19.30 Remove the lock knob retaining screw

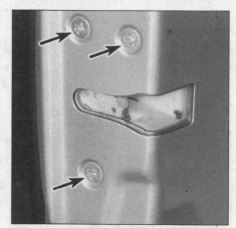

19.33 To detach the door latch mechanism from the door, remove these three bolts

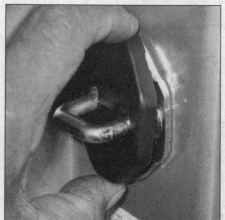

19.35 Remove the cover from the door latch striker

19.38 To adjust the door latch striker, loosen the two striker mounting bolts and move the striker left-and-right and/or up-and-down as necessary, then retighten the striker bolts

Door latch striker

Refer to illustrations 19.35 and 19.38

35   Remove the cover from the striker **(see illustration)**.

36   Remove the striker mounting bolts and remove the striker.

37   Installation is the reverse of removal.

38   To adjust the striker, loosen the mounting bolts and move the striker up-and-down and/or left-and-right as necessary to align it with the latch mechanism **(see illustration)**. When the striker is correctly adjusted, tighten the bolts securely.

20 Door window glass - removal and installation

Refer to illustration 20.2

Caution: *Wear gloves when working inside the door openings to protect against cuts from sharp metal edges.*

1   Remove the door trim panel and the plastic watershield (see Section 17).

2   Raise the window glass just enough so that you can see - and access - the two bolts that secure the bottom edge of the window glass, then remove the bolts **(see illustration)**.

3   Carefully lift up and remove the glass through the window slot. **Caution:** *Do NOT drop the glass inside the door!*

4   Installation is the reverse of removal. Make sure that, when the window is closed, there's no clearance between the glass and the glass run channel (the window glass runs up and down in a series of channels). If the window is misaligned, loosen the two window glass retaining bolts **(see illustration 20.2)** and push the window back, toward the trailing edge of the door, until it's fully seated in the run channel, then tighten the window retaining bolts securely.

5   When you're done, reset the power window control unit (see Chapter 5, Section 1).

lock cylinder **(see illustration 19.20c)**.

30   Remove the lock knob retaining screw **(see illustration)**.

31   Detach the clip that secures the inside handle cable.

32   Disconnect the two actuator electrical connectors from the latch mechanism.

33   Remove the latch mounting screws **(see illustration)** and remove the latch through the hole in the door. Be careful not to bend the lock cylinder rod, the inside door handle or the lock cable.

34   Installation is the reverse of removal.

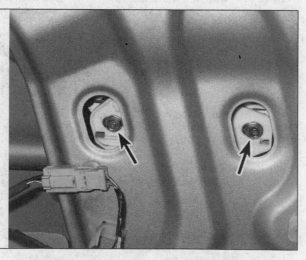

20.2 There are two access holes in the door for the two bolts that secure the lower edge of the window glass. Raise the window until you can see the two bolts, then remove both bolts

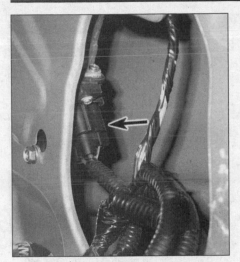

21.3 Disconnect the electrical connector from the regulator

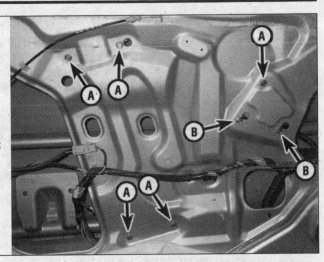

21.4 To detach the regulator from the door, remove these five mounting bolts (A) and loosen these two (B) (these two bolts are in slotted holes so you don't have to remove them, but you do have to lift up the regulator slightly to disengage the bolts from their slotted holes)

21 Door window glass regulator - removal and installation

Refer to illustrations 21.3 and 21.4

Caution: *Wear gloves when working inside the door openings to protect against cuts from sharp metal edges.*

1   Remove the door trim panel and the plastic watershield (see Section 17).

2   Remove the window glass assembly (see Section 20).

3   Disconnect the electrical connector from the window regulator motor **(see illustration)**.

4   Remove/loosen the regulator mounting bolts **(see illustration)**, then raise the regulator slightly to disengage the two loosened bolts from their slotted holes and work the regulator assembly out of the service hole in the door frame to remove it.

5   Installation is the reverse of removal.

22 Mirrors - removal and installation

2003 and earlier models

Refer to illustrations 22.1 and 22.3

1   Lower the window all the way, then carefully pry off the mirror trim cover **(see illustration)**.

2   Remove the door trim panel (see Section 17).

3   Disconnect the mirror electrical connector, then detach the harness clip **(see illustration)**.

4   Remove the three mirror retaining nuts **(see illustration 22.3)** and detach the mirror from the door.

5   Installation is the reverse of removal.

2004 and later models

Refer to illustrations 22.7 and 22.9

6   Lower the window all the way, then remove the door trim panel (see Section 17).

7   Remove the front door molding (the trim piece that frames the window glass on

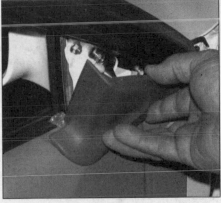

22.1 Use a small screwdriver or trim removal tool to pry off the mirror cover (2003 and earlier models)

the back, top and front of the door window). First, pry loose the two retainers, one at each lower end of the molding **(see illustration)**. After disengaging these two retainers, pop loose the six orange clips, four along the trail-

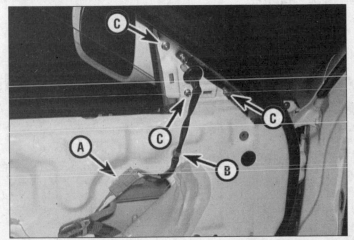

22.3 To remove the mirror from the door on 2003 and earlier models, disconnect the electrical connector (A), detach the harness clip (B) from the door and remove these three nuts (C)

22.7 Pop loose the two white fasteners from the front lower end (shown) and the rear lower end of the trim molding that runs over the top of the door, then carefully pull the molding off the door

22.9 Disconnect the power mirror electrical connector, then remove these three nuts and remove the mirror assembly

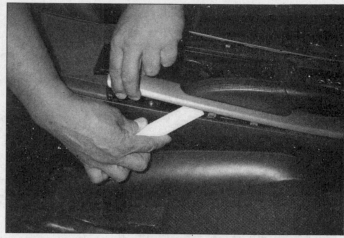

23.14 Insert a trim tool between each section of trim and the console and carefully pop loose all the clips that secure each section of trim

ing edge of the molding and two more at the front corner, just below the mirror area. Then carefully disengage the molding from the two hooks located at the upper rear corner and the lower front corner of the window opening and remove the molding.

8   Disconnect the mirror electrical connector.

9   Remove the three mirror retaining nuts **(see illustration)** and remove the mirror from the door.

10   Installation is the reverse of removal.

---

23 Center console - removal and installation

Warning: *Models covered by this manual are equipped with a Supplemental Restraint System (SRS), more commonly known as airbags. Always disable the airbag system before working in the vicinity of any airbag system component to avoid the possibility of accidental deployment of the airbag, which could cause personal injury (see Chapter 12).*

2003 and earlier models

1   Carefully pry off the console trim (the two L-shaped trim pieces that cover the left and right upper edges of the console) from each side of the console. Each trim piece has five clips.

2   Remove the two mounting screws from the left and right front corners of the rear console.

3   Open the lid on the rear console, remove the mat from the floor of the storage box and remove the two rear console mounting screws.

4   Pull up the rear console, disconnect the electrical connector for the accessory socket, and remove the rear console.

5   Remove the driver's side dashboard lower cover (see Section 25).

6   Remove the three screws, release the clips and remove the left (driver's side) front console cover.

7   Remove the two screws, release the clips and remove the right (passenger's side) front console cover.

8   Remove the shift indicator trim ring.

9   Remove the seat heater switches from the console panel tray (see Chapter 12).

10   Carefully pry out the console panel tray and release the hooks (two on each side) and tabs (two on the trailing edge).

11   Remove the four screws, release the two tabs (on the leading edge of the console panel) and remove the console panel.

12   Installation is the reverse of removal.

2004 and later models

Refer to illustrations 23.14, 23.15, 23.16, 23.18, 23.20, 23.22, 23.23, 23.24a and 23.24b

13   On manual transmission models, lower the shift lever boot and unscrew the shift lever knob.

14   Two narrow pieces of trim conceal the retaining screws for the center and rear sections of the console. Insert a trim tool between each section of trim and the console **(see illustration)** and carefully disengage all of the clips. Release the hooks at the upper end of each piece of trim and remove the trim.

15   Remove the two mounting screws from the left and right front corners of the rear console section **(see illustration)**.

16   Open the console box lid, remove the storage box mat and remove the two rear console section mounting screws **(see illustration)**.

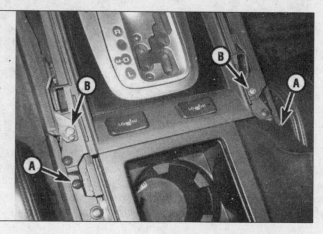

23.15 To detach the front end of the rear console section, remove these two screws (A) (right screw not visible). To detach the rear parts of the left and right console side covers from this part of the console, remove these screws (B)

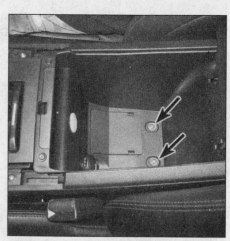

23.16 To detach the back part of the rear console section, open the console box lid, remove the storage box mat and remove these two screws

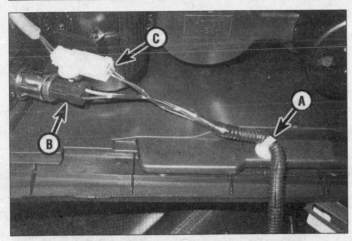

23.18 Lift up the rear console section, turn it over, detach the harness clip (A) and disconnect the electrical connectors for the accessory power socket (B) and the console illumination bulb (C)

23.20 Use a trim tool to carefully pry off the shift indicator trim ring (models with an automatic transaxle)

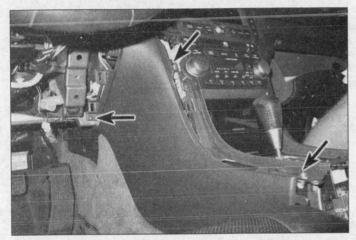

23.22 Remove the fasteners securing the console side cover (left console side cover shown, right cover similar)

23.23 To detach the upper part of the center console panel, remove these two screws

17   Slide the rear console section to the rear to disengage the two hooks.

18   Lift up the rear console section, detach the harness clip and disconnect the two electrical connectors for the accessory power socket and the light bulb socket **(see illustration).**

19   Move the seats all the way back, then remove the driver's side dashboard lower cover and the glove box (see Section 25).

20   Remove the shift indicator trim ring **(see illustration).**

21   On manual transmission models, remove the insert panel (secured by six tabs on the underside of panel, three on each side).

22   Remove fasteners from each console side cover **(see illustration),** then pull up and back on each side cover to disengage the two clips securing each cover.

23   Remove the two screws **(see illustration)** that secure the upper end of the center console panel. Pull back on the panel to release the locator pins located directly below the screws removed in Step 22.

24   Lift up the rear end of the panel and disconnect the two electrical connectors from the seat heater switches **(see illustration).** Lift up the center console a little more to disconnect the electrical connector for the accessory power socket **(see illustration),** then remove the center console panel.

25   Installation is the reverse of removal.

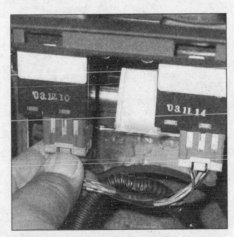

23.24a Lift up the rear part of the center console panel and disconnect the two seat heater switches . . .

23.24b . . . lift up the panel a little farther and disconnect the electrical connector from the accessory power socket

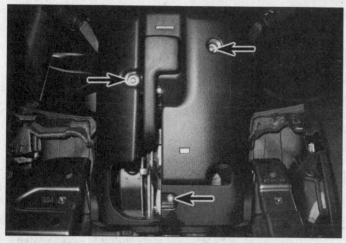

24.3 To remove the upper and lower steering column covers, remove these three screws

24.4 To separate the upper and lower steering column covers, carefully pry them apart to disengage these tabs

24 Steering column covers - removal and installation

Refer to illustrations 24.3 and 24.4

Warning: *Models covered by this manual are equipped with a Supplemental Restraint System (SRS), more commonly known as airbags. Always disable the airbag system before working in the vicinity of any airbag system component to avoid the possibility of accidental deployment of the airbag, which could cause personal injury (see Chapter 12).*

1   Disconnect the cable from the negative battery terminal (see Chapter 5, Section 1).
2   Remove the driver's side dashboard lower cover (see Section 25).
3   Remove the three steering column cover screws **(see illustration)**.
4   Separate the upper and lower halves of the steering column cover and remove the covers **(see illustration)**.
5   Installation is the reverse of the removal procedure.

25 Dashboard trim panels - removal and installation

Warning: *Models covered by this manual are equipped with a Supplemental Restraint System (SRS), more commonly known as airbags. Always disable the airbag system before working in the vicinity of any airbag system component to avoid the possibility of accidental deployment of the airbag, which could cause personal injury (see Chapter 12).*

2003 and earlier models

Instrument cluster trim panel

1   Tilt the steering wheel down to the lowest position, then remove the steering column covers (see Section 24).

2   Remove the two screws from the underside of the hood over the instrument cluster.
3   Pull off the lower edge of the cluster trim panel and release the six lower clips, then pull off the upper edge and release the three upper clips.
4   Disconnect the electrical connectors from the instrument cluster trim panel and remove the panel.
5   Installation is the reverse of removal.

Left and right dashboard end covers

Left (driver's side) end cover

6   Using a trim removal tool or screwdriver, carefully pry loose the panel and release the hook at the upper left corner and the three clips.
7   Installation is the reverse of removal.

Right (passenger's side) end cover

8   Using a trim removal tool or screwdriver, carefully pry loose the panel and release the hook at the upper right corner and the three clips.
9   Installation is the reverse of removal.

Dashboard lower cover (knee bolster)

10   Remove the dashboard left end side cover.
11   Remove the screw from the left end of the dashboard lower cover.
12   Pull down on the lower right corner of the dashboard lower cover to release the right lower clip, then pull off the cover and release the other five clips (three on the right, including the lower right clip, and two more clips on the upper edge, to the left of the steering column).
13   Installation is the reverse of removal.

Glove box

14   Open the glove box door and remove the damper screw and the damper.
15   Support the glove box door with one

hand and remove the left and right door stops.
16   Remove the two glove box screws and remove the glove box door.
17   Remove the right (passenger's side) console side cover (see Section 23).
18   Remove the right (passenger's side) end cover (see Step 8).
19   Remove the five glove box retaining screws (three screws along the upper edge and two on the left edge of the box).
20   Pull out the glove box, disconnect the electrical connectors from the trunk lid opener switch and the glove box light socket, then remove the glove box.
21   Installation is the reverse of removal.

Passenger's center vent or passenger's side vent

Note: *The following procedure applies to either of these vents; they're identical except for their different locations.*

22   Insert a taped screwdriver tip between the vent and the instrument panel at each of the two clips (one on each lower side) and carefully pry loose the clips, then pull out the lower part of the vent and disengage the two hooks on the upper edge of the vent.
23   Installation is the reverse of removal.

Side defogger vent trim

24   Insert a taped screwdriver tip between the vent and the instrument panel at the clip at the lower or trailing edge. Carefully pry loose the trim, pull out the back edge of the vent trim and release the hook at the inner upper end.
25   Installation is the reverse of removal.

2004 and later models

Instrument cluster trim panel

Refer to illustration 25.27

26   Tilt down the steering column.

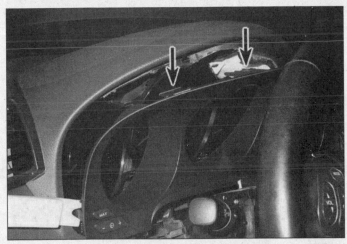

25.27 To detach the instrument cluster trim panel, carefully pry it loose with a trim removal tool. The cluster trim panel is secured by two clips (shown) on the upper edge and two more clips and a pair of hooks (not shown) on the lower edge

25.32 Remove the push fastener on the driver's side dashboard lower cover

27   There are two clips on the upper edge of the instrument cluster trim panel and two clips and two hooks on the lower edge. Using a trim tool, carefully pry loose the instrument cluster trim panel **(see illustration)** and disengage the clips and hooks.

28   Pull out the cluster trim panel, disconnect the electrical connectors from the backside of the panel and remove the panel.

29   If you want to remove or replace either the dash light brightness controller or the SELECT/RESET switch, refer to Chapter 12.

30   Installation is the reverse of removal.

Driver's side dashboard lower cover (knee bolster)

Refer to illustrations 25.32 and 25.33

31   Tilt up the steering column.

32   Remove the clip at the lower right corner of the cover **(see illustration)**.

33   Carefully pry loose the upper left corner of the cover **(see illustration)**.

34   Pull out the lower edge of the cover, detach the clips, disengage the locator pin, disconnect the electrical connectors and remove the cover.

35   Installation is the reverse of removal.

Center upper trim panel

Refer to illustration 25.36

36   To detach the center upper trim panel from the dashboard, insert a trim removal tool between the panel and the dash **(see illustration)** and carefully pry the panel loose.

37   Pull out the panel and disconnect the electrical connectors from the backside of the panel.

38   Installation is the reverse of removal.

Glove box

Refer to illustrations 25.39, 25.40, 25.41 and 25.42

39   Open the glove box door and detach the door damper **(see illustration)**.

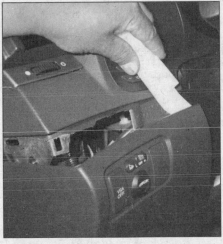

25.33 To detach the upper left corner of the driver's side dashboard lower cover, carefully pry it loose with a trim tool

25.36 To detach the center upper trim panel from the dashboard, insert a trim panel removal tool between the panel and the dash and carefully pry the panel loose

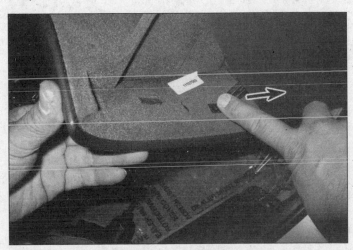

25.39 To disengage the glove box damper from the hook in the glove box door, push the lower end of the damper forward until it pops loose from the hook

25.40 To disengage each glove box stop, pull it in, toward the interior of the glove box, then push it to the rear and pull it out

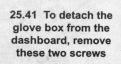

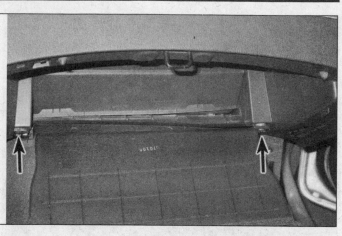

25.41 To detach the glove box from the dashboard, remove these two screws

40   Remove the two glove box door stops **(see illustration)**.

41   Remove the two glove box retaining screws **(see illustration)** and remove the glove box.

42   The glove box housing is secured to the dashboard by 10 clips, two on the left end, three on the right end, two on top and three below. To disengage the glove box housing from these clips, carefully pry out the box with a trim panel removal tool **(see illustration)**.

43   Pull out the box and disconnect the electrical connectors for the trunk lid opener switch and the glove box illumination bulb.

44   Installation is the reverse of removal.

Passenger's dashboard under-cover

Refer to illustration 25.45

45   The passenger's side dashboard under cover **(see illustration)** is secured to the underside of the dashboard by clips and a locator pin. To remove it, simply pull it

down and back. Installation is the reverse of removal.

Driver's side dashboard side vent

46   Remove the driver's side dashboard lower cover (see Steps 31 through 34).

47   Reach up under the vent from below and push up on the lower vent mounting tabs with your fingers to disengage them, push the vent up and to the right to release the tabs on the left, then push the vent up and to the left to release the tabs on the right.

48   Installation is the reverse of removal. Make sure that all the tabs snap into place.

Passenger's side dashboard side vent

49   Using a trim removal tool, carefully pry off the passenger's side dashboard trim (the horizontal trim piece that runs along the right face of the dashboard, between the glove box and the top of the dash, and directly below the passenger's side dashboard side vent).

50   Remove the screw from the mounting tab at the lower left corner of the side vent.

51   Carefully press up on the passenger's side vent from the outer lower corner, toward the interior of the vehicle, to release the two clips on the right edge of the vent. Press up on

the vent and pry it toward the door to release the two tabs on the left side of the vent.

52   Installation is the reverse of removal.

26   Instrument panel - removal and installation

Warning: *Models covered by this manual are equipped with a Supplemental Restraint System (SRS), more commonly known as airbags. Always disable the airbag system before working in the vicinity of any airbag system component to avoid the possibility of accidental deployment of the airbag, which could cause personal injury (see Chapter 12).*

Note 1: *This is a difficult procedure for the home mechanic. There are many hidden fasteners, difficult angles to work in and many electrical connectors to tag and disconnect/connect. We recommend that this procedure be done only by an experienced do-it-yourselfer.*

Note 2: *During removal of the instrument panel, make careful notes of how each piece comes off, where it fits in relation to other pieces and what holds it in place. If you note how each part is installed before removing it, getting the instrument panel back together again will be much easier.*

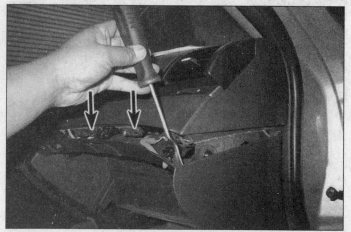

25.42 To detach the glove box housing from the dashboard, use a trim removal to disengage all 10 clips (two upper clips shown, other clips not visible)

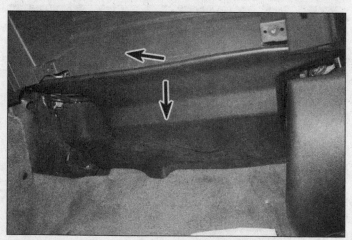

25.45 To detach the passenger's side dashboard under-cover, simply pull it down and back

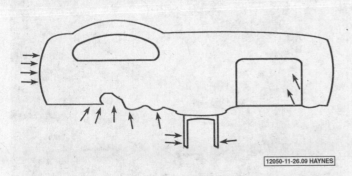

26.9 To remove the instrument panel on 2003 and earlier models, remove these 14 bolts. There are four bolts at the left end, five in the vicinity of the steering column, three at the forward end of the console and two in the right end of the glove box cavity

26.14 To remove the rear vent duct, pull the clips at the back end of the duct out of these two brackets (2004 and later models)

1   Make sure that you have the anti-theft code for the radio, then write down the frequencies for the presets.
2   Disconnect the cable from the negative battery terminal (see Chapter 5, Section 1).

2003 and earlier models

Refer to illustration 26.9

3   Remove the front seats (see Section 27). Remove the center console (see Section 23).
4   Remove all of the dashboard trim panels listed in Section 25.
5   Remove the ground bolt (on the left side, at the forward end of the center console).
6   Detach the clips and wire harness clip. On 1999 through 2002 models, remove the two mounting bolts for the Data Link Connector (DLC) bracket. Remove the DLC from the bracket.
7   Release the tabs, then remove the rear vent duct.

8   Disconnect all electrical connectors in the dash area. **Note:** *You'll have to lower the steering column to access some of the connectors.*
9   Remove the trim caps for the four instrument panel mounting bolts at the left end of the instrument panel and remove the bolts. Then, remove the other 10 instrument panel mounting bolts **(see illustration).**
10   Installation is the reverse of removal.

2004 and later models

Refer to illustrations 26.14, 26.15, 26.16, 26.19, 26.22 and 26.23

11   Remove the front seats (see Section 27).
12   Remove the center console (see Section 23).
13   Remove all the dashboard trim panels listed in Section 25.
14   Remove the rear vent duct **(see illustration).**

15   The carpet is attached to the left and right vertical stanchions below the center of the dashboard by two clips, one on each stanchion **(see illustration).** To detach the carpet from each clip, simply pull it off.
16   Remove the two rear joint vent ducts **(see illustration).**
17   Disconnect the electrical connector from the yaw rate/lateral acceleration sensor **(see illustration 26.16),** remove the sensor bracket bolts. Remove the sensor and bracket as a single assembly and set it somewhere safe. **Note:** *The yaw rate/acceleration sensor is sensitive, so be extremely careful when handling it.*
18   Disconnect all electrical connectors located in the dash area.
19   Remove the brake pedal support bracket bolts **(see illustration)** and remove the pedal support bracket.
20   Remove the parking brake handle assembly mounting bolts and remove the

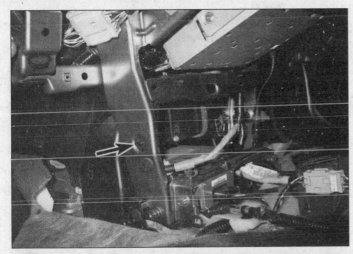

26.15 To detach the carpet from the clip, simply pull it off (2004 and later models)

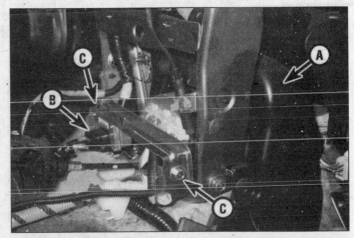

26.16 To remove each rear joint vent duct (A), simply pull them out (right joint vent duct shown, left duct identical). Disconnect the electrical connector (B) from the yaw rate/lateral acceleration sensor and remove the sensor mounting bracket bolts (C). Remove the sensor and mounting bracket (2004 and later models)

26.19 To detach the brake pedal support bracket, remove these two bolts (2004 and later models)

26.22 Remove the trim caps from the left end of the dashboard and unscrew the instrument panel mounting bolts (2004 and later models)

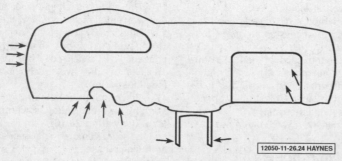

12050-11-26.24 HAYNES

26.23 To remove the instrument panel on 2004 and later models, remove these nine bolts and two clips. There are three bolts at the left end, four bolts in the vicinity of the steering column, two clips at the forward end of the console and two bolts in the right end of the glove box cavity

parking brake handle assembly and set it aside. Do not disconnect the parking brake cables from the parking brake handle assembly.

21 Remove all six center bracket mounting bolts and remove the center bracket.

22 Remove the three trim caps from the left end of the dash and remove the three instrument panel mounting bolts **(see illustration)**.

23 Remove the rest of the instrument panel mounting bolts **(see illustration)** and remove the instrument panel.

24 Installation is the reverse of removal.

27 Seats - removal and installation

Warning 1: *The front seat belts are equipped with pre-tensioners, which are pyrotechnic (explosive) devices designed to retract the seat belts in the event of a collision. Do not remove the front seat belt retractor assemblies, and do not disconnect the electrical connectors leading to the assemblies. Problems with the pre-tensioners will turn on the SRS (airbag) warning light on the dash. If any pre-tensioner problems are suspected, take the vehicle to a dealer service department.*

Warning 2: *On models with side-impact airbags, be sure to disarm the airbag system before beginning this procedure (see Chapter 12).*

Front seats

Refer to illustrations 27.2a and 27.2b

1 Disconnect the cable from the negative battery terminal (see Chapter 5, Section 1).

2 Position the seat all the way to the rear to access the front retaining bolts, then all the way forward to access the rear bolts **(see illustrations)**.

27.2a To detach the seat from the floor, move the seat all the way back and remove the front mounting bolts . . .

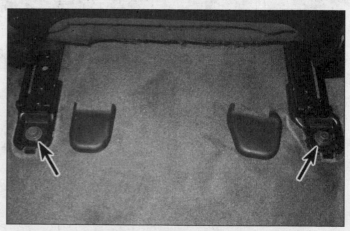

27.2b . . . then move the seat all the way forward, carefully pry off the trim caps and remove the rear mounting bolts

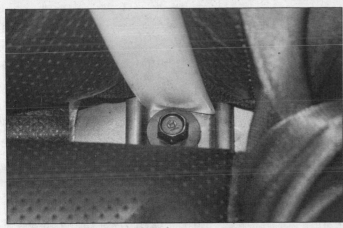

27.6 To detach the seat cushion, remove this bolt, which is located at the right end, between the back of the cushion and the lower right part of the seat back

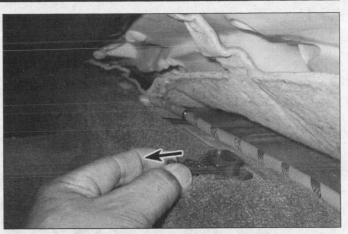

27.7 To disengage each of the seat retaining hooks (not shown) located on the underside of the seat cushion, pull each release latch forward

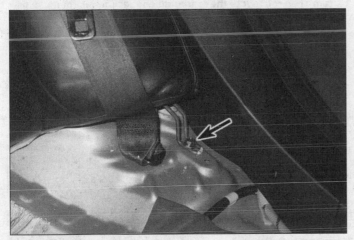

27.8a To detach the rear seat back, remove the left lower bolt . . .

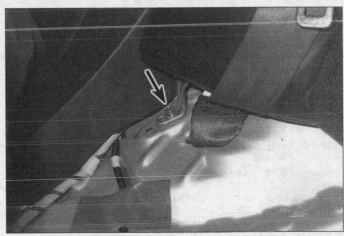

27.8b . . . the right lower bolt . . .

3   Lift up the front of the seat and tilt the seat back, then disconnect all electrical connectors.
4   Carefully remove the seat from the vehicle.
5   Installation is the reverse of removal. Be sure to tighten the seat bolts securely.

Rear seat

Refer to illustrations 27.6, 27.7, 27.8a, 27.8b, 27.8c and 27.8d

6   Remove the seat cushion bolt **(see illustration)**.
7   Release the two latches at the front of the seat cushion **(see illustration)** and remove the seat cushion.
8   Remove the five bolts **(see illustrations)** that secure the seat back, then remove the seat back.
9   Carefully remove the rear seat back.
10   Installation is the reverse of removal.

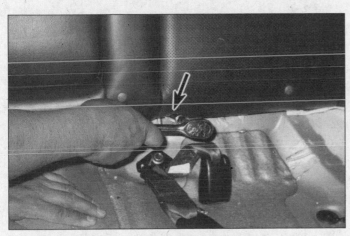

27.8c . . . the center lower bolt . . .

27.8d . . . and the two upper bolts, which are accessed through this slot in the upholstery, directly below each of the headrests

28.3 To remove each C-pillar cap, carefully pry it up with a trim tool as shown, then grasp it with your fingers and pull it all the way out

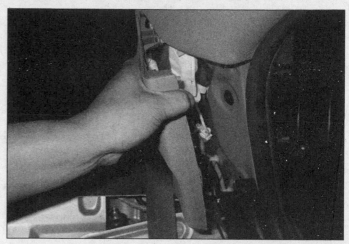

28.4 To remove the C-pillar trim, grasp the leading edge of the trim and pull it out to disengage the clips on the backside of the trim, then rotate it to the rear to disengage the rest of the clips

28 Rear shelf - removal and installation

Refer to illustrations 28.3, 28.4 and 28.5

Note: *The photos accompanying this Section depict the rear shelf on 2004 and later models, but earlier shelves are quite similar to this one, and are removed essentially the same way.*

1   Remove the rear seat cushion and seat back (see Section 27).

2   Pull out the rear door opening trim from the seat side trim hooks as necessary.

3   Remove the left and right C-pillar trim panel caps **(see illustration)**.

4   To remove each C-pillar trim, pry loose the leading edge of the trim and pull it back **(see illustration)** to disengage the five clips that secure it to the C-pillar, then remove the trim.

5   Lift up the rear shelf **(see illustration)** to pop loose the eight clips, then pull the shelf

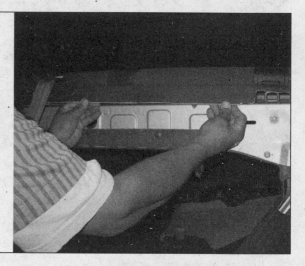

28.5 To remove the rear shelf, lift it up. The underside of the shelf is secured to the vehicle body by eight clips that pop loose when sufficient force is applied

forward to remove it.

6   If you're just removing the shelf to access something else, stop here.

7   If you're replacing the shelf, pull the seatbelts out through the slits in the shelf.

8   Installation is the reverse of removal.

Chapter 12
Chassis electrical system

Contents

1   General information

The electrical system is a 12-volt, negative ground type. Power for the lights and all electrical accessories is supplied by a lead/acid-type battery, which is charged by the alternator.

This Chapter covers repair and service procedures for the various electrical components not associated with the engine. Information on the battery, ignition system, alternator and starter motor can be found in Chapter 5.

It should be noted that when portions of the electrical system are serviced, the negative battery cable should be disconnected from the battery to prevent electrical shorts and/or fires.

2   Electrical troubleshooting - general information

Refer to illustrations 2.5a and 2.5b

1   Electrical troubleshooting is simple if you keep in mind that all electrical circuits are basically electricity running from the battery, through the wires, switches, relays, fuses and fusible links to each electrical component (light bulb, motor, etc.), then to ground, from which it is passed back to the battery. Any electrical problem is an interruption in the flow of electricity to and from the battery.

2   A typical electrical circuit consists of an electrical component, any switches, relays, motors, fuses, fusible links or circuit breakers related to that component and the wiring and connectors that link the component to both the battery and the chassis. Wiring diagrams are included at the end of this Chapter to help you pinpoint an electrical circuit problem.

3   Electrical problems usually stem from simple causes, such as loose or corroded connections, a blown fuse, a melted fusible link or a failed relay. Visually inspect the condition of all fuses, wires and connections in a problem circuit before troubleshooting the circuit.

4   Before tackling any troublesome electrical circuit, study the appropriate wiring diagrams to get a complete understanding of what makes up that individual circuit. Noting if other components related to the circuit are operating correctly, for instance, can often narrow trouble spots down. If several com-

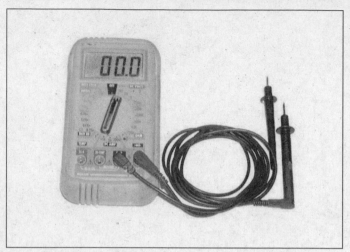

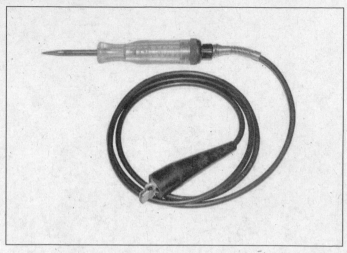

2.5a The most useful tool for electrical troubleshooting is a digital multimeter that can check volts, amps, and test continuity

2.5b A simple test light is a very handy tool used for testing voltage

ponents or circuits fail at one time, chances are the problem is in a fuse or ground connection, because several circuits are often routed through the same fuse and ground connections. If you're going to utilize test equipment and instruments, use the wiring diagrams to plan out where you will make the necessary connections in order to accurately pinpoint the trouble spot.

5   A basic electrical troubleshooting toolkit should include a test light, a circuit tester (a self-powered test light for testing circuits that are dead or disconnected from the battery), a multimeter (which includes an ammeter, ohmmeter and voltmeter), a continuity tester, a set of test leads and a jumper wire (preferably with a circuit breaker), which can be used to bypass electrical components **(see illustrations)**. Before attempting to locate a problem with test instruments, use the wiring diagram(s) to decide where to make the connections.

Voltage checks

Refer to illustration 2.6

6   If a circuit is not functioning correctly, check the voltage. Connect one lead of a circuit tester to either the negative battery terminal or a known good ground. Connect the other lead to a connector in the circuit being tested, preferably nearest to the battery or fuse **(see illustration)**. If the bulb of the tester lights, voltage is present, which means that the part of the circuit between the connector and the battery is problem free. Continue checking the rest of the circuit in the same fashion. When you reach a point at which no voltage is present, the problem lies between that point and the last test point with voltage. Most of the time the problem can be traced to a loose connection. **Note:** *Keep in mind that some circuits receive voltage only when the ignition key is in the ACC or ON position.*

Finding a short

7   If a fuse blows, check the circuit that it protects for a short. Remove the fuse and connect a test light in place of the fuse terminals (fabricate two jumper wires with small spade terminals, plug the jumper wires into the fuse box and connect the test light). There should be no voltage present in the circuit. Move the suspected wiring harness from side-to-side while watching the test light. If the test light bulb goes on, there is a short to ground somewhere in the circuit, perhaps in the area where the insulation has rubbed through.

Ground check

8   Perform a ground test to verify that a component is correctly grounded. Disconnect the battery, then connect one lead of a continuity tester (self-powered test light) or multimeter (set to the ohm scale), to a known good ground. Connect the other lead to the wire or ground connection that you want to check. If the indicated resistance is low (less than 5 ohms) on a multimeter, the ground is good; if the resistance is high (more than 5 ohms) the ground is bad. If the bulb on the continuity tester comes on, the ground is good; if it doesn't light up, the ground is not good.

Continuity check

Refer to illustration 2.9

9   Perform a continuity check to verify that there are no opens in a circuit. With the circuit off (no power in the circuit), a self-powered continuity tester or multimeter can be used to check the circuit. Connect the test leads to both ends of the circuit (or to the power end and a good ground). If the test light comes on, the circuit is passing current correctly **(see illustration)**. If the resistance is low (less than 5 ohms), there is continuity; if the reading is 10,000 ohms or higher, there is a break some-

2.6 In use, a basic test light's lead is clipped to a known good ground, then the pointed probe can test connectors, wires or electrical sockets - if the bulb lights, battery voltage is present at the test point

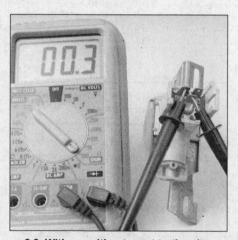

2.9 With a multimeter set to the ohm scale, resistance can be checked across two terminals - when checking for continuity, a low reading indicates continuity, a very high or infinite reading indicates lack of continuity

2.14 To backprobe a connector, insert a small, sharp probe (such as a straight-pin) into the back of the connector alongside the desired wire until it contacts the metal terminal inside; connect your meter leads to the probes - this allows you to test a functioning circuit

3.1a The engine compartment fuse and relay box is located in the right rear corner of the engine compartment on 1999 through 2003 models and in the left rear corner of the engine compartment on 2004 and later models (shown)

3.1b The under-dash fuse and relay box is located below the left end of the dashboard, behind the kick panel. There are also relays on this panel, but to access them you have to remove the left kick panel

where in the circuit. The same procedure can be used to test a switch, by connecting the continuity tester to the switch terminals. With the switch turned to ON, the test light should come on (or low resistance should be indicated on a meter).

Finding an open circuit

10   When looking for open circuits, it is often difficult to locate them by sight alone because connectors can hide oxidation, loose terminals or terminal misalignment. If the open circuit is intermittent, it's probably caused by oxidized or loose connections. Wiggling each of the connectors in an intermittently open circuit might momentarily close the circuit.

Connectors

Refer to illustration 2.14

11   Most electrical connections on these vehicles are multiple-terminal plastic connectors. The two halves of most connectors are locked together by release tabs molded into the plastic connector shells. Look for the release tab(s) or locking tab(s) on a connector and release it/them before trying to disconnect the connector. If the connector is too dirty to find the release or locking tab(s), wipe it off and/or clean it with a suitable spray type electronics cleaner. If a connector is in a dark area, use a flashlight. You might have to look closely (*very* closely!) at some connectors before you figure out how to separate the two halves, because the locking or release tabs are engaged in a way that is not immediately clear. And many connectors have multiple sets of release or locking tabs.

12   Connectors are usually locked together by release tabs that you simply depress to release, or by locking tabs that you spread apart or pry loose from some projection on the other half of the connector. Once you have figured out how to release a connector

with locking or release tabs, carefully depress the release tabs or pry the locking tabs apart with a small screwdriver, then separate the connector halves. Pull only on the connector halves. Never pull on the wires or the wiring harness, because you might damage the wires and terminals inside the connector.

13   Each pair of connector terminals has a male half and a female half. This is particularly important to remember when you look at a connector terminal guide in a wiring diagram or wiring schematic, because you need to know whether you're looking at the wiring harness side or the component side of the connector. Connector halves are mirror images of each other, and a terminal that is shown on the right side end-view of one half will be on the left side end-view of the other half. In other words, the terminal locations - and terminal numbering, if applicable - will be flipped.

14   It is often necessary to take circuit voltage measurements with a connector connected. Whenever possible, carefully insert a small straight pin (not your meter probe) into

the rear of the connector shell to contact the terminal inside, then clip your meter lead to the pin. This kind of connection **(see illustration)** is called backprobing. When inserting a test probe into a male terminal, be careful not to distort the terminal opening. Doing so can lead to a poor connection and corrosion at that terminal later. Using the small straight pin instead of a meter probe results in less chance of deforming the terminal connector.

3   Fuses - general information

Fuses

Refer to illustrations 3.1a, 3.1b, 3.1c and 3.2

The electrical circuits of the vehicle are protected by a combination of fuses, circuit breakers (see Section 4) and relays (see Section 5). Fuse and relay boxes are located in the engine compartment and underneath the left end of the dashboard **(see illustrations)**. A wide array of mini and maxi-style fuses is used to protect various circuits. These fuses,

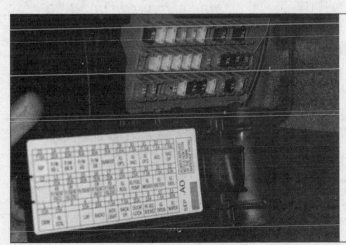

3.1c To locate a fuse on the under-dash fuse and relay panel, refer to the fuse guide on the backside of the access door

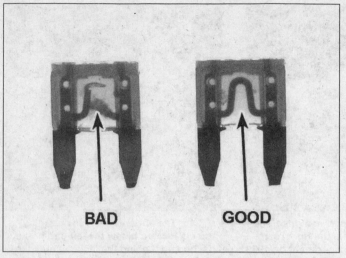

3.2 When a fuse blows, the element between the terminals melts

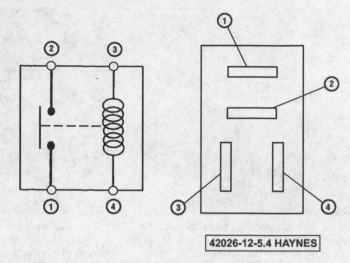

42026-12-5.4 HAYNES

5.4 Normally-open type A relay

which employ a blade terminal design, can be removed and installed without special tools. Each fuse protects a specific circuit or circuits, and the protected circuits are identified on the fuse panel cover. If the fuse panel cover is difficult to read, or missing, you can also refer to your owner's manual, which includes a complete guide to all fuses and relays in all three fuse/relay boxes.

If an electrical component fails, always check the fuse first. The best way to check a fuse is with a test light. Check for power at the exposed terminal tips of each fuse. If power is present on one side of the fuse but not the other, the fuse is blown. A blown fuse can also be confirmed by visually inspecting it **(see illustration)**.

Be sure to replace blown fuses with the correct type. Fuses of different ratings are physically interchangeable, but only fuses of the correct rating should be used. Replacing a fuse with one of a higher or lower value than specified is not recommended. Each electrical circuit needs a specific amount of protection. The amperage value of each fuse is molded into the fuse body.

If the replacement fuse immediately fails, don't replace it again until the cause of the problem is isolated and corrected. In most cases, this will be a short circuit in the wiring caused by a broken or deteriorated wire.

4   Circuit breakers - general information

Circuit breakers protect certain circuits, such as the power windows or heated seats. The number of circuit breakers employed on your vehicle depends on its electrical accessories. Some circuit breakers are located in a fuse/relay box; others are located as stand-alone units under the dash and in other locations throughout the vehicle.

Because a circuit breaker resets auto-

matically, an electrical overload in a circuit-breaker-protected system will cause the circuit to fail momentarily, then come back on. If the circuit does not come back on, check it immediately. There's probably an intermittent short or ground somewhere in the circuit that's causing the current overload, which causes the circuit breaker to cycle the circuit on and off.

For a basic check, pull the circuit breaker up out of its socket on the fuse panel, but just far enough to probe with a voltmeter. The breaker should still contact the sockets.

With the voltmeter negative lead on a good chassis ground, touch each end prong of the circuit breaker with the positive meter probe. There should be battery voltage at each end. If there is battery voltage only at one end, the circuit breaker must be replaced.

Some circuit breakers must be reset manually.

5   Relays - general information and testing

General information

1   Many electrical accessories - the fuel injection system, horns, starter, and fog lamps, for example - use relays to control current to components. Relays use a low-current circuit (the control circuit) to open and close a high-current circuit (the power circuit). If a relay is defective, the component will not operate. Relays are located in the engine compartment fuse/relay box and in or near the under-dash fuse and relay box **(see illustrations 3.1a and 3.1b)**. If a relay is suspect, test it or have it tested by a dealer service department or a repair shop. If a relay is defective, replace it. Relays cannot be repaired. **Note:** *To access the relays located at the under-dash fuse and relay box, you'll have to remove the left kick panel.*

Testing

2   There are two basic types of relays used in these vehicles: the normally-open type and the five-terminal type. To test a relay, remove it from the vehicle and use an ohmmeter to check for continuity.

Normally-open type A relays

Refer to illustration 5.4

3   Normally-open type A relays are used for:
ABS fail-safe relay
Accessory power socket relay
Air conditioning compressor clutch relay
Air conditioning condenser fan relay
Blower motor relay
Daytime running lights relay
Fan control relay
Fog light relay (2002 and 2003 models)
Fog lights/daytime running lights relay
Headlight relay 1
Headlight relay 2
High-beam cut relay (Canadian models)
Horn relay
Ignition coil relay
Navigation relay (1999 models)
PGM-FI main relay 1
PGM-FI main relay 2
Power window relay
Radiator fan relay
Rear window defogger relay
Reverse relay
Seat heater relay
Security horn relay (1999 models)
Shift lock relay
Starter cut relay
Taillight relay
Throttle actuator control module relay
Traction Control System (TCS) relay
Upstream oxygen sensor relay
Vehicle Stability Assist (VSA) relay (Type S)
Vehicle Stability Assist (VSA) throttle motor relay (Type S)

4   Normally-open type A relays **(see illustration)** have four external spade terminals: two horizontal terminals, one on top of the

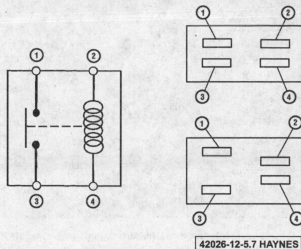

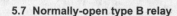

5.7 Normally-open type B relay

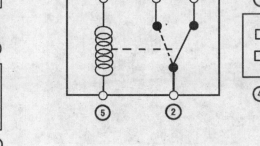

5.10 Five-terminal Type A relay

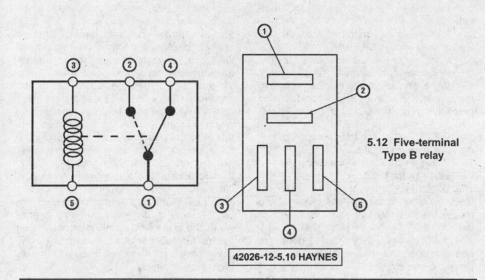

5.12 Five-terminal Type B relay

other, with two vertical terminals, side-by-side, below them.

5   To test a normally-open type relay, verify that there is *no* continuity between terminal No. 1 and No. 2 when the power is disconnected. Then verify that there *is* continuity between terminal No. 1 and No. 2 when the No. 3 and No. 4 terminals are connected to power and ground, respectively.

Normally-open Type B relays

Refer to illustration 5.7

6   Normally-open Type B relays are used for:
Anti-Lock Brake System (ABS) pump motor relay
Blower motor relay, Type 1
Blower motor relay, Type 2
Rear window defogger relay

7   Type B relays also have four external spade terminals **(see illustration)**, arranged in two parallel rows, with two terminals per row.

8   To test a normally-open Type B relay,

verify that there is no continuity between terminal No. 1 and No. 3 when the power is disconnected. Then, verify that there is continuity between terminal No. 1 and No. 3 when the No. 2 and No. 4 terminals are connected to power and ground, respectively.

Five-terminal Type A relays

Refer to illustration 5.10

9   Five-terminal Type A relays are used for the windshield wiper intermittent relay.

10   Five-terminal Type A relays have five external spade terminals **(see illustration)**, arranged in two parallel rows, with two terminals on the upper row and three terminals on the lower row.

11   To test a five-terminal Type A relay, verify that there is continuity between terminal No. 1 and terminal No. 2 when power and ground are connected to the No. 3 and No. 5 terminals. Then, verify that there is continuity between terminal No. 2 and terminal No. 4 when power is disconnected.

Five-terminal Type B relays

Refer to illustration 5.12

12   Five-terminal Type B relays **(see illustration)** are used for:
ACC cut relay
Fan control relay (Type S)
IGN 2 cut relay
Moonroof-opening relay
Moonroof-closing relay
Shift lock relay

13   To test a five-terminal relay verify that there is continuity between terminal No. 1 and No. 4 when the power is disconnected. Then, verify that there is continuity between terminal No. 1 and No. 2 when power and ground are connected to the No. 3 and No. 5 terminals.

6   Keyless entry - testing and programming the transmitter

1   Here's how the system should work:
If a door is open, you can't lock the doors and tailgate with the transmitter.
If you unlock the doors with the transmitter, but don't open a door within 30 seconds, all the doors automatically re-lock.
If the ignition key is inserted into the ignition switch key lock cylinder, the transmitter will neither lock nor unlock the doors.
On 2004 and later models, the PANIC function will not work if the ignition key is inserted into the ignition switch.

2   If the doors lock or unlock with the transmitter, but the LED on the transmitter doesn't come on, replace the transmitter.

Testing the transmitter

Note: *Make sure that all of the doors and the trunk lid are closed before starting this test. The transmitter will not lock the doors if a door or the trunk lid is open.*

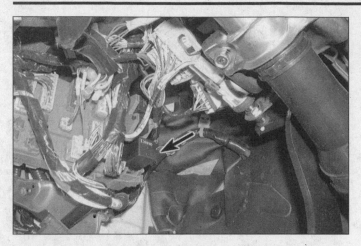

7.1a On 1999 through 2003 models, the turn signal and hazard flasher relay is located at the lower right corner of the relay panel above the under-dash fuse and relay box

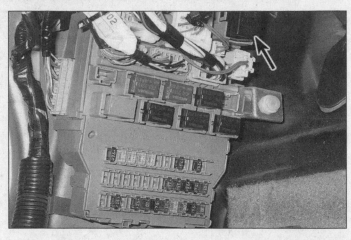

7.1b On 2004 and later models, the turn signal and hazard flasher relay is located at the upper right corner of the under-dash fuse and relay box

3   Press the LOCK or UNLOCK button five or six times to reset the transmitter. If the locks now work, the transmitter is okay. If the locks don't work, go to the next Step.

4   Open the transmitter (see your owner's manual) and inspect it for water damage. If you see water damage, replace the transmitter. If there is no water damage, go to the next Step.

5   Replace the transmitter battery with a new battery (see your owner's manual), then try to lock and unlock the doors with the transmitter by pressing the LOCK or UNLOCK button five or six times. If the doors lock and unlock, the transmitter is okay. If the doors don't lock and unlock go to the next Step.

6   Reprogram the transmitter (see Step 7), then try to lock and unlock the doors. If the doors lock and unlock, the transmitter is okay. If the doors still don't lock and unlock, replace the transmitter.

Programming the transmitter

Note 1: *This procedure DOES NOT APPLY to 2007 and later models. On those models, the transmitter must be reprogrammed by a factory scan tool, so you'll have to take the vehicle and the transmitter to a dealer service department for this procedure.*

Note 2: *Make sure that all the doors, the hood and the trunk lid are closed.*

Note 3: *You can store up to three transmitter codes in the keyless receiver unit's memory. If you exceed this number, the first code that you stored will be erased.*

7   Turn the ignition switch to ON, then within one to four seconds, aim the transmitter at the keyless receiver and press the transmitter LOCK or UNLOCK button. **Note:** *On 1999 through 2003 models, the keyless receiver unit is located inside the right (passenger's) part of the dash; on 2004 through 2006 models, it's located inside the left (driver's) part of the dash.*

8   Within another one to four seconds, turn the ignition switch to OFF.

9   Within another one to four seconds, turn the ignition switch to ON.

10   Within another one to our seconds, aim the transmitter at the keyless receiver and press the transmitter LOCK or UNLOCK button.

11   Within another one to four seconds, turn the ignition switch to OFF.

12   Within another one to four seconds, turn the ignition switch to ON.

13   Within another one to four seconds, aim the transmitter at the keyless receiver and press the transmitter LOCK or UNLOCK button.

14   Within another one to four seconds, turn the ignition switch to OFF.

15   Within another one to four seconds, turn the ignition switch to ON.

16   Within another one to four seconds, aim the transmitter at the keyless receiver and press the transmitter LOCK or UNLOCK button.

17   Verify that you can hear the door lock actuators operating, then within four seconds, press the transmitter LOCK or UNLOCK button again, or the code will not be stored. The keyless receiver is now in the programming mode.

18   Within 10 seconds, aim the transmitter at the keyless receiver unit, then press the LOCK or UNLOCK button. Verify that you can hear the door lock actuators operating after the transmitter code is stored.

19   Turn the ignition switch to OFF and pull out the ignition key.

20   Verify that the vehicle's keyless entry system operates correctly with each transmitter code.

7   Turn signal and hazard flasher relay - check and replacement

Refer to illustrations 7.1a and 7.1b

Warning: *The models covered by this manual are equipped with a Supplemental Restraint System (SRS), commonly referred to as airbags. Always disable the airbag system before working in the vicinity of any airbag system component to avoid the possibility of accidental deployment of the airbag, which could cause personal injury (see Section 26).*

1   The turn signal and hazard flashers are controlled by the turn signal and hazard flasher relay, which is located on the under-dash fuse and relay box (see Section 3). On 1999 through 2003 models, the turn signal and hazard flasher relay is located at the lower right corner of the relay box **(see illustration)**, which is located above the under-dash fuse and relay box. On 2004 and later models, the relay is located at the upper right corner of the fuse and relay box **(see illustration)**.

2   To access the turn signal and hazard flasher relay, remove the left kick panel.

3   If the flasher unit is functioning correctly, you'll hear an audible click when it's operating. If one of the turn signal indicator lights on the instrument cluster flashes more rapidly than normal, a turn signal bulb for that side has a blown filament.

4   If neither turn signal indicator blinks, the problem might be a blown fuse, a faulty turn signal and hazard flasher relay, a broken switch or a loose or open connection. If the left or right turn signal fuse has blown, check the wiring for a short before installing a new fuse.

5   If the turn signal and hazard flasher relay is bad, take it with you when buying a replacement unit. Make sure that the replacement unit is identical to the original.

8   Ignition switch/key lock cylinder assembly- replacement

Warning: *All models covered by this manual are equipped with a Supplemental Restraint System (SRS), more commonly known as airbags. Always disable the airbag system before working in the vicinity of any airbag system component to avoid the possibility of accidental deployment of the airbag, which could cause personal injury (see Section 26).*

8.4 To detach the ignition switch from the steering column assembly, remove these mounting screws (1999 through 2003 models)

8.7 To remove the clamp that secures the ignition switch/key lock cylinder assembly to the steering column, center-punch these two shear bolts, then drill out the heads (1999 through 2003 models)

1999 through 2003 models

1   Disconnect the cable from the negative battery terminal (see Chapter 5, Section 1).
2   Remove the steering column covers (see Chapter 11).

Ignition switch

Refer to illustration 8.4

3   Turn the ignition key to the LOCK position.
4   Remove the ignition switch retaining screws **(see illustration)** and remove the switch.
5   Installation is the reverse of removal.

Lock cylinder

Refer to illustration 8.7

6   Remove the retaining nuts and lower the steering column. Disconnect the electrical connectors from the immobilizer unit, if equipped.
7   The lock assembly is clamped to the steering column by two shear-head bolts **(see illustration)**. Use a center punch to make a dimple in the head of each bolt, then drill out the bolts with a 3/16-inch bit.

8   Separate the clamp and remove the assembly from the steering column. Remove the immobilizer unit, if equipped, from the old lock cylinder and install it onto the new lock cylinder. **Note:** *If the original immobilizer unit installed by the factory is replaced for any reason, the PCM must be reprogrammed by a dealer service department.*
9   Place the new lock cylinder in position without the key inserted and tighten the bolts until they are snug. Insert the key and verify that it turns in the lock cylinder. Tighten the bolts until their hex-heads break off. Reconnect the immobilizer connector (if equipped).
10   The remainder of installation is the reverse of removal.

2004 and later models

Refer to illustrations 8.13 and 8.14

Note: *The key lock cylinder/ignition switch assembly on these models is referred to by Acura as the "steering lock." It's a one-piece assembly. Neither the ignition switch nor the key lock cylinder can be replaced separately. If either component breaks, you must replace the steering lock assembly.*

11   Disconnect the cable from the negative battery terminal (see Chapter 5, Section 1).
12   Remove the steering column covers (see Chapter 11).
13   Remove the left kick panel, then trace the electrical harness from the ignition switch/key lock cylinder assembly down to the under-dash fuse and relay panel and disconnect the electrical connector **(see illustration)**.
14   Center-punch the shear bolts **(see illustration)** that attach the ignition switch/key lock cylinder assembly clamp to the steering column. Drill a hole in both bolts, unscrew them with a screw extractor, remove the clamp and remove the ignition switch/key lock cylinder assembly.
15   Install the new ignition switch/key lock cylinder assembly on the steering column without the ignition key inserted. Install the mounting clamp and new shear bolts, but don't tighten the bolts yet. Insert the ignition key and verify that the ignition key turns freely and that the steering wheel lock works correctly. Once you've verified that everything is working correctly, tighten the two shear bolts until the hex heads twist off. Installation is otherwise the reverse of removal.

8.13 Trace the electrical harness from the steering lock (the ignition switch/key lock cylinder assembly) down to the under-dash fuse and relay panel and disconnect the electrical connector (2004 and later models)

8.14 To detach the steering lock (ignition switch/key lock cylinder assembly) from the steering column assembly, center-punch and drill out these two shear-head bolts, remove the clamp and pull off the steering lock from underneath the column

9.3 To detach the combination light switch assembly, remove these two screws (steering wheel removed for clarity) (1999 through 2003 models)

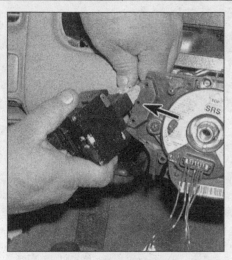

9.4 Pull out the combination switch, then disconnect the electrical connector and remove the switch (steering wheel removed for clarity) (1999 through 2003 models)

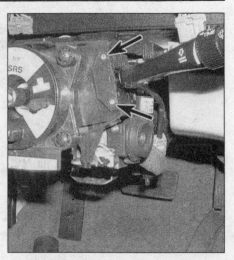

9.6 To detach the windshield wiper/washer switch assembly, remove these two screws (steering wheel removed for clarity) (1999 through 2003 models)

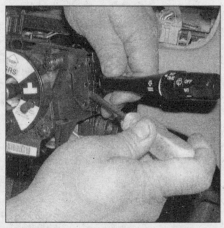

9.7a Use a small screwdriver to gently pry the windshield wiper/washer switch free . . .

9.7b . . . then pull it out of the housing and disconnect the electrical connector from the back of the switch (steering wheel removed for clarity) (1999 through 2003 models)

9   Steering column switches - replacement

Warning: *The models covered by this manual are equipped with a Supplemental Restraint System (SRS), more commonly known as airbags. Always disable the airbag system before working in the vicinity of any airbag system component to avoid the possibility of accidental deployment of the airbag, which could cause personal injury (see Section 26).*

1   Disconnect the cable from the negative battery terminal (see Chapter 5, Section 1), then wait at least three minutes before proceeding.
2   Remove the driver's side lower dashboard cover and the steering column covers (see Chapter 11).

1999 through 2003 models
Combination light switch
Refer to illustrations 9.3 and 9.4

3   Remove the combination light switch retaining screws **(see illustration)**.
4   Pull out the combination light switch and disconnect the electrical connector **(see illustration)**.
5   Installation is the reverse of removal.

Windshield wiper/washer switch
Refer to illustrations 9.6, 9.7a and 9.7b

6   Remove the windshield wiper/washer switch retaining screws **(see illustration)**.
7   Pull out the combination light switch and disconnect the electrical connectors **(see illustrations)**.
8   Installation is the reverse of removal.

2004 and later models
Combination light switch
Refer to illustrations 9.9 and 9.10

9   Disconnect the electrical connector from the *wiper/washer* switch **(see illustration)**.
10   Remove the combination light switch retaining screws **(see illustration)**.
11   To remove the combination light switch from the switch housing, push down on the retaining tab, then slide the switch out.
12   Installation is the reverse of removal.

Windshield wiper/washer switch
Refer to illustration 9.14

13   Disconnect the electrical connectors from the windshield wiper/washer switch **(see illustration 9.9)**.
14   Remove the windshield wiper/washer switch retaining screws **(see illustration)** and remove the switch.
15   Installation is the reverse of removal.

9.9 Both of the steering column switch connectors are plugged into the windshield wiper/washer switch: combination light switch connector (A) and windshield wiper/washer switch connector (B) (2004 and later models)

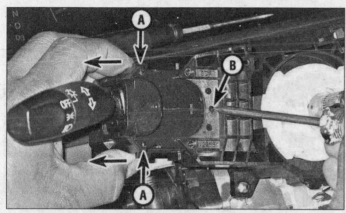

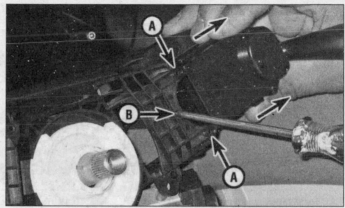

9.10 To detach the combination light switch from the switch housing, remove these two screws (A). Push an awl into this hole (B) to disengage the release tab, then slide the switch out to the left (2004 and later models)

9.14 To detach the windshield wiper/washer switch from the switch housing, remove these two screws (A). Push an awl into this hole (B) to disengage the release tab, then slide the switch out to the right

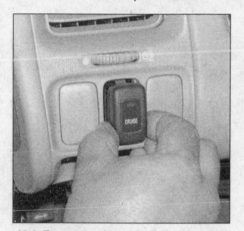

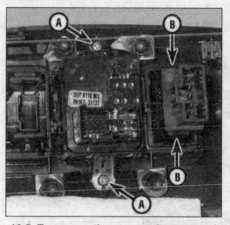

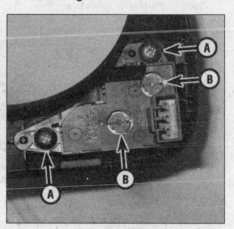

10.1 To remove the cruise control switch from the driver's switch panel on 1999 through 2003 models, pry it loose, then pull the switch out and disconnect the electrical connector

10.5 To remove the power mirror control switch from the driver's switch panel, remove the two screws (A). To remove the Vehicle Stability Assist (VSA) OFF switch, depress the two release tabs (B) and push out the switch

10.12 To remove the brightness control switch from the instrument cluster trim panel, remove the two screws (A). To replace a defective bulb (B), turn the bulb holder counterclockwise and pull it out

10 Dashboard switches - replacement

Warning: *The models covered by this manual are equipped with a Supplemental Restraint System (SRS), more commonly known as airbags. Always disable the airbag system before working in the vicinity of any airbag system component to avoid the possibility of accidental deployment of the airbag, which could cause personal injury (see Section 26).*

Driver's switch panel

1999 through 2003 models

Refer to illustration 10.1

1   To remove the cruise control switch, pry it out with a trim panel removal tool or a screwdriver (tape the tip of the screwdriver to protect the plastic). Pull out the switch **(see illustration)** and disconnect the electrical connector from the switch.
2   To remove the fog light switch or moon-

roof switch, remove the driver's side lower dashboard cover (see Chapter 11). Reach up behind the switch, depress the switch release tabs, push the switch out of the cluster trim panel and disconnect the electrical connector.
3   Installation is the reverse of removal. Make sure that the switch snaps into place when you push it into the instrument cluster trim panel.

2004 and later models

Refer to illustration 10.5

4   Remove the driver's side dashboard lower cover (see Chapter 11).
5   If you're removing the power mirror control switch, remove the two switch screws **(see illustration)** and remove the switch.
6   If you're removing the Vehicle Stability Assist (VSA) OFF switch, depress the release tabs at the top and bottom of the switch and push it out of the driver's switch panel **(see illustration 10.5)**.
7   Installation is the reverse of removal. If

you're installing the VSA OFF switch, make sure that the switch snaps into place when you push it into the dashboard lower cover.

Instrument panel brightness control switch

1999 through 2003 models

8   Remove the driver's side dashboard lower cover (see Chapter 11) and disconnect the electrical connector from the instrument panel brightness control switch.
9   Remove the two switch mounting screws and remove the switch.
10   Installation is the reverse of removal.

2004 and later models

Refer to illustration 10.12

11   Remove the instrument cluster trim panel (see Chapter 11).
12   Remove the brightness control switch retaining screws **(see illustration)** and remove the switch from the cluster trim panel.
13   Installation is the reverse of removal.

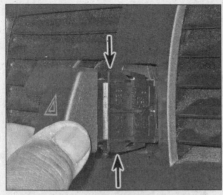

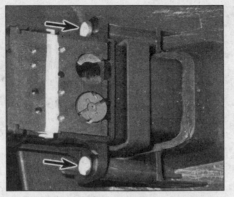

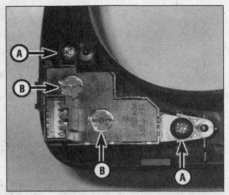

10.16 To remove the hazard flasher switch on 1999 through 2003 models with navigation, and on all 2004 and later models, depress these two release tabs and pull the switch out of the upper panel (shown) or the instrument cluster trim panel

10.19 To remove the trunk lid release switch, remove these two mounting screws (2004 and later model shown, earlier models similar)

10.22 To remove the multi-information display switch, remove these two retaining screws (A). To replace a defective bulb (B), turn the bulb holder counterclockwise and pull it out

11.2a To detach the lower part of the instrument cluster, remove these two mounting screws

11.2b To detach the upper part of the instrument cluster, remove these two mounting screws

Hazard flasher switch

Refer to illustration 10.16

14   On 1999 through 2003 models, remove the instrument cluster trim panel (see Chapter 11). On 2004 and later models, remove the center upper panel (see Chapter 11).

15   On 1999 through 2003 models without navigation, remove the two screws that secure the hazard flasher switch to the instrument cluster trim panel and remove the switch.

16   On 1999 through 2003 models with navigation and on all 2004 and later models, depress the two switch release tabs and pull the switch out of the instrument cluster trim panel (1999 through 2003 models) or the center upper panel (2004 and later models) **(see illustration)**.

17   Installation is the reverse of removal.

Trunk lid release switch

Refer to illustration 10.19

18   On 1999 through 2003 models, remove the driver's door trim panel (see Chapter 11). On 2004 and later models, remove the driver's side dashboard lower cover (see Chapter 11).

19   Remove the trunk lid release mounting screws **(see illustration)** and remove the switch.

20   Installation is the reverse of removal.

Multi-information display switch

Refer to illustration 10.22

21   Remove the instrument cluster trim panel (see Chapter 11).

22   Remove the multi-information switch retaining screws **(see illustration)** and remove the switch.

23   Installation is the reverse of removal.

Moonroof switch

24   On 1999 through 2003 models, refer to Step 2.

25   On 2004 and later models, carefully pry out the switch with a small screwdriver or trim removal tool and disconnect the electrical connector.

26   Installation is the reverse of removal. Make sure that the moonroof switch snaps into place.

Seat heater switches

27   On 1999 through 2003 models, remove the console panel tray (see Chapter 11). On 2004 and later models, remove the center console panel (see Chapter 11).

28   On 1999 through 2003 models, depress the two release tabs and pull out the defective heater switch.

29   On 2004 and later models, remove the two heater switch retaining screws and remove the switch.

30   Installation is the reverse of removal.

11   Instrument cluster - removal and installation

Refer to illustrations 11.2a and 11.2b

Warning: *The models covered by this manual are equipped with a Supplemental Restraint System (SRS), more commonly known as airbags. Always disable the airbag system before working in the vicinity of any airbag system component to avoid the possibility of accidental deployment of the airbag, which could cause personal injury (see Section 26).*

1   Remove the instrument cluster trim bezel (see Chapter 11).

2   Remove the instrument cluster mounting screws **(see illustrations)**.

3   Pull out the cluster and disconnect the

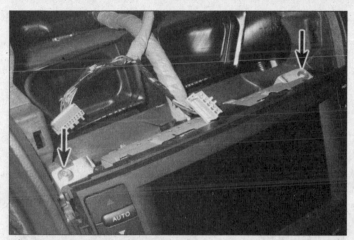

12.7a   To detach the upper end of the audio-HVAC display module, remove these two bolts (2004 and later models)

12.7b   To detach the lower end of the audio-HVAC display module, remove the bolts (left side shown)

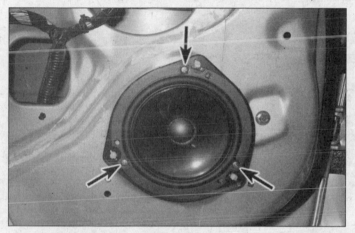

12.12   To detach a speaker from a door, remove the three mounting screws (front door speaker shown, back door speakers similar)

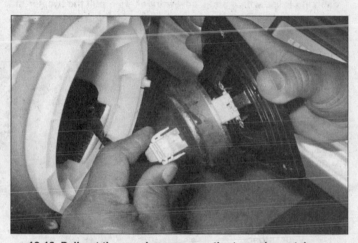

12.13   Pull out the speaker, squeeze the two release tabs as shown and disconnect the electrical connector from the speaker (front door speaker shown, back door speakers similar)

electrical connectors from the backside.

4   Installation is the reverse of removal.

12   Radio and speakers - removal and installation

Warning: *The models covered by this manual are equipped with a Supplemental Restraint System (SRS), more commonly known as airbags. Always disable the airbag system before working in the vicinity of any airbag system component to avoid the possibility of accidental deployment of the airbag, which could cause personal injury (see Section 26).*

Note: *Before beginning this procedure, make sure that you have the anti-theft code for the radio and that you have written down the frequencies for the radio station preset buttons.*

Radio

1999 through 2003 models

1   Remove the rear console and the console panel (see Chapter 11).

2   Remove all six radio mounting bolts: two

in the front (one on each side) and two on each side.

3   Pull out the radio and CD console box (models without navigation), or radio and climate control unit (models with navigation), as a single assembly and disconnect the electrical connectors from the climate control unit (if applicable) and the electrical connectors and antenna cable from the backside of the radio.

4   To separate the CD console box or climate control unit from the radio, remove the two mounting screws, one on each end.

5   Installation is the reverse of removal.

2004 and later models

Refer to illustrations 12.7a and 12.7b

Note: *On these models, the radio, the navigation display screen and the heating/ventilation/air-conditioning (HVAC) controls are integrated into a single assembly. After you remove the audio-HVAC display module, you can separate the radio from the HVAC display module.*

6   Remove the center console rear section,

the center console panel and the upper panel (see Chapter 11).

7   Remove the audio-HVAC display module assembly mounting bolts **(see illustrations)**.

8   Pull out the audio-HVAC assembly and disconnect the antenna cable and the electrical connectors from the audio unit and from the HVAC display module, then remove the audio-HVAC assembly.

9   Remove the bolts and screws from the side brackets to separate the radio from the HVAC display module.

10   Installation is the reverse of removal.

Speakers

Door speakers

Refer to illustrations 12.12 and 12.13

11   Remove the door trim panel (see Chapter 11).

12   Remove the three speaker screws **(see illustration)**.

13   Pull out the speaker and disconnect the electrical connector **(see illustration)**.

14   Installation is the reverse of removal.

12.16 To release the lugs that retain the speaker, carefully pry each lug loose with a small screwdriver, then pull the tweeter or front center speaker out of the retaining ring

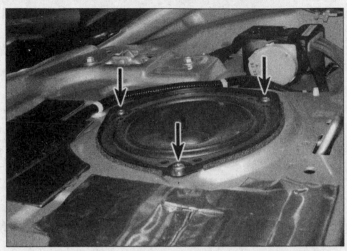

12.19 To remove a rear speaker, remove these three screws, pull out the speaker and disconnect the electrical connector

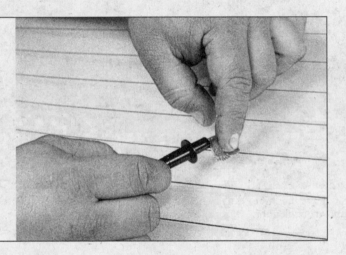

14.4 When measuring the voltage at the rear window defogger grid, wrap a piece of aluminum foil around the positive probe of the voltmeter and press the foil against the wire with your finger

Tweeters and front center speaker

Refer to illustration 12.16

15   Carefully pry up the tweeter speaker grille or front center speaker grille with a small screwdriver, then disconnect the electrical connector. **Caution:** *Tape the tip of the screwdriver to prevent scratching.*
16   Separate the tweeter from the grille **(see illustration)**. **Caution:** *The cylindrical plastic housing that surrounds the tweeter is very thin, so be extremely careful when removing the tweeter. If you damage the housing, you'll have to replace the grille.*
17   Installation is the reverse of removal.

Rear speakers and sub-woofer

Refer to illustration 12.19

18   Remove the rear shelf (see Chapter 11).
19   Remove the speaker mounting screws **(see illustration)**, pull the speaker out of its mounting hole and disconnect the electrical connector.
20   Installation is the reverse of removal.

13   Antenna - removal and installation

All models use a rear window-mounted antenna grid, which is similar to the defogger grid on the rear window. To replace the antenna, you have to replace the rear window. However, you can easily repair the antenna grid as long as the broken part is no more than one inch long. The procedure for repairing the antenna grid is identical to repairing the rear window defogger grid (see Section 14).

14   Rear window defogger - check and repair

1   The rear window defogger consists of a number of horizontal elements baked onto the glass surface.
2   Small breaks in the element can be repaired without removing the rear window.

Check

Refer to illustrations 14.4, 14.5 and 14.7

3   Turn the ignition switch and defogger system switches to the ON position. Using a voltmeter, place the positive probe against the defogger grid positive terminal and the negative probe against the ground terminal. If battery voltage is not indicated, check the fuse, defogger switch and related wiring. If voltage is indicated, but all or part of the defogger doesn't heat, proceed with the following tests.
4   When measuring voltage during the next two tests, wrap a piece of aluminum foil around the tip of the voltmeter positive probe and press the foil against the heating element with your finger **(see illustration)**. Place the negative probe on the defogger grid ground terminal.
5   Check the voltage at the center of each heating element **(see illustration)**. If the voltage is 5 or 6-volts, the element is okay (there is no break). If the voltage is zero, the element is broken between the center of the element and the positive end. If the voltage is 10 to 12-volts, the element is broken between the center of the element and ground. Check each heating element.
6   Connect the negative lead to a good body ground. The reading should stay the same. If it doesn't, the ground connection is bad.
7   To find the break, place the voltmeter negative probe against the defogger ground terminal. Place the voltmeter positive probe with the foil strip against the heating element at the positive terminal end and slide it toward the negative terminal end. The point at which the voltmeter deflects from several volts to zero is the point at which the heating element is broken **(see illustration)**.

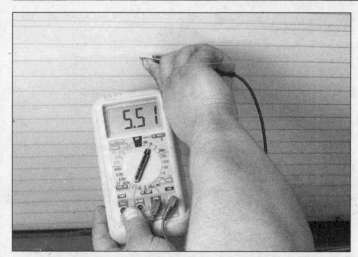

14.5 To determine if a heating element has broken, check the voltage at the center of each element; if the voltage is 5 or 6-volts, the element is unbroken, but if the voltage is 10 or 12-volts, the element is broken between the center and the ground side. If there is no voltage, the element is broken between the center and the positive side

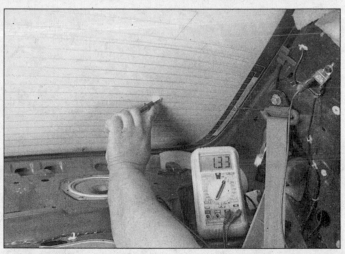

14.7 To find the break, place the voltmeter negative lead against the defogger ground terminal, place the voltmeter positive lead with the foil strip against the heating element at the positive terminal end and slide it toward the negative terminal end. The point at which the voltmeter reading changes abruptly is the point at which the element is broken

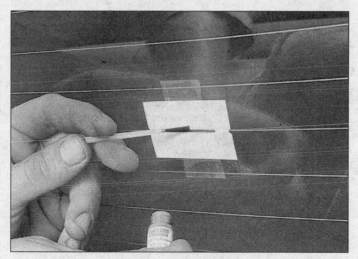

14.13 To use a defogger repair kit, apply masking tape to the inside of the window at the damaged area, then brush on the special conductive coating

15.2 To disconnect an electrical connector from a halogen headlight bulb socket, depress the release tab and pull off the connector (1999 through 2003 models with halogen high-beam bulbs only)

Repair

Refer to illustration 14.13

8 Repair the break in the element using a repair kit for this purpose (available at most auto parts stores). Make sure that the repair kit includes plastic conductive epoxy.

9 Prior to repairing a break, turn off the system and allow it to cool off for a few minutes.

10 Lightly buff the element area with fine steel wool, then clean it thoroughly with rubbing alcohol.

11 Use masking tape to mask off the area being repaired.

12 Thoroughly mix the epoxy, following the instructions provided with the repair kit.

13 Apply the epoxy material to the slit in the masking tape, overlapping the undamaged area about 3/4-inch on either end **(see illustration)**.

14 Allow the repair to cure for 24 hours before removing the tape and using the system.

15 Headlight bulb - replacement

Halogen bulbs (high-beam bulbs on 1999 through 2003 models only)

Refer to illustrations 15.2 and 15.3

Warning 1: *Except for the high-beam bulbs on 1999 through 2003 models, ALL OTHER headlight bulbs are High Intensity Discharge*

(HID) bulbs. Unless you are replacing a high-beam bulb on a 1999 through 2003 model, refer to the HID section below.

Warning 2: *Halogen gas filled bulbs are under pressure and can shatter if the surface is scratched or the bulb is dropped. Wear eye protection and handle the bulbs carefully, grasping only the base whenever possible. Do not touch the surface of the bulb with your fingers because the oil from your skin could cause it to overheat and fail prematurely. If you do touch the bulb surface, clean it with rubbing alcohol.*

1 If you're replacing the left (driver's side) high-beam headlight bulb, remove the coolant reservoir (see Chapter 3).

2 Disconnect the electrical connector from the headlight **(see illustration)**.

15.3 To remove a halogen headlight bulb socket from the headlight housing, turn it counterclockwise 1/4-turn and pull it out (1999 through 2003 models with halogen high-beam bulbs only)

16.5a To detach the lower part of the headlight housing, remove these three bolts (1999 through 2003 models)

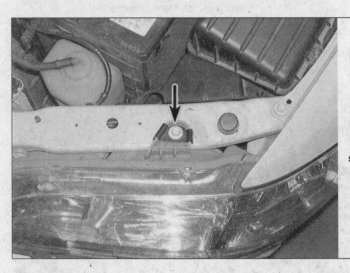

16.5b To detach the upper part of the headlight housing, remove these two bolts (one bolt not shown) (1999 through 2003 models)

3   Remove the bulb socket from the headlight housing **(see illustration)**.

4   To install a new bulb socket into the headlight housing, align the lugs on the socket with the slots in the socket mounting hole, insert the bulb socket into the mounting hole and rotate it clockwise until it stops.

5   Installation is otherwise the reverse of removal.

High-Intensity Discharge (HID) bulbs (1999 through 2003 low-beam and all 2004 and later bulbs)

Warning: *According to the manufacturer, the high voltages produced by this system can be fatal in the event of a shock. Also, the voltage can remain in the circuit even after the headlight switch has been turned to OFF and the ignition key has been removed. Therefore, for your safety, we don't recommend that you try to replace one of these* bulbs yourself. Instead, have this service performed by a dealer service department or other qualified repair shop.

16 Headlight housing - replacement

Warning: *When the headlight switch is turned on, extremely high voltage - as much as 25,000 volts - is present at a High-Intensity Discharge (HID) bulb socket. This is enough voltage to cause serious electrical shock or to electrocute you, so please carefully read and comply with the following warnings when working on HID systems:*

a) *Always disconnect the battery before removing a headlight housing (see Chapter 5, Section 1).*

b) *NEVER turn on the headlight switch before or during the following procedure.*

c) *NEVER work on the headlight housing assembly in the rain, the snow, near a sprinkler or when your hands are wet.*

d) *DO NOT TOUCH OR DISASSEMBLE the inverter unit or the igniter unit.*

e) *DO NOT attempt to power up an HID bulb with any external power source. The HID system can only be turned on and correctly controlled by the HID electrical system.*

1   Make sure that the ignition switch and the headlight switch are turned to OFF.

2   Disconnect the cable from the negative terminal of the battery (see Chapter 5, Section 1).

1999 through 2003 models

Refer to illustrations 16.5a and 16.5b

3   Remove the front bumper cover (see Chapter 11).

4   Disconnect the electrical connectors from the headlight housing. If you can't reach some of the connectors, disconnect them after you pull the headlight housing out.

5   Remove the headlight housing mounting bolts **(see illustrations)** and pull out the housing. Disconnect any remaining electrical connectors, then remove the housing.

6   Installation is the reverse of removal.

2004 and later models

Refer to illustrations 16.8, 16.9a and 16.9b

7   Remove the front bumper cover (see Chapter 11).

8   Remove the two front bumper spacer screws **(see illustration)** and remove the spacer.

9   Remove the headlight housing bolts **(see accompanying illustration and illustration 16.8)**.

10   Pull out the headlight housing and disconnect the electrical connectors.

11   Installation is the reverse of removal.

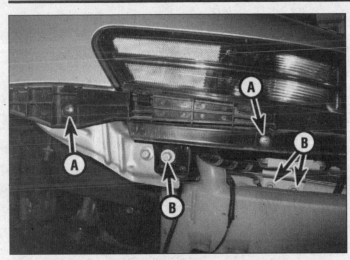

16.8 To detach the front bumper spacer, remove these two screws (A). The other three bolts (B) are lower headlight housing bolts (2004 and later models)

16.9a Locations of the lower headlight housing bolts and one of the upper housing bolts (2004 and later models)

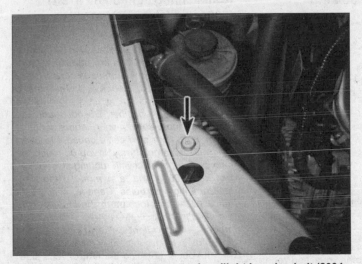

16.9b Location of the upper outer headlight housing bolt (2004 and later models)

17.1a Insert a Phillips screwdriver through this access hole . . .

17   Headlights - adjustment

Refer to illustrations 17.1a, 17.1b and 17.3

Caution: *The headlights must be aimed correctly. If adjusted incorrectly they could blind the driver of an oncoming vehicle and cause a serious accident or seriously reduce your ability to see the road. The headlights should be checked for correct aim every 12 months and any time a new headlight is installed or front end body work is performed. It should be emphasized that the following procedure is only an interim step that will provide temporary adjustment until a properly equipped shop can adjust the headlights.*

1   The vertical adjuster is located on the upper backside of each headlight housing. Use a Phillips screwdriver to turn the adjuster through the adjuster hole **(see illustrations)**. **Note:** *1999 and 2000 models also have horizontal adjusters.*

17.1b . . . and engage it with the vertical adjuster (headlight housing removed for clarity)

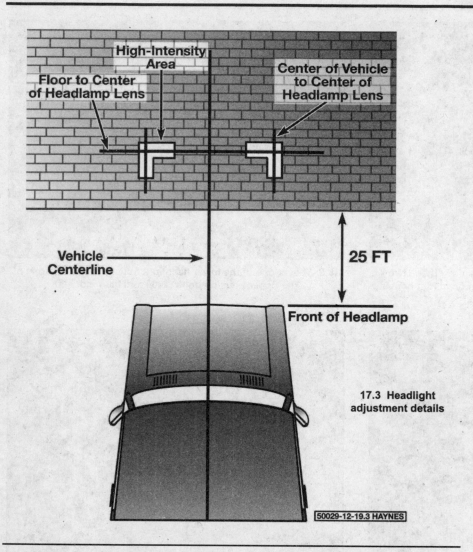

17.3 Headlight adjustment details

2   There are several methods for adjusting the headlights. The simplest method requires masking tape, a blank wall and a level floor.

3   Position masking tape vertically on the wall in relation to the vehicle centerline and in relation to the centerlines of both headlights **(see illustration)**.

4   Position a horizontal tape line in reference to the centerline of all the headlights. **Note:** *It might be easier to position the tape on the wall with the vehicle parked only a few inches away.*

5   Adjustment should be made with the vehicle parked 25 feet from the wall, sitting level, the gas tank half-full and no heavy load in the vehicle.

6   With the low beams turned on, position the high intensity zone so it is two inches below the horizontal line.

7   With the high beams on, the high intensity zone should be vertically centered with the exact center just below the horizontal line. **Note:** *It might not be possible to position the headlight aim exactly for both high and low beams. If a compromise must be made, keep in mind that the low beams are the most used and have the greatest effect on safety.*

8   Have the headlights adjusted by a dealer service department or other qualified repair facility as soon as possible.

---

18   Bulb replacement

Exterior light bulbs

Front turn signal, parking light and side marker light bulbs

Refer to illustrations 18.4a, 18.4b, 18.5a and 18.5b

1   Loosen the left or right front wheel lug nuts. Raise the front of the vehicle and place it securely on jackstands. Remove the left or right front wheel.

2   Remove the two forward fasteners securing the inner fender splash shield (see Chapter 11), then pull the splash shield back for access to the bulb.

3   The front turn signal/parking light bulb socket and, on 1999 through 2003 models, the front side marker light bulb socket, are the outermost sockets on the headlight housing. Disconnect the electrical connector from the front turn signal/parking light socket or (on 1999 through 2003 models only) the front side marker bulb socket.

4   To remove the bulb socket from a 1999 through 2003 model, turn it counterclockwise and pull it out of the housing **(see illustration)**. Remove the turn signal/side marker light bulb from the socket **(see illustration)**. To install a new bulb, align the pins with the slots in the socket, push the bulb into the socket until it's seated, then give it a clockwise turn to lock it into place in the socket. **Note:** *The pin at the bottom of the bulb must be aligned with the deeper slot in the socket.*

5   To remove the bulb socket from a 2004 and later model, turn it counterclockwise 1/4-turn and pull it out of the housing **(see illustration)**. Remove the bulb from the socket by pulling straight out **(see illustration)**.

6   Installation is otherwise the reverse of removal.

Daytime running light bulbs (Canada)/fog light bulbs (USA) (2004 and later models)

Refer to illustrations 18.9a and 18.9b

Warning: *These bulbs are halogen type bulbs. Halogen gas filled bulbs are under pressure and can shatter if the surface is scratched or the bulb is dropped. Wear eye protection and handle the bulbs carefully, grasping only the base whenever possible. Do not touch the surface of the bulb with your fingers because the oil from your skin could cause it to overheat and fail prematurely. If you do touch the bulb surface, clean it with rubbing alcohol.*

Note: *On 2004 and later models, the daytime running light bulbs (Canada) or fog light bulbs (USA) are located in the inner part of the headlight housing. On 1999 through 2003 models, the fog light bulbs are in separate housings in the front bumper cover.*

7   If you're replacing the left (driver's side) daytime running light bulb or fog light bulb, remove the battery and the battery box (see Chapter 5, Section 1), and remove the duct between the resonator and the air filter housing (see Chapter 4).

8   Disconnect the electrical connector from the daytime running light or fog light bulb socket.

9   To remove the daytime running light or fog light bulb socket, turn it counterclockwise and pull it out of the housing **(see illustrations)**.

10   Installation is the reverse of removal.

Fog light bulbs (1999 through 2003 models)

Note: *The fog light housings are located in the front bumper cover.*

11   Remove the fog light housing retaining bolt from the underside of the bumper cover, underneath the fog light housing.

12   The fog light housing is also secured to the bumper cover by a single clip that's located at the same end of the housing as the retaining bolt. Carefully pry the fog light housing loose from the bumper cover, pull it

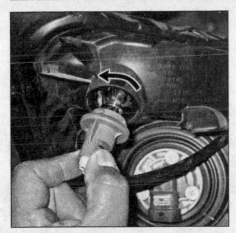

18.4a To remove a front turn signal/ parking light bulb socket or a front side marker light bulb socket from the headlight housing, turn the socket counterclockwise 1/4-turn, then pull it out of the housing (1999 through 2003 models)

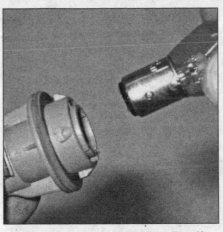

18.4b To remove a front turn signal/ parking light or front side marker light bulb from its socket, push it into the socket and turn it counterclockwise, then pull it out of the socket (1999 through 2003 models)

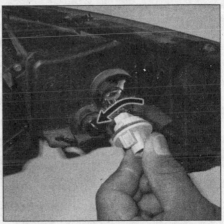

18.5a To remove a front turn signal/ parking light bulb socket from the headlight housing, turn the socket counterclockwise and pull it out of the housing (2004 and later models)

18.5b To remove a front turn signal/ parking light bulb from the socket, simply pull it straight out of the socket (2004 and later models)

18.9a To unlock a daytime running light bulb socket (Canada) or fog light bulb socket (USA), turn it counterclockwise . . .

18.9b . . . and pull it out of the headlight housing (headlight housing removed for clarity)

out and disconnect the fog light bulb electrical connector.

13   To remove the fog light bulb from the fog light housing, turn it counterclockwise and pull it out.

14   To install a new fog light bulb into the fog light housing, insert it into the hole in the housing and turn it clockwise until it locks into place.

15   Installation is otherwise the reverse of removal.

Front and rear side marker lights (2004 and later models)

Refer to illustrations 18.16 and 18.18

16   Using a small screwdriver, carefully pry out the side marker light housing until it pops loose **(see illustration)**. Be sure to wrap the screwdriver tip with tape to protect the paint.

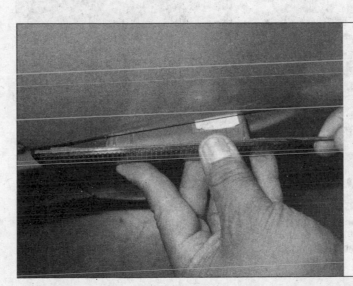

18.16 Using a small screwdriver, carefully pry out the side marker light housing

18.18 Pull out the side marker light housing and disconnect the electrical connector (front side marker shown, rear side marker identical)

18.27 Pry out this push fastener and unscrew this cargo netting hook, then pull the trunk lining forward just far enough to gain access to the backside of the taillight housing (2004 and later models)

18.28 To remove the turn signal bulb from the taillight housing, turn the socket counterclockwise and pull it out (2004 and later models)

17   If you can't pry the side marker light assembly loose, remove the front inner fender splash shield to access the backside of the front side marker, or the trunk side trim panel to access the backside of the rear side marker (see Chapter 11), and push out the side marker light.

18   Pull out the side marker light housing and disconnect the electrical connector (see illustration).

19   No further disassembly of the side marker light assembly is possible. If the side marker light is defective, replace the side marker assembly.

20   Installation is the reverse of removal.

Taillight bulbs (1999 through 2003 models)

21   Open the trunk lid and remove the push fastener on the edge of the trunk opening by turning it counterclockwise. Unscrew the cargo net retaining button and pull back the trunk lining.

22   To remove any of the bulb sockets, rotate the socket counterclockwise and pull it out of the taillight housing.

23   To remove a bulb from its socket, simply pull it straight out of the socket.

24   To install a bulb, simply push it straight into the socket.

25   Installation is otherwise the reverse of removal.

Taillight bulbs (2004 and later models)

Turn signal bulbs

Refer to illustrations 18.27 and 18.28

26   Open the trunk lid.

27   To access the turn signal bulb or the taillight/brake light LED (both in the taillight housing in the rear fender), use a trim removal tool or a small screwdriver to remove the push fastener. Unscrew the cargo net hook (see

illustration) and pull the trunk liner forward far enough to access the backside of the taillight housing.

28   To remove the turn signal bulb socket, turn it counterclockwise and pull it out of the taillight housing (see illustration).

29   To remove the turn signal bulb from its socket, simply pull it straight out.

30   Installation is the reverse of removal.

Back-up light bulbs

Refer to illustration 18.32

31   Open the trunk lid and remove the trunk trim panel (see *Trunk lid - removal and installation* in Chapter 11).

32   To remove a back-up light bulb socket, turn it counterclockwise and pull it out of the taillight housing (see illustration).

33   To remove a back-up light bulb from its socket, pull it straight out. Push the new bulb straight into the socket until it's fully seated.

34   To install the bulb socket into the back-up light housing, align the lugs on the socket with the notches in the socket receptacle in the housing, insert the socket into the housing and turn it clockwise to lock it into place.

35   Installation is otherwise the reverse of removal.

Taillight/brake light LEDs

Refer to illustrations 18.37 and 18.38

Note: *The taillight/brake light LED assembly is located inside the main (fender-mounted) taillight housing. To replace the taillight/brake light LED, you must remove the taillight housing, and to remove the taillight housing you must remove the rear bumper cover.*

36   Remove the rear bumper cover (see Chapter 11).

37   Open the trunk lid, pull back the trunk liner (see illustration 18.27), remove the turn signal bulb and socket (see illustration 18.28) and disconnect the LED electrical connector (see illustration) from the taillight housing.

38   Remove the four taillight housing mounting nuts located inside the trunk (see illustration), then, working under the back of the

18.32 To remove the back-up light socket from the back-up light housing, turn it counterclockwise and pull it out (2004 and later models)

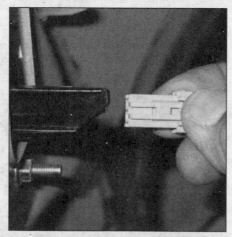

18.37 Depress the release tab and disconnect the electrical connector for the LED assembly (2004 and later models)

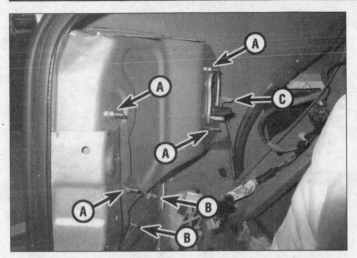

18.38 Taillight housing mounting details (2004 and later models)

A   Nuts
B   Bolts (accessed from outside, two of three shown)
C   Locator pin

18.46 Using a trim panel removal tool, carefully pry off the high-mount brake light cover (2004 and later models)

18.47 High-mount brake light details (2004 and later models)

A   Electrical connector
B   Mounting bolts

vehicle with a flashlight, locate and remove the two bolts that are screwed into the weld nuts inside the trunk. Remove the single bolt between these two bolts that's screwed into the underside of the taillight. Remove the taillight assembly.

39   To remove the LED assembly from the taillight housing, disconnect the harness connector from the LED assembly, remove the four LED mounting screws, disengage the LED assembly from the two mounting tabs and pull off the LED assembly.

40   Installation is the reverse of removal.

High-mount brake light

1999 through 2003 models

41   Using a trim removal tool, carefully pry loose the rear speaker grille from the rear shelf. The grille is secured to the rear shelf by a pair of locator pins at the front corners of the grille.

42   Lift up the rear speaker grille and disconnect both electrical connectors from the underside of the grille. Remove the rear speaker grille and place it upside down on a clean work surface.

43   To remove either of the high-mount brake light sockets, turn it counterclockwise 1/4-turn and pull it out of the grille.

44   To remove either high-mount brake light bulb from its socket, simply pull it straight out of the socket.

45   Installation is the reverse of removal.

2004 and later models

Refer to illustrations 18.46 and 18.47

46   Using a trim removal tool, carefully pry off the high-mount brake light cover **(see illustration)**.

47   Disconnect the electrical connector from the high-mount brake light **(see illustration)**.

48   Remove the high-mount brake light retaining bolts and remove the high-mount brake light assembly.

49   No further disassembly is necessary or possible. If the high-mount brake light assembly is defective, replace it with a new unit.

50   Installation is the reverse of removal. When installing the cover, make sure that the locator pins and the retaining clips are correctly aligned.

License plate light

1999 through 2003 models

51   Remove the two license plate light housing mounting screws and pull down the housing.

52   Turn the bulb socket counterclockwise and pull the socket out of the license plate light housing.

53   To remove the old license plate light, pull it straight out of the socket.

54   To install a new license plate light bulb, push it into the socket until it's fully seated.

55   Installation is the reverse of removal.

2004 and later models

Refer to illustrations 18.57, 18.58a and 18.58b

56   Open the trunk lid and remove the trunk trim panel (see *Trunk lid - removal and instal-*

lation in Chapter 11).

57   Disconnect the electrical connector from the license plate light bulb socket **(see illustration)**.

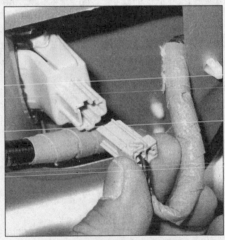

18.57 Depress the release tab and disconnect the electrical connector from the license plate light (2004 and later models)

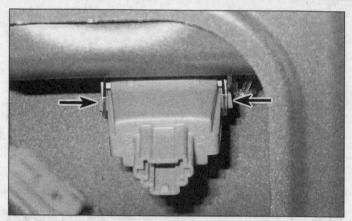

18.58a To remove the bulb socket from the license plate light housing, depress these two release tabs . . .

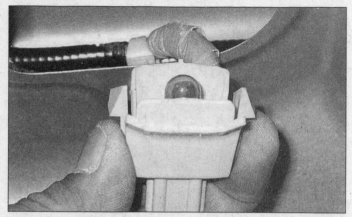

18.58b . . . and pull out the socket. To remove the bulb, simply pull it straight out

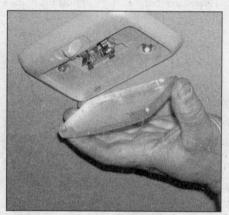
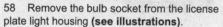

18.61 Using a fingernail file or a small screwdriver, carefully pry off the ceiling light or dome light lens . . .

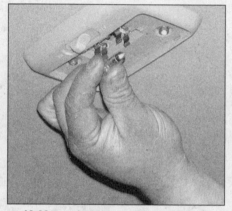

18.62 . . . then remove the bulb from its terminals

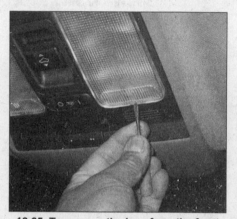

18.65 To remove the lens from the front individual map light, carefully pry it off with a small screwdriver

58   Remove the bulb socket from the license plate light housing **(see illustrations)**.
59   Remove the old bulb from the socket by pulling it straight out, then install a new bulb in the housing by pushing it straight into the socket until it's fully seated
60   When installing the bulb socket into the license plate light housing, make sure that it snaps into place. Installation is otherwise the reverse of removal.

Interior lights

Ceiling light or dome light

Refer to illustrations 18.61 and 18.62

61   Using a fingernail file or a small screwdriver, carefully pry off the lens **(see illustration)**. Be careful not to damage the plastic trim around the edge of the lens.
62   Remove the old bulb from the two metal terminals **(see illustration). Caution:** *If prying is necessary, pry only on the ends of the bulb, not on the glass.*
63   Install the new bulb.
64   Install the lens, making sure that it snaps back into place.

Front individual map light

Refer to illustration 18.65

65   Carefully pry off the lens with a fingernail file

or with a small screwdriver **(see illustration)**.
66   To remove the old bulb, pull it straight out of its socket. Insert the new bulb into its receptacle and push it straight up until it stops.
67   Install the lens. Make sure it snaps into place.

Vanity mirror lights

1999 through 2003 models

Refer to illustrations 18.68 and 18.69

68   Flip down the visor, open the cover for the vanity mirror, then carefully pry off the lens **(see illustration)**.
69   Carefully pry the old light bulb out of its receptacle **(see illustration)**. Push the new bulb into the receptacle until it's fully seated.
70   Install the lens, making sure it snaps into place.

2004 and later models

Refer to illustration 18.71

71   Using a fingernail file or a small screwdriver, carefully pry loose the housing for the vanity mirror light **(see illustration)**. Be careful not to damage the headliner surrounding the lens.
72   To remove the old bulb, simply pull it straight out of the socket. To install a new bulb

in the socket, push it into the socket until it's fully seated.
73   Install the vanity mirror light housing, making sure it snaps into place.

Rear map light (2004 and later models)

Refer to illustration 18.74

74   Using a small screwdriver, carefully pry off the lens **(see illustration)**.
75   To remove the old light bulb from its receptacle in the rear map light housing, simply pull it straight down. To insert a new bulb, push it straight into the receptacle until it's fully seated.
76   Install the lens. Make sure that it snaps into place.

Door courtesy lights

Refer to illustration 18.77

77   Open the door, then carefully pry off the door courtesy light lens **(see illustration)**.
78   To remove the old door courtesy light bulb, simply pull it straight out. To install a new bulb, push it straight into the socket until it's fully seated.
79   Install the lens. Make sure that it snaps into place.

18.68 Use a small screwdriver to carefully pry the lens off the vanity mirror light bulb receptacle (1999 through 2003 models)

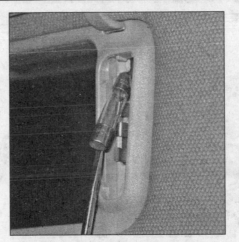

18.69 Use a small screwdriver to carefully pry out the old vanity mirror light bulb (pry only on the end of the bulb) (1999 through 2003 models)

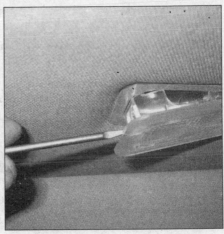

18.71 Use a small screwdriver to carefully pry loose the vanity mirror light housing (2004 and later models)

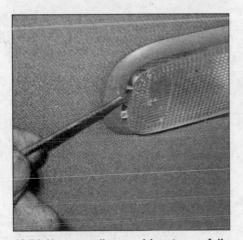

18.74 Use a small screwdriver to carefully pry loose the rear map light lens (2004 and later models)

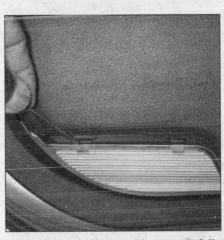

18.77 Use a small screwdriver to carefully pry loose the courtesy door light lens

18.81a To remove an illumination bulb (this one's installed in a hazard flasher switch), turn it counterclockwise . . .

Instrument panel switch bulbs

Refer to illustrations 18.81a and 18.81b

Note: *All of the illuminated instruments and switches on the dash use small replaceable light bulbs (they're actually LEDs). Although you must use the correctly rated bulb for each specific application, the replacement procedure is identical for all of these bulbs.*

80   Remove the switch with the burned out bulb (for dashboard switches, see Section 10; for instrument cluster, see Section 11).

81   To remove the old bulb, use a screwdriver to turn it counterclockwise, then pull it out **(see illustrations)**. To install a new bulb, align the two lugs on the bulb holder with the cutouts in the mounting hole, then insert the bulb into its mounting hole and turn it clockwise until it locks into place.

82   Install the dashboard switch (see Section 10) or instrument cluster (see Section 11).

Trunk light bulb

Refer to illustration 18.83

83   Open the trunk and locate the trunk light

18.81b . . . and pull it out of its switch

lens in the trunk trim panel. Remove the trunk light lens **(see illustration)**.

84   To remove the old bulb, pull it straight out.

18.83 Carefully pry down the trunk light lens

85   Install the lens. Make sure that it snaps into place.

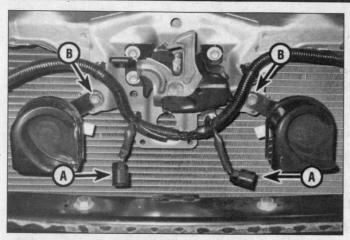

19.2 To detach the horn(s), disconnect the electrical connector(s) (A) and remove the horn mounting bracket bolt(s) (B) (1999 through 2003 models)

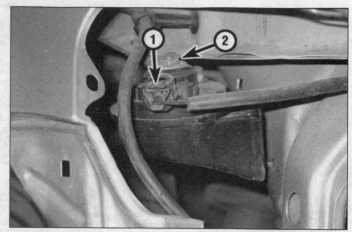

19.7 To detach either horn, depress the release tab (1) and disconnect the electrical connector, then remove the horn mounting nut (2) (right horn shown, headlight housing and front bumper cover removed for clarity) (2004 and later models)

19 Horn - replacement

1999 through 2003 models

Refer to illustration 19.2

Note: *The two horns are located in front of the radiator and condenser.*

1 Remove the front bulkhead cover (radiator cover) (see Chapter 11, Section 9).
2 Disconnect the electrical connector(s) from the horn(s) **(see illustration)**.
3 Remove the horn mounting bracket bolt(s) and remove the horn(s).
4 Installation is the reverse of removal.

2004 and later models

Refer to illustration 19.7

Note: *The two horns are located in the voids between the front wheel wells and below the headlight housings. You can access either horn by removing the left or right front wheel well splash shield, but for clarity, the accompanying photo depicts the right horn assembly*

with the headlight housing and bumper cover removed. This procedure applies to either horn.

5 Loosen the left or right front wheel lug nuts. Raise the front of the vehicle and place it securely on jackstands. Remove the left or right front wheel.
6 Remove the front wheel well inner splash shield (see *Front fender - removal and installation* in Chapter 11).
7 Disconnect the electrical connector from the horn **(see illustration)**.
8 Remove the horn mounting bracket bolt and remove the horn.
9 Installation is the reverse of removal.

20 Wiper motor - check and replacement

Wiper motor circuit check

Note: *Refer to the wiring diagrams for wire colors in the following checks. When checking*

for voltage, probe a grounded 12-volt test light to each terminal at a connector until it lights; this verifies voltage (power) at the terminal. If the following checks fail to locate the problem, have the system diagnosed by a dealer service department or other properly equipped repair facility.

1 If the wipers work slowly, make sure that the battery is fully charged and in good condition (see Chapters 1 and 5). If the battery is in good shape, remove the wiper motor (see *Wiper motor replacement*) and operate the wiper arms by hand. Check for binding linkage and pivots. Lubricate or repair the linkage or pivots as necessary. Reinstall the wiper motor. If the wipers still operate slowly, check for loose or corroded connections, especially the ground connection. If all connections look OK, replace the motor.
2 If the wipers fail to operate when activated, check the fuse (see Section 3). If the fuse is OK, connect a jumper wire between the wiper motor's ground terminal and ground, then retest. If the motor works now, repair the ground connection. If the motor still doesn't work, turn the wiper switch to the HI position and check for voltage at the motor. **Note:** *Remove the hood seal and cowl covers (see Chapter 11) and disconnect the electrical connector (see Step 8 below).*
3 If there's voltage at the connector, remove the motor and check it off the vehicle with fused jumper wires from the battery. If the motor now works, check for binding linkage (see Step 1). If the motor still doesn't work, replace it. If there's no voltage to the motor, check for voltage at the wiper control relays. If there's voltage at the wiper control relays and no voltage at the wiper motor, have the switch tested. If the switch is OK, the wiper control relay is probably bad. See Section 5 for relay testing.
4 If the interval (delay) function is inoperative, check the continuity of all the wiring between the switch and the wiper control module.

20.6a To access the windshield wiper arm retaining nut, pull off the trim cap, then remove the nut

20.6b Mark the relationship of the wiper arm to its shaft to ensure that the arm is correctly positioned on installation

20.8 Disconnect the electrical connector (A) from the windshield wiper motor, then detach the harness from the clip (B)

20.9 Windshield wiper motor and linkage bolts

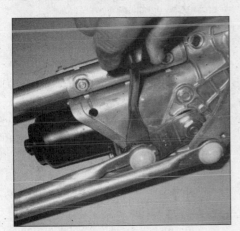

20.10 Carefully pry apart the link arm and the crank arm

20.11 Before removing the crank arm from the wiper motor shaft, rotate the crank arm so that the arrow on the arm is aligned with the center mark of the three alignment marks on the wiper motor mounting bracket

20.12 Separate the crank arm from the motor shaft

5   If the wipers fail to park (if they stop at the position that they're in when the switch is turned off instead of returning to their normal off position), turn the wiper switch to OFF and the ignition switch to ON, then check for voltage at the park feed wire of the wiper motor connector. If no voltage is present, check for an open circuit between the wiper motor and the fuse panel.

Wiper motor replacement

Refer to illustrations 20.6a, 20.6b, 20.8, 20.9, 20.10, 20.11, 20.12 and 20.13

Note: *The photos accompanying this Section depict a typical wiper motor and link assembly used on 2004 and later models. However, the unit used on 1999 through 2003 models is similar.*

6   Open the hood. Remove the covers from the windshield wiper arm retaining nuts **(see illustration)**, then remove the wiper arm retaining nuts. Mark the position of each wiper arm in relation to its shaft **(see illustration)**, then remove the wiper arms.

7   Remove the hood seals and cowl covers (see *Cowl and engine compartment covers -*

removal and installation in Chapter 11).

8   Disconnect the electrical connector from the windshield wiper motor, detach the harness clip and set the harness aside **(see illustration)**.

9   Remove the windshield wiper linkage/ motor assembly mounting bolts **(see illustration)** and remove the windshield wiper motor and wiper linkage as a single assembly.

10   Separate the windshield wiper linkage from the wiper motor **(see illustration)**.

11   Before removing the crank arm nut, make sure that the arrow on the crank arm is pointing toward the center mark of the three alignment marks on the motor bracket **(see illustration)**. This ensures that the crank arm will be at the proper angle when you reconnect the link arm.

12   Remove the crank arm nut, then pry the crank arm off the motor shaft **(see illustration)**.

13   Remove the windshield wiper motor mounting bolts **(see illustration)** and sepa-

20.13 To detach the wiper motor from its mounting bracket, remove these three bolts

rate the motor from its mounting bracket.

14   Before installing the windshield wiper linkage (especially if you're installing the old linkage), be sure to grease all the spherical bearings that connect the linkage arms.

15   Installation is otherwise the reverse of removal. Be sure to align the marks you

made between the linkage arm and the motor mounting bracket and between the windshield wiper arm and the motor shaft.

16 Turn on the windshield wipers and verify that the wiper motor operates correctly in all modes.

21 Electric side view mirrors - general information

1 Most electric rear view mirrors use two motors to move the glass; one for up-and-down adjustments and one for left-right adjustments.

2 During mirror adjustment, the power mirror adjustment switch sends voltage to the left or right side mirror. With the ignition key turned to ON (engine not running), operate the mirror adjustment switch through all of its functions (left-right and up-down) for both the left and right side mirrors.

3 Listen carefully for the sound of the electric motors running in the mirrors.

4 If you can hear the motors but the mirror glass doesn't move, there's a problem with the drive mechanism inside the mirror.

5 If the mirrors do not operate and no sound comes from the mirrors, check the fuse (see Section 3).

6 If the fuse is OK, remove the power mirror adjustment switch (see *Door trim panels - removal and installation* in Chapter 11). Have the switch continuity checked by a dealership service department or other qualified automobile repair facility.

7 Inspect the ground connections. Make sure that they're tight and corrosion-free.

8 If the mirror still doesn't work, remove the mirror (see Chapter 11) and check the wires at the mirror for voltage.

9 If there is no voltage in any switch position, check the circuit between the mirror and the adjustment switch for opens and shorts.

10 If there's voltage, remove the mirror and test it off the vehicle with jumper wires. If the mirror fails this test, replace it.

22 Cruise control system - general information

1999 through 2003 models

1 The cruise control system maintains the vehicle speed that you select until you depress the brake pedal, depress the clutch pedal (on models with a manual transaxle), shift the transaxle (models with an automatic transaxle), or turn the system off. The cruise control system consists of the following components:

Cruise control combination switch (on the steering wheel)
Cruise main and cruise control indicators (LEDs on the instrument cluster that light up when cruise control system is on)
Cruise control unit (the computer that controls the cruise control actuator)

Cruise control actuator (the electric motor that controls the actuator cable)
Actuator cable (controls the angle of the throttle plate inside the throttle body)
Brake pedal position switch (located at upper end of brake pedal; deactivates the system when pedal is depressed)
Clutch pedal position switch (located at upper end of clutch pedal; deactivates system when clutch pedal is depressed)
Transmission range switch (located on transaxle; deactivates system when automatic transaxle is downshifted)

2 When you select the speed that you want to maintain, the cruise control unit takes control of the throttle plate in the throttle body. It maintains the selected speed with the cruise control actuator, which is connected to the throttle cam on the throttle body by the actuator cable. The system maintains the selected speed until you turn it off, depress the brake or clutch pedal (manual transaxle) or shift the transmission (automatic transaxle).

3 The diagnostic procedures for troubleshooting the cruise control system are beyond the scope of this manual, but the following general procedures will help you identify common problems.

4 Check the fuses (see Section 3).

5 Have an assistant operate the brake lights while you check their operation (voltage from the brake light switch deactivates the cruise control).

6 If the brake lights don't come on or stay on all the time, correct the problem and retest the cruise control system.

7 Visually inspect the actuator cable between the cruise control actuator and the throttle cam for freedom of movement. The cable should move freely without binding or sticking. If the cable is kinked or frayed, replace it.

8 Test drive the vehicle to determine if the cruise control is now working. If it isn't, take it to a dealer service department or an automotive electrical specialist for further diagnosis.

2004 and later models

9 On these models, the cruise control system is under the direct control of the Powertrain Control Module (PCM). Under the hood, there is no actuator, nor actuator cable, because these models have an electronically controlled throttle body (no accelerator cable). When you select the speed that you want to maintain, the PCM controls vehicle speed by opening and closing the throttle plate by means of a computer-controlled solenoid (motor) on the throttle body.

10 The diagnostic procedures for troubleshooting the cruise control system are beyond the scope of this manual, but if the system can't be set, or the set speed doesn't cancel when the brake pedal is depressed, check the fuses. Start with the fuses in the engine compartment fuse and relay box, then check the fuses in the under-dash fuse and relay box.

11 Other than checking the fuses and electrical connections, the diagnostic procedures

for troubleshooting the cruise control system on these models are beyond the scope of this manual. A dealer service department or other qualified repair shop should handle any further testing.

23 Power window system - general information

1 The power window system operates electric motors, mounted in the doors, which lower and raise the windows. The system consists of the control switches, the motors, regulators, glass mechanisms and associated wiring.

2 The power windows can be lowered and raised from the master control switch by the driver or by remote switches located at the individual windows. Each window has a separate motor, which is reversible. The position of the control switch determines the polarity and therefore the direction of operation.

3 The circuit is protected by a fuse and a circuit breaker. Each motor is also equipped with an internal circuit breaker, this prevents one stuck window from disabling the whole system.

4 The power window system will only operate when the ignition switch is turned to ON. There's also a main switch at the master power window control panel (in the driver's door) which, when activated, disables the switches at the rear windows and the switch at the passenger's window. So if there's a problem with the passenger window or with either of the rear windows, make sure that it's not simply a matter of flipping the main switch before proceeding.

5 The procedures listed below are general in nature, so if you can't find the problem using them, take the vehicle to a dealer service department.

6 If the power windows won't operate, always check the fuses and relays first (see Sections 3 and 5). Also verify that there's voltage to the relay and that the relay is well grounded.

7 If only the rear windows are inoperative, or if the windows only operate from the master control switch, check the main switch for continuity in the unlocked position. Replace it if it doesn't have continuity (see *Door trim panel - removal and installation* in Chapter 11).

8 Check the wiring between the switches and the fuse and relay box for continuity. Repair the wiring, if necessary.

9 If only one window is inoperative from the main switch, try the other control switch at the window. **Note:** *This doesn't apply to the driver's door window.*

10 If the same window works from one switch, but not the other, check the switch for continuity.

11 If the switch tests OK, check for a short or open in the circuit between the affected switch and the window motor.

12 If one window is inoperative from both switches, remove the trim panel from the affected door (see *Door trim panel - removal*

and installation in Chapter 11) and check for voltage at the switch and at the motor while the switch is operated.

13   If voltage is reaching the motor, disconnect the glass from the regulator (see Chapter 11). Move the window up-and-down by hand while checking for binding and damage. Also check for binding and damage to the regulator. If the regulator is not damaged and the window moves up and down smoothly, replace the motor. If there's binding or damage, lubricate, repair or replace parts, as necessary.

14   If voltage isn't reaching the motor, check the wiring in the circuit for continuity between the switches and motors. You'll need to consult the wiring diagram for the vehicle.

24   Power door lock system - general information

1   A power door lock system operates the door lock actuators mounted in each door. The system consists of the switches, actuators, a control unit and associated wiring. On some models, the power door lock system is part of the security alarm system. On these models, the power door lock system is more complex, and more difficult to diagnose. Therefore, home troubleshooting is limited to simple checks of the wiring connections and actuators for minor faults that can be easily repaired.

2   Power door lock systems are operated by bi-directional solenoids located in the doors. The lock switches have two operating positions: LOCK and UNLOCK. When activated, the switch sends a ground signal to the door lock control unit to lock or unlock the doors. Depending on which way the switch is activated, the control unit reverses polarity to the solenoids, allowing the two sides of the circuit to be used alternately as the feed (positive) and ground side.

3   The following general guidelines should help you quickly identify and repair typical problems. If you're unable to locate the trouble using these guidelines, consult a dealer service department.

4   Always check the fuses first (see Section 3 and your owner's manual).

5   Operate the door lock switches in both directions (LOCK and UNLOCK) with the engine off. Listen for the click of the solenoids operating.

6   Test the switches for continuity. Remove the switches and have them checked by a dealer service department.

7   Check the wiring between the switches, control unit and solenoids for continuity. Repair the wiring if there's no continuity.

8   Check for a bad ground at the switches and at the control unit.

9   If only one lock solenoid doesn't operate, remove the trim panel from the door with the bad solenoid (see *Door trim panel - removal and installation* in Chapter 11) and check for voltage at the solenoid while

the lock switch is operated. One of the wires should have voltage in the Lock position; the other should have voltage in the Unlock position.

10   If the inoperative solenoid is receiving voltage, replace the solenoid.

11   If the inoperative solenoid isn't receiving voltage, check for an open or short in the wire between the lock solenoid and the control unit. **Note:** *Wire harnesses typically break between the body and door, because repeatedly opening and closing the door fatigues and eventually breaks the wires.*

25   Daytime Running Lights (DRL) - general information

The Daytime Running Lights (DRL) system illuminates the headlights whenever the engine is running. The only exception is with the engine running and the parking brake engaged. Once the parking brake is released, the lights will remain on as long as the ignition switch is on, even if the parking brake is later applied. The DRL system supplies reduced power to the headlights during daylight operation to prolonging headlight life.

26   Airbag system - general information

General information

1   All models are equipped with a Supplemental Restraint System (SRS), more commonly known as airbags. This system is designed to protect the driver, and the front seat passenger, from serious injury in the event of a head-on or frontal collision. It uses a pair of crash sensors mounted behind the front bumper. The airbag assemblies are mounted on the steering wheel and inside the passenger's end of the dash.

2   Some models are also equipped with side-impact airbags. On two-door models, the side-impact sensors are mounted in the sides of the front seat backs. On four-door models, there are side-impact sensors in the sides of the front seat backs and on the inside of the body, near the trailing edges of the rear doors. Additionally, other models are equipped with side curtain airbags, which are concealed behind the headliner and extend from the front of the interior to the rear.

Airbag module

Driver's side airbag

3   The airbag inflator module contains a housing incorporating the airbag and inflator unit, mounted in the center of the steering wheel. The inflator assembly is mounted on the back of the housing over a hole through which gas is expelled, inflating the bag almost instantaneously when an electrical signal is sent from the SRS unit (the system's processor). A clockspring on the steering column

under the steering wheel carries this signal to the module. This clockspring assembly can transmit an electrical signal regardless of steering wheel position. The igniter in the airbag converts the electrical signal to heat and ignites the powder, which inflates the bag.

4   For information on how to remove and install the driver's side airbag, refer to *Steering wheel - removal and installation* in Chapter 10.

Passenger's side airbag

5   The airbag is mounted in the upper part of the passenger's end of the dashboard, above the glove box. The passenger's side airbag is considerably larger than the steering wheel-mounted unit. The airbag trim cover on top of the dash splits open when the bag is inflated.

SRS control unit

6   This unit supplies the current to the airbag system in the event of the collision, even if battery power is cut off. It checks this system every time the vehicle is started, causing the SRS light to go on, then off, if the system is operating correctly. If there is a fault in the system, the light will go on and stay on, or it will flash, or the dash will make a beeping sound. If this happens, take the vehicle to your dealer immediately for service.

Disarming the system and other precautions

Warning: *Failure to follow these precautions could result in accidental deployment of the airbag and personal injury.*

7   Whenever working in the vicinity of the steering wheel, the right end of the dashboard or any of the other SRS system components, the system must be disarmed. To disarm the system:

 a) *Point the wheels straight ahead and turn the key to the LOCK position.*
 b) *Disconnect the cable from the negative battery terminal. Refer to Chapter 5, Section 1 for the disconnecting procedure.*
 c) *WAIT AT LEAST THREE MINUTES FOR THE BACK-UP POWER SUPPLY TO BE DEPLETED.*

8   Whenever handling an airbag module, always keep the airbag opening side (the trim, or upholstered side) pointed away from your body. Never place the airbag module on a workbench or other surface with the airbag opening facing the surface. Always place the airbag module in a safe location with the airbag opening facing up.

9   Never measure the resistance of any SRS component or use any electrical test equipment on any of the wiring or components. An ohmmeter has a built-in battery supply that could accidentally deploy the airbag.

10   Never use electrical welding equipment on a vehicle equipped with an airbag without first disconnecting the airbag electrical connectors. The connector for the driver's side airbag is located near the steering column (see *Steering wheel - removal and installation*

in Chapter 10); the connector for the passenger's side airbag is located inside the dash, near the glove box. These connectors - and all SRS component connectors - are bright yellow for easy identification.

11   Never dispose of a live airbag module or seat belt pre-tensioner. Return it to a dealer service department or other qualified repair shop for safe deployment and disposal.

Airbag module removal and installation

12   Refer to Chapter 10, *Steering wheel - removal and installation*, for the driver's side airbag module and clockspring removal and installation procedures.

Impact seat belt retractors

13   All models are equipped with pyrotechnic (explosive) units in the front seat belt retract-ing mechanisms. During an impact that would trigger the airbag system, the airbag control unit also triggers the seat belt retractors. When the pyrotechnic charges go off, they accelerate the retractors to instantly take up any slack in the seat belt system to more fully prepare the driver and front seat passenger for impact.

14   The airbag system should be disabled any time work is done to or around the seats. **Warning:** *Never strike the pillars or floorpan with a hammer or use an impact-driver tool in these areas unless the system is disabled.*

27   Wiring diagrams - general information

Since it isn't possible to include all wiring diagrams for every year covered by this manual, the following diagrams are those that are typical and most commonly needed.

Prior to troubleshooting any circuits, check the fuses and relays to ensure that they're in good condition. Make sure that the battery is correctly charged and check the cable connections (see Chapters 1 and 5).

When checking a circuit, make sure that all connections are clean and tight, with no broken or loose terminals. When disconnecting an electrical connector, do NOT pull on the wires; pull on the two halves of the connector itself.

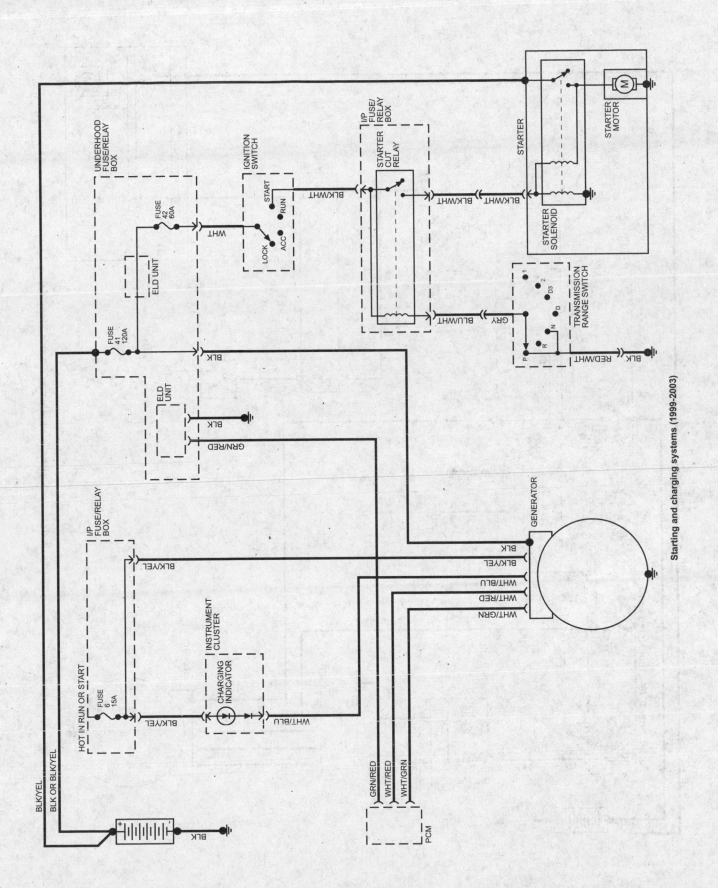

Starting and charging systems (1999-2003)

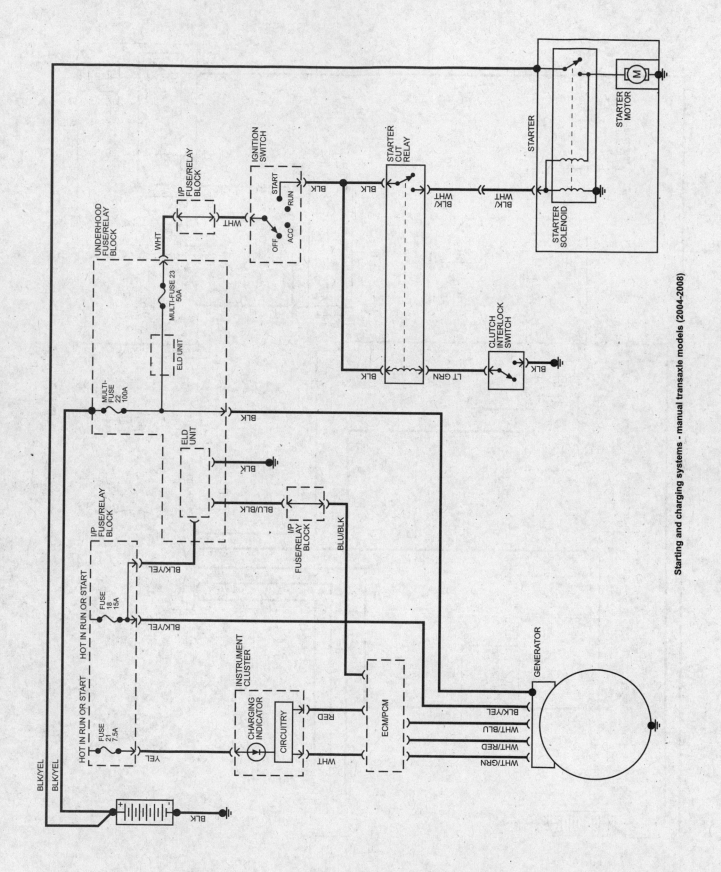

Starting and charging systems - manual transaxle models (2004-2008)

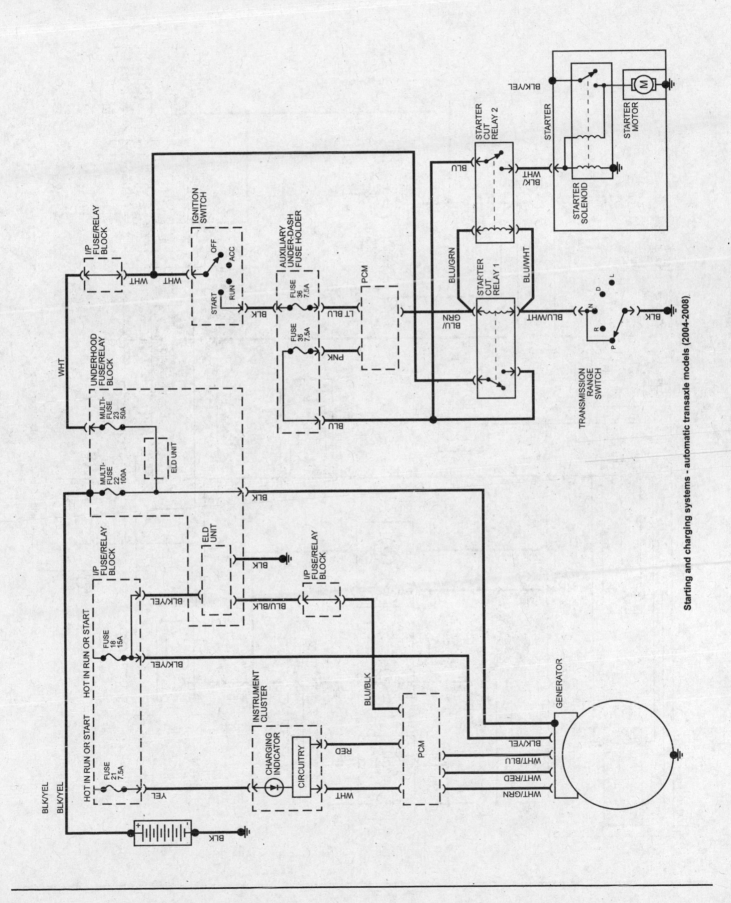

Starting and charging systems - automatic transaxle models (2004-2008)

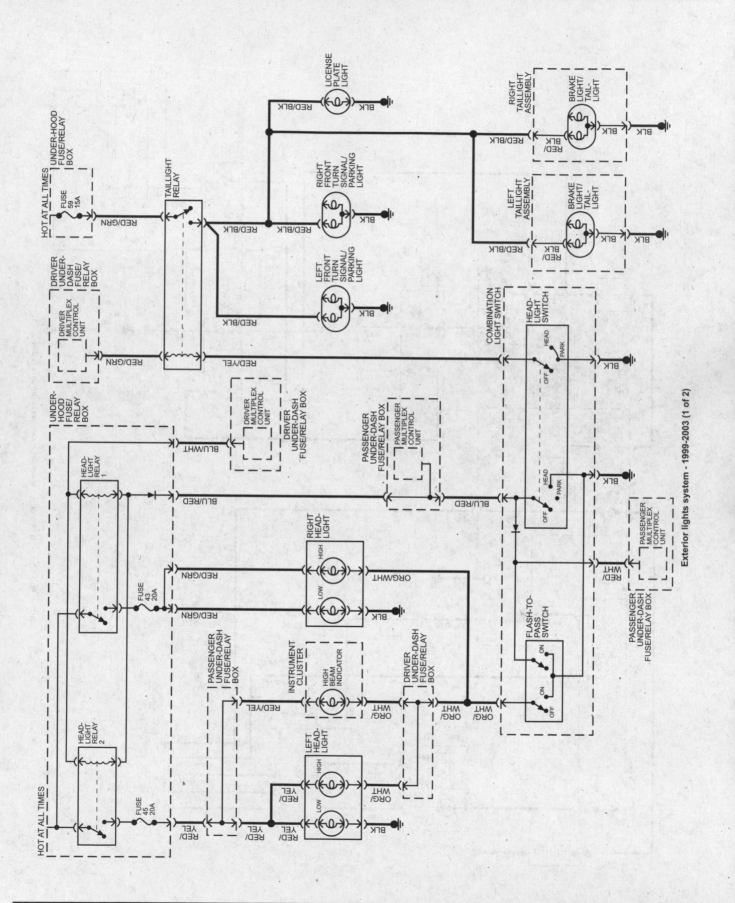

Exterior lights system - 1999-2003 (1 of 2)

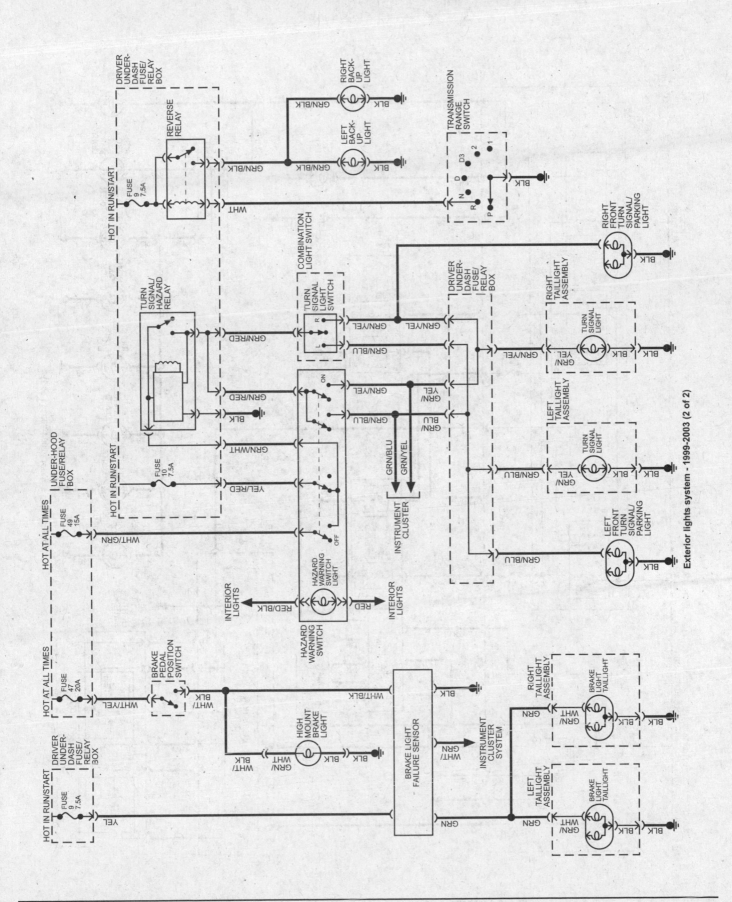

Exterior lights system - 1999-2003 (2 of 2)

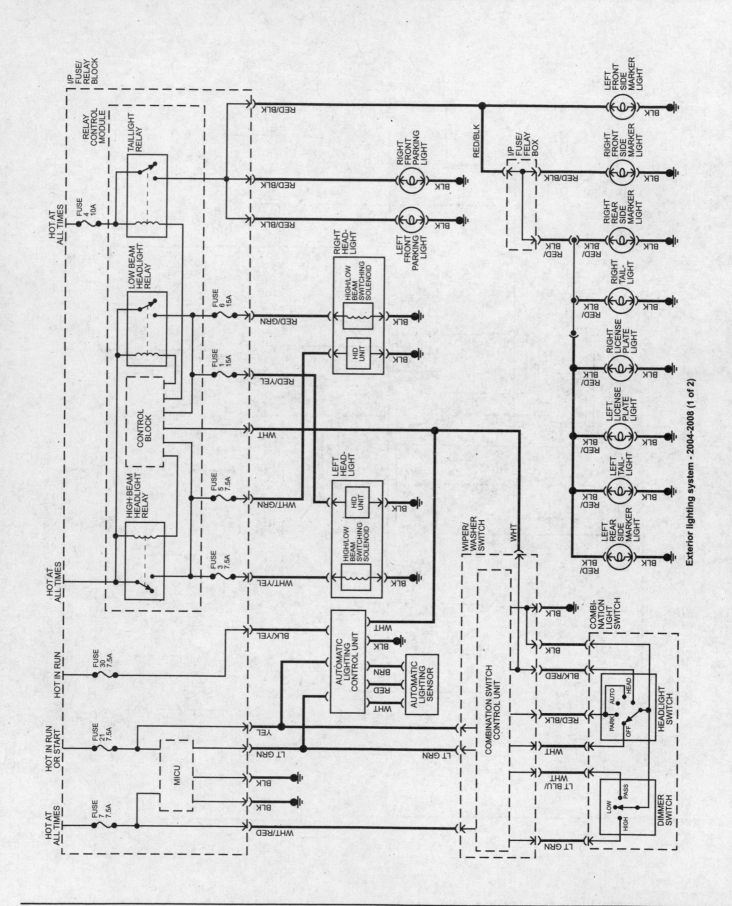

Exterior lighting system - 2004-2008 (1 of 2)

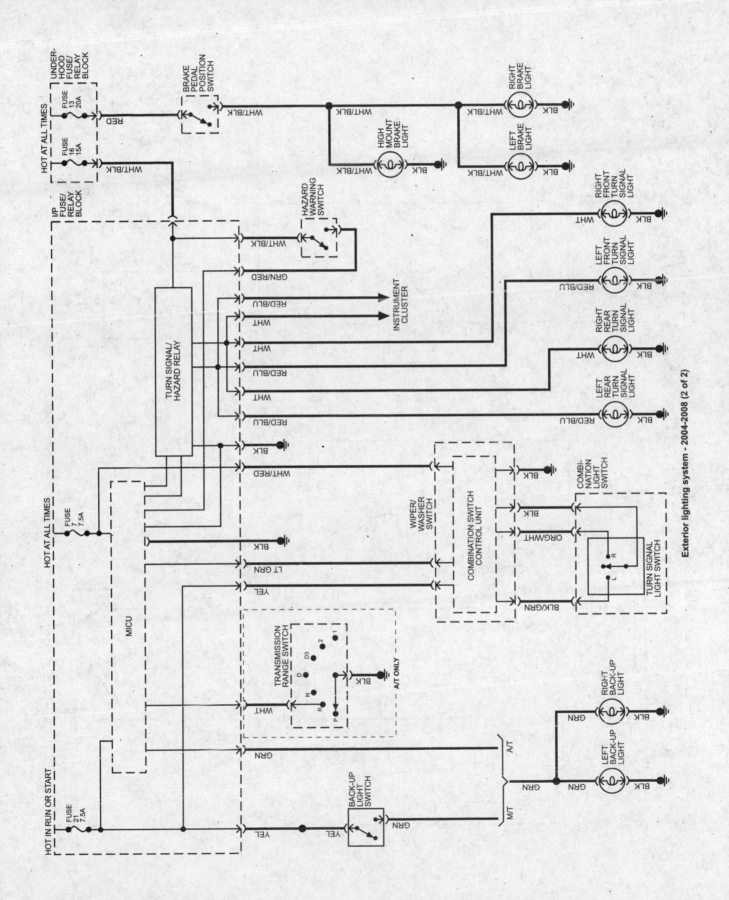

Exterior lighting system - 2004-2008 (2 of 2)

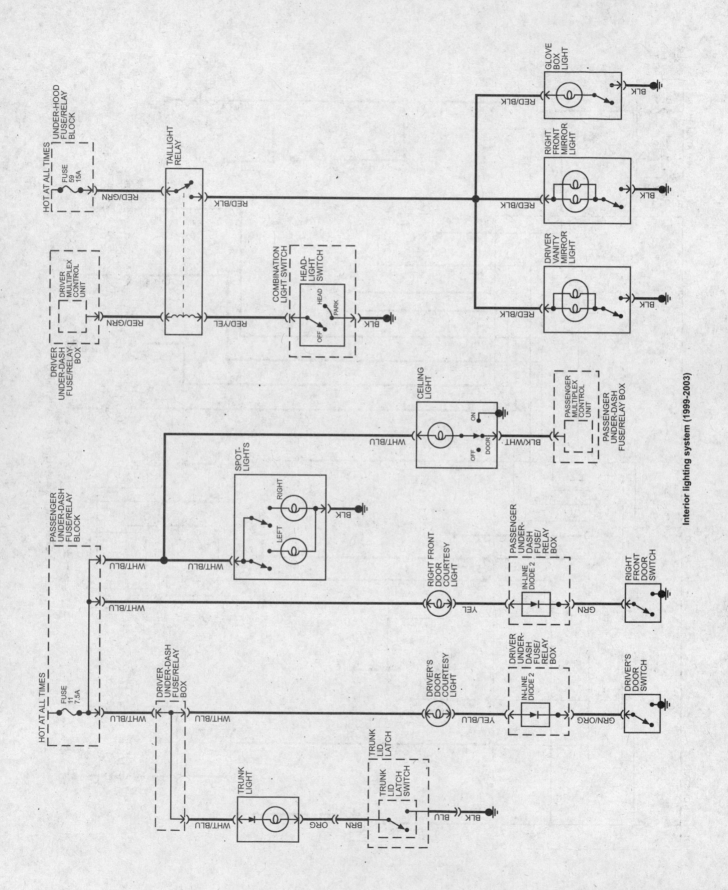

Interior lighting system (1999-2003)

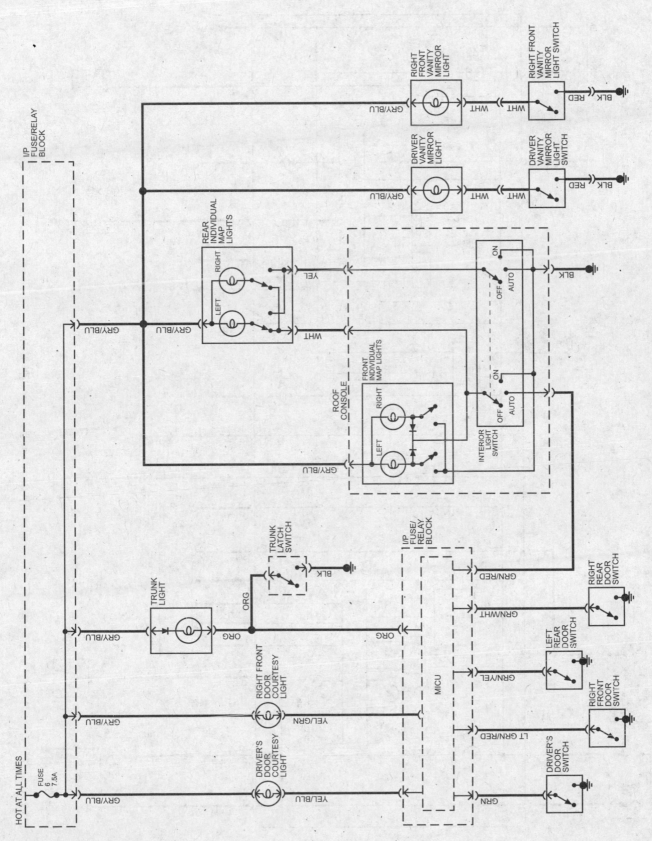

Interior lighting system (2004-2008)

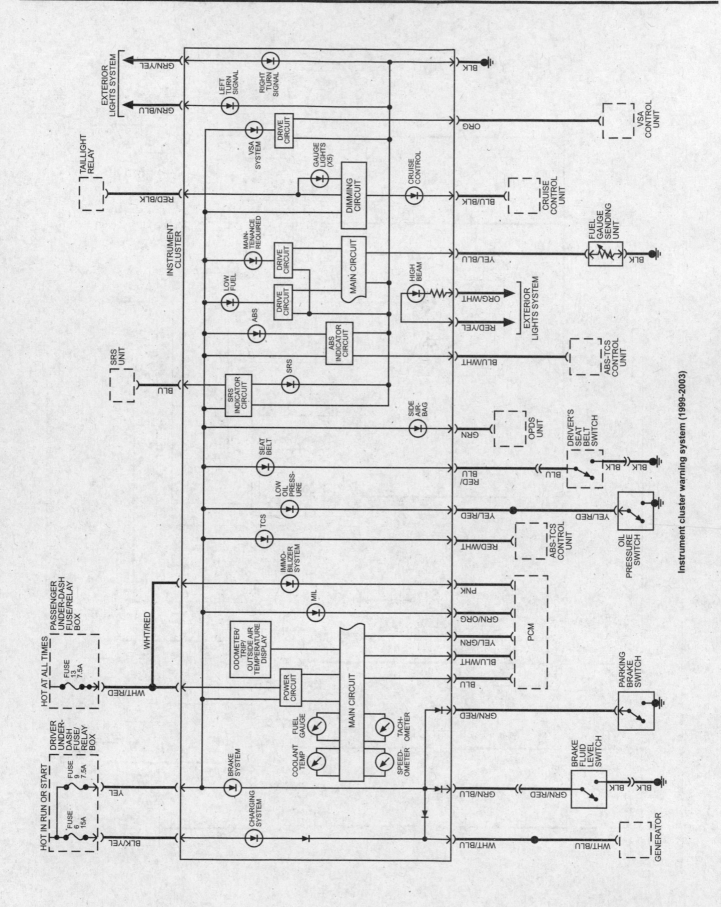

Instrument cluster warning system (1999-2003)

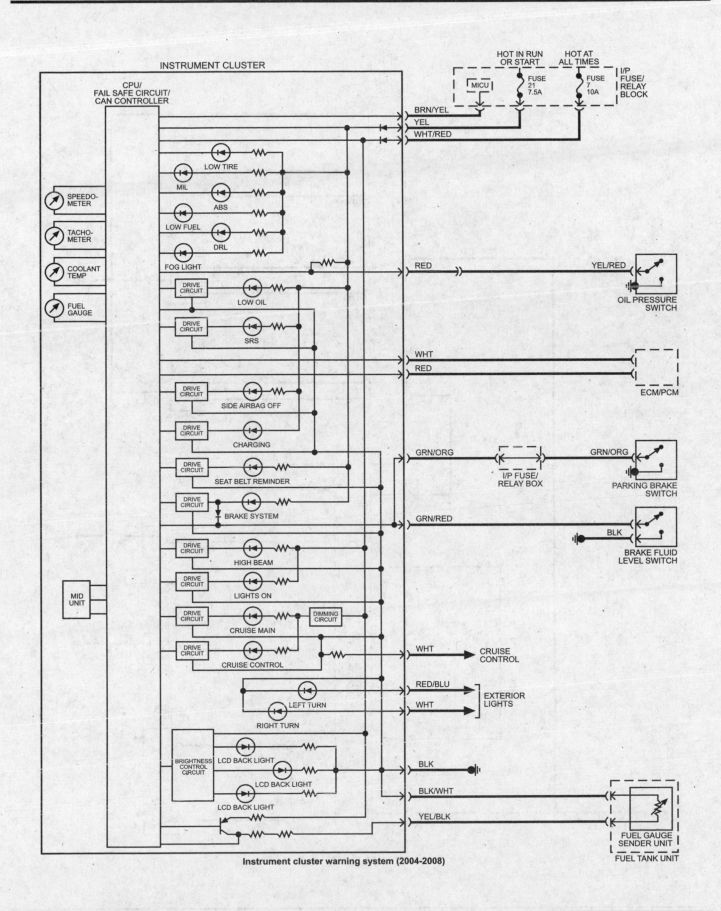

Instrument cluster warning system (2004-2008)

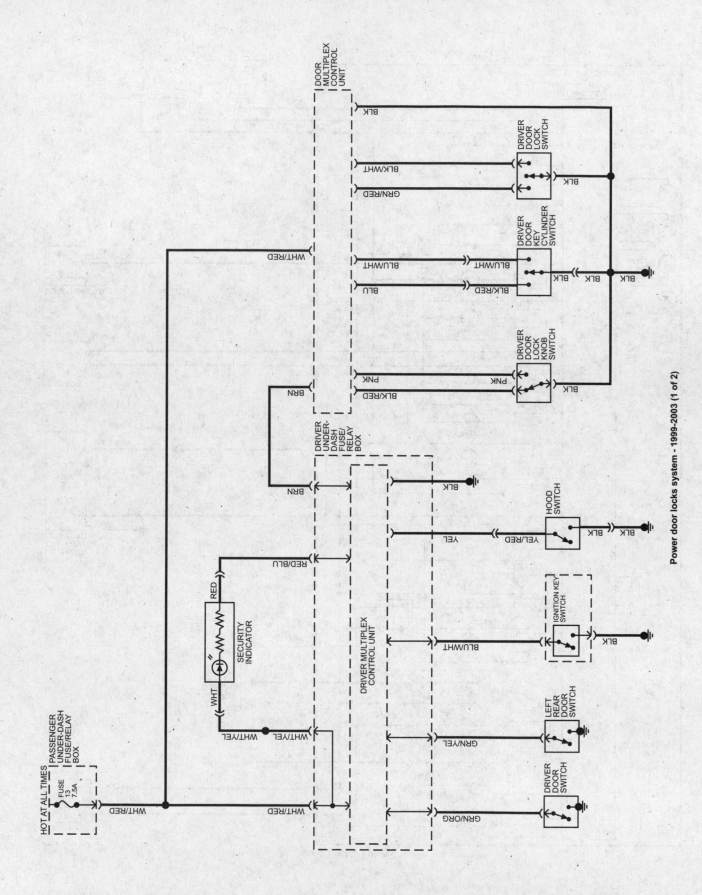

Power door locks system - 1999-2003 (1 of 2)

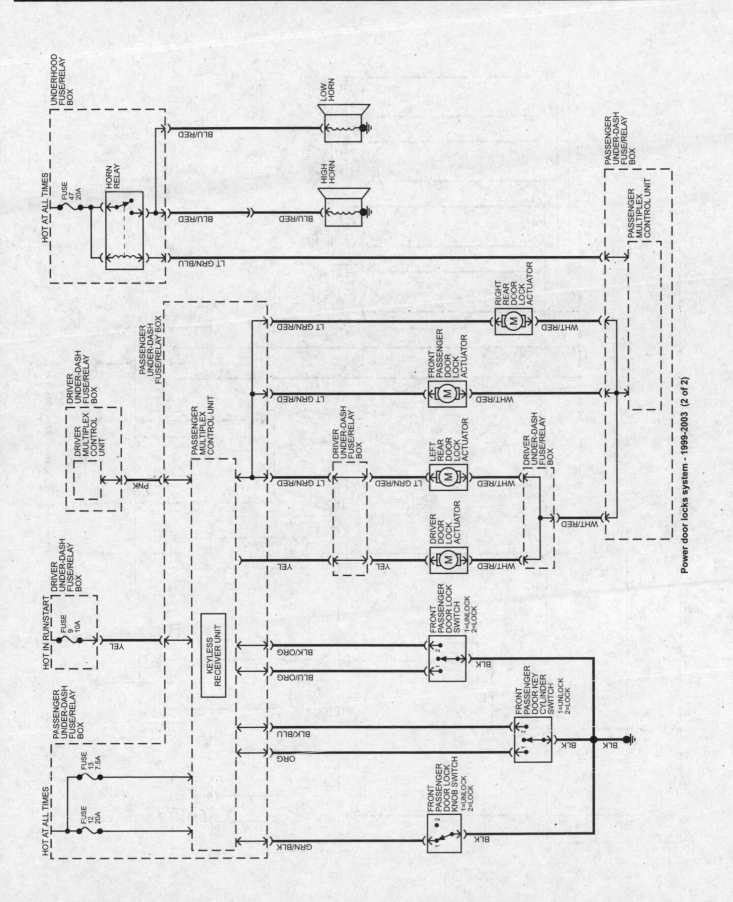

Power door locks system - 1999-2003 (2 of 2)

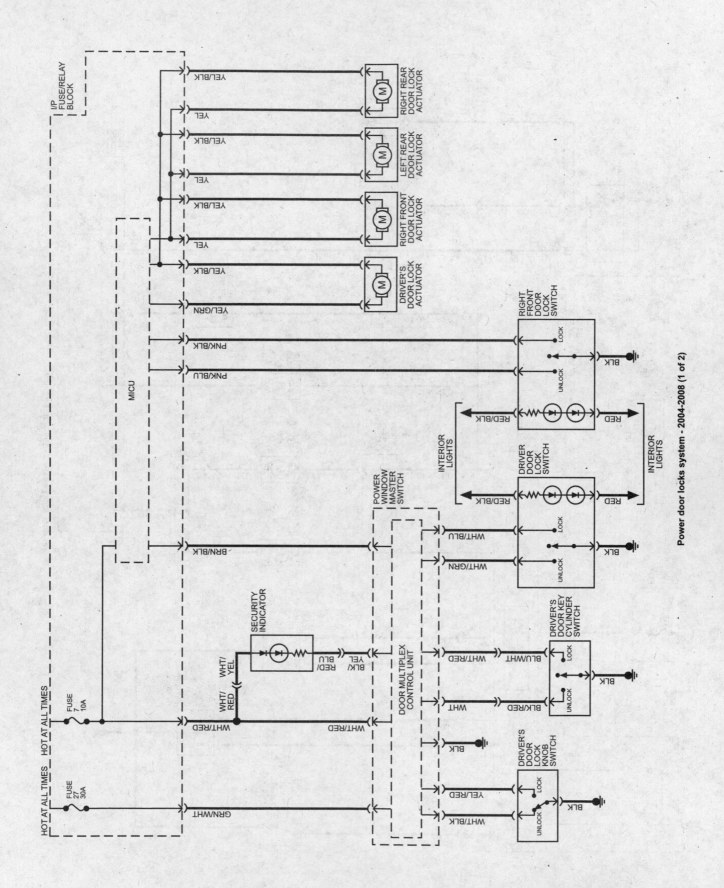

Power door locks system - 2004-2008 (1 of 2)

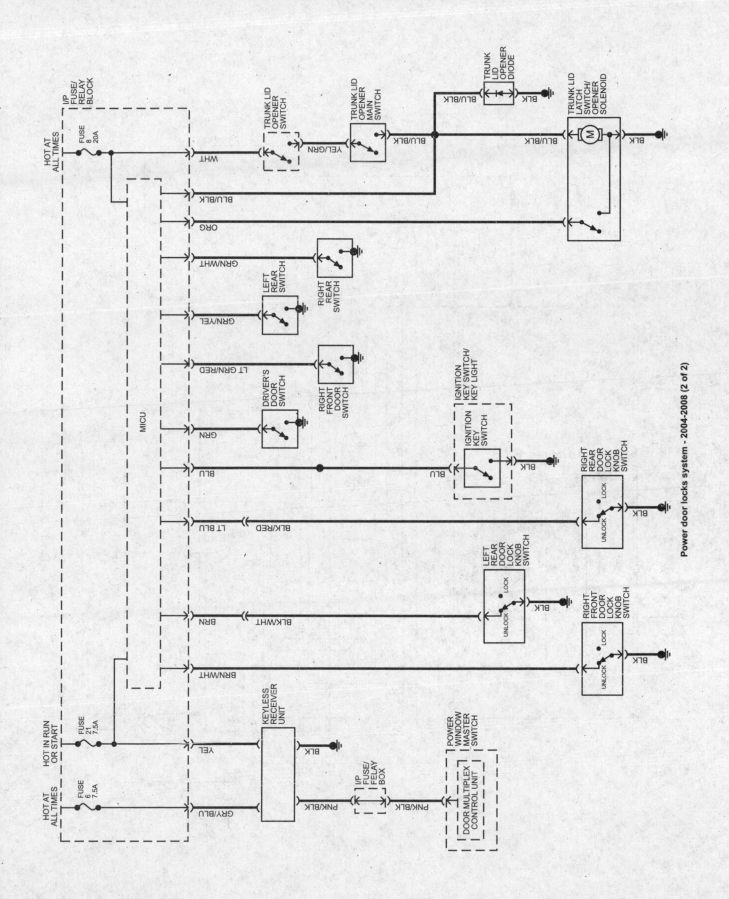

Power door locks system - 2004-2008 (2 of 2)

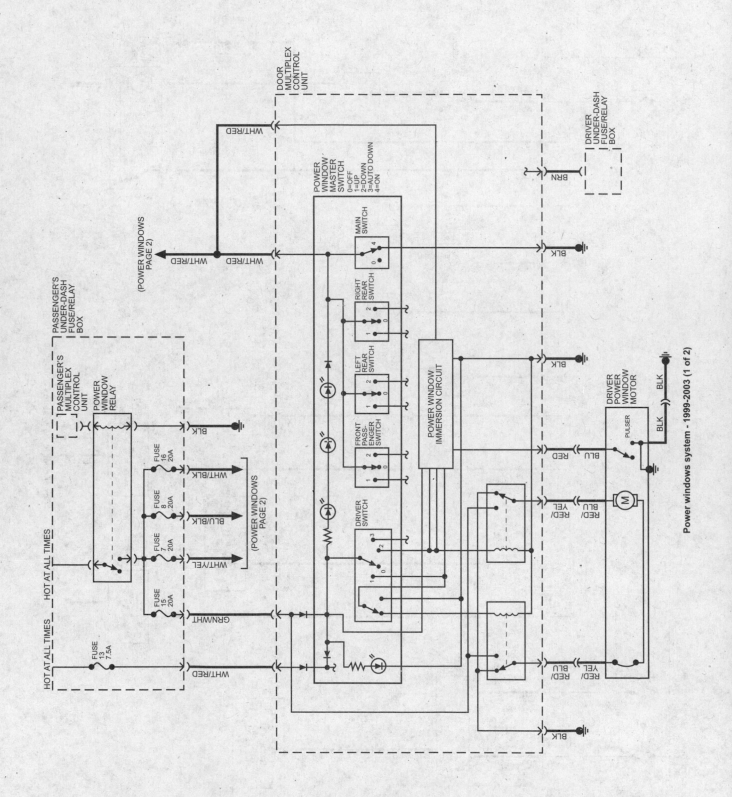

Power windows system - 1999-2003 (1 of 2)

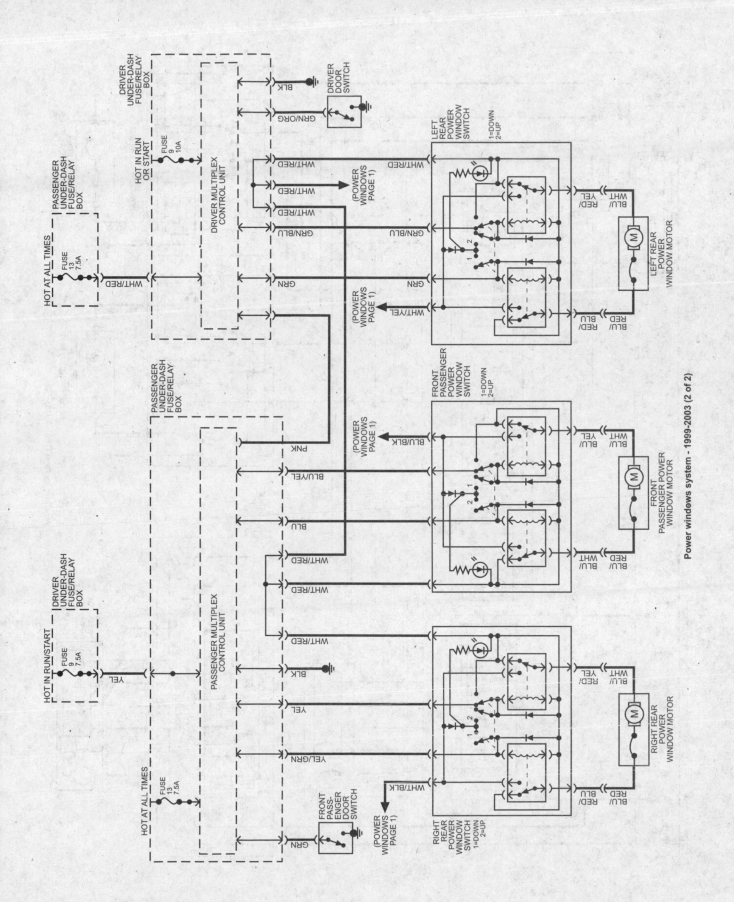

Power windows system - 1999-2003 (2 of 2)

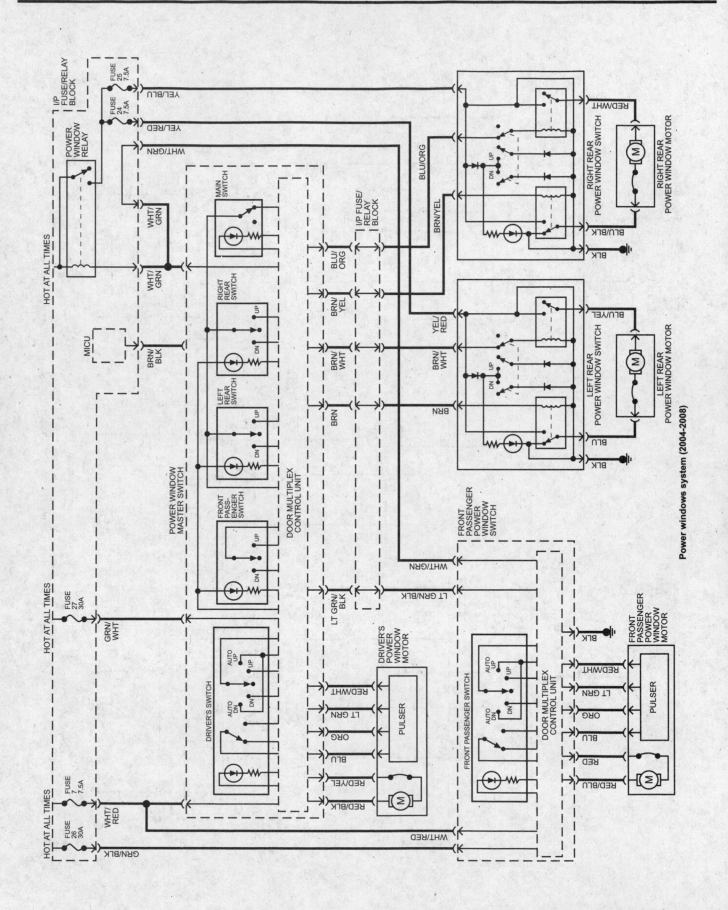

Power windows system (2004-2008)

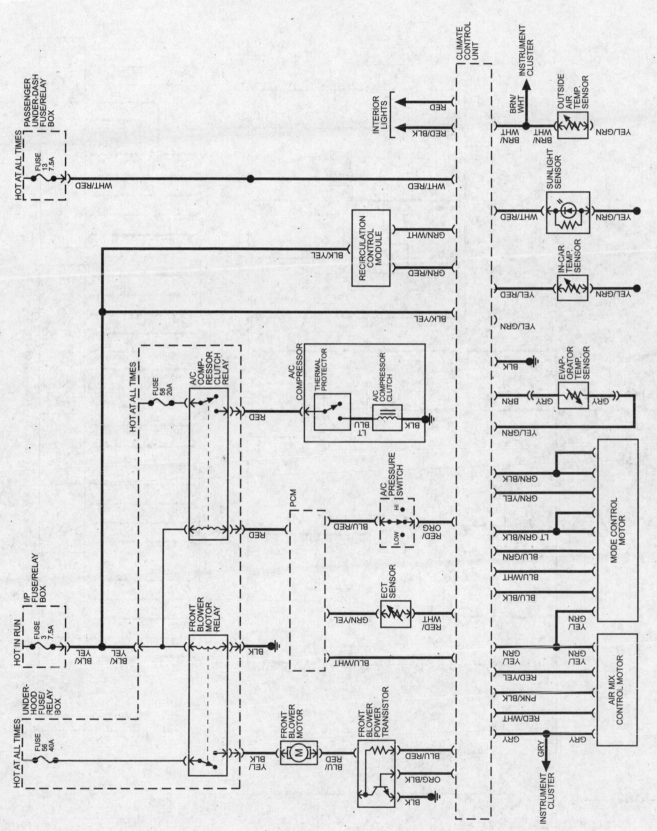

Heating and air conditioning system (1999-2003)

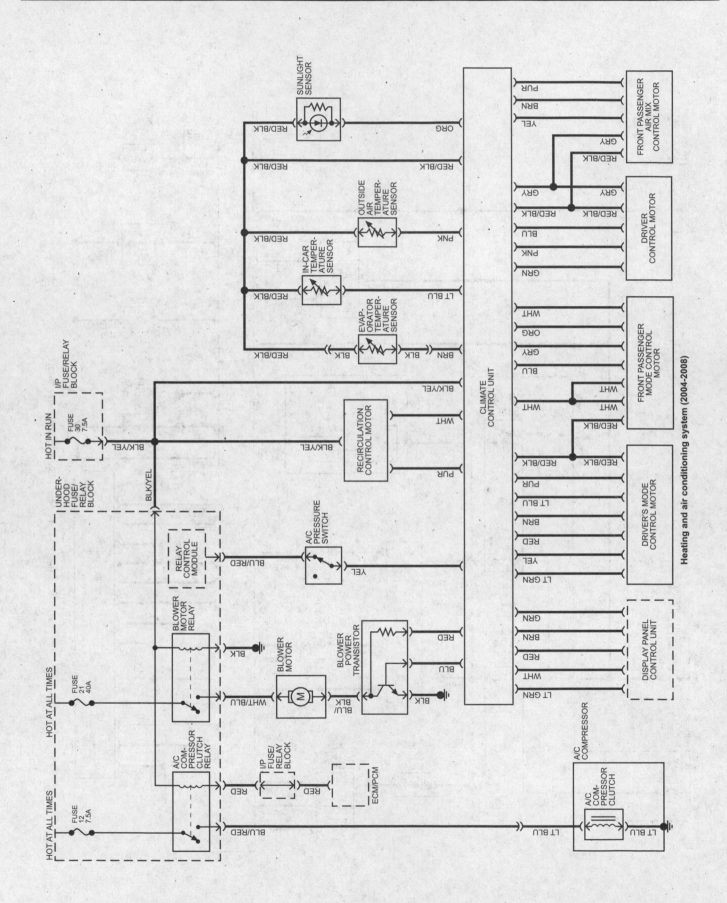

Heating and air conditioning system (2004-2008)

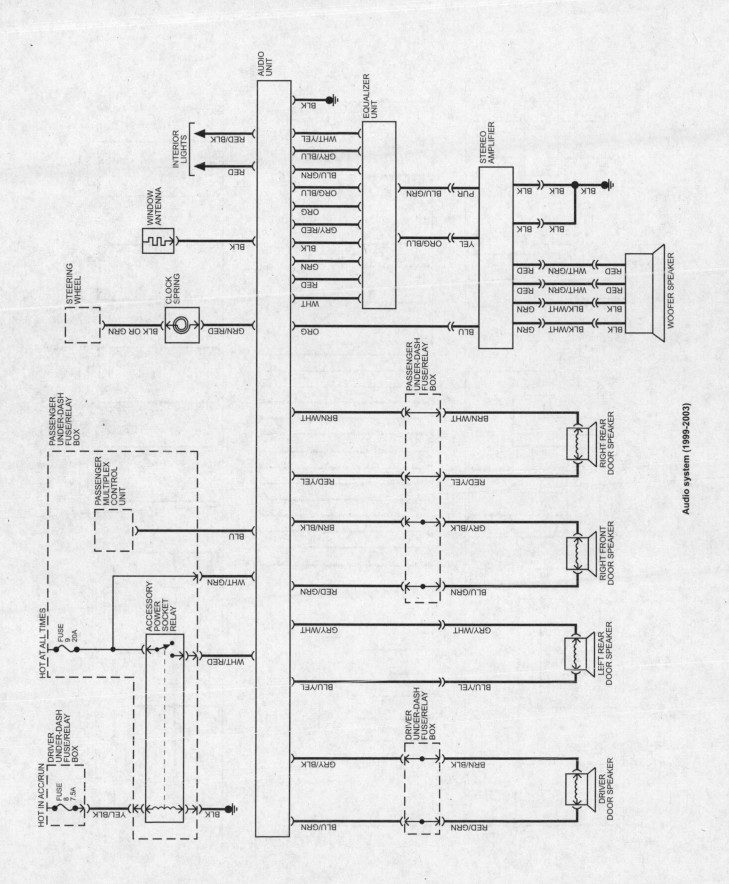

Audio system (1999-2003)

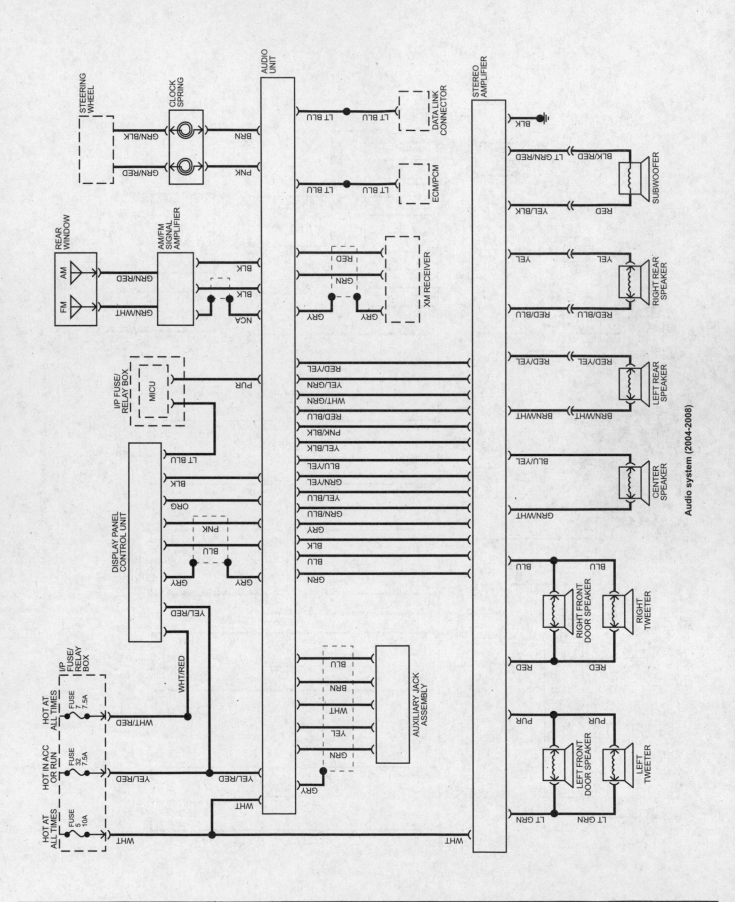

Audio system (2004-2008)

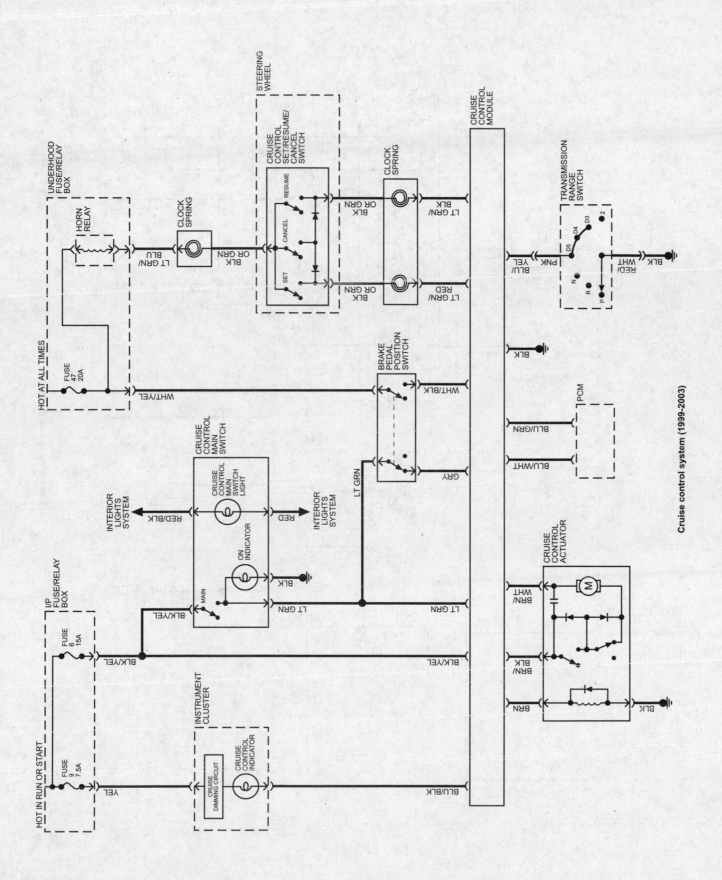

Cruise control system (1999-2003)

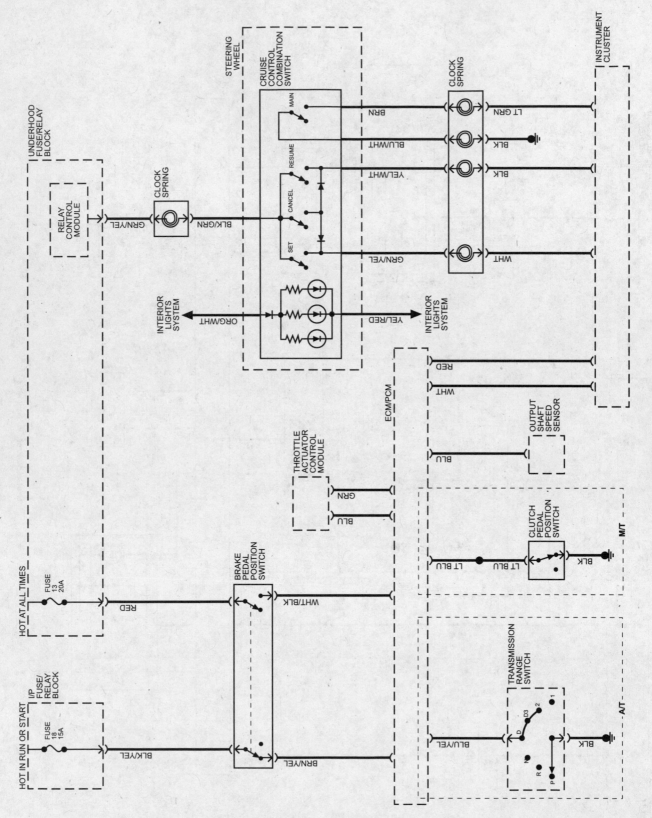

Cruise control system (2004-2008)

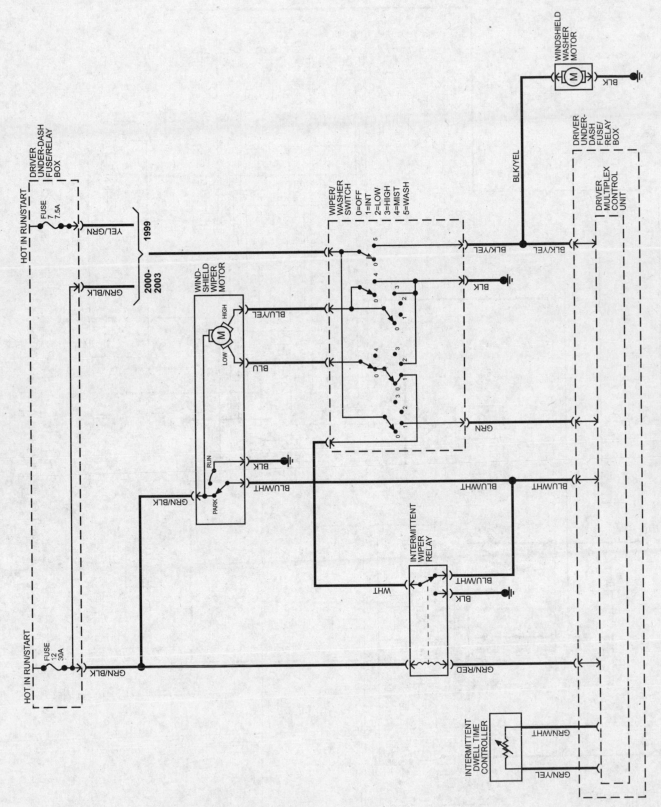

Wiper and washer system (1999-2003)

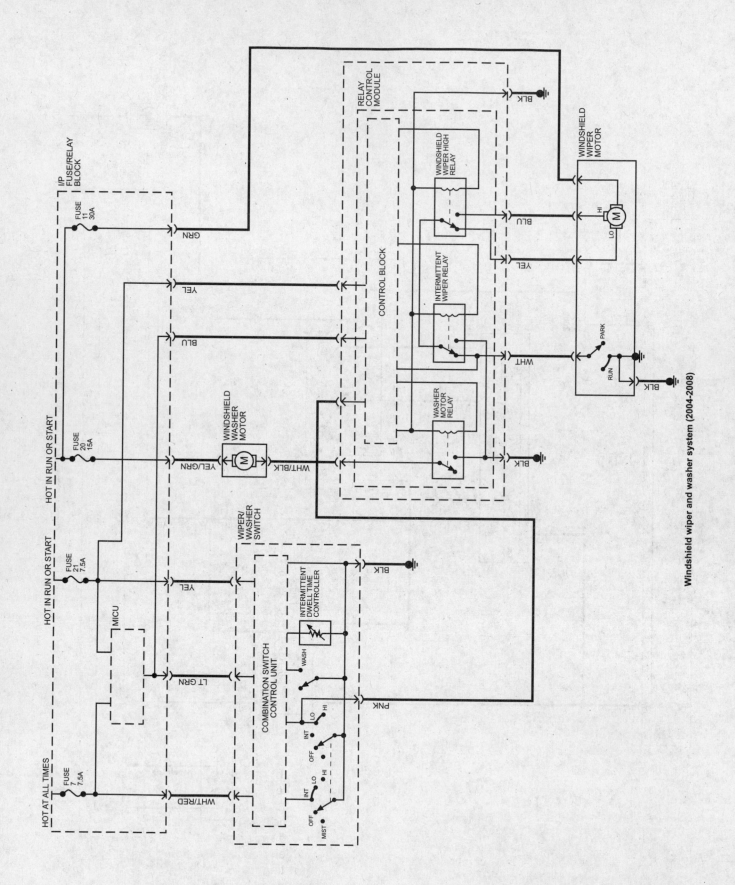

Windshield wiper and washer system (2004-2008)

Index

Notes

Haynes Automotive Manuals

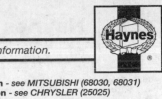

NOTE: If you do not see a listing for your vehicle, consult your local Haynes dealer for the latest product information.

HAYNES XTREME CUSTOMIZING
11101	Sport Compact Customizing
11102	Sport Compact Performance
11110	In-car Entertainment
11150	Sport Utility Vehicle Customizing
11213	Acura
11255	GM Full-size Pick-ups
11314	Ford Focus
11315	Full-size Ford Pick-ups
11373	Honda Civic

ACURA
12020	Integra '86 thru '89 & Legend '86 thru '90
12021	Integra '90 thru '93 & Legend '91 thru '95

AMC
	Jeep CJ - see JEEP (50020)
14020	Mid-size models '70 thru '83
14025	(Renault) Alliance & Encore '83 thru '87

AUDI
15020	4000 all models '80 thru '87
15025	5000 all models '77 thru '83
15026	5000 all models '84 thru '88

AUSTIN-HEALEY
	Sprite - see MG Midget (66015)

BMW
18020	3/5 Series not including diesel or all-wheel drive models '82 thru '92
18021	3-Series incl. Z3 models '92 thru '98
18022	3-Series, E46 chassis '99 thru '05, Z4 models '03 thru '05
18025	320i all 4 cyl models '75 thru '83
18050	1500 thru 2002 except Turbo '59 thru '77

BUICK
19010	Buick Century '97 thru '05
	Century (front-wheel drive) - see GM (38005)
19020	Buick, Oldsmobile & Pontiac Full-size (Front-wheel drive) '85 thru '05
	Buick Electra, LeSabre and Park Avenue; Oldsmobile Delta 88 Royale, Ninety Eight and Regency; Pontiac Bonneville
19025	Buick Oldsmobile & Pontiac Full-size (Rear wheel drive)
	Buick Estate '70 thru '90, Electra '70 thru '84, LeSabre '70 thru '85, Limited '74 thru '79 Oldsmobile Custom Cruiser '70 thru '90, Delta 88 '70 thru '85, Ninety-eight '70 thru '84 Pontiac Bonneville '70 thru '81, Catalina '70 thru '81, Grandville '70 thru '75, Parisienne '83 thru '86
19030	Mid-size Regal & Century all rear-drive models with V6, V8 and Turbo '74 thru '87
	Regal - see GENERAL MOTORS (38010)
	Riviera - see GENERAL MOTORS (38030)
	Roadmaster - see CHEVROLET (24046)
	Skyhawk - see GENERAL MOTORS (38015)
	Skylark - see GM (38020, 38025)
	Somerset - see GENERAL MOTORS (38025)

CADILLAC
21030	Cadillac Rear Wheel Drive all gasoline models '70 thru '93
	Cimarron - see GENERAL MOTORS (38015)
	DeVille - see GM (38031 & 38032)
	Eldorado - see GM (38030 & 38031)
	Fleetwood - see GM (38031)
	Seville - see GM (38030, 38031 & 38032)

CHEVROLET
24010	Astro & GMC Safari Mini-vans '85 thru '03
24015	Camaro V8 all models '70 thru '81
24016	Camaro all models '82 thru '92
24017	Camaro & Firebird '93 thru '02
	Cavalier - see GENERAL MOTORS (38016)
	Celebrity - see GENERAL MOTORS (38005)
24020	Chevelle, Malibu & El Camino '69 thru '87
24024	Chevette & Pontiac T1000 '76 thru '87
	Citation - see GENERAL MOTORS (38020)
24027	Colorado & GMC Canyon '04 thru '06
24032	Corsica/Beretta all models '87 thru '96
24040	Corvette all V8 models '68 thru '82
24041	Corvette all models '84 thru '96
10305	Chevrolet Engine Overhaul Manual
24045	Full-size Sedans Caprice, Impala, Biscayne, Bel Air & Wagons '69 thru '90
24046	Impala SS & Caprice and Buick Roadmaster '91 thru '96
	Impala - see LUMINA (24048)
	Lumina '90 thru '94 - see GM (38010)
24048	Lumina & Monte Carlo '95 thru '05
	Lumina APV - see GM (38035)

24050	Luv Pick-up all 2WD & 4WD '72 thru '82
	Malibu '97 thru '00 - see GM (38026)
24055	Monte Carlo all models '70 thru '88
	Monte Carlo '95 thru '01 - see LUMINA (24048)
24059	Nova all V8 models '69 thru '79
24060	Nova and Geo Prizm '85 thru '92
24064	Pick-ups '67 thru '87 - Chevrolet & GMC, all V8 & in-line 6 cyl, 2WD & 4WD '67 thru '87; Suburbans, Blazers & Jimmys '67 thru '91
24065	Pick-ups '88 thru '98 - Chevrolet & GMC, full-size pick-ups '88 thru '98, C/K Classic '99 & '00, Blazer & Jimmy '92 thru '94; Suburban '92 thru '99; Tahoe & Yukon '95 thru '99
24066	Pick-ups '99 thru '06 - Chevrolet Silverado & GMC Sierra '99 thru '06, Suburban/Tahoe/ Yukon/Yukon XL/Avalanche '00 thru '06
24070	S-10 & S-15 Pick-ups '82 thru '93, Blazer & Jimmy '83 thru '94,
24071	S-10 & Sonoma Pick-ups '94 thru '04, Blazer & Jimmy '95 thru '04, Hombre '96 thru '01
24072	Chevrolet TrailBlazer & TrailBlazer EXT, GMC Envoy & Envoy XL, Oldsmobile Bravada '02 thru '06
24075	Sprint '85 thru '88 & Geo Metro '89 thru '01
24080	Vans - Chevrolet & GMC '68 thru '96
24081	Chevrolet Express & GMC Savana Full-size Vans '96 thru '05

CHRYSLER
25015	Chrysler Cirrus, Dodge Stratus, Plymouth Breeze '95 thru '00
10310	Chrysler Engine Overhaul Manual
25020	Full-size Front-Wheel Drive '88 thru '93
	K-Cars - see DODGE Aries (30008)
	Laser - see DODGE Daytona (30030)
25025	Chrysler LHS, Concorde, New Yorker, Dodge Intrepid, Eagle Vision, '93 thru '97
25026	Chrysler LHS, Concorde, 300M, Dodge Intrepid, '98 thru '03
25027	Chrysler 300, Dodge Charger & Magnum '05 thru '07
25030	Chrysler & Plymouth Mid-size front wheel drive '82 thru '95
	Rear-wheel Drive - see Dodge (30050)
25035	PT Cruiser all models '01 thru '03
25040	Chrysler Sebring, Dodge Avenger '95 thru '05 Dodge Stratus '01 thru 05

DATSUN
28005	200SX all models '80 thru '83
28007	B-210 all models '73 thru '78
28009	210 all models '79 thru '82
28012	240Z, 260Z & 280Z Coupe '70 thru '78
28014	280ZX Coupe & 2+2 '79 thru '83
	300ZX - see NISSAN (72010)
28018	510 & PL521 Pick-up '68 thru '73
28020	510 all models '78 thru '81
28022	620 Series Pick-up all models '73 thru '79
	720 Series Pick-up - see NISSAN (72030)
28025	810/Maxima all gasoline models, '77 thru '84

DODGE
	400 & 600 - see CHRYSLER (25030)
30008	Aries & Plymouth Reliant '81 thru '89
30010	Caravan & Plymouth Voyager '84 thru '95
30011	Caravan & Plymouth Voyager '96 thru '02
30012	Challenger/Plymouth Saporro '78 thru '83
30013	Caravan, Chrysler Voyager, Town & Country '03 thru '06
30016	Colt & Plymouth Champ '78 thru '87
30020	Dakota Pick-ups all models '87 thru '96
30021	Durango '98 & '99, Dakota '97 thru '99
30022	Dodge Durango models '00 thru '03 Dodge Dakota models '00 thru '04
30023	Dodge Durango '04 thru '06, Dakota '05 and '06
30025	Dart, Demon, Plymouth Barracuda, Duster & Valiant 6 cyl models '67 thru '76
30030	Daytona & Chrysler Laser '84 thru '89
	Intrepid - see CHRYSLER (25025, 25026)
30034	Neon all models '95 thru '99
30035	Omni & Plymouth Horizon '78 thru '90
30036	Dodge and Plymouth Neon '00 thru '05
30040	Pick-ups all full-size models '74 thru '93
30041	Pick-ups all full-size models '94 thru '01
30042	Dodge Full-size Pick-ups '02 thru '05
30045	Ram 50/D50 Pick-ups & Raider and Plymouth Arrow Pick-ups '79 thru '93
30050	Dodge/Plymouth/Chrysler RWD '71 thru '89
30055	Shadow & Plymouth Sundance '87 thru '94
30060	Spirit & Plymouth Acclaim '89 thru '95
30065	Vans - Dodge & Plymouth '71 thru '03

EAGLE
	Talon - see MITSUBISHI (68030, 68031)
	Vision - see CHRYSLER (25025)

FIAT
34010	124 Sport Coupe & Spider '68 thru '78
34025	X1/9 all models '74 thru '80

FORD
10355	Ford Automatic Transmission Overhaul
36004	Aerostar Mini-vans all models '86 thru '97
36006	Contour & Mercury Mystique '95 thru '00
36008	Courier Pick-up all models '72 thru '82
36012	Crown Victoria & Mercury Grand Marquis '88 thru '06
10320	Ford Engine Overhaul Manual
36016	Escort/Mercury Lynx all models '81 thru '90
36020	Escort/Mercury Tracer '91 thru '00
36022	Ford Escape & Mazda Tribute '01 thru '03
36024	Explorer & Mazda Navajo '91 thru '01
36025	Ford Explorer & Mercury Mountaineer '02 thru '06
36028	Fairmont & Mercury Zephyr '78 thru '83
36030	Festiva & Aspire '88 thru '97
36032	Fiesta all models '77 thru '80
36034	Focus all models '00 thru '05
36036	Ford & Mercury Full-size '75 thru '87
36044	Ford & Mercury Mid-size '75 thru '86
36048	Mustang V8 all models '64-1/2 thru '73
36049	Mustang II 4 cyl, V6 & V8 models '74 thru '78
36050	Mustang & Mercury Capri all models Mustang, '79 thru '93; Capri, '79 thru '86
36051	Mustang all models '94 thru '04
36052	Mustang '05 thru '07
36054	Pick-ups & Bronco '73 thru '79
36058	Pick-ups & Bronco '80 thru '96
36059	F-150 & Expedition '97 thru '03, F-250 '97 thru '99 & Lincoln Navigator '98 thru '02
36060	Super Duty Pick-ups, Excursion '99 thru '06
36061	F-150 full-size '04 thru '06
36062	Pinto & Mercury Bobcat '75 thru '80
36066	Probe all models '89 thru '92
36070	Ranger/Bronco II gasoline models '83 thru '92
36071	Ranger '93 thru '05 & Mazda Pick-ups '94 thru '05
36074	Taurus & Mercury Sable '86 thru '95
36075	Taurus & Mercury Sable '96 thru '05
36078	Tempo & Mercury Topaz '84 thru '94
36082	Thunderbird/Mercury Cougar '83 thru '88
36086	Thunderbird/Mercury Cougar '89 and '97
36090	Vans all V8 Econoline models '69 thru '91
36094	Vans full size '92 thru '05
36097	Windstar Mini-van '95 thru '03

GENERAL MOTORS
10360	GM Automatic Transmission Overhaul
38005	Buick Century, Chevrolet Celebrity, Oldsmobile Cutlass Ciera & Pontiac 6000 all models '82 thru '96
38010	Buick Regal, Chevrolet Lumina, Oldsmobile Cutlass Supreme & Pontiac Grand Prix (FWD) '88 thru '05
38015	Buick Skyhawk, Cadillac Cimarron, Chevrolet Cavalier, Oldsmobile Firenza & Pontiac J-2000 & Sunbird '82 thru '94
38016	Chevrolet Cavalier & Pontiac Sunfire '95 thru '04
38017	Chevrolet Cobalt & Pontiac G5 '05 thru '07
38020	Buick Skylark, Chevrolet Citation, Olds Omega, Pontiac Phoenix '80 thru '85
38025	Buick Skylark & Somerset, Oldsmobile Achieva & Calais and Pontiac Grand Am all models '85 thru '98
38026	Chevrolet Malibu, Olds Alero & Cutlass, Pontiac Grand Am '97 thru '03
38027	Chevrolet Malibu '04 thru '07
38030	Cadillac Eldorado '71 thru '85, Seville '80 thru '85, Oldsmobile Toronado '71 thru '85, Buick Riviera '79 thru '85
38031	Cadillac Eldorado & Seville '86 thru '91, DeVille '86 thru '93, Fleetwood & Olds Toronado '86 thru '92, Buick Riviera '86 thru '93
38032	Cadillac DeVille '94 thru '05 & Seville '92 thru '04
38035	Chevrolet Lumina APV, Olds Silhouette & Pontiac Trans Sport all models '90 thru '96
38036	Chevrolet Venture, Olds Silhouette, Pontiac Trans Sport & Montana '97 thru '05
	General Motors Full-size Rear-wheel Drive - see BUICK (19025)

GEO
	Metro - see CHEVROLET Sprint (24075)
	Prizm - '85 thru '92 see CHEVY (24060), '93 thru '02 see TOYOTA Corolla (92036)

(Continued on other side)

Haynes North America, Inc., 861 Lawrence Drive, Newbury Park, CA 91320-1514 • (805) 498-6703

Haynes Automotive Manuals (continued)

NOTE: If you do not see a listing for your vehicle, consult your local Haynes dealer for the latest product information.

40030 Storm all models '90 thru '93
Tracker - see SUZUKI Samurai (90010)

GMC
Vans & Pick-ups - see CHEVROLET

HONDA
42010 Accord CVCC all models '76 thru '83
42011 Accord all models '84 thru '89
42012 Accord all models '90 thru '93
42013 Accord all models '94 thru '97
42014 Accord all models '98 thru '02
42015 Honda Accord models '03 thru '05
42020 Civic 1200 all models '73 thru '79
42021 Civic 1300 & 1500 CVCC '80 thru '83
42022 Civic 1500 CVCC all models '75 thru '79
42023 Civic all models '84 thru '91
42024 Civic & del Sol '92 thru '95
42025 Civic '96 thru '00, CR-V '97 thru '01,
Acura Integra '94 thru '00
42026 Civic '01 thru '04, CR-V '02 thru '04
42035 Honda Odyssey all models '99 thru '04
42037 Honda Pilot '03 thru '07, Acura MDX '01 thru '07
42040 Prelude CVCC all models '79 thru '89

HYUNDAI
43010 Elantra all models '96 thru '01
43015 Excel & Accent all models '86 thru '98

ISUZU
Hombre - see CHEVROLET S-10 (24071)
47017 Rodeo '91 thru '02; Amigo '89 thru '94 and
'98 thru '02; Honda Passport '95 thru '02
47020 Trooper & Pick-up '81 thru '93

JAGUAR
49010 XJ6 all 6 cyl models '68 thru '86
49011 XJ6 all models '88 thru '94
49015 XJ12 & XJS all 12 cyl models '72 thru '85

JEEP
50010 Cherokee, Comanche & Wagoneer Limited
all models '84 thru '01
50020 CJ all models '49 thru '86
50025 Grand Cherokee all models '93 thru '04
50029 Grand Wagoneer & Pick-up '72 thru '91
Grand Wagoneer '84 thru '91, Cherokee &
Wagoneer '72 thru '83, Pick-up '72 thru '88
50030 Wrangler all models '87 thru '03
50035 Liberty '02 thru '04

KIA
54070 Sephia '94 thru '01, Spectra '00 thru '04

LEXUS
ES 300 - see TOYOTA Camry (92007)

LINCOLN
Navigator - see FORD Pick-up (36059)
59010 Rear-Wheel Drive all models '70 thru '05

MAZDA
61010 GLC Hatchback (rear-wheel drive) '77 thru '83
61011 GLC (front-wheel drive) '81 thru '85
61015 323 & Protegé '90 thru '00
61016 MX-5 Miata '90 thru '97
61020 MPV all models '89 thru '94
Navajo - see Ford Explorer (36024)
61030 Pick-ups '72 thru '93
Pick-ups '94 thru '00 - see Ford Ranger (36071)
61035 RX-7 all models '79 thru '85
61036 RX-7 all models '86 thru '91
61040 626 (rear-wheel drive) all models '79 thru '82
61041 626/MX-6 (front-wheel drive) '83 thru '92
61042 626 '93 thru '01, MX-6/Ford Probe
'93 thru '01

MERCEDES-BENZ
63012 123 Series Diesel '76 thru '85
63015 190 Series four-cyl gas models, '84 thru '88
63020 230/250/280 6 cyl sohc models '68 thru '72
63025 280 123 Series gasoline models '77 thru '81
63030 350 & 450 all models '71 thru '80

MERCURY
64200 Villager & Nissan Quest '93 thru '01
All other titles, see FORD Listing.

MG
66010 MGB Roadster & GT Coupe '62 thru '80
66015 MG Midget, Austin Healey Sprite '58 thru '80

MITSUBISHI
68020 Cordia, Tredia, Galant, Precis &
Mirage '83 thru '93

68030 Eclipse, Eagle Talon & Ply. Laser '90 thru '94
68031 Eclipse '95 thru '01, Eagle Talon '95 thru '98
68035 Mitsubishi Galant '94 thru '03
68040 Pick-up '83 thru '96 & Montero '83 thru '93

NISSAN
72010 300ZX all models including Turbo '84 thru '89
72015 Altima all models '93 thru '04
72020 Maxima all models '85 thru '92
72021 Maxima all models '93 thru '04
72030 Pick-ups '80 thru '97 Pathfinder '87 thru '95
72031 Frontier Pick-up '98 thru '04, Xterra '00 thru
'04, Pathfinder '96 thru '04
72040 Pulsar all models '83 thru '86
Quest - see MERCURY Villager (64200)
72050 Sentra all models '82 thru '94
72051 Sentra & 200SX all models '95 thru '04
72060 Stanza all models '82 thru '90

OLDSMOBILE
73015 Cutlass V6 & V8 gas models '74 thru '88
*For other OLDSMOBILE titles, see BUICK,
CHEVROLET or GENERAL MOTORS listing.*

PLYMOUTH
For PLYMOUTH titles, see DODGE listing.

PONTIAC
79008 Fiero all models '84 thru '88
79018 Firebird V8 models except Turbo '70 thru '81
79019 Firebird all models '82 thru '92
79040 Mid-size Rear-wheel Drive '70 thru '87
*For other PONTIAC titles, see BUICK,
CHEVROLET or GENERAL MOTORS listing.*

PORSCHE
80020 911 except Turbo & Carrera 4 '65 thru '89
80025 914 all 4 cyl models '69 thru '76
80030 924 all models including Turbo '76 thru '82
80035 944 all models including Turbo '83 thru '89

RENAULT
Alliance & Encore - see AMC (14020)

SAAB
84010 900 including Turbo '79 thru '88

SATURN
87010 Saturn all models '91 thru '02
87011 Saturn Ion '03 thru '07
87020 Saturn all L-series models '00 thru '04

SUBARU
89002 1100, 1300, 1400 & 1600 '71 thru '79
89003 1600 & 1800 2WD & 4WD '80 thru '94
89100 Legacy all models '90 thru '99
89101 Legacy & Forester '00 thru '06

SUZUKI
90010 Samurai/Sidekick & Geo Tracker '86 thru '01

TOYOTA
92005 Camry all models '83 thru '91
92006 Camry all models '92 thru '96
92007 Camry, Avalon, Solara, Lexus ES 300 '97 thru '01
92008 Toyota Camry, Avalon and Solara and
Lexus ES 300/330 '02 thru '05
92015 Celica Rear Wheel Drive '71 thru '85
92020 Celica Front Wheel Drive '86 thru '99
92025 Celica Supra all models '79 thru '92
92030 Corolla all models '75 thru '79
92032 Corolla all rear wheel drive models '80 thru '87
92035 Corolla all front wheel drive models '84 thru '92
92036 Corolla & Geo Prizm '93 thru '02
92037 Corolla models '03 thru '05
92040 Corolla Tercel all models '80 thru '82
92045 Corona all models '74 thru '82
92050 Cressida all models '78 thru '82
92055 Land Cruiser FJ40, 43, 45, 55 '68 thru '82
92056 Land Cruiser FJ60, 62, 80, FZJ80 '80 thru '96
92065 MR2 all models '85 thru '87
92070 Pick-up all models '69 thru '78
92075 Pick-up all models '79 thru '95
92076 Tacoma '95 thru '04, 4Runner '96 thru '02,
& T100 '93 thru '98
92078 Tundra '00 thru '05 & Sequoia '01 thru '05
92080 Previa all models '91 thru '95
92081 Prius all models '01 thru '08
92082 RAV4 all models '96 thru '05
92085 Tercel all models '87 thru '94
92090 Toyota Sienna all models '98 thru '02
92095 Highlander & Lexus RX-330 '99 thru '06

TRIUMPH
94007 Spitfire all models '62 thru '81
94010 TR7 all models '75 thru '81

VW
96008 Beetle & Karmann Ghia '54 thru '79
96009 New Beetle '98 thru '05
96016 Rabbit, Jetta, Scirocco & Pick-up gas
models '75 thru '92 & Convertible '80 thru '92
96017 Golf, GTI & Jetta '93 thru '98
& Cabrio '95 thru '98
96018 Golf, GTI, Jetta & Cabrio '99 thru '02
96020 Rabbit, Jetta & Pick-up diesel '77 thru '84
96023 Passat '98 thru '01, Audi A4 '96 thru '01
96030 Transporter 1600 all models '68 thru '79
96035 Transporter 1700, 1800 & 2000 '72 thru '79
96040 Type 3 1500 & 1600 all models '63 thru '73
96045 Vanagon all air-cooled models '80 thru '83

VOLVO
97010 120, 130 Series & 1800 Sports '61 thru '73
97015 140 Series all models '66 thru '74
97020 240 Series all models '76 thru '93
97040 740 & 760 Series all models '82 thru '88
97050 850 Series all models '93 thru '97

TECHBOOK MANUALS
10205 Automotive Computer Codes
10206 OBD-II & Electronic Engine Management
Systems
10210 Automotive Emissions Control Manual
10215 Fuel Injection Manual, 1978 thru 1985
10220 Fuel Injection Manual, 1986 thru 1999
10225 Holley Carburetor Manual
10230 Rochester Carburetor Manual
10240 Weber/Zenith/Stromberg/SU Carburetors
10305 Chevrolet Engine Overhaul Manual
10310 Chrysler Engine Overhaul Manual
10320 Ford Engine Overhaul Manual
10330 GM and Ford Diesel Engine Repair Manual
10333 Building Engine Power Manual
10340 Small Engine Repair Manual, 5 HP & Less
10341 Small Engine Repair Manual, 5.5 - 20 HP
10345 Suspension, Steering & Driveline Manual
10355 Ford Automatic Transmission Overhaul
10360 GM Automatic Transmission Overhaul
10405 Automotive Body Repair & Painting
10410 Automotive Brake Manual
10411 Automotive Anti-lock Brake (ABS) Systems
10415 Automotive Detailing Manual
10420 Automotive Electrical Manual
10425 Automotive Heating & Air Conditioning
10430 Automotive Reference Manual & Dictionary
10435 Automotive Tools Manual
10440 Used Car Buying Guide
10445 Welding Manual
10450 ATV Basics
10452 Scooters, Automatic Transmission 50cc
to 250cc

SPANISH MANUALS
98903 Reparación de Carrocería & Pintura
98904 Carburadores para los modelos
Holley & Rochester
98905 Códigos Automotrices de la Computadora
98910 Frenos Automotriz
98913 Electricidad Automotriz
98915 Inyección de Combustible 1986 al 1999
99040 Chevrolet & GMC Camionetas '67 al '87
Incluye Suburban, Blazer & Jimmy '67 al '91
99041 Chevrolet & GMC Camionetas '88 al '98
Incluye Suburban '92 al '98, Blazer &
Jimmy '92 al '94, Tahoe y Yukon '95 al '98
99042 Chevrolet & GMC Camionetas
Cerradas '68 al '95
99055 Dodge Caravan & Plymouth Voyager '84 al '95
99075 Ford Camionetas y Bronco '80 al '94
99077 Ford Camionetas Cerradas '69 al '91
99088 Ford Modelos de Tamaño Mediano '75 al '86
99091 Ford Taurus & Mercury Sable '86 al '95
99095 GM Modelos de Tamaño Grande '70 al '90
99100 GM Modelos de Tamaño Mediano '70 al '88
99106 Jeep Cherokee, Wagoneer & Comanche
'84 al '00
99110 Nissan Camioneta '80 al '96, Pathfinder '87 al '95
99118 Nissan Sentra '82 al '94
99125 Toyota Camionetas y 4Runner '79 al '95

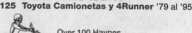

Over 100 Haynes
motorcycle manuals
also available

10-07

Haynes North America, Inc., 861 Lawrence Drive, Newbury Park, CA 91320-1514 • (805) 498-6703